WILSON'S DICTIONARY OF BIBLE TYPES

Other books by Dr. Walter L. Wilson

STRANGE SHORT STORIES

LET'S GO FISHING WITH THE DOCTOR (SOUL WINNING)

HAPPINESS IN THE HOME (FOR WEDDINGS)

YE KNOW HIM (THE HOLY SPIRIT)

GROWING UP FOR GOD

THE ROMANCE OF A DOCTOR'S VISITS

MIRACLES IN A DOCTOR'S LIFE

A SURE REMEDY, BY THE DOCTOR

REMARKABLE NEW STORIES

UNCLE WALTER'S ANIMAL STORIES

LIVELY ANIMAL STORIES

ANIMAL STORIES FOR CHILDREN

HOW TO WIN SOULS

WHOSE BODY IS YOURS?

Wilson's Dictionary of Bible Types

By

WALTER LEWIS WILSON, M.D., D.D., L.H.D.

WM. B. EERDMANS PUBLISHING CO.
GRAND RAPIDS, MICHIGAN

LIBRARY OF CONGRESS CATALOG CARD NUMBER:
57 — 14495

Sixth printing, March 1972

PHOTOLITHOPRINTED BY GRAND RAPIDS BOOK MANUFACTURERS, INC.
GRAND RAPIDS, MICHIGAN, UNITED STATES OF AMERICA
1972

INTRODUCTION

Because typology is a subject of much discussion and because there are differences of opinion concerning the meaning of types, it has seemed best to divide the material in this book into three groups.

1. The passages marked with the letter (a) are pure types, plainly described as such and referred to as such in the Scriptures. There is no question about them.

2. Those marked (b) seem to be types because of their use and because of the evident meaning they convey.

3. Those marked (c) are passages in which there may be a question as to whether or not they are types. The descriptions given of these passages are offered only as suggestions of lessons which may be learned from them. The writer claims no superior knowledge whatever in regard to their meaning and will be quite happy for others to have their own thoughts about them. There will be no spirit of criticism in the matter.

Sometimes a number of separate words are used to describe more or less the same thing. These have been designated as types, symbols, signs, shadows, representations, pictures, figures and patterns, in order to make them more lucid for the average reader. The author has refrained from making final decisions in these passages under class (c) and has left it to the student to settle in his own mind as he pursues his study.

In presenting this compendium of types, shadows, signs and symbols, an effort has been made to furnish, for the Bible student, a fairly complete explanation of the Scripture passages. I realize that the descriptions do not fully cover the subject for the Word of God is boundless, limitless and measureless.

If the reader should find other symbolical meanings than those given in the book, it will be a cause for thanksgiving. If he should differ in his opinions from those herein presented, there will be no criticism. If anyone should feel that the explanations are not sufficiently clear, then I shall hope that he will add to the information given.

A proper understanding of the meanings of types in the Bible will add greatly to the understanding of the text and will greatly increase the ability and resourcefulness of the soul winner.

This book is sent forth on its mission of helpfulness with the prayer that through its use, minds will be enlightened, hearts will be refreshed, and lives will be made more useful.

INTRODUCTION

I wish to acknowledge with gratitude the untiring efforts of my two secretaries, Miss Pearl Wisner and Mrs. Grace Longenecker, without whom it would have been most difficult for me to compile this book through the years of study and research. They were my untiring helpers.

WALTER LEWIS WILSON, M.D., D.D., L.H.D.

Kansas City, Missouri

CONTENTS

HOW TO STUDY TYPES

Lesson One

The student should first decide whether the word under consideration is used by the Spirit as a type. Not all objects are types. Care should be used in arriving at a conclusion on this matter lest one distort the Word of God and thus arrive at decisions which were never intended by the Lord.

A safe rule is to ascertain whether an object is said plainly to be a type. When Paul wrote in 1 Corinthians 10:4, "They drank of that spiritual rock . . . and that rock was Christ," we know that the rock in the wilderness was a true type of Christ.

When we read of the good and bad fish in Matthew 13:47, we know that these fish are types though the passage does not say so. The story is a parable intended to teach a lesson. It is needful therefore to learn just what they do represent and also what the net represents.

When we read of the "Red Sea" or "the Jordan," we know this to be a type just because it teaches so many very interesting and profitable lessons.

But even though we decide that an object is a type there still remains the problem of learning what it represents. Here great care is needed. Let us ask, "What constitutes a type?" Let us seek an answer by a series of comparisons:

1. There is likeness of appearance as "clouds" and "dust." (Nahum 1:3)
2. There is likeness of action as "the leopard" and "Alexander the Great." (Dan. 7:6)
3. There is likeness of effect as "rain and snow" and "the Word of God." (Isa. 55:10)
4. There is likeness of relationship as "nurse" and "Paul." (I Thess. 2:7)
5. There is likeness of value as "gold" and "the Lord Jesus." (Isa. 13:12)
6. There is likeness of position as "head" and "Israel." (Deut. 28:13)
7. There is likeness of character as "the spider" and "the sinner." (Prov. 30:28)

Lesson Two

Certain principles and processes are essential in the study of Typology. It is Scriptural to study this subject for the writers of the Scripture and our Lord Himself used types constantly for teaching great lessons. As a good knife is of most value in the hands of a skillful surgeon, so the Word of God is most effective when used by those who best understand its hidden meaning. The study of types is illuminating, for the Spirit uses the things which are seen, to teach us concerning the things which are unseen. The study of types equips us with a handy means and method of presenting the truth of God, for types are about us on every hand ready to be used.

Some suggestions for the study of types:

1. Think of the opposite of that which is under consideration; as the golden city (Rev. 21:18) and the gilded city (Rev. 18:16); the lion (Rev. 5:5) and the lamb (Rev. 5:6); the woman clothed in red (Rev. 17:4) and the woman clothed in white (Rev. 19:8).
2. Think of comparisons: great Goliath and little David; Joseph of the Old Testament and Jesus; the river in Ezekiel 47 and the river in John 7.
3. Look up the several occurrences of the type to ascertain how it is used.
4. Learn whether this type is referred to anywhere else in the Scripture as a type.
5. Consider the characteristics of the type being studied as the sea with its greatness, its depth, its restlessness, its size, its waves, its commerce.
6. Think of the lessons which may be learned from the type as the leaves in Isaiah 64:6, how they fade, how they reveal the kind of tree, how they show whether young or old, how they fall from the tree or hold on. By considering these various thoughts, the student will be enabled to quickly and easily learn lessons from the subject under consideration.

If questions should arise in regard to any of the suggestions given, the reader may feel free to address an inquiry to the author. Such communications will receive prompt attention.

Lesson Three

Quite often an object is used as the same type or a type of the same thing by several writers. This repetition confirms the object as a type and assures us of its true meaning.

Moses uses the rock as a type of Christ in Numbers 20:8. David uses the rock as a type of Christ in Psalm 18:2. Isaiah does the same thing in Isaiah 32:2. The Lord Jesus also refers to Himself as the Rock upon which the church is built in Matthew 16:18.

Balaam used trees to represent the nation of Israel, Numbers 24:6 David used a tree to represent a godly man in Psalm 1. Jeremiah follows the same plan in Jeremiah 17:8. Daniel used a tree to represent the king in Daniel 4:10. He received this message from God. Isaiah used the same type for the eunuch in Isaiah 56:3. Jesus used the tree as a type of the people of Israel in Luke 13:6.

It is well also to note that an object cannot be a type of certain things. I heard a preacher use "Joseph's coat of many colors" as a type of the doctrine of sinless perfection. It was a very grotesque comparison, utterly without foundation or truth.

Leaven is often used as a type of the gospel which, of course, it could not be. The contexts concerning leaven all through both the Old Testament and the New indicate clearly that it is a type of some evil which should be removed.

It will be most helpful for the student to ask himself certain questions in regard to the study of types and this will guide him in his investigation.

1. How is this object or subject first used in the Scripture? What meaning does it have in the first place where it occurs?
2. To what does this object or subject refer in the last passage where it occurs in the Scripture?
3. What are the characteristics of this object or subject which make it a suitable type? Christ is compared to a lion in Revelation 5. In Isaiah 53, Christ is compared to a lamb. As the characteristics of these two animals are studied, then the likeness will be more clearly understood. This plan should be followed in each case.
4. Types should be grouped according to that which they represent. There are types of Christ, Israel, the nations, the Christian, the hypocrites, the worker, the state of the soul, Satan, and many others.

5. Types may also be grouped according to their character. There are types taken from the mineral kingdom, the animal kingdom, the vegetable kingdom, the celestial kingdom, the human family, human actions, human attitudes, postures, etc. It will help the student to understand types more fully if these groupings are made while the study is being pursued.

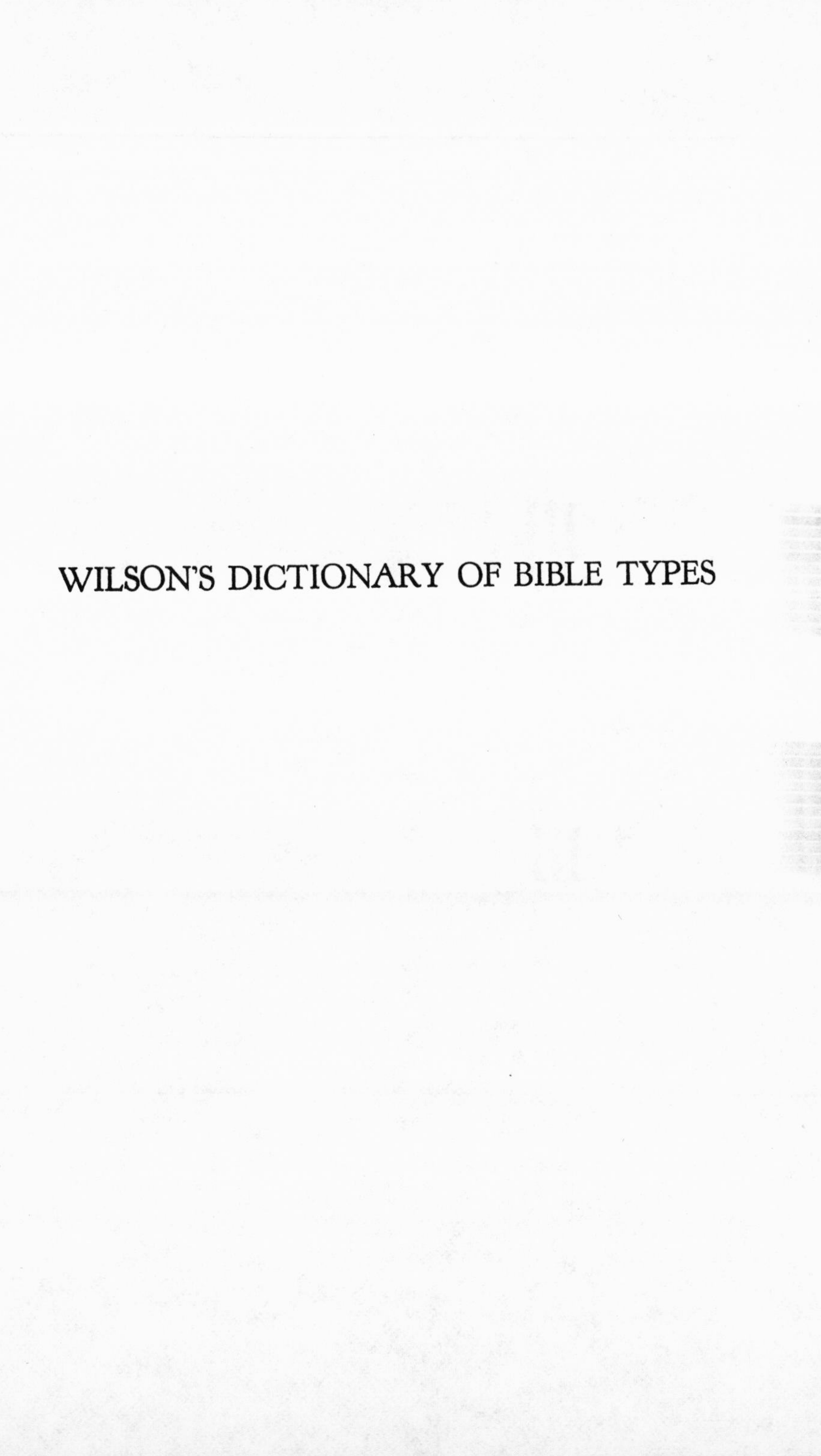

WILSON'S DICTIONARY OF BIBLE TYPES

A

AARON

Heb. 5:4 (c) Aaron is a type of Christ in many ways. As he entered into the Holy of Holies once a year with the blood of an animal, so our Lord Jesus entered into heaven by His own blood, not just once a year, but forever. Aaron bore the names of the twelve tribes on his shoulders, so the Lord Jesus carries His people and their burdens on His shoulders. Aaron bore the breastplate of twelve stones over his heart, and our Saviour bears His own children on His heart. Aaron wore a gold band on his forehead bearing the inscription "Holiness to the Lord." So our Lord Jesus was holy, pure and perfect in all His ways, words and character. Aaron pleaded with God for the people, and pleaded with the people for God. So our Lord Jesus "ever liveth to make intercession for us," and appears in God's presence for us. He also reveals God to us. Aaron was chosen by God to be the High Priest, and God chose Christ to be our High Priest. Aaron's garments were prescribed by God and were called holy garments. So the garment of our Lord Jesus is called "the robe of righteousness, the garments of salvation," Isa. 61:10.

ABRAHAM

Gen. 24:2 (c) In this passage Abraham is a type of the Father who sent His servant (the Spirit) to obtain a bride (Rebecca) for his son Isaac. The servant represents the Holy Spirit, and Isaac represents the Lord Jesus Christ. Of course, Abraham represents God the Father. Rebecca represents the Church. The Holy Spirit knocks at the heart's door, tells of the loveliness, the riches and the glory of the Son of God, and thus wins the stranger and makes him willing to leave his old haunts and companions to live for and with Jesus Christ, the Son.

Romans 4:3 (c) He is a type of the true believer from the standpoint of "faith." He was called out of idolatry by God, and so are we. He took the path of separation, and so should we. He obeyed God, and walked in a path of obedience, as we should do. He believed God about the "seed" (Christ), so do we. He was made righteous through believing in Christ. So are we. God revealed His secrets to Abraham, the man of faith, and so He does today to those who believe His Word. Abraham was the father of the faithful, and we too who believe God should have spiritual children who have faith as we have.

ABEL

Gen. 4:4 (c) He is a type of the true believer in regard to salvation. He felt his guilt, he realized his insufficiency to pay the price. He obtained an innocent lamb. He offered this lamb as a sacrifice, killing it and burning it upon the altar whereby he proved his faith in the animal who died for him, and shed his blood for him. This is the path the true believer takes today. As a sinner he feels his need as Abel did. He goes to the innocent and holy Lamb of God, Jesus Christ, by faith. He kneels a suppliant for mercy at Calvary, where the blood was shed. He believes the Word of God that the "blood of Jesus Christ, His Son, cleanseth us from all sin," 1 John 1:7. He trusts his soul and life to the living Lamb on the Throne of God who makes the death of Calvary and the shed blood effective for the one who believes.

ABSALOM

2 Sam. 14:25 (c) This son of David may be taken as a type of a human being without God. He had developed his body to perfection. Those who observed him could see nothing but physical beauty. From head to foot there was no blemish in him. With all of this, however, his heart was wicked. He hated his father David who was God's chosen king. He refused and rejected God's plan and purpose in regard to Solomon. He was fit for neither heaven nor earth, and so he died between the two of them on the tree. So is the religious hypocrite of today. He presents many aspects of beauty and characteristics of loveliness, yet his heart is not right with God.

2 Sam. 15:2 (c) In this passage Absalom is a type of the ingratitude and infidelity of professing Christians who are not really saved. When the test came he proved to be an enemy of God's king, and of God's program. He did not take his place on God's side. He wanted to assert his own sufficiency and his own supremacy.

ACCURSED

Deut. 21:23 (c) This word represents God's wrath against the sinner. It is manifest in many ways throughout the Scriptures. Sometimes it is a nation that is accursed. Sometimes it is an individual. Sometimes it is that which the world would call a "blessing," for the Lord said, "I will curse your blessings," Malachi 2:2. This passage may refer to the so-called "blessings" given by great ecclesiastical leaders which frequently are cursed by God.

Joshua 6:18 (c) In this passage all that was in the city of Jericho belonged to God. Not a bit of it was to be taken by any man. The word is used here to indicate that what is God's property becomes an accursed thing to the one who takes it unlawfully and wrongfully.

ACHAN

Joshua 7:1 (c) This man is used as a type of a selfish, wicked, religious professor. He rejected God's word about the property of Jericho which belonged to God, and took some of it to enrich himself. The ungodly who join the church, partake of the Lord's supper, and teach the Bible which they do not believe are like Achan.

Joshua 7:25 (c) Achan may be taken in this place as a type of a trouble maker who, because of his sinful, hypocritical practices in the church, causes trouble there. Because of his actions the church is in a turmoil and even perhaps may be divided because of him. Such a person is to be expelled from the church as in 1 Corinthians 5.

ACHOR

Joshua 7:24 (c) This valley represents a place of sorrow and trouble in human lives. As Achan was stoned there, and his sin put away, so in our lives times of trouble and sorrow may be called "the place of Achor." There God's remedy is to be applied to the difficulty.

Hosea 2:15 (c) The valley in this passage is described as a door of hope. When sin is judged and put away, then hope for God's blessing is revived, and joy replaces sorrow.

ADAM

Genesis 5:2 (c) This man is a type of Christ in that he was the head of the human family, and Christ is the head of God's family. Adam was sinless in the first part of his life, and then deliberately and knowingly became a partner in Eve's sin in order that he might be with her, partake of her punishment, and continue to have her for his very own. So our Lord Jesus was sinless and perfect. He willingly and knowingly took upon Himself the form of a servant, and was made sin for us that He might forever have us with Him. (See 1 Tim. 2:14). As by the sin of Adam all who are in Adam were made sinners, so by the obedience of Christ all who are in Christ are made righteous (Rom. 5:18).

Rom. 5:19 (b) Adam was the first of the earthly family and Christ is the first of the heavenly family. Our bodies are in the likeness of Adam, and in the new creation we shall be like Christ, the last Adam.

ADD

2 Peter 1:5 (b) This figure describes the growth in grace of the Christian who learns to know the ways of God as described in this passage. When any person is born again, then he changes his ways, his practices and his thoughts so that there may be in his life the graces given by the Spirit, and the knowledge of heavenly things that God desires to give to each of His children.

ADDER

Psalm 58:4 (b) This serpent is used to describe a wicked person who injures the souls and damages the lives of others by that which comes out of his mouth. That which such a person says poisons the hearts and the minds of those who hear. By this means the listeners are deceived by Satan and are led astray from God's path. False teachers who invent false religions and preach false doctrines are "adders" (See also Psalm 91:13, the open enemy and the secret foe.).

ADORN

Titus 2:10 (b) As jewels make a person more attractive, and as pictures make a room more beautiful, and as color schemes add to the delightful beauty of the room, so the Christian graces in the believer's life are an ornament of beauty to those who observe them.

These attributes from heaven make a person more attractive, and the Christian life more desirable. These "adorn" the believer.

ADULLAM

1 Sam. 22:1 (c) This cave is a picture of the refuge in the time of storm which God gives to His people. It is "the secret place of the Most High." It is the "shadow of a great rock in a weary land." It is the quiet secret place of prayer. Those who were in distress, despondent and in debt came there to David for relief. So we may go to our "cave of Adullam," into the presence of our wonderful Lord to find rest and relief from the troubles, cares, problems and griefs of life.

Micah 1:15 (c) In this passage the results of coming alone with God are described as being the blessings which those saints enjoy who hide in that secret place, and under the wings of the Almighty.

ADULTERY

James 4:4 (b) This word in this passage carries a spiritual significance. As those who are married may turn against each other secretly to find another companion, so one who is married to Christ and takes the place of being a Christian may turn against the Saviour and become a lover of the world and the things of Satan.

This is called spiritual adultery. This person professes to be a Christian, takes the place of belonging to Christ, but finds his real enjoyment, his love and his pleasure in the things that Satan offers.

ADVERSARY

Matt. 5:25 (b) The adversary in this portion evidently refers to God who sends His porter, death, to take men from this scene to the Judge, the Lord Jesus. Being found guilty, the Lord Jesus hands this wicked sinner over to one of His angels who is the officer. The angel takes the lost sinner to hell, which is God's prison house. Since the prisoner can never pay the debt he must remain there forever.

1 Tim. 5:14 (b) The adversary in this passage refers to critics of God's people who in their opposition to Christ are quick to find fault with God's people, and to call attention to the failures of Christians.

ADVERSITY

Isa. 30:20 (b) This expression represents the sorrows on which God's people will feed when they turn their backs on their Lord and become disobedient. They will feed on their difficulties and pains. They will meditate on them, talk about them, and grieve over them as though they were something to be treasured and sought after. This thought will be further developed under the word "ASHES."

ADVOCATE

1 John 2:1 (a) This title is applied to Christ in His office of pleading for us before God. He pleads for God's people in the presence of God when Satan accuses them before God. He shows His wounded hands and feet as He defends His people before the Judge of all the earth. He shows by the wounds that He paid the debt for the believer whom He represents.

AGAG

1 Sam. 15:9 (c) This King of Amalek is a type of some wicked habit or evil way which is promoted and cultivated in the life of one who knows better. Haman was a descendant of the Agag family, and caused Israel great trouble in the time of Queen Esther. Saul should have killed Agag. In that he spared his life, he is a picture of the believer who spares things in his life that are hurtful to his own soul. We should never permit any Agag to remain in our lives.

AGES

Isa. 26:4 (Margin) (a) Here we find that Christ is the One in whom men may safely trust in any age from infancy to death, or in any period of time. It also informs us that Christ may be trusted fully for every matter concerning this life or the next. Christ is able to sustain and support every person whether it be the little child, or the mature man of business. Christ may be trusted in every situation, in every circumstance, and in any time of day or night.

Eph. 2:7 (b) Reference is made here to the various periods of time which succeed each other in the course of history clear up into eternity. This passage refutes the doctrine of "soul sleeping," and the "annihilation" theory.

AGRIPPA

Acts 26:28 (c) This man is typical of a person who permits some wicked relative, or some lustful habit to keep him from trusting Christ Jesus. It probably was because of the presence of his sister Bernice and her influence upon him, that he decided to reject Christ. (See also under "BERNICE.")

AHA

Ezek. 25:3 (b) This little word is used as an expression to show contempt for the things of God. God noticed that the Ammonites and also other nations used this little word against His people, His land and His temple. That little word revealed their hatred of everything connected with the work of God and the people of God. God noticed what they said and brought His wrath upon them because they said it. (See also Ezek. 26:2)

AIR

1 Cor. 9:26 (a) This refers to the actions of one who wastes his life in busy idleness or in useless, fruitless endeavor.

Eph. 2:2 (a) Here is meant the space between heaven and earth through which the prayers of God's people must pass, and through which the saints must go on their way home to God. The Spirit of God must take our prayers through the opposition of evil spirits up to the Throne of God and the Lord Jesus. Eventually the mighty power of God must take the spirits of His people through all Satanic opposition and bring them safe home to God.

ALABASTER BOX

Matt. 26:7 (c) This may be taken as a type of man's best graces, efforts and talents which he had saved heretofore for himself, but now in consecration he brings to Jesus' feet. Some have thought that this alabaster box was the girls hope chest of the olden days. It was filled with sweet perfume of various values and sealed shut. It is said that there were several grades, cheap china, medium and expensive china. When a girl approached the marriageable age, she obtained a box according to her ability to pay and her station in life. She saved it until she found the man to whom she was willing to give her life, and with whom she desired to live. When her lover requested her hand and heart in marriage, then the girl, if she desired to answer in the affirmative, obtained the box from its hiding place and broke it at his feet. This was her declaration that her quest for a lover was ended. I cannot vouch for the truth of this statement, but it seems to fit nicely in each passage where this box was mentioned. (See Mark 14:3; Luke 7:37.)

ALIVE

Luke 15:24,32 (b) The word as used here indicates that the life of this wayward, prodigal was again what it should be. While he was in the far country living for himself and completely out of touch with his father, his condition was described as being "dead." There was no communion with his father, no contact with his home, no fellowship with his brother. He was still the child of his father. The relationship was not broken, but only the fellowship. When he ceased the life of disobedience and came back to his father, then his condition is described as being "alive." Now his life was as it once was, and as it should be.

Rom. 6:11 (a) Here the word "alive" refers to the presence of the new eternal life in the soul which is given to any person when he trusts Jesus Christ. It is the presence of this new nature that enables the believer to live for God and to understand the things of God.

1 Cor. 15:22 (a) The resurrection is in view in this passage. All who belong to Adam are dead in trespasses and sins. When these have Christ revealed to their souls by the Holy Spirit through the Word of God they are said to be made "alive" because they belong to Christ. In the resurrection we shall have a physical body which will never die.

ALMIGHTY

Gen. 17:1 (a) This is the first mention of the wonderful title of God. By this name He revealed to Abraham His power to supply every need of man, both physical and spiritual. There would be no need of any kind in any human life that could not be met completely and fully by the Eternal God who wears the Name "Almighty."

Ex. 6:3 (a) The title in this verse refers to the power of God to deliver Israel from their oppressors. He is Lord over every other lord and is able to deliver His own people from every form of oppression.

Psalm 91:1 (a) Here this title is used to describe God's power and ability to protect and preserve His children through all the vicissitudes, troubles, sorrows and problems of life.

2 Cor. 6:18 (a) This title describes the God who is able to supply every temporal need of His own people who refuse the provision of this world, and refuse to accept deliverance or provision from the children of Satan. Those who sever themselves from a place of dependence from the world and reject Satan's schemes, find that God is able to furnish them with all their necessities.

Rev. 1:8 (a) In this passage the Lord Jesus is given the title because of His sovereign ability to begin everything, and to make everything, to sustain everything, and to bring everything to an end. It describes His power to judge everything and everybody. Nothing is beyond the reach of His power.

ALMOND

Ex. 25:33 (c) The almond on the golden candlestick in the tabernacle is a type of the fruitfulness which will characterize that one who sheds abroad the light of life in his life. Each one who dwells in the holy place, holds forth the Word of Life, and brings light to those who sit in darkness, will be a fruit-bearing Christian. This almond is connected with the flower which indicates the beauty of that life and also with the knop which represents the fullness of the Christian life.

Num. 17:8 (c) Only Aaron's rod yielded almonds. Israel was to learn from this miracle that the family of Aaron was to be the fruit-bearing family in the service of the God of Israel. The other families were to have no part in the priestly ministry. He only, as a type of Christ, was to be known as the fruit-bearing priest of God. All others would be as intruders and thereby rejected. (See under "FLOWER" and "KNOP.")

Eccl. 12:5 (b) In this place the word represents the bitterness that often comes into the experiences of the aged. The almond plant itself is bitter, but the nut is sweet. Many as they enter old age carry with them bitter memories of former injustices and feel a spirit of hatred toward others.

ALMS

Matt. 6:1 (b) The word is used in a general sense here. It represents good deeds done for the blessing and benefit of others, regardless of who they were, but particularly for the poor. The lesson is that we should not be advertising our good deeds expecting that men will give us rewards. If we do tell what we do for God, then the plaudits that we receive from man is all the reward we shall have. If, however, we do these good deeds for the glory of God, then He will give us the reward in due time.

Acts 10:4 (b) In this place the word is used in regard to gifts of money given particularly for God's work and God's people. The angel carries the gift up to heaven, presents it before the Lord, and before the rest of the heavenly group so that all will know that the money placed in the collection and the money sent to missions and the money given to assist otherwise in God's work represents your interest in it.

Acts 24:17 (b) These alms refer to the sacrifices, the money, the gifts and the dues which belong to the priestly service of Israel. It may represent also those gifts which are given to preachers, missionaries and others engaged in Christian work, which is for their personal use. It may also refer to any gifts given to God's people for their relief and blessing.

ALOES

Psalm 45:8 (c) This perfume represents the worship and praise, the adoration and thanksgiving that emanates from a heart that has been touched by the love of God. It probably was one of the constituents of the perfume which was placed in the alabaster boxes mentioned in the New Testament. It is that which makes the fellowship of the Lord so fragrant and sweet to both His heart and ours. It may have been a part of those spices brought by the wise men to make His baby garments sweet. It probably was a part of the perfume brought by the woman in Luke 7, who made His traveling garments fragrant. It may have been a part of the spices brought by Mary in John 12, when she made fragrant those garments which Jesus was to wear during His last week on earth before Calvary. No doubt it was a part of the perfume brought by the unnamed woman in Mark 14, when she anointed His head two days before the Passover and made those trial garments fragrant. It may have been in the mixture that Nicodemus brought to make His grave clothes fragrant. It probably is considered as part of those perfumes which we living saints may send up to Heaven as our praises to fill the golden vials in the hands of the four and twenty elders. (Rev. 5:8)

ALPHA

Rev. 1:8 (a) In this passage our Lord Jesus Himself applies this name to Himself as He does also in verse 11. In Rev. 21:6, He again applies that name to Himself and also in chapter 22:13. He wants us to remember and never forget that He is the beginning of all literature. There would be no such thing as education, or understanding, or learning, were it not that He gave man the ability to learn, and then unveiled to man's mind the multitude of matters which we call education. All information about creation has come from Him. Those who shut Him out of their lives and thinking are in darkness, or return to darkness. He is the author of the solar system and of all chemicals. He is the designer of the earth and the heavens. He originated the plan of salvation. He is the author of every kind of life in the vegetable kingdom, the animal kingdom and the human kingdom. Christ Jesus is first, He is before all in every department of the universe. As Alpha is the first letter of the Greek alphabet, so Christ is the first cause of everything that exists.

ALTAR

Earthen Ex. 20:24 (c) This altar may represent the Cross of Calvary on which Jesus as the Lamb of God died for those who break the holy law of God. Immediately after giving the Ten Commandments, the Lord requested that this altar be built at once. He knew that His laws would be broken, He knew that men would need a sacrifice for their sins; He therefore planned that this altar should be built at once so that men could have a way of forgiveness and salvation immediately. It is called an altar of earth because it belongs strictly to this earth. God makes no provision for forgiveness and salvation after death. No sacrifice of any kind is available to the lost sinner after he dies. There is no altar in hell.

Stone Ex. 20:25 (c) This altar is to be made of stone to indicate that it is permanent, substantial, solid and cannot be tampered with by man. No tool was to be used in the making of it. Stones are made by God. It is a picture of Calvary which was God's institution. He planned it, He designed that Jesus was to die there. It must not be tampered with by man. Its blessings are eternal. Calvary came from the heart of God through the ages of eternity.

Brazen Ex. 27:1-2 (c) This may be taken as a type of the cross of Calvary, where the Lamb of God was offered as a sacrifice for original sin, and a sacrifice for sins committed, and also as a sacrifice for our own wicked selves. Christ must die for our character, as well as our conduct. On that altar, the animal represented the Saviour who died both for us and for our sins. He died for what we are as burnt offering. He died for our deeds as the trespass offering.

Golden Ex. 30:1-3 (c) This altar represents the Cross of Christ where the beautiful and perfect life of Christ was offered up to God as a sweet perfume and fragrant incense. The life of Christ which was perfect was offered to God instead of our lives which are so imperfect. It is typical also of the consecrated life of the believer from which there ascends to God as a sweet odor the sacrifices of our lips in thanksgiving, worship and praise.

Idol I Kings 18:26 (c) Here we may think of a false altar which is a type of the religious plans and schemes of men wherein they hope to appease the god of their imagination, and to obtain his favor even though what they are doing is not Scriptural.

False 2 Kings 16:10 (c) Here and elsewhere we find altars built ostensibly for the worship of God, but really for the worship of idols. These false altars are symbolical for the world's religious schemes and plans under the name of Christianity. Worldly men devise worldly plans for the worship of those who live in their sins, and yet seek a religious outlet for their feelings. Every false religion has an "altar" of this kind.

Deserted Psalm 84:3 (c) Here is brought before us clearly that God's people had forsaken both the worship and the service of the Lord to such an extent that the fires had gone out, the altar was cold, and no priest was near. The birds felt so much at home around these altars that they built their nests where the priests should have been serving, and the fires should have been burning.

Christian Matt. 5:23 (b) This probably teaches us that there is a place of worship called "the altar" to which the believer goes for worship, praise and prayer. It may be in the church building or in the home. When we come to this hallowed place, we are to come with a heart that is open and free from bitterness, free from spite, and free from grudges. We are to be a forgiving people if we expect forgiveness from heaven.

Unknown Acts 17:23 (a) This altar is probably typical of the false faiths by which people go through the motions of seeking and worshipping God, though their words and actions indicate clearly that they do not know Him, nor His character, nor His ways.

Heb. 13:10 (a) The word here probably represents the Lord's table, and all the holy associations which accompany the Gospel of Christ.

Rev. 8:3 (c) From this we learn that in some mysterious way there is such an altar in heaven. At that altar the fragrant incense of the prayers and the worship of Christians ascends to God and permeates heaven.

AMALEK

Gen. 36:12 (c) The meaning of this word is "a people that take away all." Originally Amalek was a grandson of Esau. Esau is a type of the flesh, and Amalek is also a type of the flesh which has no place in the economy of God. He was outside the family of God, and no effort was ever made to bring him into the family of

God. So the human flesh is at enmity with God. That which is born of the flesh remains flesh. The flesh never gets converted, and never becomes holy in itself. There is no help for the flesh found in the Scriptures.

Ex. 17:14 (c) Amalek was to be kept in subjection by Israel, and this is a type of our flesh which is to be kept in subjection by the people of God. As the flesh lusts against the Spirit (Gal. 5:17), so Amalek fought against Israel constantly, and the Lord declared that this battle was to continue and never cease.

Deut. 25:17 (c) Here again Amalek is represented as a type of Satan and of the flesh, both of which attack God's people, especially when they are weak, weary and sick. Those who lag behind in the service of the Lord thus separating themselves from Christians who are on the march, will find that this enemy Amalek will make inroads in their souls and lives.

AMASAI

I Chron. 12:18 (c) This man may be taken as a type of the believer who in utter consecration lays his all at the disposal of his Lord. He turns his back on the enemies of his Master. He casts in his lot with the people of God and with the Son of God who just now is despised and rejected by the world.

AMBASSADOR

2 Cor. 5:20 (a) This title is given to those Christians who carry God's message to a lost and hostile world. It probably does not apply to all believers for many of God's children are afraid to become His messengers, and they keep the good news to themselves The true ambassador comes out boldly for his king and for his country.

Eph. 6:20 (a) Paul used the title in this passage because he was representing heaven on earth. He carried the King's message to the rebels who were bent on killing him. He was God's representative to bring to men the Word of his Lord both for their salvation and their condemnation.

AMBER

Ezek. 1:4 (c) This seems to be a type of the golden glow which surrounds the person of God and presents to us in a graphic way the marvelous glory of His person. Human words do not very well describe divine glories.

AMEN

Rev. 3:14 (a) This word is a word of finality. Its actual meaning is "so be it." Christ takes this name to indicate the permanence of His decisions, the certainty of His program, and the finality of His judgment. The angels sang a song which begins and ends with this word. It is found in Rev. 7:12. There are seven glories in this prayer or song, and these describe the perfections of God. Nothing can be added to this revelation, and certainly nothing may be taken from it.

AMETHYST

Ex. 28:19 (c) This beautibul stone may be a type of the royalty and the regal splendor of those who belong to God. (See also under "TWELVE STONES" for additional meaning.)

ANANIAS

Acts 5:1 (a) This name means "graciously given of the Lord." The man in this passage proved to be one who lied to God. He had received many blessings from God and much prosperity, but he was not honest in his heart. He saw that Barnabas was highly esteemed because of his unselfish gift to the disciples. He wanted this same praise without paying the same price. The world speaks of the "Ananias Club." This Ananias represents those people who are known as proverbial liars, and whose word is always questioned.

Acts 9:10 (a) This man is a different Ananias. He was a good man who was ready to do God's will. He is a type of that servant of God who is ready to do that which he dreads naturally, and is willing to go on a moment's notice on any errand that God may request. This is a good "Ananias Club" to join.

Acts 24:1 (a) This Ananias is still a third man, not the same one as the other two. He was a high priest of Israel, and is a type of one who gains great ascendancy in a religious organization, but is an enemy of grace, is opposed to Jesus as Lord, and seeks to turn men's hearts away from the Truth into a false religion.

ANCHOR

Heb. 6:19 (a) This figure represents the firm hold that faith has in the Rock of Ages. This Rock is inside the veil with God. Our faith reaches through the waters of trouble, difficulty, darkness and despair to firmly grasp the Son of God and His Word. By this faith we are kept from being swept away in the storms of life.

ANKLE

Ezek. 47:3 (b) The river in this passage is a type of the Holy Spirit. and the ankles represent the walk of the child of God. As the Holy Spirit enters the life of the believer his walk is changed. No longer does he travel in the ways of the world, but rather he is led to the house of God, and led to walk among the people of

God. This is one of the first proofs that a man has contacted the Lord Jesus in faith, been cleansed by the blood of the Lamb, and has become influenced by the Holy Spirit who is the Living Water.

ANDREW

John 1:40 (c) This good man is typical of the believer who, in the zeal of his new experience with Christ goes out after his brother to bring him to the same Saviour. He became a fisher of men and his first catch for Christ was Peter.

John 12:22 (c) Here we find a picture of one who had the reputation of being able to bring men to Christ. He was ready to carry the petitions of men to the willing ears of the Lord. This should arouse our desire to be like him.

ANGEL

Gen. 16:7 (b) This heavenly person probably was the Holy Spirit of God because He is the Lord of the harvest. Some think that this person was the Lord Jesus. Since the Holy Spirit is the Lord of the harvest, it seems that this person must be the Spirit, because the passage refers to the harvest of lives that was to follow in Hagar's experience. It certainly is one of the Persons of the Godhead, because He said in verse 10 "I will multiply thy seed." In verse 13 she calls Him Lord. This indicates clearly that He was one of the persons of the Trinity. The name that she gave to this Lord was El-Shaddai which means "The God of the Breast," or "The God who is enough."

Gen. 22:11 (c) This person was probably a genuine angel out of heaven. He lays no claim to deity, and does not affirm his authority to do anything. The message in verse 16 of this chapter evidently is a quotation of the God of heaven, and is not a message from the angel. Some, however, think that the angel in verse 15 is one of the persons of the Godhead, and that He Himself was making the statement found in verse 16.

Gen. 24:40 (b) Here the angel is undoubtedly the Holy Spirit who leads the child of God in the ways of the Lord and brings about His desire in the world. This would seem to be confirmed by the statement in verse 7 of this chapter.

Gen. 48:16 (a) This portion brings before us the three Persons of the Trinity. The first mention of God in verse 15 refers to the Father. The second mention of God probably refers to the Holy Spirit. The third mention in which we read "The angel which redeemed" must be the Lord Jesus. The Jews in Old Testament days were Trinitarians. They all believed that there were three persons in the Godhead. Not until several centuries after Christ did the Jews become Unitarians. Most Jews have always believed that God had a Son who was to be the Messiah. They did not believe, however, that Jesus was that Son.

Judges 5:23 (b) This angel undoubtedly was the Holy Spirit. His message was in reference to the failure of the inhabitants of Meroz to come to the help of Barak when Israel was fighting the Canaanites. We must remember that the Holy Spirit curses as well as blesses. We find this truth in Isa. 40:7, as well as in other places.

Acts 8:26 (b) This one was probably the Holy Spirit who directed Philip as to his new place of service. Philip had just conducted a great campaign which was most successful, but now the Spirit took him away from that work to deal with one man down on the road to Gaza. Verse 29 indicates clearly that it was the Holy Spirit who was directing Philip in all his service and ministry. We would expect Him to do so because He is the Lord of the harvest.

Acts 10:7 (a) The angel who spoke to Cornelius was the Holy Spirit. Verse 30 reveals that this one was in the form of a man, looked like a man, had the shape of a man, and wore the clothing of a man. The angel in verse 7 who was the man in verse 30 is identified in verse 19 as the Holy Spirit. As the Lord of the harvest He told the seeking sinner Cornelius to send for the evangelist Peter. The Spirit came to Peter who wanted to be used of God and told him where to go to find a troubled soul. The Spirit said to Peter "Behold, three men seek thee; go down with them doubting nothing, for I sent them." The Holy Spirit Himself identifies the man in bright clothing as being Himself. The Spirit of God has a human form, as do the other two persons of the Trinity. He was seen plainly and rather frequently in both the days of the Old Testament and the New.

2 Cor. 11:14 (a) The passage clearly states that Satan, the Devil, is an angel of light. He takes the place of being a very good and holy person. He is called a minister of righteousness. His business is to get people to be good in order to be saved. He leads men to devise and design many kinds of religion to keep sinners away from the Saviour. He leads women to invent religions of an aesthetic character which presents beautiful phraseology, and sweet, lovely ideas, all of which is intended to keep the hearts and lives of the people away from Jesus Christ and His saving power. He never suggests that anyone will be saved by getting drunk, or gambling, or living wickedly. He knows very well that this philosophy would not appeal to the human mind. He therefore sets about to arrange a religion of good works and self-righteousness as a substitute for the Person and work of the Lord Jesus. We should be on the watch for every religion that exalts man's goodness, and detracts from the personal glory of Christ Jesus.

Heb. 13:2 (b) The angels referred to in this passage possibly may be the Lord Jesus and the Holy Spirit. They must have been the ones who came to visit Abraham and afterwards went to Sodom. They accepted the worship of Abraham and therefore they seemed to be two persons of the Trinity. It is not at all clear who the third person was. He might have been one of the archangels or another angel. Some think that all three Persons of the Trinity were there.

Rev. 1:20 (b) This word is probably the title given to the leader or the shepherd or the pastor of each of the seven churches mentioned in chapters 2 and 3. The messages were sent to these seven men who in turn were to instruct the church concerning God's Word. It seems as though the leader is held responsible to obtain special messages from God for the people that compose the flock.

ANGLE

Isaiah 19:8 (b) This action indicates that when God cursed Egypt then their labors for food and for the necessities of life would be fruitless. They would have difficulty obtaining those things which they needed for daily use. They were enemies of God, therefore His curse was upon them.

Hab. 1:15 (b) The action in this passage may be taken to mean that there are treacherous dealers who will be caught by the wicked either on their hook or in their net to their own sorrow and destruction. Because the wicked are successful in capturing their prey, they exalt and glorify the methods which they use. In the present day this may be a picture of the methods and programs used by false religious leaders to gain adherents

ANOINT

Ex. 28:41 (b). This act was a picture of that which happens to a believer who gives himself wholly and without reserve to the service of the Lord. The oil represents the Holy Spirit; the priest who applies it represents either the Father or the Lord Jesus. The believer who yields himself to God a living and willing sacrifice becomes Spirit-filled, Spirit-led, and has the unction of the Spirit upon him.

Psalm 23:5 (b) This indicates that gracious act of the Lord whereby David was caused to rejoice in being a chosen vessel of God. He thus was made to serve as a priest upon behalf of the people, and to serve as a king under the good hand of God.

Luke 4:18 (b) Here the word refers to that blessed anointing of our gracious Saviour wherein He was selected by God and appointed by Him to be the Lord of our lives and the Saviour of our souls.

2 Cor. 1:21 (a) This anointing refers to the gracious gift of the Holy Spirit to the child of God. The Spirit gives enabling power, wisdom and knowledge for the service of God, and for His glory.

I John 2:27 (a) The anointing spoken of here is that mysterious, indescribable and indispensable unction of the Holy Spirit whereby one becomes a real, true, active, earnest servant of God.

ANT

Prov. 6:6 (c) The ways and the actions of this little creature are brought before us as a lesson and a picture for our own lives. The ant is tireless, never ceasing to work. It is unselfish, always laying up food for others. It is kind, helping other ants that are in need. It is energetic, for it searches continually until it finds the food it wants. It is wise in that it prepares for the future when ice and snow will prevent foraging for food. In all of these things, we too should seek these same graces that we may not be careless and lose that reward which God wishes to give to us.

Prov. 30:25 (c) The ant in this portion is a type of those who recognize and realize their own weakness and danger. They remind us that we too are no match for our enemies and are unable to control our circumstances. They cannot prevent the winter from coming, but they do provide for that future time of storm. So we should remember that there is a coming time when old age, disease, accident and trouble may prevent us too from serving or from earning that which we need. We should prepare for that eventuality now while we may. We must prepare now in this life for death and eternity. As the ant lays up in store in its earthen nest, so we take advantage of the shelter of the Rock of Ages, and lay up treasure in heaven.

APPAREL

Isa. 3:22 (b) It is evident that the garments referred to in this passage represent and are types of the outward show with which hypocrites adorn themselves, thinking that this outward pretense and sham will influence our Lord in the time of His judgment. White feathers may cover a black skin.

Isa. 63:1-2 (b) This apparel of the Lord Himself tells us something of the story of His character. The red garments are a public announcement that the Lord God of heaven will trample His enemies under foot so that the blood will stain His garments. It is an announcement that He will not forever tolerate rebellion in the hearts of men. He will tread the winepress and shed the blood of the enemies in His anger and wrath. Christ wears that same apparel (Rev. 19:13). He wears this red garment when He comes back to earth to rule the nations with a rod of iron, and God will make His enemies His footstool.

Zeph. 1:8 (b) The word in this passage probably refers to false doctrines, false beliefs, and false faiths. In the New Testament this same truth is presented in Matt. 22, in the case of the man who wore his own garment when he should have worn the king's garment.

APPLE

Deut. 32:10 (a) The apple of the eye is the eyeball. It is very sensitive, is easily injured, and is very valuable to its owner. The expression is used as a type of the nation of Israel, which was, and is, so precious to God.

Psalm 17:8 (a) Here the Psalmist himself takes the place of being the apple of God's eye. He felt that he was so easily hurt by his enemies, and yet was so valuable to God that he dared to use that type to illustrate his own position before God.

Prov. 7:2 (a) The Law of God is here presented as being just as precious as the apple of the eye, and should therefore be guarded and preserved most carefully.

Lam. 2:18 (a) Probably the expression here represents a call from God to esteem their position as children of God, and the nation of God more highly than they were doing. Surely if Israel remembered that they were as the apple of God's eye, they would not cease weeping until they were again obeying and worshiping Him.

Zech. 2:8 (a) God is evidently notifying the world that the nation of Israel is unusually dear and precious to Him, and that He will protect that nation from every enemy. Those who touch Israel in any way to hurt them will in fact put their finger into the eye of God.

APRON

Gen. 3:7 (c) The fig leaves used by Adam and Eve are called aprons which cover only a part of the body, and are not sufficient for a complete covering. The fig leaf is soft like velvet, and under the heat of the sun shrinks to about one-forth of the original size. These leaves are a type of self-righteousness. After Adam and Eve made the fig leaf aprons they still hid from God knowing that they were still naked in His sight. No amount of self-righteous religion, church attendance, giving of money, or religious acts is sufficient to hide the sins of the heart from the face of God.

ARCHER

Gen. 49:23 (a) The word is used here to represent the ten brothers of Joseph and also Potiphar's wife and other enemies who sought to injure and in fact to kill Joseph. They were instruments of Satan to prevent the execution of God's plans.

Job 16:13 (b) The word is used in this passage to describe those who find fault with God's people. These enemies speak evil of God's servants and seek to damage God's children. The wicked words that they speak to and about the Christian are likened to arrows shot by the archer.

Jer. 51:3 (b) This is a type of God's own people who are instructed to spare no effort in attacking "Babylon." Babylon is a type of false religions (see under "BABYLON"). God's people are told to shoot at her, and spare no arrows. The true Christian should never lose an opportunity to expose the evils of the false religious sects who deceive the people and hold them in darkness and superstition.

ARK

Gen. 6:14-18 (c) This boat may be taken as a type of the Lord Jesus in His Calvary experience. As the ark was under the deluge of the downpouring rain, so the Lord Jesus suffered under the rolling billows of God's terrible wrath. This experience of Christ He calls a baptism in Luke 12:50. As those who were in the ark were saved from drowning, so those who are in Christ Jesus are saved from the wrath of God. It is the baptism of the Lord Jesus under God's anger and wrath, as described in 1 Pet. 3:20-21, by which we are saved. We are saved by baptism, but it is Jesus' baptism, and not ours.

Ex. 25:10 (c) This ark is a type of the Lord Jesus as God's perfect Son (represented by the gold), and yet a perfect man (represented by the acacia wood). The wood represented the humanity of Christ, and the golden covering both inside and outside the ark represented the deity of Christ. His perfect Godhead, and His perfect manhood are shown by the fact that the gold covered both the inside and the outside, and revealed also the purity of His outward actions and His innermost thoughts. In Him there dwelt the law of God perfectly, the priesthood of God fully, and the bread of God abundantly. He is God's mercy seat; God meets the sinner in Christ.

ARM

Ex. 6:6 (b) God's arm is used to represent His mighty power which no one can withstand. The arm "made bare" (Isa. 53:1) really represents an arm on which the sleeve has been rolled up to reveal the muscles there. The same truth is found in

Deut. 4:4. God does not always reveal His love, tenderness, patience and kindness. Sometimes He manifests His anger, His mighty power, and His ability to destroy.

I Ki. 8:42 (a) The arm in this passage represents God's unusual, miraculous work in delivering His people from enemies who were stronger and more cruel than they. It also represents His power to meet every need of Israel, and making of them a great and powerful nation. (See also Deut. 33:27)

I Peter 4:1 (b) To arm oneself is to be equipped with a knowledge of God, and of His Word in such a way that one is able to meet the arguments and antagonism of God's enemies successfully and intelligently.

ARMHOLES

Ezek. 13:18 (b) These are used as a picture of the carelessness and indolence of those who should have been actively engaged in restoring Israel to the Lord. The women were helping the men to be lazy and careless when the terrible condition of Israel should have aroused them to activity for God.

ARMOUR

1 Sam. 17:54 (c) This may be taken as a type of rejecting ability, skill, gift and manners of another person, rather than being one's own self. When we serve our Lord we should not try to be like another by imitating his ways, manners, virtues and powers.

Isa. 22:8 (c) This armor represents human powers made by human instruments for human purposes and relied upon instead of the armor of God which only He can provide.

Luke 11:22 (b) In this place the armor represents Satan's devices, arguments and reasonings which he gives to his children in order to keep them from being touched by the sword of the Spirit, which is the Word of God. Satan fills his followers with his own line of reasonings to keep them from becoming Christians. The Lord Jesus and the Holy Spirit who are stronger than Satan take away this armor and make way for the truth of God to enter the soul of the sinner.

Rom. 13:12 (b) Here the word is used for the protecting influence of light in the life of the children of God. A light is kept burning over the cash register to keep away robbers. The Christian should walk in the light of the Word of God in order to defeat Satan.

2 Cor. 6:7 (b) Here the armor represents a life of righteousness toward those whom we meet and toward God. Those who live right have no fear of accusers. They are protected from the attacks of the enemy.

Eph. 6:11 (b) The armor mentioned in this passage presents aspects of Christ: (1) We are to put on the Lord Jesus Christ (Rom. 13:14). (2) Christ Himself is the truth (John 14:6). (3) Christ Himself is our righteousness (I Cor. 1:30). (4) The gospel of peace is concerning His Son (Rom. 1:1-13) who is the king of peace (Heb. 7:2). (5) Our faith is in the Lord Jesus Christ (Acts 20:21). (6) Christ is our salvation (Luke 2:30). (7) The sword is the Word which comes from the mouth of our Lord Jesus Christ (Rev. 19:15). The helmet protects our thinking. The breastplate protects our feelings.

ARMY

Joel 2:25 (b) This word is used to describe the great hordes of locusts, caterpillars and palmer worms which God sent as a punishment on Israel.

ARRAY

Jer. 43:12 (a) When Nebuchadnezzar conquered Egypt and added it to his magnificent kingdom, God speaks of it as though the king had put on another and expensive garment. This addition was to add to the glory of the king.

ARROW

Deut. 32:23 (b) These arrows may be God's terrible judgment which He sent upon the people because of their idolatry and rebellion. (See also Num. 24:8; Zech. 9:14.)

2 Kings 13:17 (a) Here the arrow represents the power, wisdom and love of God in finding a certain and sure way of delivering the people of God from their enemies.

Job 6:4 (b) The misfortunes which God permitted to come upon Job are described as arrows.

Psalm 11:2 (a) Here the arrow represents wicked devices and evil words which the wicked use against the righteous. (See also Psalm 91:5; Prov. 25:18)

Psalm 64:7 (b) The calamity which God Himself will bring suddenly and swiftly upon His enemies is described as "arrows."

Psalm 127:4 (a) These arrows represent the children of great men who, under the training of the parents, become alert, skillful and educated men, who may be used abundantly in God's great business.

Jer. 9:8 (a) The tongue that speaks deceitfully and makes evil statements about another is described as a sharp arrow that wounds and hurts.

ASCEND

Psalm 24:3 (c) This action represents the progress of the Christian as he grows in grace, godliness and usefulness.

ASH (tree)

Isa. 44:14 (b) This tree represents the established works of men which become their idols. It may be a great, solid, substantial business, in which a man's money, fame and fortune leave him no time for God. He makes a god out of that enterprise which he has built up by his ingenuity, persistence and effort.

ASHES

Gen. 18:27 (a) By the use of this word Abraham is expressing to God his own utter worthlessness and lowliness as though he were not even worth any consideration from God.

2 Sam. 13:19 (b) Ashes on the head was typical of deep shame and mental anguish as well as repentance and sorrow.

Job 2:8 (c) The disease which afflicted Job was probably the one which we know as elephantiasis. Potash is the remedy for that disease. Job sat in the ash pile so that the potash would continually cover his limbs, and thereby he would recover.

Job 13:12 (b) These ashes represent references made by Job's comforters to the glory which he once had, but now had lost. They kept reminding him of his former position of power and wealth, which had now become a pile of ashes.

Job 42:6 (a) Job not only sat in actual ashes, but those mentioned in this passage represent also his feeling of great humility and shame. He seemed to realize his utter worthlessness before God. All of this sad experience and loss which he suffered he calls "ashes." (See also Jer. 6:26; Lam. 3:16; Ezek. 28:18; Dan. 9:3)

Isa. 44:20 (b) This refers to those who had great plenty at one time but afterwards lost their wealth. They feed on their losses, they meditate on these sorrows, they talk about the tragedies in their lives, they live on the "ashes" that are left after the destruction of their former glory and wealth. Many people talk constantly of what they once were, or what they once had.

Isa. 61:3 (b) The ashes in this passage represent the wreck of former beauty and the tragic end of former loveliness. There are those who at one time were sweet and delightful in their lives, but through calamity have been made bitter and sorrowful. When these turn back to the Lord, He restores His joy to their hearts, and His beauty to their lives.

Mal. 4:3 (b) This word is used to describe the utter and complete defeat of everything in this world that is of the Devil. The Lord will destroy the works of the Devil and will cause His people to triumph in Christ.

ASLEEP

Acts 7:60 (b) Christians who die are said to "fall asleep." This expression is used in regard to saints who die. The reason is plain; the body of the Christian will come forth from the grave to walk again with God. The body of the sinner will never be permitted to walk again in the enjoyment of God's blessings, but will awake to shame and everlasting contempt. He will be brought into God's presence for judgment at the Great White Throne, and will then be cast into outer darkness, which is the Lake of Fire.

I Cor. 15:6-18 (b) The meaning in this passage is similar to the one above. When we think of a person being asleep, we know that he will soon waken to live and walk with his loved ones. So it shall be with the believer. His very body will be raised and will be reunited with his circle of loved ones whom he knew on earth, and who were saved by grace. (See also "SLEEP.")

ASP

Deut. 32:33 (a) The effect of liquor on the soul is compared to the poison that comes from the bite of the serpent. It contaminates the blood, it affects every part of the body, it ends in death.

Job 20:14 (a) The feeling expressed by Job caused his friends to say that he was feeding from the poison that comes from the snake. Job was considering and meditating in his heart the things that were bitter, harsh and evil in his life.

Rom. 3:13 (b) This refers to the teaching and the ministry of false religious teachers whose doctrines are of the Devil. The messages which come from their mouths are as poison and they damage those who hear them. (See also Matt. 3:7.)

ASS

Gen. 49:14 (a) Here we have a type of the consecrated believer who is willing to be a burden bearer for God and for man. He bears the burdens of God's people, and carries them to God. He bears the burden of God's message, and carries it to the people. He realizes that a path of rest and peace is good for God's people, and he wants to share in the work of making it possible.

This may also be a type of the Lord Jesus Himself. Certainly He is our burden bearer; he bears the burden of our relationship to God, and also our relationship to other people. He too sees that rest is good, and calls on us to cast every burden upon Him, so that we may be free ourselves to carry the burdens of others. Certainly this is a wonderful picture of the ministry of Christ Jesus, our Lord. (See Matt. 11:28.)

Ex. 13:13 (c) The ass in this passage is typical of the sinner who must be redeemed by the death of the Lamb of God, or else be himself lost under the judgment of God.

Job 11:12 (a) The ass represents the unsaved parent who gives birth to an unsaved child (the colt). The thought of being "wild" is that the natural man wants no restraint nor does he want to be hindered in his movements. We see this plainly in the little child who wants to do as he pleases on his earliest days. It is carried out through life unless the restraining power of God is brought to bear upon him.

Isa. 1:3 (b) This ass is a type of the unsaved person and of any who are not interested in God but only want His blessings and His gifts. The ox in the passage is a type of the believer who loves the Lord and cares more for the giver than for the gift.

Zech. 9:9 (c) This ass, as the one in John 12:14, represents the believer, who being set free from his old bondage carries the Lord Jesus about wherever he goes so that others may see and know Him.

ASS (taken from "Number in Scripture")

"The 'ass' is the only animal that man is compared to: see Job 11:12, 'For vain man would be wise, though man be born a wild ass's colt.'

"In Ex. 13:13, the first-born of man is classed with the firstling of an ass. Both must be redeemed with a lamb. This is repeated in Ex. 34:20. Nothing less than a sacrificial redemptive act could bring such a being to God.

"There are 28 (4 x 7) asses separately spoken of, and with these may be compared the 28 (4 x 7) 'times' connected with 'vain man' in Eccles. 3:1-8."

1. Balaam's ass (Num. 22:21), "a time to speak."

2. Achsah's ass (Josh. 15:18), "a time to get," when she lighted off her ass to make her request and get what she asked.

3. Samson's (Judg. 15:15), "a time to war."

4. The Levite's (Judg. 19:28), "a time to be silent," when "none answered," and he sent his desperate, silent message throughout Israel.

5. Abigail's (I Sam. 25:20), "a time of peace," when she met David and made peace for Nabal.

6. Her second ass (v. 42), "a time to love," when she went to meet David and became his wife.

7. Ahithophel's (2 Sam 17:23), "a time to die," when he saddled his ass and went and hanged himself.

8. The "old prophet's" ass (I Kings 13:23, 24), "a time to kill," when he found "the man of God" killed by the lion.

9. The "man of God's" ass (v. 29), "a time to mourn," when the old prophet laid him thereon "to mourn and to bury him."

10. The Shunamite's ass (2 Kings 4:24-37), "a time to heal," when she rode to Elisha, who restored her son.

11. Mephibosheth's (2 Sam. 19:26), "a time to embrace," when he would go and salute David.

12. Shimei's (1 Kings 2:40-46), "a time to die."

13. Jesse's (1 Sam. 16:20), "a time to live" (21).

14. Moses' (Ex. 4:20-26), "a time to kill," when he incurred the judgment of Gen. 17:14, and fulfilled the truth.

15. Abraham's (Gen. 22:3), "a time to get and a time to lose," when God demanded back the son He had given.

16. The Saviour's ass (Matt. 21:5, 9), "a time to laugh," when the daughter of Jerusalem rejoiced.

17. The young, its foal (Matt. 21:5).

18-28. The asses of Jacob's sons (Gen. 44:13), filling up the other "times."

ASTRAY

Psalm 58:3 (a) The tendency to commit sin and to deceive which is inherent in the human heart from birth, this is to go "astray" from God.

Psalm 119:176 (a) Here we see the sinner's path which is not along the path of God's righteousness nor according to His commandments.

Jer. 50:6 (a) This represents the path of wrong teaching into which people are led by false shepherds.

ATHIRST

Rev. 21:6 (b) This describes the heart hunger of those who seek satisfaction from the cisterns of this world which do not and cannot satisfy the craving of the soul. The same meaning is found in Rev. 22:17.

ATONEMENT

Ex. 29:36 (b) The word literally means "to cover up." The blood of the sacrifies in the Old Testament did cover up the sins of the believers, but not until Christ shed His blood were the sins blotted out. (See also Rom. 3:25.)

AUTHOR

Heb. 5:9 (a) Christ designed, planned and executed salvation "by Himself." He presents this salvation as a gift to all who will receive Him. All other forms of "salvation" are an invention of some man or some woman, and only lead to the outer dark.

Heb. 12:2 (a) Christ produces faith in the heart as we look upon Him, think about Him, read about Him, and talk with Him. His very person causes us to believe in Him fully, and to trust in Him implicitly.

AWAKE

Psalm 44:23 (b) David speaks to God as though He were not listening and indicates that he would like to ask God to wake up and listen to the call of his heart. David was on very intimate terms with God, and sometimes asked God to wake up, sometimes to "listen," sometimes to bow down His ear, and sometimes to talk to him.

Isa. 52:1 (b) Here there is a call to the people of earth to wake up from their slumber of indifference, and to realize the wonderful gift of the garments of salvation which are offered to them. This applies particularly to Israel.

Zech. 13:7 (a) Here there is a call to God as though the sword of God, which is His wrath, were sleeping. The Lord calls on this sword to rouse itself, waken from sleep, and pierce the heart of the Lord Jesus, thus making Him the Saviour of men. The death of Christ on the cross was planned by God Himself. Christ bore the sword of God's wrath so that we might go free and be saved from wrath through Him.

Rom. 13:11 (a) The Lord's people are represented as not being active and earnest in their work and as though they were asleep in the battlefield. God asks His people to awaken from their slumber and to prepare for His coming.

Eph. 5:14 (a) In this passage the people of God have become so like the unsaved around them, who are dead in their sins, and unresponsive to God, that the Lord says His people are asleep and just as indifferent as the ungodly. It is a call to the Christian to become wide awake, alert and watchful in the service of the Master.

AWL

Ex. 21:6 (c) This may be taken to represent the permanent attaching of the saved sinner to the purposes, the person, and the service of Jesus Christ, his new Lord and Master. The ear represents the hearing or the listening for commands. There surely comes a time in the life of the believer when he decides definitely to give his whole attention, effort and work to the Master who has purchased him with His blood. (See also Psalm 40:6)

AX

Isa. 10:15 (a) This is a type of person or a nation whom God uses to punish other people or nations. Assyria was the ax in this case (v. 5) and God's hand and arm wielded the ax. Assyria is also compared to a saw, a rod, and a staff. All of these are just different aspects of the one nation of Assyria in the hand of God for the punishment of others. (See under "BATTLE AX.")

Matt. 3:10 (b) Here the ax is a type of God's judgment which will cut down the nation of Israel because of their disobedience and fruitlessness. This ax of God's wrath also cuts down individuals whose lives are not profitable to God. (See also Jer. 51:20)

B

BABE

Heb. 5:13 (a) This is typical of the child of God who has not grown in grace through the years, but must be fed on the simplest things of the Scriptures because he cannot understand the deep things of God. The same truth is found in 1 Cor. 3:1-2.

BABYLON

Jer. 50:14 (b) Throughout chapters 50 and 51 of this book, the actual city of Babylon is directly in view, but what is said about that city indicates clearly that it refers to the great religions and idolatries of the world which seek to depose God and enthrone their own philosophies. This is particularly true of chapter 51, verses 6 and 8 which evidently refer to the same situation that we find in the New Testament.

Rev. 17:5 (b) This is plainly a type of the great false religious systems of the world, particularly Romanism, which know nothing of the grace of God, nor the blood of Christ, nor the personal ministry of the Holy Spirit. It refers to those religious sects and heresies which deny the faith of our fathers, and reject the truth of God. This Babylon is represented as a woman.

Rev. 18:2 (b) As in the above Scripture we see the religious side of false religions so in this verse we find the political aspect of those great apostate religions, the political religious world. Under this description we see the wickedness of the merchants, the politics of the church, and the filthiness of her society which are all to be brought under the judgment of God. We should note that in chapter 18, verse 13, the last two items of merchandise of this great apostate religious group consists of slaves (bodies and souls of men). This is particularly true of the Romish church, whose members are slaves in body, soul and spirit to their religious leaders. This Babylon is described as a city in verse 16.

BACA

Psalm 84:6 (b) The word means "weeping," a picture of a dry, dead church or community which becomes spiritually awakened and enriched by the ministry of a Spirit-filled servant of God.

BACK

Jer. 18:17 (a) This represents the attitude of God in refusing to answer or to come to their help when idolatrous Israel was in trouble.

Jer. 32:33 (a) The word is used here to describe the attitude of Israel in refusing to listen to God or to bow to His commands.

BADGER (See under "SKINS")

BAG

Job 14:17 (a) We are to learn from this that God is keeping a careful record of every sin, none are overlooked, none are forgotten. Each one is preserved by God against the record of the sinner unless all of them are blotted out by the precious blood of Jesus.

Hag. 1:6 (b) This represents a business that failed, stocks and bonds that lose their value, barrenness in the fields caused by crop failure, the loss of sheep and cattle — generally speaking, the failure of those enterprises into which God's people put their money instead of giving it to Him. Those who rob God of that which is His due, will not profit by that which they save.

John 12:6 (a) Judas was the treasurer for the disciples and was stealing from the fund entrusted to his care. It is a lesson to us not to misuse that which belongs to the Lord, and which is in our possession for safekeeping.

BALAAM

2 Pet. 2:15 (b) This man is typical of one who claims to be a servant of God and is sometimes used of God, but for the sake of prominence and prosperity is willing to lead his flock astray and to invite worldliness to come in among the members.

Jude 11 (b) The meaning is somewhat the same as mentioned above. Balaam was willing to go wrong and do wrong so long as he received ample payment for his services. This is typical of modern-day preachers who will promote and permit wicked, worldly things and who will teach error because of the pay they receive from those who like to hear them. Read Num. 22 and 23.

Rev. 2:14 (b) Here we see a type of those in the church who invite unsaved men of the world to bring in their ideas and to lead the church to engage in things which are not according to the Scriptures, and which are quite opposed to the will of God.

BALANCES

Job. 6:2 (b) Job is indicating that God knows just how heavy each burden is and each sorrow. For this reason He knows just how much His servants can bear.

Job 31:6 (b) This figure is used to illustrate the way God estimates man's activities and motives. Only He knows the true value of our lives.

Isa. 40:12 (a) God must arrange the exact amount of weight in every part of the earth in order to keep an even balance, so that the earth may rotate on its axis evenly. He has done so and knows the exact weight of every mountain, hill and ocean.

Ezek. 5:1 (b) Here we see how God notices the smallest person and the smallest sin. He is interested in every detail of life and knows how important each movement is, whether right or wrong.

Dan. 5:27 (b) This represents God's judgment in heaven wherein He weighed the life of the king on one side of the scales, and the just demands of the law on the other side. Of course, each life in every person is found wanting and not sufficient to meet God's holy requirements. We must have the imputed righteousness and righteous life which God gives to those who belong to Jesus Christ by faith.

Rev. 6:5 (b) Here is a symbol of God's careful adjustment of earthly supplies to man's needs. In this particular case the supply was greatly cut down as a punishment on the wicked people.

BALD

Deut. 14:1 (a) Baldness in this Scripture would indicate that the people were opposed to God's judgments and God's dealings and would prove it to others by making themselves bald. (See also Isa. 22:12)

Isa. 3:24 (a) This is a sign that God had forsaken His people and left them to the will of their enemies. (See also Jer. 47:5; Isa. 15:2; Ezek. 7:18)

Jer. 16:6 (b) This is a type of despair in sorrow for which there is no remedy.

Jer. 48:37 (b) This represents great sorrow and deep grief; the loss of the hair being used as a type of long, weary lamenting.

BALM

Jer. 8:22 (b) This ointment is a figure of God's mercy and loving kindness toward His people. His precious promises are all sweet provisions to heal every hurt of the heart of His people. The words of God which bring comfort and hope are for mending the wounds which sin and Satan make.

Jer. 46:11 (a) Here we understand that there will come a time when God's healing ointment of His Word will not avail to mend the wounds of those who deliberately turn away from God.

Jer. 51:8 (a) We understand by this that God does have healing remedies even for His enemies, though they do not want His lovely provision for the needs of their hearts.

BANDS

Lev. 26:13 (a) These are hindrances and restraints placed upon the people of Israel by their Egyptian taskmasters. (See also Psalm 107:14; Jer. 2:20.)

Job 38:31 (a) There seems to be some strange, unknown influence issuing from these stars which we do not understand or comprehend.

Job 39:5 (b) Here we understand that there is no hindrance of any kind to the wickedness of the wicked as represented by the actions of this animal. This figure would indicate that there is no way of hindering the sinful actions of men except, of course, by the power and grace of God.

Psalm 2:3 (a) This is typical of the restraining laws and commandments of God wherein He curbs and retards the evil passions and cruel powers of wicked men. These heathen say that they will throw off all such restraint.

Psalm 73:4 (c) We learn from this that many wicked men die in peace with no fear of God, and no fear of punishment.

Eccles. 7:26 (b) This is a figure of the tremendous, attractive power of the evil woman who holds in the chains of sin those who yield to her evil attractions.

Isa. 28:22 (a) This solemn warning is to inform us that the evil habits of life will be made permanent if the evildoer persists in his path instead of coming to the Lord for salvation.

Isa. 52:2 (b) These bands represent the things that hinder the child of God from being a free, happy servant of the Lord. (See also Isa. 58:6.)

Ezek. 34:27 (a) This is a type of the restraints and hindrances now imposed upon Israel throughout the world by their Gentile rulers.

Hosea 11:4 (a) These are love bands that hold us to our Lord with strong cords which nothing can break.

Zech. 11:14 (a) This possibly and probably refers to the influence of relatives either good or bad. Frequently relatives are like chains around the neck to keep one from running the race for the Lord, or walking with God.

Col. 2:19 (b) This interesting use of the word teaches us that some of God's people have a ministry of restraint and hindrance which prevents enthusiastic leaders in the church from going too far, or getting out of joint. Every joint must move freely, but it must have ligaments and bands so that it will not move too far. This particular ministry is given to some of God's people.

BANNER

Psalm 60:4 (a) Evidently this is the confession which a Christian makes; it is the testimony which he bears to the truth of God and to his faith in his Lord. (See also Psalm 20:5)

S. of Sol. 2:4 (c) This banner represents the leadership of the Lord in the lives of His people. Under His guidance they march along firmly convinced and fully persuaded that everything that happens to them comes from the loving heart of their Lord.

S. of Sol. 6:4 (c) In a war where the army is composed of many allies, each nation carries its own banner, thus displaying the great resources behind the forces. In this passage the banner indicates the many divisions of God's gracious provision for his own. There is the banner of His power and also of His love, and also of His sufficiency, and also of His grace.

Isa. 13:2 (a) Probably this banner indicates that Babylon must be exposed and advertised in her true colors. Her character must be plainly manifested. It may refer actually to the city of Babylon, or it may refer to the false Babylon, which is the Roman church. and her daughters.

BANQUET

S. of Sol. 2:4 (c) A type of the happy condition of the heart of one who sits in the presence of God to feast on the precious truths of His Word, and to enjoy the blessings of His ministry.

BAPTISM

Matt. 3:11 (b) Two baptisms seem to be included in this passage. The first is the baptism of the believer in the Holy Spirit. The second one seems to be the baptism of the sinner in the lake of fire from which there is no resurrection. The Lord Jesus gives us over to the Holy Spirit when He saves us, and this seems to be called a baptism as in Acts 1:5. We should note that it is never the element that is moved, but always the person. The water is not put on the person, but contrariwise the person is always put in the water. It is the person who is put in the Spirit, or in the body of Christ, which is the church. It is always the person who is moved and placed in baptism.

Luke 3:21 (c) The baptism of Jesus certainly had nothing whatever to do with salvation, nor the new birth, nor forgiveness. He said that He did it "to fulfill all righteousness." He took His place publicly by this rite with those who were to walk in newness of life and be known as Christians, believers or saints of God.

Luke 7:29-30 (b) A type of burial wherein the believer accepts God's condemnation of himself, admits that he had to die at Calvary, and therefore should be buried out of sight in a watery grave. Thus he justifies God's diagnosis of his case, and proves it by going through this symbolical burial. Those who refuse to be baptised thereby reject God's testimony about their wickedness and sinfulness. They refuse to admit that they are so bad that they should be put to death and buried.

Luke 12:50 (a) This is the baptism of our Lord Jesus which He endured on the cross when God poured out His wrath upon Him and engulfed Him as it were in the burning billows of His anger. He had already been baptised by John in the water. Now He is baptised in the mystic fire of God's wrath. It was said by Him in prophecy "all thy waves and thy billows rolled over me." That is the baptism that saves us. He went down under the flood instead of us. He was baptised there at Calvary in our place. He is the ark of safety into which we enter for protection from the deluge of God's anger against sin.

Rom. 6:3 (b) This baptism seems to represent that mysterious and rich experience which any person enjoys in the Lord Jesus. Immediately upon trusting Christ the believer is reckoned as having been baptised in or buried with the Lord Jesus in contrast with his former position of being buried in the world. The believer is said to be "in Christ," whereas, before, he was "in the world."

1 Cor. 10:2 (b) This is the baptism accomplished in the Red Sea when the walls of water on each side, and the cloud above hid Israel from the sight of the Egyptians. They went through what was apparently a tunnel, and this is called a baptism. They were set free from the domination of Pharaoh into the leadership of Moses. They were released from the bondage of Egypt and brought into the liberty of the children of God.

1 Cor. 12:13 (b) In this place the believer is in a mysterious way put into the body of Christ, the church, by the Holy Spirit as soon as he trusts his soul to Jesus Christ. In every case the word "baptism" is used to indicate that the change or the transfer is a complete transaction which involves the entire person and personality.

Col. 2:12 (b) Here again baptism is a symbol of burial in order that the world may know that the Christian is dead and buried so far as the world is concerned. The Christian emerges from the watery grave to bear witness and testimony that he is "alive unto God" and is walking with Him.

1 Pet. 3:21 (a) We should note in this case that Noah and his family were not in the water at all. They were "in the ark," which

is a type of the Lord Jesus. Christ was baptised under the waves and billows of Gods wrath, and it is His baptism that saves, not our own baptism. The passage says "in like figure." Those who stayed out of the water were saved by the ark which was in the water. Those who are "in Christ" are saved by the baptism of Christ on Calvary. He endured the wrath of God and we who belong to Him go free.

BARLEY

Ruth 1:22 (c) This is a picture of the rich blessings that await those who come back to the Lord from their blackslidden state. In the New Testament this picture is seen in the return of the prodigal. They began to be merry, and there was no end to that merriment (Luke 15:24).

BARN

Prov. 3:10 (b) These barns represent the blessings that accumulate to God's people both for time and for eternity if they walk with God and give to Him all that He should have. It is the same truth as "lay up for yourselves treasures in heaven."

Joel 1:17 (c) We believe that this word indicates that God's curse will be upon His people for their disobedience, and no blessings will accumulate to their credit. Too many of God's dear people have empty barns.

Matt. 13:30 (c) This is symbolical of heaven where the Lord takes His own saved ones who are here described as wheat.

Luke 12:18 (c) These barns represent selfish interests and activities for personal gain. This man thought that the barns were his barns and the grain was his grain, and that the increase belonged to him. He said, "Thou hast much goods laid up for many years." He was a fool in God's sight. So is everyone who lays up treasures for himself and is not rich toward God.

BARREL

1 Kings 17:12 (c) This represents human resources. To scrape the bottom of the barrel means that we have reached the end of our assets, our resources, our wits and our wisdom. Such are just at the point of bankruptcy. Those who walk with the Lord will always find that the Lord has blessings left for the believing and trusting soul.

BARREN

Ex. 23:26 (c) Here is indicated a failure in service so that the person does not reproduce himself in others. He has no spiritual children. He has led none to Christ. That unfortunate situation will not exist in the life of one who walks with the Lord and yields to the Holy Spirit. (See also Deut. 7:14; 2 Kings 2:19; Psalm 113:9; Song of Solomon 4:2)

I Sam. 2:5 (b) Hannah is telling us in this figure that those whose hearts are right with God, and who desire the glory of God will find that the life which has been barren will now become unusually fruitful.

BASKET

Deut. 28:5 (c) Moses is telling us that God will give abundant increase for us to take home to ourselves and enjoy for ourselves if we let the Lord God command us, and if we give obedient service.

Deut. 28:17 (c) Here we find the opposite truth expressed, for if we refuse to listen to God, and to walk with Him, we shall find that God withholds the blessing, and leaves us with empty hands and desolate hearts.

Jer. 6:9 (b) The figure here is that of the enemy who invades the land and gathers into his own possession the persons and the properties of disobedient Israel.

BATHE

Lev. 15:5 (c) We have here a picture of the defiled Christian who washes his ways in the water of the Word of God as we find in Eph. 5:26. The Word of God like water removes the dirt and the soil from our lives in order that we may live clean, upright lives before men.

Isa. 34:5 (c) This strange figure indicates that Gods judgment and wrath will be righteous in character and will have the approval of the God of heaven when He punishes the inhabitants of the earth.

BATTLE

Psalm 18:39 (b) There will be a conflict in the soul of every believer between the flesh and the Spirit, between the world and God the Father, between Satan and the Lord Jesus. These three conflicts are continually being waged in the soul and heart of the children of God.

Psalm 24:8 (b) The conflict mentioned here was between the Lord Jesus and wicked men; it was also between the Saviour and Satan. It was fought on earth and Christ emerged victorious.

Psalm 55:18 (b) The word is used here to describe the conflict going on in David's life because his enemies sought to depose and dethrone him. It is also indicative of his fight with the atheists of his day, who decried and denied his religion and his God. This caused deep sorrow in David's soul.

Eccl. 9:11 (b) This is a reference to any conflict taking place between those that are enemies of God and of the people of God. He is telling us that God gives the victory and we are not to depend upon our own wits, wisdom or resources.

1 Cor. 14:8 (b) The word here refers primarily to the fight between nations and peoples. It is used, however, as a figure of the warfare that is constantly being waged between the church and the world or between the Christian and Satan.

BATTLE-AX

Jer. 51:20 (a) God uses this figure to describe the great armies of Babylon. God had used the mighty King of Babylon to destroy, to cut down, and to whip the nations of the earth.

BATTLEMENT

Deut. 22:8 (c) The thought of the passage is that we are to seek to establish preventive measures or ample protection around the church, the people of God, and the testimony of our Lord. In this way there will not be a mingling of Christians with the unsaved and no mixture of the Christian program with the world's plans and schemes.

Jer. 5:10 (b) We understand from this that the world puts up barriers to prevent the Word of God from being preached to them, and to prevent the people of God from teaching the Word to them.

BAY TREE

Psalm 37:35 (a) This tree is a type of the prosperous sinner whose business grows to tremendous proportions and whose interests enter into many departments of life, all of which are successful. God is good. He gives some men a heaven on earth because He knows they will not have one hereafter.

BEACON

Isa. 30:17 (a) Here we have a beautiful picture of the testimony of God's people. This testimony is elevated high and shines plainly so that the light from it illuminates far and wide in this world. Every church should be a beacon, and so should every saved individual.

BEAM

Matt. 7:3 (a) This represents a great fault in the life of a person who is critical and fault-finding about some small error in the life of another. He does not see his own big fault, but he quickly sees the little fault in another. See also Luke 6:41-42.

BEAR

Prov. 28:15 (b) This is a type of a wicked king, or an ungodly master who rules his people with cruel rigor and indicates no feeling in regard to the sufferings which he causes.

Dan. 7:5 (b) This animal is used as a type of the Medo-Persian empire which was the second great world kingdom to appear following the fall of Babylon. The bear raising itself on one side indicated that one of this dual empire was to prevail — the Median. The three ribs probably refer to the three great kings who had gone before, but now had been destroyed; Nebuchadnezzar, his son, and his grandson, Belshazzar.

Rev. 13:2 (b) This bear is a type of the anti-Christ who will work quickly, slyly, smoothly, quietly and apparently with no anger or hatred even as a bear which seems to be docile upon first observance.

BEARD

1 Chron. 19:5 (c) This typifies full manhood and the glory of maturity. The beard when cut subjected them to open shame and ridicule.

BEAST

Dan. 7:3 (a) These beasts represent four great kingdoms, all of them cruel, evil and Satanic in their power and influence. They caused great sorrow and desolation in the earth. These four kingdoms were the Babylonian, Medo-Persian, Grecian under Alexander the Great, and the Roman Empire.

1 Cor. 15:32 (a) The word is used here by the servant of God to indicate the character of the men who opposed Paul and persecuted him in Ephesus. We often use the term "beast" to describe men who are unusually cruel, fierce and heartless.

Titus 1:12 (a) Paul used the word "beast" to describe selfish men who lived for their own comfort and pleasure and oppressed others in order to obtain what they wanted for themselves.

2 Pet. 2:12 (b) The animal here is typical of ungodly men who live lustful, fleshly lives. They are not interested in cultivating the refining, ennobling things of life, but seek to gratify the lusts of the flesh.

BED

Psalm 41:3 (b) This is a figure of the Lord bringing comfort, peace and blessing to those who care for the sorrows of others. Someone has rendered this passage, "Thou wilt smooth out the wrinkles of his bed in his sickness."

Isa. 28:20 (b) Here is a type of man-made religious programs and humanly devised schemes of salvation on which men rest their souls for eternity. They will find in the great judgment day that this bed was too short, and insufficient.

Isa. 57:2 (a) The prophet is telling us that God's people who are the righteous ones will enter into perfect rest and peace throughout eternity.

Isa. 57:7 (b) The Lord seems to be telling us that there are those who will be at ease and comfort while they are exalted by their sins, their pride and their rebellion. (See also Psalm 73:4-6.)

Ezek. 23:17 (b) This reveals that Israel accepts all the offers and proffers of lust and profit offered by the Babylonians.

Hosea 7:14 (c) This is a picture of the rebellion of Israel even when in affliction and trouble. Though forced to their beds by illness they still rebelled against the God who could heal them.

Amos 3:12 (b) This interesting passage indicates that Israel will be at ease in comfort and asleep in the midst of sin and trouble. The expression "corner of a bed" indicates that he is sleeping on the side of the bed to make room for a companion who will share his indifference to the evils that surround him.

Mark 4:21 (b) The teaching is that we should not hide our testimony under indolence and laziness. We should be active and zealous for God even in our business and in our social life. (See also Luke 8:16.)

Rev. 2:22 (a) The indication is that God will "rub their nose in it." He will bind these to their sins and will fulfill Rev. 22:11. They will receive all the consequences of their sin.

BEDSTEAD

Deut. 3:11 (c) This is used as a symbol of the life that Og, King of Bashan, lived. The bedstead was made of iron to make it safe, because he looked after his own safety first. The great size showed that he planned for his own comfort. These two selfish purposes characterize his life and God recorded it in the story of the bedstead. Think of reading on his tombstone: "He left a bedstead."

BEES

Deut. 1:44 (b) Here is a type of the harmful enemies who can hurt and injure God's people, but cannot destroy them.

Psalm 118:12 (b) David uses this figure to describe the multitude of his enemies who annoyed him and stung him, but could not destroy him.

Isa. 7:18 (b) This is a type of the Assyrians who could annoy and injure Israel, but could not conquer them.

BEER-SHEBA

Gen. 21:31 (b) The meaning of this name is "the well of the oath." It is a type of the refreshing certainty of God's loving care and sufficient promises. (See also Gen. 22:19; Gen. 26:33; Gen. 46:1)

Amos 8:14 (b) Israel is represented as committing the sin of presumption in believing that God will not punish them for their idolatry because of the oath that he made at the well of Beer-Sheba.

BEGGAR

1 Sam. 2:8 (b) This unfortunate person warming himself on the dung heap in the backyard is a type of the sinner who seeks to find comfort from the wretched and miserable things offered by this world. He begs the dunghill for warmth and comfort, and obtains some. He is willing to endure the offensive surroundings to obtain some temporary help. When God comes into a mans life, He changes him by means of the new birth, so that he no longer wants the dung heap of this world, but sits in the presence of God in a glorious atmosphere of heavenly association.

BELL

Ex. 28:33 (c) This represents the gracious and beautiful testimony of God's people as they go about in the service of the King. (See also Zech. 14:20)

BELLY

Job 15:2 (b) This figure represents those who live on gossip, talebearing and falsehood.

Psalm 17:14 (b) The word is used to describe the innermost part of the soul which actually does feel a deep satisfaction and gratification for the blessings of life even though one does not acknowledge God, nor His claims.

Dan. 2:32 (a) The word is used here to represent the third great world kingdom mentioned in Daniel's image, Alexander the Great and his Grecian empire.

John 7:38 (b) The belly is that part of the bowels where the food, having been thoroughly mixed, saturated and changed by the juices of the digestive tract, passes through the bowel walls by the process of osmosis to be taken up by the lacteals to become blood. The Lord is telling us that what we take into our own souls, digest it, mingle and mix it with faith and trust, is ready to go forth to others and to bring the life-giving blessing to them. The ministry that we give out must first have become a very part of our own selves or else it will sound like tinkling cymbals.

BENJAMIN

Gen. 43:5, 13 (c) This person is a type of Christ in that his brothers could not see the face of Joseph unless he came with them. So it is with us; we cannot see God the Father unless Christ is with us. (See also John 14:6)

Deut. 33:12 (a) Here is a beautiful picture of the trusting and confident Christian who dwells in the presence of his Lord, is covered by God's gracious, protecting care, and like the Indian's papoose, rests securely and happily between the shoulders of his wonderful Lord. The papoose does not care how long the journey is nor how rough the road is, neither does the "Benjamin Christian" who dwells between God's shoulders.

BENT

Psalm 7:12 (b) God has His judgment prepared for the ungodly, and all the evidence against them is in His hands so that He is ready to execute His vengeance on them at the right time. (See also Lam. 2:4)

Psalm 37:14 (a) Evidently the wicked have deliberately planned and prepared trouble for the godly. They intend to injure and harm God's people in every way that they can. (See also Isa. 5:28)

Lam. 3:12 (a) Jeremiah seems to feel that God had planned trouble and sorrow for his own life for reasons which he could not understand.

Hosea 11:7 (a) The hearts of the people of Israel were inclined toward evil practices and were always ready and alert to go into things that displeased God.

BERNICE

Acts 25:13, 23; Acts 26:30 (c) This woman is surely a type of some pet sin which is nourished and protected in the life in order to keep a person from accepting Jesus Christ as his Lord and Saviour. Her name means "I give victory." It occurs just these three times with no explanation. She was the blood sister of her husband, Agrippa. They had the same father and mother. Wherever Agrippa went, she went. When he came to hear Paul preach, she was there, and she went out with him to see that he did not choose Christ, but rather remain with her. She is a type of any besetting sin in the life which demands the love of the heart, and time, and affection which should be given to Christ. Many individuals have a "Bernice" in their lives which keeps them from trusting the Saviour.

BETHEL

Gen. 28:19 (c) The meaning of the word is "The House of God." It is used as a type of God making Himself known to His people, revealing His loving care, and His mighty power. The Christian should always be dwelling in "Bethel" in the conscious presence of God. (See also Gen. 31:13)

BETHANY

Luke 24:50 (c) Here our blessed Lord reminded His disciples of incidents that had taken place in that little village. These were so important that He took them there for their final lesson before going back to His Father. He wanted them to remember, and never forget, that only the Lord Jesus Christ can give life to those who are dead. (Example of Lazarus) He also reminded them that only He Himself could dry the tears of deep and real sorrow. (Example Mary and Martha at the grave) He reminded them that only He Himself could cleanse from the leprosy of sin. (Example Simon, the leper) He would have them remember that only He Himself should occupy the heart's affections rather than the service which we render, (Example Martha who was cumbered) He wanted them to know that He desired worship above service. (Example the woman who brought the alabaster box of ointment in Mark 14:3) He wanted them to remember that they must endure the neglect of His children. (Example He returned from Bethany hungry because no one invited Him home for breakfast) He wanted them to be convinced that only He Himself could set the captive free from the bondage of tradition and habit. (Example Lazarus brought out of the tomb though wrapped in grave clothes)

BETHLEHEM

Ruth 1:1 (c) From Bethlehem to Moab represents the backsliding of a child of God who leaves the "House of Bread" (which is the meaning of the word), the place where God blesses, and travels back into the world to enjoy the things that strangers have to offer. He forgets that there are tears and graves in Moab.

BEULAH

Isa. 62:4 (c) This name probably describes the Christian life in which the joy of the Lord, the fruits of righteousness and the glories of God permeate the soul.

BIND

Gen. 49:11 (b) Joseph, in this place, was teaching Israel to cement their relationship to God firmly, and to seek their sustenance, their blessings and their joys from God only.

Job 5:18 (b) This indicates the loving care of the Lord in graciously healing His people who have been hurt and wounded in the tragedies of life. (See also Isa. 61:1)

Job 26:8 (c) Here we see God's power to carry out His own will in regard to the great, restless sea, or any other great matters.

Job 31:36 (b) Job would value a book about his life because he thought it would vindicate his integrity and uprightness. It would bring glory to him as a model man. He would cherish it as a jewel which would adorn him.

Psalm 118:27 (b) This is a picture used to describe the firm decision of the believer in being completely consecrated to God, and firmly fixed in his decision to walk only with God.

Psalm 147:3 (b) Here is revealed the wonderfully sweet influence of our Lord and His Word as He comes to help and comfort that one who has been overcome by grief and disappointment.

Isa. 49:18 (b) God is promising Israel that all the riches of their enemies shall be theirs. The enemies shall become their slaves. All the glory of the enemy will be bestowed upon them. They will take that which the enemy has and use it to adorn and glorify themselves.

Matt. 12:29 (a) Here we find that Christ will defeat Satan, will conquer him, will make him helpless, and thus deliver from his grasp those whom He calls to be His children. (See also Mark 3:27)

Matt. 13:30 (b) It seems that in eternity God will cause sinners of every kind to suffer together in groups. It may be that the gamblers will be punished together, the liquor dealers in their group, the various kinds of robbers, thieves, etc., who love to spend their time and energy together. They plan their sins together on the earth, ignoring God, and denying His claims, so God makes them suffer together in eternity. It probably refers also to those in false religions who will be punished together.

Matt. 16:19 (b) The teaching here is that the servant of God filled with the Spirit of God, and knowing the mind of God, will be led by the Spirit to the right person who is ready for the message. The Spirit will direct the soul winner to a husband who is to be won for the Saviour, but will ignore the wife who may be near. The Spirit will lead the Christian to talk to one clerk in the store, and leave the other clerks untouched by the Gospel. The Christian worker will lead one brother to Christ, and leave the other brother in his sins. The Spirit will lead a soul winner to the person with whom the Holy Spirit is dealing, and will keep him from talking to that one in whose heart the Lord is not working. It may mean also that the servant of God will be in such close communion with heaven that he will know God's thoughts, and will therefore do the things that have been decided upon in heaven, and will carry out the plan that has been devised in heaven.

Matt. 22:13 (b) This man was depending upon his own ideas about the wedding garment and thought that he could provide his own suit of clothes. It is a picture of that person who thinks that he can clothe himself in his own robe of righteousness by his good works, and his religious activities. With his hands he did good deeds; with his feet he ran on good errands. The works of his hands and of his feet are represented by the suit which he wore at the wedding. For this reason the Lord instructed the angels to tie those hands and feet to show that God would not have any of his deeds, nor his work, nor his walk as a passport to the king's palace and the wedding feast. We must wear the imputed righteousness of God in order to enter heaven. We cannot wear our own. (See Romans 4:5-6.)

Matt: 23:4 (b) Churches make rules for their members which are irksome, burdensome, and really have no value in God's sight. This Scripture refers to man-made commandments such as abound in false religions, particularly in Romanism. None of these have any value in God's sight. None of these are found in the Bible. These are not issued from God's Throne. These have no value in obtaining forgiveness, nor acceptance with God. They do not bring about favor from God. (See Matt. 15:9)

BIRD

Lev. 14:5-6 (c) The dead bird represents Jesus on the cross as the dying Saviour. The live bird represents the Lord Jesus on His throne as the living Lord.

I Kings 17:4 (c) The raven is an unclean bird. It is very selfish. The Lord, however, chose it to be His servant and to give the food out of its own bill to Elijah. It was a converted raven, changed to be God's servant to man. So God changes unclean men into godly men who execute His plans and carry out His purposes.

Isa. 31:5 (c) This passage may refer to the use of airplanes and was literally fulfilled when General Allenby captured Jerusalem in World War I.

Isa. 46:11 (b) This represents the great and strong nation of cruel soldiers who would invade Israel and destroy the country.

Ezek. 39:4 (b) A type of the cruel nations that pounced upon Israel and tore her to pieces. It refers particularly to the nations used by God to execute His wrath.

Hosea 9:11 (b) The actions of the bird in flying away are compared to the way in which the pomp, power, glory, and wealth of Israel was to pass away. (See also Prov. 23:5)

Matt. 13:32 (b) Satan and his angels are compared to birds in this place. They are at home in the great apostate church where the devil and his angels rule and reign.

Rev. 18:2 (b) As described under "Babylon," this passage represents the great religious and political combination which has spread over the whole earth — a mixture of religion and politics in which evil spirits (birds) of every kind revel and dwell. It is a well-known fact that "wicked spirits are in heavenly places." In many pulpits where God should be honoured, wicked spirits (the "birds") teach their doctrines and bring destruction to human souls.

BIRTH

2 Kings 19:3 (b) The figure is used to describe the great distress of Hezekiah and the people of Jerusalem when they were surrounded by their enemies. They should have deliverance, as the mother has deliverance when her baby is born; however, they were still harassed and persecuted by their enemies. They were praying to God to deliver them out of their present difficulties, and this is compared to the birth of a child. (See also Isa. 37:3)

Psalm 58:8 (b) In this place is a plea that the plans of the wicked not be allowed to prosper, but rather to be defeated before they were put into practice.

Eccl. 6:3 (b) The frustration of a life of disappointment is compared to a baby that is born dead. That little one has less trouble than the one who lives a life full of trouble.

Isa. 66:9 (b) God in this place is promising a full deliverance eventually for Israel so that she will emerge from her captivity as a full-grown nation.

John 3:3 (a) This figure is used to describe the miraculous change which takes place when a person is saved by the Lord Jesus Christ. The Christian is brought out of bondage into liberty, out of darkness into light, out of helplessness into usefulness, out of death into life.

Gal. 4:19 (a) The soul exercise of Paul over the needs of the Galatians for full consecration to the person of Jesus Christ is compared to a birth. Works, deeds and philosophies were occupying the minds and hearts of those in the church at Galatia while Christ was being ignored and displaced from His lordship. Paul wanted Christ to be reinstated in their thinking so that He would be paramount in their love and devotion.

Rev. 12:2 (b) This difficult passage may refer to the sorrows of Israel in their slavery under the Romans at the time that Jesus was born.

BIRTHRIGHT

Heb. 12:16 (a) This is an illustration of that to which every believer is entitled, the very best of heaven and the sweetest blessings of earth. When a person becomes God's child through faith in Christ Jesus, he receives certain birthright privileges and the Lord wants him to take hold of these and to possess them in his daily life.

BISHOP

1 Pet. 2:25 (a) This title is given to the Lord Jesus in regard to His right to rule over the religious life and affairs of the church.

BITTER

James 3:11 (a) No one's lips should both bless and curse. If the heart is right with God, then all that comes out of it will be blessed and good. If bitterness comes out, it is because the heart is contaminated.

BLACK

Job 30:30 (a) Job's skin must have been actually and literally black, or at least dark enough to be called black. Judging from the symptoms described in the book, he had an oriental disease which we know as "elephantiasis." Those who suffer from this trouble do have a very dark skin covered with an odious eruption. (See under "ASHES")

Song of Solomon 1:5 (c) This probably represents the Saviour as He appears to unsaved people. To them He is unattractive, with no beauty and no value.

Song of Solomon 5:11 (c) This black hair is probably a type of the eternal youth, vigor and strength of our Lord as a young king thirty-three and a half years old. (See also Song of Solomon 7:5; Rev. 1:14)

Lam. 4:8 (b) Here is described how completely the Nazarites of Jerusalem had turned away from the beautiful life they were supposed to live, and had become sinful and wicked in their manner of living. The black is descriptive of their character.

Jer. 8:21 (a) Here is described Jeremiah's feelings concerning Israel's relationship to him. He thought that Israel despised him, had no use for him, and saw no beauty in him, which probably was true. He reproved them for their sins, and warned them of their punishment. This, of course, made the nation despise him.

Jer. 14:2 (c) If the Word "they" refers to the gates, it would indicate that they were damaged by fire, and were being destroyed. If, however, the word refers to the people then probably the famine and the sufferings had brought about the blackened condition of their skin.

Zech. 6:2 (b) These horses probably represent war and famine with the terrible results of both. They are described as being "black" because of the fearful condition of the people under those circumstances. It is said that these also are the four winds (R.V.) as described in verse 5. It may be that the black horses represent the power of God in causing wars, tumults and famine to rage upon the earth. It seems as though this power was against the enemies of God.

Rev. 6:5 (b) This black horse probably represents the famine and the sorrow which would prevail on the earth as a punishment for the wickedness and the evil being practiced. You will notice that the balances are for weighing the food because it is so scarce. This seems to be confirmed in verse 6.

BLEMISH

Lev. 21:18 (c) The word is used to remind us that the believer must have a sacrifice that is absolutely perfect in every respect. The only sacrifice that God will accept as being perfect is the Lord Jesus. Nothing else and no one else can be truly perfect.

2 Pet. 2:13 (b) This reference is to those people who are unsaved and therefore untaught in the Word of God who come among God's people bringing damage, hurt and injury to God's program.

BLEW

Matt. 7:25 (c) This tells us of the overwhelming power of trouble, calamity and disaster which envelops a human life to destroy it. If that person had founded his faith on the Rock of Ages, he would not be shaken by these winds of adversity.

BLIND

Ex. 23:8 (a) If the judge is bribed with gifts, then he fails to execute true judgment and his decisions are not righteous. You will note that when "Justice" is seen in sculpture or in painting, she has no hands and her eyes are blindfolded. This is to teach us that justice takes no bribes, and is not affected by the standing or the relationship of the person who is being judged.

Lev. 19:14 (c) This describes the condition of those who teach wrong doctrines or evil practices, especially those who are ignorant of God's Word and God's ways.

Isa. 29:18 (b) These people are those who have eyes to see, but do not have the necessary information nor understanding. Somehow or sometime they shall have their understanding enlightened so that they can see and know God's truth. (See also Isa. 35:5; Isa. 42:7)

Isa. 42:16 (a) We learn here that God leads those who do not see clearly. They have willing spirits and honest hearts. but they have not been taught nor informed by godly teachers. These are described further in verses 18 and 19.

Isa. 43:8 (b) This figure describes those who have heard the Word of God, have been reared in Christian surroundings, but have failed to see either their own need or the provision that the Lord has made.

Isa. 56:10 (a) These people are religious leaders who are ignorant of God's plans and do not understand God's words. (See also Matt. 15:14; Matt. 23:16; Luke 6:39)

John 9:39 (a) The time may come in a human life, or in national life when God will hide Himself because of the constant and definite rejection of His Word. He binds men to their decisions. He hides Himself from those who continually reject Him.

John 12:40 (a) God closes the mind and the understanding of those who willingly remain ignorant of God's truth, and do not want God's revelations. (See Rom. 11:7, 25)

Rom. 2:19 (b) This describes those who are groping for the light and need someone to teach them the truth and to guide them to Jesus Christ.

2 Pet. 1:9 (b) This is the description of one who has been instructed in the way of righteousness, has learned the precious provisions of the Lord but has failed to take advantage of the blessings thus offered.

Rev. 3:17 (a) There are those who pretend to know God's truth, and yet are in the darkness of ignorance. These invent new religions based on their own philosophies. They have never seen the light of life.

BLINDNESS

Rom. 11:25 (a) This describes the condition of the minds of Israel in that they could not and did not understand the person and the work of Christ and the fulfillment of the provision made by God. The same meaning applies in 2 Cor. 3:14.

Eph. 4:18 (b) As in the former Scriptures, their minds were blind so that their thoughts were perverted. In this passage, the heart did not understand the things of God, therefore the feelings were perverted.

2 Cor. 4:4 (b) This is a picture of the effect that Satan produces on the minds of people when he presents to them false teachings, erroneous doctrines, and baseless theories.

BLOOD

Gen. 4:10 (c) This is symbolical of the death of Abel by the hand of Cain, his brother. The actual blood shed by Abel and lying on the ground called loudly for the punishment of the murderer.

Ex. 12:13 (a) Here is a proof that those in the house had believed God's Word and had offered the proper sacrifice. The lamb and its blood are types of Christ and His blood. (See 1 Cor. 5:7.)

Lev. 20:9 (a) Here is pictured the fact that God will fasten upon the guilty person his guilt and his punishment. The law-breaker shall receive the due reward of his deeds. (See also verses 13 and 27; Ezek. 18:13; 33:5)

Deut. 17:8 (a) The words used here refer to relatives who are quarreling among themselves. Those of the same blood are brought before the judgment seat for the adjustment of their difficulties. (See 2 Chron. 19:10)

Job. 16:18 (a) Job is making a call for a great inventory of his own life. He is inviting an investigation of his own character. He is really asserting that he has lived a righteous life.

Psalm 58:10 (b) This is a description of the joy of God's people when the wicked are conquered and the enemy is under the feet of the Lord. (See also Psalm 68:23)

Isa. 1:15 (a) Probably this is a figure which describes the guilt of these people in murdering their fellowmen and murdering their children for idol worship.

Ezek. 16:6 (a) This probably refers to the early days of Israel's history in the time of Abraham followed by the times of Isaac and Jacob. The nation was formed with difficulty and trouble which is compared to the birth of a baby whereby blood is shed.

Joel 2:31 (c) It is not clearly understood whether the moon will actually become red, or whether men because of strained eyes see the moon as red, or whether the tumult of earth's sorrows changes man's vision. Evidently it refers to a time of great and miraculous happenings because of the powerful operation of the Spirit of God in human affairs. (See also Rev. 6:12; 8:8; 16:3.)

Matt. 16:17 (a) This represents human reasonings, philosophies and deductions or conclusions. Nothing within the human heart or mind ever reveals anything of God or of the Deity of Christ.

John 1:13 (a) This is a definite statement that no one becomes a child of God because of his parents, or through any blood stream. Salvation or Christianity is not passed down to the children through the blood stream of the father or the mother. Each child and each relative must experience the will and the power of God in his own personal case in order to become a child of God. This relationship only comes about through personal faith in Jesus Christ.

John 6:54 (a) The blood in this case is a type or a picture of the life and death of Christ and the Person of Christ appropriated by the believer for salvation. It represents the receiving by faith of the sacrifice of Christ for forgiveness and cleansing. It is a figure of speech which we commonly use when one expresses his love for another by saying, "I could eat you up." Sometimes the expression is used, "I lapped it up as a cat laps milk." The thought is the same. The believer embraces by faith with no question or doubt the value of the person of Christ and the efficacy of His work for our souls. See also I Cor. 11:25, 26.

Acts 17:26 (a) This blood is a type or a symbol of the universal character of human beings as distinguished from all animal life. All human beings are made of the same kind of blood. It is different from animal blood, but it is always human blood. This links all human beings together as a separate group from all the animal creation and proves the fallacy and the false character of the hypothesis of "evolution."

Acts 20:26 (a) The word in this case is used to represent the fact that Paul would not be held responsible for the death, the second death, of any of those whom he had contacted in his travels and preaching. The appearance of blood indicates death. Paul so preached Christ and the Gospel that none of those who heard His Word need never die in their sins and be sent to the Lake of Fire, which is the second death. Paul felt that he had completely cleared himself of all responsibility in connection with the salvation of those people.

1 John 1:7 (a) The blood here represents the sacrifice of Christ at Calvary with all the saving power connected with it. When we believe in and trust the Lord Jesus Christ, God and Christ apply His sacrifice to our record of sins, and to ourselves in order to blot out all these sins and iniquities. God has made a "blood bank." Any person who believes in and accepts the Lord Jesus Christ may and does receive the benefits of that precious blood.

Rev. 14:20 (c) This is a picture of the complete victory of the Lord Jesus over all His enemies and the vindication as well as the culmination of the wrath of God against all His opponents.

Rev. 17:6 (b) This blood represents the death of multitudes who have been slain by this wicked church under the guise of serving God. That evil monster, the apostate church, was and is responsible for the death of many thousands of true believers who were burned at the stake, tortured in cages, torn by the rack, and otherwise killed by extremely cruel means. This church revelled in this carnage, and still rejoices in every opportunity to injure and destroy true believers in the Lord Jesus Christ. (See also Rev. 18:24)

BLOSSOM

Isa. 5:24 (b) God is thus informing Israel that there would be no blessing waiting for them in future days. The fact that there were no flowers indicated that there would be no fruit.

Isa. 27:6 (b) The restoration of Israel is to be a slow process as in the formation of fruit. First, there is the bud, then the bloom, and then the fruit.

Ezek. 7:10 (b) As the blossom is an evidence of future fruitfulness, so on a rod it indicates the coming of God's punishment on His people. It presages fruit. In this case it is foretelling that the fruit will be of the kind that hurts and harms Israel.

Hab. 3:17 (b) Flowers always indicate that fruit is to follow. Flowers raise the hope of the farmer for a bountiful crop. In this case since there were no flowers it would indicate clearly that there would be no future fruit, but rather famine and sorrow. Even though this was the case, the prophet would rejoice and sing.

BLOT

Prov. 9:7 (b) The Lord is telling us that when an outsider interferes with the evil actions of another, he is quite apt to receive an injury to himself, which may be seen also by others. It becomes a blemish on his life.

BLOW

Job 20:26 (b) This represents the terrible judgment which God will bring on a disobedient person without a human instrument. It is a divine punishment sent by God Himself.

Song of Solomon 4:16 (b) This is symbolical of the ministry of the Spirit in giving or withholding or in providing what is needed to make the garden fruitful. The "wind" is a type of the Holy Spirit in His ministry. (See also John 3:8)

Haggai 1:9 (b) Here we see a type of God's punishment and curse upon that which disobedient Israel sought to accomplish. See also Isa. 40:7 and 24; Ezek. 21:31; 22:21.

BLUE

Ex. 25:4 (c) Blue threads were woven into the various parts of the tabernacle to remind Israel that though they were traveling on earth their destination was heaven. The color "blue" is used throughout the Scripture to remind the people of their heavenly character. The blue yarns were woven in with the red yarns to remind Israel that they were forgiven and were made fit for heaven by the shed blood of the sacrifice. Linen yarns also were woven with these to remind the people of God of God's righteousness given to them as a gift to make them acceptable to God. Purple yarns were to remind Israel that they were a part of the royal family of heaven. The cherubims were to remind them that one day they would be associated with angels. See also Ex. 26:1; 39:3.

Ex. 26:31 (c) The colors in the veil were to remind Israel that they could not enter the holy place, nor have the full enjoyment of God's fellowship except by the graces and privileges represented by these.

Ex. 26:36 (c) The blue in these door curtains was to remind Israel that they could always enter into God's house and God's fellowship by means of that heavenly revelation and heavenly salvation provided through the blood of the lamb.

Ex. 28:31 (c) This color on Aaron was to remind him that he was always to be enveloped with a heavenly deportment. It would also remind him and Israel that he was a heavenly man living in heavenly places and occupied with heavenly business.

Num. 15:38 (c) The sabbath breaker had just been stoned (see vs. 35), so God told His people to put this ribbon of blue on the bottom of their garments to ever remind them that they were to obey the message from heaven, and not live by their own ideas, and conclusions.

Esther 1:6 (c) The wicked king seeking to justify his sins had the blue woven in the curtains so as to connect his evil orgies with something of heaven and heaven's business. Most wicked practices have in some way a religious tinge to their ceremonies. The most wicked institution in the world, the apostate church, has a great religious program in order that they may cover up their evil doings by it.

Esther 8:15 (c) It is evident that Mordecai was God's man for that particular time. The blue would remind all who saw him that he was carrying out God's plan, and accomplishing God's purposes.

Ezek. 23:6 (c) The Assyrians clothed themselves in garments of blue probably to imitate the priesthood of Israel and thus give a religious touch to their evils. Thus with a pretext of being a godly people, they would deceive Israel and gain their confidence. Wicked religions still follow this plan.

BLUNT

Eccl. 10:10 (b) This figure is used to teach us that our knowledge of the Word of God must be fresh, clear and forceful. We must be quick-witted. We must be alert and well trained in the art of affecting the hearts of others. The work of God is easily accomplished when we have been whetted on the emery wheel of Scriptural truth.

BOARD

Ex. 26:15 (c) This board may be used as a type of a saved person. It was once a tree in the woods and of no value as a dwelling place for God. The tree had to die. It was cut down, made into boards, dressed, planed, and fitted. Even yet, it was not useful to God nor could it be placed in His holy temple. It must have silver tenons on the bottom to rest on in the sand. Silver speaks of redemption. It must have a covering of pure gold all over to hide the wood. Then it was fit for the tabernacle. (Eph. 2:22) So it is with the sinner. He must be cut down. He must die in the person of his Substitute, the Lord Jesus Christ. He must go with Christ through the sufferings of Calvary, his burial and resurrection, and then be clothed with the golden robe of righteousness, the beauty of his Saviour. He must rest on redemption ground and be joined to the other "boards." Then he helps, with them, to form "a habitation of God by His Spirit."

Song of Solomon 8:9 (b) The board here represents a type of all believers standing together "fitly joined together," Eph. 4:16, in order to make a Church which is God's dwelling place.

BOAZ

Ruth 2:1 (c) This is a type of the Lord Jesus who owns the field and who marries those who were formerly foreigners and strangers, but who put their trust in Him and become His bride, the church.

BODY

John 2:21 (a) In this passage, the body of the Lord Jesus is represented as a temple in which God dwells.

Rom. 6:6 (b) Here the word is used as though sin itself owned the body as, in fact, it does in some instances. The entire body, from head to foot, is used by some to serve sin.

Rom. 12:5 (a) All the Christians bound together by the Holy Spirit are referred to here as forming the body of Christ. The believers on earth are called His very body because they are so precious to Him, and because of His utmost care for them. His life indwells all His church.

Eph. 1:23 (a) The body is used here in the sense that all the members of the body of Christ, those who are saved by grace, belong to one another. As the parts of the body belong to one another and are made to serve one another, so each member of the body of Christ serves each other member. No part of the body is independent of any of the rest of the body and so it is among true believers.

BONDS

Psalm 116:16 (c) These bonds are a description of the habits, customs, and traditions that bind the Christian before the truth of God sets him free to serve in God's way. The same picture is seen in the case of Lazarus. The grave clothes of death held him as the old habits and ways of people hold them. Christ sets free.

Jer. 5:5 (b) The bonds in this passage are the legitimate and rightful laws of God in His path, but the leaders had thrown away these restraining influences of the work of the Lord.

Luke 13:16 (b) The sickness which this woman suffered is described as a bond because it hindered her from living a normal life.

Acts 8:23 (b) This man, because of avarice and desire to buy spiritual power, was said to be bound by the bond of iniquity — an unholy desire.

Col. 3:14 (b) Love is described as a bond which holds us in the right relationship to God and to others and makes us what we should be.

BONDAGE

1 Cor. 7:15 (a) This refers to the burden of trying to observe a course of conduct when it is really unnecessary to do so.

Gal. 5:1 (a) Here we see the burden of trying to keep the law to be saved when there is always a conscious knowledge that it is being broken.

BONE

Gen. 2:23 (c) This indicates the very intimate relationship which exists between Christ and the church. The church in a figure was made possible by His wounded side. As Adam may be taken as a type of Christ, so Eve being taken out of him as a very part of him, is a type of the church which owes her very existence to the pains, the suffering and the glory of the Lord Jesus Christ. This refers only to the true Church of true born-again believers, and not to the great false church which has been made by men.

Num. 19:16 (c) Here is a type of anything that is dead. God does not want His people to be occupied with the dead things of this world, but with the living things of heaven. The pleasures and the processes of this world are dead in the sight of God and have no spiritual value whatever in the Christian life. We are no longer dead in sins, but alive unto God.

Judges 9:2 (b) Abimelech is telling the people that he is related to them by blood, being born of and in the nation of Israel. It is a type of intimate relationship. (See also 2 Sam. 5:1, 19:13, 1 Chron. 11:1)

Psalm 38:3 (a) The innermost being of the Psalmist would rejoice in God's delivering power but, instead, he was filled with sorrow.

Psalm 42:10 (a) David felt it deeply and keenly that God's enemies should be able to question God's care for him.

Psalm 51:8 (a) By this figure David describes the misery of his heart because of his sin. He is hurt by his conscience as the pain of a broken bone hurts the body. (See Psalm 6:2; 31:10; 32:3; 102:3)

Psalm 141:7 (b) This is a picture of the utter desolation and hopelessness of Israel when they turned their backs on God.

Prov. 3:8 (a) By this symbol Solomon assures that if they will walk with God they will be a strong, vigorous, active people, a nation of conquerors.

Prov. 12:4 (a) The sorrow caused by the unfaithfulness of the wife is compared to a disease that eats away the very vitals of the blood stream, and weakens the whole person.

Prov. 14:30 (a) Envy is compared to a disease which destroys the very foundations of faith and leaves the person spiritually sick and weak. Since the red blood cells come from the marrow of the bones, so rottenness in that substance destroys the vitality of the body. Envy has the same effect on the soul. It is a hidden malady in the life.

Prov. 15:30 (a) Good news is compared here to the life-giving effect and power of healthy bones. The good news brings new life and strength into the heart and soul. (See also Prov. 16:24; Isa. 58:11; Isa. 66:14)

Prov. 17:22 (a) Diseased bones are a type of the bad news that causes the heart to faint, the strength to fail, and joy to cease. This is also a picture of the unhappy effect upon a person who is wholly occupied with his deep sorrows and his broken spirit.

Prov. 25:15 (b) Here is indicated that a kind answer will soften the hard heart of an enemy and will break down his resistance.

Isa. 38:13 (a) The pain which the king suffered, both physical and spiritual, hurt him so deeply he felt as if his bones were broken.

Jer. 20:9 (a) The prophet was so obsessed with a desire to serve God and to testify of and for Him that it stirred his whole being and he felt it as though the bones of his body were affected.

Jer. 23:9 (a) The prophet's whole body, as well as his mind, was deeply moved by the words of God given in power. He felt it especially because of the great failure of the prophets of Israel.

Jer. 50:17 (a) These bones represent the elders and rulers of Israel who were conquered by Nebuchadnezzar.

Ezek. 24:4 (b) This figure is a prophecy that God will gather the choice men, the leading men of Israel, together for judgment because they forsook Him.

Ezek. 37:11 (a) These dry bones are used as a type of the condition of Israel when she had departed from God. The bones were dead, dry, useless, ugly and disjointed. God saw them as though they were all in one valley, though actually Israel was scattered over the world. All the bones were there, even the tiny ear bones. No bone was missing. This is a type of the fact that throughout the world God has His people in training so that when the nation is revived under God's hand and restored to His favor there will be every kind of person there necessary for the operation of the fully equipped empire. He will have electricians, printers, teachers, scientists, physicians, dentists, navigators, farmers, machinists and every other form of human activity. When these bones come to life through the operation of the Spirit of God they become mature men, fully equipped for the purposes of God. Every bone must be there in order to produce this result. These bones represent the fact that there was a former life which had disappeared. We do not read of the bones of any other nation. God still reckons that the Jewish people are one nation, one people, and are to be again His own chosen people.

Zeph. 3:3 (a) The prophet uses this figure to tell us that the rulers of Jerusalem were deliberate in their wickedness and went about their sinful practices leisurely.

Matt. 23:27 (a) These bones represent the old dead traditions of Israel which were worthless and useless as a means of godliness, but which were handed down from generation to generation for strict observance.

Eph. 5:30 (a) This indicates the very intimate and sweet relationship which exists between Christ and His church.

BOOTH

Lev. 23:42 (c) This may be taken as a type of the transient character of our lives here on earth in order to remind us that we are pilgrims and strangers.

BORN

Isa. 66:8 (a) The nation of Israel was really born on the evening of May 14, 1948. This was immediately at the close of the British protectorate under the Balfour Declaration. Look up the history of Israel currently for the details of the birth of this great new nation.

Ezek. 16:4 (a) This expression is really an allegory to tell how God found Israel in Egypt a confused mass of inexperienced slaves with no order and no political standing. Then God delivered them from that condition and changed them into an orderly and powerful nation. It may be taken as a picture of the experience of a lost, undone and unclean sinner living in the bondage of his sin and afterward delivered by the Lord through the Gospel to become a useful servant of God.

John 3:3 (a) The transformation which takes place when a lost sinner trusts Jesus Christ is compared to the birth of a child. A new life is given him, with new desires, new knowledge, new hope, new habits, and a new nature. Now he is able to know and to understand God. The inward change is revealed by the outward actions.

I Pet. 1:23 (a) This also is a statement concerning the wonderful transaction that takes place when the Word of God reveals to a soul the value of Christ Jesus the Lord.

BORNE

Isa. 46:3 (a) This is a figure to describe the way in which Israel was protected, preserved and provided for by God through the difficulties, trials and wars of generations.

Lam. 5:7 (b) This figure evidently represents the fact that the children suffered the effects of their fathers' sins.

Matt. 23:4 (b) Here is described the great difficulty which the people had in trying to be good, and to observe all the traditions of the scribes and Pharisees in order to be saved. They made their religious life a burden and a grief instead of a joy and a blessing.

BOSOM

Num. 11:12 (a) This is a type of Moses' great heart of love. He complained that it was just too much for him to assume and carry the burdens of three and one-half million people as a mother carries a baby on her breast.

Isa. 40:11 (a) This represents the daily care of God for the people of Israel, His own lambs.

Luke 6:38 (b) This is just a sweet way of saying that kindness shown to those who have shown kindness fills the heart with sweet joy.

John 1:18 (a) Christ uses this figure to tell how near He is to God's heart and how welcome He is in God's presence.

BORROW

Ex. 3:22 (a) The Hebrew word for "borrow" is rendered *ask* eighty-five times and is rendered borrow five times. The real word for borrow, as we understand the meaning of it, is found in Deut. 28:12; Neh. 5:4; Ps. 37:21. Israel did not *borrow* from the Egyptians only that to which they were entitled as wages for four hundred years of slavery. There was no indication nor suggestion that repayment would be made. It was a plain solicitation of that which was rightly their due for years of service with no pay.

BOTTLE

1 Sam. 10:3 (c) Probably this bottle represents the gift of the Holy Spirit. They would be strengthened, cheered and refreshed as only the Holy Spirit can do. The three men may represent the Father, the Son and the Holy Spirit.

Job 38:37 (a) This is a type of the storehouse of the sky from which the rain pours upon the earth from time to time.

Psalm 56:8 (b) This is a very sweet request for the Lord to keep a record of all the tears that David shed for the people of God, and the work of God.

Jer. 19:1 (a) This vessel represents the believer. The potter represents the Lord. First, He finds us just as a shapeless lump of clay. Then He takes us and puts us on the wheels of adversity and of strange experiences, molds us and makes us into a vessel fit for His use.

Jer. 48:12 (b) Here is a symbol of the granaries, wine vats and other depositories of food products, all of which were to be destroyed and emptied by the enemies of Israel.

BOUGH

Gen. 49:22 (a) This is a picture of the blessed and fruitful influence of Joseph in the life of all nations when he was governor of Egypt. It is also a picture of the blessed effect that his life and his words were to have on following generations. It also indicates that no servant of God should confine his gifts and talents to one group of believers. All of God's servants are to serve all of God's people as much as possible.

BOUND

1 Sam. 25:29 (b) This figure describes the safety and blessedness of Christian unity with our wonderful Lord.

Psalm 107:10 (b) Here is described the hindering effects of sorrow and trouble in the life which prevent one from doing many things that he would like to accomplish.

BOW (RAINBOW)

Gen. 9:13 (a) This is a symbol of the beautiful and variegated care of God. It is a token of the truth and uncertainty of His Word. It is the evidence of His oath, which He will certainly perform.

Job. 29:20 (b) Here we find a figure of the strength and power which once belonged to Job when he had many possessions and a position of honor.

Psalm 11:2 (b) The reference is to the attacks his subject constantly made against David both by their subtle intrigue, and by their wicked words.

Rev. 4:3 (b) This rainbow is all green. Only one color is left now because the days when God's people need His care have gone forever and they are now at home with Him. The rainbow tells of His mercy and grace which is now to be everlasting in its duration. The green tells of perpetuity. This is the only full rainbow of which there is any record. So far as known a complete rainbow has probably never been seen on earth. There is always a break somewhere near the bottom. The reason for this is that no one on earth has ever seen or known all the fullness of God's grace and mercy. The rainbow is a testimony, a proclamation of the grace and goodness of God toward evil men. In eternity, however, this fullness will be known and therefore the rainbow is seen in its completeness. It is around God's Throne — not any other throne — because He only is the author of grace, mercy and peace.

Rev. 6:2 (b) This is a type of the strength and power given to this world ruler. It is not a rainbow.

BOWELS

Gen. 43:30 (b) The word is used to signify the innermost part of a person where the deepest feelings seem to lie. It is the same kind of expression as "from the depths of my heart."

Lam. 1:20 (b) This refers to the deep trouble in his innermost soul. Because of Israel's condition, the very vitals of his life were touched.

Phil. 1:8 (b) Here is a reference to the deepest Christian experience which Paul manifested in his earnest love for these Christians.

Philemon:7 (b) The expression in this passage refers to a full-hearted joy which the saints experienced when Philemon ministered to them and brought a blessing from God to them.

1 John 3:17 (b) Here the word is used to express feelings of sympathy, not on the surface, but deep in the heart. Much of so-called Christian living is a surface matter. The word "bowels" in-

dicates in all these passages the very deepest feelings of the believer.

BOWL

Ex. 25:31 (c) The bowl held the surplus. It indicates by figure that the Lord wants His light bearers to have a large amount of surplus ministry to give to God's people at all times.

BOX

Matt. 26:7 (See full description under "ALABASTER".)

BRACELET

Gen. 24:22 (c) This probably is teaching that when the Spirit of God takes possession of us for Christ, our hands are to become His in useful and beautiful service.

Ezek. 16:11 (b) This is descriptive of the beautiful adornment that is given to one who trusts the Saviour and who becomes wonderfully useful in the service of the King.

BRAMBLE

Judges 9:14 (b) Jotham used the bramble as a type of Abimelech, presenting him as a little, insignificant, inconsequential man who would be untrue to them and would be a sticker in their sides.

Isaiah 34:13 (b) This is a graphic picture of the deserted and forsaken land when God's curse fell upon it. In figure, it represents the wretched, unhappy, miserable condition of one who shuts God out of his life. (See under "THISTLE".)

BRANCH

Gen. 49:22 (b) The word refers to the beneficent relationships of Joseph which were to extend beyond the boundaries of his own land, and of his own people. It gives us a picture of the Lord Jesus whose grace, love and mercy were to extend beyond the boundaries of Israel to all people on earth.

Prov. 11:28 (b) The righteous will flourish from his union with God as a branch flourishes from its union with the vine.

Isa. 4:2 (a) The prosperity of Israel in the day of the Lord is compared to the beautiful growth and rich fruit of the branch of a fruit tree. Christ also is called "the branch" in five Scriptures. In each of these passages He is called the *branch* for a different reason. In this particular Scripture Christ is the *branch* springing from the Father to reveal in His life, His actions and His words the beauty and the glory of the Father. Christ is more beautiful than any of the things which He has made. He is the express image of the beauty of the unseen God.

Isa. 9:14 (a) Here the *branch* represents the affiliations, relationships and associations of the people. The entire "plant" of Israel was to be cut down.

Isa. 11:1 (a) The Lord Jesus is compared to a *branch* of the tree, and Jesse is the trunk of the tree, for Jesse was in the direct line of Christ, one of His ancestors. The Lord Jesus came from Jesse, and yet as the root down out of sight, He was before Jesse, and Jesse came from Him. The *branch* here reveals the eternal character of Christ. He is like the Father in this respect. The *branch* is always of the same character, appearance, substance and essence as that from which it comes. So Christ in every respect is exactly like His Father. He was before Jesse in His deity, and He came from Jesse in His humanity.

Isa. 17:9 (b) Several lessons may be learned from this branch. One is that the cities of Israel would be completely destroyed. There will be ruin but not extermination. Another lesson may be that some of the principal men of Israel will be left alive to continue the testimony of Israel.

Isa. 60:21 (b) Israel here is represented as a remnant. The tree is largely gone, and only a small *branch* remains. The Lord will plant that *branch* so that it may become a tree again.

Jer. 23:5 (b) Again Christ Himself is compared to a *branch*, David being the tree, and the Lord Jesus springing out of the line of David. It reveals His union with David. (See Jer. 33:15) In this place also Christ is represented as being exactly like His Father in His righteous character. He is absolutely holy and pure, as is God the Father. This *branch* has all the characteristics of the tree (the Father) in being perfectly sinless, perfectly righteous in every thought, word and deed.

Jer. 33:15 (b) Strangely enough in this Scripture Israel is said to have the same name and the same character as the *branch* of Jeremiah 23:5. You will note that the passage records "this is the name whereby SHE will be called." The reason for this is that the bride always takes the name of the one she marries and becomes a partaker of his character, his riches in glory, and his position. The queen rules in equality with the king. The passage reveals the wonderful union between Christ and His church. It reminds us of the marvelous truth of imputed righteousness. See Rom. 4:6.

Ezek. 17:22 (b) The word in this passage indicates the king of the country, the one who is the highest among the people.

Zech. 3:8 (a) This gives us another picture of the beauty of Christ Jesus our Lord. God Himself is the tree and the Lord Jesus is the *branch*. The type in this passage represents Christ as being the servant of God who will do everything that the Father wants done, and in the way the Father wishes to have it done. By His words and His work He reveals exactly the character and conduct of the Father. The *Branch* is of course, as in the previous references, exactly the same in essence, in substance, in character, and in appearance as His Father.

Zech. 6:12 (a) Again the Holy Spirit is revealing to us that the Lord Jesus, the *branch*, is the one who carries out exactly and in detail the will of His Father. What the Saviour did in building His church is exactly what the Father wanted done. He is a priest upon His throne. The priest is from the tribe of Levi, and the king is from the tribe of Judah. No one in Israel could be both a priest and a king, for the tribes were not permitted to cross with each other. The Saviour brought in a new dispensation. God the Father made Him head of the church, and also the King of the Kingdom of God. This was God's will. It is beautifully illustrated in the picture of the *branch* and the tree.

John 15:2 (a) This branch is a picture of the Christian, who, because he is joined to Christ Jesus the vine, lives the kind of a life that Christ the vine lived. The *branch* lives because the vine lives. (John 14:19) When any person trusts Christ Jesus with his soul and receives Him (John 1:12), he becomes at once a member of God's church, a part of Christ's body. The Holy Spirit accomplishes this miracle. Uzziah tried to be both a priest and king, and God smote him with leprosy as a punishment. (2 Chron. 26:16) King Saul tried to be both a priest and a king, and God punished him by taking away the Kingdom of Israel from him. (I Sam. 13:9)

BRAND

Zech. 3:2 (a) The word represents something that is to be burned, not a seal to be placed upon an object. It refers to Joshua who, in his natural state, was fit only for the burning of hell; but by the grace of God was saved from that condition and position and was made a priest of God. This is sovereign grace. This has been the experience of every born-again Christian.

BRASS (BRAZEN)

Ex. 27:2 (a) This metal is used as a type of severe judgment in righteousness. In this Scripture, the righteous judgment of God upon the sinner is pictured by the punishment of the animal as a substitute. God's righteous wrath against the sinner's sin was satisfied by the suffering and death of the animal. We should note that the brass covered the acacia wood which was beneath it. The wood represents the humanity of Christ which in itself might not be able to stand fiery judgment. The brass representing the character and righteous judgment of eternal God is a picture of the deity of the Lord Jesus combined with His humanity.

BRASS (BRAZEN)

Lev. 26:19 (c) Probably the meaning of this picture is that the earth will become hard, fruitless and unresponsive to the efforts of men so that no crop can grow, even as nothing could grow on brass. By using the metal "brass," the lesson probably is that the drouth and the dearth are a result of God's judgment on the land for the sins of the people.

Num. 21:9 (a) This serpent was made of brass to represent the Lord Jesus who, under the divine judgment of the God of heaven, was made sin for us on the cross. It was made of brass to inform us that the judgment which He endured was right and true, and came from the God of heaven. (See John 3:14; 2 Cor. 5:21)

Deut. 28:23 (a) The Lord is informing us by means of this metaphor that the ungodly, the disobedient, the rebellious will not be able to send their prayers through to God. He will not hear when they cry to Him. The heavens will not respond to their petitions.

Deut. 33:25 (b) This is a very apt description of the way our Lord prepares us for life's travel over rough roads, sharp thorns and stones. He equips us with the kind of disposition and nature, with that kind of faith and trust which does not mind the roughness of the way.

Job 6:12 (a) Job was pleading for relief and reminding his enemies that he could feel the shame and could suffer physical pain. He was not made of hard metal, that had no feelings.

Psalm 107:16 (a) God is affirming to His people that He had performed many wonderful miracles for them, and had delivered them from many embarrassing situations. (See Isa. 45:2.) He also made the same statement about Cyrus.

Isa. 48:4 (b) This represents a bold, heartless condition of soul which rebels against the will of God.

Isa. 60:17 (a) God is reminding His people that He will add greatly to the blessings of His people, bringing to them valuable treasures instead of less consequential things. He promises to make their blessings to increase in quantity and in quality.

Jer. 1:18 (a) God has promised to His servant that he would be strong, invincible and unmovable in the presence of his enemies. He would be able to withstand all their assaults against him. (See also Jer. 15:20)

Dan. 7:19 (a) The metal in this place indicates that the fourth beast which was the Roman empire would be a grasping, destructive nation with hard, cruel power over all her enemies. History proved that this was the case.

Dan. 10:6 (a) In this vision it may be that we are given a description of the Lord Christ as to His power, purity and position.

His arms would tell us of His service, His feet would represent His accomplishments. The fact that they were polished would indicate that all His word, His way, His will and His walk would be true and perfect in every respect.

1 Cor. 13:1 (a) The use of the metal here evidently indicates that there are those hypocrites who would be bright, beautiful and vocal, but would have no true value.

Rev. 1:15 (a) The feet of the Lord Jesus are represented by this metal because He walked in a righteous path of pure and perfect judgment. (See also Rev. 2:18)

BREACH

Job 16:14 (a) Here we learn that God had broken down all the defense that Job had set up. That in which Job rejoiced, his many friends, his family, his farm, and his business were all taken from him, and in his poverty and loneliness he was exposed to his enemies.

Psalm 106:23 (a) Israel by their sins had opened the way for God to come in and punish them; then Moses prayed and prevailed for them. (See Isa. 30:13,26; Lam. 2:13; Jer. 14:17)

Prov. 15:4 (b) An evil tongue opens the way for the human spirit to get in trouble. It disturbs and distracts the heart.

Isa. 58:12 (b) Those who prevail with God in prayer and walk with Him in fellowship will mend a rift in the church and will bring God's divided people together.

Amos 4:3 (b) The Lord is telling Israel here that He will break open the defenses of Samaria, and the idolatrous inhabitants would be made to flee for their lives.

BREAD

Gen. 49:20 (b) Here we find a figure of the profitable and useful things which occupy the life of this man. He took unto himself only those things which would make him worth while and useful. In our day we would say that he did not spend his time reading trash, watching worldly pictures, or gossiping with his neighbors. He was busy learning a multitude of interesting and profitable things which would be useful in his daily life.

Num. 14:9 (a) We are to learn here that the enemies of Israel would be easily whipped and would be consumed as bread is consumed by the hungry man.

Judges 7:13 (b) This cake of barley bread represents Gideon who, though weak and lacking in military skill, would win a great victory for Israel and for God.

1 Sam. 10:3 (c) Probably in this passage the Lord is referring to King Saul, that all his needs will be met by the Father, the

Son and the Spirit which are represented by the three loaves. We know that Christ is the bread of life. We also understand that both the Father and the Spirit meet the heart hunger of the one who belongs to them. Certainly three loaves were more than Saul could eat at one meal, and he would have enough left over for future needs. It is a beautiful picture of the sufficiency that we find in the triune God.

Psalm 80:5 (a) There are those who feed upon their sorrows. They continue to weep over former griefs. They meditate on their afflictions and talk about them to others. Because of Israel's disobedience, He permitted them to have plenty of tears, and plenty of cause for tears. They would not have God's comforting care.

Prov. 9:17 (b) This is probably a type of some sin or sins which at first seem pleasant and satisfying but afterwards result in punishment. (See also Prov. 20:17)

Prov. 31:27 (b) This probably represents those who think that it is sweet, good and profitable to sit around doing nothing. They are lazy and useless. God condemns this form of life.

Eccl. 11:1 (b) Here the figure is used to represent good desires, acts and words. As these are given out to the needy, a full reward will return to the one who is so doing even though it may be after a long time. The waters represent all kinds of people. As we do good to others the blessing will return upon our own heads in the coming days.

Isa. 30:20 (a) God makes trouble and sorrow to be like a loaf of bread. It must be eaten. We must partake of it as we journey through life. God sees that we have this loaf, and plenty of it. It should strengthen our faith, increase our confidence in God, and keep us from seeking to build a nest in any earthly tree.

Isa. 55:2 (a) The things that most people seek for and think that they will be satisfied when they obtain them, find that these are not bread at all, but only look like bread. Christ is the bread of God, nothing outside of Him, nothing that omits Him, can ever satisfy the need of the human heart and life. God the Father provides in the triune God that which is needed by the triune man, his body, soul and spirit. This truth is illustrated by the Lord Jesus in Luke 11:11.

Luke 11:3 (b) This must primarily refer to the physical bread which we eat, and which must be given to us through the kindness, wisdom and goodness of God. It may also refer to every other ministry from heaven which we need for the many exigencies that arise in our lives from day to day.

Luke 11:11 (a) In our prayers we often ask for that which we think is good for us and will be a blessing to us. We go by the sight of our eyes and the reasonings of our minds in deciding what is best for us. The gracious Father in heaven, however, knows exactly the condition and the character of that for which we ask. In some cases He sees that the thing we request is like a stone. It would not harm us, nor hurt us, but it would be of no value whatever to us. We could not eat it, we could not use it, we would not be blessed by it. For this reason, He has to say "no" to our request.

John 6:33 (a) Throughout this chapter bread is typical of the Lord Jesus Himself.

When He is received by faith into the heart, soul and life of a believer, He satisfies, gratifies, strengthens, blesses and gives life more abundant to those who feed upon Him and rejoice in His love and grace. It is not enough just to know about Christ, nor even to believe all that may be read about Him. The baker would die of starvation in the midst of his breads, cakes and pies if he did not eat them. It is the personal appropriation of the Lord Jesus that conveys and imparts eternal life to the soul.

1 Cor. 10:17 (a) This bread as a loaf represents the true Church of God on earth. As the loaf contains many grains (no one knows how many), so the Church contains many members, and no one knows how many. It is true, however, that the loaves contain nothing but wheat. No sand or cinders are there, no sticks or stones will be found there. God's true Church contains only true believers, saints of God. Man's churches contain all kinds of grain, and other substances. Gamblers, saloon keepers, liquor dealers, tobacco slaves, thieves, murderers, and all kinds of hypocrites may be found in man's organizations. God's true Church, however, contains, as members, only those who belong to Jesus Christ by faith.

BREAST

Gen. 49:25 (c) The teaching here probably is that the Lord will grant fruitfulness and that the children given by God's kindness will be fed, well cared for, and will grow to maturity as they should.

Ex. 29:27 (c) This part of the animal is typical of our affection and love offered to God, waved before Him as a memorial, and to remind Him that we love Him above all others. We believe that all the "burnt" offerings teach this same truth.

Job 21:24 (a) We are taught by this figure that this person retained his vigor, power and resourcefulness until the end of his days.

S. of Sol. 1:13 (b) Here is a picture of the perfect love, sweetness and satisfaction which exists between the Lord and His bride, the children of God.

S. of Sol. 4:5 (b) This will remind us of the sufficiency, devotion and activity of the love of the children of God for the Lord Jesus Christ. (See also Chap. 7:7-8)

S. of Sol. 8:8 (b) This peculiar picture will remind us that the Christian may lose his love and affection for the bridegroom, the Saviour. Or it may be that this bride is a very young bride who has not yet learned to love, worship and adore as she should. Love grows as it is practiced. It may also be that this is the Christian who has lost his first love, and is not now as affectionate as she should be. Evidently this lack is made up and is restored as described in verse 10.

Isa. 28:9 (a) We learn from this comparison that some of God's people grow up to maturity as Christians. They no longer need to feed on milk, but are able to eat and digest strong meat. Paul mentions this same truth in I Cor. 3:2. Christians should grow in the knowledge of the things of God until they become matured Christians. (See Eph. 4:13)

Isa. 60:16 (a) God's people were to obtain the best and richest treasures of their enemies. Their enemies would be made to give up their very living to Israel.

Isa. 66:11 (a) This is a prophecy of the restoration of Jerusalem when Israel will again rejoice in the abundant blessings of God as the babe is satisfied with the mother's milk.

Ezek. 23:3 (a) This is a terrible accusation against Israel because they had permitted the wicked people around them to take liberties with them to satisfy all their evil desires. Israel committed horrible sins with the wicked nations around them. In verses 8 and 34 we find that these same nations punished Israel severely.

Hosea 2:2 (a) God presents to us a graphic picture of the wicked associations of Israel with the idolatrous nations around her. God would not ignore these evil associations. We find this same sin presented in all of its evil in the church of Rome today. They have partaken of the idolatrous practices of almost every known evil religion. They nourish every form of evil and sin and promote every kind of wicked association with the world.

Hosea 9:14 (a) God is warning Israel that He will punish them by preventing the blessings which they expected to receive and would dry up their natural resources of sustenance.

Nahum 2:7 (b) Here we find revealed that in the day of God's judgments many will be calling for help and will cry out for relief when none is available.

Rev. 15:6 (a) This probably teaches us the fact that these angels had their loyalty, their love and their devotion bound up in the golden bands of purity and holiness. They were entirely loyal to God, He had their love and affection.

BREASTPLATE

Ex. 25:7 (c) The high priest wore a breastplate in which were brilliant stones, each one bearing the name of one of the tribes of Israel. This is a figure of the nearness to God and dearness of each believer wherein his own High Priest carries him on His breast close to His heart.

Isa. 59:17 (c) Here as in Ephesians 6:14 (a) the breastplate is a type of a righteous life. Those who live right fear no wrong. Their hearts are protected. Their feelings are protected. They have done that which is just and they are not afraid of evil consequences.

1 Thess. 5:8 (a) This breastplate of faith and love guards the believer from being hurt or hindered by the shafts that may be shot at him from enemy sources. Faith in God and love for his fellowmen keep him from getting his feelings hurt.

Rev. 9:9 (c) The references here may be to the modern tanks used in battle. They are protected with great plates in front. Their motors make a terribly loud sound. They have cannon in the rear as a tail. It is no doubt a figure of speech with regard to the great tribulation day when terrible damage will be done by men against the people of God.

BREATH

2 Sam. 22:16 (a) The wrath of God is compared to His breath. No special effort is required to breathe. Wrath is a natural attribute of God which is continually manifested against sin and sinners. In anger the breath comes strong and vigorous. (See also Job 4:9; Psalm 18:15)

Isa. 11:4 (b) The wrath of God is executed by the Holy Spirit. (See also Isa. 40:7)

Isa. 30:28, 33 (b) The Holy Spirit is compared in these passages to a river. He is constantly operating. He is always in the divine channel. He is always bringing the purpose and plans of God into human hearts. (See also Ezek. 47:5; John 7:38)

Isa. 33:11 (a) Israel will destroy themselves by the way they live. Their sins and their daily activities will bring destruction upon them. (See this thought also in Hosea 13:9)

Ezek. 37:9 (a) The breath also in this place is a type of the Holy Spirit. Breath is often associated with this Person, as when Jesus breathed on them and said, "Receive ye the Holy Spirit." (See also Job 33:4; 37:10; 41:21; Psa. 33:6)

BREECHES

Ex. 28:42 (c) This is probably a figure of the righteousness which should characterize the priest of God with regard to his walking, his downsitting, and his uprising.

Ezek. 44:18 (b) This garment is a type of human righteousness, self-made and self-applied. We are not to confess that we are saved by grace but kept by works. These are not to be mixed. Sweat is a product of the exertion of the human body. God wants nothing that comes out from us spiritually when we take the place of being His servant. We must display for Him only that which He has given us. God's righteousness and our own righteousness are not to be mixed in our conversation and profession. See also Deut. 22:11. There are those religions which teach that we are saved by grace, but we are kept saved by works. Other religions teach that we are saved partly by faith, and partly by works. Both of these theories are false in God's sight, and are not to be believed nor accepted by any who want God's favor, His salvation and His approval. Nothing that emanates from our own spirits or originates in our own minds is acceptable with God when it is a matter of salvation or of our relationship to God. (See Isa. 64:6) Just as nothing that comes out of our bodies can be pleasing to another person, so nothing that emanates from our spirits is acceptable to the great Spirit.

BRICK

Gen. 11:3 (c) This is a type of man-made religious programs which lack the consistency, strength and durability of the Rock of Ages. No religion of any kind that has its origin in the mind of a man or a woman will pass God's judgment. Salvation is of the Lord, and not of some group of men or women. Salvation is of the Jews, and therefore cannot come through any Gentile source. All false religions are as "bricks." They are designed and conceived in human minds and are not based on the Word of God, nor the will of God.

Isa. 9:10 (b) Israel found that if their first efforts in following idols should fail, then they would devise ways and means of sinning in a more durable and lasting way.

Isa. 65:3 (b) Here we find a picture of the wickedness of Israel. They should have made altars of stone. Stones are made by God. Instead of that they made altars of brick, and bricks are made by men. They substituted their own works (bricks) for and instead of God's works (stones). (See also Ex. 20:25)

BRIDE

Isa. 62:5 (a) This is a term applied to Israel in the rejuvenation, when Israel returns to the Lord and Christ reigns in Jerusalem.

John 3:29 (a) This is a picture of the Lord's disciples and Himself.

Rev. 21:2 (a) This is a picture of the whole church of God gathered together in glory for the wonderful meeting with her Lord, the Bridegroom.

BRIDEGROOM

Isa. 61:10 (a) In this and in other passages, the Bridegroom is the Lord Jesus Himself. In the Old Testament, the Bride is Israel and the Bridegroom is the Father, but in the New Testament, the Bride is the church, and the Bridegroom is the Lord Jesus. (See also Matt. 25:1)

BRIDLE

2 Ki. 19:28 (a) This is a figure to represent the restraining, guiding and compelling power of God in making nations obey His will. (See Jer. 50:9; 51:7, 11, 20)

Job 30:11 (a) Perhaps this represents the criticism which Job's friends loosed upon Him without restraining. These friends wanted Job to express himself freely without hindrance, hoping thereby to catch him in his words.

Job 41:13 (a) If this has a typical meaning, it might refer to God's restraining power over both the body and the soul.

Psalm 39:1 (b) This represents the restraining influence which David brought to bear upon his own mouth in order to prevent him from saying things which should not be said.

Isa. 30:28 (a) The bridle represents the power of God to make men do His will. He binds men to the choice which they make. The bridle reveals God's control over His enemies in making them continue in a path of disobedience. This thought is also found in Isa. 66:4, and 2 Thess. 2:11.

Isa. 37:29 (a) This indicates God's warning to Sennacherib that He would take charge of the affairs of this king in such a way that he would be forced to turn away from Jerusalem and return to his own land. God's methods, means and plans are referred to as a bridle.

James 1:26 (a) Men are expected to control and to hold in check the tongue and the talk. No one should speak loosely and carelessly. The speech should always be with grace, seasoned with salt.

James 3:2 (a) God expects that man will control all the notions, desires and motions of the flesh.

BRIER

Isa. 5:6 (b) Briers are symbols of the little bothersome troubles that hurt and hinder God's people. God promised to send them on Israel because of their disobedience. Briers are small, not as large as thorns, but they are very painful and troublesome. (See also under THORNS, THISTLES, NETTLES and BRAMBLES. See also Isa. 7:23; Isa. 32:13; Ezek. 28:24.)

Isa. 9:18 (b) God's wrath is to be kindled so greatly that He would cease dealing with His people by small punishments, but rather would abandon them to their enemies. (See also Isa. 10:17.)

Isa. 27:4 (b) Man's antagonism to God is compared to the little brier which is so easily destroyed, and which is so inconsequential. (See also Ezek. 2:6)

Isa. 55:13 (c) Here the brier is a type of human troubles which are to be replaced by God's blessings. (See under THISTLE.)

Micah 7:4 (a) The brier in this case represents a little, weak, frail man who thinks he is somebody, when he really is a cipher (Gal. 6:3) This man sets himself up against God, and God in derision compares him to the little, weak, troublesome brier that is soon destroyed.

Heb. 6:8 (b) Briers in this case represent hateful, harmful and hurtful expressions that come from the heart of one who knows better, and who should be producing fruit and flowers for God. God does not bless briers. The one who produces them will surely come under the curse of God.

BRIGHT

Acts 10:30 (c) This tells of the glory and the heavenly character of this Person, the Holy Spirit.

Rev. 22:16 (a) Describes the beauty, the sinlessness, and the glory of Christ.

BRIMSTONE

Isa. 30:33 (a) This reveals the terrible and destructive power of the wrath of God when it is poured forth.

Rev. 9:17 (b) Here is a picture of the fierce anger and destructive power of God's army as they attack their fellowmen who are enemies of God.

BROAD

Job 36:16 (a) By this is declared the liberty, largeness, and freedom of that one who is blessed by the Lord.

Matt. 7:13 (a) Here is indicated the widespread popularity of the path that leads to hell.

Matt. 23:5 (a) This indicates the desire of the hypocrite to advertise his pious character.

BROKEN

Lev. 21:19 (b) The spiritual teaching probably is that this man cannot walk with God properly nor serve God acceptably. The broken foot indicates a bad walk. The broken hand indicates ineffective work. The Lord wants us to walk well with Him and work well for Him.

Job 22:9 (a) This is a picture of the helplessness of orphans when some cruel man has taken from them their living.

Psalm 31:12 (a) This is descriptive of the feelings of one who is reproached, neglected and laid aside.

Prov. 15:13 (a) Here is a crushed spirit from which pride and antagonism have been removed.

Eccl. 12:6 (b) This describes the end of life when the hand and the heart fail. In this passage we may consider that the silver cord is the spinal cord, the bowl is the brain, the pitcher is the heart, and the wheel is the nerve center.

BROOK

1 Sam. 17:40 (c) This may be taken as a figure of the Word of God from which we may take portions and passages (stones) to hurl at God's enemies.

1 Kings 17:5 (c) This may be taken as a picture of the temporary character of the pleasures and programs which the world offers to the soul.

Job 6:15 (b) Here we have an indication of the vacillating character of human relationships. The best of friends separate. The sweetest fellowships often turn to bitter animosities.

Psa. 42:1 (b) This is a type of the rich blessings found in the Word of God, and in His fellowship by those who seek Him with the whole heart.

Psa. 110-7 (b) Possibly this brook refers to the intimate fellowship that Jesus had with His Father as He communed with Him in prayer, and learned of Him in His study of the Word.

Prov. 18:4 (b) Here is described the refreshing, life-giving character of man's helpful counsel to his fellowmen.

Isa. 15:7 (c) Possibly this is a reference to the transient character of possessions which will soon be carried away by the stream of time. We too should remember to keep short accounts with God. When we fail or falter, when we drift around and wander, let us come back to Calvary and look up to that precious One who is living on the Throne and whose blood cleanseth from all sin. There is no excuse for any Christian remaining out of fellowship with God.

BROTH

Isa. 65:4 (b) This term is used to describe the evil mixture of lust and pleasure which Israel was enjoying in her rebellion against the Lord.

BROTHER

1 Kings 20:33 (b) The ungodly enemy king took the place of being a relative of Ahab, the King of Samaria. Ahab accepted the suggestion. He therefore linked himself with one who was a bitter enemy of God and whom God had ordained for destruction. Christians are not brothers of the unsaved. Christians are children of God, while the unsaved are children of Satan. God cursed Ahab for his action in this matter.

Job 30:29 (a) Job felt so disgraced, so discouraged, and so wretched that he claimed kin with animals. He felt that he was not worthy to be called even a human being.

Psalm 49:7 (b) The word is used to describe any friend or relative who shows a helpful interest in time of distress. The passage particularly refers to the false teachings of Romanism, with its masses for the dead, and Mormonism with its baptism for the dead. No human being can do anything whatever to help the souls of those who have died.

Prov. 17:17 (c) This title refers to any person who loves, cares and shares with one who is in adversity, trouble or sorrow. God always provides someone who will help in time of sorrow.

Matt. 5:22 (b) The teaching evidently is that if any person should mock at or scoff at a Christian who is seeking to live a separated life, and thereby fulfill God's will, that person is in danger of eternal punishment because he sides in with Satan and takes sides against God.

Matt. 7:3 (a) This name is applied to any person with whom one is in close association and fellowship.

Matt. 12:50 (a) This person is a true believer in the Lord Jesus, who has received the gift of eternal life, and thereby has entered the family of God. It also describes the very close and precious relationship which Jesus maintains toward those who love Him and obey the Father.

Rom. 14:10 (a) In this passage the word refers to any believer or even one who claims to be a believer against whom another Christian may show a hostile attitude.

1 John 2:9 (b) This title is given to any real believer, a true Christian, one who has been born again, and is really a child of God.

BRUISE

Gen. 3:15 (b) This prophecy informs us that Satan would succeed in wounding the Lord Jesus which he did at Calvary.

2 Kings 18:21 (b) Here is described some of the weaknesses of the armies of Egypt, which were not always to be invincible. The

Lord was indicating clearly that already Pharaoh's armies were injured and hampered.

Isa. 1:6 (b) The word indicates the damage to the life and character of Israel caused by the storms, the wars and the conflicts which they suffered in their daily experiences. The word indicates that Israel has had many tragic experiences that have injured the country, wrecked the morals of the people and caused a condition of sinfulness that is obnoxious to God.

Isa. 42:3 (b) Here is presented a beautiful revelation of the tenderness of the Lord Jesus. He would not hinder any believer who was struggling in grace and usefulness. He would not speak disparagingly of anyone whose service was not perfect. He would not hinder nor crush any person who was trying to do his best.

Jer. 30:12 (b) This is probably a type of deep-seated wickedness in Israel's manner of living.

Ezek. 23:3,8 (b) This indicates clearly that the people of Israel when carried into Egypt were permitting and promoting lustful and wicked relations with the Egyptians.

Dan. 2:40 (b) This informs us that the fourth kingdom, the Roman Empire, would injure and damage many nations, but would not completely destroy them.

Nahum 3:19 (b) This word is used to describe the permanent and deep-seated wickedness in the hearts of the men of Nineveh which caused God to utterly destroy the city.

Luke 4:18 (a) This is a type of the injury caused by sin in the lives of men and which would be healed and mended by the wonderful grace and power of the Lord Jesus Christ.

Rom. 16:20 (a) This expression is used to inform us that God will enable His people to keep Satan in subjection, although we are not able to destroy him.

BRUIT

Jer. 10:22 (b) Here is a comparison of the great judgment of Israel to the roaring of falling waters.

Nahum 3:19 (b) Here is a graphic description of the howling, wailing, and crying of Nineveh in her judgment.

BRUTE

Jer. 10:8 (b) This describes the lusts and fleshly desires of a worldly people.

Jer. 51:17 (b) This indicates that man's whole thought and desire is for earthly things.

2 Peter 2:12 (a) By this is described leading men of the church who desire only those things which satisfy the natural cravings of the human heart and mind.

Jude: 10 (a) This is an assertion that these evil leaders knew nothing of spiritual things but only the things of this earth.

BUCKET

Num. 24:7 (b) As a gardener waters his garden with buckets of water, so Jacob or Israel would bring blessing to every part of the earth.

Isa. 40:15 (b) In this way is described the insignificant character of the great nations of the earth. The earth is compared to a bucket.

BUCKLER

2 Sam. 22:31 (b) This is a beautiful type of God's protecting care over those who hide themselves in Him.

Job 15:26 (b) This may refer to the excuses, reasonings and arguments of the ungodly who want none of God in their lives.

Psalm 18:2, 30 (a) This is a description given by David of the Lord who was protecting and preserving him from the attacks of his enemies.

Psalm 91:4 (a) God's Word was Moses' buckler. He hid himself behind and within God's failthful promises and invites us to do the same. (See also Prov. 2:7)

BUD

Num. 17:8 (c) This indicates that God can bring life out of death and to cause that which is helpless to become prosperous.

Psalm 132:17 (b) Here is a beautiful way of saying that the throne of David would again be set up and dead Israel would again become a living nation.

Isa. 27:6 (a) This is another prophecy that the nation of Israel which has been crushed and made fruitless will again flourish and bring forth fruit. (See also Ezek. 29:21)

Ezek. 7:10 (a) Evidently Israel was boasting and exhibiting pride of position and power. It is compared to the budding of a plant which would afterwards become fully developed.

Ezek. 16:7 (a) Here is a type of the freshness and loveliness with which God endowed the nation of Irsael under the reign of David and Solomon.

BUILD

Psalm 89:4 (a) Here is revealed the blessings that God will yet bring upon Israel in causing the scattered people to grow up again into a strong nation.

Psalm 127:1 (a) This is a plain statement that God must work in any church or Christian movement or nation if the desired results are to be obtained.

Prov. 9:1 (c) Probably this is a type of the Lord Jesus under the name of "Wisdom." He causes individuals to grow up into full maturity as Christians and nations to develop fully as godly nations.

S. of Sol. 4:4 (c) This may represent or describe the firm conviction of the church, her stamina, and her purpose of heart to serve God only.

Isa. 66:1 (a) The thought expressed in regard to this building is found also in Job 22:23, Acts 7:49, Acts 20:32, 1 Cor. 3:12 and Col. 2:7. It is the thought of developing in the life all various departments that make for a full, mature, Christian growth. There must be a good foundation and then a heating plant to keep the soul warm for God. There must be a place for meals, the dining room, for we must feed on the bread of life. A music room should be built, so that the heart will keep singing. Of course, there will be a library, for we are to keep studying, learning and reading. A bedroom is necessary so that we may rest, as He invites us to do. Besides this, there must also be light, water, the bath and the attic for storage. We should see that all these are developed as we grow in the knowledge of God and the service of the King.

Matt. 7:24 (a) We have a picture here of man's faith and works founded only upon the Lord Jesus, the Rock of Ages. In verse 26 the opposite is true.

Matt. 26:61 (b) Here the reference is to the resurrection of the Lord Jesus, wherein His body, so badly disfigured on the cross, would be restored in three days to full strength and power.

Luke 14:28 (a) God expects that each of His children will endeavor to serve Him so that definite accomplishment will be left behind in that Christian life. Moody built a tower, the Moody church and school. Livingston built a tower in Africa, the opening up of the dark continent to God. Dr. Bingham built a tower, the Sudan Interior Mission. Hudson Taylor built a tower, the China Inland Mission. What tower are you building for God?

Rom. 15:20 (a) Paul describes his work and ministry as a work of building. Those who heard him speak grew in grace as a building grows under the hand of the workman.

Gal. 2:18 (b) This is a reference to the growth in grace and knowledge, as well as in fellowship and service which these people enjoyed to whom Paul preached. He said that he was not rebuilding the old faith of Israel, but was really building the new faith of the church.

Ephesians 2:22 (a) Here is represented the work of the Spirit of God wherein Christ is revealed to the heart, and the individual becomes one of God's children, a stone in the building of His mystical church.

Heb. 3:3 (a) It is evident that Christ planned Israel's program and outlined the course they were to pursue in history.

BUILDERS

Psalm 118:22 (a) These were the leaders of the nation of Israel. They were the scribes, the Pharisees, the Sadducees, and the Herodians. They refused to have Christ as the cornerstone for the life of faith, they despised Him and rejected Him. (See also Matt. 21:42; Mark 12:10; Luke 20:17; Acts 4:11; 1 Pet. 2:7)

Ezek. 27:4 (c) The city fathers planned the building of the city of Tyrus, but did not take God into their consideration. They built without the Lord, and the Lord destroyed their works.

I Cor. 3:10 (a) Paul was the builder of churches. He did not carelessly organize these churches, he planned them carefully and according to the will of God. The word "church" does not refer to a building of wood and stone, but refers rather to the people who constitute the Church of God.

Heb. 11:10 (a) The Lord Jesus said "I will build my church." He is both the architect and the contractor of this world, and of the next. He designed everything that exists in the universe, and then He made it. Only He has and had the power to do it.

BUILDEST

Ezek. 16:31 (a) These evil men definitely planned and constructed places for sinning throughout the city.

Matt. 27:40 (a) The enemies of the Lord Jesus were referring to His own statement which they quoted in regards to the raising up of His own body from the grave after the enemy had so cruelly disfigured it.

BUILDETH

Prov. 14:1 (a) This figure is used to describe definite planning in the home so that there will be provision for the knowledge of God, education, culture, food, rest and pleasure. (See also Jer. 22:13)

Amos 9:6 (a) Only the eternal God with His unlimited and indescribable power could have made the heavens, and the heaven of heavens, so intelligently and so perfectly. He made everything with design. We read: "He made the stars also."

I Cor. 3:10 Paul was the builder and planned the formation of the many churches of Asia. Other servants of God came along with their ministry and continued to build up the saints of God.

BUILDING

2 Chron. 3:3 (c) This is probably a type of the Lord Jesus Christ who was the most magnificent and the most glorious person ever to dwell on earth.

1 Cor. 3:9 (a) This is plainly a type of the church of God, which is the dwelling place of God on the earth. It does not refer to any denomination, nor any building of wood or stone. It refers to the gathering together of those who are saved by grace, washed in the blood of the Lamb, redeemed by power, and are actually and truly the children of God.

2 Cor. 5:1 (a) This type is used to describe the new body which each believer will have after the resurrection.

Eph. 2:20-21 (a) In this place the building is used as a type of the church which the Lord is constructing by saving souls, bringing them into His family, and attaching them to each other by invisible bonds. Christ is constructing for Himself a dwelling place on earth among His own children. This is called "the church" of which He Himself is the cornerstone, He is the architect and the contractor.

Heb. 9:11 (a) The type here evidently refers to the personal body of the Lord Jesus. He calls it a temple which men would seek to destroy, but which He would raise up in three days. (See also John 2:19)

BUILT

Psalm 89:2 (a) The Psalmist seems to be expressing his confidence that God's mercy toward him would increase and abound in the coming days. It may be that he also was expressing his intention of having a greater comprehension or knowledge of God's mercy than he had ever known before. God's mercy is always like the ocean for its fullness, but we must learn to understand it, appreciate it, and appropriate it more fully.

Jer. 31:4 (a) In this graphic way the Lord assures Israel that He will restore their national position and power by making their land again the "glory of all lands."

Ezek. 13:10 (a) This figure represents the building of false claims in a false religion by false leaders. Examples are Mormonism, Russellism, Seventh Day Adventism, Roman Catholicism, Unity, Christian Science, and many others.

I Cor. 3:14 (a) Here we find represented a substantial work of God erected by a saint of God on the person and work of Jesus Christ. An example of this is the Sudan Interior Mission by Dr. Bingham, and the China Inland Mission by Hudson Taylor.

1 Pet. 2:5 (a) By this figure we see the work of God in constructing for His glory a group of Christians both local, national

and international, which will be known as "His body, His house, His church, His family."

BULL

Psalm 22:12 (b) This name is applied by the Saviour to those who in violent hatred surrounded the cross to kill Him. They acted like infuriated animals. They released their hatred in violence against the precious Son of God.

Psalm 68:30 (b) This is a type used to represent the strong, active, vicious enemies of Israel. (See also Isa. 34:7)

Isa. 51:20 (a) The type here is used to present the people of Israel who were furious against God because He had poured out His wrath upon Jerusalem.

Jer. 50:11 (a) The enemies of God are compared to these violent wild animals who would gloat over Israel in their victorious march through the land.

BULLOCK

Ex. 29:36 (c) This animal is used as a type of Christ in all His greatness and wonderful sufficiency. It was the largest of the offerings. The other two offerings were the lamb and the pigeon. These three offerings probably represent different concepts of Jesus as the sacrifice. Some know little about Him — just enough to trust Him — the pigeon aspect. Others know more about Him and His work, and therefore trust with more knowledge — the lamb aspect. Some who have been raised in Christian circles have heard much about Christ, and have read their Bibles more often so that they have a very large conception of His sufficiency — the bullock aspect. In this passage the animal represents the Lord Jesus as a sin offering. No other sacrifice is acceptable for sin except the perfect Lamb of God who perfectly met our need at Calvary. (See also 2 Cor. 5:21.) In Lev. 1:5 the burnt offering also is typical of Christ offered for us. (See under "OFFERINGS".)

Lev. 16:27 (c) The animal here is a type of the Lord Jesus in His greatness and completeness. Because of this He is able to make the believer fit for heaven, and heaven fit for the believer.

Deut. 17:1 (c) This animal is a picture of Christ Jesus in His sacrificial office as burnt offering. He is the only perfect one who could make a perfect sacrifice. All other sacrifices made by men are tainted and defiled with sin. God will have only a perfect offering. None can provide this except Jesus Christ Himself.

Jer. 31:18 (b) The speaker is Ephraim which is a name given to Israel when they were in a backslidden condition and were walking in disobedience to God. They complained of the punishment God was sending upon them, although they brought punishment upon them, by their own disobedience. They compared themselves to the bullock, which was being beaten for its idleness. It should have been in the yoke serving God.

Jer. 46:21 (a) Here we find a type of the leaders of Egypt. They had grown rich, proud and strong, but their end was to be punishment from God.

BULRUSH

Isa. 58:5 (a) This is a type which describes the bowed head, the heavy heart, and the distressed spirit of one who has been crushed by his circumstances.

BULWARK

Isa. 26:1 (a) This presents a beautiful aspect of God in His care for His people and in His protecting power over them.

BUNDLE

I Sam. 25:29 (b) This is another name for the precious fellowship into which believers are brought with their Lord, safe and secure.

S. of Sol. 1:13 (c) All of God's gracious lovingkindnesses and mercies are grouped by the Psalmist, as a bundle is wrapped together.

Matt. 13:30 (a) This represents unsaved people bound together according to their associations on earth — gamblers with gamblers, thieves with thieves, harlots with harlots, etc. Each kind is bound together and made to suffer together in hell. They fellowshipped together on earth in their sins — now they are bound for punishment in eternity.

BURDEN

Gen. 49:14 (a) This beautiful metaphor presents the believer as a bearer of the sorrows and griefs of others. One burden is the load that the Christian has for the glory of God and His work; the other is the burden He has for man's need of salvation and relief. He couches down to show His perfect willingness to bear these loads, and to have this yoke put upon his neck. He is described as being strong because the Spirit of God gives the strength necessary bearing both of these burdens.

Perhaps this is also a beautiful illustration of the Lord Jesus. He too bowed down to bear the burden of God's relationship to the people and the relationship of the people to God. He bore God's righteous character and revealed God's judgments while He made provision for man's terrible need because of his sins.

Num. 4:15-19 (c) This was a God-given load to bear for the glory of the Lord. Some burdens are liabilities — some are assets.

Deut. 1:12 (b) Moses thus describes the great weight of responsibility that was upon him because of the problems connected with the tremendous host he was leading to the promised land.

Psalm 38:4 (b) The word is used to describe the load of sin which crushed David's spirit.

Psalm 55:22 (b) This is a description of any weight of grief or sorrow, any distressing problem or situation which should be brought to the Lord for His sustaining grace and power. (See also Eccl. 12:5.)

Psalm 81:6 (b) This is a beautiful way of saying that God sometimes leaves the load of grief, sorrow and trouble which weighs down the heart and spirit, but removes the person from under the weight of it. In this case, the burden was left but the person was removed from it, and became a singing, rejoicing believer even though the burden remained. This is one of the three ways in which the Lord relieves His distressed children. As an example, we may think of the father and mother who have an afflicted child. There is no way of removing that burden, but God does provide that the hearts of the parents may be radiant, happy and trustful even though the sorrow remains.

Isa. 9:4 (b) Here we find that God delivers His people from the grievous yoke of the enemy so that they may be free to serve Him.

Isa. 15:1 (a) Here the burden is the sad story of God's judgments upon Moab. Frequently when God told of the punishment He was preparing to mete out to the enemy, the story is described as a "burden." (See Isa. 17:1; 19:1; 21:1, 11, 13; 22:1, 25; 23:1; 30:6)

Isa. 46:1-2 (b) Probably the Lord is telling us that the sins, sorrows and sufferings of these wicked people were like a heavy load on the hearts and the lives of every living thing in the land.

Jer. 23:33 (b) The question is asked concerning what message there is from the Lord about punishment and retribution. (See also vss. 36 and 38)

Lam. 2:14 (b) The word is used here to describe the false information given by false prophets to bring fear upon the people.

Ezek. 12:10 (b) Here is a message concerning punishment and judgment against the leaders of Israel. (See also Hosea 8:10; Nahum 1:1; Zech. 12:1; Mal. 1:1)

Matt. 23:4 (b) The word is used in this case concerning religious laws, rules and programs formulated by false religions and forced upon the worshippers in that faith. (See also Luke 11:46)

BURN

Gen. 44:18 (a) Judah did not want Joseph's anger to be aroused and inflicted upon him. He remembered his treatment of Joseph in former days.

Ex. 3:2 (c) This expression is a picture of God's presence and power in the midst of Israel and also in the midst of His church. God's people are really blessed by His presence and are not destroyed.

Job 30:30 (b) Job let his extreme pain and suffering as he sat in the ashes as though a fire was kindled in his body.

Psalm 39:3 (b) The spirit was thoroughly aroused and stirred because the feelings were repressed and held in.

Psalm 89:46 (b) The Psalmist did not want God's anger to be increased and poured out upon the people.

Isa. 1:31 (b) This is a description of the fierce wrath of God which will destroy the enemies of Israel.

Isa. 3:24 (b) This is a description of the fever, the pain and the sorrow in the human body that destroys its beauty.

Isa. 4:4 (b) This undoubtedly refers to the cleansing power of the Spirit of God when He comes forth in judgment. (See also Matt. 3:11, Acts 2:3)

Isa. 10:17 (a) Here is described the punishment which God would execute upon the King of Assyria.

Isa. 27:4 (b) Here is a picture of the destructive power of the Lord God Almighty who will conquer every enemy.

Isa. 40:16 (b) This wonderful passage tells us the story of the insufficiency of all man's sacrifice and offering. Lebanon is a mountain six miles wide and fifty miles long. It was covered with a very thick forest of trees of many kinds, principally cedars. It was a hunter's paradise, for the thick undergrowth harbored many kinds of wild animals. In this Scripture the Lord is telling us that if all the burnable materials on that mountain, trees, bushes, vines and grasses, were to be piled up to make one great bonfire and then if all the animals were killed and placed upon the top of that bonfire to be offered as a sacrifice to God, this would not be sufficient to put away the sins of Israel. The greatest thing that any man can do is not sufficient to save his soul. Only the sacrifice of the Lord Jesus Christ is sufficient to satisfy God's demands.

Lam. 2:3 (b) God is informing us that He was filled with just anger against the evil doings of His people.

Mal. 4:1 (b) We learn from this type that a terrible day of retribution and judgment is ahead when God will come forth in power to punish His enemies. It has no reference whatever to the "annihilation of the wicked" in eternity. It refers to the destruction of nations from this earth. This was done in the case of the Canaanites, Philistines, Amalekites, Jebusites and other enemies of Israel. They have been blotted from the earth, and so far as we know there are no descendants to be found.

Matt. 3:12 (a) This refers to the literal fire of hell in which sinners must spend eternity.

Luke 12:35 (a) This term is used to describe a clear, bright testimony for God, which would illuminate and inspire those who came under its influence.

Luke 24:32 (a) The warm and delightful feeling produced in the heart when God speaks words of comfort and love to His people is thus described.

John 5:35 (a) This refers to the active, forceful testimony of John the Baptist. His messages entered into the souls and hearts of the people and left a permanent impression.

Rom. 1:27 (a) The word is used here to indicate a wild, unrestrained desire that was fed and nourished by the sinner.

1 Cor. 7:9 (b) In this way is described the torment or unsatisfied passion in the body.

2 Cor. 11:29 (b) The word in this passage describes the deep desire in the soul of the servant of God for the blessing of others.

BURNT OFFERING

Gen. 8:20 (c) This offering represents the perfect life and the perfect person of the Lord Jesus offered up to God in the place of and instead of our imperfect character and unholy life.

Lev. 1:4 (c) The offering in this Scripture is the first in the five offerings. It represents our entire self being acceptable to God in the person of the perfect Lord Jesus Christ. He makes us acceptable to God by the sacrifice of Himself, and then our service can be acceptable to God. Christ had to die for our character as well as our conduct.

Ezra 3:2 (c) Here this offering represents the person and work of the Lord Jesus offered to God for the nation of Israel. By this sacrifice the nation would be acceptable to God in the new enterprise of rebuilding Jerusalem.

Psalm 51:19 (c) By this means David indicated that after confession and cleansing he would be acceptable to God — this is typical of the perfection of the Saviour offered in our stead.

Isa. 40:16 (c) If all the thousands of animals on the broad slopes of Lebanon were gathered together to make a burnt offering to God, this tremendous sacrifice would not be sufficient to put away one sin, nor would it equal the offering of the Lord Jesus Christ for our sins. (See also OFFERING)

BURST

Prov. 3:10 (b) This is a picture of the great material blessing that God would give to His obedient people.

Jer. 2:20 (b) Here is a figure to represent God's delivering hand for Israel from her enemies, the Assyrians. (See also Jer. 30:8; Nahum 1:13)

Jer. 5:5 (b) Here is the story of the great men of Israel who refused to bow to the law of God and threw off the yoke of the Lord that they might be joined to idols.

BURY

Rom. 6:4 (b) This probably means that the convert is placed under the waters of baptism as a public confession that he died with Christ, was placed in the tomb with Him, and rose again with Christ to walk in newness of life. It is a testimony of identification with Christ in His death, burial and resurrection. (See also Col. 2:12)

BUSH

Ex. 3:2 (c) This is descriptive of the nation of Israel in which God dwelt and yet which suffered from the persecutions of many enemies, yet was not consumed or destroyed.

Deut. 33:16 (b) It refers to the unusual character of God's presence on the earth as contrasted with the greatness of heaven.

Luke 6:44 (b) This is descriptive of a small character who never gives out blessing but injures and damages those who come near him.

BUSHEL

Matt. 5:15 (b) A type of business affairs under which some Christians bury their testimony. (See also Luke 11:33)

BUSINESS

Eccl. 5:3 (a) This is typical of active, ambitious enterprises which bring dreams of wealth and greatness.

Luke 2:49 (a) The work of serving His heavenly Father and doing all the things His Father sent Him to do is thus described.

Rom. 12:11 (a) It may refer to one's secular occupation but more likely refers to the work of the Lord in all of its many phases.

1 Thess. 4:11 (a) This refers to any work which is honest and honorable and through which remuneration is received for living expenses.

BUTTER

Job 20:17 (b) Butter and honey are the products of living animals. The Lord is telling us in this passage that the blessings of the living God for and upon the one who daily trusts Him and loves His will will be copious and constant. The living Lord gives His richest blessings to His people who know Him as the living Lord. There are those Christians who live around the cross and forget that Christ is now the living Son of God in His human body on the throne of heaven. Those who have daily fellowship with the Lord Jesus in heaven are said to be living on milk and honey.

Job 29:6 (b) This is a type of great prosperity and abundant riches in the things of earth. These are had because the living Lord of heaven commands His daily blessing of His obedient child.

Psalm 55:21 (a) This is a type, because of its slippery and greasy character, of the deceitful and clever statements made by the ungodly in order to mislead the hearer.

Isa. 7:15 (b) This rich food here represents the abundant blessings which Jesus received from His heavenly Father in great quantity even while a child on earth.

BUY

Isa. 55:1 (b) This represents the laying of one's life at the Lord's feet in utter abandonment and full devotion in order to obtain the fulness of His blessing.

Rev. 3:18 (b) Here is described the attitude of helpless dependence upon God for those blessings which will transform the life and make it worthwhile.

BY-WORD

Deut. 28:37 (a) Here we find that in the day of Israel's rejection and disobedience she would be called by hateful names which the natives of different countries would apply to her in the various places where she would be scattered. (See Jer. 24:9)

1 Kings 9:7 (a) Here is another prophecy from God that the Jews would receive sneers and be called hateful names by their neighbors. (See also 2 Chron. 7:20; Psa. 44:14)

Job 17:6 (b) Job's name was ridiculed among his acquaintances because of his misfortunes. See also chapter 30, verse 9.

C

CABIN

Jer. 37:16 (a) This is really a dungeon or a prison cell for prisoners.

CAESAR

Matt. 22:21 (b) He represents anyone who rightfully rules over us and to whom certain obligations are due.

John 19:12 (c) Here he is a type of any earthly relationship which replaces or displaces the Lordship of Christ.

CAGE

Jer. 5:27 (b) This is a name given to a home, synagogue, or temple where Satan's deceits are housed and protected, as the church building of a cult which is anti-Christian.

Rev. 18:2 (a) It reveals that there are religious systems which house Satanic forces and hold them in such a grip that no gospel and no emancipating power from heaven is permitted to enter and deliver.

CAIN

Gen. 4:5 (c) He is a type of a self-righteous person who disdains the sacrifice of the Lamb and offers to God the labor of his own hands for his sins. He is one who believes in salvation by works and character building.

Heb. 11:4 (c) He represents any person who offers to God the products of his own life, imagination, and thought as a sacrifice for his sins instead of the blood of the Lamb.

1 John 3:12 (a) He indicates any person, who, in order to sustain and maintain his own evil ways, desires by hook or crook to get rid of his righteous and godly associates.

Jude 11 (a) This is a picture of those who reject the sacrifice of Christ, pursue a path of religious activity, and offer it to God instead of the merits of the Saviour.

CAKE

Exod. 12:39 (c) Christ is thus pictured as One in whom there is no sin and of whom we may eat as the Bread of God.

Judges 7:13 (b) This cake represents Gideon and his weak, little army of three hundred men. They are compared to a small cake with reference to their weakness but they are compared to a barley cake to describe their value.

Hosea 7:8 (a) The nation of Israel is the cake. They were kind and good to their neighbors but were not obedient and good to God. Also represents a sinner who is beautiful in his attitude to his fellowmen (the under side or human side) but raw toward God (the upper side).

CALDRON

Ezek. 11:3-7 (a) This is a type of Jerusalem. As broth boils in the kettle, so the inhabitants of Jerusalem were to suffer under the fire of cruel invaders.

Micah 3:3 (a) This caldron is a picture of the terrible boiling, burning troubles that were to come upon the people because of the wrath of God. They were as helpless to get out of their trouble as the contents of the kettle were unable to get out of it.

CALF

Ex. 32:4 (c) This was worshipped as an idol because it represented food to eat and work to profit thereby. It was worshiped in Egypt as a god, and Israel had been so many years there, that they turned to this false god when their hearts were not right with the true God.

Lev. 9:2-3 (c) This may be taken as a type of Jesus in His youth and His humility. He was led as a lamb to the slaughter. He was a young man, and this calf is a fitting symbol of the young king.

Psa. 29:6 (c) The type in this case may represent youth, vigor, activity and a carefree life.

Jer. 34:18 (b) This is certainly a type of the death of Christ who passed through the furnace of God's wrath, suffered in the darkness, and yet was "the light of life." (This was called a heifer in Gen. 15:9)

Ezek. 1:7 (a) Here we find a type of the Lord as He walked significantly, surely, certainly and with a definite plan and purpose.

Hosea 8:5 (a) The Samaritans made a calf their god. It could not and did not deliver them from their enemies, but caused God's wrath to fall upon them.

Hosea 14:2 (b) From this we learn that the offering of praise, thanksgiving and worship from their lips would bring joy to the heart of God, as though Israel offered a calf on the altar.

Mal. 4:2 (a) From this we learn that Israel's blessings under the good hand of God were that they were fed by the Lord, protected by the Lord, and grew greater, stronger and more useful under God's good hand.

Luke 15:23 (c) This represents the fullness of Christ's sufficiency and His ability to supply the needs of the repentant sinner.

Rev. 4:7 (b) No doubt this is a type of our Lord Jesus who served both God and man. See under "OX."

CALLING

Rom. 11:29 (b) A word applied to invitation from God for His special service with which He also grants the gifts and the power to do that service.

1 Cor. 1:26 (b) Indicates God's choice of an individual and His plan and purpose for him regardless of his qualifications or position.

1 Cor. 7:20 (c) The word here evidently refers to the kind of business in which the person was engaged when he was saved by grace. Undoubtedly it is taken for granted that this is a legitimate work and not something that is illegitimate and ungodly.

Eph. 4:4 (c) This calling is out of darkness into light; out of Satan's kingdom into God's kingdom; out of the devil's family into God's family.

Heb. 3:1 (c) This word refers to the new economy, the new life of God, the new association with the things of heaven.

2 Peter 1:10 (b) Here is a request to examine one's self carefully and thoroughly to see whether the gift of eternal life has really been implanted in the soul and whether the person is really saved.

CALM

Psalm 107:29 (b) Describes the peace and tranquillity of one who has called on the Lord in the storms of life and His Word has removed all fear from the soul.

CAMEL

Isa. 60:6 (b) This animal is used to describe in picture the business, the activity, the merchandising and the prosperity that should come upon Israel when that nation is restored again to her place in the world.

Ezek. 25:5 (a) This is a type of the destruction and desolation which would come upon the Ammonites under the wrath of God. Their busiest city was to become a place for stabling animals on their journey and a grazing place for flocks.

Matt. 19:24 (a) The camel is a literal one and the eye of the needle is a literal eye of a literal needle. This is no figure of speech. The parable reveals the impossibility of a sinner to enter into heaven by any works or wealth of his own.

Matt. 23:24 (a) Our Lord compares a small, insignificant story to a gnat, and a great and preposterous yarn to a camel. People doubt and question the truth of God, but will readily believe any kind of a statement by any kind of religious teacher no matter how absurd the statement is. Jacob readily believed the lie told to him by his ten sons about the death of Joseph. He refused to believe the truth that these same men brought to him informing him that Joseph was alive. (See also Mark 10:25; Luke 18:25)

CAMP

Heb. 13:13 (b) The great religious groups of the world established by human agencies and teaching men's theories are called a "camp."

Rev. 20:9 (b) A term used to describe the armies of Israel encamped in and around Jerusalem.

CAMPHIRE

Song of Solomon 1:14 (c) Christ and His love toward the Church are compared to the sweet perfume of camphire. See also 4:13 where our love for Christ is to Him as the fragrance of camphire.

CANAAN

Gen. 17:8 (c) This describes this country and compares it to the life of victory which should be the portion of every believer. In Canaan, the Lord gave rich possessions and fought all their battles for them. Many Christians stop at Jabesh-Gilead and never cross over Jordan to the land of grapes, figs, olives and victory. Canaan is called in several Scriptures the land that floweth with milk and honey. It probably represents typically the victorious life of the happy, radiant, conquering Christian. This person lives in constant fellowship with the living God and Father, has conscious communion with Christ Jesus, and receives daily blessings from the Holy Spirit. He has crossed over Jordan out of the desert into the life more abundant, the life that is life indeed.

CANDLE

Job 18:6 (b) This is a type of the personal testimony of a man during his daily life. (See also chapter 21:17, and Prov. 31:18)

Job 29:3 (b) God's care and God's comfort, together with the light brought about by God's presence in the soul are compared to the candle.

Psalm 18:28 (a) The Psalmist is telling us that God will give him a bright testimony so that others might learn to know God through his ministry and messages. God certainly did it.

Prov. 20:27 (a) This is probably man's spirit enlightened by God and called by men "an enlightened conscience." It reveals the thoughts and intents of the heart. (See also chapter 24:20.)

Zeph. 1:12 (a) Here we learn of the meticulous care of God in all His detail of searching out the things He must expose.

Matt. 5:15 (b) This is a type of man's testimony hidden in his business (the bushel), or dimmed by laziness (the bed). Some splendid Christians are either so busy in their work, or so filled with the desire for ease and pleasure that they do not testify for their Lord as brightly and as constantly as they should, and could.

Rev. 18:23 (b) Since this candle indicates man-made religious life, the Lord is informing us that all such idolatry and false pretense, as well as all human religious inventions will be utterly abolished, when God judges these false religions.

Rev. 22:5 (b) These candles are a type of human, man-made religions and revelations. In heaven there will be no need of any man-made ideas or notions, only God's truth will remain.

CANDLESTICK

Exod. 25:31 (c) This is a type of the Holy Spirit illuminating all the things of God. The pure gold represents the purity of the Spirit and of His Word. The seven branches or stems represent the fullness and completeness of the revelation of the Spirit. The bowls represent the great provision of the Spirit. The flowers represent the beauty of the Spirit. Some Bible expositors feel that the candlestick also represents God's people, and certainly it does in the book of Revelation.

Rev. 1:20 (a) Here we certainly find a type of the church as she gives light on the Scriptures and reveals Christ by her ministries. The Lord Jesus Himself said that the "seven candlesticks are the seven churches." These candlesticks reveal that the seven lessons given through the seven churches present full and complete light on what the Spirit says to us about God's will. Each church is to present an unsullied, pure light from heaven to a dark and sinful world.

Rev. 2:5 (a) This is clearly a type of the testimony of an individual or of a church wherein the person and work of Christ no longer are properly presented to the public.

Rev. 11:4 (a) These are two mysterious men sent from God with great power to make known His judgment on the earth sometime in the future days. They will give the light of God to the enemies of God. They bear God's testimony in a hostile land. Some think these are Moses and Elijah. The context clearly indicates that these candlesticks are types of real men.

CANKER

2 Tim. 2:17 (b) This describes the damaging, deadening, harmful results of the words spoken by these two men. This word "canker" is better translated by the word "gangrene."

CANKER WORM

Joel 1:4 (c) This is the third in a series of punishments sent by God upon the nations as a reward for their wickedness.

Nahum 3:15 (c) It represents any evil calamity that may be sent by God to punish His people as individuals or as a company.

CAPTAIN

2 Chron. 13:12 (a) One of the many positions taken by our Lord for the blessing of His people. We are soldiers of Jesus Christ as we find in Hebrews 2:10. See 2 Tim. 2:3.

CAPTIVE

Isa. 51:14 (b) This is typical of any Christian who is a slave to any form of evil or uncleanness. (See also Isa. 52:2)

Luke 4:18 (b) Here is a type of those who are bound by Satan in false doctrines, false beliefs and evil practices. (See also Isa. 61:1)

Eph. 4:8 (a) These captives are the Old Testament believers who took advantage of the sacrifices, were protected by the blood of those offerings, but were held in paradise as captives until the blood of the Lord Jesus would blot out their sins. Immediately after Calvary, Christ went down to paradise and took all of these Old Testament believers up to heaven to be with God. The blood of bulls and of goats covered their sins, but it took the blood of Jesus Christ to blot out their sins.

2 Tim. 3:6 (b) This name is given to those who are held in bondage by Satan as they listened to false teachers who lead them into false faiths.

CARCASS

Jer. 19:7 (a) A term of derision used against the people of Jerusalem who, because of their wickedness, were to fall under the sword of their enemies.

Matt. 24:28 (a) Here we have a reference to any corrupt community, city or nation which God must of necessity disapprove and remove. The vultures represent God's judgment upon the corrupt and dead condition that exists among these people.

CARE

Matt. 13:22 (a) This refers to the problems of daily living which become so burdensome that there is no heart for the things of God.

1 Peter 5:7 (b) It is any problem in the life which hinders the soul and weighs down the spirit.

CARMEL

1 Kings 18:42 (c) This is a place of retreat for prayer, meditation, and communion with God.

2 Kings 19:23 (b) By this is indicated the extent of God's judgment which reaches even to the finest and best that the enemy controls.

Song of Solomon 7:5 (b) This indicates that the beauty of God's people is as great, colorful, delightful, and attractive as this wonderful mountain.

CARNAL

Rom. 7:14 (a) It refers to anything and everything that pertains to human flesh and the human mind.

Rom. 8:7 (a) This describes a mind which thinks only of temporal and physical things.

1 Cor. 3:1 (a) The Corinthians were still occupied with the things which they could see and handle. They had not yet learned to live in the atmosphere of God.

2 Cor. 10:4 (a) This refers to human weapons such as swords, spears, and other physical force.

CARPENTER

Zech. 1:20 (b) Here is an agency God uses to tear down or to build up His work among men.

The four horns mentioned in the previous verses may indicate the great Gentile kingdoms of Babylon, Persia, Greece and Rome. They of course were very destructive to Israel. Probably the Lord sent along the four carpenters to repair the damage done by the four horns. God always has a remedy for every difficulty and defeat.

CARRY

Psalm 90:5 (b) This is descriptive of the transient character of human life which exists for a short while, and then disappears.

Isa. 41:16 (b) This figure indicates the case in which the enemies of Israel shall be dispersed and scattered.

Isa. 46:4 (b) We are informed here that God will protect and provide for the care and comfort of those who put their trust in Him.

1 Cor. 12:2 (b) By this we learn of the tendency of the human heart to go astray from God.

CART

1 Sam. 6:7 (c) This is a type of man's schemes for doing God's work. God had said that the priests were to carry the ark on their

shoulders. The Philistines substituted a cart for the ark. God had not told them how to carry it. God was displeased and trouble came. God's work must be done in God's way. If the right thing is done in the wrong manner, God will not accept it. God demands that His service shall be carried on according to His plan and program. We must not substitute the ways of the world for the ways of God. In raising money for the church, or in providing amusements for the young, or in carrying on our services, or in our method and manner of using the house of God, we must not resort to the ways of the ungodly, the plans and programs of those who are strangers to God, for God will not add His blessing to it. See 2 Sam. 6:7 and compare with 1 Chron. 15:13.

Isa. 28:27 (b) This passage teaches that our Christian work is not all to be done by one pattern. Each type of person must be dealt with in a different manner. The cart wheel worked on some grain but not on others.

Amos 2:13 (a) God compares Himself to a cart on which a great load (a volume of blessings for His people) has been placed. They did not want God nor His blessings.

CASSIA

Psalm 45:8 (c) This tells of the sweet worship and adoration which proceeds from the lips of God's people (probably the ivory palaces), to the praise and the glory of the Lord Jesus.

CAST

Job 18:8 (b) Here is a description of the sudden calamity that comes upon one who is engaged in wicked practices.

Psalm 22:10 (b) This describes the dependence of Jesus upon His Father.

1 Pet. 5:7 (b) By this we are told to throw all our problems, difficulties and griefs at the feet of the Saviour. Someone has said, "Take your burden baggage to God's depot, and check it."

CASTLE

Prov. 18:19 (b) This figure describes the position and resentful arguments of an unsaved person whose heart has been hardened through mistreatment and unwise dealings.

CATERPILLAR

Isa. 33:4 (a) The people of Israel, swarming over the country gathering in the spoil, are likened to the caterpillars eating vegetation.

Jer. 51:14 (a) God compares with caterpillars the invading hosts of men who would attack and capture Babylon.

Joel 2:25 (a) This wonderful promise from God is given to encourage those who have wasted their lives and then come back to serve God in fellowship with Him. He will make that life doubly fruitful to make up for the wasted years.

CATTLE

Psalm 50:10 (b) This represents the great wealth and resources of God which are for the blessing of His people.

Isa. 43:23 (b) This tells us that God notices when even the smallest offerings are not brought to Him.

Jonah 4:11 (c) This indicates that God cares for everything that He has made.

CAVE

1 Sam. 22:1 (c) It is a type of the hiding place of God's people when they are persecuted, oppressed, and distressed. They flee to the "secret place of the Most High."

Psalm 57 (Title) (c) This indicates that when God's people are in the most difficult positions and in distressing situations, they may still sing and express their faith in the living God. See Psalm 142 (Title).

Isa. 2:19 (a) This is not a figure but will actually take place when the great men of the earth seek to hide from God. (See Rev. 6:15.)

CEDAR

Psalm 29:5 (b) This is a type of proud, prominent persons who take a stand against God, His Word and His work.

Psalm 92:12 (a) Here is a picture of the believer who in the midst of drouth, death, dearth and desolation fixes his faith and trust down deep in the living promises of God and flourishes for Him, in company with other believers. Cedars grow in forests and help each other to stand the storms. Cedars represent collective Christian testimony. The palm tree in this verse represents the individual testimony.

Zech. 11:2 (b) This is a type of the great nation of Israel which had grown to be a world power and then because of disobedience to God was cut down and destroyed as a nation. This passage was read at Spurgeon's funeral to teach that the lesser preachers mourned over the death of this great preacher (the cedar).

CEPHAS

John 1:42 (a) This name means a "rock" or a "stone." The bit of stone that is chipped off from the great rock is of the same texture and chemical composition as the one from which it comes. Peter belonged to Christ and therefore was recognized by God as a part of Christ. The name "Peter" has the same meaning.

CHAFED

2 Sam. 17:8 (a) By this word is represented the condition of mind of David and his soldiers because of the great loss they had suffered in Jerusalem.

CHAFF

Job 21:18 (a) As chaff has no value to the farmer, so the wicked have no value to God. Because they are worthless and are not stable, nor useful in God's program of life, they must be sent to the fire.

Psalm 1:4 (b) Here we have a type of certain kinds of people who have no value to God because of their wickedness. As chaff contains no chemicals that can be used by the farmer in any way, so the wicked are lacking in any value to God, and so are shut out from God's presence because of their worthlessness (See Matt. 3:12)

Isa. 33:11 (a) By this term the Lord reveals to us how worthless to Him are the ideas, schemes, and programs of the religious movements of this world.

Jer. 23:28 (a) This is a symbol of the worthlessness of men's dreams and their idle reasonings. God makes foolish the wisdom of this world (See also 1 Cor. 3:19)

CHAIN

Prov. 1:9 (a) In this passage, wisdom, knowledge, and the law of God are compared to three golden links which adorn those who possess them.

Lam. 3:7 (b) Jeremiah compares his many sorrows to links in a chain which weigh him down and prevent his progress.

Ezek. 7:23 (b) The combination of circumstances and conditions which the Lord would bring upon Israel in punishment are compared to links in a chain to bind His people.

Rev. 20:1 (b) God's commandments restrict, prohibit, and defeat Satan and are compared to links that form a chain for his utter punishment. (See 2 Peter 2:4; Jude 6)

CHAMBER

Prov. 7:27 (b) A description of the departments in hell where sinners are punished according to their deserts.

Song of Solomon 1:4 (c) The different experiences of blessing in the Christian life are compared to chambers in the palace of the king.

Isa. 26:20 (b) This refers to those times in the believer's life when he retires from the busy public life to be alone with the Lord.

Matt. 24:26 (b) Here is indicated that rumors should spread abroad that our Lord had hidden Himself in some secret place on earth in order to appear suddenly in judgment.

CHARGES

1 Cor. 9:7 (b) This is an indication that the believer will be supplied from heaven with all the equipment necessary for Christian work.

1 Tim. 1:18 (a) These are the instructions given by Paul to Timothy concerning his ministry.

CHARIOT

Psalm 20:7 (b) It indicates that some people trust in human expedients and schemes of their own for deliverance. We trust *not* in our own resources, nor wits, nor wisdom.

Psalm 76:6 (b) This is a type of the power of God to overcome man's resistance and rebellion.

Psalm 104:3 (a) The clouds are described as the vehicles upon which the Lord is carried whithersoever He will.

Jer. 4:13 (b) This is a description of the invincible power of God. Just as man cannot control the coming and the going of the clouds, so man cannot control God's movements.

CHEEK

S. of Sol. 5:13 (c) Solomon is pouring out his love and praise to his Lord. He describes each part of His body as being wonderfully attractive to him.

Matt. 5:39 (b) This may be taken as a sign of humbleness and meekness in the presence of those who are the opposite.

CHEEK BONE

Psalm 3:7 (b) David is indicating that God has already whipped Absalom and broken his power. He would, therefore, prevent any damage to come from Absalom's insurrection.

CHEW

Lev. 11:4 (c) (See under "CUD")

CHICKEN

Matt. 23:37 (a) The Lord Jesus compares Himself to a mother hen and the individual Israelite to the baby chicken whom He desired to protect, preserve and provide with every need. In Luke 13:34, where the word "brood" is used instead of the word "chickens," we learn that in the early part of His ministry, Christ intended to gather all of Israel under His wings. However, toward the end of His ministry, as we find it in Matthew, He called individual Israelites to come to Him for protection, for in the meanwhile, the nation had rejected Him as their Lord, their King, and their Messiah. No longer does He endeavor to call the whole nation to Him, but now calls individual persons.

CHILD

Isa. 9:6 (a) The word "child" refers to size and age, rather than to relationship. The word "son" refers to character and likeness. In the New Testament the Greek word for "child" is "teknon" which indicates a physical relationship between a parent and the offspring. Jesus was never called a child of Joseph, nor the child of man, nor the child of God. The Greek word "huios" meaning "son" or "likeness to another" is always used about Christ. He is the *Son* of Man and the *Son* of God. He is not the *child* of man nor the *child* of God. A Christian is called a "child of God" (teknon) because of his faith and trust in Christ Jesus as in Gal. 3:26. He is called a "son of God" (huios) only as he is like God more or less in his actions. He is a son of God (huios) if he is a peacemaker (Matt. 5:9 R. V.). He is a son of God if he forgives his enemies (Matt. 5:45 R.V.). He is a son of God if he lives a separated life (2 Cor. 6:18). When Jesus was referred to as a child in Luke 1:59, Luke 2:27 and other passages, the word used is "paidion" which means "a little lad." Even here the word is not the word for relationship but refers to size.

Jer. 1:6 (a) It is here used by the prophet to describe his feeling of helplessness in the face of a great work of God.

Jer. 31:20 (a) God very tenderly refers to the people of Israel as being members of His own family, young, helpless, and in need of paternal care.

Matt. 23:15 (a) Those who are led astray by false teachers are described as being related to hell and belonging there.

Acts 13:10 (a) This man was so wicked and so hostile in his attitude toward God that Paul told him he belonged to the devil's family and had a devil's nature.

Rev. 12:5 (b) This man child is the Lord Jesus brought forth from the nation of Israel to rule all nations.

CHOICE

1 Sam. 9:2 (a) This word indicates that this young man was bright, attractive, talented, brave, lovable, tender-hearted, and thoroughly trustworthy.

CHOKE

Matt. 13:7 (a) This is a graphic way of stating that the sorrows and cares of this earth may drive out the influence and the effect of the Word of God in the soul.

CHRIST

Some types of Christ:

Aaron,	Ex. 28:2 (c)
Adam,	Gen. 5:2 (c)
Ark, (covenant)	Ex. 25:10 (c)
Ark, (Noah's)	Gen. 6:14 (c)
Ass,	Gen. 49:14 (c)
Author,	Heb. 5:9 (c)
Bishop,	1 Pet. 2:25 (a)
Body,	1 Cor. 12:12 (a)
Branch,	Zech. 3:8 (a)
Bread,	John 6:51 (a)
Bridegroom,	Matt. 25:1 (b)
Bullock,	Lev. 1:5 (c)
Burnt Offering,	Lev. 1:3 (b)
Calf,	Rev. 4:7 (b)
Captain,	Heb. 2:10 (a)
Chief,	Song of Sol. 5:10 (b)
Commander,	Isa. 55:4 (b)
Cornerstone,	Isa. 28:16 (a)
Covert,	Isa. 32:2 (a)
David,	2 Sam. 19:10 (c)
Day,	Psa. 118:24 (b)
Door,	John 10:9 (a)
Eagle,	Rev. 4:7 (b)
Flour,	Lev. 2:1 (c)
Foundation,	Isa. 28:16 (b)
Fountain,	Zech. 13:1 (b)
Garment,	Isa. 61:10 (b) Rom. 13:14.
Gate,	Psa. 118:20 (b)
Gold,	Isa. 13:12 (a)
Headstone,	Psa. 118:22 (b)
Heir,	Heb. 1:2 (a)
Hen,	Matt. 23:37 (a)
Hiding Place,	Isa. 32:2 (a)
High Priest,	Heb. 4:14 (a)
Isaac,	Gen. 24:36 (c)
Jacob,	Gen. 32:28 (c)
Jonah,	Matt. 12:40 (a)
Joseph,	Gen. 37:7 (c)
Joshua,	Josh. 1:1 (c)
Judge,	Acts 17:31 (a)
King,	Psa. 2:6 (a)
Lamb,	Rev. 5:6 (a)
Leaves,	Rev. 22:2 (c)

Light,	John 8:12 (a)
Lily of the Valleys,	Song of Sol. 2:1 (c)
Lion,	Rev. 5:5 (a)
Manna,	John 6:32 (a)
Master of the House,	Luke 13:25 (b)
Meal,	2 Kings 4:41 (c)
Mediator (umpire),	1 Tim. 2:5 (a)
Melchizedek,	Gen. 14:18 (c)
Merchantman,	Matt. 13:45 (b)
Owl,	Psa. 102:6 (a)
Ox,	Ezek. 1:10 (b)
Passover,	1 Cor. 5:7 (a)
Peace Offering,	Lev. 3:1 (c)
Pelican,	Psa. 102:6 (a)
Physician,	Jer. 8:22 (c)
Pigeon,	Lev. 12:6 (c)
Propitiation (mercy seat),	Rom. 3:25 (a)
Ram,	Gen. 22:13 (a)
Rock,	Matt. 16:18 (a)
Rock of Ages,	Isa. 26:4 (margin) (a)
Rose of Sharon,	Song of Sol. 2:1 (c)
Root,	Rev. 22:16 (a)
Sabbath,	Col. 2:16-17 (b)
Seed,	Gen. 3:15 (a)
Serpent,	John 3:14 (a)
Shepherd,	John 10:11 (a)
Sin,	2 Cor. 5:21 (a)
Sin Offering,	Lev. 4:32 (c)
Solomon,	1 Kings 10:13 (c)
Sower,	Matt. 13:37 (a)
Sparrow,	Psa. 102:7 (a)
Star,	Rev. 22:16 (a)
Sun,	Mal. 4:2 (a)
Temple,	John 2:19 (a)
Thief,	Rev. 3:3 (a)
Tree,	Rev. 22:2 (b)
Trespass Offering,	Lev. 5:6 (c)
Turtle dove,	Lev. 1:14 (c)
Vine,	John 15:5 (a)
Worm,	Psa. 22:6 (a)

CHURCH

Some types of the Church:

Body,	John 15:5 (a)
Branches,	Eph. 1:23 (a)

Bride,	Rev. 21:9 (a)
Building,	Eph. 2:21 (a)
Candlestick,	Rev. 1:20 (a)
Eve,	Gen. 3:20 (c)
Family,	Eph. 3:15 (a)
Household,	Eph. 2:19 (b)
Jewels,	Mal. 3:17 (b)
Light,	Eph. 5:8 (a)
Loaf,	1 Cor. 10:17 (margin) (a)
Lump,	1 Cor. 5:7 (a)
Olive tree,	Rom. 11:17 (a)
Queen,	Psa. 45:9 (b)
Rib,	Gen. 2:21 (c)
Seed,	Matt. 13:38 (a)
Sheep,	John 10:11 (a)
Stones,	1 Pet. 2:5 (a)
Temple,	Eph. 2:21 (a)
Virgin,	2 Cor. 11:2 (a)
Wife,	Rev. 21:9 (b)

CINNAMON

Ex. 30:23 (c) This is typical of the delightful fragrance of the life of Christ before His Father.

Prov. 7:17 (c) This is typical of the enticements and allurements of sin.

CIRCUMCISION

Jer. 4:4 (b) Here is a type which compares the physical circumcision with the spiritual act of reckoning one's self dead unto sin and of laying aside the desires of the flesh. (See also Col. 2:11.)

CISTERN

Jer. 2:13 (b) It is a type of human provision and self-made supplies for satisfaction, comfort, and preservation substituted for trust in the living God who is the source of all blessing.

CITY

Prov. 25:28 (a) The Christian is compared to a city filled with treasures, jewels and valuables. His treasures are patience, love, peace, zeal, et cetera, which, unless guarded, will be taken from him by critics, enemies, fault-finders and gossips.

Rev. 18:10 (a) This city is a figure of the religious-political groups of earth which build huge buildings, manifest outward piety, have a mixture of Christian doctrines with heathen practices. This "city" is engaged in the business of buying and selling every kind of merchandise, and ruling in the affairs of men. Their merchandise includes the bodies and the souls of men (Rev. 18:13 margin). God is telling us here that He will visit such religious movements in judgment, and will pour out His wrath upon them. This "city" is said to be decked or guilded with gold, whereas God's true city is said to be pure gold. (Compare Rev. 18:16 with Rev. 21:18)

CLAD

Isa. 59:17 (a) This is a description of the complete abandonment of the Lord Jesus to the work of His Father and to His service for men.

CLAP

Psa. 98:8 (b) This is an expression used to describe the joy that shall fill the whole earth when Christ rules and reigns. (See also Isa. 55:12)

Lam. 2:15 (b) It is used to express utter disgust, contempt and hatred. (See also Ezek. 25:6)

CLAY

Isa. 45:9 (b) This is typical of human beings who are shaped and molded in the hands of the Lord. (See also Isa. 64:8)

Jer. 18:6 (a) It represents Israel as a nation in the hands of the Lord for Him to alter, mold and make as He pleases.

Dan. 2:42 (b) Here the "clay" represents the friability and inconstancy of the nations at the end of the age. They will be easily broken and will have little cohesion with other nations as clay is easily broken and will not adhere to iron.

John 9:6 (c) This probably indicates the fact that the Lord shuts our eyes effectually to the things of this earth that He may open them to see His face and rejoice in His presence, and enjoy spiritual realities.

CLEAN

Job 11:4 (b) This word is used to indicate a life that was not soiled by sinful or selfish actions.

Job 17:9 (a) These hands have not been soiled with sinful and wicked practices.

Psa. 19:9 (b) The Lord is telling us that the Word of God produces in the life purity and godliness.

Psa. 51:7 (a) David uses the word to inform us that he wanted to be pure in God's sight. All his sins, iniquities, guilt, trespasses and transgressions would be blotted out from the sight of God if God cleansed him. (See verse 10)

Psa. 73:1 (b) This describes the condition of a heart that has been washed by the blood and made white before the Lord.

Prov. 14:4 (b) There are those who are more interested in formalism than they are in results. They want solemnity without life. The Lord is condemning the program.

Prov. 16:2 (b) This indicates that a man has examined his own way of living and has come to the conclusion that his way is quite right for both man and God. This man is his own judge and jury. He decides his own character and comes to the conclusion that he is quite fit for God's presence. He is not interested in God's thoughts about himself nor God's judgment upon himself. (See also Prov. 14:12)

Matt. 8:2 (a) Lepers are made "clean," they are not said to be "healed." Leprosy is evidently a type of the defiling influence of sin. After being cleansed he no longer defiled others, but can mingle freely with others, without injuring them.

Luke 11:41 (b) The term indicates that things which are used for the glory of God and for the blessing of His people are acceptable to God.

John 15:3 (b) Here is revealed that the life of a man is attractive to God when he believes and practices the Word of God.

Acts 18:6 (b) Paul asserts that he has properly warned the people, earnestly presented the Gospel to them, and therefore cannot be blamed if any are lost.

CLEAVE

Psa. 22:15 (b) This is a description of the terrible results of the suffering of Christ on the cross.

Psa. 44:25 (b) Here is a graphic story of the utter depression which comes upon those whom God forsakes.

Psa. 119:25 (b) In this way is described the feelings of the psalmist when sorrow had overwhelmed him.

Matt. 19:5 (b) It is a figure to show how closely related and attached a husband and wife are in the sight of the Lord.

Rom. 12:9 (a) This is a strong expression to show how fully we should be given over to the good things of God.

CLOAK

Matt. 5:40 (c) This is an expression, both literal and figurative, to show how willing we should be to go the second mile for those who are in need.

1 Peter 2:16 (a) It refers to hypocrisy and pretense.

CLOSET

Matt. 6:6 (b) This is any quiet place where one may retire from the busy world to be alone with the Lord.

Luke 12:3 (b) Here is a figure to describe that the secret things of life shall become public property in the sight of the Lord.

CLOTH

Matt. 9:16 (b) This is a beautiful figure to show us that God does not patch our old nature nor try to add good deeds and characteristics to the old man. Instead, He gives a new nature, a new hope, and a new life. God does not patch the sinner. He gives the sinner a new birth.

CLOTHE

Prov. 6:27 (b) This figure reveals the fact that a man's hidden life surely affects his public activities.

Ezek. 16:10 (b) Here is an illustration of the way the Lord enriched Israel and took her from being a base nation to make her a glorious people.

Haggai 1:6 (a) This is typical of man's provision to cover his own need. He is left quite unsatisfied. This was illustrated in the story of the fig leaves.

Matt. 6:30 (b) Clothing the grass with flowers is a figure of the way in which our blessed Lord covers His people with salvation and with the fruit of the Christian life, as well as temporal mercies.

Mark 5:15 (c) This is a type of the robe of righteousness given to the sinner when he trusts the Saviour.

CLOUD

Isa. 44:22 (a) This is a type of the multitude of sins in the sinner's life. They are so many that they resemble a thick cloud in God's sight.

Hosea 6:4 (a) It is descriptive of the evanescent and transient character of the good deeds of these people. Their goodness passes away quickly as a cloud is dispersed by the early sun.

Joel 2:2 (b) This is typical of the shades and shadows of sorrow which often come quickly into human life and hide the sunshine. More directly, a type of the day when the enemies of Israel would overwhelm her and destroy her land.

Nahum 1:3 (b) This indicates the presence of God when sorrows and difficulties appear in our lives. These are compared to clouds of dust that are raised on a country road when a traveler passes by. The dust indicates the presence of the person. So when we see the difficulties, problems and distresses arise in our lives we may know that our Lord is there, and is in control.

1 Thess. 4:17 (a) As the cloud of dust in the road tells that someone is coming, so it may be literal in that we actually are (and of course shall be) caught up through the clouds when we go to meet our Lord. It may be figurative indicating that there will be a group or a "cloud" caught up from the different communities, cities, and cemeteries, there being so many that they will resemble clouds.

Heb. 12:1 (a) This cloud evidently refers to the group of witnesses mentioned in the previous chapter. There were all of these and more — so many that they are compared to a cloud.

CLOUDY

Ezek. 34:12 (b) Here is a type of the days when sorrows, shadows, and difficulties seem to overcast the sky and the heart is sad and lonely.

CLOVEN

Lev. 11:3 (c) A divided hoof represents a divided walk. It indicates that the person has left the broad road, the path of sin, and is now walking on the narrow road with God, and among God's people. This reveals the fact that he has been made clean in his walk, and if he "chews the cud" it indicates that his talk is also clean. The animal which had both the divided hoof and chewed the cud was a picture of the believer whose walk and talk are Scriptural.

Acts. 2:3 (c) This probably represents the messages which the Holy Spirit brings, one to the saved, the Church, and the other to the unsaved, the world.

CLUSTER

Deut. 32:32 (b) Here is described the terrible amount and character of God's wrath against His people when they turn from Him.

Song of Sol. 1:14 (a) The Lord by this illustration reveals to us the great abundance of love that exists between the Saviour and His Church. (See also chapter 7, vs. 7)

Rev. 14:18 (b) It seems as though sinners are grouped together for punishment throughout eternity. The gamblers are grouped together, also the drunkards, the harlots, the thieves, and religious hypocrites. This picture is also seen in Matt. 13:30. The contrast to this may be seen in Mal. 3:17 in which God's people as jewels are placed together in eternity in beautiful arrangement for God's pleasure.

COAL

Psa. 120:4 (b) The evil words of hostile enemies are compared to coals that burn and hurt when they strike.

Prov. 6:28 (b) This is a figure to describe the fact that those who live in sin are defiled and hurt by sin even as those who walk upon coals are burned by them.

Isa. 6:6 (b) The purging power of a live coal which destroys germs and corruption is here used to illustrate the effect of the Lord Himself in touching human life to purge, cleanse, and blot out the sins.

COAT

Gen. 3:21 (c) We usually use these coats of skins to represent the imputed righteousness of God which is given to us through the death of the Lord Jesus Christ. The animal died so that the skins could be used for clothing. Just as human babies are born with no clothes and must obtain clothing from an outside source so new babes in Christ have no garment of their own, but must receive the garment of salvation, the robe of righteousness from God through faith in Jesus Christ. This truth is illustrated in Matt. 22:11-12.

Job. 30:18 (c) The disease which Job had, which was probably elephantiasis, fastened itself upon his body tenaciously and clung to him as a garment.

COCKATRICE

Isa. 14:29 (b) This represents the cruel and evil result of plans which are promoted by Satan and carried out by wicked men. (See also Isa. 59:5)

COLD

Jer. 18:14 (b) God's Word and His messages from His prophets are compared, or rather contrasted, with the sweet, cold, refreshing streams from Lebanon as against the brackish, stale waters that come from earth's cisterns. (See Jer. 2:13)

Matt. 10:42 (a) The Lord specifies cold water to indicate that some effort has been made to prepare this drink and make it both palatable, attractive and satisfying to the thirsty.

Matt. 24:12 (a) Cold love is an indifferent love. The soul is not aroused and the heart is not stirred, even though there is a mental attitude of love toward another. (See also Rev. 3:15)

COLOR

Lev. 13:55 (c) Probably this represents the various aspects of sin. Sometimes things that are not wrong appear to be wrong; sometimes things that are wrong appear not to be wrong.

Num. 11:7 (b) The Lord is informing us that both the value and the beauty of this manna was unexcelled, and was excellent for food. The manna changed its color in the eyes of the Israelites. That which was very attractive to them at the first became dull and unattractive at the last. So holy things may become common if they are handled carelessly. Compare the next verse with Exod. 16:31)

Isa. 54:11 (b) This figure reveals how beautiful God will make the nation of Israel when he restores them to their full glory.

Ezek. 16:16 (b) Here we see a type of the beauty and attraction that Israel made for themselves in order to invite heathen neighbors into their fellowship and fold.

Ezek. 17:3 (b) This presents a description of the greatness and beauty of the King of Babylon who came to destroy Israel.

Acts 27:30 (b) The hypocritical acts of these sailors are represented as a color; as when a wax apple is colored red to make it appear to be a real apple.

COLT

Gen. 49:11 (b) This picture is presented to teach us that God's people, especially young Christians, are to be bound to the Lord and to His words. The vine represents the Lord. They are bound to the vine so they will be well nourished and become fruitful.

Mark 11:2 (c) This type represents a young Christian who is loosed from the world and its evil habits in order to be the servants of the Lord Jesus, to take Him wherever He wants to go.

COMELINESS

Dan. 10:8 (a) A word used to describe the virtues and excellent qualities in Daniel's life which became utterly vile to him when he was brought into the conscious presence of the Lord.

COMPASS

Job 16:13 (b) The suffering saint felt like his sorrows were as enemies shooting arrows at him. (See chapter 19, vs. 6)

Psalm 49:5 (b) The sins of the Psalmist's life seemed to be like witnesses against him accusing him.

Isa. 50:11 (b) This is a description of those who have a false religion and false doctrines, and who think that these are a light to them for eternity.

Jer. 31:22 (b) This may be a picture of the Church gathered around her Lord as His lovers.

CONCEIVE

Psalm 7:14 (a) This indicates that the iniquity of the heart produces sin in the life. (See also Isa. 33:11; Isa. 59:4; James 1:15)

Jer. 49:30 (b) The king had devised in his mind and heart a complete plan for conquering Israel.

Acts 5:4 (a) Ananias and his wife had concocted the plan of lying to the disciples and had agreed together what they would say.

CONIE

Prov. 30:26 (c) A type of the weak Christian who, feeling his weakness and helplessness, clings the more closely to Christ and hides in Him, the Rock of Ages.

CONFLICT

Phil. 1:30 (b) Describes the battle that was constantly going on in Paul's heart and life because of the evil forces and persecutions which came upon him from both Jewish religious leaders and Gentiles.

CONTEND

Jer. 12:5 (b) A remarkable picture which illustrates the conditions of religious professors. If these worldly religionists are made weary by the feeble Christian influences around them here, what will they do when they are really in the presence of the Lord? "Footmen" represent Christians in this world who have a feeble, halting walk and yet live very much better lives than the ungodly. "Horses" refer to fully developed Christians who live wholly for the Lord. Christians on earth are the "footmen" and Christians in heaven are the "horses." If these empty professors cannot endure the presence and the ministry of the Christians who surround them, then how would they ever endure being with God, with Christ, and with fully developed Christians? (See under "JORDAN.")

Jude:3 (a) This describes the attitude that believers should take toward unbelievers in regard to the ministry and propagation of the Word of God. Believers should stand actively, boldly, and constantly for the "faith of our fathers."

CORD

Josh. 2:15-21 (c) It is a symbol of the precious blood of Christ. As this red cord hanging from Rahab's window announced her faith in God, in His Word, and His promises, so the precious blood applied to our hearts by faith announces this same truth for us.

Job 30:11 (c) This cord represents those bonds and bands which bound Job to God in sweet favor and rich prosperity. The Lord loosened the bands and permitted Job to fall into affliction and poverty.

Psa. 2:3 (b) It refers to the restraining influence of God which the wicked kings of earth desire to dispel. They wish to live and do as they please and to be free from the restraint of God and His Word. Such examples are Russia and Germany.

Eccl. 4:12 (b) Three persons whose hearts and lives are bound together in love and in happy fellowship are compared to a three-fold cord or rope which has more strength than either one strand or two strands.

Isa. 5:18 (b) This is a type of the evil desires of the human heart which crave wicked and sinful practices.

Hosea 11:4 (b) This is a type of those lovely and gracious attributes in God's heart which draws other hearts to Him.

CORN

Job 24:24 (b) This is a picture of the fruitless and useless life of the wicked whose plans are frustrated by God.

Psalm 4:7 (b) This type indicates the temporal prosperity of the people of this earth. They are happy when their crops increase. David was more happy than they with just the presence of God in his life.

Psalm 65:13 (c) This may be taken to indicate God's great blessing upon His people and His loving care for them.

Psalm 72;16 (b) Probably this represents the great blessing that shall come upon Israel and which will radiate out to the nations of the earth when God restores His people to be the head of the nations. Christ is the principal grain. It may be that this blessing refers also to the Word of God.

Prov. 11:26 (c) This is a type of the blessed ministry of the Word of God, its promises, its assurances, and its gospel messages, all of which are for the rich blessing of men. Those who fail to distribute the precious things from the Scripture are compared to persons who withhold corn when the people are hungry.

Isa. 36:17 (b) This type is used by the King of Assyria to assure Israel that they would be contented in his land of Babylon even though they were strangers.

Hosea 2:22 (b) The figure here describes the blessing that will come to Palestine when Israel is fully restored as a nation.

Hosea 14:7 (a) As the grain comes up freshly in the spring, so Israel will again grow as a thriving nation.

Amos 9:9 (a) This is a prophecy concerning the scattering of Israel among the nations. He will not overlook a single grain.

John 12:24 (a) This is plainly a type of the Lord Jesus who had life in Himself and who, when buried, could not be kept down but rose the third day. It is a type also of the believer who has God's eternal life in him. The Holy Spirit is the gardener who takes the grain of corn, the Christian, plants him in His harvest field where He wants him to be, and places him where he will produce the best crop. (See Matt. 13:38)

CORNER

Isa. 11:12 (b) This expression is used to describe every part of the earth. It is an idiom easily understood. (See also Ezek. 7:2; Rev. 7:1)

Matt. 6:5 (b) This indicates any place of prominence which a religious person takes for his own advantage.

Matt. 21:42 (a) This refers to the foundation of the church, and in fact all of God's purposes. Everything that God does rests and centers in His Son, the Lord Jesus. As a stone we see His permanence in strength. He remains unchanged through the centuries. (See also Psalm 118:22; Mark 12:10; Acts 4:11; 1 Peter 2:7)

Acts 26:26 (a) This type is used to illustrate the fact that Paul's work was not done slyly, secretly nor quietly, but out in the open and before the public. Neither did Christ live, suffer and die hidden in obscurity. All of this was done openly and plainly in the sight of all the people.

CORNERSTONE

Psa. 144:12 (b) This represents the place of prominence which the women of Israel would have when the Lord made them beautiful in their obedience and lovely in their faith.

Isa. 28:16 (a) Here is a type of the mainstay and foundation of the church. As the cornerstone of a building indicates its official character and its permanent construction, so Christ is to the church. He is the principal stone, the main foundation, the center One in all of God's purposes and plans. (See also Matt. 21:42; Eph. 2:20)

CORRUPT

Prov. 25:26 (a) This is a picture of what God thinks of one who by virtue of his position and knowledge should be giving out blessings to the people, but instead is giving out that which defiles the people.

Ezek. 20:44 (a) Here is described the wicked actions and sinful practices of the people of Israel, and these are compared to things that are rotten, spoiled and decayed.

Matt. 7:17 (b) This is God's description of a professing Christian whose testimony and ministry are not according to the truth of God.

1 Cor. 15:33 (a) This expression describes the unsavory and defiling influence of wicked companions. (See also Jude 10)

2 Cor. 2:17 (a) The Word itself cannot be changed, but the use of it may be a misuse whereby Scriptures are made to teach evil doctrines or practices. (See also Mal. 2:8)

CORRUPTION

Isa. 38:17 (b) Hezekiah is comparing hell to a place of seething rottenness, filled with terrible wickedness, from which he has been graciously delivered.

Dan. 10:8 (a) When Daniel examined his own life, faith, and many virtues in the light of God's presence, they seemed wholly filthy and vile.

Rom. 8:21 (b) The bondage of living in this world of sin and death is compared to vile, rotten, evil things. (See also 2 Peter 1:4)

COUNTENANCE

Num. 6:26 (b) The countenance is the expression of the face. In this Scripture the sweet experience in the heart and soul which comes from seeing and knowing the loving fellowship of God is described as His countenance. (See also Psalm 89:15)

Prov. 15:13 (c) Here is indicated that the burden has been lifted from the soul and the heart has been made glad. (See also Prov. 27:17)

Isa. 3:9 (a) This remarkable statement reveals one of the miracles which may be seen constantly. The form of the face of the Jew identifies him at once in every part of the world.

Matt. 28:3 (b) This refers to the unusual brightness which surrounded and covered the face of this angel from God.

COUNTRY

Luke 4:24 (a) This refers to the locality or the neighborhood in which a person lives.

Luke 20:9 (b) The word is used to describe heaven where Christ has gone to live with His Father until He returns to earth again.

Heb. 11:14 (b) Probably this refers to the eternal state where we shall live together in happy fellowship with no debts, no death, no despair, but only the peace of God and His presence.

COURT

Psalm 84:2-10 (b) This refers to the presence of the Lord in which the Christian delights to live. It also refers to the beautiful place Christ has gone to prepare for the eternal home of the soul.

Psalm 92:13 (b) The term is used to describe the throne room of God where the believer presents petitions for himself and for others, and prospers in his heavenly ministry of prayer.

COVERT

Psalm 61:4 (b) This is a beautiful picture of the protection and loving care of the Lord for His own children who come to rest under His wings, and in His presence.

Isa. 4:6 (b) The term is used to describe the safety and comfort of those who in the day of the Lord's glory and His reign on the earth, will be found among His people and will walk in His fellowship.

Isa. 32:2 (a) We find here a picture of comfort, safety and blessing enjoyed by the one who trusts his life and his soul to the Lord Jesus. This person begins to walk with God and to live for His glory.

CRACKLING

Eccl. 7:6 (b) This is a description of the fruitlessness and uselessness of the sport of fools.

CRANE

Isa. 38:14 (a) Hezekiah uses this word to illustrate the emptiness of his heart and the loneliness of his spirit when he was on his sick bed.

Jer. 8:7 (a) Israel is said to know less about God's dealings than the crane knows about her own life. The crane knows what to do and when to do it, but Israel did not seem to know.

CREEP

Acts 10:12 (b) This is a type of worldly people who are so attached to this earth and its affairs that they never appreciate spiritual values. But they were cleansed and saved.

Jude 4 (a) The writer describes the subtle, clever, insidious ways of the enemies of God who get in among God's people to make known their evil doctrines and to turn away the people from the true faith in God.

CRIB

Prov. 14:4 (b) Where no work is undertaken for the Lord, there is no trouble and no blessing. If work is undertaken for the Lord, though it entails much labor, pain and trouble, great blessings will follow.

Isa. 1:3 (b) The Lord is teaching us that the ox, which represents the Christian, knows and esteems the one who owns him, as the Christian knows and loves his Lord. The ass, however, who represents the ungodly, the unsaved, is only interested in the gifts that he may receive from his master. The crib is used to represent earthly blessings which earthly people receive and return no gratitude to the God who gives them.

CRIMSON

Isa. 1:18 (b) This is a type of the extremely permanent effect of sin upon the soul. The word really means "a double dye," or "a repeated dipping in dye" until the substance is thoroughly and fully dyed. Thus the Lord is telling us that no matter how deep the sinner may be dyed in his sins, the Lord is able to blot them out, and to make him white and clean.

CROOKED

Job 26:13 (c) This word probably describes the wicked, cruel ways of Satan.

Eccl. 1:15 (b) This refers to things in our life which cannot be straightened out by men. An illustration would be a child that is born deformed, or blind, or with a defective mind, and this cannot be altered nor changed. It evidently refers to things that are wrong, either in the body, or in our circumstances, or in our relationships, which are unhappy, unfortunate and tragic, and which are of such a nature that they cannot be remedied. (See also Eccl. 7:13)

Isa. 40:4 (b) Our Lord is promising that things in this world, or in the life of His child which may be unrighteous, ungodly, harmful and hindering may be straightened out by His power and be made to fit into God's plan.

Phil. 2:15 (a) This describes wicked people whose lives do not measure up to the teaching of the Word of God.

CROSS

Matt. 10:38 (b) This is always a symbol of suffering and of pain and sorrow. To take up the cross means to deliberately and willingly enter into a path of obedience to God and service for God that perhaps may entail the loss of earthly possessions and of friends and the enduring of hardships and difficulties of a severe nature. It means self denial and self abnegation. It means a willingness to lay aside opportunities for earthly advancement and be willing to live in more or less of obscurity if that is the will of God. It means the denying of luxuries, self-interests and ambitions in order to enter fully into a walk with the rejected Christ in a hostile world.

1 Cor. 1:17 (b) In this passage the cross represents the preaching of those truths which condemns men, reveals their unsaved condition, exposes the wickedness of their hearts, makes known their inability to save or help to save themselves. Men do not want the story about their own wicked and helpless condition. The cross reveals that all that God can do with any person of any kind, anywhere, is to put him to death. No person is fit to live in God's presence without the Saviour. It is the preaching of this truth which men call "foolishness."

Gal. 6:14 (a) In this interesting passage the cross has several implications. When the Lord Jesus was made sin for us, took our place under the wrath of God, identified Himself and His life with ourselves and our lives, God caused Him to be crucified; God poured His wrath out upon the One who was taking our place. The world crucified Christ, and that makes the world an enemy of every Christian. But since Jesus was dying for the individual, the cross means that this individual has been put to death by the world that crucified Christ; therefore, he is dead to the call and the attractions of the world. This truth should cause us to live in separation from that which is so full of enmity against our lovely Lord.

CROWN

Psalm 103:4 (a) This is the blessed gift of God's loving kindness and tender mercy resting upon the subject of His grace. This loving care of God and the rich reward He gives is compared to a beautiful and valuable crown.

Prov. 4:9 (b) Here is a description of the blessing which comes upon one who uses wisdom in his living and grace in his actions.

Prov. 14:24 (c) This probably is a type of the power, glory and position which riches give to their possessors.

Prov. 16:31 (a) The honor and respect due to old age is represented by this beautiful white hair.

Phil. 4:1 (a) The Christians at Philippi who were saved through Paul's ministry were described as a crown for his head in the day when the Lord gives rewards. (See also 1 Thess. 2:19.)

CRUCIFY

Rom. 6:6 (b) This expression is used to impart the wonderful truth that when the sinner believes God, confesses his need, and trusts in the Lord Jesus Christ, God reckons that he died with Christ on the cross, and therefore has been punished in the person of Christ for his sins.

Gal. 5:24 (b) Here the word indicates an act in the mind and heart of the Christian wherein he lays aside and refuses to obey the sinful desires that arise within him.

CUCUMBER

Isa. 1:8 (b) This vegetable is used by the prophet to remind Israel that their heart's desire had led them into a life of worthless, useless activity such as they had experienced in Egypt. Cucumbers have no food value, and were one of the principle foods in Egypt. God let them have their desire and sent leanness into their souls.

CUD

Lev. 11:4-6 (c) The act of chewing the cud is probably a method of describing a good conversation such as should characterize true Christians. A true Christian will talk right (chewing the cud), and will walk right (dividing the hoof). Those animals that did both of these were called clean animals, and could be eaten. (See Deut. 14:6-8) Chewing the cud and dividing the hoof go together in the Scriptures. Both of these must characterize the animal that God calls "clean," and which might be eaten by the people. Chewing the cud refers to meditating on the Scriptures, and talking about the things of God and the things that are pleasing in God's sight. It refers to godly meditations as in Psalm 1:2; Psalm 63:6; Psalm 143:5; I Tim. 4:15. God told Joshua to meditate on the Word of God. Josh. 1:8. The right talk, however, must be accompanied by the right walk. Enoch walked with God. Demas walked with the world. God calls on us to separate the precious from the vile. Jer. 15:19. We are to live a separated life as in 2 Cor. 6:17. If we walk with the Lord, and talk about the things of God, then we are "clean" Christians, and acceptable in God's sight.

CUMMIN

Isa. 28:25-27 (c) Probably in this story the wheat represents the gospel message, while the other four grains represent other truths that should and do accompany gospel preaching. In all of our preaching and teaching the good news about the rich provision the Lord Jesus makes for the soul should have the principal place. Other things that accompany this message may be prophecy, history, personal experience, godly living. Certainly there are many such truths to be found in all good teaching and preaching, but these are not to replace the gospel of God's grace.

CUP

Psalm 16:5 (b) This figure describes the blessings which satisfied David's heart and soul.

Psalm 23:5 (b) By this figure David described the fullness of joy and peace which was his portion because of the Lord's goodness to him.

Isa. 51:17 (b) This type is used to describe the action of our Lord in pouring out His wrath and indignation upon the peoples of Jerusalem who were forced to submit to His punishment. (See Hab. 2:16)

Matt. 26:42 (b) This probably represents God's wrath, judgment and punishment handed to the Lord Jesus for Him to drink when He was nailed to Calvary for us. Probably the cup was the agony endured by Christ when He was made sin for us. (See 2 Cor. 5:21)

1 Cor. 10:16 (b) This indicates that the Lord expects His own people to drink and to make a part of themselves the forgiveness, redemption and cleansing that comes through the precious blood of Christ. It also represents the cumulative blessings that come through fellowship and association with God's people as they meet together.

CUT

Jer. 50:23 (b) This is a type of the judgment of God upon Babylon. God used Babylon as a hammer to punish the earth and having done so He sent another nation to destroy Babylon. To illustrate this He used the picture of the hammer being cut in two parts and broken to pieces.

Matt. 24:51 (b) This figure is used to describe the helplessness and the hopelessness of one whom God casts into the lake of fire.

Mark 5:5 (c) By this picture is described the damage that the unsaved to do their hearts and lives when they wander from God among the cares, sins and sorrows of this world.

Luke 13:7 (b) This probably is a type which describes the death of one who lives a fruitless and useless life in God's sight. More particularly it depicts the destruction of Israel after God had done so much to make her fruitful and useful.

Acts 7:54 (a) This is a graphic way of stating that Stephen's words went home to the hearts of his enemies and convicted them of their wickedness.

CYMBAL

Psalm 150:5 (c) This indicates that our praise and worship should not be of a subdued character but should be loudly proclaimed so that all may hear.

1 Cor. 13:1 (a) We are being warned by the Lord that though we may make a loud noise in the service of the King, and be heard for our much speaking, it will be in God's sight only as the noise of the metal if it is not promoted and produced by a heart filled with love for God.

D

DAINTIES

Gen. 49:20 (b) The messages and the ministry which Asher would give to others would be of such a delightful nature, so sweet and precious to the hearers, that Jacob compares them to a specially rich and attractive food.

Psa. 141:4 (b) David indicates that the pleasures of sin which are offered by evil men are the Devil's delicious and delightful foods. They come from Satan and damage the soul. (See also Prov. 23:3-6; Rev. 18:14)

DAMSEL

Ruth 2:5-6 (c) This girl may be taken as a sample or a type of the member of your church. As Boaz expected his farm manager to know who the girl was, so probably God expects the pastor, or the Sunday School teacher to know who each person is who is laboring and serving in his fellowship.

DANCE

Job 21:11 (b) This is used as a type of the careless, indifferent lives of the ungodly.

Eccl. 3:4 (b) By this is indicated that there is a time when cares and burdens should be laid aside and there should be freedom of spirit.

Matt. 11:17 (c) By this our Saviour describes the indifference of people to His commands and invitations.

(DARKNESS)

DARK

These words are used to describe four different kinds of mental comprehension, or physical experience. In the Scriptures which are used, an attempt will be made to suggest which kind of darkness is indicated.

Matt. 22:13 (a) Here we find a tragic description of the eternal condition of those who are lost. This is "eternal darkness." The soul who turns his back on God and rejects Jesus Christ who is the light of life enters eternity with no light and shall remain in utter darkness and outer darkness forever.

Matt. 27:45 (c) On this occasion the darkness was "actual" and "literal." It may be taken as a warning to sinners that all of those who crucify Christ, who reject Him and turn their backs on Him will be forever in the outer dark. This same picture was given in Egypt when the plague of darkness fell upon the people. The idolators and all of those who rejected God in Egypt were enveloped in the dense darkness which could be felt while there was light in all the houses of Israel who believed God. "Mental darkness" is probably referred to in the following Scriptures: Prov. 2:13; John 1:5; Acts 26:18; 2 Cor. 6:14; 1 John 2:11; Isa. 50:10. "Eternal darkness" is undoubtedly the meaning of the passage in Matt. 8:12 and in Matt. 25:30; Job 10:21.

For other examples of "mental darkness," see Matt. 6:23; Psa. 69:23; Rom. 11:10; Zech. 11:17; Rom. 1:21; Job 38:2; Amos 5:18. For other examples of "spiritual darkness," see Psa. 107:10; Psa. 112:4; Isa. 5:20; Isa 9:2.

Eph. 5:11 (b) This work describes "social" darkness. It refers also to social service performed by religious groups in which God and Christ and the Bible are omitted and only the welfare of human beings is considered. These works leave the beneficiaries greatly helped physically, but they remain in the dark spiritually. No light from heaven has come, no information from the Bible, and no knowledge from God. (2 Pet. 1:19)

Eph. 6:12 (b) This is evidently "mental darkness," for Satan is busy blinding the minds of them that believe not lest they should be saved. The unsaved have no true light on the Son of God and His wonderful work of Calvary. They cannot and do not understand the Bible. (See also Eph. 5:8; Col. 1:13.)

DART

Prov. 7:23 (b) This describes the shaft of sorrow and disaster which suddenly overtakes one who lives a wicked life.

Eph. 6:16 (b) This is a type of Satan's arguments and reasonings, as well as his seductive statements which lead the soul astray.

DAUB

Ezek. 13:10 (b) This act is used as a type of the work of that preacher or teacher who mixes together various religious doctrines, philosophies and deductions with which to organize and build a so-called Christian work, a religious work. This is typical of all the many false religions that have been propagated in the last few decades. (See also Ezek. 22:28)

DAUGHTER

Isa. 10:32 (b) This term is used to represent the Jewish people, particularly those of Jerusalem. The word is also used to describe the descendants or the adherents of other nations. (See also Judges 11:40; Psalm 48:11; Ezek. 16:57, etc.)

2 Cor. 6:18 (b) This term is applied to those women who are God's children who live and work as their Father desires them to do. They are not only related to the Father because of salvation, but they resemble their Father in their life of separation.

1 Pet. 3:6 (b) This name is given to the descendants of Abraham who enjoyed the faith of Abraham, and practiced it. (See also Luke 13:16)

DAVID

Ruth 4:22 (c) He is a type of the Christian and of Christ who lives for God in his youth, is persecuted and rejected by his brethren, is tempted in the wilderness, but finally is exalted on the throne.

DAY (SABBATH)

Jer. 17:21 (b) This time of rest was a picture of the real and true rest which the believer has in Jesus Christ. Christ is the true Sabbath. All the other sabbaths were a picture of Him. They pointed forward to Him. In these days Christ Jesus invites us in the words, "Come unto Me — I will give you rest." This rest is described more fully in Hebrews, chapter 3 and chapter 4. (See also Col. 2:16, 17)

DAY (of wrath Job 20:28); (of temptation Heb. 3:8); (of trouble Psa. 102:2); (of the Lord 1 Thes. 5:2). All of these days represent an unspecified length of time in which certain conditions exist as described by the word that is used. The expression "day of the Lord" refers particularly to the time when the Lord Jesus is ruling and reigning, exercising His authority. He calls this "my day" in John 8:56.

DAY (numerical) For an explanation of the expression "forty days" and other expressions wherein other numbers are used, see under "NUMBERS."

Eccl. 7:1 (c) This probably refers to the time when the blessings of life have accumulated and the rewards for faithful service are given the Christian. Death takes him to his reward.

Isa. 7:17 (c) Probably this refers to times when the wicked prosper, the sun is shining, the birds are singing, and there seem to be no signs of sorrow.

John 9:4 (b) Here is a reference to the few years in which the Saviour lived on earth. He walked among men as the light of life and gave light on the mysteries of life.

1 Thess. 5:4 (b) By this is indicated the time when our Lord shall return to earth as the Sun of Righteousness to scatter the clouds of unbelief and the dark shadows of sin.

DAYSMAN

Job 9:33 (a) This name is given to our Lord Jesus who is the only mediator between God and man, the only intercessor, and the only advocate. Job sought to know such a person. Having come, Christ is that to us.

DEAD

Psa. 115:17 (b) Probably this refers to unsaved people who are dead in their sins. For those who are spiritually dead, see Luke 9:60; 1 Tim. 5:6; Eph. 2:1; 2 Cor. 5:14; Jude 12.

Matt. 8:22 (b) Here those who are spiritually dead are requested to bury those who are physically dead. The undertaker may be dead to God, having no Saviour, no eternal life, and has never been born again. He is described as dead to God. The friend whom he is to take care of in death is physically dead. That one lies helpless in the casket. So he, the undertaker, pays no attention to God.

Luke 15:24 (b) The word is used here to describe the separation and the break in fellowship that occurred between a loving father and his rebellious son. Selfishness and a desire for sinful pleasure caused the son to turn away and go into the far country. The communion was broken. The boy was still the child of his father, but was a rebellious son. This aspect of "death" is found also in Rev. 3:1.

Rom. 6:11 (a) This word is used to describe the attitude of a true believer toward sin, wickedness and evil. (See also Col. 3:3, 1 Pet. 2:24)

Col. 2:13 (a) Again as in Matt. 8:22, the Holy Spirit describes the condition of the unsaved soul in the sight of God. God speaks to the sinner, but there is no response. He calls him, but there is no reply. He commands him, but there is no obedience. He loves him, but receives no affection in return. The soul is dead toward God.

Heb. 6:1 (a) These works are those which have no value in God's sight, and do not produce God's life in the experience of others. They are nearly always religious works, which are observed by those in false religions. They have no spiritual value whatever. (See also Heb. 9:14)

Rev. 20:14 (a) When the soul is forever cast out of God's presence after the final judgment of the Great White Throne, this is characterized as "the second death." The first death is the physical death when the soul is separated from the body, and can no longer go to church services, nor hear songs, nor see the flowers, nor mingle among Christians. The second death takes place when that disembodied soul which has been in hell since its first death, is taken out of hell, is reunited with his body in the second resurrection, is judged at the Great White Throne in his body, and then both body and soul are cast into the lake of fire, to be punished forever in conscious torment. Never again can that person see or have any relationship whatever with the God and the Saviour who would have saved him had he trusted Him. In this passage the figure used by the Holy Spirit is "the container for the thing contained." The "grave," called in this passage death, gives up the body and hell gives up the soul. Just as the believer in the first resurrection goes to the Judgment Seat of Christ in his body to be judged, so the sinner in the second resurrection and in his body is judged at the Great White Throne and forever cast out of God's presence.

DEAF

Psalm 58:4 (b) In this interesting way God describes the wicked sinner who refuses to hear the call of God's voice and will not respond to God's Word.

Isa. 42:18 (a) The word is symbolical of people of today who do not hear God's call, probably because they have no interest in spiritual matters. They are called upon to pay attention to God's Word, but they ignore it.

Isa. 42:19 (b) This is a description of the child of God who refuses to listen to the call of the world and of sin. He will not listen to Satan's arguments. (See also Psa. 38:13)

DEALER

Isa. 21:2 (a) This undoubtedly refers to the teachers, preachers and spiritual guides in all false religions who lead their hearers astray, and charge a good price for their services. They sell their doctrines to their people and collect the wages. (See also Jer. 6:13; Jer. 8:10; Isa. 24:16; Isa. 33:1)

DEATH

Rom. 7:13 (a) This describes the effect of wickedness and sinfulness upon the natural human heart and soul in the sight of God. Our sinful natures in our natural state send up sins, trespasses, transgressions, evils, wickedness and iniquities until they form a thick, dark cloud between the soul and God. (See Isa. 44:22.)

Rom. 8:6 (a) Here we see the result of setting the mind on the things of earth so that it cannot receive nor comprehend the things of heaven.

2 Cor. 4:12 (a) Paul uses the word here in order to describe the crushing and destructive effects of persecution and prosecution of his own life.

1 John 3:14 (a) This describes the state of being unsaved and without eternal life. (See also under "DEAD.")

Rev. 20:14 (a) The first death is the death of the body because of which the person cannot longer enjoy the earthly blessings of life. This second death is called by that name because the body and the soul have at the Great White Throne been brought before God for a final judgment. The individual is taken away from this short appearance in God's presence to be eternally and forever shut out of ever seeking God again.

Here are some references to death as used in the Scriptures:

Dead to sin — Rom. 6:2	Dead with Christ — Rom. 6:8
Dead in sin, — Eph. 2:1	Dead to the world — Gal. 6:14
Dead to God — Luke 9:60	Dead works — Heb. 6:1;
Dead to this life — Rom. 5:12	Heb. 9:14

Paul said "I die daily," 1 Cor. 15:31. By this he was showing that he himself was fulfilling Rom. 6:11. The meaning of all of this evidently is that the believer in Christ Jesus takes his place with Christ in His rejection from the world, and identifies himself with this rejected Lord. He does not now take part in, nor love, the things that this world offers to the unsaved.

DECAY

Heb. 8:13 (b) The Lord uses this strange word to describe the condition of the Old Testament plan and method of dealing with men according to "the law of Moses." The plan failed because of the evil hearts of men. (Heb. 7:18-19) Men could not, would not, and did not keep the law. The rebellion in their hearts and the sinfulness of their natures prevented the law from doing for them what should have been done. For that cause the loving God of heaven arranged a new plan entirely and sent Christ Jesus to give the gift of eternal life so that men would be made right inside. Then the outside actions would be according to the Word of God.

DEEP

Psa. 36:6 (b) This word describes the mysteries of God which cannot be fathomed.

Psa. 69:2 (b) Here is a description of the terrible sufferings of Christ.

Dan. 2:22 (b) This is a figure to describe the marvelous mysteries of God which cannot be discovered or understood except by divine revelation.

Rom. 10:7 (a) Undoubtedly this word refers to "Sheol" of the Old Testament.

DEN

Matt. 21:13 (a) Here is a type of the desperate condition of the temple, filled with cheating, lying, deceitful merchants bartering their wares.

DESERT

Isa. 35:1 (c) This is typical of the marvelous change in a dry, barren human heart when Christ comes in to dwell and the living water flows freely.

Isa. 43:19 (c) The blessing of God will remove all barrenness and relieve all drouth when once He is admitted to rule and reign in the heart.

Jer. 17:6 (c) A type of the surroundings in which one gets no blessing for his soul, no food for his heart, no light for his mind — a religious desert.

DESTROY

Psa. 63:9 (c) This means to kill the body so that the soul has no body in which to express its desires. (See Matt. 10:28)

Eccl. 5:6 (c) It means to ruin for the purpose for which it was intended.

John 2:19 (a) It means to tear down and wreck so that it is no longer useful.

1 Cor. 10:9 (a) This is a type of physical death due to poison from the serpents. You will note from the above Scriptures that the word "destroy" never means "annihilation" nor "obliteration" as is taught by some. It always means to "spoil for the use for which it was intended."

DEVICE

Psa. 21:11 (a) This describes the schemes and plans of wicked men to attack God and His people.

Dan. 11:24 (b) This refers to the wicked plans of men who have a desire to shut God out from their arrangements.

2 Cor. 2:11 (a) This describes the devil's clever schemes to prevent Christians from walking with the Lord in happy fellowship and profitable service.

DEVIL

Job. 1:6 (a) (Satan) As a mighty commmander-in-chief of all evil forces Satan was and is permitted to come before God to accuse the believers. (See also Rev. 12:10)

Matt. 12:24 (a) (Beelzebub) This name describes a false leader who is occupied with a clean-up campaign of the soul. Under this name the devil seeks to get his followers to put away evil habits and wicked ways and become a clean, upright, moral person. This person remains a lost sinner, although the devil has enabled him to put away many evil characteristics.

Matt. 12:29 (b) (Strong Man) Here the Lord Jesus refers to the devil as one who has mighty power and is able to hold his followers firmly a prisoner in his grasp. He does this by tradition, by fear, by wrong teaching, and by ignorance.

2 Cor. 11:14 (a) (Angel of Light) The devil is very clever at presenting various and sundry religions to deceive human hearts. He brings about a new religion which claims to give light to those who believe and follow the teachings of that false leader. The devil seems to be a heavenly person in this role. He presents a method of living that is clean, upright, moral and attractive, but which eliminates Christ Jesus and Calvary.

Eph. 2:2 (a) (Prince) As a prince the devil seeks to obtain the throne of the heart and become a king. He wants to rule this world and render no account to God. Somehow the God of heaven has permitted Satan to have pretty much his own way in the lives of individuals and in the affairs of nations.

1 Pet. 5:8 (a) (Lion) Under this title the devil is presented as one who is fierce, strong, malicious and cruel. In this character he is contrasted with the angel of light in 2 Cor. 11:14. The lion character may be seen emanating from Moscow. The angel of light character may be seen emanating from Mrs. Eddy at Boston.

Rev. 9:11 (b) (Apollyon) This word and the Hebrew word Abaddon describe the devil as being the sovereign ruler over sin, and able to deceive the world, whereby many are sent down to hell.

Rev. 12:9 (a) (Dragon) The devil is presented in this horrible character as one who has no regard whatever for the lives nor the property of those with whom he comes in contact. This characteristic of the devil is perfectly exhibited in the history of the Roman Catholic Church.

Rev. 12:9 (a) (Serpent) The cunning of the devil and his clever subtlety is compared to the snake. By beautiful phraseologies and clever manipulation of the Scriptures he entices many to follow his wicked ways, thus deceiving them into hell.

DEW

Job. 29:19 (b) A symbol of the gracious, refreshing blessing of God that was upon Job's life and efforts at one time.

Psa. 110:3 (b) This is a beautiful type of the freshness, vivacity and glow of youthful vigor in our Lord Jesus when He was on earth.

Prov. 19:12 (b) This describes the gracious acts of a kind and thoughtful king.

Hosea 6:4 (b) This is descriptive of the transient character of the prosperity of the nation of Israel. They quickly lost their place of favor and blessing.

Hosea 14:5 (a) Here God compares Himself and His ministration of grace to the "dew of the morning."

DIAMOND

Jer. 17:1 (a) This is a figure of the indelible record which sin makes upon the pages of God's book, and upon the heart, soul and life of the wicked person.

DIE

Gen. 2:17 (b) The word is used here to describe various experiences of human beings. (1) The death of the body to this world. (2) The death of the soul to God. (3) The death of the Christian to worldly and wicked desires. (4) The final separation from God when the soul and body together are cast into the lake of fire to be forever punished.

1 Cor. 15:31 (a) Paul is telling us here that it is his daily experience to consider himself dead to sin and to the sinful calls of the world. It is his constant experience for sin is constantly appealing to us for satisfaction.

2 Cor. 6:9 (a) The word refers to the experience of laying aside the things that displease the Lord and becoming unresponsive to the calls and demands of sin.

DIM

Lam. 4:1 (b) Here is shown the falling away of former glories in the life of either a nation or a man who once walked with God and then turned away.

DISEASE

Ex. 15:26 (c) The word may be used to symbolize the wicked habits and ways that this sinful world fastens upon those who belong to it but from which the Christians are delivered.

Psa. 103:3 (c) Here it is indicated that every wrong, harmful and hurtful thing in the Christian's life will come under the beneficent and blessed healing power of the Lord Jesus, if he wills it so.

DISTILL

Deut. 32:2 (a) Here is shown the widespread and delightful influence of all the words of God upon the hearts who receive them.

DITCH

Job 9:31 (a) This is an expression which describes the utterly abject condition of one whom God casts down in derision and despair.

Psa. 7:15 (a) Here is a figure of speech to describe the trap made by the enemies of God's children into which they themselves fall.

Prov. 23:27 (a) This is a terrible description and indictment of an evil woman. She is compared to a place of degradation and shame.

DIVIDE

2 Tim. 2:15 (a) This indicates the need to make proper comparison of Scripture with Scripture and join together the thoughts that are related.

DOG

2 Sam. 9:8 (a) This poor man felt so desperately unworthy that he compared himself to this animal.

Psa. 22:16 (a) These were Jesus' enemies who wandered around the cross gaping at Him and desiring to injure Him.

Isa. 56:10 (c) These were the leaders of Israel who refused to warn and to protect them from their enemies; or it is any unsaved religious leader who fails to be a blessing to God's people.

Matt. 15:26 (a) This troubled woman accepted the place Christ gave her and compared herself to a dog waiting to be fed with the crumbs.

Phil. 3:2 (b) This is a reference to unsaved, religious leaders whose only purpose is to feed themselves and bark out their feelings which give no enlightenment or help to others.

2 Pet. 2:22 (b) This refers to a religious leader who gets nothing from God but gives out that which he has mixed up and concocted within his own mind. He feeds on this himself and offers it to others.

Rev. 22:15 (a) God is informing us that false leaders, evil teachers and other similar characters who are described as "dogs" in the Old Testament and the New, will not be permitted to enter heaven.

DOOR

Gen. 4:7 (b) Living animals which were available and acceptable for sin offerings were to be found everywhere and Cain needed only to step out of his own door to find a satisfactory sacrifice that would have met his needs.

Ex. 12:23 (a) This door is a symbol of the soul of a man. By faith the individual is to take his place under the precious blood of Christ, applying it to his own heart by faith and acknowledging to God that he is taking refuge under the shed blood of Jesus Christ, the Lamb of God.

Ex. 21:6 (b) This is typical of consecration. The believer now is to devote his ears to hearing only the Word of God and the truth of God. (See also Deut. 15:17; Psa. 40:6 (Margin).

Psa. 78:23 (b) Here is a type of the wonderful way in which God poured out rich blessings on Israel from His heavenly storehouse.

Prov. 26:14 (a) This indicates the fruitless, worthless life of the lazy man.

Ezek. 47:1 (b) The Lord Jesus is the door, and the river represents the Holy Spirit. Christ Jesus gives the Spirit as recorded in John 7:37-39.

Micah 7:5 (a) This indicates a comparison of one's lips to a pair of doors which should be closed on certain occasions.

Matt. 6:6 (b) The expression here refers to the shutting out of one's thoughts all useless things when in prayer.

Matt. 25:10 (b) This solemn warning is to inform us in plain language that the opportunity to be saved has been ended. The door of mercy has been closed. Those on the outside are lost forever. (See also Luke 13:25)

Luke 11:7 (b) The thought seems to be that the unseen God in heaven hears the cry and the supplication of His child who desires to be useful in helping others.

John 10:1 (a) Entrance to heaven can be obtained only by and through the Lord Jesus Christ. There is no other way to enter heaven. No other person can have anything whatever to do with the saving of the soul. Only Christ can make us fit to go to heaven, and then take us there. (See also vss. 2, 7, 9)

Acts 14:27 (a) This represents the opportunity and the privilege of hearing the Word of God and of being saved through the Gospel of the grace of God.

1 Cor. 16:9 (a) By this figure Paul expresses the opportunity and privilege of preaching the Gospel in other places. (See also 2 Cor. 2:12; Rev. 3:8)

Col. 4:3 (b) This is a description of liberty of thought and freedom of speech, a quick mind, a retentive memory, and ability to speak well for the Lord. God makes the opportunity for ministry.

James 5:9 (b) Here is indicated the immediate presence of God, the Judge, when we are dealing with one another.

Rev. 3:20 (a) The word here describes the entrance to the heart as though the heart were a house and the owner of it must make it possible for the Lord to enter and abide there. Also refers to God's desire to enter into the church to rule and reign there.

DOORS

Job 3:10 (a) This is a graphic way of saying that Job was sorry that he was born, that he proceeded out of his mother's womb, and was delivered as all babies are.

Job 38:8 (a) Here is a reference to the boundaries of the sea as though they were doors through which the sea could proceed no further. (See also vs. 10)

Job 38:17 (a) The departure out of this life into eternity is described as though the soul were passing through a door.

Job 41:14 (a) The mouth of the great monster referred to in this passage is described as a door through which the food enters the body.

Psa. 24:7 (a) This is a figure of heaven as though it were a castle of magnificent structure into which entrance is made by doors, as was the case in ancient history. The doors of many of those castles lifted straight up into the air to permit the proper persons to enter. Then the gates were lowered straight down. The Psalmist is telling us that when the Lord Jesus returned to heaven after the victory of Calvary. He received a royal welcome as King returning from the conflict to re-enter his own palatial grounds. (See also vs. 9)

Psa. 78:23 (a) This expression is used as a figure to describe the bountiful giving of God from above to His people on the earth below. The same figure is used in Mal. 3:10 where "windows" are used instead of doors.

Prov. 8:34 (a) This figure is used to describe the attitude of a Christian in prayer who kneels in the presence of God, feeling at home with God, and presenting his petitions directly to God.

Isa. 26:20 (a) By this figure the Lord is calling His people to a spirit of humbleness, and an attitude of submission because of the terrible wrath which God will execute against His enemies, and by means of which Israel will be restored.

Isa. 57:8 (b) The Lord is using this illustration to show the tremendous apostasy of Israel in the home, out in public, and in their relationships with other nations. They had sold out their lives to the wicked people around them.

Zech. 11:1 (a) The Lord is telling us that the enemy will be able to enter Lebanon freely and without opposition, as one would enter a house through an open door.

Matt. 24:33 (a) This refers to the close proximity of the return of our Lord after the nation of Israel has been formed anew and established in Palestine. (See also Mark 13:29)

DOORPOST

Ex. 21:6 (c) (See under "DOOR")

Deut. 11:20 (c) This is a call for the people of God to publicly announce to neighbors, friends and those who pass by that those in this home are believers, who accept the Word of God as their law of life, and express thereby their faith in God.

Isa. 6:4 (c) Perhaps this is a typical way of expressing the fact that the whole of heaven responds to the command, the Word and the glory of Christ Jesus.

DOUBLE HEART

1 Chron. 12:33 (a) A heart which is divided in its loyalty and fealty is referred to here. These men were not partly for David and partly for Saul. They were all for David only.

Psa. 12:2 (a) This describes the hypocrite's heart. He pretends to love his neighbor but secretly works against him.

DOUBLE MIND

James 1:8 (a) A mind that is partly devoted to God and partly to something else is described here. (See Prov. 3:5; Jas. 4:8)

DOUBLE TONGUE

1 Tim. 3:8 (a) This describes a tongue that speaks both good and evil about the same person.

DOVE (TURTLE)

Gen. 15:9 (c) This covenant was instituted by God with Abram; and the animals used in establishing the covenant were to assure Abram that though his people would be in the furnace of Egypt suffering under the lash and slavery, yet through it all the sacrifice would be effective for them, and they would be able to maintain a light for God through all their tribulation. Probably the various animals mentioned represent different aspects of the value of the sacrifice in the eyes of men. (See also Lev. 12:6; Lev. 14:22)

Lev. 1:5, 10, 14 (c) This small offering, the dove, may represent a small view or knowledge of Christ, which is often the case with some converts. They only see that Jesus saves, and they trust Him to do it. Other converts have a greater knowledge of Christ, the "lamb" understanding of the value of Christ. Others have a very large grasp of the truth when they are saved, and this is the "bullock" aspect.

Psa. 74:19 (a) Asaph, the song leader for David, compares himself to this weak, powerless and defenseless bird. He desired the protecting care of the Almighty God because of his own weakness.

Isa. 38:14 (a) This is a type of one who is depressed, discouraged and disconsolate.

Jer. 48:28 (b) Here is a type of one who has tried every refuge and then finally flies to Christ to hide under His protection and care.

Matt. 3:16 (a) Here is represented the manner in which the Spirit descended. The Spirit did not look like a dove, neither did Jesus look like a sheep. The Spirit descended in great sweeping spirals as a dove descends and rests upon the ground. The passage refers only to the action and the manner in which the Spirit descended, and does not refer to the shape of the Holy Spirit for none of the persons of the Godhead are shaped like the animal with which they are compared or contrasted. (See also Mark 1:10, Luke 3:22, John 1:32)

S. of Sol. 2:14 (a) Some believe that the church is referred to in this passage, and others believe that it is the Lord Jesus. It seems more likely to be the church, for the church is weak and helpless, and the rock probably represents the Lord Jesus in whom we Christians hide. (See also chap. 5:2; chap. 6:9.)

Hosea 7:11 (a) Ephraim is a name applied to backsliding Israel. In this passage she is compared to this poor, simple, helpless bird which is a prey to every enemy. (See also chap. 11:11)

DRAG

Hab. 1:15-16 (a) By this time we understand that God refers to the methods, plans and means which were used by wicked men to gather in helpless and deceived souls to themselves. It refers no doubt to the schemes and plans used today by professing Christian leaders who inveigle men and women into a religious life by various methods and means.

DRAGON

Deut. 32:33 (a) The counsel of wicked leaders and teachers is compared to the poison of cruel animals.

Job 30:29 (a) Job compares his companions to evil, ugly, horrible animals who brought only dismay to his heart.

Psa. 44:19 (a) The writer compares his spiritual condition with the dark, dank place inhabited by wild animals.

Psa. 74:13 (b) These dragons probably refer to the enemies of Israel whom they met on the way to the promised land. The "waters" represent peoples, nations and tongues, all of whom God subdued before His people who were marching to Canaan.

Psa. 91:13 (a) Here is a type of the public enemies of Israel who were openly and outwardly enemies of God and of His people. The adder represents hidden dangers and seductive sins that do not operate openly.

Psa. 148:7 (a) It is quite evident that God will make all the great nations of the earth (the dragons) to bow the knee, to acknowledge the Lord, and to yield to His power.

Isa. 13:22 (a) This is probably a type of the powers, such as Babylon, Egypt, Assyria, who invade Jerusalem and take up their dwelling places in the palaces of the God's city. (See also Isa. 34:13; Jer. 9:11; Jer. 10:22; Jer. 49:33; Jer. 51:37; Mal. 1:3)

Isa. 35:7 (a) These are the great leaders of foreign countries who have been taking their places in the palaces of Jerusalem, but now are cast out, and the blessing of God has taken their place.

Rev. 12:3 (a) This is a picture of Satan, in his cruelty, wickedness and evil actions. He is the enemy of Israel, of the Church, and of Christ.

Rev. 13:2 (a) This reveals the anti-Christ who exercises tremendous power over the people of the world, and he receives this power from the Devil. He is like a leopard because of his swift and cruel actions. He is like a bear because of his subtlety. He is like a lion because of his tremendous strength.

DRAW

John 12:32 (a) This word is used throughout the Scripture to indicate an unseen power which pulls men by an irresistable force either to do good or to do evil. (See S. of Sol. 1:4.) The context will always indicate whether the power is from God, or from some evil source. In some cases, it refers to an actual physical act, as in 2 Chron. 5:9. This should be contrasted with Ex. 25:15 where Israel was instructed not to draw out the staves from the ark. In the time of Exodus, the ark was in transit, Israel was traveling from place to place, and this may represent the vacillating life of most Christians. In 2 Chron., however, the ark was in its final resting place in the temple of God, and it was to be carried about no more. This may be taken to represent the position of consecration in which the believer hands himself, his body, soul and spirit over to the Holy Spirit to wander no more, but to walk only with God.

DREAM

Job 20:8 (a) By this figure is described the evanescent and transient character of the wicked man who appears on earth for a little while, and then disappears. (See also Isa. 29:7.)

Psa. 73:20 (a) All the prosperity and activity of the wicked has no more value in God's sight than a dream has to any person after he awakens.

Psa. 126:1 (a) The marvelous transformation of Israel, from being the tail of the nations to being the head, did not seem to be a reality. They could hardly believe it was true.

Jer. 23:28 (a) The vagaries and mental wanderings of ungodly, religious leaders are called "dreams" and are contrasted with God's Word. Dreams are like the chaff, having no value whatever. God's Word is like the wheat, which contains life, and gives life.

DREAMERS

Jude: 8 (a) The reference is to wicked men who imagine evil devices and arrange wicked programs for God's people. These come from the minds of the wicked leaders, and are not the true revelations of God.

DREGS

Psa. 75:8 (a) This is a picture of the bitterness of the wrath of God in its worst form and character. The teaching that a "loving God will not punish sinners" is repudiated by this statement. The wicked will suffer the punishment of God to the last drop.

Isa. 51:17,22 (a) In this place the fury and the wrath of God have been poured out on Jerusalem to the last drop. God punished Israel in great wrath because they turned against Him in such a wicked and evil way.

DRY, DRIED, DRIETH

Num. 11:6 (a) This is the experience of the soul when disappointed and disgusted with conditions, and there is no refreshing thought in the soul to keep the heart happy.

2 Ki. 19:24 (a) The boastful King of Assyria uses this figure to describe how he has conquered other countries, hindered their water supply, and cut off their living. (See also Isa. 37:25)

Job 18:16 (a) The figure used here by Bildad represents the complete cutting off of the blessings of life when one lives a sinful life, and is an enemy of God.

Job. 28:4 (a) Job uses this figure to describe the utter sorrow and lack of blessing that comes in the life of one who, as he, had lost everything in life except his own personal life.

Psa. 22:15 (a) Our Lord in this passage indicates that His whole body is filled with utter weakness and every human blessing had been taken from Him, including His physical strength. He was drained of His blood which left Him utterly helpless from the physical standpoint.

Psa. 63:1 (a) The emptiness of a hungry heart and the disappointment of a soul when present blessings fail are compared to a dry, barren desert.

Psa. 107:33,35 (a) This is a beautiful picture of the way our Lord is able to take all the pleasure and joy out of a life, or to give the sweetest joys possible to a human life. He can both give and take away, so that the soul and the heart are either radiant or barren.

Prov. 17:22 (a) Just as the bones supply the blood with invaluable ingredients, so a happy heart supplies the spirit and the soul with radiance, vigor and vision. When the bones are actually not operating sufficiently through the marrow, the whole body suffers with anemia.

Isa. 44:3 (a) That person who is filled with sadness and sorrow, and in whom there is no joy or peace is referred to in this passage. God is able to give that one the living water in abundance, so that his life will become radiant and fragrant.

DRY, DRIED, DRIETH

Isa. 53:2 (a) By this type we understand the poverty of the parents of Jesus, and also the destitute condition of the nation of Israel who were slaves of Rome. The Lord Jesus, who is the Lily of the valleys, came out of those unhappy conditions. The unsaved see no beauty whatever in Christ, and some Christians see very little of His value.

Ezek. 19:13 (a) This is a picture of the nation of Israel as they are scattered throughout the nations of the world where they have no king, no prince, no priest, no temple, and no sacrifice.

Ezek. 37:2 (a) This figure represents the spiritual and national condition of Israel today. There is nothing about them that reveals the life of God, or that they belong to the Lord, or that they are God's people. Their constant conversation is about money, society, pleasure and health, but no desire for God.

Hosea 9:16 (a) The foundations of the very national existence in Israel (Ephraim) were destroyed by the enemy through the will of God so that they cease to be a national power. (See also chap. 13:15)

Joel 1:10 (b) This refers to the absence of any blessings to fill the heart with joy.

Zech. 11:17 (b) This expression is used to illustrate the fact that the leaders of God's people because of their apostasy would be unable to serve or work acceptably.

Matt. 12:43 (b) An evil spirit when not permitted to work in a human heart is quite unhappy and distressed by his lack of human cooperation. Demons must work through human beings.

Luke 11:24 (a) Evidently this refers to the fact that demons are not "at home" outside the human body. This evil spirit left the man of his own accord. He was not cast out by the power of God. Evidently when Satan sees that a person is in soul trouble, he leaves that person for a season in order that that one may clean up his habits, add some religious ways, and try to make himself fit for heaven without Christ, and without the blood. This man becomes religious, joins the church, quits his filthy ways and evil habits, so that the world thinks he is a converted man. After some time, Satan returns to this man. He finds that his old habitation is empty, for Christ has not entered, nor is the Spirit of God there. He finds that the man has taken on some beautiful and attractive ways called "garnish." Since the house is empty he has no trouble re-entering and again controlling the actions and the life of that person. The unlearned Christian and the worldling say, "See, that man was gloriously converted, and now he is a lost man." The man never was converted, he was only polished, cleaned up and made religious.

Luke 23:31 (b) The word here contrasts the time when Jesus was on earth, the Scriptures were available, and the sanctuary of

God was still standing, with the time when all religious freedom will be denied and only Satan's influence and power will be seen in the earth. When Satan rules, there is no blessing from God.

DRINK

Matt. 6:25 (b) God condemns the placing of human and temporal desires above spiritual values.

John 6:55 (a) This is a graphic way of telling us to take richly the blessing and the virtues of Christ into our souls. The believer must be constantly partaking of the loveliness, the greatness, and the sufficiency of Christ Jesus. As the Word of God describes Him to our hearts, we accept the message and appropriate all of Christ for all our needs.

John 7:37 (a) This shows the need of appropriating the Holy Spirit for fruitful service. (See also 1 Cor. 12:13) The Holy Spirit is the "Living Water." He only makes the Christian fruitful, opens the understanding for the Scriptures, and enables one to be a spiritual Christian. We therefore drink Him into our souls as the Living Water, and as the Lord Jesus requests us to do.

1 Cor. 10:4 (a) The word is used as a type of filling up the heart, soul and life with the values offered by the Lord Jesus from heaven.

DRINK OFFERING

Gen. 35:14 (b) The expression here typifies the giving to God of even that which seems to be essential for our own lives.

Lev. 23:13 (c) This drink offering of wine represents the things that bring joy into the heart and life and even these are offered to the Lord in utter consecration.

Phil. 2:17 (b) (Margin) If Paul's life should be poured out for the Philippians and he should be killed while seeking to serve them, he would consider it an honor.

DROMEDARY

Jer. 2:23 (a) Israel is compared to this animal as she takes her own way through a desert land, independent of all other things. A type of Israel in her independence from God and in her rebellion.

DROP

Deut. 32:2 (a) The word is used to illustrate the falling of God's Word upon the heart and the production of abundant good works as a result.

Isa. 40:15 (a) This is a type of the insignificance of the nations.

Amos 7:16 (a) This is a description of preaching and ministry to God's people.

DROSS

Psa. 119:119 (a) This shows the worthless character of the ungodly.

Prov. 26:23 (b) The expression here typifies hypocrisy — a beautiful silver covering on a worthless bit of broken pot has no value.

Isa. 1:25 (b) The word here describes those unhappy and deceitful things in the life of Israel which God would take away by His various cleaning processes. (See also Ezek. 22:18)

DROUGHT

Psa. 32:4 (b) Here we see the dearth in David's soul which followed as a result of his sin.

Isa. 58:11 (b) This shows a condition which sometimes exists in a Christian's life whenever things around him are discouraging and the outlook is dark.

DRUNK

Deut. 32:42 (b) This is a figure to describe the excessive destruction that will follow the wrath of God upon Israel or the nations in their disobedience.

2 Ki. 19:24 (a) The conquering heathen king by this figure describes the victory he obtained over his enemies and the joy that he had in conquering them. (See Isa. 37:25)

S. of Sol. 5:1 (a) Solomon is expressing by this means the exquisite pleasure he had in reveling in all the good things of life which he had so abundantly.

Isa. 51:17 (a) Here we find a type of the experience of Israel, the inhabitants of Jerusalem, in being forced to absorb the anger of God and the pouring of His wrath upon them.

Isa. 63:6 (b) This is a picture of the terrible condition of the people when God's anger is once released against them.

Jer. 46:10 (a) By this figure we are told that the land of Egypt was completely overwhelmed and overcome by the sword of God's wrath through His servant, Nebuchadnezzar. (See also Jer. 51:57 where the same truth pertains to Babylon.)

Ezek. 34:18 (a) The Lord is reproving the shepherds of Israel because they took for themselves the best of the land, its riches and its increase, while neglecting to care for the flock of God.

Rev. 17:2 (a) The great false church, particularly Romanism, has offered to the world freedom of lust, liberty in sin, cruelty in action, and the great powers of the world have reveled in these liberties, so that the nations that are controlled by this church act accordingly. Those who are under the domination of this wicked influence live in ignorance and poverty and revel in their evil ways.

Rev. 17:6 (a) This no doubt refers to the wicked practices of the great false religions of the world, particularly the Roman Catholic Church, which through the centuries has reveled in the blood of saints and martyrs. Even to this day, those who love our Lord Jesus Christ are murdered by orders of this church in those countries where they control the government.

Rev. 18:3 (a) In this passage it is the nations who are made to drink the hatred of this abominable church, and cannot escape. It should be noted that all nations suffer from the overruling and overriding power of their apostate religion.

DRUNKARD

Nahum 1:10 (a) The Lord is informing us that He will completely conquer and destroy those who have filled their lives with hatred for Him and love for the wines of iniquity. This refers to Nineveh.

DRUNKEN

Lam. 3:15 (a) The prophet thus describes his upset and disconcerted soul. He has been bewildered by the sorrows and troubles which have overcome him, and by the terrible treatment given him by God's people.

Lam. 4:21 (a) The Edomites were to be overcome by the wrath of God, were to be humiliated in the presence of their enemies, and finally be destroyed.

DUMAH

Isa. 21:11 (a) The meaning of this word is "the burden of silence." Since there is no sound from heaven, no voice from God, no expressions from eternity except what we find in the Bible, the prophet was troubled about it. His trouble made him ask the question, "What of the night?" Few ever ask, "What of the light?", or "What of heaven?" Many ask, is there a hell? but no one asks, is there a heaven? This silence is not broken by audible sounds, but is certainly broken by the Word of God.

DUMB

Isa. 35:6 (a) Israel has no song while they are scattered over the world, and are subject to the rule of other nations. Individuals have no song while they are oppressed with sin, and are servants of Satan. Then, when the Lord gives deliverance and salvation, the song begins in the heart, and the soul rejoices afresh.

Isa. 53:7 (a) The Lord Jesus standing before His accusers would not reply to their accusations, for He was taking our place, He was our substitute. We were so very guilty that our substitute made no answer to His accusers. (See Acts 8:32)

Isa. 56:10 (a) False leaders of God's people are described as dogs. They had no message for God's people; they were false prophets; they were wicked leaders; and they failed either to warn Israel, or to encourage, or to help them back to God.

Ezek. 3:26 (a) The Spirit of God forbade the prophet to speak to the people. The silence of the prophet was due to the commandment of God, the Spirit, and not to any failure of his own. (See also Ezek. 24:17-18, where God released his tongue; see also chap. 33:22.) Paul had a similar experience. (See Acts 16:7)

DUNG

2 Kings 9:37 (a) The word here compares the dead body of a wicked queen to the filth of the earth. A figure to express God's utter abhorrence of Jezebel.

Jer. 8:2 (a) It is God's description of how despicable the leaders of Israel were in His sight because of their wickedness.

Mal. 2:3 (a) God in this way expresses His utter abhorrence of the religion of apostate Israel. He thus describes His abhorrence of the religious ways of the priests and leaders of Israel because of their wickedness and sinfulness.

Luke 13:8 (b) In actual life, dung is used as fertilizer. In this parable, dung probably represents things in this life which are used to promote and help the growth of the things of God.

Phil. 3:8 (a) Paul uses this figure to show his utter contempt for the things in the world — things which he formerly had thought were profitable and helpful to him.

DUNG GATE

Neh. 3:13 (c) Probably this figure is used to describe the care we should exercise in ridding ourselves of those unhappy things in our lives, bad habits, evil ways, harmful practices, that should not be permitted either in our words or actions. We make ample provision to take care of that which we cast off from our bodies, and we should also make ample provision to get away alone somewhere and get rid of the filthiness of our spirits. (See 2 Cor. 7:1)

DUNGHILL

Psa. 113:7 (b) In the Orient, extremely poor people would bury their arms and legs in the dung heap in order to keep warm in cold weather. This is typical of the people of the world who bury themselves in the pleasures and practices of the wicked in order to obtain joy, peace and pleasure. (See also 1 Sam. 2:8)

Lam. 4:5 (b) This typifies the rich who, in their degenerate aristocracy, are no longer able to enjoy the palace but now seek pleasures in the offal which the earth produces.

DUST

Gen. 18:27 (a) This is an expression to describe the utter humiliation and feeling of insignificance which filled Abraham's heart in the presence of God.

Num. 23:10 (a) This figure is used to represent Israel numerically, as well as Israel which was to be scattered throughout the whole world, as dust is scattered. As dust is found everywhere on the land areas, so Israel may be found in every country. (See also Gen. 13:16; Gen. 28:14; 2 Chron. 1:9)

Job 4:19 (a) This represents the frailty of the man whose only hope is in this life. He is on his way to the grave where his body will return to dust, and he cares not that there is another life beyond the tomb. (See also chap. 16, v. 15)

Job 42:6 (b) The word is used here to express Job's feeling of weakness and inferiority when he saw the Lord in His glory.

Psa. 7:5 (a) The word is used here to describe the humiliation and shame that David would endure if it could be proved that he had lived a life of disobedience to God.

Isa. 2:10 (a) This represents the humble place we should take in the presence of the Lord, for dust is often used as a type of humiliation.

Isa. 26:19 (a) This probably refers to those who are the righteous dead, as they come out in resurrection to sing and worship God.

Isa. 29:5 (a) The Lord uses this figure to describe the thorough whipping and punishment which He will administer to the enemies of Israel.

Isa. 47:1 (a) This is a prophecy that proud Babylon would be reduced to poverty, humiliation and destruction.

Nahum 1:3 (b) Here we see the clouds compared to the dust of the road on which our Lord walks. Clouds which to us represent power, wind, rain, storms are only as dust under God's feet. Clouds of dust upon the country road indicate the approach of a visitor. So clouds that may arise in our lives may indicate the proximity of our Lord on His way to deliver us.

Lam. 3:29 (a) This is a picture of the voluntary humiliation of a true worshipper as he realizes his own sinful condition and appreciates the kindness and love of God.

Micah 1:10 (a) The word "Aphrah" means "dust." The prophet is describing the anguish of spirit that will characterize the people of that city when God judges and punishes them. (See Nahum 3:18)

DWELL

Matt 10:14 (a) This figure illustrates that the disciples were to completely eliminate all association with the enemies of God when they left the city in which they were not welcome. (See also Mark 6:11; Luke 9:5)

Acts 13:51 (b) This portrays an act of utter contempt and complete rejection of the people of Antioch.

DWELL

Psa. 91:1 (a) The word here indicates the manner of life of the believer who walks with God.

E

EAGLE

Ex. 19:4 (a) God compares Himself to an eagle in His work of taking Israel safely through the sorrows, dangers, and distresses of the wilderness journey.

Psa. 103:5 (a) The strength and vigorous care given to the believer who walks with the Lord is compared to that which the eagle possesses. The Christian thus blessed is able to mount up above his surroundings and circumstances.

Prov. 30:17 (a) By this figure we are informed that this particular type of sinner may not die a natural death, but will be subject to an unusual punishment which is unnatural.

Isa. 40:31 (a) Under this figure, the Lord describes the ease and joy with which Christians rise out of their distresses and are set free from their surroundings when they look to the Lord earnestly for His blessing.

Ezek. 1:10 (b) One of the four aspects of the Lord Jesus, His deity, is represented here. This character of Christ is described particularly in the Gospel of John. (See also chap. 10:14, and Rev. 4:7).

Ezek. 17:3 (a) The King of Babylon is represented by the eagle in this verse. The description concerns his invasion of Palestine and his victory over the King of the Jews. In verse 7 the eagle represents the King of Egypt. This is plainly seen by reading the rest of the chapter. These Kings are represented as eagles because they ruled over other kingdoms, they were swift in their invasions, and they were cruel in their afflictions of their conquered peoples.

Ezek. 17:7 (a) The King of Egypt also is compared to an eagle because he too was just about equal in power to the King of Babylon and ruled over kings and nations.

Dan. 7:4 (a) The King of Babylon is described as an eagle in this passage, because of his supreme power, his swiftness, and his superiority. He is also described as a lion in the same passage. This refers to his mighty strength, for he did have more actual military power than the nations who followed him.

Hosea 8:1 (a) Here is a reference to the swiftness with which the enemy of Israel would invade the land and conquer the people of God because of their disobedience.

Micah 1:16 (a) This peculiar figure probably describes an Oriental custom of magnifying the grief of those who sorrow. They wear unusual garments, eat unusual food, wail in an unusual loud fashion, and otherwise seek to let the world know of their grief.

Matt. 24:28 (b) This is a description of the cruel, devouring nations who will pounce upon Israel in the time of her downfall and will carry away all her treasures. (See also Luke 17:37)

Rev. 12:14 (a) This seems to be a prophecy concerning the special provision God will make to preserve a remnant of Israel from the terrible scourge and persecution that will arise against that people in the great day of God's wrath.

EAR

Ex. 21:6 (c) This describes the binding of the Christian to his Lord for permanent obedience wherein his ears are open only to the call of God. (See also Deut. 15:17)

Ex. 29:20 (b) In this and other passages we find a type concerning the consecrated hearing of the believer. As in the case of the piercing of the ear, which is described in Ex. 21:6, the anointing of the ear carries the same truth. The ear that has been touched by the oil is now to be devoted only to listening to God's messages, and is to refuse the call of all other leaders. (See also Lev. 8:23, Lev. 14:14)

Deut. 32:1 (a) The people of the earth are evidently indicated by this passage, and the Lord wants all people of every kind, everywhere, to listen to His voice, and hear His message. (See also Isa. 1:2; Joel 1:2)

2 Ki. 19:16 (a) This is a request from the man of God for God to listen closely to his petition. It reveals a very close and intimate fellowship with God. In many places in the Scripture this same truth is mentioned, and men who knew God intimately wanted to be sure that His ear was open to their cry. God also asks us for our ears, meaning that He desires to have us listen closely to His Word, and understand fully the meaning of His message. It will not be necessary to enumerate the various Scriptures, for there are many which reveal these two truths. The reader will find them quite obvious as he studies the various passages. (See also Deut. 1:45)

Psa. 40:6 (b) This is one of the prophetic Psalms in which it is indicated that the Lord Jesus Christ was a permanent servant of God the Father, and that His ears were only open to God's call. It is a fulfillment of Deut. 15:17.

Psa. 45:10 (a) The Lord hereby expresses a deep desire for Israel to listen to His message sent from heaven. (See also Rev. 2:11, 17, 29; Rev. 3:6, 13, 22)

Isa. 48:8 (a) It is quite evident that God knew before Israel became a nation that their ears would be closed many times to His call and they would refuse to listen.

Isa. 50:4 (a) This passage is spoken prophetically of our Lord Jesus. Christ is saying that He was constantly listening for His Father's voice, and the messages from His God.

Isa. 59:1 (a) We are assured that God does not close His ears to the cry of His children, but is always listening for any message that truly comes to Him from our hearts.

Jer. 6:10 (b) These hearers had not been turned away from the things of the world and therefore were not wholly devoted to God. God expects His people to cut off the hearing for voices other than His.

Jer. 7:24 (a) Animals are able to turn their ears one way while their faces are in an opposite direction. People cannot do so. Our ears are stiff. God has so made us that when our ears are turned toward any sound, the face also must be turned in the same direction. When God speaks to us He wants us to be looking at Him. In this passage, the rebellious people of God refused to turn their faces toward the Lord. Therefore, their ears were not turned toward Him. They were listening to other voices. (See also chap. 25:4; 34:14; 35:15; 44:5; 2 Chron. 24:19; Neh. 9:30)

Amos 3:12 (a) This prophecy is to tell us that one day Israel will walk with God again (the two legs), and will also again listen to God's voice (the ear). This will occur when Israel is again restored to their national position at Jerusalem.

EARLY

There are several meanings applied to this word and this action. We shall list them and give just a few Scriptures under each one, for the reader can readily notice by the context which meaning is intended.

EARLY IN LIFE — Psa. 90:14 (a)

EARLY IN THE DAY — John 20:1 (a); Judges 7:3 and 19:9; 2 Ki. 6:15; Psa. 57:8; 1 Sam. 17:20

EARLY IN THE PROJECT — Psa. 46:5; Psa. 63:1; Psa. 78:34; Psa. 101:8

EARLY IN THE DISTRESS AND NEED — Prov. 1:28 (a); Prov. 8:17; Isa. 26:9; Hosea 5:15; Psa. 78:34

EARNEST

2 Cor. 1:22 (a) The thought is that the Holy Spirit is given as a pledge, or as a down payment. God gives a foretaste of greater blessings that are to follow. (See also 2 Cor. 5:5; Eph. 1:14)

EARRING

Gen. 24:22 (c) The jewelry given to Rebecca is a picture and a type of the blessings which God gives in this present world through the Holy Spirit, a sample of the greater riches that await us when we actually meet the Lord face to face. The Holy Spirit gives us samples of joy, peace, rest, zeal, vision and divine understanding, so that we too may be drawn to that unseen Lord with whom we shall spend eternity.

Prov. 25:12 (a) This is a type of an ear that accepts reproof and instructions from another, and is glad to have constructive criticisms about his ways.

Ezek. 16:12 (a) We learn from this that the Lord gave His people ears that love to hear His voice, and desire to know His Word and to obey His will. This is described as ornaments of the ears.

Hosea 2:13 (a) The figure is used here to describe those who make themselves attractive to the world and to God's enemies, and turn their affections to those things and those people who do not love the Lord, nor want His presence.

EARTH

Ex. 15:12 (a) This statement probably refers to the incident in the life of Moses when the earth opened up a cavity and Korah, Dathan and Abiram went down alive into hell. (See Num. 16:29-33)

Deut. 32:1 (a) The word refers to the peoples of the earth in every nation, for it is the desire of our Lord that all shall hear His Word. (See also 1 Chron. 16:31; Job 20:27; Psa. 96:11; Isa. 24:4; Isa. 45:22)

Psa. 63:9 (a) This statement clearly indicates that hell is in the heart of the earth. There are many other passages that confirm this truth. (See under "HELL")

Matt. 13:5 (c) The teaching probably is that there was nothing in the heart of the hearer, nor in his mind, which would enable him to receive or understand God's Word. (See also Mark 4:5)

EARTHLY

John 3:31 (a) A term to describe one whose life, ambitions, and desires are connected wholly with the things of this life.

EARTHEN

2 Cor. 4:7 (b) A term used to describe the frail character of the Christian's body. (See also Lam. 4:2)

EARTHQUAKE

1 Kings 19:11 (c) Probably this is telling us that great calamities and sudden tragedies do not always bring a message from God to the heart. It is the Holy Spirit who imparts divine impressions to the soul.

Matt. 28:2 (c) It is symbolical of the fact that things which the world calls "real" are not very stable. The One who made the world is able to shake it. The foundations of this earth will come under the judgment of God to be destroyed and the inhabitants will be punished. (See also Matt. 27:51; Acts 16:26)

EAST

Gen. 3:24 (c) The direction of the sunrise is probably to keep ever before the people the fact that Christ will arise as the Son of Righteousness with healing in His wings. The gate to the tabernacle was on the east side and so was the door to the tabernacle. Evidently this is typical of the truth concerning the return of our Lord.

Psa. 103:12 (b) Since there is no measurement between these distances, this is typical of the complete removal of the sins of the believer.

EAST WIND

Job 15:2 (b) This figure is used to express Job's opinion of the vain talk and the useless conversation of his three friends, and of others who talk vaguely of God's business.

Isa. 27:8 (b) In this way God expresses His power to control the storms of life and the vicissitudes of our daily experience. His dealings with men are compared to various kinds of winds according to the character of those dealings.

Hosea 12:1 (a) In this passage again the Holy Spirit is comparing the vain talk of men with the various kinds of winds. (See also under "WIND")

Hab. 1:9 (a) A description of this figure is more fully given under the word "WIND."

EAT

Prov. 4:17 (b) This describes the act of appropriating and reveling in wicked things with all the heart and soul.

Jer. 15:16 (b) This is typical of the act of appropriating the truth of God and making it a part of one's soul and life.

John 6:50 (a) The Lord describes the appropriation of Himself, His love, His words, and His grace, as the act of eating.

2 Tim. 2:17 (a) The Spirit is telling us in this passage that the words sometimes used will damage the soul, the heart and the mind as a canker damages the physical body.

James 5:3 (b) The thought probably is in this passage that those who spend their time seeking to get rich and avoid or evade the Word of God and the Saviour of God will throughout eternity suffer the anguish with which their memory will plague them.

EDEN

Gen. 2:15 (c) Here is a type of the condition of bliss and blessing that is the portion of the consecrated, trusting Christian in this life and of the eternal richness of the next life.

EDIFY

1 Thess. 5:11 (c) This is the thought of enriching the life, inspiring the heart, and enlightening the mind of the children of God

EGG

Luke 11:12 (b) The teaching in this passage concerning the bread, the fish and the eggs is the same in all three. The wee little child thinks that what he sees is good for him to eat. He sees the round brown stone, and it looks quite like the loaf of bread his mother has taken from the oven. He sees the snake in the grass and thinks it is the same as the eel which his mother cooked in the skillet. And now he sees the scorpion and thinks it is an egg because of its size and shape when rolled up ready to strike. The Lord is teaching us that He must say "no" to some of our requests when He sees that the thing we are asking for would not help us, but would really hurt us.

EGYPT

Heb. 11:26 (c) A type of the world with its riches and opportunities.

Rev. 11:8 (a) Because Jerusalem was given up to business pursuits, idolatry and pleasure, it is compared to Egypt.

EIGHT

The number which indicates something new.

1 Sam. 17:12 (b) David was the eighth son and he began a new dynasty in Israel.

Eccl. 11:2 (c) Seven, being the number of perfection, this is an invitation to go further than the full amount required. The fulfillment of the expression "go the second mile."

John 20:26 (b) This is a new revelation to Thomas and a new confession from him.

1 Pet. 3:20 (c) The eight souls in the ark represented a new manifestation of God's grace, a new exhibition of His terrible judgment, and a new message to the world. The number "eight" always represents something new. This is true both in Scripture and in nature. The chapters numbered "eight" contain a new revelation not previously found in the Scriptures. The eighth note on the piano begins a new octave. The eighth day of the week begins a

new week. There are just seven colors in the rainbow; the eighth color begins a new spectrum.

Genesis 8 — is the beginning of a new generation of people on the earth proceeding from Noah and his family.

Exodus 8 — is the performing of a miracle which had heretofore been unknown in the history of man.

Matthew 8 — is the first instance of the miraculous cleansing of the leper by the word and the touch of another.

Luke 8 — is a new revelation of relationship between Christ and those who hear His Word; a new experience of seven demons cast out of one person.

Acts 8 — is a new experience of Phillip in personal work, the leading of the Spirit, and the conversion of an Ethiopian.

Romans 8 — brings a new revelation of the leading of the Spirit.

Hebrews 8 — shows a new revelation of God's covenant.

Revelation 8 — gives a new vision of the ministry of angels.

All the other chapters *number eight* in the Bible express something new as these do.

EIGHTEEN

Judg. 3:14 (c) *Ten* is the number of human weakness and defeat, *Eight* is the number of a new beginning. The number of "eighteen," therefore, indicates deliverance from defeat and the beginning of new liberty.

Judg. 10:8 (c) The Philistines and the Ammonites "oppressed the children of Israel eighteen years." This period of weakness was ended by the beginning of victory and deliverance.

2 Ki. 24:8 (c) This lad was eighteen years of age. He had the years of weakness and he had the beginning of something new, for the King of Babylon came and carried him into captivity.

Luke 13:11 (c) This woman also had a period of helplessness and had the joy of seeing a new experience come into her life and soul when Jesus spoke. See also vs. 4. When their sinning ended, their suffering began.

ELEVEN

Gen. 37:9 (a) The eleven stars represent the eleven brothers of Joseph who were to bow down to him as they afterward did. (See Gen. 42:6; 43:26; 43:28; 44:14; 50:18)

2 Ki 23:36 (c) The eleven years represent the number *six* which is the number of man's sufficiency joined with the number *five*, the number of human weakness. He had the ability to reign but did not have the heart to walk with God.

Matt. 28:16 (c) The number eleven reminds us that these men had sufficient instruction from Christ, sufficient inspiration from the Holy Spirit, and sufficient knowledge of God, yet they failed in so many respects. There should have been twelve patriarchs all working together but one was missing for many years. There should have been twelve disciples working together, but one proved to be a traitor. The number *eleven* reminds us of the failure even of that which is planned and ordained of God while it is in human hands.

ELIEZER

Gen. 24:2 (c) (Gen. 15:2) If this eldest servant was named Eliezer, then he is a type of the Holy Spirit who was sent after a bride for Isaac. Abraham represents the Father; Isaac the son representing the Lord Jesus; Eliezer represents the Holy Spirit. The Spirit is on earth gathering out from among the people a church, the bride of the Son. He is now dealing with us, communing with us, giving us gifts, and leading us along the way until He brings us to the Son at the great marriage feast.

ELIJAH

1 Ki. 17:1 (c) He is a type of Christ as Lord, as King, as the Lion, and as the Eagle. The word means "God is the Lord."

ELISHA

1 Ki. 19:16 (c) He is a type of Christ as the Saviour. The word means, "God is the Saviour."

EMBRACE

S. of Sol. 2:6 (c) This is typical of the close fellowship which the Lord Jesus has with those whom He loves and who have learned to trust Him. It speaks also of His protecting care as a mother holds the child to her bosom.

Heb. 11:13 (c) This is a figure to describe the appropriation of the Word of God with all the heart and soul.

EMERALD

Ex. 39:11 (c) This green stone represents praise, worship and adoration which begins now and lasts throughout eternity. Judah which means "praise" had his name graven on the emerald stone on the breastplate of the high priest.

Rev. 4:3 (c) This complete rainbow was given this color to typify the eternal character of God's grace and the everlasting nature of God's covenant of mercy. It was "green" to signify eternal praise.

EMPTY

Matt. 12:44 (c) The word is used to describe the condition of the unsaved person who has had a reformation in his life but has never received the Lord Jesus to fill his heart and soul.

Mark 12:3 (b) This is the condition of a servant of God who should have received the best from those to whom he ministered, but instead, he received the worst.

Luke 1:53 (b) This describes the condition of a person who hears the Word of God with pre-conceived ideas and with no heart hunger. He returns to his home from the service having received no blessing.

ENCAMP

Job 19:12 (b) The sorrow and trouble which came upon Job are compared to soldiers who surrounded him in order to remove from him all his pleasure and comfort.

Psa. 34:7 (a) The angels of the Lord surround the saint of God to protect and preserve him and to provide for his every need.

ENCHANTMENT

Lev. 19:26 (a) This refers to tricks and schemes to alter people's lives in an unnatural and unrighteous way.

Num. 24:1 (c) These enchantments are evidently pictures and types of the schemes and plans of Satan which are contrary to the will and way of God.

END

Num. 23:10 (a) He would like to die as a righteous man though he had not lived as one.

Deut. 32:29 (a) This refers to the outcome of Israel's disobedience and path of rebellion.

Psa. 37:37 (a) This end is death or the manner of death.

Psa. 73:17 (a) This describes the outcome of the sinner's life even though it be a life of prosperity and financial success.

Isa. 45:22 (a) The ends of the earth are those countries, nations and tribes which are farthest removed in every direction from Palestine. The word is used to illustrate the wide scope of the love of God.

1 Cor. 15:24 (a) The word here refers to the very end of the history of this earth and all that pertains to it.

ENSIGN

Isa. 5:26 (b) This is typical of a banner at the head of victorious troops conquering the enemy. God does this for His people.

EPHOD

Ex. 25:7 (c) This garment represents part of that wardrobe described in Isa. 61:10 as the "garments of salvation." It was on this garment that the twelve stones were set in the breastplate and fastened to the garment. It may represent that part of our Christian experience in which and through which we show forth the virtues of our Lord Jesus Christ. The ephod contained gold, blue, purple, crimson and cotton. These colors and materials represent the various and glorious characteristics of our Lord Jesus, and are imparted and imputed to us when we are made children of God. On the shoulder pieces of this garment were two large stones on which were engraved the names of the twelve tribes, six on each stone. All of this refers in some way to our Lord Jesus who carries us on His shoulders and on His breast.

EPHRAIM

Hosea 7:8 (a) This is another name for the nation of Israel, and was used about Israel when she turned her back on God to serve idols and live in rebellion. Israel as "Ephraim" is pictured as "a cake not turned." This refers to the fact that Israel or any individual for that matter might be splendidly related to the things of earth and to fellowmen, which would represent the lower side of the cake where it is well cooked. The upper part, however, which is raw, represents the state of Israel or an individual toward God, if that individual is an unsaved, self-righteous person. This is a type of the religious man of the world whose human attitudes are above reproach, but who has not a proper relationship to God. (See the thirty-five other times this name is mentioned in Hosea. See also Psa. 78:9.)

ESAU

Gen. 25:25 (c) This is a type of the flesh and the life of selfishness in contrast with Jacob and the life of faith. (Heb. 12:16)

ESPOUSE

2 Cor. 11:2 (a) Paul brought the Church of Corinth before God in prayer for Him to love them. He brought Christ before the Church that they might love Him.

EVE

Gen. 3:20 (c) A type of the church as Adam is a type of Christ. As she was made out of a part of Adam, so the church is a part of the Lord Jesus. The church is called His Bride as Eve was Adam's bride.

EVENING

Eccl. 11:6 (b) The evening time in the life is the time when the shadows fall, the day's work is ended, sorrows and weakness have come, and hope has faded. We should be as busy serving God in the later years as we are in the early years of life. Sometimes the dark times precede the bright times. We read that the evening and the morning were the first day. The darkness preceded the light. (See also Ex. 16:12; Num. 9:21) We read in Ezek. 24:18 "in the evening, my wife died, and in the morning I did as I was commanded." We should not permit sorrow and difficulty to hinder our service. It may be taken also as a picture of the fact that our time on earth is the evening time, followed by the morning in glory, a morning without clouds.

EXAMPLE

James 5:10 (c) Bible characters are examples of certain truths and the patterns of certain attributes which James asks us to consider. Here are a few:

Abel, the model speaker
Enoch, the model walker
Noah, the model worker
Job, the model of patience
Moses, model of faithfulness
Joseph, the model of piety
David, the model of praise
Jonathan, the model friend
Abraham, the model of faith
Samuel, the model of godliness
Elijah, the model reformer
Elisha, the model helper
Ebedmelech, model of kindness
Nehemiah, model man of business
Daniel, the model of decision
John the Baptist, the model of devotion
Paul, the model of earnestness
Peter, model of impulsiveness
Jesus, model of every virtue

EYE

Psa. 17:8 (b) The psalmist compares himself, in regard to his need for protection, to an eye in the head. He feels that he must be well sheltered by the Lord in order to keep from being hurt by the people.

Psa. 32:8 (a) The Lord promises to direct His children by His look. Of course, His child must keep looking into His face in order to learn what His eye expresses. This is done by prayer and Bible study.

Eccl. 1:8 (b) This is typical of the failure of things of earth to satisfy the craving of the heart.

Lam. 2:18 (a) This represents a call for all Israel to weep bitterly and constantly about their sins, showing a spirit of repentance and a desire to return to God.

Lam. 3:51 (b) What we see certainly affects our desires and our actions. As we gaze upon Christ Jesus we desire to be like Him, and we purpose to live for Him. We purchase clothing because we see, and it appeals to us. We purchase a house because we see, and it meets our desires. In our early days we see a companion and he or she attracts our heart's affections and we marry that person. So the eye affects the heart. Let us therefore look unto Jesus.

Ezek. 1:18 (b) These eyes probably represent the omniscience of the Spirit of God. When it is written that there are seven "eyes," it no doubt means that there is perfect vision and understanding on the part of this wonderful Person. (See also chap. 10:12.)

Dan. 7:8 (a) This probably is a figure of the unusual vision and knowledge of this king. It may represent some great world power, whether religious or political, whose spies are everywhere, learning the secrets of nations, of clubs, or associations, to use for the profit of this cruel ruler. This truth is indicated in verse 7. (See also v. 20.)

Zech. 2:8 (a) This term is used to express the great value of Israel to God. If anyone touched His people to persecute or injure them, He felt it keenly and would come to their rescue.

Zech. 3:9 (b) The stone represents the Lord Jesus Christ. The seven eyes represent the person of the Holy Spirit in His omniscience. Christ was fully Spirit-filled, Spirit-led, Spirit-guided. The seven eyes represent the perfections of the Spirit of God, all of which perfections were manifest in Christ Jesus. (See also Rev. 5:6)

Zech. 11:17 (a) This is figurative of the removal of power and of vision from false leaders. When God arises to execute vengeance, He will strip from His enemies their power of vision and strength.

Matt. 5:29 (a) It is an actual eye but figuratively it means that if we are so intent on seeing things we should not see that we cannot and will not trust the Saviour, then it is better to have the eye removed so that the soul may not be hindered in following the Lord fully.

Matt. 6:22 (b) The Lord is telling us that we are to look straight forward and have an eye "single for His glory." We are to look off from every other attraction to Jesus only. Our eyes affect our hearts, therefore we are to let only those things enter our minds and hearts through the eye gate that will bring glory to God and blessing to us.

Matt. 7:4 (a) This is typical of the little things in the life of the other person which we may see and dislike while we at the same time overlook the big things which are wrong in our own lives.

Eph. 1:18 (a) It is typical of our inability to understand and to grasp spiritual truths offered to us from God, unless the Lord explains and teaches us.

EYELIDS

Job 41:18 (c) This is a poetical description of an unknown animal, and the words are God's words. He probably is telling us that the opening of the eyes by the raising of the eyelids of this monster is comparable to the rising of the sun in the morning which illuminates our way, and enables us to live intelligently.

Psa. 11:4 (b) The expression of the eyes tells a wonderful story to those who watch the eyes. Since the Lord guides us with His eye, as in Psalm 32:8, we need to keep our eyes upon His eyes to see what is His pleasure and so be directed by Him.

EYE SALVE

Rev. 3:18 (a) This is a type of the teachings of God's Word that enables us to see things as God sees them, and to evaluate things in the light of eternity.

F

FACE

Ex. 10:5 (b) The surface covering of the hills, valleys, and plains, etc., is described in the Scripture as the "face of the earth." This expression occurs in many places.

Num. 6:25 (a) Lest we should be so occupied with our blessings that we forget the Blesser, our attention is called in this prayer to the fact that after we are made rich by the blessing of God, then we are to gaze upon His lovely face, and thus be occupied with Him. (See also Psa. 31:16; Psa. 67:1; Psa. 69:17; 80:3; 143:7.)

Psa. 27:8 (b) To seek the face of the Lord means to come into His presence in confession and contrition, to believe His word and to seek His fellowship until there is a consciousness in the heart that there is nothing between the soul and the Savior. Then one may commune with Him freely.

Isa. 3:15 (b) The expression here refers to the suppressing of the poor until their faces show the anxiety and the distress that they are suffering from such oppression.

Isa. 25:7 (a) This may refer to the shadow of death which hangs over all people. Or it may refer to the unbelief that shrouds people's hearts in darkness.

Ezek. 1:6 (b) These four faces represent four aspects of the Lord Jesus Christ. These four figures were embroidered on the four banners which were displayed in the four camps of Israel as they encamped around the tabernacle, three on each of the four sides. These four aspects of Christ characterize the four gospels. Matthew explains the lion characteristics of Christ; Mark describes the ox character; Luke presents the human character; and John represents the Deity of our Lord. (See also Ezek. 10:14; Rev. 4:7)

Ezek. 38:18 (a) This is the picture of a man whose anger is seen in his countenance as the face reddens and the mouth tightens. God uses this picture to describe His feelings.

FADE

Isa. 28:1 (a) The glory of Israel had departed and their country had been ravished and destroyed. The word "fade" is used to describe that desolation.

Isa. 40:7-8 (a) When the curse of God is on the people, all their blessings depart and drouth, pestilence and the sword destroy all signs of prosperity. The word "fade" is used here to describe that scene of desolation.

Isa. 64:6 (a) This is a marvelous comparison of the autumn leaves with people who have reached old age. Some leaves fade into sear, yellow, curled, worm-eaten objects which no one admires. They are raked and burned. Other leaves fall and are more beautiful than when they were on the trees. The beautiful crimson, scarlet, or golden tints, the orange shades, the glossy surface, make some leaves a beautiful work of art. These leaves are often saved because of their beauty. So it is with people; some, as they grow older, become crabbed, sour, and most difficult to live with. When they die, they are hurried away. No one cares. Others grow more beautiful and more delightful as the years go by. They are a joy to all who know them. When they die, they are sadly missed and their memory is cherished. (See also Isa. 1:30.)

Ezek. 47:12 (a) Here is a graphic picture of a church or a community in which the Spirit of God is working unhindered. The trees represent the Godly leaders, the preachers, the teachers, who are feeding the saints of God with heavenly manna, and whose testimonies (leaves) are bright, constant and unfailing.

James 1:11 (a) As the flower wilts and withers when there is no rain and the sun is hot, so the rich man will droop as age comes on and the pleasures of life fail.

1 Pet. 1:4 (b) This is an expression used to compare the earthly inheritance that shrivels and shrinks with the heavenly inheritance which grows brighter and better.

FALL

Esther 6:13 (a) This expression is used to describe the defeat of Haman at the hands of the Jews. He would be deposed from his high and exalted position in the kingdom. This of course took place soon. (See Psa. 5:10; 141:10.)

Esther 9:3 (a) The word is used to describe the great fear and apprehension that fell upon the people because of the power given to Mordecai, the Jew.

Prov. 26:27 (a) This act is used to describe the conditions of that one who is caught in his own evil schemes and is injured by the plot which he intended for others.

Heb. 6:6 (a) The action referred to in this passage has no reference whatever to a Christian. It refers to one who has attached himself to Christianity as glasses are attached to the face, or as earrings are attached to the ears. The ears never fall away, nor does the nose, for they are a part of the body. The Christian is a part of the body of Jesus Christ, as is described fully in Ephesians. Professing Christians are attached to the church, or the people of God, as Judas was, but they are not a part of that living group known as the Church of Jesus Christ, or the body of the Lord Jesus. There are those who profess to be saved but have never really been born again. They pretend to adhere to the doctrines of Christ, but under pressure and persecution they turn their backs on Christ and repudiate that which they pretended at one time to believe.

FAMILIAR

1 Sam. 28:7 (a) It was generally thought that certain witches, necromancers, soothsayers, magicians and astrologers were in intimate association with certain spirits in the other world. This group of people taught that those with whom they communicated in the other world would listen to their call and come back to earth with a message. These folk claimed to be able to reach out into eternity and call for the appearance of anyone they desired. It was a devilish program which was condemned severely by God. The Lord said, "Should the living seek to the dead?" Isa. 8:19. We cannot be on familiar terms with anyone who has died except our Lord Jesus Christ for He came back from the dead and called on us to have fellowship with Him.

FAMILY

Eph. 3:15 (a) God's people are represented as a family for fellowship. This is one of the six aspects of the church found in the book of Ephesians. As a "family" we serve together and play together. We study and work together in happy relationship. Each one helps and loves the other. Each one shares the problems, the defeats and the victories of the others in the family. So it should be among God's people.

FAMINE

Amos 8:11 (a) This is symbolical of the lack of the Word of God as the Bread of Life. When the Scriptures are ruled out, then the people perish, the vision is gone, hope fades, and there is a general declension.

Luke 15:14 (b) The gifts of God may be used up, but the love of God never fails. This boy left his father's home, which is a type of walking with and loving our Lord, to seek his pleasures in the far-off country, which represents the world. He found that all that the world offered him soon failed. Nothing that the world gives can satisfy the craving of the human heart. The world with its pleasures and its pursuits fails to satisfy the craving of the heart. The person must return to God, he must come again under the protection of the sacrifice of the Lamb of God, and thus enjoy fellowship with God.

FAN

Isa. 41:16 (a) God would use Israel to blow away their enemies and to have the victory over those who oppressed them.

Jer. 4:11 (a) This is not a constructive wind, as when the chaff is fanned out from the wheat, but it is a destructive wind to increase the damage, as when a wind causes the fire to scatter through the forest or to spread from house to house. The enemy would destroy Jerusalem.

Jer. 15:7 (b) This represents the great power of God's destructive wrath. As one fans a fire in order to make it burn more brightly, so the Lord will watch over His wrath to make it burn more fiercely upon those who forsake Him.

Jer. 51:2 (a) The process of punishment is reversed in this Scripture and the enemies of the Jews are being punished themselves. Babylon is conquered and scattered by her enemies. God really did wipe out that great city with a destroying wind. (See Jer. 51:1.)

Luke 3:17 (b) This is descriptive of a farmer who, with his fan and the wind produced by it, separates the chaff from the wheat. So Christ will separate those who are His from those who are not, in the great day of judgment. (See also Matt. 3:12) The chaff referred to in this passage are those folk who are of no value at all to God. (See under "CHAFF.")

FAST

Isa. 58:6 (a) The description given in this passage reveals that true fasting is not necessarily abstaining from food. The abstaining from food in itself evidently has little, if any, value in God's sight. It is the leaving of the duty of preparing and eating the meal, so that there may be time for serving others, for prayer for others, and for enriching the soul from God's Word. Several hours a day are consumed in preparing and eating meals. That time may well be used once in a while for more profitable service and devotion. From five to seven hours a day are consumed in preparing meals, eating them, and in cleaning up after them. Fasting eliminates the loss of that time, so that the person may devote himself fully to the things of God, both for his own blessing, and the blessing of others. (See Matt. 6:17; Mark 2:19; Luke 18:12; Acts 13:2.)

FASTEN

Eccl. 12:11 (a) This refers to the permanent effect in the heart and mind of messages which may come from God, or from other sources. They make a permanent impression on the one who hears them.

Isa. 22:23 (a) God has set Christ securely in history and in prophecy, so that He can never be avoided, evaded, nor obscured.

Luke 4:20 (a) The audience gazed intently upon our Lord so as to miss nothing that was said or done by Him. (See also Acts 11:6.)

FAT

Gen. 41:20 (a) This is a type of the seven prosperous and fruitful years which were to precede the seven years of drouth and dearth.

Gen. 49:20 (a) What Asher appropriated, received and enjoyed was for his blessing and profit. Because of this that which he gave out to others was profitable and helpful to them. The lesson for us is that if we would give out that which brings joy, gladness and help to others, we must ourselves feed on the Living Bread, and drink the Living Water.

Lev. 3:16 (c) This may be taken as a type of the rich blessings of life, health, money, gifts and talents which may be the portion of a Christian. All these should be recognized as gifts belonging to the Lord and Saviour, and not used or appropriated for ourselves.

Deut. 32:15 (b) This word is used to express the fact that when Israel (Jeshurun) became powerful with a great army, then they rebelled against God, kicked over the traces, and began living a life of rebellion. (See Deut. 31:20; Prov. 13:4; 15:30; 28:25.)

1 Sam. 2:29 (a) These wicked sons were making themselves rich and wealthy by taking that which belonged to the Lord because it had been dedicated to the Lord. They were stealing from God. (See Psa. 22:29)

2 Sam. 1:22 (b) Jonathan conquered the power of the enemy though they were great, strong, mighty and wealthy. (See also Isa. 5:17.)

Isa. 6:10 (a) This is a type or a picture of a good thing in a wrong place. Fat in or on or around the heart hinders its beating, and its proper operation. So when one's riches, power and position control the heart and life, that person is hindered in his service for and devotion to the Lord.

Isa. 34:6 (a) Here we find a type of the success of God's avenging hand in destroying the land and the people who rebelled against Him.

Isa. 58:11 (a) This is a beautiful type of the goodness of the great God of heaven in enriching the lives of those who walk with Him, and obey His Word. (See also Gen. 45:18)

Ezek. 34:14 (a) This is a figure of the blessing of God upon the fields, the homes, the business and the lives of those who love Him, walk with Him, and obey Him. (See also Num. 13:20; Neh. 8:10; 9:25; Isa. 25:6; Isa. 28:1; Isa. 30:23)

FEATHERS

Lev. 1:16 (c) These represent hypocrisy, for the gay feathers of birds, colored and attractive, may hide the true nature of that which is beneath.

Psa. 91:4 (b) They represent the protecting care of God over His children as the hen covers her baby chicks.

Ezek. 17:3,7 (a) This is a picture of the fanciful spread, or gaudy show made by these two kings. They clothed themselves with pomp. The display of beauty and wealth on the outside covered the wickedness of their hearts on the inside.

FEEL

Gen. 27:12 (c) Isaac did feel his son Jacob and was deceived by his feelings. (See v. 21.) We should be warned by this picture against trusting in our feelings in those matters which pertain to God, and to faith, and to God's Word. We are to live and understand by faith, not by feeling.

Judg. 16:26 (c) Samson felt the pillars, he realized their strength and their size, but was not dismayed by that. He believed God, and because of his faith he accomplished his purpose. Let us also consider every situation in life, and then look to God to work the necessary miracle. (See Rom. 4:19.)

Psa. 58:9 (b) Thorns were used to make a fire beneath the pots. They were fit for nothing but burning. The Lord is describing the suddenness with which His wrath would come upon His enemies. There would not be a gradual approach to the storm, as would be when the thorn fire gradually heats up the pot.

Acts 17:27 (a) Our Lord indicates that men are blind and therefore cannot see God as they should. They therefore reach out the hand of faith and find God by faith. Then He opens their eyes to see, and know, and understand Him.

FEET

1 Sam. 2:9 (a) By this we are taught that God will direct the walk, the ways, the service, and the lives of His people.

2 Sam. 22:34 (a) Here we find a picture of the way God equips His children for the rough paths of life. Sometimes He smooths out the road. Sometimes He removes mountains, exalts the valleys, and makes the crooked places straight. However, sometimes He leaves the road filled with stones, and the mountains steep and apparently inaccessible, but He fixes up His child to enjoy the difficulties, and to surmount them easily. The hind is a mountain deer with small feet. It feels quite at home among the cliffs and chasms of the mountain range, and has no difficulty traversing them. So the Lord equips His people to overcome obstacles, and to live happy lives in the

midst of difficulties. (See also Psa. 18:33, 36; 2 Sam. 22:37; Hab. 3:19)

1 Ki. 2:5 (a) This is a reference to the evil way of Joab in killing those whom he thought might hinder his leadership, and replace him as the general of the army.

2 Ki. 9:35 (b) This is a three-fold picture. The skull represents the thoughts and the teachings which this wicked woman established in Israel. Her feet represented her evil ways and wicked walk which still were copied by the people of Israel after she was dead. Her hands represented her wicked works which still afflicted Israel.

Job 12:5 (b) By this picture we may understand one who is willing to go astray in paths of sin and wants no one to enlighten him on the error of his way, nor warn him of its consequences.

Job 29:15 (a) Job is using this illustration to describe his ministry as a messenger to those who could not walk. He took food and supplies to those who could not otherwise obtain them. He is telling us that he was a friend, and a liberal friend, to the poor.

Job 30:12 (a) This describes to us those young people who were insulting the old servant of God, and who rejected both his company and his counsel.

Job 33:11 (a) God had so afflicted Job that he could not go about his business as he would like, nor enter into the activities of life.

Psa. 25:15 (a) David pictures himself as a bird caught and entangled by his enemies in great difficulties. God would save him out of these perplexities by His wonderful love and power. (See Psa. 31:8 Lam. 1:13.)

Psa. 40:2 (a) This is a type of the solid foundation for our faith and our safety, Christ Jesus, the Rock of Ages.

Psa. 66:9 (a) By this is represented the safekeeping from God of those who walk with Him in fellowship and obedience.

Psa. 73:2 (a) Asaph was so confused by what he saw of the prosperity of the wicked that he contemplated going into wicked ways himself. God, however, preserved and kept him from following such a path, and revealed to him the end of the road which the wicked take.

Psa. 74:3 (a) This great singer is calling upon God to hurry to Jerusalem with His delivering power because of the dire need and the wretched condition of Israel.

Prov. 6:13 (a) The wicked man leads others to walk in wicked ways with him. He invites his friends to go astray in paths of sin with him.

Prov. 6:28 (a) This is a type of the damaging effects of sin in a man's life. The hot coals represent sinful deeds, and the one who plays with them will surely suffer from them.

Prov. 19:2 (a) This represents a warning to consider carefully the walk and the way in which we go as to whether it is right or wrong, and whether it has the approval of God.

Prov. 26:6 (a) Here we find a picture of failure. If we want to accomplish our ends we must not commit the work to one who is irresponsible.

Prov. 29:5 (a) This is an injunction to help our neighbor to live a good and useful life by not feeding his pride.

S. of Sol. 7:1 (a) By this we are taught that our walk must be made safe and comfortable, as well as beautiful and attractive through the death of our Saviour. Shoes are made from the hide of a dead animal. So our natural walk must be covered over with the life of our lovely Lord, so that we may "walk with the Lord in the light of His Word."

Isa. 6:2 (b) Even these heavenly beings felt that their walk and way were not fit to be seen by the Lord. How much more do we need to be covered by the blood of Christ and by His robe of righteousness.

Isa. 7:20 (a) In this way God is warning Israel that He will send the King of Assyria to execute terrible vengeance on them, even to the smallest details of their lives.

Jer. 13:16 (a) This is a picture of the confusion and chaos that would come on Israel if they turned their backs on the God of heaven who is the light of life.

Ezek. 1:7 (a) All of this passage depicts the Lord Jesus in several aspects. These feet are typical of the straight and sure and godly walk of Christ as He lived on earth. It may mean also that as the feet of the calf lead it to the altar for sacrifice, so the feet of the Lord Jesus led Him to Calvary to die for us.

Ezek. 16:25 (a) This figure is used to express the sinful lusts of Israel as they invited their neighbors, who were really their enemies, to come in and to bring with them evil pleasures for the enjoyment of Israel.

Ezek. 32:2 (a) Pharoah provided for the people that which defiled them, and enabled them to live in wicked practices. (See also chap. 34:18.)

Dan. 2:33,42 (a) These represent a kingdom ruled over by ten kings. This kingdom would be on an insecure foundation. It would be made up of elements that would not work together. It may be that this kingdom is the revived Roman Empire. If so, it is mentioned also in chapter 7, vss. 7 and 19.

Dan. 10:6 (a) Here is a type of the perfect walk of our Lord. His walk and His way were bright in effect, solid and substantial in purpose. (See also Rev. 1:15; 2:18.)

Nahum 1:3 (a) This is a figure from country life. When clouds of dust arise in the road, we know that someone is coming along the way. So, clouds of trouble in the life of a believer tell us that God is near. He said, "When thou passeth through the waters, I will be with thee." He also said, "I will be with him in trouble." He has not promised to keep His children out of trouble. He has promised to preserve us when we go through the trouble.

Nahum 1:15 (c) This indicates that the pathway of the gospel messenger was blessed of God to bring joy to many hearts. (See also Romans 10:15.)

Hab. 3:19 (a) The prophet is telling us that the Lord fixed him up in such a way that difficulties, obstacles, and mountains in his path were easy to traverse and a delight to his heart as the mountain deer (hind) delights in the cliffs and chasms of the mountain.

Eph. 6:15 (b) We cannot live the gospel. We can, however, and should, walk in such a way that people will listen to what we say. The feet are not shod with the gospel. That must come from our lips. The feet (our walk) should be of such a character that it will make it easy for people to believe what we say when we give them the gospel.

FEET (Under)

2 Sam. 22:10 (a) This figure is used to describe the complete control that God will have and does have over His enemies. No one can successfully fight against God. In His own good time, He triumphs completely and every enemy is crushed. (See also Psalm 18:9.)

2 Sam. 22:39 (a) The thought in this passage is quite similar to the one above. God controls the actions of His enemies, as He pleases, and forces them to obey His will. This truth is to be seen in the case of the King of Babylon whom God described as His "battle ax" to subdue the nations. Having accomplished this purpose, God destroyed the Babylonian empire. (See also Psa. 91:13.)

Psa. 8:6 (a) God has made the Lord Jesus Christ the sovereign Lord over all creation. Every knee must bow to Him, and every tongue must confess to Him. Every voice is to acclaim Him Lord of all. (See 1 Cor. 15:25-27; Eph. 1:22; Heb. 2:8.)

Rom. 16:20 (a) God will yet triumph over all the plans of the devil, and will subdue Satan and his hosts. (See also Gen. 3:15.)

Rev. 12:1 (a) Probably the description that is given is to inform us that this woman is the nation of Israel. This nation began as we read in Gen. 37:7,9. In this passage, the sun represents Jacob, the father, the moon represents Joseph's mother, the stars represent the other brothers. For that reason in the passage before us, the Lord is identifying the woman as the one represented by those figures way back in Jacob's day.

FEET (Wash)

Ex. 30:19 (c) Perhaps this figure indicates that our work and our walk must be clean as we enter into God's service. (See v. 21; chap. 40:31.)

Psa. 58:10 (b) This unusual picture describes the complete victory that God's people will eventually have over all their enemies. It may be that this refers definitely to the time when Israel will be the head of the nations, having conquered and subdued all her enemies.

S. of Sol. 5:3 (c) In this passage we may see the utter devotion of the child of God to his Lord. He has removed his coat for whole-hearted work in the harvest field, and he has cleansed his feet from evil ways that he may walk humbly and softly with God. Certainly no other walk would be desirable nor permissible between these two lovers.

John 13:5-14 (b) By this service we are to learn that the Lord Jesus took the humble place, and so should we. He served the disciples in lowliness of mind, heart and position, and so we should serve each other. He indicated by this service that He would cleanse our ways for us, that we might walk in a clean path. He also assured Peter that He would continue this service from heaven and that we also should help to encourage each other in paths of godliness. (See also Psa. 119:9; Eph. 5:26; 1 Tim. 5:10.)

FELL

Matt. 7:25,27 (a) Christ is warning us in this passage that if we build in this life on any other foundation than Himself, we shall not be able to stand in the Judgment Day. He is the Rock of Ages, the Cornerstone, the rock foundation. Good works, religious observances, church activities, gifts of money, and all other such activities, if depended on for salvation, will be like the sinking sand, and the sinner will not be able to endure the storm of God's judgment if he depends upon these. (See Luke 6:49.)

Matt. 13:4 (a) This parable represents the ministry of God's Word by the servant of God. The action of the seed falling represents the Word of God, coming upon the ears of listeners. The various attitudes of heart to those messages are represented by the various kinds of soil on which the seed is placed. (See Mark 4:4; Luke 8:5.)

Luke 10:30 (b) This picture probably represents the treatment that the world gives to most of its own people. The world takes from its followers their money, their health, their time, and oftentimes their lives. The world gives nothing in exchange for this robbery, but leaves the victim half dead. The person is spiritually dead, but physically alive.

Acts 1:25 (a) Judas was in an exalted position, being called by Christ to be one of the twelve. When he turned against the Saviour, denied Him, and sold Him, then he lost that exalted place, and became the world's worst.

Rev. 6:13 (a) Stars in the book of Revelation represent great personalities. There comes a time when God cleans out the heavens of all these powerful, wicked ones and they are cast to the earth. Satan himself is one of the stars. Of his own free will he strikes down upon sinners from heaven as lightning strikes suddenly and destructively. (See Luke 10:18.) God permits the devil to exercise his power from heavenly places so that he strikes as lightning strikes, but no one can possibly say "I have him under control." In the passage under consideration, as also in Rev. 8:10, we are informed that these mighty and wicked angelic beings are permitted to come upon this earth from their position of power to injure and harm the inhabitants.

FENCE

2 Sam. 23:7 (a) We are informed by this type that many wicked men are so dangerous, so strong, and so resourceful in their evil that those who approach them need to be well guarded lest they be greatly injured. This is certainly true of many of our great underworld characters.

Job 10:11 (a) Because of Job's great troubles, trials and suffering, he wanted to die. He was not able to die, and so he describes the limitations of his body by this figure.

Job. 19:8 (a) Job felt that his hope of escape could not be found. All his resources were gone, his friends failed him, his health had departed, and he was left alone. He describes these experiences as being a fence which held him to his ash pile.

Psa. 62:3 (a) There is some irony in this Scripture and some misery with it. David asks his enemies whether they regard him as a bowing wall or a tottering fence which they can easily destroy. He reminds them that this is not true, and that God will destroy them instead of they destroying him.

Isa. 5:2 (a) This figure represents the protection that God gave to Israel when he brought them into the land of Canaan and put His fear upon the nations round about so that they could develop themselves into a mighty kingdom. Instead of appreciating this wonderful protection, they discarded His care, and became followers of the idolatry of the neighboring nations.

Jer. 15:20 (a) God assured Jeremiah that when he stood as a warning against Israel and reproved them for their sins, he would be fully protected and preserved by the God who sent him on this mission.

FEVER

Matt. 8:14 (c) Here is a type of the worries and difficulties which bother many hearts and hinder their usefulness. The touch of Christ on the life will bring peace. (See also John 4:52.)

FIELD

Lev. 19:19 (c) The Lord uses this figure to warn us against seeking to teach the truth in any group where falsehoods are taught. Teachers who teach God's gospel of grace sometimes think they can succeed in their ministry while teaching in a group where the Word of God is denied, and the gospel is perverted. The Lord warns against any such mixture of teaching. Wheat and cockleburrs should never be sowed together in the field. The weeds will take the crop. (See Deut. 22:9.)

Psa. 96:12 (c) This probably is a picture of the blessed condition of this earth during the millennial reign of Christ. There will be no weeds, no burrs, no poison ivy, but the fields will be fertile, and will abound with flowers, grains and those things which bring joy to the heart of man.

Isa. 16:10 (c) This probably is a picture of the famine, dearth and drouth that would overtake Israel, or Moab, or any other nation when they become worshippers of idols and have no love for the God of heaven.

Ezek. 17:5 (a) Babylon in this case is represented as a field into which the King of Babylon took the leaders of Israel and most of the people. There they were to grow and become strong again before returning to Israel.

Matt. 13:38 (a) This is a name given to the various countries of the earth in which there is a harvest of souls to be gathered for the Lord.

John 4:35 (c) It is used here to describe the crops of grain upon which the reaper was to work. The grain represents people with whom the Spirit has been dealing and has made ready for salvation.

FIERY

Deut. 33:2 (a) In God's law He revealed His justice, His righteousness and His power. As fire destroys burnable materials, so the law of God destroys all that opposes God. and all that promotes sin.

Psa. 21:9 (a) By this picture we learn that God will punish His enemies eternally in the lake of fire. Even in this life the ungodly suffer the consequences of their disobedience to God. They will be in pain as a burning from the results of their sins. (See Heb. 10:27.)

Isa. 14:29 (a) Though the King of Assyria should depart from them, his posterity would yet pursue and injure Israel, destroying their land, and appropriating their property.

Dan. 7:9-10 (a) This is a type of the severity and certainty of God's judgments wherein He executes wrath upon all the guilty.

Nah. 2:3 (Marg.) (a) Some think that this is a definite reference to the operation of motor vehicles by electricity. It may refer to the speed with which they would operate, as well as the power of operation.

Eph. 6:16 (a) Here is a picture of the fierce attacks which Satan will make on God's people by the malicious tongues of his followers, and by persecution.

1 Pet. 4:12 (a) By this is indicated the time of suffering and persecution that awaits God's people from Satan and his followers.

FIG (LEAVES)

Gen. 3:7 (c) These leaves may be a type of human righteousness which is used as a shield to hide human sins. The fig tree produces beautiful, large, soft, velvety leaves which are very attractive and lovely to feel. Man's religion is quite like that. He knows he is not fit to stand in the presence of God, and so he manufactures a religious program and thinks that this will be sufficient. Fig leaves shrink very quickly and reduce in size to about one-fourth their original size. Thus they fail to hide the parts as they should. So it is with human religions. They are not sufficient to cover man's sin and need. Only the blood of Christ is sufficient as a covering that satisfies the demands of God.

FIG (TREE)

Judges 9:10-11 (b) This is an allegory. Gideon was the fig tree. Jotham his son was the vine, Abimelech was the bramble. Jotham in speaking to Israel reminded them that while both he and his father really cared for the blessing and the good of the nation, Abimelech would not be a blessing, but would be to them a curse and would bring only sorrow and trouble to them.

1 Ki. 4:25 (c) This is an interesting type of general prosperity. There would be no mortgages and no debts, but each man would own his own property and be able to recline at ease in his own home. (See also Micah 4:4; Zech. 3:10)

2 Ki. 18:31 (b) This is a promise from the King of Babylon that if the Jews would come over to him, surrender to him, and yield themselves to him, he would take them away to a fruitful land and give them their freedom. (See also Isa. 36:16)

S. of Sol. 2:13 (a) This is a type of the prosperity of Israel as a nation. Their fruit trees would abound in fruit, and their fields would be fertile and productive.

Isa. 34:4 (a) This represents the result of God's curse on the nation. He will cause all blessings to cease so that the land will be barren. (See Jer. 8:13; Hab. 3:17)

Nah. 3:12 (b) This is a type of the curse that is to come upon Nineveh. Their riches and their treasures would fall an easy prey to the invader.

Hosea 9:10 (a) God chose Israel in the beginning as a nation which would be full of possibilities for His glory; it would be a nation giving Him an opportunity to manifest His wisdom, His power, and His grace.

Joel 1:7 (b) The Lord uses this type to describe the action of the enemy in their damage to Israel so that she could not, and would not, bring forth fruit unto God. However, in 2:22 God promises a restoration.

Hab. 3:17 (b) Here we find a picture of utter desolation. The lack or the absence of flowers was certain evidence that there would be no fruit in the future. The lack of grapes on the vines indicated a present need. The efforts of the olive trees to become fine fruitful trees would fail, and there would be no oil for the use of the owner. The barren fields would tell the story of dearth and drouth. The flock cut off from the fold would indicate either the invasion of the enemy who would steal the cattle, or else the prevalence of a disease which would kill off the animals. The empty stalls would assure them that there would be no milk, no meat, and no supply for their needs. In spite of this absence of all prosperity, the heart of this servant of God would still sing and rejoice in God. (See Hag. 2:19)

Matt. 21:19 (b) Here as usual the fig tree is a type of the nation of Israel in its political aspect. The Lord cursed the fig tree, but not an olive tree. The olive tree represents Israel from the religious viewpoint. Paul tells in his epistle that the believers are grafted into the olive tree, not into the fig tree. We do come to Israel's God, but we do not become a part of the nation of Israel. You will note that this passage does not say that Christ expected to find figs, but it says "if haply He might find." It was not the season for figs actually, and neither was it the season for blessing in Israel, for they were slaves to Rome, and were living in rebellion and hypocrisy to God. The cursing of the fig tree was really not a curse. All the Saviour said was, "No fruit grow on thee." Peter considered this a curse. This was really a type of the coming destruction of the nation of Israel as a political power. This was accomplished at the time of the destruction of Jerusalem.

Matt. 24:32 (a) The budding of this tree refers to the beginning of the restoration of the nation of Israel as a political power. We see these "buds" appearing today. The nation has been formed in Palestine. A good part of the country is controlled by the Jews. They have their own government, postage, coinage and educational institutions. All of this is just an evidence of the coming greatness of that great nation. One day they will conquer Jerusalem entirely, will expel all foreign influences, will destroy the Mosque of the Mohammedans, and will establish their king again upon his throne in that great city. (See also Luke 21:29)

Luke 13:6 (a) This fig tree represents Israel as a political nation. During the three years that Christ was preaching on the earth, He sought to bring them back to God by His ministry. He sought to restore the real worship of the true God. There was no response to these efforts of His. They repudiated Him, they rejected His Word, they renounced His claims, they refused to return to the God of their fathers. All the efforts He put forth, plus those of His disciples, are represented in this parable by the efforts made to fertilize the tree. Because of their failure to respond, Israel was doomed by the Lord to be dispersed among the nations.

FIGHT

2 Chron. 20:17 (c) This is a splendid illustration of the provision God has made to meet all our need in this life. He would have us trust Him daily for daily needs, and for salvation from daily troubles. At Kadesh-Barnea, Israel refused to permit the Lord to become their captain and to fight their battles. So they were made to wander in the wilderness thirty-eight years. We too will find it necessary to wander in defeat unless we permit Him to fight the battle for us.

Acts 5:39 (a) This figure is used to describe the persecution of God's people by their enemies, and the refusal of these enemies to bow to God's Word through the teaching of Christ and His disciples. (See also Acts 23:9.) Fighting God's people is fighting God. (See Matt. 25:45.)

1 Cor. 9:26 (a) By this strong word, Paul describes his resistance to sin, to Satan and to the world. Paul had strong convictions about living a holy and godly life. He would battle with Satan, and in every possible way win the victory through Christ.

1 Tim. 6:12 (a) The figure is used here to describe the firm stand that Christians should take for that which is right, and that which is true. We are to uphold the gospel. We are to stand against the attacks of the world, the flesh and the Devil at every opportunity.

FILTHINESS

2 Cor. 7:1 (a) This describes the character of a bad disposition, selfishness, egotism, sarcasm, criticism, meanness, rancor, bitterness and assertiveness. None of these should be permitted to exist in the heart of God's child.

FILTHY

Col. 3:8 (a) The word here describes lewd language, contaminating conversation, "racy" stories, and all evil communications. (See 2 Pet. 2:7)

1 Tim. 3:3 (a) By this word we understand "tainted" money. This refers to money used for wrong purposes, or to obtain evil ends. (See also v. 8; Titus 1:7, 11; 1 Pet. 5:2)

Jude 8 (a) This is a figure of men who imagine evil things about God's people to further their own lustful desires. (See Rev. 22:11)

FINGER

Ex. 8:19 (a) Here is a mark of the power of God. Only His finger was needed in order to do great things, and to perform marvelous miracles. We are reminded by this that if so much could be done by one finger, what tremendous things would be done by His whole person.

2 Sam. 21:20 (a) The presence of six fingers and six toes would mark this man as a "superman." Six in the Bible represents the number of man's sufficiency and supremacy.

1 Ki. 12:10 (a) The king by means of this figure told the people that the least of his laws of oppression would be worse than the greater laws of oppression which were enforced by his father Solomon. He assured the people that he would be more oppressive and more cruel than his father had been.

Isa. 58:9 (a) The pointing of the finger was a gesture of impudence and scorn against God. This was to be discontinued entirely. and the attitude of Israel was to be completely changed into one of devotion, acceptance and friendliness.

Dan. 5:5 (c) This is a picture to show that God uses human instruments to pesent divine truths. He used only a man's fingers because He did not need man's brains, nor his mind in order to make or reveal His decisions. The man's fingers simply wrote the story that God had devised in His own heart.

Luke 11:20 (a) Probably the Lord Jesus was referring to the Holy Spirit as a part of Himself. He said on one occasion that He cast out demons by the Spirit of God. It may be also He used the finger to indicate that this was only a very little of His power. When He uses greater power the demons and the Devil himself will be cast into the lake of fire to be forever punished.

FIR (TREE)

2 Ki. 19:23 (b) This is a type of the finest and best of Israel's men. (See also Isa. 37:24)

Isa. 14:8 (b) Probably this refers to the millennial time when Satan will be cast down and will be unable to bring trouble on the earth. The fir tree is a type of the happy life of a believer. It is a picture of joy particularly when found in the life of a leader. So these leaders may rejoice in peace when Satan is cast out of the earth and chained for the thousand years.

Isa. 41:19 (c) This is a picture of the joy of the Lord that fills the believer's heart when he is in the midst of distressing and disturbing conditions.

Ezek. 31:8 (a) This is a type of the great men of Assyria who excelled in might, power, pomp and dress. They were not like the great men of Israel, but were more beautiful and attractive in their appearance and demeanor.

Hosea 14:8 (c) By this figure is represented a happy Christian life, a life of usefulness for the Lord, and a happy situation.

Nahum 2:3 (b) By this figure is indicated that the great men of Israel, the leaders of their worship and service, were to be humbled and defeated by God's command.

Zech. 11:2 (b) The comparison here is between the size of the little fir tree and the great cedar tree. The lesser person weeps and grieves when the greater person dies or falls in the battle. This Scripture was used at Spurgeon's funeral.

FIRE

Gen. 22:6 (c) This represents the judgment of God. Abraham representing God, the Father, was going forth to sacrifice His son. Isaac in this case represents the sinner. The fire and the wood represent God's wrath poured out at Calvary. The ram represents the Lord Jesus who took the place of Isaac (the sinner) and died in his stead. Fire when used as a type usually indicates wrath, judgment, punishment or other expressions of anger. (See also Num. 11:1-2; Num. 21:28; Judges 6:21; Isa. 10:16; Jer. 4:4; Isa. 66:15.)

Ex. 3:2 (c) This may be taken as an illustration of the fact that Israel, though under the judgment of God from time to time, was not and would not be destroyed by the Lord. He punished them severely with the fire of His wrath many times, but He has never cast them off completely nor caused them to cease from being His own people.

Ex. 12:8 (c) We may understand this to represent the judgment of God on the Lord Jesus at Calvary when He went through the burning billows of God's wrath against sin and sinners. When fire is mentioned in connection with sacrifice, it represents the judgment of God upon the animal for our sakes. The animal in each case represents in some manner the Lord Jesus who is the Lamb of God. (See also Lev. 1:8, 12, 17; chap. 3:5; chap. 9:24; Judges 6:21.)

Ex. 19:18 (c) Probably we may take this to mean that God dwells in the midst of the holiest of judgment. His glory, His brightness, His justness destroy all evidences of sin, evil, wickedness and every other thing that does not conform to His holy character. (See Deut. 4:11; 9:15; 18:16; Isa. 47:14.)

Lev. 6:9-13 (c) Our Lord is telling us by this message that Calvary was to be always effective day and night. Any time any person wants to come to the Lord Jesus to be saved, He will find that He is ready any hour of the day or night, and that the precious blood of His sacrifice is available on every occasion, no matter when nor where.

Lev. 10:1 (c) We may understand from this expression "strange fire," human energies, human devices, human judgments, human exercises, human decisions which did not come and do not come from God. We see this graphically displayed in the expression "They shall put you out of the synagogues: yea, the time cometh, that whosoever killeth you will think that he doeth God service." John 16:2. The true fire is mentioned in Num. 16:46. That fire was taken from off the altar of incense for that fire came down from God, and was holy fire. The two sons of Aaron should have used that fire for their censors. Instead of this they rebelled against God, they refused to obey God's rule and follow God's order. They substituted their own judgment and desires for the plain command of God. They were earnest, they were zealous, they were apparently doing that which priests should do, but the fact that they used unlawful fire, strange fire, proved that their hearts were wrong.

Lev. 10:2 (c) It is only natural that the judgment of God should have fallen on these two men who, as leaders of Israel, were apparently carrying out God's will, and yet in their hearts were rebels against God's law. God will not have as a substitute for His Word any of our schemes, plans and zealous efforts. When we substitute our judgment for God's judgment, we may expect only the wrath of God. (See also Num. 3:4; Num. 26:61; 2 Ki. 1:10 12.)

Lev. 16:13 (c) Here we see the sweet savour of the sacrifice of Calvary. This lovely perfume caused by the offering up of Christ Himself on the Cross fills heaven, the holy of holies. It also fills the hearts of those who have enthroned Christ as Lord and King.

Num. 16:46 (c) This unusual passage reveals in more detail the same truth that we found in Lev. 10:2 We find in chap. 16, vss. 6 and 7, that the rebellious men took censers, placed in them incense of their own making, and fire of their own procuring. Aaron took his censer, placed the holy incense in it, and put the holy fire from off the altar in it. All those with the false fire and the false incense were killed, while Aaron with the true incense and the true fire, lived.

Notice this same truth also described in 1 Chron. 15:13. Judgment fell upon Uzza as described in 1 Chron. 13:10, because he and David imitated the Philistines in handling the ark of God. In 1 Chron. 15:13 David discovered his mistake in following the plan of the heathen in doing the work of God. He therefore corrected it.

Judges 6:21 (c) This fire indicates the judgment of God expressed through Christ Jesus, the Rock, which tries every man's work to see of what sort it is, and this takes place at the judgment seat of Christ. (See 1 Cor. 3:13.)

Judges 9:15 (b) The anger of Abimelech was to be poured out on Israel. He would prove to be their enemy after they appointed him their leader.

1 Ki. 19:12 (c) Three great calamities are mentioned in this passage, and each one represents some form of the judgment of God. The Lord is telling us that He does not speak to people through such calamities, but rather through His Word. It is the Word of God which brings conviction of sin. Calamities only bring the fear of death and the fear of punishment. Great calamities cause "the cry of distressed nature." The Word of God causes the cry of a convicted soul who realizes his sin against God.

2 Ki. 2:11 (c) This strange picture probably teaches us that those of us who go to heaven go because of and by virtue of the wrath of God which fell upon the Saviour, thereby bringing to us forgiveness, cleansing and fitness.

Job 18:5 (c) This probably refers to the usefulness and the ministry of wicked men, all of which shall be brought to an end, and their works burned up.

Job 41:19 (c) This metaphor may describe the terrific power and the force of the jaws of this tremendous animal. Or it may refer in prophecy to modern weapons of war which actually do spout fire, both from the front and from the rear.

Psa. 39:3 (b) This is a type of the strong desire in the heart of the Psalmist to make known God's goodness, and His grace. He just could not keep still.

Psa. 66:12 (b) Here is described the great sufferings and tribulations of the people when they disobeyed the Lord.

Prov. 6:27 (b) In this way the Lord is telling us that the secret life is revealed by its effects on the outward life. That which men see outwardly is a result of what is done secretly. (See also Isa. 9:18.)

Prov. 16:27 (b) By this figure we understand that the words of this person injure and harm the hearer.

Isa. 9:5 (b) Here is indicated the fact that the coming of Christ would mean sorrow, division and trouble on the earth. (See also Matt. 10:34)

Isa. 31:9 (b) This is a type of the judgment of God which rested in Zion, the place where God put His Name. God deals with the nations according to the manner in which they dealt with Israel. (See Matt. 25:41-46; Isa. 33:14.)

Isa. 33:14 (a) No doubt this is a plain reference to the fires of hell. Men have made a type out of it saying it refers to a burning conscience. Nowhere is this indicated in the Scripture. The fire is always presented to us as real flame, both in hell and in the lake of fire.

Isa. 43:2 (b) Here the word is a genuine type and it refers to earthly sorrows, sufferings and difficulties. God has not promised to keep us out of the fires of difficulty. He has promised to preserve us from any injurious effects when these tragedies come into our lives.

Isa. 50:11 (b) This is a type of self-illumination, home-made philosophy, individual reasonings. All such end in disappointment, for only God's Word and God's plan would endure.

Isa. 66:24 (a) No doubt this actually represents the eternal judgment of God in the lake of fire. There is literal fire in hell, which is in the heart of this earth. There is literal fire in the lake of fire, where sinners are sent after the judgment of the Great White Throne. Here is expressed to the fullest extent the righteous justice and judgment of God, whereby the sinner suffers forever because of his wickedness, his rebellion, and his refusal to believe God.

Jer. 5:14 (a) This is a type of the power of the Word of God when spoken by a servant of God in the power of the Spirit of God. The Word of God destroys the enemy. The word spoken by the Saviour in Gethsemane caused the enemy to fall backward to the ground. The Word of God spoken by Peter caused Ananias and Sapphira to die. (See also Ex. 20:19; Deut. 5:25; Heb. 2:2-3.)

Jer. 20:9 (a) When Jeremiah decided that he would not speak again for God, he found that the Word of God hidden in his heart and mind was just too valuable and too precious to keep. He must speak to be refreshed. It was a burning in his soul. (See also Psa. 39:3)

Jer. 48:45 (a) Here is a type of the hatred of the enemies of Moab who planned the destruction of that nation.

Jer. 51:58 (c) Probably this represents the vain labors of the inhabitants of Babylon as they sought to prevent its destruction by the invading enemy.

Ezek. 1:4 (b) This may be a picture of the mighty power, the destroying force of God in His righteous anger and judgment. The four living creatures are four symbols or types of Christ. (See v. 13)

Ezek. 10:6-7 (b) No doubt this fire represents the consuming power and judgment of God which was to be poured out on disobedient Israel. (See also chap. 21:31; 22:20; 24:12; 28:18; Amos 5:6; Amos 7:4.)

Ezek. 36:5 (a) This is a type of God's wrath against the enemies of Israel for their hatred of His people. (See also chap. 38:19.)

Dan. 7:9 (a) Wheels always represent motion or progress. This fire must represent the action of God in judging the people. His righteousness and His holiness destroy all pretense, hypocrisy and sin before Him.

Dan. 10:6 (a) By this is represented the piercing look of our Lord in the day of judgment, He destroys all hypocrisy by the look of His eye. (See also Rev. 1:14.)

Hosea 7:6 (a) This is a type of the burning passion of sin which ruled the lives of the people of Israel.

Obad 18 (a) By this is represented the wrath of Israel against the people of Esau, their enemies. This same kind of truth is found in Zech. 12:6, where Israel punishes all her foes.

Hab. 2:13 (a) By this figure God is telling us that those who build up violence and hatred in their sinful rebellion shall not see their labor succeed.

Zech. 3:2 (a) The unclean sinner (Joshua) is taken out of the company of those who are under the wrath of God, and who are to be punished by God. He is clothed in God's righteousness after being delivered, and becomes one of God's servants, a priest of and for God. It is a picture of that blessed experience which we call the "new birth"; we too are made priests of God.

Zech. 13:9 (c) Probably this is a picture of the destruction of Jerusalem when most of Israel were slain and only a few survived. Titus slaughtered the Jews on that terrible occasion. Those living in the country districts escaped.

Mal. 3:2 (a) This is a type which represents the way God puts His people through trouble and sorrow in order to make them pure, in order to remove evil from their lives.

Matt. 3:10 (b) Here is a real type of the genuine and real fire in hell into which all hypocrites and professing Christians will be sent for eternal punishment. (See also chap. 7:19; 13:42,50.)

Matt. 25:41 (a) This fire is not a type but is real, literal fire of hell. (See also Matt. 18:8; Mark 9:44)

Luke 22:56 (c) This may be taken as a type of a backslider who having lost his love for the Lord seeks to warm himself by the attractions of the world. He seeks satisfaction in the pleasures, the business, and the various pursuits of the men of this world.

John 15:6 (a) This fire is used by the Lord Jesus to describe the fierce criticism and the repudiation which fellow-men will give to those who profess to be Christians, but live like sinners. Such men who take the place of belonging to Christ, but do not walk with the Lord, are repudiated as Christian leaders. It is men who gather them, and men who burn them. This has nothing whatever to do with the salvation of the soul, nor with eternal conditions. It relates entirely to this life, and to the rejection which is given to a Christian leader who lives for the Devil.

Acts 2:3 (b) This may be taken as a symbol of the power and the anointing of God by the Spirit. This purging, cleansing power is for both saint and sinner, therefore the tongues are cloven. The Spirit of God convicts both the sinner and the Christian and He reveals the will of God to both.

1 Cor. 3:13 (a) Here we find a type of the judgment and the discerning power of God at the Throne. By means of His piercing investigation and His thorough understanding, all that is not profitable to God will be burned up.

1 Cor. 3:15 (a) People are saved by grace alone, with no reference of any kind to merit or to good works. There are those whose works after they are saved are not what they should be. Sometimes the works are really wicked, sometimes they are just injurious, and sometimes they are just of no value at all to God or man. Sometimes these works are works of charity, in which God is omitted, and therefore have no value to God. At the judgment throne, all such works are burned up. The person, however, is saved (by the skin of his teeth). He gets into heaven because he trusted the Lord Jesus Christ, and the sacrifice of the Saviour made it possible for God to blot out his sins. He lives in heaven with no crown, no reward, no works to his credit. He is there wholly on the basis of God's grace, but receives no reward for service rendered.

Heb. 1:7 (a) The angels of God permit no foolishness nor pretext. They demand honesty and genuineness. Therefore, they are compared to flaming fire which destroys all dross, and leaves only that which has God's approval.

2 Thess. 1:8 (a) The Lord Jesus is described in this passage as returning to earth with omnipotent power, with holiness and purity. His presence will destroy every form of evil, wickedness and sin. His righteousness will take vengeance on the unrighteous sinners who had no use for Him on the earth. This will be a terrible day of judgment when sinners receive from the reigning Christ that just due which rebels should receive.

Heb. 11:34 (a) This type reveals the severe persecution which was endured by faithful men of God in the Old Testament. (See Dan. 3:17.)

Jas. 3:6 (a) By this type there is revealed the destructive power of an evil tongue. The tongue of the ungodly, and sometimes the tongue of the godly, sears and injures the hearts, the souls and the lives of others. Words are sometimes like poisoned arrows. They injure and destroy those who hear them.

Jas. 5:3 (a) This represents the terrible remorse that shall burn the heart and the soul of the one who rebels against God.

1 Pet. 1:7 (a) Here is represented the persecution which is to be endured in the life of that one who will live godly in Christ Jesus. The world does not want him. Society will not receive him. The business world sneers at him.

Jude 23 (a) Probably the meaning of this is that there are those who are close to eternity, very near to being sent to hell. They are about through with this life. These are to be reached for the Lord, even though their lives have been wasted. Let us remember that in the Gospel work, as long as there is life there is hope.

Rev. 3:18 (a) The Lord is telling us by this picture that all the blessings which He is offering to us have been tested through the centuries, and are worthy of our complete trust.

Rev. 4:5 (a) The Holy Spirit is presented to us in this manner, both because of the illumination which He gives in a seven-fold manner, and also because of His power which is seen in seven ways. (See also chap. 1:4)

Rev. 8:5 (c) This may represent the terrible judgment of God, and His fierce wrath against sin and sinners. He sends His angels to execute His decrees upon men. The mountains in verse 8 are a figure to represent the amount and the stupendous volume of the wrath of God which men must endure who reject him.

Rev. 9:17 (b) By this type there is probably conveyed to us some idea of the burning and destroying power of these messengers of God. The breastplate was for keeping God's servants from being injured. The fire from the mouth describes the withering power of their words as they spoke God's messages. (See also chap. 11:5.)

Rev. 15:2 (b) By this type is described the transparent judgments of God. There is no trickery or hidden evidence here. There is no hypocrisy in God's presence. God's fierce anger is displayed in all its justice, righteousness and purity.

Rev. 20:10 (a) This reference, as all other references to fire in hell, indicates literal, actual fire. This is not a type. (See vss. 14 and 15: also chap. 21:8. The fire described in Luke 16:24 is literal fire. Those who seek to spiritualize the word, and make it mean the "torment of a conscience" have no ground whatever for their philosophy.)

FIRE IN COMBINATIONS

FIRE (KINDLE)

Deut. 32:22 (a) The evil actions of men provoke the burning wrath of God into severe action. (See also Jer. 15:14; 17:4)

2 Sam. 22:13 (c) It may be we are to be impressed with the tremendous brightness of God which would dispel all darkness, and would bring judgment upon all that this fire would reveal.

Psa. 57:4 (a) The wrath and the hatred of Saul and his army is thus described by David.

Psa. 78:21 (a) This is a type of God's anger and wrath against His own people of Judah and Israel because of their sins. (See also Isa. 10:16; Isa. 42:25; Jer. 6:1; Jer. 11:16; Jer. 17:27; Jer. 21:14; Lam. 4:11; Ezek. 20:47; Ezek. 24:10; Hosea 8:14; Amos 2:5.)

Isa. 50:11 (a) This is a type of man's wits and wisdom, wherein he seeks to build up a religion and a line of "thinking" that is contrary to the will and the word of God.

Jer. 43:12 (a) Here we find a splendid type of God's power to punish all His enemies and especially those particular enemies which are mentioned in each of the following passages: Jer. 49:27; Jer. 50:32; Ezek. 30:8, 14, 16; Ezek. 39:6; Amos 1:4, 14; Amos 2:2.

Luke 12:49 (a) This is a striking illustration of the trouble that comes into a home, a family, or a society when Christ is received into the heart by any person. When the Lord Jesus takes possession of a person's soul, then trouble begins. There is a division at once in the family between the saved one who wants to live for God, and those in the family who have no interest in Christian things. The house is divided, enmity of a real kind develops. The Christian who wishes to walk with the Lord in business finds there is a gulf between his manner of life and the lives of the others who wish to have their wild parties, gain customers by liquor, and spend their time smoking or playing cards, and other things which the world offers to the Devil's children.

Jas. 3:6 (a) The tongue that is inspired by Satan to speak and say things that are cruel, hateful and sinful is described as a burning flame that injures, harms and hurts those who hear it. How careful we should be that the words we speak are full of grace and truth.

FIRE (PILLARS)

Rev. 10:1 (a) This seems to represent one who walks in a godly path in the presence of God, and stands firm for the truth of God.

FIRE (SEND)

Lam. 1:13 (a) The deep sorrow and trouble that filled the life of the prophet in the midst of a disobedient and hostile Israel is compared to the burning pain caused by the flame.

FIREBRAND

Isa. 7:4 (a) These two kings were trouble makers. They sought to destroy God's people and God's heritage. Their desire was to leave behind them only the debris of God's wonderful kingdom of Israel.

Amos 4:11 (a) Israel was so sinful and rebellious that she should have been punished as a firebrand. Instead of this, God sent mercy, goodness and grace many times so that He saved them, instead of destroying them.

FISH

Num. 11:5 (c) This is a symbol of the good things offered by this world to attract and entice God's people away from God's path of separation. They all leave a bad odor and have little food value.

Ezek. 29:4 (b) The king and his people are compared to fish. They will adhere to their king in his disobedience to God; all of them together will be destroyed.

Ezek. 47:9 (b) By this is indicated that where the Spirit of God has His own way, many souls will be saved. The fish represent the unsaved who are caught by the Gospel and thereby are brought to the Lord.

Jonah 1:17 (c) This is a type of the Gentile nations who have absorbed, but have not digested, the Jewish people.

Hab. 1:14 (a) By this is described men and women who are caught by the sophistries of wicked leaders and are thus deceived and led away from God.

Matt. 7:10 (b) This figure represents something which, in our estimation, seems to be very good and profitable for us to possess, but which God sees would be injurious and harmful to us. (See also Luke 11:11.) The child saw a snake and thought it to be an eel and good to eat.

John 21:6 (c) Some say that these fish represent the miracles performed by our Lord Jesus Christ while He was on the earth. Others think that the giving of the number of the fish indicates the care with which God looks after each deed that we do for Him. Still others think that these fish, and the number of them, represent God's abundant care for His own. There were far more fish than the seven men could possibly eat for themselves. This of course is true of God's provisions for us.

FISHERS

Jer. 16:16 (a) These are messengers of God sent throughout the world to find His people, the Jews, and bring them to Him for judgment.

Ezek. 47:10 (a) This is a striking illustration of the power of the Spirit of God to make soul winners out of those who permit Him to dominate their lives. These fishers are men who, with the story of God's grace and love, are raised up in those happy surroundings where the Holy Spirit is Lord, is recognized and is trusted. In those churches where the Holy Spirit is free to work, men and women develop into personal workers who are successful in catching men and women for Christ. (See also Matt. 4:19; Mark 1:17; Luke 5:10.)

FISH GATE

Neh. 3:3 (c) This may be taken as a figure of the fruitful life of the one who has entered through the sheep gate into God's Kingdom. (See Neh. 12:39; Zeph. 1:10.)

FISHHOOKS

Amos 4:2 (a) God will use means to catch the people of Israel from all over the world in such a way that they cannot escape the punishment He will pour out on them.

FISHPOOLS

S. of Sol. 7:4 (b) This is a poetic figure of the enticing beauty of the clear, deep eyes of the lover, so full of expression and passion.

FIST

Prov. 30:4 (a) By this figure is illustrated the hold that God has on the wind, controlling its force and its movement. (See also under "WIND.")

FITCHES

Isa. 28:25 (b) In this passage types are used to illustrate the preaching of the gospel, the harvesting of souls, and the use of the person after he is saved. The fitches represent some of the things that accompany the Gospel. The wheat represents the saving message of the gospel. The four other grains may represent songs, prayers, humbleness of mind, and acceptance of the Word, all of which do usually accompany the preaching of the gospel. God's gospel must occupy the principal place in all of our ministry to the lost. For that reason, the wheat is to be planted in the principal places in this allegory.

FIVE

A number that describes the weakness of every human being. Every chapter number *five* in the Bible contains some story of man's weakness and inability.

Examples:

Genesis 5. Although men lived many years, they must eventually die.

Exodus 5. God's people in their weakness were crushed under their oppressors.

Leviticus 5. God recognizes the poverty and inability of His children and gives them the privilege of bringing turtle doves which cost nothing instead of larger offerings which cost much.

Esther 5. The weakness of Haman is revealed in his inability to conquer Mordecai.

Mark 5. Men were too weak to conquer or control the man in the tombs.

John 5. The man at the pool was too weak to enter and his friends were too weak to help.

Revelation 5. No man was found who was able to open the book.

All the other chapters in the Bible numbered *five* contain some mark and proof of human weakness and inability.

Matt. 14:17 (c) The five loaves were certainly an insufficient supply to feed the great multitude.

Matt. 25:15 (c) The five talents only produced another five talents. They represent an insufficient amount in the hands of an insufficient man. He only produced an amount equal to that which he began. Man cannot be trusted with very much.

Luke 16:28 (c) These five brothers were helpless to keep themselves out of hell.

John 4:18 (c) The five husbands were not enough to satisfy this woman and to fill her heart with the peace and the joy that she craved.

1 Cor. 14:19 (c) Five words fitly spoken are valuable but it takes a great many more than that to reveal God's will and to instruct the Christian properly. Man has five fingers on the hand, five toes on the foot, and five senses. He is weak and impotent.

FLAME

Ex. 3:2 (c) Probably this teaches us the lesson that God would dwell among His people Israel, would deal with them severely when they sinned, but would never destroy them.

Job 15:30 (a) By this figure is represented the calamity which did overtake him and the terrible curse which did destroy his work and his efforts.

Job 41:21 (b) It may be that this is a prophecy of the modern tank with its power to destroy both from the guns in front and those in the rear. Or, it may be just a poetic form of expressing rage.

Isa. 10:17 (a) This terrible figure is used to describe the wrath of God against Jerusalem when He directed the enemies of God to burn and destroy the city. (See Isa. 29:6; 47:14; Ezek. 20:47.)

Isa. 30:30 (a) This represents the outpouring of God's wrath against Assyria.

Isa. 43:2 (a) The Lord is telling us that great troubles and sorrows shall not destroy Israel, for God will bring them through it all safely.

Jer. 48:45 (a) By this type is represented the fierce, burning anger and power of the enemies of Moab.

Dan. 7:9 (a) This figure indicates God's justice and righteousness against all evil, sin and hypocrisy.

Obad. 18 (a) God will make His people a powerful scourge to defeat the people of Esau.

Heb. 1:7 (a) This is typical of the destroying power of angels as God's messengers of judgment. (See also 2 Ki. 19:35.)

Rev. 1:14 (a) This type is used to reveal the power of the Lord to discern the thoughts, motives and intents of the people when brought to the judgment. (See also Rev. 2:18; 19:12.)

FLAMES

Psalm 29:7 (a) Probably this represents the judgment of God against both saint and sinner. He knows who are His, He knows how to judge both kinds, and will do so righteously.

Isa. 13:8 (a) Hatred and fierce cruelty shall characterize the people who besiege and destroy Babylon.

Isa. 66:15 (a) By this we are told that God's burning anger will be poured out upon all the enemies of His people. (See Ezek. 20:47.)

FLAT

Lev. 21:18 (c) The nose is the organ of discernment. With the nose we may tell whether a substance is spoiled or fresh, whether it is old or new, whether it is alive or dead. If the nose is broken and mashed flat, then this power of discernment is obscured or is absent. So it is in the Christian life. That one who is unable to distinguish between what is from God and what is from Satan, what is right in the sight of God, and what is unscriptural, what is true and what is false, cannot be a servant of God, for he would not know God's truth from Satan's deceiving lies.

FLAX

Isa. 42:3 (b) This interesting type is used to illustrate the struggling Christian who is endeavoring to serve the Lord to the best of his ability, but is not doing it very well. This one is not to be discouraged by those who are better taught. (See also Matt. 12:20.)

FLEA

1 Sam. 24:14 (a) David thus describes his own insignificance, weakness and worthlessness in his own sight. (See chap. 26:20)

FLEE

Jer. 48:6 (a) In this passage the Lord is urging us to make haste and leave those situations in which the soul is not being fed nor watered, and to make our way to that place where the soul will be refreshed and blessed. There are those who are in modernistic churches where the Word of God has been supplanted by human expedients and they are not learning to know the Lord, nor His ways. They should leave the group and find a fellowship where the Holy Spirit is working and the Word is loved. (See under "HEATH.")

Matt. 3:7 (a) John is warning the people to make haste in getting to the Saviour and thus escape the terrible wrath of God that will be executed against all the ungodly. If men believe God's Word and realize that outside of Christ they will be forever punished in the lake of fire, there would certainly be a rush to get to the Saviour.

FLESH

Psa. 56:4 (a) By this figure human power is contrasted with divine power.

Psa. 63:1 (b) David uses this expression to describe the longing of his soul for the fellowship of God, and to see God develop His purposes and plans.

Jer. 17:5 (b) This figure refers to human power, man-made expedients and remedies, as well as the results of human effort in contrast with the deliverances that God prepared for His people.

Ezek. 16:26 (b) This term is used to express the great lustfulness of the Egyptians and also of the Israelites. Their immoral practices were the prime occupation of their lives. It represents the natural, evil human heart as in Ezek. 36:26.)

Matt. 16:17 (b) This term is used as a reference to the human mind, the educational values of the mind, and human religious reasonings.

John 1:13 (b) Salvation is not a decision on the part of a human being wherein with his mind he decides to become a Christian and step out of darkness into light. Salvation is of God, and only God can save by revealing Himself to the soul. No action of the person (the flesh) can give eternal life to a lost man.

John 3:6 (a) This refers to all that pertains to the human body. The body is never transformed, nor born again, nor converted. It remains "flesh" until it dies, or until the Lord returns in person to change our bodies.

John 6:52 (b) This expression occurs several times in this chapter. It refers to an appropriating of the Lord Jesus by faith so that the soul, the mind, and the heart are filled with His own lovely Person, and the heart is satisfied with Him. That interpretation which causes men to try to turn bread into the physical body of Jesus is utterly false, is an invention of the Devil, and is being used throughout the world to deceive the ungodly.

Rom. 7:5 (a) This expression is used to describe those who do not have the Spirit of God, are not saved, and are called "sensual" in the book of Jude. Their flesh dominates their lives, and they are occupied with what they can see, hear, taste, smell and feel. (See chap. 8:8-9; 2 Cor. 10:3)

Rom. 8:12 (b) This is a type which describes the lusts, desires and affections created by the human body. (See also chap. 13:14; 2 Cor. 10:2; Gal. 5:13-17; Gal. 6:8; Eph. 2:3; 2 Pet. 2:10; Jude 23)

Eph. 5:30 (a) This figure indicates that we are joined to Christ in a very real and eternal union by faith in Him.

James 5:3 (a) Probably this represents the remorse felt by a lost man because of a greedy and avaricious life.

FLIES

Eccl. 10:1 (b) This is a type which represents an evil deed done by a godly man. A lovely life may be stained by an ill-advised action or some wicked work.

Isa. 7:18 (a) This type is used to describe the army of Egypt which would persecute and annoy Israel.

FLIETH

Psalm 91:5 (b) This is a figure of open antagonism aimed at the child of God.

FLINT

Deut. 8:15 (b) The flint rock is probably the hardest of all the rocks. By this picture the Lord is telling us that He is able to bring great blessing to us out of impossible situations. He often brings deliverance from sources that we never thought of. He is able to use strange circumstances and unknown assets to bring to us the relief that we need. (See Deut. 32:13; Psalm 114:8.)

Isa. 50:7 (a) By this term the Lord is telling us of His determination to go to the limit for our salvation and our blessing. Nothing would swerve Him from this purpose.

FLOCK

Psa. 77:20 (a) The people of Israel are compared to sheep under the leadership of the Lord God of heaven. (See also Isa. 40:11; 63:11; Jer. 13:17; 23:2; 25:34; Ezek. 24:5; Micah 2:12; Matt. 26:31)

Luke 12:32 (a) This refers to the followers of the Lord Jesus. He is the shepherd, those who love Him are His sheep.

Acts 20:28 (a) In this passage the church is compared to sheep. It refers to the true church of God, consisting only of believers, born-again people. It does not refer to those great national and international organizations which call themselves "The Church." (See 1 Pet. 5:2.)

FLOOD

Gen. 6:17 (c) This is emblematic of the great judgment of God upon those who are out of Christ, even as this flood came upon those who were out of the ark. (See also Psa. 90:5.)

Psa. 29:10 (c) Perhaps this indicates the great, surging mass of humanity over which our Lord Jesus rules, reigns and controls.

Isa. 28:2 (a) This word graphically describes the overwhelming wrath and power of God in punishing Israel.

Isa. 59:19 (b) From this we understand something of the great force and power of the wicked who seek to overthrow God's people and to hinder God's work.

Jer. 46:7 (a) The power of Egypt is thus described. (See also v. 8; 47:2; Amos 8:8; Amos 9:5.)

Dan. 9:26 (a) By this we understand the power of the army of the Romans who destroyed Jerusalem.

Dan. 11:22 (b) This type describes the power of the anti-Christ as he seeks to destroy all that belongs to Christ Jesus, and to establish Satanic rule.

Nahum 1:8 (a) Thus is described the power of the invading army that conquered the city of Nineveh. Jonah was sent to Nineveh with a warning, and the people repented. About seventy-five years later Nahum wrote his prophecy of the destruction of Nineveh because they had réturned to their wicked ways.

Matt. 7:27 (a) This word is a type of the adversities, oppositions and sorrows which suddenly overwhelm and overcome those who are not resting on the Rock of Ages, Christ Jesus. (See also Luke 6:48.)

Rev. 12:15 (a) This word describes the terrible persecution of Israel by satanic forces which made them slaves for many years, and finally scattered them throughout the world. During the tribulation Israel will again suffer persecution.

FLOODS

2 Sam. 22:5 (a) This is a prophecy concerning the mob that surrounded Jesus at the trial and at Calvary. (See Psa. 18:4)

Psa. 24:2 (a) By this we understand that God's Word is made permanent and sure for all peoples, nations and tongues.

Psa. 32:6 (b) The Lord is telling us here that in times of great trouble God will protect and preserve His people.

Psa. 69:2 (a) Thus Christ describes in prophecy His own deep and severe trouble at Calvary.

Psa 93:3 (b) The word is used to describe the volume of difficulties, sorrows and troubles raised by the enemies of God.

Psa. 98:8 (b) This is a call for all people to join in praising God for His righteous judgments.

Isa. 44:3 (a) This word beautifully illustrates the way that God will pour out His abundant blessing upon the soul and the heart that is thirsty for Him.

FLOOR

1 Ki. 6:30 (c) The floor of the tabernacle was the dirt and the soil of the desert. This reminded Israel of their pilgrim character. The floor of the temple was covered with gold to remind His people that they were pilgrims on the way home to the eternal glory of God.

Isa. 21:10 (c) This is a heart cry concerning the loss of that which had been gathered in from the harvest, but was never enjoyed.

Jer. 51:33 (a) Here is a type of the severe threshing that God would give Babylon when He sent the enemy to destroy it.

Dan. 2:35 (a) This is typical of the day of God's judgment when the saved and the unsaved will be separated as the farmer separates the wheat and the chaff on the threshing floor. (See also Matt. 3:12.)

Hosea 13:3 (a) The judgment of Israel is described by this figure. The people are the chaff to be destroyed because they are of no value to God, and have no interest in God's affairs. (See also Micah 4:12; Luke 3:17)

FLOUR

Ex. 29:2 (c) This is no doubt a type of the beautiful white, smooth life of Christ in which there was no sin, nor evil. His life was pure grace, pure love, pure holiness and pure beauty.

FLOW

Joel 3:18 (a) This is a picture of the abundance of God's blessings poured out on the people from the living God when the Holy Spirit is loved, honored and trusted. (See also Ex. 3:8; 13:5; Lev. 20:24; Josh. 5:6; Ezek. 20:6.)

FLOWER

Ex. 25:33 (b) By this figure is represented the beauty of the testimony of the church, of the individual Christian, and of the Holy Spirit. Those who testify to the things of God should live beautiful lives and thus exemplify the doctrine. (See Ex. 37:19; 1 Ki. 6:18.)

Job 14:2 (a) Man's birth is thus compared to the development of the flower. After certain processes the full bloom appears. First there is the development of the bud in various stages, and finally the full bloom.

Job 15:33 (a) In this way the Lord describes the failure of the hypocrite to succeed in life, and to develop into that which God would like him to be.

Isa. 18:5 (a) In this way God describes the destruction of Egypt in her industries and in her efforts to build up a world-wide power.

Isa. 28:1-4 (a) This is a promise from God that He will destroy the beauty of Israel, the cities, villages, valleys and fields because of their evil doings.

Isa. 40:6-8 (a) This word is used to describe man's best works, and his greatest achievements. (See also James 1:10-11; 1 Pet. 1:24)

FLOWERS

Lev. 15:24, 33 (b) The term is used to describe the monthly sickness, the menstrual period to which all women are subject.

FLY

Job 5:7 (a) As the sparks ascend heavenward from the fire, so we should speed our way at once to God when trouble comes.

Psa. 18:10 (a) This figure represents the speed with which God will come to the rescue of David when in trouble. (See also Dan. 9:21; Isa. 6:6; Isa. 60:8; Luke 15:20. Some think this passage may refer to the airplane.)

Prov. 23:5 (a) Here is a very fine picture of the way that our money and other assets disappear. Usually it is a slow disappearance. When the eagle flies away toward heaven it gets smaller and smaller to our vision until finally it disappears. So sometimes our health and our wealth gradually disappear until we are left hopeless, hapless and helpless.

Jer. 48:40 (a) By this expression the Lord is describing the speed with which He would destroy the country of Moab.

Ezek. 13:20 (c) This may represent the wiles of evil women who would and did lure men from God's path of righteousness.

Hab. 1:8 (a) This is the way God describes the speed of the Chaldeans when they invaded Israel.

FLYING

Isa. 31:5 (b) This figure describes the wisdom and power of God in defending Jerusalem. Some scholars think this passage may refer to the airplane.

Zech. 5:1-2 (b) This represents the great volume and power of God's wrath which will come upon all the earth from heaven. The roll contains the records of God's decisions and judgments. The little book in Rev. 10:2 contains the description of His wrath which is to be executed against the ungodly of all the earth.

FOAL

Gen. 49:11 (b) This figure is used to teach us that Judah wanted his posterity to be firmly joined to the Lord. It was his desire to keep the nation of Israel as a producing vine for the glory of God.

FOAM

Hosea 10:7 (a) This is a symbol of the lightness, frivolity and worthlessness of many of earth's great men, as God viewed their lives.

Jude 13 (a) This type describes the expressions of the ungodly in word and action. They make a great noise and a great appearance, and then subside into silence and oblivion.

FOOL

1 Sam. 26:21 (a) This is a type of one who has heard the Word of God but has deliberately refused to obey it.

Psa. 14:1 (a) This indicates God's thought about the man who, in spite of all the evidence available, denies the existence of a personal God.

Prov. 12:15 (a) The one who rejects the revelation of God and assumes his own thoughts and deductions about his path of life is a fool in God's sight.

Matt. 5:22 (a) The man who mocks at the Christian who desires to live all out for God, and out and out for Christ in separation and consecration, and calls that Christian a fool for doing so, is condemned by God. He is opposed to God's plans.

FOOT

Deut. 32:35 (a) In this way the Lord is indicating that the enemies of God will be cut off and die.

Deut. 33:24 (a) By this we learn that the walk of the Godly man shall be a spiritual one filled with the richness and sweetness of God's blessings.

Psalm 68:23 (a) This type is used to describe the victory over their enemies of those who walk in fellowship with God.

Psalm 94:18 (b) David uses this type to describe his feeling that he was drifting away from God's path.

Eccl. 5:1 (b) By this figure we are admonished to watch the walk and the manner of life.

Isa. 1:6 (c) The whole person is evidently wicked and vile in God's sight. Men are mad in their walk and their thought. The feet represent our walk, the head represents the thought. There is nothing at all in a human being that is acceptable to God until we trust Jesus Christ and become God's children.

Ezek. 1:7 (b) These are types of the walk of our Lord Jesus Christ. The calf is sure-footed and leaves a definite imprint where it steps. So Christ Jesus walked in a sure and certain path without sin, and left the imprint of His holiness wherever He went.

Matt. 5:13 (a) Here we find a type of the actions of the world against the professing Christian who claims that he belongs to the Lord, yet shows no proofs of it in his daily life. Neither the world nor the church has any confidence in that man, and refuses to receive his testimony. This truth is also found in John 15:6.

Matt. 18:8 (b) In this way the Lord is telling us that if we want to walk in the ways of the world so that the feet take us astray to the picture show, the tavern, the dance, it is best to cut off that foot so that such desires cannot and will not keep us away from Christ. (See also Mark 9:45)

Matt. 22:13 (c) In many places in the Bible what we do, what we say, and how we walk and work are compared to garments or robes. Evidently the teaching in this passage is that this man wanted to be at the king's banquet in his own self-righteousness. Since this self-righteousness comes from the hands (what we do), and from the feet (how we walk), the Lord is indicating how worthless these are by telling the servant to bind him "hand and foot," and to cast him out of His presence.

1 Cor. 12:15 (b) This is a type of a Christian, any Christian. The Lord is telling us here that no part of the body is independent from the rest of the body. Every Christian is essential to the entire church of God. No believer, no matter how humble or obscure, is overlooked by the Lord, either as to his care or his usefulness.

Heb. 10:29 (b) Here is a picture of the hatred that some had and some now have toward the person of our Lord Jesus. It is a picture of utter contempt for Christ, and a desire to crush Him.

Rev. 10:2 (b) This figure represents the absolute power and authority of our Lord over all nations and His ability to punish all people.

FOOTED

Lev. 11:3 (c) The divided hoof is a symbol of a separated walk. Chewing the cud is a symbol of Godly conversation and confession. Both must go together. Our walk and our talk must agree. If we walk well in a path of separation, but our conversation and language does not honor the Lord, we will not be accepted by God. If we talk well, but we walk contrary to the Word of God, we shall likewise be rejected. The walk and the talk must both be acceptable to God.

Lev. 21:19 (c) This figure represents the man whose walk is not pleasing to God, is not upright and Godly.

FOOTMEN

Jer. 12:5 (c) The word represents ordinary Christians who walk with God and serve the Lord and His people. They may have very little of the glory of God about them, and not much holiness. If they make the man of the world weary so that his company is not desired, then what would the worldling do if he were taken to heaven where Christians were glorified and are perfect and holy? Horses represent perfect Christians in heaven.

FOOTSTEPS

Psalm 17:5 (b) David calls upon the Lord to keep him in the way he should go, so that he may walk constantly in the presence of the Lord, and not wander away.

Psalm 77:19 (b) The Lord uses this figure to reveal the fact that God's ways are not known to men, for He does not reveal them to men. These are the secrets of His own heart. Read the special case about Moses in Psalm 103:7. Here we find that the people saw what He did, but Moses understood why He did it. (See also Job. 33:13.)

Psalm 89:51 (b) Here we learn that the ungodly scorn the way of the righteous and sneer at the Godly.

Song of S. 1:8 (c) This is probably a call for Christians to walk together in happy fellowship.

FOOTSTOOL

1 Chron 28:2 (a) David compares the temple of God to a resting place for the Lord.

Psalm 99:5 (b) This figure represents the attitude of one who comes into the presence of God to pray, to worship and to commune. It is a picture of one kneeling at the foot of the king on the throne seeking some favor from him. (See Psa. 132:7)

Psalm 110:1 (a) By this type the Lord is informing us that He will subdue all His enemies and will put His feet on their necks in derision, in the day of judgment. (See Matt. 22:44; Mark 12:36: Luke 20:43; Acts 2:35; Heb. 1:13; Heb. 10:13.)

Isa. 66:1 (a) This earth which seems so great to us is only as a small cushion in the sight of God on which His feet. (See also Matt. 5:35; Acts 7:49.)

Lam. 2:1 (a) The land of Israel is thus compared. God cursed the land.

FOREHEAD

Ex. 28:38 (c) This type describes the open confession and open acknowledgment of one's condition or position. (See also Rev. 14:9)

Jer. 3:3 (a) God compares the people of Israel to a wicked woman who is bold, brazen and unashamed in her sins.

Ezek. 3:8 (b) God promised to His prophet Jeremiah that strength would be given Him and courage to stand against the looks and the words of his enemies.

Ezek. 16:12 (a) A picture of the loveliness and the beauty which God put on Israel when He gave them to be the head of the nations, and placed them in Canaan which He calls the glory of all lands. (See chap. 20:6.)

Rev. 7:3 (a) Probably this is a literal mark put on the literal forehead. We do not usually consider this as a type, but rather as an actual fact. God will mark His children for public identification. The Devil uses this same plan to identify his children. (See the following passages in this book of Revelation: 9:4; 13:16; 14:1-9; 17:5; 20:4; 22:4.)

FOREIGNER

Eph. 2:19 (a) This describes the spiritual condition of those who have never accepted Christ Jesus and therefore do not belong to God's family, God's church, nor the "holy nation" of the saints.

FORESKIN

Jer. 4:4 (a) This indicates that the heart's affection for worldly and sensual things has never been cut off nor removed. The heart should love only the Lord and the things that are for His glory. (See also Gen. 17:11. Deut. 10:16.)

FOREST

Isa. 32:15 (a) This type is used to describe the abundant blessing that accompanies the unhindered ministry of the Holy Spirit. When He is recognized, is present and is working in power, then there is an abundance of life, hearts are enriched, souls are saved, and Christians become fruitful.

Isa. 44:23 (b) This is a picture of the rich blessing that the earth will enjoy when the Lord Jesus Christ returns to earth to reign on the throne of David. (See Psa. 29:9.)

Jer. 5:6 (c) The forest is probably a type of the great group of nations of the world, out of which would come a conqueror. (See also Ezek. 15:6.)

FORNICATION

2 Chron. 21:11 (a) The word is used to describe the wickedness of a people who forsake the true God, and the blessings which He gives in order to follow the attractions of the ungodly world, and of false gods. (See also Isa. 23:17; Ezek. 16:15, 29; Jude 7; Rev. 2:21.)

Rev. 17:2-4 (a) God thus describes the wickedness of that which claims to be the Church of God as it supports and invites wicked men of the world to join with them, and to partake of their religious exercises. (See chap. 18:3; 19:2.)

FORTRESS

2 Sam. 22:2 (a) This describes a blessed hiding place in God, which the believer enjoys when he goes to the Lord in prayer and commits his case into His hands. (See also Psa. 18:2; Psa. 31:3; 71:3; 91:2; 144:2; Jer. 16:19.)

Jer. 6:27 (a) God promised to Jeremiah that he would be a strong and fearless witness which his enemies could not overcome.

FORTY

The number represents testing in human life.

Gen. 7:4 (c) Noah's faith was tested and found to be all that it should be.

Ex. 16:35 (c) God's faithfulness was tested and found to be sufficient for all the needs.

Ex. 24:18 (c) Israel's faith and trust were tested and failed. (See Ex. 32:7.)

1 Sam. 4:18 (c) Eli was tested. He had judged Israel and failed at the end.

1 Sam. 17:16 (c) Israel was challenged and was proved to be utterly unworthy and cowardly. Saul reigned forty years and was deposed as a failure.

2 Sam. 5:4 (c) David reigned forty years and ended his rule gloriously.

1 Ki. 11:42 (c) Solomon reigned forty years and ended his period of testing in idolatry.

Matt. 4:2 (c) Jesus was tested forty days and forty nights. He came back more than a conqueror. Jesus revealed Himself to His own for forty days after His resurrection so that they could endure the tests through the years. (See Acts 1:3.)

FOUL

Rev. 18:2 (a) In this way God reveals His utter hatred for the wicked practices and the evil beliefs which prevail in those great world systems of religion which are described as Babylon. In these religious systems every evil known to man prospers and is promoted. Men and women are held as slaves in darkened buildings. Many are not permitted to even speak. They are bound to permanent silence. Others have physical afflictions imposed upon them in the name of God. History reveals the burnings, the tortures, the imprisonments, and the lustful practices of these great religions. The followers are kept in abject slavery, and therefore the verse describes the situation of the wicked leaders as being in a cage and a prison cell. Luther and others were blessed of God in breaking open many of these prison cells, and setting great multitudes free from the tyranny, the wickedness, the evil of the monster that held them captives.

FOUNDATION

2 Sam. 22:8 (b) This is a poetic picture from David's fertile mind of the great answer he received from God to his petition. (See v. 16, and Psalm 18:7, 15.)

Psa. 11:3 (b) This is a type of the basic doctrines of the Christian faith on which the believer rests his soul for eternity.

Psa. 87:1 (b) Probably this represents the central truth, and the basic reasons for God's activities on the part of Israel.

Prov. 10:25 (a) This is a picture of the eternal safety of one who has been made righteous by the living God. (See Eph. 2:20.)

Isa. 28:16 (a) God has appointed the Lord Jesus Christ, His Son. to be the One on and in whom all His works rest. Christ is the beginning, the author, the first and the last, the Alpha and Omega, and the hope of God's people. The whole structure of the Church rests on Him (See Psa. 118:22; Luke 6:48; Eph. 2:20.)

Rom. 15:20 (a) The pioneer work of a missionary or a Christian worker is compared to a foundation upon which he builds and prepares the people for further development in the Christian life.

1 Cor. 3:10 (b) No doubt this refers to the gospel that Paul preached and to the doctrines which he ministered. By these the Corinthians were established in the faith. Other men of God came along and added to the knowledge and the faith of these believers.

1 Tim. 6:19 (a) By this is meant the true faith, intelligent trust and a clear understanding of God's truth on the part of God's children.

2 Tim. 2:19 (a) By this type we are assured that those who belong to Christ Jesus may rest safe and secure on God's Word about us, and to us.

Heb. 6:1 (a) The six experiences mentioned here represent the bedrock of Christian faith. From these we grow up into a greater temple of God as we learn additional truths, and enter more and more into the knowledge of God's work, His Word, and His way.

FOUNDATIONS

Psa. 82:5 (a) It seems that our Lord must have used this figure to indicate that the basic principles of humanity were being violated throughout the earth. Hatred was replacing love. Dishonesty was replacing integrity. Idolatry was replacing the true worship of God. Certainly this could be true, as it is so largely true today.

Isa. 54:11 (b) This seems to be a beautiful and poetic description of the coming glories of the nation of Israel when restored to their own land, and to their power and authority.

Ezek. 30:4 (a) This is a prophecy concerning the destruction of Egypt. It was certainly fulfilled to the letter.

Heb. 11:10 (b) Here is a reference to the eternal character of the heavenly Jerusalem in contrast with the transient character of the cities of the earth.

Rev. 21:14, 19 (a) The new city, the eternal state, the eternal dwelling place of God's people, will be characterized by solidity, beauty, holiness and purity. It will rest upon the teachings and the experiences of the twelve tribes of Israel, and also upon the experiences and teachings of the twelve apostles of the Lamb.

FOUNTAIN

Lev. 20:18 (a) By this word is described the monthly period which is common among women.

Deut. 33:28 (a) By this type we understand the continual, abundant harvest of grain and fruits.

Psa. 36:9 (a) This is a prophecy, or a picture, of the blessed source of both our physical and our spiritual life. (See Psa. 68:26.)

Prov. 5:16 (a) The Lord is using this figure to express His desire that each one of us who knows our Lord should be a source of blessing, comfort, help and joy to those around us.

Prov. 5:18 (a) Here is probably a reference to the fertility of a normal man in his marital relationships.

Prov. 13:14 (a) By this figure we are instructed to observe God's rules, and His desires toward us so that we may enjoy life to the full. (See chap. 14:27.)

Prov. 25:26 (a) This situation is unnatural and breeds trouble in a home, or in a nation.

Eccl. 12:6 (c) This may be taken as a picture of the end of life. The silver cord may refer to the spinal cord which no longer operates normally. The golden bowl may be the brain which is no longer active. The pitcher may refer to the heart which no longer pours out the blood. The fountain may refer to the blood stream in the arteries and the veins, as well as the heart. The wheel probably refers to the inability of the nervous system to function properly. All of this is a picture of old age.

Isa. 41:18 (a) The Lord is telling us that in the valleys of despair and sorrow He will bring sweet rich blessings for the heart. He will cause His mercy, love and grace to fill the soul of that one who in the hour of need turns to Him for solace. It is also a picture of the great blessings that God will send upon this earth in the millennial age.

Jer. 2:13 (a) Here is a type, a splendid picture of God as the source of life and all things that pertain to life and godliness. We should never turn away from the living God. (See also chap. 17:13.)

Hosea 13:15 (a) The curse of God will cause the blessings of Ephraim to cease.

Joel 3:18 (a) By this we see the abundant blessings that God will pour out on His people in a coming day. It may be a prophecy concerning the coming of Christ, as in Zech. 13:1.

Rev. 21:6 (a) This fountain represents the Holy Spirit. The Lord Jesus is the giver of that lovely Person. He is also referred to in John 4 as a well of water, which has the same meaning (See John 4:14).

FOUR

This number denotes God's government of men and affairs upon the earth. Israel was to encamp in the form of a square. The tabernacle rested in the center with three tribes on each of the four sides. This indicated God's governing power and care over the nation of Israel. In the Scripture, the eternal city, the everlasting abode of the saints, is a city four-square because there God alone is the Lord, and there is no other ruler. (See Rev. 21:16)

1 Ki. 18:33 (c) This number of barrels probably was intended to remind Israel that God was sovereign Lord, and able to reveal His power in sending down the fire. (See under "TWELVE")

Prov. 30:15 (c) These four things represent God's sovereignty in earthly affairs and their inability to satisfy the heart.

Prov. 30:18 (c) These four things represent God's sovereignty in controlling actions.

Prov. 30:21 (c) These four things represent God's sovereignty in His permissive will.

Prov. 30:24 (c) These four things represent God's sovereignty in leadership.

Prov. 30:29 (c) These four things represent God's sovereignty in power, and also these are four aspects of Christ's superiority.

Jer. 15:3 (c) By this we may understand that God intended to reveal His eternal power as sovereign Lord in punishing His enemies. (See Ezek. 14:21)

Ezek. 1:5 (b) These creatures represent four aspects of Christ Jesus as the Lion, the Ox, the Man and the Eagle. In all four of these aspects Christ Jesus is supreme Lord. As the lion, the Lord Jesus is the King of kings and Lord of lords. He rules over all other powers and enemies. He is the Supreme Commander, the Chief, the Almighty One. He is unconquerable and unavoidable. Matthew describes Christ in this aspect. As the ox, Christ is the servant of God, and the servant of men. God calls Him his servant. This is illustrated in the story of the washing of the feet in John 13. Jesus said, "I am among you as one that serveth." The ox exists only to serve men. Mark describes Christ in this aspect.
As the man, the Lord Jesus is a lover, a friend, a companion, an associate, and a leader. He was made man so that we could have fellowship with Him, and He could mingle with men in all their human experiences. Luke describes Christ in this aspect. As the eagle, the Lord Jesus is God Himself. He is Deity, eternal, all-powerful, and rising above all obstructions, hindrances, storms, in complete control of every force. His deity is fully described in the Gospel of John. These four aspects of the Saviour are revealed again in Ezek. 10:14; Rev. 4:6.

Ezek. 37:9 (c) This is emblematic of God's power to give life even in hopeless cases. In this particular case it reveals the power of the Holy Spirit to bring Israel back into true fellowship with God, giving them the gift of eternal life when they accept Jesus Christ, and trust Him as their Messiah and their Saviour.

Dan. 3:25 (c) The number here represents God's power to overrule the king, and to quench the violence of fire, and to deliver His own children.

Dan. 7:2 (c) By this we understand that God had power to raise up kingdoms, and to destroy kings as He wills. (See v. 3) All the kingdoms were destroyed by God's Word. They were enemies of Israel, and of the God of Israel. (See v. 17)

Dan. 8:8 (c) The great horn was Alexander the Great. The four horns were his four generals who took over the kingdom when he died. God overthrew all of these, but saved Israel, His people, from destruction. (See v. 22, chap. 11:4.)

Amos 1:3 (c) In each of the eight times (two times four) that this expression occurs in chapters 1 and 2, God is showing His supreme power to punish every enemy, including these who are named in each instance. Notice that Judah and Israel are included in the list, for they had rebelled against God and were following the ways of the heathen around them.

Zech. 1:18 (c) The number in this case reveals that God had supreme power to send other nations to punish His own people.

Zech. 1:20 (c) By this we learn that God had the power to mend and build up that which He Himself had destroyed. The four-fold destruction in v. 18 was to be repaired by the four carpenters in v. 20.

Zech. 6:1 (b) The number in this case represents God's supreme power to punish Israel in four different ways, as described or illustrated by the four horses. (See under "HORSES".)

Matt. 24:31 (c) The number in this case reveals that God is the Lord and Master of every part of the world. (See also Mark 13:27.)

John 11:17 (c) Here we see God's power over death, the greatest enemy of all. The Jews thought that after four days the spirit of the dead person left, never to return. They thought that this spirit hovered around the person for three days before leaving permanently on the fourth day.

John 19:23 (c) The garment torn into four pieces is just a figure of their utter disregard for His claim to Lordship in their lives.

Rev. 7:1 (c) By this is revealed the power of God over angels, and over the earth.

Rev. 9:13 (c) In this way we understand God's power over all forms of religion.

Rev. 21:16 (c) As in the old days Israel camped four-square to reveal God's authority and power over them, so in the new world the city four-square reveals to us that God the Lord will have absolute control and authority in this new life.

FOURTEEN

Since the number *seven* is the number which indicates God's perfections in His creation activities, the number *fourteen* may be used to represent that same precious truth doubled or repeated.

Gen. 31:41 (c) It may be used as a type of the wonderful and complete service of our Lord in calling, preserving, and maintaining both Israel and the church.

1 Ki. 8:65 (c) This indicates that the worship of God's people was full and complete both for their salvation and their preservation.

Matt. 1:17 (c) This reveals God's great accuracy and perfection in controlling the genealogy of Christ.

Gal. 2:1 (c) This reveals that Paul was unusually careful to take the full time necessary to prepare himself adequately for the service of his Lord.

FOWL

Gen. 15:11 (c) These are a type of Satan and his angels who are always enemies of any sacrifice for sin, and especially for any types or shadows of Calvary. Satan was defeated at the Cross, and he ever tries to get men's minds to be occupied with every other kind of remedy for sin, except the one remedy of the blood. In this particular case, Satanic powers wanted to hide from Israel the value of God's preserving care, and His rich provision for their needs.

Dan. 7:6 (b) Here is a type of the swiftness with which Alexander's four armies and generals would progress in their campaign to conquer the earth.

Matt. 6:26 (b) The Lord calls our attention to His care for the bird family so that we may realize His care for us. We are more precious than the birds, and all of the children of God have His promise that He will preserve and provide for them.

Matt. 13:4 (a) Here is a type of evil spirits who pounce upon the Word of God when the sinner hears it in order to take it out of his heart and mind. (See also Mark 4:4; Luke 8:5.)

Mark 4:32 (b) These birds represent evil spirits who make their home and perform their activities in religious systems. (See also Matt. 13:19.)

Acts 10:12 (b) These birds represent unclean people who were saved by grace, washed in the blood of the Lamb, and thereby made fit to live in heaven. The Lord is telling us that when He saves any kind of a wicked person, He makes that person a fit subject for heaven, the company of angels, and the presence of God. (See chap. 11:6.)

Rev. 19:21 (b) By this type we understand the destructive and consuming power of the armies who would destroy their enemies.

FOX

Luke 13:32 (a) A type of the crafty, cunning and wicked cruelty which characterized the life of Herod.

FRANKINCENSE

Matt. 2:11 (c) This is a type of the fragrant love and the precious worship of those who came to adore and honor Christ Jesus.

FROG

Ex. 8:2 (c) Probably this is symbolical of those wicked, filthy, repugnant habits and ways which Satan brings into men's lives for dishonorable purposes. (See also Rev. 16:13)

FRUIT

Gen. 1:29 (c) This type may be used as a symbol of the blessed results which come from preaching the gospel. The tree bearing fruit may represent great Christians with great visions and talents. The bushes and herbs may represent lesser ones not so widely known but who also bear fruit after their kind. The grass may be taken to mean the great mass of obscure Christians who tell the story in their own way and win hearts for Christ in their own sphere. The fruit is those who are saved. (See verses 11 and 12.)

Gen. 4:3 (b) By this type we probably understand that it represents our own self-made righteousness. It was the product of his own efforts.

Num. 13:26 (c) We may understand this to be a type of the blessed results of walking with God in the promised land.

2 Ki. 19:30 (a) By this type is revealed that in the restoration Israel will be firmly rooted and grounded in their relationship to God, and they will be useful and fruitful in their relationships to the other nations.

Psa. 92:14 (a) This is a word of encouragement to those who have come to advanced age in that they will still be useful, and be blessed in their ministry as they come to the end of the journey.

Prov. 8:19 (b) We may understand from this picture the spiritual graces which God gives to the believer. It may also include rich and fruitful work in which the Christian engages, such as soul winning, Christian edification, missions and other ministries which flow from the hearts of those who are saved by grace.

Prov. 10:16 (b) By this type God describes the results of wicked living and sinful practices.

Prov. 11:30 (b) In contrast to the above, the Lord uses this type as a picture of the results of Godly living and Christian practices.

S. of Sol. 2:3 (b) This is a symbol of the precious fellowship and the gracious results which come from feeding on Christ and His Word.

Jer. 17:8 (a) This wonderful type is used to reveal the success that will follow a Godly walk in fellowship with the Lord, and a constant abiding in the Holy Spirit, and a constant feeding on the Word of God.

Matt. 3:8 (a) This is a type of those works which prove that one is born again and has received the gift of eternal life. (See also Luke 3:8.)

Matt. 12:33 (b) Here is a type of the Godly actions and desires that emanate from the heart of the Christian.

Matt. 13:23 (a) By this type is meant a Godly, fruitful life which brings glory to God and blessing to others.

Matt. 13:26 (a) Here we see the Christian life in full bloom, so that it is well recognized. The hypocrites, however, are exposed and denounced.

Matt. 21:19 (b) By this type the Lord is revealing His disappointment in the useless life lived by the nation of Israel. No good results followed in their train.

Matt. 21:34 (b) This type represents good and blessed results that should have been found in the experience of Israel when the Lord Jesus came to live among them. Instead of being thus welcomed, exalted and received, He was rejected and despised.

Luke 13:6 (b) By this type we learn that there should be more in the life of the professing Christian than merely a profession. There must be the manifestation of the life of the Lord in our souls.

John 4:36 (a) Fruit in this place is also a type of the good results which follow in the service of the King. (See also Mark 4:20; Rom. 1:13; Rom. 6:21; Rom. 15:28; Phil. 4:17; James 3:18.)

John 12:24 (a) This type represents the wonderful results that have come through the centuries from the death of the Lord Jesus at Calvary. Many have been saved, lives and homes have been enriched, the gospel has been preached, the poor and the unfortunate have been relieved.

John 15:2, 4, 8 (a) In this case "fruit" is a type and an emblem of good and profitable works, holy endeavors and Christian activities which should normally come from the life, the heart and the soul of a saved person. (See also Matt. 3:10; 7:17, 19; Luke 3:9; Luke 8:14.)

Rom. 1:13 (b) This symbol represents the salvation of souls, the upbuilding of Christians, the restoration of the backslider, and the teaching of God's people.

2 Cor. 9:10 (a) This type indicates the good results of the labors and the efforts of Christians. By their prayers, their activities, their gifts, and their influence, they bring glory to God, and blessing to men. (See also Phil. 1:11.)

Gal. 5:22 (a) Here we find a type of the results which are manifest in the Spirit-filled life wherein the Holy Spirit has His place as the Lord of the life. Thereby He is permitted to produce the results God desires to have manifested.

Heb. 12:11 (a) This type represents the results of godliness and godly living. It is pleasing to God, it brings glory to His Name, and brings blessing to our fellowmen. (See also Col. 1:6.)

Jude 12 (a) The type is used here to represent the evil results of the life lived by the ungodly, who care not for the instructions of God's Word. These evil men produce no good results in the sight of God.

FUEL

Isa. 9:5, 19 (a) By this figure the Lord is describing those ungodly, rebellious folk who are material for the fires of hell. (See Psa. 9:17; Ezek. 15:4,6.)

FURNACE

Gen. 15:17 (b) By this type we learn that the experiences of Israel in the land of Egypt would be one of suffering and of shame, of pain and of anguish as the Egyptians treated the Israelites as slaves. (See 1 Ki. 8:51; Jer. 11:4.)

Deut. 4:20 (a) Here again the Word is used to describe the sorrows of Israel which they suffered through the four hundred years of their slavery.

Psa. 12:6 (a) This symbol represents the testings and examinations of the Scriptures by wicked, hostile men as they sought to destroy God's words. It is a picture also of the carefulness and thoroughness with which God chose His words as they were placed in the Scriptures.

Isa. 31:9 (a) This picture is used to illustrate the terrible destruction which Judah and Jerusalem would bring upon Assyria.

Isa. 48:10 (b) The type in this place describes the great trials and sorrows that Israel would experience through and during her national history.

FURROWS

Psa. 129:3 (a) This is a remarkable type used to describe the beating which the Lord Jesus received on His back when He was tormented before He went to Calvary. (See also Hosea 10:10). Let us notice that Israel and Judah were to be punished together.

G

GALL

Jer. 8:14 (b) A word which is used as a type of the bitterness in life's experiences. In this case it was bitterness because of the oppression and the destruction from invading armies. There are those who live on the bitterness of past experiences. They carry hatred in their hearts because of former injustices. They keep these evil things alive in the heart. So they are said to "drink gall."

Lam. 3:19 (c) This may be taken as a prophetic utterance concerning the bitter experiences of the Saviour on Calvary.

Amos 6:12 (a) Strangely enough men's hearts are so wicked that they turn God's blessings into curses. That which God does for their good they renounce and feel bitter at God because of His actions. (See under "PLOW.")

Acts 8:23 (b) By this word is described the unhappy and wretched condition of this man who was deceived about the Holy Spirit.

GAP

Ezek. 13:5 (a) In a peculiar way the Lord is describing certain conditions in the national life of Israel wherein their sins made openings for Satan to enter, and the emissaries of Satan to destroy.

Ezek. 22:30 (a) Probably it is a type of the gulf between the Lord and His sinning people. Christ Jesus came to fill up this gap and to bring us to God. In those days perhaps it referred also to the lack of a high priest who would be faithful to God, or also to a Godly king who would stand between an angry God and a disobedient people.

GARDEN

Num. 24:6 (a) A word which is used to describe the fragrant and fruitful nation of Israel as seen by the Lord through the eyes of Balaam from the mountain top. God looked down through the smoke of the sacrifice. He did not see the iniquities and evils of Israel, but rather describes them in this beautiful way.

Job 8:16 (a) By this term Bildad describes the beautiful life filled with radiance and fragrance of that one who walks with God, and lives for His glory.

S. of Sol. 4:12 (c) We may take the expression as a picture of the Church in which God's people are the flowers, and their worship is the fragrance. (See also Chap. 5:1; 6:2; 11.)

Isa. 1:8 (a) Here is a type which describes the woeful conditions of the nation of Israel which should have been filled with useful and beautiful fruit, but instead produced only a strange, worthless, useless fruit of the cucumber vine. The cucumber was one of the articles of food that Israel had to eat in Egypt when they were slaves. It is not a stable fruit as apples, but soon decays, and even while it is in good form it is of little use for sustaining life. This is like the pleasures which the world offers. Sports exhilerate for a few moments, but leave no permanent value in the lives of those who see them. The pleasures which God offers are for evermore. (See also verses 29 and 30.)

Isa. 51:3 (a) Here we find that the Lord gives His definite promise that the nation of Israel which now is of so little use to God will one day be a fruitful nation blessing the earth, and bringing joy to the heart of God.

Isa. 58:11 (a) Here we see a beautiful type of the happy condition of the soul of that one who walks with the Lord, learns from His Word, and rejoices in the presence and the ministry of the Holy Spirit.

Isa. 66:17 (b) Probably this type refers to the lives of those who live in wealth with plenty for their bodies to enjoy, while their souls are in rebellion against God.

Jer. 31:12 (a) By this type the Lord is describing to us the blessing that will rest upon the nation of Israel in the millennium when they have turned back to God, and He has removed all cause for the grief and sorrow.

Lam. 2:6 (b) In this way the Lord is referring to the transient character of Israel. He is telling us that He will remove the nation as the small shelterhouse in a garden is easily removed and destroyed.

Luke 13:19 (b) Here is a picture of the fair earth in which foul religions develop. It is also a picture of the nation of Israel in which false beliefs and practices arose and flourished.

John 19:41 (c) Joseph of Arimathea, a rich man, had a garden in which Calvary was located. It was not a bare hill as we often sing. No garden is a bare, rocky, lonely hill. It was a beautiful place in which the cross was erected. Men sometimes build gardens for themselves with a mansion, flowers, and all the peculiar treasures of the wealthy, but arrange no place for Christ. He is crucified afresh. He is not permitted to rule and reign.

GARLIC

Num. 11:5 (c) This is typical of the best things which this earth supplies for the children of this world. Those who partake of the world's goods bear the odor and the influence of them in their lives.

GARMENT

Gen. 49:11 (a) By this type the Holy Spirit is informing us of the wonderful and rich blessing which Judah would enjoy from God. His vines would produce so abundantly that he could use the wine for every purpose; figuratively he could use it for laundry purposes. This is just a picture of the great abundance which God would give to this wonderful man.

Psa. 69:11 (c) These are the prophetic words of our Lord in which He stated that from head to foot He was covered with grief and sorrow because of our sin and iniquity.

Psa. 73:6 (c) This refers to the fact that evil and hostile actions against the things of God completely envelop the one who does them, as a robe covers the entire body.

Psa. 102:26 (a) By this type our Lord is describing the eventual destruction of this physical earth, as well as the heavens. He will discard them, He will destroy them, and will not try to mend them. (See also Heb. 1:11; Isa. 50:9; Isa. 51:6, 8.)

Psa. 104:2 (a) By this picture we see the complete envelopment of the Lord in light effulgent. The Saviour was covered with this light on the Mount of Transfiguration.

Psa. 109:18 (a) This is a description of Judas Iscariot. The cursing was not with oaths but rather it was his curse upon Christ, wherein he consigned the Lord Jesus to the wrath of His enemies, and wished for His destruction. He did it with his whole person. From his feet which carried him to the garden to the lips which kissed the Saviour, his whole person was involved in his wicked action.

Prov. 30:4 (a) This type represents the boundaries of the ocean or the lakes or the rivers whereby God controls the extent of their influence and their power.

Eccl. 9:8 (c) This word typifies the religious profession and confession which are made by Christians before the world. They are to live lives that are unspotted, unstained and unreproachable.

Isa. 59:6 (a) The Lord uses this term in regard to the efforts made by men to weave their own garments to cover their own nakedness. All men's efforts to protect themselves from the gaze of God's righteousness will be unavailing. All such man-made righteousnesses are of no avail.

Isa. 59:17 (a) This figure represents the anger of God against a disobedient people. His whole being is aroused to take vengeance on those who know not God, and obey not His gospel.

Isa. 61:3 (a) In this beautiful way the Lord describes the radiance, the happiness and the sweetness that fills the heart and the life of the child of God who loves the things of God, and lives for the glory of God.

Isa. 61:10 (a) That eternal life which God gives to us whereby He makes us His child is a complete covering for the Christian. All of his own natural person is covered by the Lord Jesus Christ so that we are found "in Him," not having our own righteousness, but the righteousness of God which is by faith of Jesus Christ. We read that this righteousness "is for all, and upon all them that believe." In this way it is compared to a garment.

Ezek. 16:18 (a) This word undoubtedly refers to the grandeur, the glory, and the beauty that God gave to the nation of Israel when they flourished so wonderfully under previous leaders. They took these riches and gave them to their enemies as they joined up with their neighbors in their wicked practices.

Zech. 3:3 (a) We think that Joshua in this verse is a type of the nation of Israel and that the garments are a type of the wicked ways, actions and deeds of these people. He stood before the Lord of heaven who took pity upon him, removed the filthy garments and gave him heavenly robes. This is probably a picture of the redemption of Israel when God again works on and in this great people to make them a holy and righteous people when they accept the Messiah.

Matt. 9:16 (b) This represents the old nature of the unsaved man. The Lord does not patch the old nature and try to make it better. He gives a new nature that needs no patching.

Matt. 22:11 (b) The type in this Scripture represents the covering of imputed righteousness which the King of heaven, God the Father, gives to every one who trusts His Son, the Lord Jesus. This man would not have God's robe. He came into the presence of the King wearing his own robe, which is a figure of human, self-made righteousness. The King rejected him because of his refusal to lay aside his own self-made righteousness and receive the righteousness which is God's gift. (See Rom. 5:17; Rom. 10:2-3.)

James 5:2 (b) The type in this Scripture refers to the evanescent and transient character of the position and power which riches give in this life. These rapidly disintegrate as the trials of this earth and the disappointments of life eat them away.

Jude 23 (b) This garment refers to the righteousness which must be worn in the presence of God. It must be entirely from heaven, and not be tainted in any way by human works, merits, or activities.

Rev. 3:4 (a) This is a type of the profession, confession and public life of certain Christians in Sardis. They kept themselves clean, upright, honest and undefiled in their daily lives. (See chap. 16:15.)

GARNISH

Job 26:13 (a) This word is used to describe the beautiful and artistic decorations of the heavens in the arrangement of the stars, constellations, sun and moon.

Matt. 12:44 (b) This type describes the professing Christian who "goes forward," joins the church, but who does not know the Saviour personally. He gets rid of the evil things in his life and takes on some of the lovely things of the church. He becomes an usher or he sings in the choir. He participates in the activities and gives of his money. As he puts on all these things, the Saviour calls it *garnish.* The evil spirit comes back to such a man because he is empty — Christ has not entered; the Holy Spirit has not come into his life. (See also Luke 11:25.)

Matt. 23:29 (b) This is a description of the flowery words used by the Pharisees to describe the virtues of the dead prophets while they themselves rejected the teachings of those same prophets.

GATE

There were thirteen gates to Jerusalem. Twelve of them are described in Nehemiah and the thirteenth, called the "new gate," is found in Jer. 26:10. They are listed as follows:

Valley Gate Neh. 2:13 (c) This gate portrays the humbleness of heart and mind which is essential before one can be saved. We must accept God's judgment against ourselves.

Fountain Gate Neh. 2:14 (c) This represents the fountain opened for sin and for uncleanness whereby the sinner may be saved through the shed blood of Jesus.

Sheep Gate Neh. 3:1 (c) We are assured here that having been humbled and washed in the fountain, we now are His sheep. We are His sheep by the new birth.

Fish Gate Neh. 3:3 (c) This gate represents fruitfulness. Those who are saved go after others for Christ.

Old Gate Neh. 3:6 (c) We are warned here against new-fangled religions and the Christian is encouraged to stay by the old Book and the old path.

Dung Gate Neh. 3:14 (c) There are always things to be removed from the life. We should make provision to keep ourselves clean for God.

Water Gate Neh. 3:26 (c) There is living water to drink (the Holy Spirit) and there is water for cleansing (the water of His Word).

Horse Gate Neh. 3:28 (c) The Christian here is called to the service of the King and to hard work for Him in His vineyard. Horses are types of work and power.

East Gate Neh. 3:29 (c) The Son of Righteousness will arise. Christ is coming back again. We shall hail His return.

Miphkad Gate Neh. 3:31 (c) The word means "registry." God has registered the believer's name in the Book of Life and will look after all who are listed there.

Ephraim Gate Neh. 8:16 (c) Ephraim is the name applied to Israel when she was in a back-slidden state. This is the gate by which the backslider may return to God. What an encouragement for us to go after those who have drifted away from God's fellowship.

Prison Gate Neh. 12:39 (c) This reminds us that there is a rebel within each of us, who is to be kept down under lest he injure and harm the work of God.

New Gate Jer. 26:10 (c) The Christian is to be constantly entering into new experiences of God's grace and new fields in God's service. We are to "enter into His gates with thanksgiving." There are many of them, so that one may be sure to get in and none need be shut out.

Gen. 22:17 (a) Since the gate is the entrance to the walled city, the possession of the gate indicates victory over the enemy and the conquering of his city. (See also 24:60.)

Ruth 4:1, 11 (a) The gate in this place is a type of the principal place of business in various cities, but especially in the land of Israel. Here business was transacted, contracts were made, and judgment was executed. (See also Deut. 21:19; 22:24)

Psa. 24:7, 9 (a) This type is used to express the glorious entrance into heaven of our wonderful Saviour when He returned from Calvary to glory. It is a figure to describe the triumphal entry of the Lord Jesus into His Father's presence and the palace of the King.

Psa. 100:4 (b) By this expression we understand that we come in prayer and praise by faith before God to worship and to adore Him.

Psa. 118:20 (b) Here we find a picture of the Lord Jesus through whom we enter into the courts of God and by whom we reach the palace of the King. He is the gate and the door. (See Gen. 28:17.)

Prov. 8:34 (b) By this type we understand God's thoughts about the portals of heaven, the entrance into God's presence. The Christian waits before the Lord on his knees, and watches before the

Lord as he reads the Scriptures and enjoys a sweet tryst with Him.

Prov. 17:19 (b) This type is used to express self-exaltation, personal emulation, and egotistic assumption, of power, authority and position.

S. of Sol. 7:4 (b) This gate is the entrance to Heshbon. Just beside that gate were two beautiful pools. These pools are compared to the two eyes of the lover, clear, sparkling, beautiful, attractive.

Isa. 3:26 (a) This represents the utter desolation of Jerusalem. She was to be destroyed by her enemies and the gates burned with fire.

Isa. 14:31 (a) By this figure God is revealing to us the terrible sorrow and pain which will fill the hearts of His people when the country of Palestine is destroyed.

Isa. 24:12 (a) Here again we find a description of the terrible destruction of Jerusalem. Her gates will be destroyed so that there is no defense against the enemy.

Isa. 26:2 (a) This is probably a millennial scene in which Jerusalem having been rebuilt will welcome all nations who fear God. (See also Isa. 60:11; 62:10.)

Isa. 45:1-2 (c) It may be that the gates in this passage represent both Judah and Israel, both of whom were to be conquered by the invading army. God often chose heathen kings as His instruments for whipping Israel. The brass indicates strength and judgments.

Isa. 54:12 (c) Probably this type represents the glory of Jerusalem after it is rebuilt by our Lord and becomes again the head of the nations.

Lam. 5:14 (b) This picture reveals the fact that the fine leaders of Israel had ceased to serve and to judge so that a state of chaos existed in the city.

Nah. 2:6 (b) Probably this refers to the control of the rivers. It may be noted that on several occasions rivers were diverted or changed in order to accomplish certain purposes.

Matt. 7:13 (b) The strait gate is the way of salvation by the cross. It is God's only way. It is too narrow to admit both the sinner and his opinions or the sinner and his merits. It is just wide enough for the sinner himself to enter naked, empty, bankrupt and guilty.

Matt. 7:13 (b) The wide gate represents the way of the world. It includes all the many human religions that entice men to enter and promise them eternal life. It leads to destruction.

Matt. 16:18 (a) No doubt this figure is used to describe the power of Satan and of sin, the power and influence of every kind of evil.

No influence from hell and no drawing power of the wicked one can affect the Church of God.

Heb. 13:12 (a) As in the Old Testament the sacrifices for sin were carried outside the camp, away from the sanctuary of God, so the Lord Jesus, when He was made sin for us, and became an offering for us, suffered outside Jerusalem on the hill of Calvary. He fulfilled fully the types in the Old Testament.

Rev. 21:12, 21, 25 (c) These gates are no doubt poetic figures to represent the fact that only through Israel in the Old Testament as twelve tribes, and the disciples in the New Testament, as twelve men, does any person have any opportunity of entering into God's Kingdom. Through the Jews we receive our Bible, our Saviour, and all the revelations of spiritual truths. Through the twelve disciples or apostles we receive all knowledge of our Lord Jesus, and His way of salvation, except as typically described in the Old Testament. It is through the ministry and the teaching of these twenty-four men that we have our information, our knowledge of God, and learn the way to God.

GATHER

Isa. 5:2 (b) In this way the Lord tells us that when He established Israel in their new land of Canaan, He destroyed the enemies, He removed the opposition, and He gave them the land prepared for their use.

Matt. 3:12 (a) This action is used as a type of the work of our Lord when He brings together His own people to dwell in His eternal Kingdom. The Christians are the wheat. All others are the unsaved who are chaff, tares, etc. (See also Luke 3:17.)

Matt. 12:30 (a) The Lord uses this term to indicate the cooperation and fellowship of His own servants who work with Him and for Him, and according to His instructions. They are bringing into the Kingdom, into the Church, believers from many fields. (See also Luke 11:23.)

Matt. 13:28 (a) By this type the Lord is telling us of the day when He will separate the unsaved from the Christians in order that His children may be with Him and all the ungodly sent off to their eternal punishment.

Matt. 24:28 (b) This expression is used to describe the great hordes of the ungodly who will gather over and around the dead bodies of those who oppose God's people, God's gospel, and God's Word. The picture is that of the eagles, or the vultures who assemble around the carcass of an animal to devour it. (See also Luke 17:37.)

John 11:52 (a) Our wonderful Saviour is telling us in this way that one day He will bring together Jews and Gentiles to make one worshipping body of people who will own Him as their Shepherd. (See also Psa. 50:5.)

John 15:6 (b) By this term is indicated the way that men will unite in their thinking against those who profess to be Christians, but whose lives deny it. Those who presume to teach and preach the tenets of religion must themselves show the effects in their own lives, or else they will be rejected by men as imposters.

GIBEON

Josh. 9:3 (c) These people are a type to us of those who beguile Christians, deceive them, and offer them various kinds of allurements to win their sympathetic cooperation and fellowship. The world has many ways of enticing God's people to join up with them. Quite often this may be seen in so-called "charity movements." The world puts on great programs for the relief of humanity, and in which they ask the Christians to join, while at the same time they will not permit the name of Christ, nor the Word of God, nor the message of the gospel to have any place in their plans and solicitation. Christians who join up with the ungodly in those enterprises which will not permit Christ nor God to have any place will suffer for it.

GHOST

Mark 15:37 (a) Here and elsewhere the word should be rendered "Spirit." It is the same word rendered "Spirit" in all the other places where "Spirit" is used.

GIDEON

Judges 6:11 (c) The name means "cutting off iniquity." He is a type of a humble, industrious Christian who yields himself to the Lord of the harvest, affiliates with others of God's children, claims God's promises, and expects the Lord to manifest Himself in power. Also a type of one who displays implicit and explicit obedience and depends on the Lord for results.

GIFT

Ex. 23:8 (a) This refers to any bribe of any kind whatsoever that would cause the recipient to be warped or to be partial in his judgment.

Psa. 68:18 (b) This refers to the talents and various abilities given to Christians to fit them for special and efficient service. (See also 1 Cor. 12:4; Eph. 4:8.)

Prov. 18:16 (a) This gift may refer to money. The giving of money obtains a hearing among great people of the earth and the wealthy are given places of honor which are not granted to the poor.

(b) It may refer also to the talents and attainments of an individual through the exercise of which he becomes famous. Edison exercised his gift of invention and was brought before great men; Houdini exercised his gift of magic and appeared before the wealthy; Paderewski exercised his musical talent and played for royalty. So the Christian may develop a gift for God under the leadership of the Spirit and be greatly in demand by those who are seeking for the best in Christian service. Some are gifted to teach prophecy or to unfold the Scriptures analytically or to develop and promote Sunday School work or to lead young people in their Christian ministry or to sing God's praises. All of these gifts give one a great place among the people of God and are in demand for the ministry and service of the King.

Prov. 25:14 (a) A reference to one who boasts of an ability which he does not possess.

GIFT is used as a type for a number of rich blessings from God. The Holy Spirit is called a gift. Eternal life is called a gift. Special blessings and equipment for service are called gifts. Money is also called a gift. Some of these are listed as follows:

THE GIFT OF THE HOLY SPIRIT

John 4:10; Acts 2:38; Acts 8:20; Acts 10:45; Acts 11:17.

In 2 Cor. 9:15 we read about the "unspeakable gift." This is usually described as referring to the Lord Jesus Christ. All Bible students do not agree with this, but rather think that it refers to the Holy Spirit. The word "gift" that is used in this passage is the Greek word that is always used in those passages which plainly state the Holy Spirit is a gift. The word "unspeakable" is a difficult one to analyze. The Lord Jesus spoke often, and so did the Holy Spirit speak often. Neither of these two persons could be adequately described by human speech. We get no help from this word in deciding who is under consideration in this statement. Some think it may refer to "eternal life." The word that is used, however, probably indicates that the Holy Spirit is the one under consideration.

THE GIFT OF ETERNAL LIFE, SALVATION, RICHTEOUSNESS

Rom. 5:15-18; Rom. 6:23; Eph. 2:8.

THE GIFT OF SPECIAL BLESSINGS AND EQUIPMENT FOR SERVICE

Rom. 1:11; 1 Cor. 1:7; 1 Cor. 7:7; 1 Cor. 13:2; Eph. 3:7; Eph. 4:7; 1 Tim. 4:14.

THE GIFT OF MONEY

2 Cor. 1:11; 2 Cor. 8:4; Phil. 4:17.

GIN

Job 18:9 (a) This figure is used to describe a trap laid for him by his enemies. Men are always seeking to find ways and means of tripping up God's children. (See also Psa. 140:5; 141:9.)

Isa. 8:14 (a) This figure is used to describe a trap. This trap, however, was prepared by the Lord for the punishment of His people at Jerusalem.

GIRD

2 Sam. 22:40 (a) This is a figure of a soldier binding on his armour. This illustrates the spiritual strength and power that God gives for the difficulties of life.

Psa. 30:11 (b) By this figure David is describing the joyful life which he received from his Lord and which was so precious to him that he compares it to a garment that surrounded him and strengthened him.

Psa. 45:3 (a) By this figure David requests his God to reveal His strength and power on the behalf of His servant.

Psa. 109:19 (a) This figure is used about Judas whose bitter attitude of cursing toward Christ, and the hatred of his heart toward his Master is compared to this garment which surrounded his whole person and influenced his whole life.

Isa. 45:5 (a) The Lord in this way illustrates the truth that He gave to Cyrus the strength and the power which was necessary for conquering the world.

Ezek. 16:10 (a) Here the Lord gives us a picture of the way He protected, surrounded and preserved Israel in the early days of their national existence.

Luke 12:35 (a) By this is indicated that the Christian should be ready for the service of the Lord day or night. He should be filled with enthusiasm and able for the battle.

GIRDLE

Isa. 11:5 (b) This is a symbol of a righteous life and a faithful spirit which encompasses a person to make him a useful and dependable servant of God. No doubt it is primarily a prophecy concerning the Lord Jesus Christ.

Jer. 13:1, 10 (a) The Lord tells us in this story that the girdle represents Israel in her decadence, her wickedness and weakness. God had intended Israel as a wonderful nation, but she mingled with the world around her and became a rotten, useless people.

Rev. 1:13 (c) This golden garment over the heart or the breast of the Lord indicates the purity, beauty and value of the love of Christ for His people.

GIRT

Eph. 6:14 (a) By this type we learn that God's Word gives strength and power to His people.

GLASS

1 Cor. 13:12 (b) Here we may learn the lack of vision and inability to understand spiritual verities as one should.

2 Cor. 3:18 (a) This no doubt is an illustration of the fact that we look into the Word of God and behold there the true picture of ourselves. God describes us perfectly in His Word. Having seen our need we hurry to the Saviour for cleansing. It probably also means that in the Word of God, which is the glass, we behold the beauty of the Lord, the precious Person of the Holy Spirit, the wonders of God the Father, and so we ourselves become more Godly, more holy, more like Christ.

James 1:23 (b) This is a way of saying that a man sees in the Scripture the spots and the blemishes of his life but does not use the remedy to get rid of them.

Rev. 4:6 (c) It probably indicates that the throne of God rests upon and is surrounded by such holiness and purity as is best illustrated by clear glass through which everything may be seen and nothing is hidden.

Rev. 15:2 (c) God's angels and God's wrath are without spot, shadow, or sin of any kind. Everything about God's punishment of men is above reproach and is perfectly clear, clean and transparent.

Rev. 21:18 (c) The misuse of gold on earth is often connected with wickedness, sinfulness, hypocrisy and pretense. This city of God is quite the opposite. The gold of that city covers no evil and hides no wickedness. Everything is transparent and the bottom may be seen from the top.

GLEAN

Judges 8:2 (a) By this figure Gideon was telling the men of Ephraim that they had reaped a greater harvest by capturing Oreb and Zeeb than he had obtained in capturing or killing the rest of the army.

Jer. 6:9 (b) This figure represents the thorough work of the enemies of the people of Judah when they invaded the land and carried them away as prisoners.

GNAT

Matt. 23:24 (a) The Lord Jesus used this insect as a type of the estimation we place upon sins or unpleasant things in our own lives; or little things in the lives of others to which we do not object. This is in comparison with the big animal, the camel, which represents the same kind of things in the lives of others, which we do not condone.

GOLD — GOLDEN

Job 23:10 (a) Job is in this way describing the severity and yet the value of the sufferings through which he was passing. He is telling us that these sufferings are like the fire in the furnace that refines the gold to remove the dross. He expects that the sufferings, sorrows, pain and disappointments will remove from him any wickedness that might be there, any evil ways, anything that displeases God, and he would emerge from this time of trial more pure and more godly than he had ever been before. (See Prov. 17:3; 27:21)

Psa. 19:10 (a) This figure indicates that the precious truths of the Bible are more valuable, more useful and more to be desired than the finest metal that earth can produce.

Psa. 45:13 (b) This type is used to describe the righteous acts of the people of God. Their deeds are compared to garments made of golden threads woven together through the life by kind words and godly deeds.

Psa. 68:13 (a) This figure indicates that the people had been living in a dirty, filthy way in their sins, but now had been redeemed from that kind of life, and were living beautiful lives, attractive in every way both to God and to man.

Prov. 11:22 (a) By this type we learn the lesson that ungodly actions in the life of a beautiful woman are as inconsistent as to see a jeweled ornament placed in the snout of a pig. The same thought is expressed in a different way in Eccl. 10:1.

Prov. 25:11 (b) By this figure we learn of the great value of words that are well spoken and timely. They have a beautiful effect upon the soul.

Isa. 13:12 (a) Gold adorns, but Christ adorns much greater. Gold buys one's way into earthly places but Christ brings one into the throne room of heaven. Gold meets the requirements of this life but Christ equips for the eternal life. Gold settles quarrels between men but Christ settles the quarrel between God and man. Gold saves the life from many discomforts, but Christ saves the life from eternal loss. The man in the passage is the Lord Jesus. He is better than gold which is used as a standard for purity on the earth.

Lam. 4:1 (a) In this way the Lord describes the departing of the glory of Israel. During the reign of Solomon the glory of Israel reached its highest point. Afterward, because of the evils which crept in, and the idolatry which abounded, the glory, position, power and wealth gradually disappeared. We should notice that the expression is "the gold is become dim." The gold has not entirely disappeared, it has not been completely abolished. It is rising again to shine with even greater glory when Christ Jesus, the Messiah, returns.

Ezek. 16:13 (a) We learn from this that Israel was made wealthy, beautiful, great and powerful by the hand of God who gave to them liberally of the blessings of heaven and earth.

Dan. 2:38 (a) The King of Babylon is described by this figure because of his great wealth and his world-wide power. All the other kingdoms were inferior in wealth and power to his kingdom. He was the supreme ruler of the earth. He was so flattered by being given this position that he decided he should be better than all the rest of the kingdoms, and so in the next chapter, 3:1, he made an image that was all of gold. He felt it was humiliating to him to be only the head of gold. This egotistical pride came to an end when he was made to eat grass like the cattle. God revealed to him that in the sight of the Lord he was neither the head of gold, nor the rest of the body of gold.

Zech. 4:2-6 (a) This candlestick is a type of the Holy Spirit, both beautiful, useful, valuable and enlightening. He is the author of the light that comes from heaven through the Lord Jesus Christ. He reveals the truth about ourselves, and the truth about the Saviour.

1 Cor. 3:12 (a) The deeds which are done by Christians for the glory of God, and the blessing of men are compared to this precious metal. Much of our service is of little or no value to God. It is the desire of our Lord that our works should have His approval, and should be actuated and activated by the Holy Spirit.

2 Tim. 2:20 (a) All kinds of vessels are necessary in the house of God. Some are very fancy, delicate, expensive, and more ornamental than useful. Such is the beautiful vase that adorns the mantel in the parlor. It represents the attractive gold, cut glass or ornamental pieces that beautify the parlor of the home. There are other vessels, however, which are called vessels of dishonor. These are the kitchen utensils, the skillet, the pans, the coffee pot. Most folks would like to be the golden ornament in the parlor, but those in the kitchen are more useful. The purging from "these" is not purging the golden vessels from the kitchen vessels, it refers to purging oneself from the evils mentioned in the previous part of the chapter. If one does this, then the Lord can use him wherever He wishes, perhaps in the parlor, or perhaps in the kitchen. He will be subject to the will of his Lord.

Heb. 9:4 (b) Probably the precious metal is used in this Scripture as well as in Exodus to describe the Deity of Christ, and His divine character. As Moses' ark was covered both within and without by the golden plates, so Christ Jesus was pure holiness in His outward actions, and in His inward being, in His private life and in His public actions. He was sinless, holy, pure and divine. There were no shadows in His life.

Rev. 3:18 (a) Those invaluable graces which we may receive from the Lord are compared to this precious metal. These blessings from heaven enrich the life on earth, and will enrich the soul for eternity.

Rev. 5:8 (a) The value of the prayers of God's people is revealed by the use of this type. It is as though when the prayers of the Christians ascend to God, He places them in these golden vessels because they are as valuable and fragrant to Him as perfume is fragrant to us.

Rev. 9:7 (b) The locust probably represents men filled with evil spirits and who are given authority as kings and rulers to oppress their fellowmen. Perhaps it may be done in the name of religion. This may be the thought in making the crowns of gold.

Rev. 15:7 (b) The value of the wrath of God may be understood by the fact that His wrath is in these priceless vases. Only valuable things would be put in such a valuable vessel. We elect judges in order that they may punish the evil doer. We value the service of that judge who brings the vengeance of the law upon the lawbreaker. We do not expect the judge to set the lawbreaker free.

Rev. 17:4 (b) The false woman represents and is a type of the great world-wide religious system, that denies the truths of the gospel, and substitutes for God's Word the traditions of men, the teachings of religious leaders, and gaudy presentations that appeal to the eye and the ear. Because this great apostate group controls almost unlimited wealth, they offer to the world a false peace which invites their confidence and seals their doom for eternity. All of this display of wealth, power and beauty is covered by the figure of gold. She appears to be the genuine church of God by her protestations, but actually she is "the habitation of demons, the hold of every foul spirit, and a cage of every unclean and hateful bird." Rev. 18:2 She holds out to the world the promise of forgiveness, absolution, and a method of cleansing, all of which are represented by the type of "a golden cup."

Rev. 18:16 (b) The great false religious group called Babylon in the previous chapter and under the type of a "woman" is represented in this chapter as a city because of her tremendous commercial activities. She buys and sells by the millions of dollars in constructing and equipping great cathedrals, schools, convents, palaces, art galleries, museums, etc. This entices the merchants of the earth to seek her favor because of the remuneration to be gained. Thus this great church seems to be a golden source of profit. We should notice that in verse 13 this city trades in the bodies and the souls of men.

Rev. 21:15 (a) The measuring reed is represented as being golden to remind us and to assure us that all of God's measurements and weights and decisions are without stain of sin, without deceit, and without misrepresentation.

Rev. 21:18-21 (b) The city of God which is represented by the figure of "pure gold" is in contrast with the false city, the false religious empire built up by Satanic power, and which pretends to be gold, but is really only "gilded with gold." No one should be deceived by this golden appearance. We should ascertain what lies beneath and composes the real body of that which appears to be golden.

GOMORRAH

Gen. 13:10 (c) The word means "a rebellious people" and may be taken as a type of the people of the world who refuse and reject Christ and His Word and prefer to live in their sins and iniquities. Their judgment is assured.

Deut. 32:32 (a) The Lord applies this terrible name to the nation of Israel when they turned away from His love and grace to worship idols, and to live in sin. Since they were living like the inhabitants of Sodom and Gomorrah, the Lord applies that name to them as being most appropriate.

GOODS

Matt. 12:29 (a) This figure is used to describe the unsaved, the ungodly, the non-Christian who are in the grasp of Satan, and are described by Jesus Himself as "children of the Devil." He holds absolute power over them, and they carry out his will and plan. They can only be released from Satan's chains by the power of the Lord Jesus Christ through His gospel, and by the convicting power of the Holy Spirit. (See Mark 3:27; Luke 11:21)

Matt. 25:14 (b) Jesus thus describes the business of God, the work and labor of the gospel, and all Christian ministry as God's "goods." These are entrusted to us to invest well for Him. It refers also to the talents, gifts and various abilities of the people of God which should be invested for the Lord. It refers also to the temporal possessions, such as money, the hospitality of the home, and other such things, which also should be invested for the glory of God.

GOURD

Jonah 4:6 (c) This is a type of some gracious provision of God which is temporary in character and is intended to serve only for a certain purpose. The Lord gives and the Lord takes away and we should rejoice in both instances.

GRAPES

Num. 13:23 (c) This lovely fruit may be taken as a type of the rich blessings which may be found across the Jordan of spiritual death, in the promised land in which the Christian should live after he has died with Christ at Calvary and been raised to walk in newness of life. It represents the precious blessings that fill the life of that one who walks with God in constant fellowship with Him, loving Christ and obeying the Holy Spirit. This life is the iife that is life indeed.

Deut. 32:32 (a) The good God of heaven is reminding Israel of the tremendous contrast between the grapes of Eschol and the grapes of Gomorrah. The sweet blessings that come from walking with the Lord, in obedience to His Word, and in loving fellowship with Him, are to be contrasted with the bitter fruits that come from the pleasures of sin which last but for a season. For one hour of pleasure men will barter heaven and insure to themselves an eternity in hell.

Judges 8:2 (a) The two princes of the Midianites are compared to the grapes which Ephraim gathered. (See chapter 7:24,25)

Job 15:33 (b) Eliphaz uses this type to illustrate his thoughts about Job. He is stating that Job is a hypocrite and will never be able to produce good fruit in his life.

S. of Sol. 2:15 (b) This is typical of the delicate and delightful fruits of a human life such as kindness, love, patience, etc., which may be spoiled and damaged by little habits and ways that are mean and obnoxious.

Isa. 5:2 (a) Here, the fruit represents the attributes of Israel and their attitude toward the Lord. They should have loved Him, worshipped Him, walked with Him, glorified Him, and thus have yielded good grapes. Instead, they dishonored Him, hated Him, disobeyed Him, and grieved Him. Their evil actions are compared to wild grapes.

Jer. 31:29 (a) God is telling us in this way that the life of the father is reflected in the character of the child; the actions of the child are a result of the life and the atttitude of the father. (See Ezek. 18:2.)

Obad. 5. (b) The people of Israel are represented as grapes. The Edomites who dwelled in a high, rocky, inaccessible fort made forays against the Israelites, capturing them on the highways and killing them in the fields. They left none, young or old. The Lord contrasts this with thieves who steal grapes but who will leave some on the vines for the owners of the vineyard. The Edomites were worse than the thieves.

Matt. 7:16 (b) We learn from this figure that evil lives cannot produce good fruit for God. Those who belong to the Devil are not bearing fruit for the God of heaven. (See also Luke 6:44.)

Rev. 14:18 (b) This figure represents the people of the earth who are the product of wicked leaders, evil teachers and false faiths.

GRASS

Psa. 37:2 (a) This is a type of the weakness, instability and transient character of the ungodly, who soon die and are forgotten. (See also Psa. 90:5; Psa. 92:7; Psa. 103:15; Psa. 129:6)

Psa. 72:16 (a) By this figure the Lord is telling us of the great growth of the nation of Israel numerically. When the blessing of God rests upon that nation, then they will flourish again as they once did.

Isa. 40:6 (a) In this passage the Lord is reminding us that the honors which men bestow, and the position of prominence to which men attain, soon disappear. These are not permanent. The rich man loses his riches; the influential man loses his power; the prominent man becomes obscure, but God's gifts are permanent. (See Isa. 51:12)

Isa. 44:4 (a) This strange type indicates that God's people will grow beautifully among the many people of the world where they are scattered. It indicates that they will be a spiritual people who will be of noble character and godly attributes. This certainly is the future of Israel when they turn again to the Lord.

Jas. 1:11 (a) The rich man in this passage is compared to the grass of the field. His riches disappear, and he himself fades into obscurity. He must lie in the grave side by side with the poor, for there is no difference in death.

1 Pet. 1:24 (a) The permanent character of the Scriptures is contrasted with the very short life of grass.

GRASSHOPPER

Num. 13:33 (a) These spies felt weak and insignificant when they compared themselves with the giants and considered the power of these mighty men in Canaan.

Judg. 7:12 (a) The invading hosts of the enemies of Israel are compared to an invading plague of grasshoppers. It is a picture of the quantity of the enemy, rather than the quality or character. (See Jer. 46:23)

Eccl. 12:5 (b) The aged person cannot endure the slightest burden. To an ordinary person the grasshopper would hardly be noticed if it should alight on that person. It comes suddenly, and is gone quickly. It remains only a little time. So it is in the lives of the aged. A slight difficulty arises quickly, and is soon gone, but it seems to be a tremendous load to the old grandmother or grandfather. The mole hill becomes a mountain in the older days.

Isa. 40:22 (a) By this figure the Lord is describing His thoughts about the people of the earth, whether they be prominent or obscure. None of them are very important in God's sight. They are small and insignificant when compared to the greatness and the power of God.

Nah. 3:17 (a) The great men of Nineveh flourished in times of prosperity and peace. Afterwards God saw that they were destroyed and their memory perished.

GRAVEN

Isa. 49:16 (a) The indelible and ineffaceable marks of Calvary are forever to be seen in the hands of the Lord Jesus Christ. They are a constant reminder of our tremendous need and Christ's sufficient supply for that need.

Jer. 17:1 (a) The sins of Israel are indelibly written upon the pages of history and can never be erased or effaced from their persons.

GRAVES

Ezek. 37:13 (a) This is a picture or a figure of the condition of Israel when scattered among the nations. The national character of this great people is buried beneath the nationalities of other kingdoms.

1 Cor. 15:55 (a) This is a symbol of death which claims the body. When the Lord Jesus returns to earth the grave will neither get nor hold the body of the living Christian, for he will be transported to heaven without dying.

Rev. 20:13 (R.V.) (a) By this symbol the Lord is telling us that the grave gives up the body, and hell gives up the soul of the unsaved. These are reunited at the great white throne, and are judged before being sent to the lake of fire.

GREASE

Psa. 119:70 (a) This is a picture of pride, opulence, egotism and self-satisfaction. These make a person proud, insolent and self-sufficient.

GREEN

Job 8:16 (b) This type is used to describe the hypocrite who is unstable and is soon destroyed.

Job 15:32 (b) By this figure we see that the man who is deceived and is not true to God's Word, and is not really linked up with God, will not prosper, and shall not be productive in his life.

Psa. 52:8 (a) This type indicates a fresh, happy spirit, full of life, vigor and growth.

Jer. 17:8 (a) This symbol represents youth, life, freshness and vigor. This is a Christian who is spiritual, zealous, active for God.

Hosea 14:8 (a) By this type we understand life at its best. Such a life is filled with joy, gladness, singing and service.

Luke 23:31 (b) This is a figurative way of saying that if Israel was so rebellious and so hostile when the Lord Jesus was with them, what would they be like when Christ was gone from them. When they were free to read the Scriptures and to worship in their temple (all of which is compared to a green tree), what would they be like when they had no temple, and their enemies came in like a flood, and they had no Scriptures from which to read. This time is compared to the season of a dry tree.

GREYHOUND

Prov. 30:31 (c) This is a type of the Lord Jesus in His swift actions both of judgment and of blessing. (See under "GOAT")

GRIND

Job 31:10 (b) This is a symbol of subserviency and recompense.

Isa. 3:15 (b) By this symbol is indicated the cruel hardships placed upon the poor by the powerful rich.

Matt. 21:44 (a) This figure indicates the power of God to punish His enemies and the power of Christ to punish those who reject and refuse Him. (See Luke 20:18)

GRINDERS

Eccl. 12:3 (a) This name is given to the teeth of the aged. In old age the teeth are gone, having decayed or been extracted, and so they can no longer chew their food.

GRISLED

Zech. 6:3 (b) It is quite evident that these horses of various colors represent various types of God's curse and judgment. They probably represent the same four judgments that are mentioned in Ezek. 14:21. It is difficult to state definitely which judgment is represented by the grisled horses. Certainly it is something that is a curse to Israel.

GROUND

1 Sam. 3:19 (a) By this type the Lord is promising to Samuel that all his words will be used to profit the hearers, and that none of his sayings will be wasted.

1 Sam. 14:45 (a) In this peculiar way and by this figure the people are asserting that no harm of any kind shall come to Jonathan who had won such a great victory over the Philistines.

Eph. 3:17 (b) This figure is used to describe the deep-seated faith and trust of one who believes God and believes fully God's Word.

Col. 1:23 (b) By this figure is indicated a firm conviction and a true faith in the teachings of God's Word, God's Truth.

1 Tim. 3:15 (a) This describes the permanency, the stability, the reliability of the true church of God established by Christ, and of its members who are saved through His blood.

GROVE

Ex. 34:13 (a) The groves which are described in this passage and in the others which are given in this paragraph represent an unusual planting of branches of trees or saplings carved into shapes for immoral purposes. As in most cases of idolatry, immorality is quite evident, so in this case. Men and women approach these groups of planted sticks to arouse their passions and to gain some unnatural satisfaction. (See Deut. 7:5; 12:3; 16:21; Judges 6:25; 2 Ki. 13:6; 2 Ki. 18:4; 2 Chron. 34:3; Micah 5:14.)

2 Ki. 23:6 (a) It should be noted that these plantings of items to encourage immorality were found inside the temple of God. They were small in size so that they could be placed in the building. They were to be removed from the temple, burned, and, if they were covered with metal, that was to be ground up and scattered. (See vs. 14.) The grove mentioned in Deut. 16:21 and the groves planted by Abraham were normal and natural groups of ordinary trees.

GUEST

Matt. 22:10 (b) These guests are those who hear God's invitation to belong to His Son, they accept the call, they trust the Saviour, and they are admitted to the wedding of the Son of God. Some think these guests are the believing Israelites of the Old Testament.

H

HABITATION

Psa. 74:20 (a) This expression describes the dens of iniquity, both religious and irreligious, in which evil people live their wicked lives.

Psa. 91:9 (b) This is a picture of the precious experience of one who walks with God and dwells in His presence by faith. It is actually the story of the life of the Lord Jesus who lived in the presence of God from a past eternity, and walked with His Father during His sojourn on earth.

Psa. 97:2 (a) The type is used here to describe the atmosphere of righteousness and judgment in which God dwells.

Jer. 9:6 (a) The Lord is using this figure to describe the surroundings in which Jeremiah lived, for the people were cruel, deceitful and wicked, among whom he must make his dwelling.

Hab. 3:11 (a) In this way we are informed that the sun, the moon and the heavenly bodies all dwell in that which would be called "home" to them.

Luke 16:9 (a) Probably this is an expression of derision on the part of the Lord. Those who live with and for the unrighteous on the earth may expect to spend eternity with them in hell.

Acts 1:20 (a) The word is used in this passage to indicate the home in which Judas and his family lived. The whole family was blotted out by the Lord, and Judas and his family had no successors. (See Psa. 109:6-19)

Acts 17:26 (a) The word is used in this passage to describe the countries in which great races are supposed to live and stay. China should be for the Chinese, the United States should be for the white people. Africa should be for the black people. Evidently it was never God's plan to have the races mixed and mingled, as is now being done. Much national and international trouble would be avoided if this particular verse was observed, and the will of God in this matter was carried out.

Eph. 2:22 (a) The plan of God is to make out of each group of Christians a dwelling place for the Holy Spirit. A godly church is the holiest place on earth. It is God's dwelling place on earth. Every true church of God should be like this.

Rev. 18:2 (a) This type is used to describe the great apostate church and other religious bodies that offer spiritual guidance contrary to the Word of God. In these religious groups, Satan and his angels are at home. They set their thrones in these evil churches. They promote cruelty, wickedness, sin and all the evils that accompany idolatry and liquor. There is no opposition to their operation. They are permitted and encouraged to grow in number and in power. These demons are free to do as they wish in these apostate groups.

HAIL

Job 38:22 (c) This scourge represents the wisdom and the power of God in judging His enemies and punishing those who refuse His Presence, and His Word.

Isa. 28:2 (a) By this type we are taught that the judgment of God which man cannot hinder nor prevent will whip His enemies, and spoil their labor. God is a righteous God and will judge His foes with dire punishment.

Isa. 32:19 (a) The Lord is informing us by this type that when He judges and punishes His enemies, His own people will be safe and secure. This condition existed in Egypt when the hail destroyed the crops of the Egyptians, but did not spoil the crops of the Israelites.

Rev. 8:7 (a) Here is described another of God's judgments on men, and it probably is a literal judgment, with literal ice falling with tremendous force to destroy the works of men. (See also chap. 11, v. 19; 16:21)

HAILSTONES

Psa. 18:12-13 (a) This type represents the words of our Lord. By this poetic language the Psalmist is describing the power and fierce anger of God in judgment. The words of God are compared to may things in the Scriptures; sometimes they are for blessing, and sometimes for condemnation.

Ezek. 13:11 (a) The type is used in this passage to reveal the power of God by which He will smash and destroy the works of His enemies. (See chap. 38:22)

HAIR

Judges 16:22 (b) Samson's long hair revealed his belief and trust in the commandment of God. As a Nazarite, he was wholly given over to God, and this included wearing long hair. He was really discarding his oath and his position as a Nazarite. When he permitted the hair to grow again, this was his testimony that he again was returning to the God of his youth, and was now to be obedient to God's Word. (See chap. 13:5.)

2 Sam. 14:26 (c) Since Absalom was God's enemy, God could find little that was good to say about him. He had very beautiful

long, heavy hair, and so the Lord records this fact. It was the only commendable thing that could be said about him, for he was very wicked in his character and conduct.

S. of Sol. 4:1 (a) The mixture of white hair with dark hair as age progresses is compared to the white goats and dark goats mingled together on the hillside as seen from afar.

S. of Sol. 5:11 (b) The black hair of our wonderful Lord Jesus was an indication of his youthful character, His power, vigor, vision and activity as a rich young king.

S. of Sol. 7:5 (b) The purple hair of our Lord Jesus is a picture of His royal character, being the Son of God, in the royal family, and with all the royal prerogatives of the living God.

Isa. 7:20 (a) This strange figure is used to describe the "trimming" that the King of Assyria would administer to Israel. He would not and he could not destroy them, but God would let him take away much of that which belonged to Israel, desecrating their land, and wrecking their homes.

Jer. 7:29 (a) By this figure the Lord is describing the attitude of repentance and humbleness that Israel should take before Him. Jeremiah's heart was fully set on seeing Israel break down in their spirits and humbly seek the God of their fathers.

Ezek. 5:1 (a) This strange picture represents God's people in their weakness, insignificance and uselessness. They had wandered so far from God that they were no more important than a few hairs from the body. The hairs represent the people of Israel.

Hosea 7:9 (a) This figure is used to describe the fact that God's people may grow weak, old and helpless without recognizing the fact. Israel had drifted from the Lord, had forsaken the fountain of living waters, and had lost their power, but they were not aware of it. Samson too lost his power, and did not know it until he was overcome by the Philistines.

John 11:2 (b) Since the hair is given to a woman for her glory, this was a picture of Mary laying her glory at Jesus' feet. (See also Luke 7:38; 1 Cor. 11:15.)

Rev. 1:14 (b) The white hair of the Lord Jesus is a picture of His eternal character ever living with God, ever ruling and reigning through all the eternities. It indicates that the Lord Jesus is the ancient of days filled with wisdom, knowledge, understanding and discretion.

HAMMER

1 Ki. 6:7 (c) By this figure the Lord is informing us that the house of God is to be a divine institution, built in the quiet of His presence, and because of the still small voice teaching us. There

is to be no dissension nor quarreling in regard to it. The Lord Himself makes each living stone a part of the building, and then He brings us together to form the local church made up of sinners already saved by grace. God's church is not a product of man's ideas.

Jer. 23:29 (a) The Word of God is thus represented. There are many kinds of hammers such as the hammer of the blacksmith, the goldsmith, the carpenter, the stone mason, et cetera. Some are for heavy, rough work, others are for fine delicate work; so the Scriptures are used for every kind of need or purpose in life.

Jer. 50:23 (a) This type is used to describe Babylon. God picked out the armies of Babylon to punish and to destroy the nations of the earth. He used Babylon to whip Israel and Judah. God has a perfect right to choose any one He pleases, saved or unsaved, to carry out His purposes and His plans.

HAND

The word "hand" occurs about 1046 times in the Bible. It is used in approximately 20 different ways as types of various attitudes and actions. The Scriptures are too numerous for us to list them all, but we will seek to arrange them in groups in a way that will be helpful and profitable to the reader. The arrangement will not be an alphabetical one, but will rather be placed as the thoughts are found in the Scriptures. A typical Scripture reference will be used in each case.

The Hand Represents Human Power. Gen. 9:2; Gen. 39:6.

The Hand Represents Divine Power. Ex. 6:1; Ex. 13:3.

The Hand Represents Conquering Power. Ex. 14:8; Num. 33:3.

The Hand Represents a Position of Service. 2 Ki. 3:11.

The Hand When Washed Represents Innocency. Deut. 21:6; Matt. 27:24.

The Hand When Kissed Represents Loving Affection, or Deceitfulness or Hypocrisy. Job 31:27.

The Hand When it is the Right Hand Sometimes Represents Honor and Favor. Psa. 110:1; Rom. 8:34.

The Hand When it is the Right Hand May Indicate Security and Peace. Psa. 16:8; Psa. 109:31.

The Hand When it is Given is a Sign of Friendship, Confidence and Trust. 2 Ki. 10:15.

The Hand When it is Lifted Up May Represent an Act of Supplication to God, and of Dependence on God. Ex. 17:12; 1 Tim. 2:8.

The Hand When Laid On, Indicates the Imparting of Spiritual

Gifts on the Part of a Leader of God's People to One Who Is Less Able and Less Prominent. Acts 6:6;

1 Tim. 4:14. This seems to have been done only by Apostles and those in authority.

The Hand When Stretched Out Indicates that Mercy Is Extended and Offered. Prov. 1:24; Rom. 10:21.

The Hand When Leaned Upon is a Type of Confidence and Familiarity. 2 Ki. 7:2; 2 Ki. 5:18.

The Hand When it is God's Hand May Signify Divine Power. Acts 4:28; probably the Holy Spirit, Acts 8:18; divine retribution Judges 2:15; sovereign disposition Psa. 31:15; divine sufficiency Psa. 104:28; 145:16.

The Hand When it is Man's Hand May Represent Evil Power. Ex. 18:9; personal possessions 1 Ki. 11:31; counsel or agreement 2 Sam. 14:19; personal sufficiency Prov. 3:27.

Isa. 49:16 (a) This shows the wonderful love and the constant care of God for those who have trusted their lives and their souls to Him. His wounded hands are ever before Him to remind Him of the children of God whom He has saved. The work which He does is always connected with His people. The engraving on those hands was done by the nails at Calvary.

Isa. 59:1 (a) This is a picture of the blessed, far-reaching power of God to save both the soul and the life of every one who believes God.

Isa. 65:2 (a) Here is a figure of God's constant call to His enemies to come unto Him for salvation and restoration.

Heb. 10:31 (a) This figure reveals the terrible sufferings of that one who fails to kneel as a suppliant for mercy at the feet of the Lord Jesus. The terrible wrath of an angry God will fall upon him in judgment.

HANG(ED)

Psa. 137:2 (a) This figure is used to describe the discouragement of Israel and the disheartening experience which they went through while slaves in Babylon. No song was left in their hearts. They laid aside their harps.

Isa. 22:24 (a) This figure is used to describe the work of God in placing on the Lord Jesus all the majesty, glory and honor which is due to Him. God ascribes power and beauty to His Son, and so do all of those who know and love Jesus Christ.

Matt. 22:40 (a) By this type the Lord is telling us that all of God's plans for men and His purposes depend upon the two great commandments which He mentions.

Heb. 12:12 (a) Here we see a picture of the discouraged and defeated Christian who is called upon to look up to His Lord, and to take fresh courage.

HARDEN (the heart)

Ex. 7:13 (a) By this type is described that one who deliberately refuses to listen to God's Word, or to obey His voice. This rebellious spirit shuts God out of his life deliberately. The expression occurs in many places, and we give just a few of the references. Ex. 9:12; 10:1; 11:10; Deut. 2:30; Matt. 19:8; Mark 3:5.

2 Ki. 17:14 (a) Reference is made by this figure to the way that a horse stiffens its neck so that the driver cannot guide the head to the right or to the left. The horse usually does this when it is frightened or angry, takes the bit firmly in its teeth, stiffens the neck and then runs away out of control. The Lord does not want us to act toward Him that way. (See Neh. 9:16.)

Job 9:4 (a) This word describes the firm determination of any person to rebel against God, to refuse the teaching of His Word, and to reject God's counsel. Such a one cannot expect the blessing of God either in this life, or the next.

Job 39:16 (a) In this figure we see that the mother bird has lost her love for her babies and goes away to leave them without care, food or protection. This is most unnatural, and it is unnatural that one who enjoys the blessing of God should turn away from that wonderful Lord.

Dan. 5:20 (a) By this word is described a mind that has turned against God and is opposed to God's thoughts and God's will. It is the mind of an egotist who relegates all power and glory to himself in rebellion against the living God.

Heb. 3:8 (a) We may refuse to bow to God's promises of deliverance, refuse to let Him be our Deliverer, reject Him as our Captain, and try to run our own lives by our wits and wisdom. This is the meaning of "harden." (See chap. 4:2.)

Acts 19:9 (a) In this way the Lord is telling us that, after hearing the preaching of the Word, some decided not to accept it, but rather to oppose it. This kind of heart is sometimes called a "stony" heart. (See Ezek. 11:19)

Heb. 3:13 (a) Sin tends to turn the heart from God, and to keep the soul from being influenced by the Holy Spirit. The heart ceases to respond to the love and the grace, and the mind ceases to believe and obey God's will.

HARDENETH

Prov. 21:29 (a) This person shows in his face that he is an enemy of God. His countenance is fierce, angry and hateful.

Prov. 28:14 (a) The man who refuses God's Word, and rejects His commandments is warned by the Lord. God is telling him he will be punished for his rebellion. (See Prov. 29:1)

Rom. 9:18 (a) The truth of this passage is denied by many. We should note, however, that wax in the sun gets soft and clay in the sun gets hard. We should note, also, that the rain falls on one piece of ground and weeds grow. The same kind of rain falls on another piece of ground, and flowers grow, and also grain and vegetables. Men harden their hearts, they turn against God, they refuse God's leadership and His right to rule over them. After these tendencies are revealed in the soul and life, then God takes these men at their word and seals their decisions upon themselves. Pharaoh had lived many years as a rebel idolator before we read that God had hardened his heart. Jacob and Esau had lived their lives, and 2000 years had passed by before God said, "Jacob have I loved, and Esau have I hated." God is not unjust, nor unrighteous. He is always kind to those who seek for Him.

HARDER

Jer. 5:3 (a) These rebellious people had set their hearts against God, against His temple, against His sacrifices, and against His law. This rebellion was revealed in their faces. They showed the hatred of their hearts by their countenances.

Ezek. 3:9 (a) God gave to His servant, the prophet, needed grace to face his enemies with a calm, quiet, peaceful countenance. God enabled him to do this quietly and with confidence. This was revealed in his face.

HARE

Lev. 11:6 (c) This little animal may be used to represent the professing Christian whose talk is orthodox, but whose walk is heterodox. The hare of the Bible, or the rabbit, did chew the cud (the talk), but did not divide the hoof (the walk). It does not walk smoothly, nor evenly, but by jumps. Its color blends with its surroundings. So the professing Christian who is not really born again seeks to live and act as a real Christian, when he is in that environment, and vice versa. The walk and the talk must both be according to the Word of God, and produced by the Spirit of God.

HARLOT

Isa. 1:21 (a) This word is used to describe Jerusalem when she was living in idolatry and in corrupt relationship with the rich nations around her. The affections of her heart were taken away from the living and the true God, and she became enamoured of the idols of other peoples. (See also Jer. 2:20; Ezek. 16:15; Hosea 2:5.)

Rev. 17:5 (a) Babylon is a type of the Roman Catholic Church. This is so stated by many historians and scholars who are authorized to explain the Scriptures. Many large denominations have hived off from this church, and have carried with them many of the traditions and practices of the mother church. Many of these follow the practice of the mother church in seeking the favor and the gifts of the world.

HARNESS

1 Ki. 20:11 (a) This figure describes a very evident truth. The one that enters into the battle is not to give the victorious shout, but rather the one who comes out of the battle as the victor. The one who begins a race is not to be commended, but rather the one who ends the race as a successful contestant.

HARP

Isa. 5:12 (b) This is a symbol of joy, praise and worship. When Israel was captive in a foreign land, their song ceased, and the musical instruments were laid aside. (See Psa. 137:2.) In this passage the musical instruments are mentioned to describe the hilarity and riotous music that comes from those who follow wine and strong drink. They are full of joy, praise and worship for their false gods.

HART

Psa. 42:1 (a) David uses this animal and its habit to describe his own deep longing for the living God from whom comes the living water. This heart desire of David is expressed in several ways, and by several figures. (The hart is the male member of the red deer family. The hind is the female of the species.)

Isa. 35:6 (a) Isaiah uses this type to show the great grace and power of God in making a poor, lost, helpless sinner to rejoice in a new-found Saviour, and in His forgiveness.

Lam. 1:6 (a) By this figure the prophet is telling us that the nobles and the leaders of Israel have become wanderers with no certain dwelling place, and with no provision for their comfort.

HARVEST

Jer. 8:20 (b) This is a description of the end time when the Lord will judge the earth and gather into heaven believers who are profitable to Him (the grain), but will shut out of heaven the weeds and the tares which have no value to Him. We see this on the farm constantly. That which is useful to the farmer he gathers into his barns. The vines and the stubble remain in the field to rot.

Jer. 51:33 (a) This is a picture of the judgment of this great city when God would cut her down and destroy her because of her iniquity.

Matt. 9:37 (a) This is a type of the great number of people who are interested in their souls' welfare, are hungry for deliverance, and are waiting for someone to lead them to Christ Jesus, the Saviour.

Matt. 13:39 (a) By this figure the Lord is telling us of the judgment at the end of this age when the Lord will separate His people from the ungodly, will reward the Christian, but will punish the sinner.

Rev. 14:15 (a) This is a picture of the Great Tribulation when the end comes and God comes forth in mighty judgment and terrible wrath to punish the wicked and the rebellious people of earth.

HAWK

Lev. 11:16 (c) This is a type of wicked men who prey upon widows, orphans and other unfortunates in order to obtain what they have for their own enrichment.

Job. 39:26 (b) This is a symbol of the unsearchable ways of God which cannot be controlled nor understood by men.

HAY

Isa. 15:6 (c) This is symbolical of the desolation in the lives of those who are disobedient to God, and to His Word.

1 Cor. 3:12 (a) Here is a type which represents the worthless character of many religious works done in the name of the Lord as religious enterprises. Many of these activities in the name of Christianity will not stand the test of God's judgment, but will be destroyed in the day when God judges the secrets of men by Jesus Christ.

HEAD

This word is used as a type of many and varies things in the Scriptures. Since it occurs so often, and in so many ways, it will not be possible to give all the Scripture references pertaining to it. The typical meanings most used are presented with a few Scriptures as examples.

Gen. 3:15 (b) This is a type of the utter defeat that shall be brought upon Satan by the Lord Jesus Christ.

Gen. 49:26 (a) This type is used to represent the superiority of this great man of God. He was to receive the best of God's blessings above his brethren, as in the dream the sheaves bowed down to his sheaf, and the stars made obeisance to him. (See Deut. 33:16)

Ex. 29:10 (a) The figure in this case indicates that the entire animal is to be taken as an offering, as the head is the important and directing power of the body. (See Lev. 4:4; Lev. 8:14)

Deut. 28:44 (b) By this figure we understand that the nations were to rule over Israel and the people of Israel were to be slaves to their neighbors.

Josh. 2:19 (b) The type in this passage is one that is quite often used throughout the Scriptures indicating that the whole person is to blame and is guilty in the sin that is committed. The head is taken as a type of the entire person, his body, soul and spirit. (See 1 Sam. 25:39; 2 Sam. 1:16; 2 Chron. 6:23.)

2 Sam. 1: 2 (c) The placing of earth upon the head was a sign of deep grief, sorrow, shame and humiliation. It was commonly practiced by the Israelites and by others. (See 2 Sam. 15:32; Josh. 7:6)

2 Sam. 22:44 (2) This passage is evidently a type or picture of the crowning glory of the Lord Jesus. David often speaks in this manner about the Messiah. Christ is to be supreme, He is to be the sovereign over all the creation. The word is used often about the Saviour in His glory, grandeur and majestic power.

2 Ki. 2:3 (c) The type is used in this place to describe the leadership of Elijah over Elisha. Elisha was subservient to Elijah. His life was directed by Elijah. Now the master of Elisha was to be taken away from him.

2 Ki. 19:21 (b) Here we see a picture of the contempt with which Assyria was to be held by Israel. God compares Israel to a weak young woman, and her attitude as that of showing perfect disdain for the great nation and army of Assyria. (See also Isa. 37:22)

2 Ki. 25:27 (c) This is a beautiful way of saying that the imprisoned king was released from his confinement, and was given, just out of courtesy, a throne on which to sit in Babylon. No power accompanied this honor, it was only a mark of the king's favor.

Psa. 3:3 (c) By this figure David is expressing his belief in the God of heaven, and his confidence that his God would restore him to his throne.

Psa. 22:7 (c) This action on the part of those who surrounded the cross indicated their contempt of the Lord Jesus. It showed how they despised Him in their hearts.

Psa. 23:5 (b) David uses this type to show that God Himself had made Christ the Lord of heaven and earth, a King and a Priest. It also indicates that David gave God the credit for making him the King of Israel.

Psa. 24:7 (b) This picture is taken from the records of wars. When the conqueror came back to the walled city the gate of the city was raised to admit the victor. So David is describing the return to glory of the Lord Jesus after His success at Calvary.

Psa. 44:14 (b) This action on the part of the nations among whom Israel is scattered indicates their contempt of the Jew. These unfortunate people throughout the world are the objects of derision. and this is indicated by the action mentioned.

Psa. 60:7 (c) This strange passage may mean that God's constant acts of forgiveness toward Ephraim, and the many times He restored the nation to a place of prominence prove the character of God, and magnified His righteous acts and judgements.

Psa. 68:21 (b) Here we see a type of the complete mastery that God would have over the enemies of Israel.

Psa. 110:7 (a) This type asserts without question that Christ Jesus will be on the throne of the world and will rule and reign without competition.

Prov. 25:22 (a) There was a custom in Palestine which is referred to by this type. When the fire in one home went out, the friend would go to a neighbor carrying an earthen vessel on the head, and would borrow a few coals of fire with which to rekindle his own fire. If the neighbor was unusually kind, he would not give his unfortunate neighbor just a few coals, but would give him a good quantity. These would be carried back in the vessel on the head. The Lord takes advantage of this custom to remind us that when our neighbor is in an unfortunate position mentally or otherwise, we are to be unusually kind and liberal with him. Then he will find it difficult to hold a grudge against one who has been so helpful. (See Rom. 12:20)

S. of Sol. 2:6 (c) A figure of the tender love of the Lord Jesus for His church. (See also Chapter 8:3.)

S. of Sol. 5:2 (c) This probably is a picture of the diligence and constancy of the Lord Jesus in serving His people, the Church, all day and night.

S. of Sol. 5:11 (c) The beautiful purity of Christ, as well as His supreme value, are represented in this picture. The same figure was used in regard to the image which Nebuchadnezzer saw and in which he was the head of gold. This indicated that His kingdom and has own personal self were to be the finest, the greatest, the most powerful of all kingdoms mentioned or represented by the the image. So Christ Jesus and His kingdom, His gospel, His business, and everything connected with Him is supreme purity, marvelous power and magnificence.

S. of Sol. 7:5 (c) Here Christ Jesus is represented as being the supreme authority and power, having the ascendancy over all others. Carmel is probably the greatest mountain ridge in Palestine. It was on this peak that Elijah and Elisha saw the mighty power of God, and the enemies of God saw the wrath of God, as well as His wonderful display of vengeance. Christ Jesus embodies all the fullness of the Godhead bodily. To Him has been given all judgment. Because of this He is likened to Mount Carmel.

Isa. 1:5 (a) This is a type of the mind and the thoughts. The Lord is telling us that all the thoughts, plans and meditations of His people were evil, therefore their hearts or their feelings were evil as well.

Isa. 59:17 (a) God has in a wonderful way made provision in Christ Jesus for protecting the thoughts which emanate from the mind. Christ is our salvation. As we put on Christ He turns our thoughts to heavenly things, and enables us to think God's thoughts after Him. (See Eph. 6:17.)

Dan. 2:38 (a) This is a type of Nebuchadnezzar and his kingdom, which was more excellent than any of the other world kingdoms that would follow.

Hab. 3:13 (a) By this figure the Lord is informing us that He will destroy the leaders of His enemies so that their kings and their captains will go down in utter defeat. It may also be taken as a prophecy of the destruction of Satan.

Matt. 21:42 (a) Christ is the chief of all Christians. He is the originator, the designer and the builder of His church. All the structure of God's church rests on Jesus Christ, His Word, His work, and His character. Any building outside of Christ is a structure on sinking sand. (See Mk. 12:10; Lu. 20:17; Acts 4:11; 1 Pet. 2:7.)

Matt. 27: 39 (b) This action indicated the derision of the people against the Saviour. It showed that they held Him in contempt. (See Mk. 15:29.)

Luke 7:38 (a) This is a type of great humility for the hair of the woman is her glory. She took that which was most precious to her, that which marked her beauty and her sweetness, bowed her head at Jesus' feet, and wiped the tears with her hair. By this act she revealed her utter humiliation in His presence, and her trust in Him.

Luke 21:28 (b) This is a picture of victory, joy and anticipated blessing. It is a figure that represents courage, hope and expectancy.

John 13:9 (b) Evidently Peter wanted his thoughts, his works, and his walk to be, all of them, cleansed by our precious Lord. The feet represent the walk, the hands represent the work, and the head represents the will. Peter would have all of this in complete submission and subjection to His blessed Lord.

1 Cor. 11:3-4 (a) The Lord Jesus is the sovereign Master of every Christian, and also of the Church. In the home, and a godly

home is intended in this passage, the man is the authority in charge, but not as a "boss," but rather as a leader and guide for the family. The Lord Jesus came as a servant of God, though He Himself was God and so He followed out all the will, plan, and purpose of God, His Father.

1 Cor. 12:21 (e) Here we see a picture of Christian relationships. The leader of the church, or the pastor, cannot get along without the janitor, the organist, the usher, and all the other various members of the church.

Eph. 1:22 (a) This figure represents the Lord Jesus as the reigning power in the church. His Word is supreme, His will is sovereign. Every other person who claims to be a lord over the church is a usurper, a traitor to Christ, and a curse to men. (See Eph. 4:15; Eph. 5:23; Col. 1:18; Col. 2:10.)

Col. 2:19 (a) This is a true type of Christ Jesus, the founder, the leader, and the Lord of the church.

Rev. 1:14 (a) By this we learn of the age of our Lord Jesus who was "from the beginning," and who is the "Ancient of days." We learn from this that the Lord Jesus has eternal experience, good judgement, wonderful discretion, and therefore knows exactly what to do under every circumstance.

Rev. 9:7 (a) Here we see a type of the host of warriors led by men who have received their power from God to punish the inhabitants of the earth.

Rev. 9:19 (a) This sounds very much like a picture of our modern tanks. They shoot from the front and also from the back It quite evidently refers to tremendous power emanating from the forefront of these battle instruments.

Rev. 13:1 (a) This hydra-headed monster represents the anti-Christ. The seven heads probably represent the seven hills of Rome from which there emanates the tremendous power of the great apostate church. It seems from this figure that the anti-Christ will emerge from the Roman power under the leadership of ten mighty men, and that by these the world will be brought into complete subjection with the exception of God's people who refuse to thus bow.

Rev. 17:9 (a) We are told quite plainly here the meaning of this type. The Roman power is situated on seven hills,, and is already ruling with despotism and cruelty over many millions of helpless subjects.

HEADSTONE

Psa. 118:22 (a) This is a type of the Lord Jesus. He is both the cornerstone and the headstone. He is the beginning of the church, and the end the church. The beginning of the Christian life is brought about by trusting the Saviour. The end of the Christian life is to live with the Saviour.

HEAL

Deut. 32:39 (b) This type teaches the spiritual lesson that the Lord is able to mend the troubles that come in among God's people.

2 Chron. 7:14 (b) Here is a promise from God that He will remove the curse, the drouth, and the famine from the land of Palestine and cause it to become fruitful again.

Psa. 147:3 (b) By this is revealed that the Lord, by His words of comfort, His messages of mercy, and His promises of peace, will remove the sting and the hurt from human hearts.

Jer. 3:22 (a) This is a promise from God that He will repair the damage that has been done by and in Israel when they return to the Lord their God, and in humility walk again with Him.

Jer. 17:14 (a) In this way Jeremiah expressed his great desire for the Lord to minister comfort to his heart; his spirit was sore broken by the way he had been treated by the people whom he came to help. He needed the comfort of his God.

Jer. 30:17 (a) This is a promise from God that He would repair the broken-down cities, cause the ground to be fertile, restore the rains, and make Israel again a healthy and happy nation of people.

Lam. 2:13 (a) The Lord indicates quite clearly that nobody on earth could restore Israel to her former state of health, holiness and power, except the Lord of glory Himself. (See Hosea 5:13; 6:1)

Hosea 14:4 (b) The God of love offers in this passage to restore the land of Israel, to bring the hearts of her people back to Himself, and to repair and remove the damage done by invaders, and brought about by her idolatry.

Zech. 11:16 (a) The Lord indicates here that He will raise up a ruler over Israel who will pretend to be a shepherd, but will really be an idolator who will deceive Israel, and will work for their eventual ruin.

Matt. 13:15 (a) God expresses His desire to restore Israel, but they reject His offer and prefer to stay as slaves to the invader and live in rebellion to their Lord. (See John 12:40; Acts 28:27)

HEALTH

Psa. 42:11 (a) This word is used to express the joy of the heart and the peace of the soul which are so easily reflected in the face. It tells of the splendid condition of the heart and life of that one who becomes a victorious and praising Christian. (See Psa. 43:5)

Psa. 67:2 (a) This type is used to indicate the fact that the prosperity which God gives because of Godly living gives strength and blessing to those who are walking with the Lord. The society and the business life of these will be in happy, strong, excellent condition.

Prov. 12:18 (a) By this figure we understand that those who speak wisely and well to others bring blessing to the hearers so that they rejoice in life and are prosperous in their souls. (See also Prov. 13:17)

Isa. 58:8 (a) This is a description of the healthy, holy and Godly person who fulfills the description found in verse 7 and so reveals the fact to others that he is growing in grace and in the knowledge of God and in usefulness.

Jer. 8:22 (a) By this figure we understand that although God had remedies for Israel's needs, these remedies were not used and so the nation was weak, sickly and depressed.

HEAP

Prov. 25:22 (a) There was a custom in Israel of lending coals of fire to a neighbor with which to rekindle a fire which had been allowed to die out. The neighbor carried the clay vessel on the head. When the neighbor desired to show special kindness to the one who wanted the coals, she would give an extra amount of these hot coals and fill the vessel that was carried on the head of her neighbor. By this she revealed her desire to be more than an ordinary helper. The Lord asks us to do this for those who need our help even though they be very unfriendly toward us. This act of kindness will win their friendship. (See Rom. 12:20)

Hab. 2:5 (a) Here we are taught that some one will gather followers around himself who agree with him and his leadership.

2 Tim. 4:3 (a) We learn by this figure that a false leader will invite folk to follow him, and those who are in false doctrines will invite false leaders to minister to them.

HEAR

Isa. 55:3 (a) This is a call from God for His people to listen intently and carefully. We are to pay close attention to His words. We are to listen with a desire to understand God's will, and with an intention of obeying that will. (See also John 5:24, 25, 28; John 8:43, 47; John 9:27; John 10:8; Acts 3:23)

HEART

The word "heart" is used in the Scriptures to indicate many attitudes of the mind and many various kinds of affections and reactions. It is described as being *deceitful* in Jer. 17:9. This evidently means that it will lead us astray by its feelings and its attitudes so that we must not trust in our own desires, but rather be led by the Word of God.

We read that the Lord *searches* the heart, Jer. 17:10. By this is indicated that the Lord examines our motives, desires and feelings to see if they agree with His will.

In Joshua 24:23 we read about the heart that is *inclined* to the Lord.

Our Lord spoke of being "in the *heart of the earth*." Matt. 12:40. This does not refer to the grave which is on the surface of the earth. It refers to hell, which is actually in the center of this earth. The Lord Jesus did go down to that part of hell where the Old Testament saints were kept in conscious comfort until the Lord Jesus would shed His blood for them. After Calvary, He went down into this place and "led a multitude of captives captive." They were now ready to go into God's presence because His blood had blotted out their sins. The blood of the sacrifices which they had brought only covered their sins.

There is an *honest* and *good* heart described in Luke 8:15. This refers to that sweet attitude of confidence and trust in God wherein the person listens with a hunger and a thirst for the revelation of God's will through His Word. It indicates that this person loves to receive God's instructions, and to accept God's provisions.

A *broken* heart is described in Psalm 34:18, and Psalm 51:17. By this expression is meant that deep grief has fallen upon that friend, tears have flowed, the shadows have fallen, and grief has stricken the spirit.

In Heb. 3:12 we read of an "*evil* heart of unbelief in departing from the living God." Those who are afflicted in this way are those who doubt God, refuse to believe His promise, and seek relief from some other source. They do not believe that God is a living Person who will actually work on their behalf.

At the end of the Old Testament in Malachi 4:6, we read of a heart that is *turned* unto the Lord. This is a work of the Spirit of God in causing the mind and the desire of the person to come back to God from paths of disobedience and sin.

The *stony* heart is described in Ezek. 11:19, and chapter 36:26. This describes the person who steadfastly and stubbornly refuses to believe God's Word, and will not have the authority of God in his life. He is not moved by any preaching, nor stirred by any invitation. The Word of God makes no impression on his soul.

The heart that *fails* describes that one who is overcome with fear, horror and despair. He has no strength left for the conflict. He is made weak. He seems to be helpless and hopeless. This heart is described in 1 Sam. 17:32, and in Luke 21:26.

We read in 2 Cor. 3:3 of the *fleshy* heart. This passage really refers to the physical heart which is made of flesh. Somehow and in some mysterious way the Spirit of God works in our souls to bring about deep feelings of worship, love and devotion. One really does feel it in the bosom when those emotions arise.

The *understanding* heart is mentioned in 1 Ki. 3:9, 12. The thought is that there is a deep and confiding trustful interest in God and in His Word. The figure is in contrast with a simple, mental knowledge which does not affect the life nor the actions.

The expression found in Luke 24:25 "*slow* of heart" refers to that attitude of the heart wherein the person questions the truth of God's statements, and hesitates about believing in the Word and work of Christ Jesus.

One miracle of God's grace is found in the expression "the multitude was of *one* heart." Acts 4:32. By this we understand that all this great crowd thought alike, felt alike, acted alike, and planned alike. What a wonderful church this would make.

The expression "*lay* it to heart" describes that attitude in which one will accept the Word that he hears, and will apply it to his own soul. He will make the message a personal message to his own self, and will seek to act upon it. This is true in Eccl. 7:2; Isa. 47:7; Mal. 2:2.

Gen. 6:6 (a) This represents God's innermost feelings in regard to His dealings and relationships with men.

Job 23:16 (a) The troubles and sorrows that had come upon Job caused him to be very tender and soft in his spirit so that there was no pride, hardness, nor self-sufficiency in his heart.

Prov. 16:1 (a) By this figure is represented the feelings and the desires of men.

Jer. 17:9-10 (a) This type represents the purposes and the desires which actuate the thoughts and actions of men.

Mark 7:21 (a) This figure represents the soul and mind of a human being, his innermost self, his real self.

HEAT

Eccl. 4:11 (c) This type is used to represent the fact that whether it be in the service of the Lord, in the duties of the church, or in any other enterprise, it is better for two to work together for they will encourage each other, assist and help each other to be enthusiastic in the work.

Jer. 17:8 (b) We learn from this that those whose faith is founded on the Word of God, and whose lives are controlled by the Spirit of God, will be constantly radiant and zealous for the Lord, even though very adverse conditions may arise.

Ezek. 3:14 (a) Here we find a type of anger, bitterness and hatred.

HEATH

Jer. 17:6 (a) This figure represents a worthless, useless Christian. He lives in a desert, with no joy of the Lord, none of the peace of God, and does not bring a blessing to God's people.

Jer. 48:6 (a) It is said that the heath in this verse represents the tumble weed of the western plains in our own country. It is about the same size and shape. It bears a small bloom. It flourishes in the wet season in southern Palestine. When the dry season comes, the entire plant shrinks, the roots shrink in the ground so that it is only loosely held in place. When the wind comes, it blows the whole plant out of the ground, it rolls along before the wind until it finds a marsh, or a swamp. Here the roots take hold, replant themselves, and the plant again broadens out its little branches and blooms. (I have not seen this plant, but have read this description given by others.) The lesson it teaches us is that if the Christian finds himself in that society or association where the Word of God is not loved and preached, where the Spirit of God is grieved and quenched, where the soul is drying up for lack of the living water, then he should loosen his hold on that place, or that association, and let the Holy Spirit take him into a new association where the living water abounds and the work of God is prospering.

HEAVE

Num. 15:20 (c) The lifting and moving back and forth of the sacrifices of the Israelites was called heaving. It represents the Christian holding up before the Lord figuratively and waving back and forth before His face the beauty and loveliness of Christ, the blood of Christ, the sacrifice of the Saviour, so that he calls attention to the virtues of His Son, rather than to any merits of his own. (See also Num. 18:19)

HEAVEN

The word is used to identify certain spaces or certain conditions. Since it is used in so many ways, we will in this paragraph just list a few, and these will cover a majority of the Scripture references.

1. The place where the birds fly (Gen. 1:20; Lam. 4:19)
2. The place in which are located the sun, moon and stars (Gen. 1:14-17)
3. The place where the clouds are seen (Gen. 7:11)
4. The place from which the lightnings come (Gen. 19:24; Luke 9:54; Luke 10:18)
5. The place where God dwells (Gen. 21:17; Gen. 22:11)
6. The place where dew originates (Gen. 27:28; 39)
7. The place from which angels come (Gen. 28:17)

8. The place from which rain comes (Deut. 11:11; 1 Ki. 8:35; 2 Chron. 6:26; Jer. 10:13)
9. The place which describes Israel's dispersion (Deut. 30:4; Neh. 1:9)
10. The place where the blessings of earth originate such as rain, dew, heat and cold. (Deut. 33:13)
11. The place where storms form with thunder, lightning and wind. (Job 26:11)
12. The place where manna, the heavenly food, came from. (Psa. 78:24; John 6:31, 41)
13. The place which describes the supreme seat or throne of God. It is above all the other heavens. (1 Ki. 8:27; 2 Chron. 2:6; 2 Chron. 6:18)
14. The place where the believer, the Christian, the saved person, goes in his spirit when he dies. We never read in the Bible that the believer "goes to heaven." Probably the reason is that the Holy Spirit never calls our attention to the place where we are going, but always to the Person by whom we go, and to whom we go. We are said to be "absent from the body, and present with the Lord." We also read, "I have a desire to depart and to be with Christ, which is far better." Jesus said, "I will receive you unto Myself." We should notice that it is always the Person, and never the place that gives comfort to the heart.

HEDGE

Job 1:10 (b) This figure represents God's protection and care for Job, His servant.

Psa. 80:12 (b) This is an illustration of the way God took care of Israel, and hindered her enemies from overcoming her. He removed His protection later on because of her disobedience and wickedness.

Prov. 15:19 (a) The word describes the hateful and hurtful ways of some people who thus injure and harm others. The wicked words, ways and works of the ungodly are as thorns and briers in the lives of those they intend to injure.

Eccl. 10:8 (b) By this figure we understand that if one breaks down the fence of the neighbor or in any way trespasses on his neighbor's rights, he will be made to suffer for it.

Isa. 5:5 (b) This is a picture of the protective measures taken by God to preserve Israel from their enemies when they came to dwell in the promised land. The hedge is the fence that is mentioned in verse 2. When Israel became disobedient and rebelled against God's law, He removed every hindrance and His protecting arm, and gave them over to their enemies. (See also Psa. 80:12; Psa. 89:40; Matt. 21:33; Mark 12:1)

Job 3:23 (a) This represents those hindrances which God puts around a man to close him in and prevent progress. (See Lam. 3:7)

Jer. 49:3 (c) We may learn from this that the enemies of God will seek hiding places from God and from His anger poured out. They find, however, that these places of refuge prove to be places of thorns, briers and hardship. (See Nahum 3:17)

Ezek. 13:5 (a) By this figure we understand that the prophets were not protecting God's people as they should by proper teaching, leading and example.

Ezek. 22:30 (a) This unusual passage teaches us that while God gives divine interference in order to protect and guard His people, He also needs Godly men who will stand with Him and on His side to prevent the entrance of evil doctrines, evil programs, and evil teachings among the people of God.

Hos. 2:6 (a) This type reveals that God will surround the people with troubles, sorrows, griefs and pains so that they can hardly escape and must be punished.

Luke 14:23 (b) This type represents the difficult places in our cities and villages where it is hard to find people for the Lord, and one is quite apt to have his feelings hurt, and sometimes his body as well, he seeks to reach hearts for Christ in the ungodly districts of the city.

HEEL

Gen. 3:15 (b) This figure indicates that Satan would hinder the Lord Jesus in His earthly walk and would hurt Him but could not destroy Him.

Gen. 25:26 (c) Probably this may be taken as a type of the power that Jacob was to have over Esau because of the blessing which his father gave.

Gen. 49:17 (a) We may learn from this figure that Dan would be deceitful and underhanded in his dealings with others so that he would be a hinderer, a disturber of the peace, and would prevent the prosperity and progress of others.

Job. 13:27 (c) This may be taken as a figurative statement that our walk is marked before God, and so that the walk of each person is different from every other person. It also has the actual meaning that every heel print is different from the print of every other heel. No two are alike. In some hospitals the feet of new-born babies are pressed upon carbon paper, and then upon wax, to leave a perfect imprint of those feet. No other baby will have prints similar to these.

Job 18:9 (b) By this we understand that the evildoer will be caught in his sin in various peculiar and unknown ways.

Psa. 41:9 (b) By this we understand that Judas secretly and deceitfully betrayed Jesus to His enemies. (See also John 13:18)

Psa. 49:5 (b) This evidently refers to the evils which were felt and remembered by the sons of Korah in their path and in their walk on previous occasions. (See Jer. 13:22)

HEIFER

Gen. 15:9 (c) In this way we may understand the service character of the Lord Jesus Christ. He served as a young man. He was crucified after He had been only three and one-half years in public ministry. The Jewish priest began to serve at thirty.

Num. 19:2-4 (c) This may be taken as a picture of the Lord Jesus Christ as a strong, vigorous youth. The red may represent the precious blood of Christ. Both the Saviour and His work at Calvary are necessary to separate us from the world. (See Heb. 9:13)

Isa. 15:5 (a) This is an interesting type of the Moabites who. though strong, active and energetic, will need to flee for their lives because of the invading enemy. At three years of age, the heifer is reckoned to have reached his maturity, and is ready for breeding purposes, or other acts which can only be given to a matured animal. (See Jer. 48:34)

Hos. 4:16 (a) The heifer evidently is difficult to break for work. This is a picture of this young animal sitting down on her haunches, planting her feet in the ground, and trying to prevent the cowboy from pulling her along. It was God's desire to bring Israel back into a place of blessing, but she resisted, refused and held back.

Hos. 10:11 (a) This type represents Israel in her true condition of sincere service to God, and her spirit of obedience.

HEIGHT

2 Ki. 19:23 (b) This proud ruler was boasting of his great power in conquering mighty kings, and powerful nations. (See Isa. 37:24)

Ezek. 19:11 (b) By this figure we understand that the nation of Israel had risen above all the nations about her, both in strength, power and riches. Then because of her sinfulness, God permitted her to be broken down and withered.

Ezek. 31:5, 10, 14 (a) Assyria is thus represented as being at the top of the nations. She revealed her pride of position and power. (See also Amos 2:9)

Ezek. 32:5 (a) Hereby we learn that God will humble and bring down in defeat and humiliation Pharaoh, the King of Egypt.

HELMET

Isa. 59:17 (a) A symbol of the blessing that comes to the one who is saved. His thoughts are guarded and his decisions are in the fear of God.

Eph. 6:17 (a) This represents the provision God has made in His salvation for protecting the mind, the thoughts, and the mental processes. The mind is renewed by the Holy Spirit. It is enlightened by the Word of God and all of this is compared to a helmet. (See also 1 Thess. 5:8)

HEM

Matt. 9:20 (c) This may be taken as a picture of implicit faith in Christ, even though it be just to come near and to touch that which belonged to Him. Christ rewards true faith, though it be feeble, and not too intelligent. (See also Matt. 14:36)

HEMLOCK

Hos. 10:4 (a) This tree is bitter and poisonous and causes damage to those who drink the extract from it. So Israel had made judgment an unrighteous, unholy, and wretched procedure in the land. The judges took bribes and were not honest in their decisions. (See also Amos 6:12)

HEN

Matt. 23:37 (a) This is a type of the tender care and protection which the Lord Jesus offered Israel. Christ Himself is compared to the mother hen and the chickens represent the Israelites and the Christians of today.

Luke 13:34 (a) In His early ministry, the Lord Jesus compared Himself to a mother hen calling her brood (the whole nation of Israel) to come to Him and trust Him. Quite some time later in His ministry, He repeats the same verse in Matt. 23:37, but He changed one word. Instead of calling the "brood," He called the "chickens" — the individual persons of Israel. The events which transpired between these two passages reveal that Israel as a nation had rejected Christ, therefore at the end of His journey, He made His appeal for individuals rather than for the whole nation.

HERB

2 Ki. 19:26 (a). This figure represents the weakness and helplessness of the nations which were destroyed by Rabshakeh. (See Isa. 37:27)

HEWED

Jer. 2:13 (b) By this figure we understand that Israel had planned schemes and programs for pleasure and profit which omitted God, and which were contrary to God's Word and God's will.

HID

Deut. 33:19 (a) This figure is used to illustrate the fact that Israel would find and appropriate the wealth of many nations. The nations are compared to sand.

Job 3:23 (b) Job bewails the fact that although he is well educated and enlightened, yet he cannot use this knowledge while he is an outcast and despised. He seems to refer to this in verse 20.

Psa. 17:14 (b) God blesses the wicked rich with good things, and with things that most people never can possess. He gives to the ungodly rich a heaven on earth, for frequently they want none beyond the grave. (See also Job 21:2-13; Psa. 73:3-17)

Isa. 29:14 (b) God is informing us concerning the hypocrites in Israel that He will confound the wisdom of their wise men, and remove their power to understand and to invent.

2 Cor. 4:3 (a) The unsaved do not understand God's gospel, nor His ways. The things of God are a mystery to him. Satan blinds the minds so that the unbeliever makes wrong conclusions concerning God's Word, and God's will.

HIDE

Psa. 17:8 (a) This is a beautiful picture of the confidence that David had in the love and care of his Lord. He pictures himself as one of the little chickens or a little bird which in time of fear or danger hurries beneath the mother's wings. (See also Psa. 91:4)

Isa. 29:15 (a) Here we see a picture of those who try to run their own way, "paddle their own canoe," seek to manage their own affairs, without consulting God, or caring for God's will.

Isa. 49:2 (a) This is an expression which indicates the safety and peace of the one who realizes that he is hidden in the hollow of the Lord's hand as a precious coin or jewel is held in the hand of its owner. The thief must kill the owner before the jewel in his hand can be taken from him.

Hos. 13:14 (a) This type informs us that God will no more alter His plan or purpose to give to Israel everlasting blessings. He will resurrect the nation from throughout the world where the people have been scattered, and will fulfill His Word spoken to them through the prophet. This truth is indicated in John 11:25-26.

Nahum 3:11 (b) Probably this figure indicates that Nineveh was to be so completely destroyed that no one would ever be able to find her and to rebuild her as a city.

HIDING PLACE

Psa. 32:7 (a) An illustration of the confidence of the Christian who finds a quiet place where he may kneel and pour out his heart to God in prayer and commit to Him the protection of his life and the problems he faces.

Isa. 32:2 (a) This man is the Lord Jesus who protects and preserves His children from the storms of life and gives them calm and peace in the midst of turmoil and trouble.

Hab. 3:4 (a) God has power in His hands, and it is hidden power. The world generally thinks of Him as being a careless, indifferent person, who can be easily avoided and carelessly disobeyed. When he opens His hand He will display that power to conquer every enemy, and to punish every sinner.

Zeph. 2:3 (a) This is a great promise concerning the Godly people who have submitted their hearts and lives to the Lord of heaven. It assures them that they will be protected from the wrath of God in the great day of judgment, because they repented.

HIGH

This word refers to many different positions and situations. A few of these are listed here:

1. Any elevated place (Job 11:8)
2. Exalted in importance (Psa. 62:9; John 19:31).
3. A proud person (Psa. 101:5); Prov. 21:4)
4. A place of power (Ex. 14:8; Psa. 97:9; Isa. 6:1; Ezek. 1:18)
5. A place of leadership (Deut. 26:19)
6. A place of honor (1 Ki. 9:8; Psa. 149:6; Isa. 52:13)
7. Having unusual knowledge (Psa. 131:1; 139:6; Prov. 24:7; Rom. 12:16)

HIGHWAY

Prov. 16:17 (a) This describes the path of uprightness and godliness in which the people of the Lord will walk. (See also Isa. 35:8)

Isa. 40:3 (a) By this figure we understand that God's people should and will make it easy for God to work among the people. By their ministry and example they will prepare the hearts of the people to hear God's Word, and to talk with Him. (See also Isa. 62:10; Jer. 31:21)

Matt. 22:9 (a) This probably refers to the prominent places in the city or country which are easy to reach, and where there are many people to whom the invitation may be given. (See also Luke 14:23)

HILL

Psa. 2:6 (a) This is a clear reference to the Mount of Olives on which the Lord Jesus will stand when He returns to this earth to set up His kingdom. (See also Zech. 14:4)

Psa. 3:4 (a) This word is used as a type of the high and holy place where God sits upon His throne in heaven.

Psa. 24:3 (b) By this we understand the action of that one who seeks to come into God's presence in prayer and worship. He must be cleansed by the precious blood, and must be washed by the Word of God.

Isa. 40:4 (c) This probably refers to real hills which prevent so much of this earth from being usable and tillable. Also may be a type of the difficulties, obstructions and hindrances in the Christian pathway which the Lord removes as it pleases Him. (See also Luke 3:5)

Isa. 40:12 (c) Chemical elements are combined by weight rather than by volume. All mountains and hills are made of many chemical elements which have been put into combinations by the Creator, our Lord. God must know the weight of each mountain and hill in order that these may be balanced against the weight of the water in the oceans. A pint of water weighs a pound, so our Lord measures the waters in order that He may know their weight. The earth is a ball which rotates upon its axis and therefore it must be balanced, or else it would fly to pieces. God therefore does measure the waters, weigh the hills, and weigh the mountains so that the weight would be equally distributed throughout every part of the earth. The Lord is telling us this great fact so that we may reverence Him, worship Him, and rejoice in the God who can do it, and does do it for our blessing. He is perhaps teaching us that He knows all the troubles, sorrows, disappointments and victories of our lives, and knows how to balance them perfectly to give us a wonderful experience of living.

Psa. 68:16 (b) Here is a picture of the joy and gladness which fills the hearts of the rulers of Israel when God rules and reigns in Jerusalem.

Psa. 114:6 (b) We probably are to learn from this that difficulties and problems, large and small, are no problem to God. He removes all hindrances easily.

Matt. 5:14 (b) This is a type of the blessed influence a Christian exerts when he takes an out and out stand for Christ so that the world can see and recognize his faith.

HIND

Gen. 49:21 (a) This is a picture of the freedom, liberty and enjoyment which this tribe would have in life. Those whom the Lord sets free are free indeed.

2 Sam. 22:34 (a) The hind is the female of the red deer. It is noted for its fleetness and its sure-footedness. The Psalmist is using

this as a type of the ability which God gave him of avoiding King Saul, and other dangerous enemies. It is a picture also of the ability God gives His children to travel easily over the rough paths of life, and to feel at home among the difficulties of life. The hind enjoys the rough mountain terrain. She is sure-footed, she does not seek easy paths. (See also Hab. 3:19; Psa. 18:33) (The "hart" is the male member of the red deer family)

HINGE

1 Ki. 7:50 (c) The hinges tell of the motives which actuate the life of the Christian. The inner motives of the private life, and the outer motive of the public life are to be pure, rich, and valuable as gold is valuable and rich.

HOLE

Isa. 51:1 (a) Evidently this picture represents the depths of sin, evil and wickedness into which a human being may descend.

Hag. 1:6 (b) By this we learn how impossible it is usually to make things go well in this life, to make proper investments and to heap up riches. Somehow or other they leak out, slip away and disappear.

HONEY

Ex. 3:8 (b) Honey and milk are the products of life. The one comes from the living bee, the other from the living cow. The land of Canaan represents that place in the Christian's life wherein by utter consecration he begins to receive his richest blessings from the living Lord on the throne. (See Deut. 8:8)

Deut. 32:13 (a) The rock represents the Lord Jesus, and the honey represents the sweetness, the loveliness and all those precious graces which one receives from Christ by faith.

Lev. 2:11 (c) Here honey represents natural human sweetness. In the sacrifices to the Lord, nothing is acceptable to God except the virtues of Christ. All the natural graces which we admire in one another are to be completely omitted from everything that pertains to sacrifice for sins or for merit before the Lord. Honey is a type of all that is good and best in the human heart and which some desire to offer as a sacrifice for sin.

Judges 14:9 (c) The lion represents the Lord Jesus and the honey represents the lovely and delightful sweetness which the believer enjoys as he comes and takes out of Christ's heart and life the blessings which are so freely given.

Job 20:17 (b) This evidently refers to an abundance of comforts, the luxuries of life, things over and above the natural blessings.

Psa. 19:10 (b) The Word of God is to the soul what honey is to the body. The Scriptures are frequently referred to as honey and the honeycomb. (See Psa. 119:103; Ezek. 3:3; Rev. 10:9.)

HONEYCOMB

Psa. 19:10 (a) The honeycomb seems to be a bit more sweet than the honey which it contains. Perhaps it is the drippings of the honeycomb that are especially sweet. The Word of God is described as this honeycomb. It refers to God's truth as revealed in His Word. The sweetness and the attractiveness of the Word of God are revealed in this passage, and the Song of Solomon 4:11. The kind expressions of helpfulness which are revealed in the Word are indicated in Prov. 16:24 and Prov. 24:13.

Prov. 27:7 (c) Probably the meaning of this passage is that one might become righteous overmuch, as is described in Eccl. 7:16. Sometimes passages are used out of their connection, or magnified beyond their purpose, and this is not profitable nor helpful to those who are occupied therein. The passage also means that if one is not hungry for the things of God, he will not want any help from God. If a person feels that he has enough of religion, or of the knowledge of God, or of salvation, and needs no more, then the finest preaching and teaching will do him no good.

HOOF

Lev. 11:3 (c) The teaching of this passage may be that the hoof which is divided represents a walk that is divided. Those who walk with God should not pretend to be walking with the world. Those who walk with the world should not pretend to the walking with God. The Lord calls us to a path of separation. We are to walk in the Spirit as a consecrated people. Otherwise, we are not true to our Lord.

HOOK

2 Ki. 19:28 (a) This type is used by the Lord to describe His power and ability to return Sennacherib back to his own land, and the ease with which He would do it. It is as though God put a bridle on Sennacherib and directed him back to his own land. It might be described as a farmer putting a ring in the nose of a bull, or a fisherman catching a fish with a hook and line. (See vss. 35 and 37; Isa. 37:29; Prov. 21:1.)

Ezek. 29:4 (a) This figure represents the power of the enemy to subdue and conquer Pharaoh. Assyria was probably the one who used the hook, and the hooks were his various types of warfare and war machines. He chained his captives. The same figure applies to Gog and Magog in Ezek. 38:4. Here it refers especially to that great day when God will come to judge the nations of the earth and to tame their wrath.

HORN

The horn is used as a symbol of power, strength, honor and grandeur. Sometimes it is a good power, and sometimes an evil power. Sometimes it refers to the strength of a nation, other times to the ruler of a nation. Sometimes it refers to a position of elegance and popularity with pride. Only a few cases will be listed to illustrate these truths.

Deut. 33:17 (a) Type of the strength and the power of the two tribes of Joseph.

1 Sam. 2:1 (a) Type of the feelings of victory of Hannah because she was a new mother.

2 Sam. 22:3 (a) Type of God as the power who placed David as King over Israel.

1 Ki. 22:11 (b) Type of the power of the King of Israel in conquering Syria.

Job 16:15 (b) Type of the humbling experience of Job when he lost his all.

Psa. 18:2 (a) Type of the power of God which gave David his position.

Psa. 22:21 (a) God's power is compared to or contrasted with the power of the unicorn which perhaps was the rhinoceros.

Psa. 75:4 (a) Type of the proud rich who wished to exalt their own strength and whom God would humble. (See vs. 10)

Psa. 89:17 (b) Type of the blessing of God because of which the power and excellency of Israel will one day be exalted. (See vs. 24; Psa. 92:10; 112:9; 132:17.)

Psa. 118:27 (c) Probably this means that God will bind us to our decisions when we consecrate our lives to Him.

Lam. 2:3, 17 (b) This is a type of the power of God to reduce the strength of Israel and to increase the power of the enemy.

Jer. 48:25 (b) This is a picture of the power of Moab both for offense and defense, which God took from them and made them weak.

Ezek. 29:21 (b) This is a type in prophecy of the restoration of Israel as a world power.

Ezek. 34:21 (b) A figure of the power of the leaders of Israel who were persecuting the poor.

Dan. 7:7 (b) Here and throughout this book horns are a sign of both men and nations in their power to rule or misrule. The little horns represent kings or generals, or men who rise up out of obscurity and are not well known. The big horns represent mighty kings who become world rulers, such as Alexander the Great.

Dan. 8:3 (a) These two horns represent the two kings as are mentioned.

Dan. 8:8 (b) This figure describes a prominent and well-known ruler.

Amos 6:13 (b) A type of the great power which the people claimed they had created by their own wits and wisdom.

Micah 4:13 (b) By this type God indicates that He will make Israel again a great and strong nation.

Hab. 3:4 The word here is a mistranslation, and it should read "bright beams." It probably indicates that there is power in the light of God and in His wonderful hands of strength.

Zech. 1:18 (a) Here we see four Gentile powers which persecuted and scattered Israel.

Luke 1:69 (a) This is a type of the Lord Jesus by whom and through whom sinners are saved from the wrath to come.

Rev. 5:6 (a) These represent the seven-fold aspect of the Holy Spirit in His power as the seven eyes represent the seven aspects of the Spirit's knowledge.

Rev. 12:3 (a) The figure represents Satan and his mighty power in controlling men.

Rev. 13:1 (a) This type represents Satan's anti-Christ who will have power over the nations.

Rev. 13:11 (a) The type in this case represents the false prophet. Because there are two horns we understand that he has power to exalt the Devil, and also to curse men.

Rev. 17:3, 12 (a) These are the evil powers of the world as represented in the ten kings.

HORSE

Psa. 32:9 (a) This is a warning that the believer should use good judgment, think for himself, and not be just as an animal that must be guided by another.

Psa. 33:17 (b) This is a type of any human resource in which people trust for deliverance instead of in the living God.

Jer. 12:5 (c) This is a peculiar type — the footmen represent ordinary Christians living ordinary Christian lives. They make the unsaved man weary and he wishes to get away from their influence and company. The horses represent Christians who have come to full growth even perhaps those who have already been taken to heaven. If the weak Christian wearies the sinner, how much more will those Christians who have been made like Christ and have been brought into perfect manhood and full stature for God? The sinner would not be able to stand their presence at all.

The horses in Zech. 1 and Zech. 6 probably represent great movements wrought by God in dealing with men.

Zech. 6:2 (b) The red horse — a type of the destructive power of war. (See also Rev. 6:4)

Zech. 6:3 (b) The black horse — represents world-wide famine which naturally follows great wars both international and internal. (See also Rev. 6:5.) Each person receives his food by weight.

Zech 6:3 (b) Bay horse — probably represents the scourge of pestilence and disease which follows upon the famine that follows the war. (See also Rev. 6:8)

Zech. 6:3 (b) The white horse — probably represents a man-made peace which will be forced upon the world by the anti-Christ under the guise of religion and righteousness. It will be a false peace which will not stand. (See also Rev. 6:2)

Rev. 19:11 (b) The white horse — typical of the great power which the Lord Jesus will exhibit in righteousness and justice when He comes forth from heaven as the Almighty Conqueror.

HOUSE

Deut. 7:8 (a) This is a reference to the nation of Egypt. (See also 8:14.)

Deut. 25:10 (a) The type here is used to describe a family or the line of generation. (See also Ruth 4:12; Judges 8:35; 9:6; 10:9; 1 Sam. 3:14; 2 Sam. 3:1.) In quite a number of places throughout the Scriptures the word "house" is used as a reference to a family in various generations, or to a nation.

Isa. 66:1 (b) This is a type of the building which the Lord expects each believer to construct in his life for the glory of God and the blessing of men. This house must have a right foundation, Jesus Christ: a heating plant to keep the heart and soul on fire for God; a kitchen so that the food may be prepared for the soul; a library for the education and instruction of the mind; a music room to keep the heart singing; a parlor for hospitality; a bedroom for rest; a bath room for cleansing; an attic for storage; and also the light of the Word and the water of the Spirit.

Matt. 7:26 (a) Refers to the kind of life one builds for eternity. If he builds on Christ, his life will stand the tests of time and eternity. If he builds on character, morals, tradition or false religions, it will be destroyed under the storm of God's wrath.

2 Cor. 5:1 (a) This refers to the physical body in which we live.

1 Tim. 3:15 (a) This is a name applied to the entire church of God composed of all believers.

2 Tim. 2:20 (b) This type refers to the church of God in which there are some who are very valuable, and other people who do not seem to be so important. In every home there are beautiful vases, and other valuable vessels in the parlor. They are expensive, attractive, and receive much attention from the visitors. In the kitchen of the same home there are the skillet, the teakettle, the baking pans, and other such inferior vessels. They are just as essential, or more so, than those in the parlor. We could keep house without those in the parlor, but we would not get along very well without those in the kitchen. Our Lord is telling us that if we purge ourselves from the sins that are mentioned in the early part of this chapter, the entangling with the world, the attractiveness of sins, the mishandling of the Word of God, profane babbling, and false teachings, then we shall be vessels unto honor. Some of us will serve in the kitchen, and others in the parlor.

Heb. 3:5-6 (b) In verse 5 the type represents the nation of Israel. In verse 6 it represents the church of God, of which the Lord Jesus is the head.

HUNGER

Isa. 49:10 (b) This refers to the time when Israel is restored as a nation and will be satisfied again with God, His Word, and His ways. Their desire for peace, comfort and prosperity will be gratified. (See John 6:35)

Matt. 5:6 (b) This represents a deep desire for God, as David so often desired. (See Luke 1:53)

Luke 15:17 (b) the prodigal could never find heart satisfaction away from his father's house. He felt deeply the need of the blessings that came from being associated with his father. So the child of God must be in fellowship with God to be happy.

HUNGRY

Psa. 107:5, 9 (a) This type represents the deep heart desire which comes in a human heart when it realizes the need of God. The soul reaches out after God, and is only satisfied when it finds in Him that which fills the need of the soul.

HUSBAND

Jer. 31:32 (a) God uses this type to illustrate His deep love for Israel, and His devotion to their needs. He protected them, preserved them, and provided for them. Instead of a response from their hearts of loving affection, they turned against Him to worship idols. (See also Hosea 2:2)

2 Cor. 11:2 (a) By this we understand the relationship of the Lord Jesus to those who are saved by His grace, and who constitute His bride.

HYSSOP

Ex. 12:22 (c) A type of faith in action wherein the precious blood of Christ is applied to the door of the heart.

Psa. 51:7 (b) A type of the blessed work of the Lord wherein He applies to us the precious blood and cleanses from all sin.

I

IDLE

Matt. 12:36 (a) The words mentioned here are spoken words which do no good work for God or man. Idle men are men who are not working. Idle words are words that are not working. They are words which when spoken have no value whatever to either God or man.

Matt. 20:3 (b) This is a picture of Christians who have not taken up any definite work for God but who are spectators in the game of life so far as the church and the gospel are concerned.

Luke 24:11 (b) These tales are stories that have no usable point, give no information, and have no value for their hearers.

IDOL

Jer. 22:28 (a) This type refers to a man who had been extolled by the people and then had been cast down. The hopes of the people were wrecked with his downfall.

Zech. 11:17 (a) This is a reference to a religious leader who, after winning the hearts of his people, deserts them and leaves them empty, hungry and helpless.

1 John 5:21 (b) An idol in the Christian's life is anything or any person that takes the heart and love away from the Lord or that comes between the child of God and God. It may be money, fame, pleasure, companionship, or even a religious activity.

INCENSE

Ex. 30:1 (c) A figure of the sweet, fragrant life of the Lord Jesus offered up to God during His life of suffering and death of agony wherein and wherewith God was well pleased.

INCENSE (Strange)

Ex. 30:9 (c) In this case, the strange incense is a figure of human activities and religious performances which are offered to God for His acceptance in competition with and instead of the life of the Lord Jesus. It is human merit substituted for Christ's merit.

INK

2 Cor. 3:3 (b) As in physical life, ink is used to make impressions upon paper, so in spiritual life, the Holy Spirit is the medium by and through whom impressions are made on human hearts. The ink is in contrast to the Holy Spirit.

INN

Luke 10:34 (c) The inn is a type of the church which should be full of Christians to nurse the new-born babes in the spiritual realm and to bind up the wounds of those who have been hurt in life's battle.

INVENTION

Psa. 99:8 (b) The habits and ways of men which are not of God but which gratify the animal lust in man are called by this name.

Eccl. 7:29 (b) Men have devised and contrived schemes and plans to gratify and satisfy their sinful cravings. Such was never intended by God.

IRON

Psa. 2:9 (b) This evidently refers to the severe judgment that the Lord Jesus will execute against all His enemies.

Eccl. 10:10 (c) We understand by this that if the mind is not acute, and the spirit of man is not alert, and if the understanding is not clear, then more effort must be put into the work that is being done. It probably has a direct reference to the fact that those who teach and preach must know the subject well, must be enthused in the matter, must have original thoughts, and must know how to present the subject to others in an effective way.

Isa. 10:34 (b) This picture represents the irresistible power of God to destroy all wicked leaders and evildoers.

Isa. 45:2 (b) By this we understand that God will destroy every opponent and remove every hindrance to His will.

Isa. 48:4 (a) This type represents the hard, stiff, unbending attitude of Israel toward God in that they refused to obey Him, and to walk in His ways.

Jer. 1:18 (a) God promised the prophet that he would be able to stand and to withstand all the opposition of the enemies of God in Israel.

Jer. 15:12 (b) This question refers to the fact that Israel as iron would be able to conquer and destroy two northern kingdoms which would be very strong in themselves. These two kingdoms may be the Syrians and the Chaldonians.

Jer. 28:13 (b) As wood is easily broken, but iron cannot be broken, so the oppression of former invaders would not be as severe and difficult as the oppression brought by Nebuchadnezzar.

Ezek. 4:3 (b) This strange passage may have several meanings. It may refer to the fact that the kingdom which shall come to besiege Jerusalem will be hard and irresistible. Or, it may mean that the prophet's message would not reach the hearts of the people in Jerusalem because of the hardness of their hearts, and their resistance to the things of God.

Dan. 2:33 (b) This represents the strength that will characterize the world empires.

Dan. 7:7 (b) This is a picture of the fierceness and power that will characterize the revived Roman Empire.

Amos 1:3 (a) The type in this passage represents the power and strength of the invaders from Damascus.

Micah 4:13 (b) By this figure is described the victorious power of the conquering armies of Israel.

1 Tim. 4:2 (a) As heat destroys the feeling in any part that is burned, so sinning dulls the conscience about God and His Word.

Rev. 2:27 (b) This indicates the stern force that our Lord Jesus will use in conquering the rebellious nations of earth. (See also Psa. 2:9; Rev. 12:5; 19:15.)

ISAAC

Gen. 22:9 (c) He is a type of the Lord Jesus being offered up by His own Father for the sins of man. He is also a type of the sinner who should be punished for his sins but who finds a substitute in the Lord Jesus, represented by the ram caught in the thicket.

ISRAEL

Gen. 32:28 (c) In that this is a new name given to Jacob, it is a type of the new relationship of the believer when he trusts Christ and becomes a Christian. Israel has been used as a type of the church because they were under the blood of the Passover Lamb, they had a High Priest, they were separate from the nations, and they confessed that they were pilgrims looking for a city with foundations.

Some types which represent Israel in various aspects:

Adulterers, Hosea 7:4 (a)
Bride, Isa. 62:5 (a)
Brood, Luke 13:34 (b)
Cake not turned, Hosea 7:8 (a)
Caldron, Ezek. 11:3 (a)
Calves of the stall, Mal. 4:2 (a)
Cedar Trees, Num. 24:6 (b)
Chickens, Matt. 23:37 (a)
Dust, Gen. 13:16 (a)
Fig Tree, Matt. 24:32 (b)
Great Lion, Num. 23:24 (b)
Heifer (backsliding) Hosea 4:16 (a)
Jonah, Jonah 1:17 (c)
Lign aloes, Num. 24:6 (a)
Olive tree, Rom. 11:17 (b)
Sand, Gen. 22:17 (a)
Seething pot, Jer. 1:13 (a)
Sheep of His hand, Psa. 95:7 (a)
Sheep of His pasture, Psa. 100:3 (a)

Silly dove, Hosea 7:11 (a)
Spring of water, Isa. 58:11 (a)
Stars, Gen. 22:17 (a)
Trees, Psa. 104:16 (b)
Unicorn, Num. 24:8 (a)
Vine, Ezek. 15:6 (a)
Virgin, 2 Kings 19:21 (b)
Watered garden, Isa. 58:11 (a)

ISSACHAR

Gen. 49:14 (c) He is a type of the Lord Jesus bearing God's burden for man and man's burden for sin, thus making it possible for man to rest. Also a type of the Christian who bears God's burden for the lost and man's burden in his need of rest and redemption.

ITCHING

2 Tim. 4:3 (b) This refers to teachers who utter things which they know will please the people so that the people will praise them for their messages and their ministry. It probably refers in this place to teachers of false doctrines, and platitudes which please the hearers. It may mean that the people want to hear what pleases them.

IVORY

Psa. 45:8 (b) Some think that this refers to the mouth, the ivory being the teeth, and the fragrance, the praise and worship that comes from the mouth.

Song of Sol. 5:14 (c) This describes the unusual value and the striking beauty which the bride saw in the bridegroom. Words that lovers use are not always first class diction. The heart pours out its affection in words that best express the feelings. (See also chap. 7:4)

Amos 3:15 (b) This is descriptive of the destruction that awaits the wealth and the provisions for ease and comfort made by the ungodly.

J

JACOB

Gen. 25:26 (c) This is a type, throughout his life, of the Christian who, though he fails and falls, quickly builds an altar, brings the Lamb of God by faith, and hides under Calvary and the precious blood for every sin. Though Jacob often wandered, he returned to God at once. He wanted to know God. He wrestled during the season with God. He gave liberally to God. God is "the God of Jacob." (See also chap. 49:24, and other places.)

JASPER

Rev. 4:3 (c) Probably a very valuable stone, translucent or transparent, typical of the preciousness of our God in whom there is no flaw, defilement, evil, nor spot of any kind. He was beautiful, precious, valuable and attractive. (See also Rev. 21:11).

JAW

Job 29:17 (b) A graphic description of the way Job hindered the wicked from injuring the poor, the widows, and others who were helpless.

Prov. 30:14 (b) Solomon describes the cruel wickedness of the oppressors of his day who sought to injure the poor and needy.

Isa. 30:28 (b) In this case, "the people" are the nations that oppress Israel. They are compared to a horse. God's power controls them as a driver controls the horse by the bit and the bridle. God will lead them to listen to bad counsel and to carry out wrong plans so that they will be defeated in their purposes.

JERICHO

Luke 10:30 (c) In this passage, Jerusalem represents the place of Christian privileges and Jericho represents the way of the world. The verse presents this trip as a path downward.

JERUSALEM

Gal. 4:26 (a) This is a type of the true faith of God. Also a type of the free life by the Son through His Truth.

Heb. 12:22 (a) The name given to our eternal home in glory and also to the present church.

Rev. 21:2 (a) A description of the place in which we shall live and dwell in happy fellowship with God and His Son through eternity.

JEWEL

Gen. 24:53 (c) In this passage the servant represents the Holy Spirit who brings gifts from the Father and the Son to the bride who will one day be at the marriage supper of the Lamb. Jewels are made by God. Men polish them and make them fit to be worn by the queen. These gems represent people which have been taken by the Lord, worked upon by Him, and prepared to bring joy to His heart throughout eternity. Only the Holy Spirit can do this work in the heart and life of a believer.

Prov. 11:22 (a) This gem represents the attractiveness, loveliness and beauty of an unsaved woman. The swine with the snout represents the unrighteous life which this beautiful woman may live. The woman herself needs to be saved, and become a child of God, then these gems of beauty will really adorn the person.

Prov. 20:15 (a) Beautiful and wise words adorn the lives of those who walk with God, and seek to please Him in their conversation.

Song of Sol. 1:10 (c) This is a lover's comment on the beauty and the sweetness of the one to whom he is attracted. (See also chap. 7:1; Isa. 61:10.) The joints represent her graceful movements and actions, making her attractive in all her work and ministry for her lover. Her words from the mouth are beautiful and her ways are also attractive.

Ezek. 16:12 (a) In this way is described the graces and beautiful characteristics which God gave to Israel in her balmy days of prosperity. (See also vss. 17 and 39; chap. 23:26.)

Mal. 3:17 (b) God's people are compared to beautiful gems. Through the vicissitudes of life they are polished and made fit for His presence. In heaven God puts together for eternity those Christians who seem best suited to each other, whose nature makes them beautiful together, and probably they were those who lived and served together on the earth. Tares were bound in bundles to be burned, while God's people were arranged together to be honored and blessed.

JEZEBEL

Rev. 2:20 (b) She is a type of religious groups which teach and practice things opposed to the truth of God and which lead to a dissolute and wicked life.

JOB

Ezek. 14:14 (a) An example of one who can and did pray the prayer of faith which moved God to perform miracles. (See also James 5:11.)

JONAH

Matt. 12:40 (a) This figure is used by the Lord as a type of Himself in that He was to be three days and three nights in the heart of the earth, as Jonah was three days and three nights in the whale's belly.

Also a type of the believer who, being given a commission by God, seeks to avoid it and evade it, but eventually is brought back into God's path (Jonah 3:3)

Also a type of Israel the nation now scattered among the nations but who will be cast out by them so they may return to their own land. (Jonah 1:17)

JORDAN

Psa. 42:6 (c) This represents a beautiful Christian life in which the stream of God (the Holy Spirit) refreshes the soul and enriches the life.

Jer. 12:5 (b) This verse is very appropriate in these days. The river probably refers to the time of death. It is usually taken as an emblem of the stream which separates us from the city of God. The argument evidently is that if in this life the people of this world are wearied with the realities of eternity, what would be their condition if they were transported across the river into heaven, where there are none of the things that attract the unsaved. If, in the company of believers here, with their anemic and emanciated type of Christianity they are disgusted, what would these people do when brought face to face with death, and the realities that must be faced after death.

JOSEPH

Gen. 37:9-10 (c) This character is a type of the Lord Jesus in many respects. Forty-two different aspects of Christ may be seen in his life. In this Scripture, Joseph is a type of Christ in that he is honored by his father and mother. They and all of his brothers must bow down in obeisance to him, as every knee shall bow to Christ.

Gen. 43:3 (c) Here Joseph is a true type of God, the Judge, and Benjamin is a type of the Lord Jesus. It is almost a repetition of that beautiful truth in John 14:6. No man can see the Father's face unless he comes with the Lord Jesus, the elder brother.

Gen. 49:22 (c) This is a type of the fruitful Christian who, though persecuted and hindered by others, nevertheless continues to bear fruit in the regions round about as well as in the home parish. Israel was to be a blessing to Gentiles.

JOSHUA

Josh. 1:1 (c) He is a type of the Lord Jesus who, as the Commander and Leader of His people, conquers their enemies and leads them in triumph into blessed resting places.

JOT

Matt. 5:18 (a) This is "jod" of the Hebrew alphabet. It occurs just before Psalm 119:73. It has a numerical value of ten and is used in the Hebrew language both as a letter and as a number and also as an article by which the value and meaning of another letter is changed. It is the smallest letter in the Hebrew alphabet. Our Lord uses it to show the very great care which He exercises over the smallest details of the Scripture.

JOY

Neh. 8:10 (c) This is symbolical of the great satisfaction in the heart of our Lord over the victory made possible by His provision for sin and for the sinner. He was well pleased with His work in creation. He is well pleased with His work in salvation. He will be pleased in the final consummation. We are strong in His victory.

JUDAS

Matt. 26:47 (c) He is generally used as a type of the ingrate who turns traitor to the friend he should love and becomes an enemy of one to whom he is deeply indebted.

JUNIPER

1 Kings 19:4 (c) This is a tree which probably represents a defeated spirit, a disappointed life, and a depressed soul. We should always have an axe handy to cut down the juniper tree.

Job 30:4 (c) This indicates that these disappointed and depressed people were feeding on their miseries.

K

KEY

Isa. 22:22 (b) By this figure our Lord is describing the right of Jesus Christ to rule and to reign. He only can consign men to heaven or to hell. He has never delegated this power to another. (See Rev. 1:18)

Matt. 16:19 The two keys given to Peter were evidently the two gospels: one gospel for the Jews which included baptism for the remission of sins; the other gospel for the Gentiles in which salvation is by faith alone. By means of these two gospel keys, Peter was used of God to bring thousands to Christ.

Luke 11:52 (b) This key is probably the person of the Lord Jesus Himself for when He is ignored, overlooked, or denied in the Scriptures, then there can be no knowledge of the truth of God, nor of the will of God.

Rev. 1:18 (a) The Lord Jesus controls the destiny of the soul. He alone can send a man to hell. He alone decides the day of one's death. His will and decision in these matters is described as a key.

Rev. 3:7 (a) This represents the right of the Lord Jesus to erect the throne of David again, to sit upon it, and to execute sovereign powers. This right is described as a key.

Rev. 9:1 (a) The key in this passage represents the divine right and power given by God to the angel to open and close the pit of hell in order that the purposes of God might be performed.

KICK

1 Sam. 2:29 (b) This represents the attitude of God's people as they complained against God's rules of living.

Acts 9:5 (b) By this we understand the actions of Paul as he opposed the Lord Jesus and the new revelations which Christ brought. Paul was only hurting himself, injuring his soul, and fighting against God by his opposition.

KICKED

Deut. 32:15 (b) Israel refused to work for God and they rebelled against His restraint and His program.

KID

Deut. 14:21 (b) This is a type of the life of a young person. The milk which should have sustained the little kid was used instead to boil it. The Lord does not want us to use for destructive purposes that which He has given us for constructive use. The practice of stewing the kid in the mother's milk was observed by oriental farmers as a means of blessing on their crops. They would make the stew, mix water with it to give volume, and then sprinkle this over the fields in order to make them fertile and more productive. The Lord warns people not to resort to these heathen expedients but rather to look to Him and depend upon Him for blessing on their fields and crops. (See also Ex. 23:19 and Ex. 34:26.) (See also under MILK.)

1 Sam. 10:3 (c) This is probably a type of the Lord Jesus, the young man, offered as a sacrifice. As each of these three men had an entire kid for himself, so each believer may have all of the Lord Jesus for himself. Christ is not divided. All of His ministry, all of His work, all of His grace is for each individual believer.

Luke 15:29 (c) This is a type of the Lord Jesus unrecognized, unused, and unappreciated by those who should have known Him best.

KIDNEY

Ex. 29:13 (c) This figure probably indicates those secret activities of the life which are occupied with unpleasant things which should not be made known, and yet are necessary and must be given into.

KINDLE

Isa. 50:11 (b) This is a graphic description of the formation of human opinions, the building up of human religious plans, and the designing of human experiments in spiritual things.

Jer. 17:4 (b) This is a type of the initiation and growth of wicked devices which arouse God's anger.

Ezek. 20:47 (b) This represents the forming of God's wrath against those who rejected His Lordship and refused His sovereignty.

Luke 12:49 (b) This marks the beginning of the constant turmoil and trouble which is always present when Christ is loved by some and hated by others.

James 3:5 (b) This represents the beginning of a great time of trouble caused by some little word or thoughtless expression which separates friends and begins a time of strife between hearts.

KINE

Gen. 41:2 (a) These represent seven years of plenty which were shortly to come. Verses 3 to 7 represent seven years of famine and want.

Deut. 28:4 (c) By this it is indicated that the labor of the godly will be blessed and will be very fruitful.

Amos 4:1 (a) Here is a type of the proud, wealthy and wicked rulers of Israel.

KINSMAN

Ruth 4:14 (c) This may be taken as a type of our Redeemer, Jesus Christ, who bought us with His blood and has taken us to be His bride.

KING

Song of Sol. 1:4 (c) In this way we see the Lord Jesus Christ in His glory as the sovereign ruler of His church.

KISS

This is a sign of trust and affection, either true or false. A few Scriptures are given herewith to show the many ways in which the word "kiss" is used in the Scriptures:

Gen. 27:26 (c) Kiss of devotion
Gen. 45:15 (c) Kiss of reconciliation
Gen. 50:1 (c) The farewell kiss
Ruth 1:14 (c) Kiss of desertion
1 Sam. 10:1 (c) Kiss of honor
1 Sam. 20:41 (c) Kiss of confidence
2 Sam. 15:5 (c) Kiss of treason
2 Sam. 20:9 (c) Kiss of hypocrisy
Job 31:27 (c) Kiss of connivance
Psa. 2:12 (c) Kiss of trust
Psa. 85:10 (c) Kiss of justice
Prov. 7:13 (c) Kiss of impudence
Prov. 27:6 (c) The enemy's kiss
S. of Sol. 1:2 (c) Kiss of affection
Luke 7:45 (c) Kiss of gratitude
Luke 22:48 (c) Kiss of betrayal
Acts 20:37 (c) Kiss of sorrow
Rom. 16:16 (c) Holy kiss of saints

KNEE

Isa. 45:23 (a) A type of submission to Christ in the day of His power. (See also Phil. 2:10.)

Ezek. 47:4 (b) The Holy Spirit affects our life of devotion.

Heb. 12:12 (b) This is a picture of the week, depressed and distressed Christian.

KNIFE

Prov. 23:2 (b) Type of self-restraint and the crucifixion of fleshly desires.

KNIT

Judges 20:11 (c) Typical of union and cooperation between all the forces.

1 Sam. 18:1 (a) This is a beautiful picture of hearts that are joined sweetly and firmly together. (See also 1 Chron. 12:17.)

Col. 2:2 (b) This figure indicates that each was willing for the other to be "on top" part of the time. In knitting, the threads take turns being "over" and "under" each other.

Col. 2:19 (b) This is a figure to describe the fellowship of believing hearts. In knitting, one thread is over and then under, then over, then under. It indicates a willingness to be humbled and to have the low place part of the time, and to let the other person be exalted part of the time.

KNOP

Ex. 25:31 (c) These knops were ornaments on the candlestick. They represent those beautiful traits of character which should adorn the Christian life and cause the Christian's faith to be admired by others.

L

LADDER

Gen. 28:12 (c) We are made to realize that there is a way to glory from earth. There is a way for us to approach to God in prayer, and then return to the fields of labor bringing with us heaven's blessings.

LADY

Isa. 47:5 (b) This name is a description of the city of Babylon. It had been a beautiful city, with hanging gardens, parks, and very gorgeous robes on its soldiers. This verse is prophesying that it will no longer have that grandeur, but will be brought down to desolation and destruction.

LAMB

Gen. 22:7 (b) It is quite evident that this lamb is a type of the Lord Jesus Christ who was described by John as "the Lamb of God." Abraham's reply indicates the same truth, for he said "God will provide Himself a lamb for a burnt offering." It does not say He will "provide for Himself." The Lord Jesus was and is one of the persons of the Godhead, and He gave His own self to be a sacrifice.

Ex. 13:13 (b) In this place again the Lord Jesus is evidently the anti-type, while we are represented by the ass. The Scripture says "man is born a wild ass's colt." Each one of us must be redeemed by the blood of the Lord Jesus, the Lamb of God, or else we shall be punished ourselves.

Lev. 23:12 (c) The Lord Jesus was inspected before He was offered as the Passover Lamb. Pilate's wife inspected Him socially. Pilate inspected Him for the civil government. Herod inspected Him for the military government. Judas inspected Him from the standpoint of personal fellowship. The Centurion inspected Him as a law-enforcement officer. All of them found Him without a blemish, and therefore fit from the human standpoint to be the Lamb of God.

Prov. 27:26 (c) It may be that this also is a picture of the Lord Jesus in that we must be clothed with Him as the Scripture says, "Put ye on the Lord Jesus Christ." The garment of salvation, and the robe of righteousness are just His own wonderful self given to us to cover all our sins and discrepancies.

John 1:29 (a) The Lord Jesus is often compared to a lamb, and for many reasons. The lamb was used for food, and the Saviour has told us to eat of Him. The lamb is used for growing wool to make warm garments, and so we are clothed with Christ that we may be accepted by God in Him. The lamb was an acceptable sacrifice to God, and so the Saviour offered Himself to God as our sacrifice. The lamb was used as the Passover sacrifice, and the Scripture says, "Christ our Passover is sacrificed for us." The lamb is a gentle creature, and our Lord said he was "meek and lowely in heart." The lamb does not object to being sheared or killed, and so "He was led as a lamb to the slaughter, and as a sheep before her shearer is dumb, so He opened not His mouth."

Rev. 5:6 (a) Throughout the book of Revelation, the Lord Jesus is presented under the type of "a lamb as it had been slain." It appears that Christ constantly bears the marks of the crucifixion, and that He still has the wounded hands, feet, side, back, head and face. God will never let us forget that the Lord Jesus became a sacrifice for our sins, and for ourselves. He is called "the Lamb" in order to keep this truth constantly before the hearts and minds of saved and unsaved in eternity. The sufferings of the lost are said to be "in the presence of the holy angels, and of the Lamb."

LAME

Lev. 21:18 (c) Undoubtedly the lame man in this passage is a type of the Christian or the professing Christian who does not walk in a straight path and in fellowsip with God. Such a one would not be suitable as a servant of the Lord, or a leader of the people.

Deut. 15:21 (c) The sacrifice that is offered to the Lord must be perfect. Every sacrifice which man offers outside of Christ is defective, and cannot stand divine inspection. Christ alone is the only perfect sacrifice.

2 Sam. 9:3 (c) Many evangelists use this figure as a type of all sinners. Everybody is lame on the feet in a spiritual sense. The walk is not what it should be. The ways of men are not perfect and godly as they should be. We therefore receive "the kindness of God," the feet are put under the table out of sight, while we sit at the King's banquet, and enjoy His fellowship after the King accepts us.

Prov. 26:7 (b) Our Lord is describing to us the fact that we naturally go wrong and walk in a crooked path. Very few men, if any, can walk in a straight path where the footprints can be seen, as in the snow. One leg is longer than the other. All of us are lame in the spiritual sense. It is a natural thing with everybody.

Isa. 33:23 (c) Here is a very beautiful way of telling us that those who realize their weakness and their insufficiency are usually those who come to God for help and receive from Him the blessings He gives.

Heb. 12:13 (b) Men are not always strong and vigorous in their spiritual life. Some are weak Christians and stumble along the way instead of being able to stand for the faith, resisting the enemy. We are called upon to so walk, live, act and talk that weak Christians will be strengthened in their faith and made to stand strong for the Lord.

LAMP

Gen. 15:17 (c) Here we find a picture of the experience of Israel in Egypt. They were to have terrible oppression and suffering which was described as a smoking furnace, but in the midst of this they were to have the Word of God and the teaching of God's truth which is represented by the burning lamp. God never failed even in the darkest hour to send the light of His truth to the people.

Ex. 25:37 (c) The lampstand had seven branches, and these are generally taken to represent the seven-fold Spirit of God who is the Spirit of light. It is also taken by some to represent the perfect testimony of the Word of God. Others think that they represent the ministry of the church which gives out the light of the gospel. All three may be true, for certainly these golden lamps do represent all these three sources of light.

Judg. 7:16 (c) In this account the pitcher probably represents the believer. The lamp probably represents the light that is in the believer, the indwelling Spirit of God, and the wonderful light-giving Word of God. The pitcher must be broken that the light may shine out. The believer must be broken in spirit, humble and contrite, that the light may shine from him. Nothing earthly must interfere.

1 Ki. 15:4 (b) Here is a figure of the testimony and life of King David. These were left to his children. They were to exhibit the faith which David had and to carry on the testimony which David maintained. (See also Psalm 132:17)

Job 12:5 (b) This lamp represents the Word of God and the counsel of the Lord. That person who is ready to leave the path of righteousness and walk with the world does not want counsel or advice either from the Word of God, or from the child of God. He despises both.

Job 41:19 (c) Probably this is just a poetic way of telling of the terror produced by the hideous noises that come from the mouths of enraged animals. It may have a counterpart somehow in describing the vile and wicked expressions that come from the mouths of the ungodly who seek to destroy much good.

Psa. 119:105 (a) The Word of God is the lamp which lights the way through life and illuminates the path to glory. Those who walk in the light of the Word of God live godly, consecrated lives which are fruitful, helpful and pleasant. (See also Prov. 6:23)

Prov. 13:9 (b) The Lord tells us in this passage, as well as in other portions, that the influence of the wicked, and the memory of them, as well as their public testimony, will be blotted out, for they have no value to God. (See also Prov. 20:20)

Isa. 62:1 (a) The gospel of God's grace began at Jerusalem with our Lord Jesus and has spread throughout the world. Thus this Scripture has been fulfilled.

Ezek. 1:13 (a) The living creatures represent four aspects of the Lord Jesus Christ. The fire represents the judgment that emanates from Him as the Judge of all the earth. The lamps represent the Holy Spirit of God in His seven aspects, and as coming from the Lord Jesus who is the giver of the Holy Spirit.

Dan. 10:6 (a) This may he another representation of the Lord Jesus Christ whose eyes shine with the glory of God, and penetrate the heart and soul of those with whom He deals.

Matt. 25:1 (a) It is generally believed that these lamps refer to the testimony of these virgins. Some testimonies are beautiful explanations and expressions of human experiences, but which lack the Spirit of Life. Others give testimonies in which it is clear to be seen that the Holy Spirit indited both the experience and the expression. The oil represents the presence of the Holy Spirit Himself, and when He is present the testimony of the one who speaks savors of heaven and presents a spiritual tone which is absent in other testimonies.

Rev. 4:5 (a) The passage tells us that these lamps do represent the Holy Spirit in His wonderful sevenfold aspect. The Spirit gives light and life. He directs the way. He teaches the truth of God. He anoints for service. He reveals wicked ways and evil doctrines. He guides the feet in the way of peace. He illuminates the soul with the light of heaven.

Rev. 8:10 (a) The lamp which fell from heaven was either an angel or a superman. The lamp represents the testimony and the message which that unusual person brought to the earth. The message which he gave was bitter as wormwood and deadly in its effect on the souls of men.

LANTERN

John 18:3 (c) This figure may be used as a picture of the intellect of man seeking to find out God and Christ by searching. Man brings his light in an endeavor to find God. Christ is the Light of Life. All of man's intellectual lightness falls into an eclipse in the light of the Son of God. Man cannot find God by reasonings or deductions.

LANDMARK

Deut. 19:14 (c) This may be used as a figure whereby we are to recognize the rights of others, and not defraud our neighbors. (See Deut. 27:17)

Prov. 22:28 (c) We should learn by this that we are to see and ask for the old paths which God has set by His prophets and apostles. Let us beware of new religions invented by men and women. (See Prov. 23:10)

LANES

Luke 14:21 (c) The streets refer to the public places, and the lanes refer to the out-of-the-way places where people live in more or less obscurity. This is also described as "highways and hedges." This refers to the easy places to reach and the difficult places to enter. (See vs. 23)

LAPPETH

Judges 7:5 (b) Evidently those who thus drank were on their feet ready to go. They were ready for the war at a moment's notice. The others who go on their knees were off-guard and not ready to go. This is a picture of being ready "in season, out of season."

LATCHET

Gen. 14:23 (c) Abraham thus shows his disdain for the slightest favor which might be offered him by an idolatrous king. He would not accept the slightest gift from one who was an enemy of God.

Mark 1:7 (c) John uses the least of the things on the person of Jesus to illustrate his own feelings of utter unworthiness in the presence of his Lord.

LATTICE

S. of Sol. 2:9 (c) It may be that this indicates an obscured vision of the Lord. Some do not see clearly the value of Christ. This probably is because of either bad teaching, or no teaching. The lattice will be taken away if we study the Word of God, under the teaching of the Spirit of God. We shall then see our lovely Lord clearly.

LAUGH

Psa. 2:4 (a) By this is indicated God's complete supremacy as He looks with scorn on the feeble efforts of man to reject His Son from being ruler of this world. (See also Psa. 37:13)

Prov. 1:26 (a) By this is described the terrible condition of one who invites God's rejection, repudiation and wrath in the day when he needs the Lord the most. There is no mercy after death.

LAVER

Ex. 30:18 (c) This may be used as a type of the Word of God. (See Psa. 119:9, Eph. 5:26.) No size is given for the laver, nor do we know how it was carried. We do not know the depth, the scope, nor the value of the Word of God. There is no rule about how God's Word is to be carried here and there from heart to heart. The laver is a beautiful picture of all of this.

LAW

Also called testimony, commandments, statutes, precepts, judgments, the Word, and words.

Called "Law of Moses" 1 Ki. 2:3

Called "Law of the Lord" 2 Ki. 10:31

Called "Law of God" Rom. 7:22

Called "Law of the Spirit" Rom 8:2

Called "Law of Righteousness" Rom. 9:31

Called "Law of Liberty" Jas. 2:12

Jas. 2:12 (a) This is the law that operates when there is no restraint nor hindrance. We judge a lion by the way he would act if free, and not by the way he acts in the cage. So God will judge people by the way they act when they are free to do as they please, and no one sees or knows of their actions.

God's law is like a light Psa. 119:130

God's law is like a lamp Psa. 119:105

God's law is like a hammer Jer. 23:29

God's law is like a fire Jer. 23:29

God's law is like a seed Luke 8:11

God's law is like water Eph. 5:26

God's law is like a sword Heb. 4:12

LEAD (metal)

Zech. 5:7 (b) The ephah is a unit of measure. The size of it was according to God's command, as in Ezek. 45:11. God measures and weighs every part of the earth. This weight of "lead" assures us that God will hold down or preserve honesty in measurements throughout the earth when His people (Israel and the church, the two women) shall be fully controlled by the Holy Spirit (the wind), and shall be established among men.

LEAF

Gen. 3:7 (c) These leaves represent the actions and ways of human beings who attempt to hide their sins under their own righteous acts and deeds. As Adam and Eve made these transient coverings for themselves, and used the things which would soon shrink and fade, so self-righteous sinners try to cover up their evil deeds and wicked ways by good works and religious performances. You will note that Adam and Eve hid from God after they made the fig leaf aprons. They themselves realized that the aprons did not hide them from the eyes of God. Only the precious blood of Christ avails to hide our sins from a holy Judge.

Psa. 1:3 (b) This type illustrates the bright, attractive, happy life which is lived by that individual in whom is the life of God. As the leaf reveals the kind of tree that it is on, so the life of the individual reveals whether or not he belongs to Jesus Christ. Leaves usually represent a profession, but not necessarily the possession of eternal life.

Isa. 6:13 (b) By this we are taught that though one may be a Christian and have the real gift of eternal life, he may be having a winter-time in his experience, when the leaves are not to be seen. A live tree may have no leaves on it because of the conditions that exist.

Isa. 64:6 (a) As leaves fade, so the human life fades. Some grow more beautiful as they grow older. They become more attractive with age. As many leaves grow more beautiful, waxen, and tinted when they are ready to fall, so some lives are more glorious in their closing days. Other leaves, however, fade in a most unattractive way. They are sear, yellow, worm-eaten, curled, shrunken, and very unsightly. No one wants them. They are quickly swept up and burned. Many lives are like that. The individual grows sour, fault-finding, critical, demanding, and there is no grief when he falls and is swept away into eternity.

Jer. 17:8 (b) By this figure we are taught that the person who walks with God in happy communion with Him will be a constant testimony and will continually bear fruit for God. The leaves represent both confession and profession. The godly Christian will never hide his identity with Christ, but will always be confessing Him.

Ezek. 17:9 (b) In this graphic way the Lord is telling us that in the time of persecution Israel would lose her identity with God and would no longer profess to be the people of God. They do retain their physical identity but their spirituality has disappeared. The present nation of Israel is a godless nation, with no recognition at all of the great truths of the sacrifices, the temple, and the Lord God.

Ezek. 47:12 (b) Here we see a type of the constancy, beauty and certainty of the profession and confession of the real child of God. The believer is represented as God's tree, planted in God's Word, and permeated by the Spirit of God.

Dan. 4:12-21 (b) By this figure we are told that the profession and identity of the great king were clear, plain and definite until God cast him down from his throne.

Matt. 21:19 (b) In this way we learn of the empty profession of the nation of Israel who claimed to be God's people. Their hearts were not right with God, and they produced no fruit for His glory. This figure also may apply to individuals who are members of some church, are active in the Christian life, and yet are not themselves saved by grace, and redeemed by the blood.

Rev. 22:2 (b) This is probably a type of the blessings and graces of Christ which are innumerable in number. They have their source in God's heart, and bring the blessings of heaven to those who belong to the Lord.

LEAN

S. of Sol. 8:5 (c) This may be taken as a picture of the Church. God's people are just now traveling through this wilderness world on the way Home to glory. Along the way we are trusting on, believing in, and loving the Lord Jesus who is our Bridegroom.

Prov. 3:5 (b) The Lord uses this figure in order to warn us against trusting in our own mental processes, rather than in the revealed Word and will of God.

Isa. 36:6 (b) This is symbolical of Israel trusting in the help of the armies of Egypt as a man leans on a crutch or a staff to help him along a difficult way. Egypt would fail Israel, and prove to be a hindrance instead of a help. (See also Ezek. 29:7)

Micah 3:11 (b) These hypocrites were professing to trust in the Lord while in their actions they were denying Him. They were hypocrites. They really did not expect nor desire to walk with God.

LEAN (adjective)

Job 16:8 (a) This figure is used to illustrate the faint heart and the drooping spirit of this poor, weary man in his misery. When trouble overtakes God's people they are no longer "fat and flourishing" in their attitude, nor their actions.

Psa. 106:15 (a) God definitely uses this figure to indicate the terrible spiritual condition of Israel after they turned away from trusting in the Lord, and appointed a king for themselves in whom they would put their trust. (See also Isa. 10:16; Isa. 24:16)

LEAVEN

(b) In every place where leaven is mentioned, it is a type of evil teachings, evil doctrines and evil practices. It is always to be put away and cast out as an unclean thing. The gospel is never called leaven. Nothing good is ever compared to leaven. Nothing good is ever said about leaven. In every place it is mentioned, leaven is defiling and is to be put away. (See Ex. 12:15; Lev. 2:11; 1 Cor. 5:6)

Matt. 13:33 (a) The leaven in this case is a type of evil doctrines, taught by the apostate church. The woman is the apostate church, the meal is the Word of God, the leaven is wrong and evil teachings concerning the Word of God. Every false religion mixes false teachings in with the Scriptures and thereby poisons those who eat it. The leaven is never the gospel. There is no place in the Bible where leaven is spoken of in an approving way, nor is it ever related to anything good.

LEBANON

Isa. 40:16 (b) This wonderful picture tells a remarkable story of the inability of the best efforts of the sinner. Lebanon was a mountain about six miles wide, and about fifty miles long. It was covered with beautiful, magnificent, stately cedar trees. There were also the pine, the box, the fir and other trees. There were bushes, vines and grasses. In the midst of all this tangled forest, there were many wild animals of many varieties. It was a hunter's paradise. The Lord is telling us by this figure that though a sinner in his desire to obtain forgiveness should gather together in one pile all the burnable material on this huge mountain, and then kill all the animals that lived on that huge mountain, that sacrifice would not be sufficient to put away one sin. God is telling us by this wonderful figure that man's best and greatest efforts are not sufficient, and do not avail for the putting away of any evil or any sin in a human life. Only the blood of Jesus is sufficient.

LEEK

Num. 11:5 (c) The six vegetables mentioned in this passage refer to six kinds of pleasures with which the Egyptians regaled themselves. None of them are stable, none of them are very profitable, all of them have an unhappy odor, none of them are a source of strength for the body. These are used as types of various kinds of pleasures and pursuits offered by the world to those who belong to this world and have never tasted the heavenly manna. The things which the world offer hardly satisfy for more than one day at a time. The game played today does not satisfy the craving for tomorrow. The music played today is not acceptable tomorrow. The show that is seen today has no attraction for tomorrow.

LEES

Jer. 48:11 (b) These refer to the sins of Moab. The lustful practices of these people and their wicked ways had been disturbed by their enemies and so had accumulated as settlings do in the bottom of the wine jar. The same truth applies to Israel. (See Zeph. 1:12)

LEFT (hand)

I Chron. 12:2 (c) This figure is used to illustrate the unusual care with which these men equipped themselves to serve their king. The lesson for us is that we should cultivate those talents in which we do not naturally excel, and make our obscure gifts as useful as our natural talents.

Eccl. 10:2 (c) Since the heart of man is universally found on the left side of the chest, and not on the right side, the lesson to be learned is that all men are fools in the sight of God while in their natural state.

LEG

Ex. 29:17 (c) This type probably teaches the lesson that the walk of the child of God, as well as his inward desires, feelings and thoughts must all be cleansed with the washing of water by the Word of God. All must be laid at the feet of the Lord in sacrificial service. The walk must be clean.

Psa. 147:10 (c) Here is a figure of the walk of men in their business pursuits and their lives of pleasure. God takes no pleasure in that which is strictly human, but takes pleasure only in His Son and in those who walk with His Son.

Prov. 26:7 (c) By this we understand that the reason for the ungodly walk of the wicked is because their nature is sinful. All unsaved people walk in a crooked path because they have an uneven disposition and lack divine life.

S. of Sol. 5:15 (b) In the world of sports the leg and its strength and power to endure are prime requisites for success. The prize fighter who wins is the one who can keep his legs strong and stiff to the end. The runner must have legs that will keep up the stride to the end of the race. In the Scripture before us, the legs are used as a type of the wonderful power, stability and endurance of our precious Lord. They are made of marble to show the beauty of this precious Saviour. And they are made of marble in order to show their strength and permanent power.

Dan. 2:33 (a) These legs represent the Roman empire which was unusually strong and durable both in its civil power and its military might. The nation was upheld in its position as a world ruler by these two elements of strength.

Amos 3:12 (a) This probably indicates that God, the Shepherd, will deliver His people so that they may walk with Him again, and listen to Him as they should.

LEOPARD

Jer. 5:6 (b) This animal which is so quick in its actions and so swift in its pursuit is a picture of the swift destroyers mentioned in the passage. They would come suddenly with fierceness and attack with cruelty.

Jer. 13:23 (a) The spots on the leopard are from birth. It is an inherent marking. So the sinner is born with evil and wicked tendencies which are permanent in his life. He cannot change them nor obliterate them in any way. Only a divine power could remove them. The sinner is helpless in his sins. Only the divine Son of God can change him and make him whiter than snow. This animal represents also the sinner who admits he has "spots of sin" on him, but thinks there is lots of good in him. God will not save him, until he admits he is *all* bad.

Hosea 13:7 (a) In this passage the lion represents power, the leopard represents swiftness, the bear represents silence and certainty, and these are characteristics of the God whom they abandoned.

Rev. 13:2 (a) This animal represents the anti-Christ, who though pretending to be a man of peace will really be a cruel monster, killing all his enemies, violating his oath and showing swift and certain vengeance on those who belong to Jesus Christ.

LEPER

Ex. 4:6 (b) This disease is a type of sin from the standpoint of its being incurable and defiling. In nearly every case of healing, the leper is said to be "cleansed." One of the outstanding features of this disease was its defiling influence on others. The leper must live a separated life. He must wear a cloth over his mouth and cry "unclean." He must be shut out of the camp. All of this is true about an unsaved man as regards his relationship to heaven. He cannot enter heaven because of his defilement which is hopeless. Only God can remove it, only God has the remedy.

Lev. 13:13 (b) In this peculiar passage the leper is pronounced clean if he is entirely covered with leprosy from head to foot. This is probably a picture of the condition of an unsaved man when he finds out and is fully convinced in his own heart that he is utterly bad, completely lost and entirely without hope. Whenever one reaches that place he is right at the door of heaven. The Lord Jesus reveals Himself to that heart. The Holy Spirit gives him faith, and he passes from death unto life.

Lev. 13:44 (b) It is quite evident that the decision concerning the state of any man must come from the High Priest Himself, Jesus Christ. No pope, nor bishop, nor ecclesiastical authority of any kind can decide the spiritual status of any person. Only the High Priest, Christ Jesus, has the right, the power and the privilege of doing this. Only He can know the human heart.

Lev. 14:2 (b) Every sinner must come to Jesus Christ for cleansing. There is no other way. Christ Jesus must pronounce him clean. No Catholic priest can do it, no bishop can do it, no protestant preacher can do it, no Jewish rabbi can do it. Jesus Christ alone has the final and the official word. He Himself is the one who has told us "He that believeth on the Son hath everlasting life." John 3:36

LEVITE

Luke 10:32 (c) This sect may be taken as a picture of the lay workers of many churches who know almost nothing about soul winning, and care less. They are busy with the physical and social affairs of the church, but not the spiritual.

LICK

Num. 22:4 (b) This is an illustration of the complete and thorough work that the armies of Moab expected Israel to do in conquering them and in overrunning their country.

Psa. 72:9 (a) By this we understand the complete defeat which God would bring upon His enemies causing them to fall prostrate in the dirt.

Isa. 49:23 (a) This represents the humiliation of a defeated enemy and the complete elimination of their power. (See Micah 7:17)

LIFT

This action represents in most cases a restoration of power or place, authority or influence. It may represent also the restoration of a radiant spirit and a happy heart. It sometimes means a return to confidence in God, and a new trust in His power. We shall consider a few of the various places in which the expression occurs.

Gen. 40:13 The head, a restoration to power.

Num. 6:26 The expression of the face, showing approval.

Num. 16:3 Exalting to a place of power.

Num. 23:24 Israel restored to a place of leadership.

2 Ki. 19:4 The prayer ascending to God acceptably (See Isa. 37:4)

2 Ki. 25:27 The restoration to a high position, though in mockery.

1 Chron. 25:5 The sounding forth of the music.

Ezra 9:6 The upward look of dependence on God.

Job 10:15 An expression of shame and confusion (See Zech. 1:21).

Psa. 7:6 The manifestation of God's power publicly.

Psa. 24:7 A figure of triumph when the conqueror returns.

Psa. 25:1 The act of bringing oneself into the presence of the Lord by prayer and faith.

Psa. 93:3 An expression of the uprising of the people as a mob against God.

Psa. 110:7 It represents the constant, buoyant, radiant faith of the Lord Jesus Christ as He walked on earth among His enemies. He enjoyed the presence of His Father, and communed with Him day and night.

Heb. 12:12 This is an encouragement to keep the spirit trusting in the Lord, the heart glad in Christ, and the faith active in His word.

LIFT (Up)

This action is used by the Holy Spirit to describe many situations and conditions throughout the Bible. It expresses the act of bringing one's self into the presence of the Lord by prayer, by faith and by listening to Him, as we find in Psalm 25:1. The following are some of the ways in which it is used:

Lift up my hands Psa. 28:2 This is for supplication in prayer.

Life up Thy people Psa. 28:9 Bring them out of slavery and poverty.

Lift up thy feet Psa. 74:3 A call to action by the Lord.

Lift up the horn Psa. 75:4 Obtaining power to curb Israel.

Lift up thy waves Psa. 93:3 Raise up and train great leaders.

Lift up his head Psa. 110:7 Christ raised from Calvary to the Throne.

Lift up mine eyes Psa. 121:1 Where shall we look for help?

Lift up a companion Eccl. 4:10 To restore to spiritual health.

LIGHT

This word is used in many ways in the Scripture. Sometimes it refers to man's intellect as in Isa. 50:11. Sometimes it refers to the Word of God, as in Psa. 119:105. Sometimes it refers to false doctrines as in Matt. 6:23. It is also a type of the Christian who walks with God, as in Eph. 5:8. It refers also to the testimony of the Christian, as in Matt. 5:16. It is a figure of the state of the believer after he leaves Satan's kingdom of darkness, and is brought into God's Kingdom. (Acts 26:18) It refers to the walk of the believer in which he serves the Lord in a godly way, and directs his life according to the Word of God, as in 1 John 1:7. It refers to the defense of the believer who lives above reproach and has a godly testimony before his neighbors, as in Rom. 13:12. Christ Jesus Himself is the light of the world, as He affirms in John 8:12 (a). In some strange way the entrance of Christ into the life and heart enables the mind to become intelligent and intellectual. Only where Christ Jesus is loved and His Word is preached do we find minds active for the blessing of others, and alert in inventing that which will be a blessing to mankind. The blessings which we enjoy in civilization, such as electronics, transportation, communication, refrigeration, manufacturing, agriculture, chemistry, physics and institutions of learning are all products of protestant countries where Christ Jesus is permitted to rule and reign in the heart of people, and the Word of God is read, preached and taught publicly, and without hindrance. (See John 1:4)

LIGHTNING

Zech. 9:14 (b) This is a severe picture of God's avenging wrath and righteous judgment on His enemies. No one knows where it will strike, nor when, nor what damage will be the result.

Luke 10:18 (a) The disciples thought they had conquered Satan. Our Lord is assuring them that this is not the case. Satan occupies heavenly places. He strikes in people's lives wherever and whenever he pleases. No one can put Satan down nor conquer him. He daily attacks people where and when he pleases. This passage does not refer to Satan's fall from heaven, but rather to his daily attacks on the people on earth.

LILY

S. of Sol. 2:1 (b) This flower is a type of Christ in His beauty and loveliness. We should notice that the word "valley" is in the plural. The Lord knew we would have many valleys between the cradle and the grave, and would need the Saviour in His beauty and sweetness in every one of them. This lily is a type of Christ, first. because it is always pure white. Then, it is always fragrant, with an unusual sweetness of its own. It is also a universal flower, found wherevan man lives and vegetation can grow. It always droops with its beautiful little bells hanging toward the ground; one must be low and lowly, and then look up into the beauty of Christ in order to enjoy Him. This lily does not live on public highways, but is found in sheltered nooks. So it is with Christ Jesus. He is not found in the public markets, nor in the busy throng, but in the secret place of the Most High, under the shadow of the Almighty. Some think that this lily is a type of the Bride, the Church of Christ.

1. Because it grows on the earth and though the earth is black, the lily grows up white, thus showing the transforming power of the Lord.
2. Because it brings joy to the heart of its owner by its beauty and fragrance even as the church brings joy to the Lord.
3. Because there are so few of them compared with the number of weeds and worthless plants even as the Christians are few in number compared to the sinners.

Hosea 14:5 (a) This is a type of Israel in the regeneration when they will be restored to the Lord and shall bring joy to His heart by the beauty and fragrance of their testimony.

Luke 12:27 (a) Here we see a picture of God's gracious care for each child of God. God beautifies them and supplies their needs. They, in turn, give forth loveliness and perfume for the blessing and the joy of God.

LINEN

Lev. 6:10 (c) This symbolizes the beautiful gift of righteousness given by God to those who come in simple faith and trust Him with their souls. It is the "robe" of righteousness, the "garment" of salvation. It is always pure white.

Deut. 22:11 (c) By this figure God reveals His displeasure at man's schemes and plans to make a different robe of righteousness from that which He has ordained. Linen is a man-made product. After the Lord Jesus saves us and makes us Christians, then we begin to live a life of righteous acts, deeds and godliness which is compared to a linen robe. Wool is a product of God's power and ingenuity. No man can make wool. The Lord is telling us that we must not mix God's provision for a garment with man's provision. The wool represents God's grace. It is altogether "of God." Linen represents man's works. By this picture God condemns the mixture of grace and works in the matter of making the robe to wear for eternity. We are not saved by grace, and then kept by works. We are not saved partly by grace, and partly by works. God expects us to wear all linen as regards living for His glory and honoring His Name. He expects us to be clothed altogether by wool when it is a matter of relationship to Him, and being saved by Him.

Rev. 19:8 (b) The garment of the bride here is a type of her own righteous acts, accomplished because she was the bride, and not in order to be a bride. The garment mentioned in Psalm 45 is made of gold, and that one was provided by the Lord Himself.

LION

This animal is used as a figure or a type of power, sagacity, strength, wrath and ability. Sometimes the lion represents Christ Jesus. Sometimes it represents Satan. It always represents tremendous power and strength.

Gen. 49:9 (b) Emblematic of the power, strength and cunning of Judah for God because he came from God. The "lion" refers to God. Judah as the whelp is the offspring.

Judges 14:8 (c) This is sometimes taken as a type of Christ. Out of His death comes the sweetness of God's grace, and the blessings of salvation.

2 Sam. 17:10 (b) This is the estimate of David's power and boldness as given by Hushai. He uses this figure to describe the mighty fighting power of David.

1 Ki. 7:29 (c) These figures represent various aspects of the Lord Jesus Christ. They are to be seen in connection with the character of Christ, both in Ezekiel and in the Revelation. Over the grave of Bobby Burns in the castle at Dumfernlin in Scotland there is a wooden canopy upheld by four posts. On the top of these posts there appear the four figures which Solomon mentions and which are also mentioned in Ezekiel — the lion, the ox, the man, the eagle. These indicate the four great attributes and characteristics of the Lord Jesus Christ.

1 Chron. 11:22 (c) This may be used as a type of Satan. Though every condition was favorable to the lion, this bold servant of David took his life in his hand and killed the beast. So our Saviour with everything against Him overcame Satan at Calvary when it seemed as though He could not possibly come out of the conflict a victor.

1 Chron. 12:8 (a) The face of the lion is under perfect control of the spirit of the lion. No one can tell the feelings of the lion by observing the face. Even when ready to attack, the face remains placid and calm. This figure used in connection with the Gadites indicates that these were men of might as the lion, men of fight as a lion, men of flight as a lion, and always with perfect control of their actions and their feelings.

Psa. 22:13 (a) The maddening throng around the Cross resembled lions in their hatred, their vociferous shouts and their anger against the Son of God.

Psa. 35:17 (b) This is a cry of the Lord Jesus for God to preserve Him from the fierce attacks of the enemies around Him.

Eccl. 9:4 (b) This is a very graphic way of telling us that a great and mighty powerful man is of no value when dead. Nero, Napoleon, Stalin and Hitler have lost their power. The least of all living persons is better than the greatest of dead conquerors.

Jer. 12:8 (a) This represents God's own people who should have been of the sheep of His pasture, but instead turned against Him in hatred and rebellion.

Ezek. 1:10 (b) This is one of the types of the Lord Jesus in which His great strength, power, majesty and sovereignty are represented. (See also Rev. 4:7 and Rev. 5:5)

Ezek. 19:2 (a) The nation of Israel was compared to this animal. The leaders represent the parent animals. Their offspring are the cubs, but all of them are fierce and cruel in their attitude toward God and His prophet.

1 Peter 5:8 (a) Satan is thus described. This animal cannot be tamed to become a servant of man. Its nature cannot be changed. It is never constructive, but always destructive in all its actions. It is never a friend of man, but always his enemy. He is said to be roaring because he is always hunting up victims. The lion roars only when it is hungry. Satan is never satisfied. He is always in the business of devouring and destroying and is never a blessing to men.

Rev. 5:5 (a) Christ Jesus is the King of kings as the lion is the king of beasts. He is unconquerable and unavoidable. He cannot be defeated. He is afraid of no enemy. He cannot be hindered by any circumstances. He is always able to do whatever needs to be done for the glory of God and the blessing of men.

Rev. 13:2 (b) This animal reveals the terrible power the anti-Christ will have to tear, destroy and hurt God's people and all who will not bow to his sovereign sway.

LOAF

Lev. 23:17 (c) (Wave) These particular loaves of bread represent godly, human efforts for the glory of the Lord. They were mixed with leaven, because all human efforts have sinful and evil characteristics. Nothing that we do or give is pure. The loaves of bread that represent Christ have no leaven in them whatever, but these loaves that represent us and our own human offerings did have leaven. Christ only is the pure bread of life.

But these wave loaves may also represent Jesus Christ our Lord as the One who was made sin for us. He went through the furnace of God's wrath, and this destroyed all the sin which He had taken upon Him for us. We come before God presenting as our sacrifice the Lord Jesus in His perfect beauty after He came through the furnace and became to us the bread of life.

1 Sam. 10:3 (c) The three types in this verse are as follows: a kid for each man represents the individual sacrifice of Christ for each one; the loaf for each man represents the personal appropria-

tion of Christ for each heart; the bottle of wine for all the men represents the joy of the Lord which cannot be measured but which is available for everyone and for all who will come.

1 Sam. 10:4 (c) In that Saul was given two loaves of the bread, it may indicate that he was to have a double portion now, both as a king and as a prophet. He was to guide God's people in temporal things, and also in spiritual. He was to be a double example to all of Israel of a godly and a holy king. It may teach us also that those who have bread should share it with others. One of the men gave nearly all the bread he had. This should characterize each Christian.

Matt. 15:34 (c) This is a type of God's enriching grace which is sufficient for one's own heart and for supplying the needs of others. The Lord would have His own examine themselves to see if they have any good blessings from heaven to give to those whom they meet along the highway of life. Each Christian should have plenty of bread for all whom he meets — biscuits for the children, loaves for the grown folks, soft bread for those who cannot chew, hard rolls for those who wish something upon which to exercise their thoughts. The Christian should go forth to the day's work with his bread basket filled for the hungry.

Luke 11:5 (b) This parable is concerning the soul winner. The first friend is the Lord Jesus. The second friend who comes at midnight is the troubled soul who comes to your door selling brooms. He is in the darkness of unbelief and is seeking something for his soul. The Christian may feel that he has nothing to give to this inquiring person. He realizes that he needs bread for this hungry man. Christ is telling us that we may come to Him to get what we need for the occasion. We may think we just want three loaves, but the Lord may see that we need much more. He will therefore give to the seeking Christian all the living bread that is needed for the seeking sinner. No Christian needs to permit any inquiring soul to depart unsatisfied.

1 Cor. 10:17 (a) (Margin) (1) This is a symbol of the whole church of God which is like a loaf of bread. It contains only wheat grains. It has no sticks or stones nor foreign substances but only wheat. Only true, born-again believers are in the church of God. Hypocrites and professing Christians may be in the visible church, but none are in Christ's mystical body, the invisible church.

(2) This loaf is a complete loaf separated from everything else in the house. This is a picture of the church which should be separated from every worldly thing, every worldly association, and is a separate distinct institution in this world. By looking at it one may see that it is a complete, self contained unit, it is one body in Christ.

(3) As no one knows how many grains are in the loaf, so no one knows how many Christians compose the church.

(4) As the grains in the loaf are combined with one another so the Christians in the church are bound together in sweet and holy communion with one another.

(5) As the purpose of the loaf is to bring a blessing to those who have it, so the church is to bring joy and honor to Christ and be a blessing in every way to the people of earth who surround it.

LOCUST

Psa. 109:23 (a) This is emblematic of the weakness and the helplessness of our blessed Lord as He was sent from one persecutor to another just as the wind blows the locusts about.

Prov. 30:27 (c) This is a figure used to illustrate the blessedness of mutual fellowship regardless of leadership. Also that the problems of life require united effort though there be no adequate leadership.

Rev. 9:3 (c) Here we see a type of some form of curse which God will send upon the earth against His enemies. It may refer to tanks or some similar weapon of war which will be used to destroy God's enemies.

LODGE

Isa. 1:8 (a) The lesson to be learned from this type is that the people of Israel had forsaken the gardens of God, the flowers and fruits of God's love and grace, and preferred to dwell among the pleasures of this world. Cucumbers were one of the foods of the Egyptians. They contained no nutriment, had little food value, and perish quickly. Israel seemed to prefer that kind of a life rather than the rich pasture provided by God Himself.

LODGE (verb)

Matt. 13:32 (b) Here we see a graphic picture of the terrible state of the apostate church. The birds represent evil spirits. The tree with its many branches represents an unnatural growth in which wicked spirits feel at home in the various divisions of the great apostate religious world. The mustard seed never should produce a tree. This is an unnatural growth. So the present religious institutions filled with all sorts of evil doctrines, worldly practices and unsaved persons is not according to the will of God. The devil has his throne in the apostate church, as we read in Rev. 2:13. He and his evil angels are represented by the birds that lodge, make their nests and feel at home in the various branches of this huge, religious institution.

LOINS

Ex. 12:11 (c) By this figure the Lord was instructing His people to be ready to go, packed up, all ties broken off, and the journey begun for an unknown land. It is a splendid picture of "readiness."

1 Ki. 12:10 (a) Here we see a comparison between the oppression with which Rehoboam would afflict the people, as compared with the much lesser affliction which Solomon brought upon the people. (See also 2 Chron. 10:10)

Psa. 66:11 (b) The loins are used in the Scripture as a picture of strength, power, vigor and maturity. In this passage God weakened the strength of His people and made them incapacitated as a nation.

Isa. 11:5 (b) This picture is given us to describe a godly life, an upright character and an honest heart in business. It is also used to describe the character of God, all of whose power and work would be absolutely righteous in character.

Isa. 45:1 (b) The Lord is informing Cyrus that He will weaken the strength of kings and nations who oppose him in order that he may conquer and subdue every enemy.

Jer. 30:6 (b) This represents a condition of despair, weakness, helplessness and hopelessness throughout Israel because of their sins, and because of the wrath of God.

Ezek. 47:4 (b) Look under "ANKLES" for a rather full description of this parable. The loins represent vigor and power of a man controlled by the Spirit of God, and therefore brought into useful channels that are profitable in the sight of the Lord.

Dan. 10:5 (b) In this vision the heavenly messenger had divine strength, power and ability that was pure as the gold, and beautiful in appearance. He was God's messenger with God's message, for God's servant.

Luke 12:35 (a) Here we find an exhortation to every believer to bring all his powers, talents and gifts into the service of the King, with a ready heart, and a willing mind.

Eph. 6:14 (a) If we know God's truth from His Word, we can and will be bold and aggressive in the battle of faith, and in the service of the King.

1 Pet. 1:13 (a) It is quite evident from this figure that the Lord is referring to our powers to think, analyze and consider by our mental processes the things of time and eternity. The Lord expects us to think through in regard to His work and service, to be resourceful, energetic and vigorous in preaching the Word and in carrying out His plans as He reveals them to us.

LOOK

Psa. 18:27 (b) The word here is used to indicate pride, egotism and self-sufficiency, all of which are to be brought down in humiliation and shame by our wonderful Lord. (See Psa. 101:5; Prov. 6:17; Prov. 21:4; Isa. 2:11; Isa. 10:12)

Ezek. 2:6 (a) The type here indicates a fierce, angry countenance gazing in hatred against God's child. (See chap. 3, v. 9)

Dan. 7:20 (b) This figure also represents a fierce countenance of severe determination which is intended to frighten and to bring dismay.

LOOSE

Gen. 49:21 (b) Here we see a picture of freedom of thought, expression and of action on the part of the people in the tribe of Naphtali. (See Deut. 33:23)

Lev. 14:7 (c) This probably represents the living Christ now appearing in the presence of God for us. We are saved both by the death of Christ for us, and also by the life of Christ before the Throne. He died to pay the debt of our sins as in Rom. 5:6, and we are saved by His life as we read in Rom. 5:10. This same truth is found in Lev. 16:15. One goat died for the sins of the people, and in v. 21, another goat lived for the salvation of the people. Christ at Calvary is represented by the dead bird or the dead goat. Christ on the Throne, as our Advocate with the Father, is represented by the living bird and the living goat.

Job 12:18 (b) By this we learn that God is able to weaken the strength of oppressing rulers, and to deliver the captives from their power. He is able to control the powerful actions of great kings and rulers.

Job 30:11 (b) Job is complaining about his condition. He felt he was forsaken and turned over to wander in the darkness of confusion, with no guide to lead him.

Psa. 102:20 (b) Probably this refers to the conversion of the sinner. He has been on his way to the second death, which is the lake of fire. Then he hears the call of God, believes the gospel of God. and is set free by the truth of God. It is probably a fulfillment of Luke 4:18.

Psa. 146:7 (a) This action probably refers to the work of God in delivering those who are bound by Satan and setting them free. It is probably a fulfillment of Matt. 12:29, or Isa. 61:1, or Luke 4:18.

Eccl. 12:6 (b) This strange figure is probably a picture of the spinal cord, which ceases to operate properly and does not function as it should. It is one of the marks or evidences of old age.

Isa. 5:27 (b) This beautiful picture tells the story of Israel restored to the Lord when the Messiah returns and rebuilds the nation of Israel and Palestine. Their strength will be renewed and their power will be enhanced.

Isa. 33:23 (b) We are being told here that when we are weak, then we are strong, as in 2 Cor. 12:10. When Israel as a nation, or when any individual, confesses his weak and helpless condition, then he may look to the Lord and find adequate provision for his need.

Isa. 51:14 (b) The lost sinner bound by evil habits, wicked ways, and hindered by sinful companions has a deep desire to be delivered from this bondage, so that he may live a life of freedom with God and may enjoy the blessings of God. (See also Psa. 68:18; Zech. 9:11; Eph. 4:8,9)

Isa. 52:2 (b) Here we find a call to Israel to take advantage of God's grace, power and goodness and to appropriate for themselves the rich provisions God supplied for them.

Isa. 58:6 (b) Here is a call to remove those cruel laws that bound burdens on the poor, and to substantiate those blessings which will bring joy and gladness to the oppressed.

Matt. 16:19 (a) This passage is quite similar and carries the same meaning as Matt. 18:18 and John 20:23. We should note that the binding and the loosing are products of the power of God in the heart and soul. God gave the keys of the kingdom of heaven, one key for the Gentiles and one for the Jews. That tells the source of the power. The passage in John tells us of the force that is behind the power, and that force is the Holy Spirit as revealed in the passage. The passage in Matt. 18:18 reveals the operation of that power; it is because God's people agree together in their prayer life, and in their decisions. That one who has received the Spirit of God as his Lord, and as according to John 20:22, will find the same result as described in v. 23. The Spirit-filled and the Spirit-led man will take God's emancipating gospel to a husband and will leave the wife in the dark. He will lead a brother to Christ and leave the other brother in his sins. He will speak helpfully to one clerk in the store, and have no message for the other clerk. Where the Spirit is Lord in the life, then the individual Christian worker is led to the person with whom God is working, and will be kept away from the disinterested soul. He brings the message of deliverance and salvation to the one who is ready for it, but the Spirit keeps him away from the person who is to remain in his sins.

Matt. 21:2 (c) Here we find a picture of a lost mother and her son who are in the dark spiritually, and do not know which way to turn. One road leads to heaven, and the other road leads to hell. Tradition and fear hinder their making any progress. At the Master's call and command a messenger came with a sweet message from that wonderful and precious Saviour which released them so that they could come to the Lord Jesus and have the great honor of carrying Him wherever He wanted to go. (See Mark 11:4-5; Luke 19:31)

Lu. 13:12-16 (a) This woman was bound physically as well as spiritually. Somewhere in her life Satan had led her into some kind of evil that left its mark on her body. When Jesus came, her body was immediately healed, made whole, and she herself delivered from Satan's bondage to be a follower of the Lord Jesus Christ.

John 11:44 (c) It is sometimes the case, and quite often it is true, that a man will find the Saviour, be really born again, and yet carry with him in his new life some of the old ways, habits, traditions and customs which hinder him from living a happy, free, Christian life. The grave clothes are a type of those hindrances. God's children have the privilege and the duty of helping that friend to get rid of the old customs and habits and set him free for the service of the King.

Acts 2:24 (a) Death binds men permanently. Only God can break those bands and bring back to life again. This was done in the case of our Lord Jesus Christ.

Rev. 5:2 (c) It may be that this big book contains the story of human lives. No man lives such a clean life, free from sin, that he is worthy to open and to read the lives of others. Only Christ Jesus meets these requirements. He was sinless, therefore He was worthy. He can break the seals so that the book may be opened by Him and read by Him.

LOP

Isa. 10:33 (b) God is telling us that He will cut off and destroy the enemies of Israel, the Assyrians. (See v. 24)

LORD

This title is very widely used for many purposes and reasons. We shall enumerate some of these so that the reader may acquaint himself with the many different ways in which God is Lord, and in which various kinds of people, nations and rulers are lords.

The Lord He is God Deut. 4:35
He is Lord of lords Deut. 10:17
He is Lord of all the earth Josh. 3:11
The Lord is King Psa. 10:16
The Lord is a refuge Psa. 14:6
The Lord is my portion Psa. 16:5

The Lord is my shepherd Psa. 23:1
The Lord is my light Psa. 27:1
The Lord is my salvation Psa. 27:1
The Lord is my strength Psa. 28:7
The Lord is my shield Psa. 28:7
The Lord is good Psa. 34:8
The Lord is terrible Psa. 47:2
The Lord is our defense Psa. 89:18
The Lord is upright Psa. 92:15
The Lord is merciful Psa. 103:8
The Lord is gracious Psa. 103:8
The Lord is thy keeper Psa. 121:5
The Lord is thy shade Psa. 121:5
The Lord is around us Psa. 125:2
The Lord is righteous Psa. 129:4
The Lord is nigh us Psa. 145:18
The Lord is far off Prov. 15:29
The Lord is our Maker Prov. 22:2
The Lord is that Spirit 2 Cor. 3:17
The Lord is at hand Phil. 4:5
He is the Lord our righteousness Jer. 23:6
He is the Lord of kings Dan. 2:47
He is the Lord of the sabbath Mark 2:28
He is Lord and Christ Acts 2:36
He is Lord of all Acts 10:36
He is Lord of the dead and the living Rom. 14:9
He is the Lord of glory 1 Cor. 2:8
He is the Lord from heaven 1 Cor. 15:47
The Lord is the avenger 1 Thes. 4:6
The Lord is faithful 2 Thes. 3:3
The Lord is pitiful Jas. 5:11

This title is given to us in His Word in order that we may learn to know Him more intimately and trust Him more intelligently in the many vicissitudes of life.

LOSE

Matt. 10:39 (a) The Lord uses this word to describe the results of a wasted life in which there is no profit to God and no profit to the man for eternity. One may be a wonderful man of business or religion, or a prize-winning athlete, and yet have nothing for God or eternity. That life is said to be one that is lost. (See Matt. 16:25; Mark 8:35; Luke 9:24; John 12:25)

John 6:39 (a) We learn from this that the Lord Jesus saves the soul, and then keeps that one after salvation so that he never goes to hell. He is so powerful and His work is so perfect that the sinner is saved for eternity.

LOSS

1 Cor. 3:15 (a) This word is telling us that the believer's life should be filled with profitable and useful works so that he will receive a full reward at the judgment day. It has no reference whatever to the salvation of the soul. It refers only to a failure to receive a reward for faithful service. It is the reward that is lost, not his soul.

Phil. 3:7 (b) Paul indicates plainly that all those religious observances which he practiced before he was saved, before he met the Lord Jesus, were only a liability to him, and not an asset. He was glad to get rid of all his beliefs and practices as a Pharisee in order that he might enjoy the liberty and the loveliness of Christ Jesus, his new Lord. The old things as a Jew were a liability to him. The new things as a Christian were an asset to him.

LOST

Matt. 18:11 (a) We should note that in this Scripture the word "seek" does not occur. It is speaking of a child that is not saved, but is in sin. He sins because he is born as a sinner, and the word "lost" indicates that he is outside the family of God and on the way to a lost eternity.

Luke 19:10 (a) The unsaved person in this verse refers to an adult. That one needs to be sought after as well as needs to be found. He has deliberately gone astray and turned to his own way. God seeks him out as a shepherd seeks out the lost sheep, or as Saul sought the lost asses. The lost man is unsaved; he is in his sins; he does not know where he is going; he does not know God; he is in the dark. (See Eph. 2:12)

2 Cor. 4:3 (a) The word is used in this passage in the same way as in the former passages. We learn here of a different characteristic of the unsaved man, i.e., he does not understand God's Word or God's gospel. He can talk intelligently about business or pleasure, science or arts, but has no understanding of God's truth, God's gospel, and God's Son. For this reason he is said to be lost, he is on his way to hell.

LUKEWARM

Rev. 3:16 (a) Here God gives us a type which describes the unhappy state of one who is indifferent to the claims of God, indifferent to the needs of the church, indifferent to the needs of his own soul, and who travels along life's pathway with no definite decision in regard to eternity.

M

MAN

This name is used as a type of all mankind, both men and women It is also used as a type of God Himself. It is the name given to the new nature which we received at conversion. It typifies also the physical body in which the person lives. It represents the mind and thoughts of men. Some of the places in which these types are used will be found in the following list:

Man of War Ex. 15:3
Man of the Earth Psa. 10:18
Man of Peace Psa. 120:7 (R.V.)
The Man John 19:5
The Inner man Eph. 3:16
The Double-minded Man James 1:8
Man of the Heart 1 Pet, 3:4
Man of God Deut. 33:1
The New Man Eph. 2:15
The Outward Man 2 Cor. 4:16
The Vain Man James 2:20
The Hidden Man 1 Pet. 3:4

MAN OF GOD

There are several men in the Scripture to whom is applied this type. Each one receives this designation because of some characteristic in his life. We shall see this in the list that follows:

Moses, the Model of Intercession Jer. 15:1
The Angel of the Lord, Model of Sufficiency Judges 13:6
The Pre-existent Christ, Model of Justice 1 Sam. 2:27
Samuel, Model of Understanding 1 Sam. 9:6
Shemaiah, Model of Counsel 1 Ki. 12:22
Elijah, Model of Faithfulness 1 Ki. 17:18
Elisha, Model of Kindness 2 Ki. 4:7
Ahijah, Model of Severity 2 Ki. 23:16
David, Model of Praise 2 Chron. 8:14
Isaiah, Model of Spirituality. 2 Chron. 25:7
Igdaliah, Model of Consecration Jer. 35:4
Timothy, Model of Holiness 1 Tim. 6:11
You, the Saint of God, Model of Godliness 2 Tim. 3:17

MAN (FIRST)

I Cor. 15:47 Adam is used in this case under this title as the beginning of the human race so that every person on earth partakes of the characteristics of that first man. Physically we are all made like he was made. We have the same members and faculties. He began the human race, and was the first one of that race.

MAN (SECOND)

1 Cor. 15:47 Christ Jesus is called the second man because He began a new race of heavenly people. He was the first one of that marvelous family called the "Church," or the "Body," or the "Kingdom," or the "Family" of God. All those who belong to Christ Jesus have come to Him for the beginning of a new life, and have received that new life, are like Him in some respects and will eventually be fully conformed to His image. Each of these men, Adam the first, and Jesus the second, began a new race of people. The first one is earthly in character, and the second is heavenly in character.

MANNA

Deut. 8:3 (a) This bread is a type of Christ, the living Bread. God gave it to Israel in a miraculous way. He is the living bread which sustains the lives of God's people. It was always pure white. It was sweet. There was enough for all. (See also John 6:49; Heb. 9:4)

Rev. 2:17 (a) This bread is a type of some sort of unseen and unknown blessings which are given by God for the blessing of His people when they live victorious lives for Him. It is a gift that is lovely, precious, attractive and satisfying, but the character of it is unknown.

MANSION

John 14:2 (b) Our blessed Lord used this word to describe the wonderful place He is preparing in glory for His own children. We do not know what it is like, nor just where in glory it will be located, but we do know that if the architect of the universe is making it, it will be gorgeous, glorious and marvelous.

MANTLE

2 Ki. 2:14 (c) This is an emblem of authority. Elijah, who was the master of Elisha, left this garment for Elisha, so that all would know that Elisha now was the successor to Elijah, and could and would exercise all the powers of Elijah. It may be understood as a type of spiritual power conveyed from the greater to the lesser

MARBLE

S. of Sol. 5:15 (c) This beautiful stone is a symbol of strength, vigor, stamina and symmetry. Soldiers, prize fighters, sailors. mountain climbers and foot travelers know the need of strong, durable legs. The picture is given to us by Solomon to represent the

Lord Jesus who would always walk with us and never tire. He would fight for us and never lose. He would go with us and never fail.

MARK

Gen. 4:15 (c) Cain received this sign from God which was to tell the world that this man was a sinner, a murderer. Since that time sin has left its mark upon the human body. The face tells the story of the drunkard. The eyes tell the story of jealousy and hatred. The body is influenced by the sins which are committed.

Ezek. 9:4 (c) By this God indicates that He marks His own people with those blessed attributes of God which distinguish them from all others as the people of God. (See Rev. 3:12)

Rev. 13:16-17 (a) Since God marks His children with a distinctive brand of some kind, so the Devil, imitating God, puts a mark on all of his children. No one knows what the mark is, and all conjectures are in vain. This brand by the devil is put on the forehead where everyone can see it, or in the hand where it can be hidden. This sign distinguishes the devil's children from God's children, and will probably be branded upon all the unsaved during the tribulation days.

MARRIAGE

Isa. 54:1 (a) This situation is described more particularly in Gal. 4:27. The Lord is telling us that Israel is married to God, and is "the wife" of God. God calls Himself "her husband." The ungodly are those who have no relationship to God. Their number far exceeds the number of those who belong to God. Those on the broad road are many, while those on the narrow road are few. This is also the story of the difference between Israel and the Church. The laws of Sinai produced a few followers, but the love of Calvary has produced a multitude of followers. The Jewish nation has remained few in number, while among the Gentiles the gospel has brought multitudes into the family of God.

Isa. 62:4 (a) The time is coming when Israel, God's people, will again own all their own land to the east of the sea, they will walk with God, they will live godly lives, they will love the God of their land, and He will again be able to shower upon them the blessings of heaven, both spiritual and physical.

Jer. 3:14 (a) In this place God is calling His people Israel to return to Him in sweet fellowship and confiding trust so that He may again be to them all that a husband should be.

Mal. 2:11 (a) The affection of Judah for idols is compared to a marriage wherein the heart that should have been joined to the Lord turned away from Him to be joined to idols.

Rom. 7:4 (a) This is a beautiful type of the blessed relationship which is brought about when the sinner trusts the Lord Jesus and is born again. It is the act of being saved wherein the sinner gives himself to Christ and Christ gives Himself to the sinner in a very sweet, eternal and devoted union.

Rev. 19:7 (a) In this way is described that precious, mysterious union which will take place some day in the sky between the Lord Jesus and His bride, the Church. Individually, we are married to Christ at the moment we are saved. Collectively, we will enjoy this precious mutual event some day above the clouds when all the Church of God is united together, differences are forgotten, sectarian lines are eliminated, and the saints go marching in to the marriage supper of the Lamb.

MARSH

Ezek. 47:11 (b) This word describes the lives of certain people. They live in the lowlands of life where the stinging, crawling, evil varmints of sin make their habitation, and where dirt abounds in the life, the soul and the words of those who live there. The gospel never reaches them. The light of heaven is shut out. The story of God's grace is not permitted. They live in the mire and the muck of filth, sin and wickedness, and are never changed, except by the Spirit of God.

MAST

Prov. 23:34 (b) Here we see a type of the condition of a drunken man who reels to and fro and has no certain standing. He is blown about easily by the winds of lust, and is carried away by his own evil mind.

Isa. 33:23 (b) This type represents the helplessness of God's people to handle their own affairs properly. They must depend fully on the guidance of the Lord for their daily path.

MAUL

Prov. 25:18 (a) A false friend is compared to this instrument which is used to crush, damage and injure that upon which it is used.

MEAL

2 Ki. 4:41 (c) This meal may be taken to represent Christ Himself, or it may be the Word of God. Both Christ and His Word are able to dispel all poisonous thoughts in the life, and to deliver safely from the evil doctrines and teachings of false religions. Since the meal offering represents the life of Christ offered to the Father instead of our own, we are rather inclined to believe that this meal may represent the blessed Person of our Lord Jesus who delivers from all evil doctrines, and every poisonous faith.

MEASURE

Psa. 39:4 (b) This figure probably represents the value of a person's time. Much time is wasted each day we live. We should evaluate both our time and our actions to see of what value these are, either to God or to man. If we do so we shall live useful lives, profitable in every way.

Matt. 7:2 (b) It is quite evident that our Lord knows exactly how much reward to give and also indicates that men know how much reward to give. A man will receive what he is worth, both from the hands of men and from the Lord. (See also Mark 4:24; Lu. 6:38)

Matt. 23:32 (a) By this figure we learn that the evil deeds of the fathers are brought to full completion in the lives of their children. The evil that the fathers failed to do were committed by the children.

Luke 6:38 (a) Here we learn of the abundant reward that is given in large quantities to those who themselves minister blessings to others.

John 3:34 (a) The Father does not give the Holy Spirit on the installment plan, nor just in partial portions, but He gives His entire Holy Spirit to the Lord Jesus, but also to any other true believer who desires to be Spirit-filled.

Rom. 12:3 (a) All do not have the same mental capacity. Some are more well developed mentally than others. The Lord is telling us by this figure that He is able to supply the graces of heaven to every person according to their capacity.

Rev. 6:6 (a) By this we learn that the blessings of God will be measured out to men, and there will not be an abundance of supply, but rather a meager supply in the time of God's wrath.

Rev. 21:17 (b) There are many standards of measurements in the earth used in different countries. In this case the Lord is giving us the elements that will be used for determining human conditions of human hearts and lives.

MEAT

Judges 14:14 (c) The lion is the eater and the honey is the meat. It is a lovely picture of the sweet, precious and delightful food which we find in the Lord Jesus Christ as we partake of Him for the blessing of our souls.

Psa. 42:3 (a) There are those who feed upon their sorrows. Their griefs are never comforted, and their conversation is continually about the troubles they have had. They are never satisfied unless they weep over former losses.

Psa. 69:21 (a) When our Saviour was hanging on the cross, hungry, thirsty and torn with grief and sorrow, they gave Him the bitter gall instead of the comfort and the water that He so much needed.

Prov. 23:6 (a) The wicked seem to have every kind of blessing that the heart desires. Often these riches have been obtained by dishonest means and methods. The Lord wants us to be satisfied with that which He provides, and which we obtained by honest efforts. Let us not crave to have that which the devil gives.

Dan. 1:8 (c) The rich food which came from the king's table had been offered first to an idol. Daniel would have none of that which was highly esteemed among men, and especially among royalty. It was defiled food. Let us remember that the finest that the world can give is not the portion of God's people.

John 4:32, 34 (a) Our Lord indicates by this type that the will of God satisfied the longings of the heart of the Son of God, and that he flourished and grew on the service of His Father. We too should feed on the will, the words and the work of God.

John 6:27 (a) The Lord is using this figure to indicate worldly gain and worldly goods upon which men feed for satisfaction. Rather He offers us the blessings of the Christian life as food for our souls and hearts.

John 6:55 (a) This passage refers definitely to a very intimate association with Christ wherein He Himself in His own person becomes priceless and precious to our hearts' affections. The mother says to her baby, "I could eat you up!" It is a figure which indicates that the heart, soul and life are wrapped up in the Son of God.

1 Cor. 8:13 (a) It is quite evident that Paul uses this figure to show that he would not do anything which his own soul desired, if the doing of it would hurt the heart and the feelings of one of God's dear children.

Heb. 5:12 (a) The word in this passage is used to illustrate the deep truths of the Word of God. Those Christians had to receive the simplest kind of teaching because they had not learned to think through the doctrines and the philosophies of the Word of God.

Heb. 13:9 (a) The heart is not to be influenced by human arguments, man-made theories, and various religious devices. God wants our souls to be strong and healthy because we are resting upon the facts of the Scriptures, and not on the fancies of men.

MEDICINE

Jer. 30:13 (a) The Scriptures are used as a type in this place because they heal the broken heart, they mend the wounds that sin makes, they bind up the bruises that are incurred in wandering away from God's path.

Jer. 46:11 (a) The many means and methods used by Israel to help in their troubles and sorrows are described by this type. Men are still evading God's remedy and trying by legislation and by religious programs and by social service plans to relieve the wickedness and sin of men. None of these remedies are successful. Every one fails. Only that which is provided by God through Jesus Christ, and administered by the Holy Spirit will succeed in curing the ills of society.

MELCHIZEDEK

Heb. 7:1 (a) Scholars disagree on the position occupied by this priest. Some are quite sure that he was an Old Testament incarnation of Christ Jesus Himself. Others believe that he was a strange, unusual character who was a type of the Saviour. The evidence is not too clear, and the reader may use either conclusion that he feels the Scriptures justify.

MELT (and forms)

Ex. 15:15 (a) The inhabitants were to be made weak and helpless with fear because of the power of God. (See also Josh. 2:11; Josh. 14:8; 2 Sam. 17:10; Isa. 13:7)

Judg. 5:5 (b) In this song Deborah uses many figures of speech to indicate the overwhelming power of God. She is indicating that heaven and earth all combine in revealing the victorious power of the defender of Israel. It also may be considered as a figure of the way great difficulties, hindrances and impediments disappear when God moves for the blessing of His people. (See Psa. 46:6; Psa. 97:5; Isa. 34:3)

MEPHIBOSHETH

2 Sam. 9:6 (c) This interesting person has been taken as a type of all those whose walk is imperfect, their way of life is crooked, but they heard the call of the Lord, came to Him, were forgiven, were brought into His family, and their crooked feet were hidden under the table of His bounty, grace and mercy. This is such a wonderful type of the Saviour receiving the sinner, that the Queen of England recommended to Charles Stanley that he carry this message to all the armed forces.

MERCHANDISE

2 Pet. 2:3 (a) This is a very real and true figure or picture of that which happens in many religions. The devotees of many religious sects are absolutely bound to the rule and laws of their re-

ligion. Their leaders can do anything they wish to them, even to the suffering of the body. Men are only free in those groups where the Lord Jesus Christ is loved and trusted, and His Word is believed, accepted and practiced. There are religious slaves by the millions (See Rev. 18:13 Marg.)

Matt. 22:5 (c) This is a type of any kind of business which allures and entices one away from the Lord Jesus and His fellowship.

John 2:16 (c) We see here a picture of any worldly enterprise brought into the house of God wherein His house loses its holy character and becomes a place for commercial enterprise.

Rev. 18:12-13 (b) This is a word to describe the great traffic carried on by the church, principally the Roman Catholic Church, which buys and sells vast quantities of various articles for the promotion and maintenance of its many activities. Included in this merchandise are the bodies and the souls of men which the Roman Catholics buy and sell for a profit.

MERCY SEAT

Ex. 25:17 (a) Here we see a type of the Lord Jesus Christ in Whom centers all the mercy of God and through Whom we reveive mercy from God. He is called the "propitiation" in Romans 3:25 which is understood to be the same as the mercy seat. The expression "mercy seat" means "propitiatory." We come to the Lord Jesus, both as our High Priest, and also as our Mercy Seat, that we may confess our failures and receive again the cleansing of the precious bood. Mercy abounds there. Mercy meets the needs and requirements of justice.

MIDNIGHT

Luke 11:5 (c) The term describes the deep perplexity and distress of a soul that has come to the end of his resources and is in soul trouble about his path and his future. It represents the man or the woman who calls at your door selling some article, but in his heart there is conviction of sin, and a realization of his need. You are supposed to have the Bread of Life to give to him in his deep distress.

MILE

Matt. 5:41 (a) The term is used to describe those actions wherein we do more than is expected of us. We give more than is requested of us. We show an interest beyond that which is required.

MILK

Ex. 23:19 (c) This is a warning against using the precious Word of God to injure or destroy that which it should build up and strengthen. The milk is a type of the Word of God. The milk should have been used to cause the kid to grow into a large, strong, healthy animal. Instead it was used to destroy the tender, young animal. God is telling us that we should not take that which He gives to us for constructive purposes and use it for destructive purposes. Baptism is an example. It was given to the church as a blessing, but has been used to destroy many churches, homes and lives. The heathen also had a custom of sprinkling the broth made in the above manner over their fields in order to make the fields fertile. The Lord condemns this custom of the heathen, and assures His people that blessing on the fields comes from Himself. (See under "KID." Also Ex. 34:26; Deut. 14:21; 34:26)

Num. 13:27 (b) This is a type of the multitude of blessings that abounded in the land of Palestine.

Isa. 55:1 (b) Here we find a type of the sweet richness which awaits the soul who places his faith and trust in the living Lord.

1 Cor. 3:2 (a) Here is a picture of the simpler truths of the Scripture which most anyone can grasp without particular study and without much help. These truths are contrasted with the deeper and more difficult truths of the Word which are compared to meat. (See also Heb. 5:13; 1 Pet. 2:2)

MIRE

Job 30:19 (b) Job's sorrow, trouble, and poverty are compared to mud which is so unpleasant and so hard to get out from when one is submerged in it.

Psa. 69:2, 14 (b) This is a type of the deep trouble, the great sorrow, and the anguish of heart of the Lord Jesus Christ as He went through Gethsemane and Calvary.

Isa. 57:20 (a) The filthiness in many human lives is compared to the dirt cast up constantly by the restless sea.

Jer. 38:22 (b) This is a type of the great difficulties into which Israel was plunged because of her iniquity and sin.

2 Pet. 2:22 (b) Here we see illustrated what God thinks of a life of worldliness. The pig represents an unsaved person who has cleaned up his life, perhaps has joined the church, and then has turned back into living his own way and enjoys the pleasures of sin.

MOAB

Ruth 1:2 (c) Moab may be taken to represent all that is outside of Christ in this world. Canaan or Palestine was God's country, and all other countries were heathen countries. Naomi and her husband left God's people to go down and live among the idolators. They found there were graves there, sorrow and tears abounded there. They were worse off in Moab than they were in Israel. Let us never think that we can find more blessing in the world among God's enemies than in the church among God's people.

MOCK

Prov. 1:26 (a) We can hardly understand God mocking the sinner when the anguish and pain of God's wrath overtakes him. It has the thought of mimicking as God sees the suffering of those who rebel against Him.

MONEY

Isa. 55:1 (a) This type condemns every religion that offers salvation by works. The type represents everything considered of spiritual value by human beings if it is used to purchase forgiveness, and obtain entrance into heaven. Salvation is not for sale. It cannot be bought, nor earned, nor merited by any person, or in any way.

Matt. 22:19 (c) This represents legitimate things which should be given to those with whom we are associated on earth. We should give to the family, to the community and to the government.

Matt. 25:18 (b) This word is typical of any gifts or talents given to a person by the Lord and which should be invested for Him in His service.

MOON

S. of Sol. 6:10 (c) This orb is probably a type of the church. It may also be considered as a type of the Christian. It shines in and upon a dark world as we should do. It has no light of its own, but reflects beautifully the light of the sun. We have no light of our own, but reflect the light of the Son of God. When the shadow of the earth gets in the way, the light of the moon is hindered. So when worldliness enters and clouds the church, the light of her testimony is obscured.

MORNING

Gen. 1:5 (c) We may consider that every day of the life will be filled with shadows (the evening), and sunshine (the morning). There will be sadness followed by gladness in each day. The morning times seem to represent the happy times of life when there are no griefs, sorrows nor troubles. It is the time when everything is going well. There is plenty of money available. The home is a happy home, and the business is prospering. It may also represent the coming of our Lord, which is described as "a morning without clouds." It is probably the time referred to by Isaiah when he said, "The morning cometh, and also the night." Christ is described as the Morning Star, for He will shine in His glory when He returns with power and great glory.

Psa. 30:5 (c) This probably is a picture of the return of the Lord, the rapture of the church, and the beginning of a new day for God's people. (See also Psa. 49:14)

Eccl. 11:6 (c) This represents the bright times in life when the sun is shining, the birds are singing and the soul is filled with hope and joy.

Isa. 14:12 (b) The word is used in this place to describe the bright glories in the pre-earth days, when Satan was one of God's chief angels, clothed in the glory of heaven, and living gorgeously in the light of God.

Isa. 21:12 (b) Here we find described the great rapture of the Church, the morning time for God's people, in contrast with the night of darkness and trouble in which earth will enter.

Rev. 2:28 (b) Here is a description of the Lord Jesus as the One who shines brightly before the eternal dark overtakes men. He is the One who will direct the way when the shadows fall across the path.

Rev. 22:16 (a) By this figure the Lord describes the primal presence of Christ. It is a beautiful description of His deity.

MORSEL

Prov. 17:1 (b) This figure is used as a type of earth's poorest possessions. It is better to have a very little of anything with a quiet heart, than to have a great supply of everything with a troubled heart.

MOSES

Ex. 2:10 (c) He is sometimes considered as a type of Christ in that he was the mediator between God and Israel. He was rejected and repudiated by Israel the same number of times that Jesus was rejected while on earth. He was somewhat clothed with glory on Mount Sinai, as Jesus was clothed with glory on the Mount of Transfiguration. (See also Deut. 18:15 which indicates this truth.)

MOTE

Matt. 7:3 (b) This word describes what may be a very small and inconsiderate flaw in the life of another person, whereas the critic may have faults and flaws far greater than in the one he observes and criticises. The mote is in the flaw in the other person's life, while the beam is the flaw in our own lives.

MOTH

Job 4:19 (b) This insect which weighs very little is used as a type of God's wrath in its least and lightest form. This, falling on mortal man, crushes him and wrecks him.

Psa. 39:11 (a) In this passage natural human beauty is compared to this insect in that it is quickly and easily lost, crushed and destroyed, even as this insect may be easily destroyed.

Isa. 50:9 (b) This type indicates the way the Lord uses little things to remove great things. Little troubles, little difficulties, little adversities destroy peace, joy, zeal, earnestness and even faith, just as a little moth will destroy a large, expensive garment.

Hos. 5:12 (a) The destructive insect eating away at the cloth is a picture of the way our Lord would quietly and slowly deal with Israel, taking away his blessings, one by one, and leaving them as a damaged garment, with no strength, no beauty and no power.

Matt. 6:19 (c) By this is represented decay in the animal kingdom from the moth, decay in the mineral kingdom by the rust, decay in the human kingdom by the thieves. All of these ruin and destroy the things we lay up for ourselves on the earth.

MOTHER

Judg. 5:7 (a) Deborah as the deliverer of Israel took care of the people of God as though they were her own children.

Isa. 50:1 (a) Israel as a united nation is compared to a wife or a bride who begat the great multitude of the people of Israel. The nation had turned away from God as a wife turns away from her husband. (See Hosea 2:2; 4:5; 10:14)

Jer. 50:12 (a) Those who founded and established the great city of Babylon are described in this manner. They formed this mighty, powerful group, they nourished the Babylonians, and taught them to war. The Lord describes the heathen gods and their customs as having been those who moulded Israel into their present evil condition. They followed the gods of the Hittites and the Amorites.

Ezek. 19:2 (a) The strong, able founders of Israel are compared to a mother lion. The nature was fierce, and their attitude cruel. They were no longer the sheep of His pasture.

Ezek. 23:2 (a) This type probably refers to the one kingdom which existed under Solomon. It was afterwards divided into two kingdoms, which are mentioned as the two daughters.

Matt. 12:49-50 (a) Our Lord indicates that there is a very close and sweet relationship between Himself and those who love Him enough to leave all other associations just to live with and for Him.

Rom. 16:13 (a) The servant of God who leads God's people has that sweet, tender care for them and looks after their best interests as we find in the family relationship.

Rev. 17:5 (a) This term probably refers to the Roman Catholic church. Most of the large denominations have emerged from that tremendous system, and have carried with them some of the grave clothes, the habits, the ways and the customs of the Roman church. Some of these "daughters" are so near like the mother church that it is difficult to distinguish them from her.

MOUNT (and forms)

Deut. 1:6 (c) This may be taken as a picture of the Christian who stays all the time around Calvary, or the story of his conversion, and makes no progress in the Christian life. He is occupied only with the death of Christ, and does not see the value nor the power of the risen Christ. He does not grow in grace nor in the knowledge of the Lord Jesus. The Lord wants us to go on and grow unto full stature for our Lord.

Psa. 11:1 (b) The figure here is used to represent some kind of refuge or protection which is outside the realm of God's provision. It refers to human plans and expedients for the protection and welfare of the person. He expects us to fly to Himself for refuge, and this picture is seen in Jer. 48:28.

Psa. 30:7 (b) David is referring to his strong position as king and ruler over a great and mighty nation. He gives God the credit for maintaining him in this exalted position.

Isa. 14:13 (a) This figure is used to express the devil's determination to ascend above God in power and in glory. He planned to be at the very top of all excellence and authority. It may refer to the ambitions of any person to be the greatest, the highest and the best in satan's kingdom.

Isa. 30:17 (a) The type is used in this place to represent the supreme place of authority on the earth among the nations which Israel will occupy some day when Christ is King.

Isa. 40:4 (a) By this delightful figure the Lord is encouraging us to know that He will remove obstacles and hindrances in the Christian's life so as to make His yoke easy and His burden light in the service which we render.

Matt. 17:20 (a) Our Lord is telling us the same message that He told to Zerubbabel in Zech. 4:6-7. Troubles, hindrances, problems and difficulties are represented in the Bible as mountains. Those who know the Lord intimately and believe Him fully may address themselves to these problems and see the Lord solve them and remove them. Spirit-filled men see miracles happen in their lives. (See also Matt. 21:21; Mark 11:23)

Gal. 4:24 (a) Sinai was the place where the law was given to Moses. He brought the law down to the people. It revealed the perfect will of God, and God's thoughts and plans about man's holiness. These laws are permanent, inflexible and solid as the mountain.

MOUTH

Num. 16:30 (a) By this figure is described the opening up of the crust of the earth which permitted Korah, Dathan and Abiram and their properties and families to go down into the heart of the earth, or hell. (See also Num. 26:10; Psa. 69:15 Deut. 11:6)

2 Sam. 22:9 (a) This is a poetic expression used by David in the rejoicing of his heart. He is describing the greatness of God, the power of his Lord, and the judgments decreed by the great Judge when He pours out His wrath upon His enemies. (See Psa. 18:8)

2 Ki. 4:34 (c) We should learn by this figure that we are to talk to others in the language and in a manner which they can understand. This older prophet talked to the young man (in figure) in a way that a boy could understand the meaning. We should learn to do this also in our teaching and ministry.

Job 5:16 (a) The reference here is to the fact that the evil thoughts and desires of the heart find expression through the words that are spoken. The Lord by His grace and power prevents wicked people from saying evil things.

Job 31:27 (a) In this peculiar figure, Job describes the fact that he did not say one thing, and do something entirely different. There was no disagreement between his statements and his doings whereby he could deceive others. He was no hypocrite.

Job 41:19 (a) God is describing in poetic language the tremendous strength and fierce power of this animal which may have been one of the prehistoric monsters whose skeletons have been discovered.

Psa. 22:21 (b) This is a type of the cruel power, the blasphemous statements and the cutting words spoken by the enemies of Christ as they surrounded the cross on which He hung.

Isa. 5:14 (a) Hell is ever ready to receive all who are sent there by Christ, the Judge. The gates are never closed; the entrance is never barred. There is no limit to the number that she may take into her pit of torture.

Isa. 6:7 (c) Here we find that which may be used as a description of the cleansing power of God on the speech, the language and the conversation of men who trust in Him.

Isa. 9:12 (b) This type represents the power of the enemies of Israel to come with damage and cruel hatred to invade the land and destroy the inhabitants.

Isa. 11:4 (b) The reference no doubt is to the word that shall issue from the mouth of the Lord Jesus when He comes to judge the earth in righteousness and to punish His enemies. The rod is also mentioned as a sword proceeding from the mouth of the Lord Jesus

Christ. His word is sufficient to judge and condemn. (See also Isa. 49:2; Rev. 2:16; Rev. 19:15)

Dan. 7:5 (b) The prophet is describing in an interesting way the King of the Medio-Persian empire, Darius. That nation, with the Medians in supremacy, destroyed the kingdom of his three predecessors in Babylon. He is represented as devouring that which had been built up by the three great kings of Babylon.

Dan. 7:8 (b) The proud and boastful language of the Roman emperors is thus described by this figure. It refers to the great leaders of the mighty Roman empire, which is represented by this fourth beast. (See also v. 20)

Amos 3:12 (a) In this case the lion represents the invading hosts of the enemies of Israel who almost completely destroy the people of God. Very few of the Jews are left, and they are in hiding in any place they can find, such as under the bed, or hiding in a couch under the blankets. Only a very insignificant part of Israel is left after the enemies finish their attack. Not much is left with which Israel can walk and work, and not much is left of their power to hear the call or the will of God.

Nahum 3:12 (b) By this we understand that Nineveh would become an easy prey to an invading army, who would destroy her inhabitants and carry away her possessions. The eater is the enemy that shall come to conquer Nineveh.

Zech. 5:8 (b) The ephah was a measuring vessel. It was open at the top. The women probably represent commerce and business. They have wings to show that they may traverse the entire world if they wish. The woman in the midst may represent the fact that commerce and business have invaded society, and in a large measure controls the morals and actions of people everywhere. The lead weight placed on the opening at the top of this vessel probably indicates that God Himself seals men to the decision which they make, so that they are unable to extricate themselves from the chaos, the deceit, the wickedness in which they find themselves.

1 Cor. 9:9 (a) The ox represents the Christian worker who is entitled to proper remuneration for the labor which he gives to God's people, and to the church. He brings spiritual blessings to the saints, and they should give temporal blessings to him. (See also 1 Cor. 9:11)

2 Tim. 4:17 (a) Paul describes his enemies as lions who would by their words and by their power hinder his testimony and destroy his person.

Rev. 1:16 (a) This figure is often used about the words that come from the lips of our Lord. What he says is piercing, cutting and forceful. (See also Heb. 4:12; Rev. 19:15)

Rev. 12:15 (a) By this figure is represented the power of Satan by which he endeavors to destroy the nation of Israel, and to blot out all trace of the Lord Jesus Christ. Probably he does most of this by his words, false teachings, false doctrines, and false religions which are in fact destroying millions of souls, and keeping them from Christ Jesus.

Rev. 13:2 (a) This beast is the anti-Christ from whom there comes announcements that create great hopes and words that create great fears. He is described as a monstrous wild and fierce animal who by his messages destroys millions. (See also Rev. 9:19)

MULE

Gen. 36:24 (c) If this word is correctly translated, then there is a wonderful lesson to be found in this passage. Mules were found in the wilderness because the asses had been mingling with the horses and producing these fine work animals while it was all unknown to the owners. It is the story of "unearned increment." It is the story of God granting rich blessing and increase without our definite planning or knowledge. God does this for His children frequently.

2 Sam. 18:9 (c) In this story we see a picture of the disappointment which comes to those who trust in human devices and rest their hopes on earthly provisions. Absalom had hoped to use the mule either to carry him to victory, or else to carry him to safety. He was disappointed in both cases, and the mule became the means of his death. It is a warning to us not to place our confidence in any means or methods provided by earth's resources. The animal represents any doctrine, or theory, or religion which is man-made, and on which one often depends for salvation and deliverance. It will fail us in the hour of need.

MUSTARD (Tree)

Matt. 13:31 (a) This figure represents the great religious group called "the church." It began with a very small group, but has spread all over the earth, and has become a monstrosity. Its members include Atheists, idolators and evildoers of every kind. Its branches reach out into every part of society, and in every nation. The birds in this church tree represent evil spirits ruling in church councils. (See also Mark 4:31; Luke 13:19)

Matt. 17:20 (Seed) (a) This figure is used to represent the individual believer. It does not refer to the size of his faith, for the Lord always condemned little faith. Little faith means big doubts. The Lord condemns these. He is telling us that though one may be obscure, unknown, uneducated and unimportant in life, yet if that person is full of faith as the seed is full of mustard, then he may see miracles performed in his life. (See also Luke 17:6)

MUZZLE

Deut. 25:4 (a) This word has two meanings. The first is that we are to know that the servant of God, which is represented by the ox, should be free to tell the story of God's grace in his own way, and not be hindered by any rules or regulations of men. It also means that the servant of God is entitled to receive the benefits in a material way of his ministry. He should be given remuneration for his work. He is entitled to receive the food, the clothing and the other necessities of life because of his ministry. (See also 1 Cor. 9:9; 1 Tim. 5:18)

MYRRH

Psa. 45:8 (c) This type represents the fragrance of Christ to God in His sacrificial death. His death went up to God as a sweet smelling savour, which is most blessed both to God and to man. (See also John 19:39)

Prov. 7:17 (c) This may be taken as a picture or a type of the enticing, alluring schemes and plans of the harlots to attract men to their homes, and to a life of sinful pleasure.

S. of Sol. 1:13 (c) By this figure we understand the feelings of God's people concerning the loveliness of Christ to their hearts. The beauty, the fragrance and the attractiveness of the Lord Jesus are compared to the sweet odors arising from precious spices.

Matt. 2:11 (c) This perfume is the third of the gifts mentioned, which were brought to the Lord Jesus Christ by the wise men. It typifies the beauty and the value of Christ as He gave His life for us. The gold is a type of His perfection and loveliness in His prenatal days. The frankincense may be taken as a type of the beauty and loveliness of Christ during His life on earth. The myrrh may remind us of the preciousness and sweetness of Christ in His death.

MYRTLE

Isa. 41:19 (c) The seven kinds of trees mentioned in this verse may be taken as types of seven kinds of Christian experience. The myrtle tree usually represents the happy, radiant Christian life which remains green and beautiful even through the winter months.

Isa. 55:13 (b) No doubt our Lord is teaching us that when we walk with Him, believe His Word, and live for His glory, our lives will be filled with joy and gladness, instead of with sorrow, grief and pain such as the thorns produce. The brier represents the sorrows, pains and griefs of life, while the myrtle represents the joys, the beauty and happiness of life.

Zech. 1:8 (b) By this picture we may understand that our Lord coming forth in power and having upon Him the blood of His enemies because He trod the winepress alone is found mingling and mixing among a happy, radiant people of God in God's country.

N

NAAMAN

2 Ki. 5:1 (c) He may be taken as a type of a lost sinner who realizes his need but goes to the wrong place and the wrong person for the remedy. This man did not listen well to his instructions. He went to the king instead of to the prophet. After learning his mistake, he then went to God's man, the prophet, who gave him God's remedy. At first, he rejected God's remedy because it did not agree with his own ideas. Through the persuasion of his servant, he decided to obey the man of God, and when he followed those instructions he received the cleansing he desired.

NABAL

1 Sam. 25:25 (c) We take this to be a type of the foolish man who is so in love with his sins that he has no time for God's message, God's messenger, nor God's ministry.

NAIL

2 Chron. 3:9 (c) The fact that the weight of the nails is given may be taken as a picture of the value God puts on unseen acts and deeds. He knows that which is done in obscurity, privately and without publicity. He weighs our words and deeds as they are used for His glory.

Ezra 9:8 (b) This represents the fixed and permanent position of the people of Israel when God returns them to their own land.

Eccl. 12:11 (a) Wise words fasten themselves in the heart and the mind. They remain there for a blessing in days to come.

Isa. 22:23 (a) By this picture we see the permanent and secure position of Christ, the Messiah, as He sits on the throne of His kingdom. Temporarily the nail and the place have been removed, but He is still Lord, and will resume His position as the King of Israel in the day of His power.

Zech. 10:4 (b) This figure indicates that it is God Himself who has made Christ to be King and Sovereign. He establishes both Israel and the Church under His permanent and eventual rule.

Col. 2:14 (a) We have revealed to us in this picture the act of God in putting our sins on Jesus, so that He bore them "in His own body on the tree."

NAILS (animal claws)

Dan. 7:19 (a) These represent the terrible power of the Roman empire to grasp, hold and destroy her enemies. It is the claws of the wild beast that are so greatly feared.

NAKED (and forms)

Gen. 3:7 (c) We may learn from this figure that nothing is hidden from God. All things are open to His eyes, and nothing can be covered up. There was no hypocrisy here, for they knew all about each other, and God knew all about them.

Gen. 42:9 (a) Joseph accused his brethren of being spies who came to see the military installations, the defense measures, and the riches of the land, with a view to invading and conquering Egypt.

Ex. 20:26 (a) In climbing steps, any physical disability or defects could be seen by observers. God does not require public demonstrations of the faults and failures of those who come to worship Him.

1 Sam. 20:30 (b) Saul is accusing Jonathan of insulting his mother, and denying his birthright privileges by his loyalty to David. Jonathan was the heir to the throne and therefore would inherit the glory, the power and the wealth of his father if he remained true to his father.

Job 1:21 (c) This is one way of saying that he came into the world owning nothing, and possessing nothing. He would leave the world with nothing. (See Eccl. 5:15)

Job 26:6 (a) We have not seen hell, but God has seen it, for He made it; therefore, everything about hell is clearly seen and understood by the Lord.

Isa. 47:3 (b) The prophet is telling the Babylonians that they will lose all their wealth, their ornaments and that their defense will be taken from them, and they will be left helpless.

Lam. 1:8 (b) The nations have seen Jerusalem punished by God, and stripped of her power, beauty and place of honor.

Lam. 4:21 (a) The Edomites will give themselves over to sin and wickedness without pretense or shame.

Ezek. 16:8 (a) This word occurs in several places in connection with Israel, and of other nations. It describes a state of exposure of all the nation with no deception, no pretense, no covering up of any sin or evil. It represents also the loss of all assets, power, strength and defense. (See v. 36; Ezek. 23:10; Nahum 3:5; Hab. 2:15)

Amos 2:16 (a) The judgment of God on Israel will be so severe that none will have any goods or possessions left. Everything will be lost. This has been literally fulfilled.

Micah 1:8 (b) The prophet thus describes the utter desolation of Israel. By this unclothed illustration, Israel was to know of that which was to happen to them. (See v. 11)

Hab. 3:9 (a) God's words of judgment were clearly revealed without camouflage or deception.

2 Cor. 5:3 (a) Since we cannot take any garments with us when we die, we must have His robe of righteousness, or else we would be in the presence of God without a garment. We cannot come into God's presence unclothed. God has provided a robe of righteousness, and a garment of salvation. It may be also that the Lord is referring in this passage to the changed bodies which we shall have in the resurrection. It will be identical with the present bodies which we own, but will be incorruptible, and will be free from all pain, suffering and deterioration. (See also Rev. 3:18)

Heb. 4:13 (b) The Lord is telling us again the same truth that He gave us in Gen. 3:7. He tells us very clearly that nothing can be hidden from God. He can see through any covering, any false religion, any false teachings, any excuses that the sinner may use to cover his sins, iniquities, trespasses and transgressions.

Rev. 3:17 (a) God is telling these people that their real condition is seen and known by Him. Nothing about them or their lives is hidden from His eyes.

Rev. 16:15 (a) God sees these people as having no covering at all, unless it is the robe of righteousness which He gives to those who trust in Him, and belong to Him.

Rev. 17:16 (a) The false church is to be stripped of all her pretense and false claims, and will be seen in all her wickedness. All her evils will be exposed.

NAME

2 Sam. 7:9 (a) This represents a great and good reputation. It means the same in most of the passages in which it is mentioned, as in Isa. 55:13, and Jer. 13:11.

Prov. 22:1 (a) The good reputation of a man is of more value than earthly possessions. (See Eccl. 7:1; Isa. 56:5; Isa. 63:12; Jer. 32:20; Zeph. 3:20)

John 1:12 (a) We are not told in this passage which name the Lord is referring to. The Lord Jesus has somewhere around two hundred names in the Bible. Each name indicates an office which He bears, and a service which He renders. The Lord is using a common principle in this passage, for if we are sick we seek for one whose name is physician. If the teeth need attention, we seek for a dentist. If the car needs fixing we seek for a mechanic. The name indicates the work which the person can do, and is really a title. Probably in the passage we are considering the name referred to is

"Saviour." As we pass along the streets of life and realize that we need to be saved from our sins, and from the penalty of them, we find this wonderful Man whose Name is Saviour, and we at once commit our cause and our case to Him. He does the saving, and therefore we prove that we believe in His Name when we take advantage of that name or title and trust our all to Him.

Rom. 10:13 (a) Again in this passage we do not find mentioned what name we call upon. It may be that it is the name "Lord." Certainly we are saved when Jesus Christ becomes our Lord. His lordship is put first, ahead of His other many names. Those who appeal to Him in this way find He is ready and willing to save.

NAOMI

Ruth 1:2, 20 (c) This is the type of a backslider who, having enjoyed the blessing of God, leaves the fellowship of God to go into the world. Afterward she returns from the far country suffering the consequences of disobedience In the beginning she is the backslider going away, but in the end she is the backslider restored to the fellowship of God.

NAPKIN

Luke 19:20 (b) This is a type of the preparations made by gifted Christians for keeping and preserving their gifts, instead of using them for the blessing of others. There are those who are well taught in the Scriptures. They listen well to sermons, but none of their talents and gifts are used for the blessing of others.

John 20:7 (b) Probably this is a picture of the separation that was to take place between Christ, the head of the Church, and His followers who constituted His Body. By this means the Saviour is telling that He was to leave this earth, leave the Christians behind, and ascend to His Father. The head was to be in heaven, while the Church, which is His Body, was to remain on earth. Mary did not want Him to leave, and so she tried to hold Him here. For that reason the Lord forbade her to hold Him.

NARROW (and forms)

Prov. 23:27 (b) The man who gets led astray by such a woman finds himself become a slave to her. His freedom of movements in life is hindred. He cannot make the progress in business, nor society that he should.

Isa. 28:20 (a) By this type is described the religious plans of men and other human devices by which they expect to provide safety, comfort and protection for themselves, for this life and the next.

Isa. 49:19 (b) This presents a picture of the flourishing condition of Israel, when they are restored to their land. They will increase in number until they fill the land, and will need more space for expansion.

Matt. 7:14 (a) Our Lord in this way pictures the path of the believer. The world thinks that God's people are fanatics because they do not follow the ways of the world in sin of many kinds. Because the believer does not spend his time, talents and funds in the ways of the world, they think that the Christian is restricted and hindered. The Christian really is brought into a broad place.

NATION

1 Pet. 2:9 (a) The Church of God is thus named. All who are saved are in the kingdom of God where Christ is King over them. As such we are to trade together, promote the welfare of each other, and speak the same language.

NAVEL

Prov. 3:8 (b) This type represents the seat of digestion, health and strength. This is used just as we speak of the heart as the seat of affection and joy.

Ezek. 16:4 (b) In this place it is a type of that which holds one to the world, and to things which attract the soul, and keep one from living entirely for God.

NAZARITE

Num. 6:2 (c) This type represents one who willingly takes the path of separation to live only and constantly for the glory of God. (See also Judg. 13:5)

NECK

Gen. 27:40 (b) Here we find a type of the position of servitude. The yoke on the neck indicates subjection to another. The yoke broken from the neck indicates deliverance from the condition of servitude. (See Deut. 28:48; Jer. 28:10; Jer. 30:8; Acts 15:10)

2 Chron. 36:13 (b) In this passage, as in many others, the stiff neck, or the hard neck, represents a rebellious spirit which refuses to bow to the will of God. It is equivalent to the expression we use about the horse, who "takes the bit in his teeth." The horse refuses to be guided by the driver. So there are those who refuse to be guided by the Lord, either in their faith or in their practices.
(See also Psa. 75:5; Isa. 48:4; Jer. 17:23)

Prov. 29:1 (a) That person who refuses to listen to God's Word, and rejects the guidance of the Spirit will be surely punished by God.

NEEDLE

Matt. 19:24 (b) The Lord uses this little article to illustrate the impossibility of entering heaven by one's own resources. The needle mentioned in Luke 18:25 is a surgeon's needle, for Luke was a physician. The meaning, however, is the same in both cases. No one can be saved by his own merits, or assets, or resources, or religious activities. Christ only is the way to God.

NEEDLEWORK

Psa. 45:14 (b) This type illustrates the various beautiful works performed by Christians, whereby they weave a robe of righteousness against the day of their meeting with Christ in the judgment. The Christian has two robes. The one in Psa. 45 made of golden thread is the product of God's own rich provision. This robe entitles us to come into God's presence. It is described in verse 13, of this 45th Psalm. The robe which is described in verse 14 is a different robe entirely, and is a robe which we make by good works after we are saved. It is described in Rev. 19:8. That robe of fine linen is made of the righteous acts of the saints. We ourselves weave this robe day by day by our Christian activities for our Lord. The first robe of wrought gold we receive by faith when we trust Jesus Christ, and make Him the Lord of our lives. The second robe we receive at the marriage supper of the Lamb, and is made up by us in our many words and deeds done for the glory of God. The garment mentioned in Matt. 22:11 is the garment of wrought gold which is the gift of the mighty God to those who heed His call, and come to Him.

NEIGH

Jer. 5:8 (a) The horse calls for his mate for he wishes companionship and association. There is no real relationship between these animals, and the Lord is calling upon men to remember divine relationships which have ordained human relationships and thus to maintain a godly, consistent life. He is not to be constantly seeking for alliances which are not just and true. (See also Jer. 13:27)

NEST

Num. 24:21 (a) These people lived in a stronghold in the mountains and thought that they were secure. As the eagle builds where she thinks she is perfectly safe on the high cliff, so these people planned on safety from their situation. They did not know they were to be destroyed eventually, their stronghold would be conquered and they themselves would be annihilated. (See Jer. 49:16; Hab. 2:9)

Deut. 32:11 (a) This is a description of the home life as it existed in Egypt among the Israelites and out of which they were emptied at the Passover. They had to leave their dwelling place and take the long journey through the wilderness. It is also a description of the personal life in the home, in the business, or in the church, out of which the Lord sometimes thrusts His children in order that they learn to know His power, and trust His love.

Job 29:18 (a) Job uses this term to describe his own lovely, comfortable home life before he was attacked by Satan.

Isa. 10:14 (a) The King of Assyria used this expression to describe his palace and his city which were filled with great riches and treasures which he had obtained by war.

Jer. 48:28 (a) This type represents the believer who finds his home, his life, and all his affairs wholly resting in the Lord Jesus Christ, the Rock of Ages.

Jer. 49:16 (a) In this way the Lord describes the sinner who seeks to make for himself a comfortable place in which to live, but who omits God from his life. (See also Oba. 4)

NET

Job 19:6 (a) Job's circumstances, troubles and disasters which befell him on every hand are compared to a net which catches fish or animals, and makes them helpless.

Psa. 9:15 (a) In this way the Lord is telling us that the schemes and plans of the wicked, whereby they hope to enmesh and catch Christians, have turned about to be a snare for themselves, their own devices work against those who made them. (See also Psa. 25:15; 31:4; 35:7; 57:6)

Psa. 141:10 (b) These nets may be the wicked designs and evil traps prepared by David's enemies to catch him. The case was reversed and they fell victims to their own evil plans. (See Hab. 1:15)

Prov. 1:17 (a) The Lord is evidently warning us against the hidden snares, pits and traps of the enemies of God. They use hidden schemes and plans, veiled or camouflaged in order to deceive and thus seduce God's people. We are to be diligent, vigilant and alert of these devices of the Devil. (See also 2 Cor. 2:11.)

Eccl. 7:26 (a) In this way the Lord is warning us against the tricks and traps of Satan who would like to destroy the testimony of the people of God.

Isa. 51:20 (a) It is evident that our Lord is thus describing the defeat of His people who will be captured and bound by their enemies in the streets of the city, when God pours out His wrath upon them.

Ezek. 12:13 (b) This figure is used to describe the way in which the King of Babylon will capture the King of Israel as a bird is caught in the net.

Matt. 4:21 (c) These nets may be taken as a type of the schemes and plans of many religious leaders to capture souls for the church. They need mending constantly, but they should be forsaken.

Matt. 13:47 (b) In this parable the net represents the great religious plans and programs of Christendom which are used to gather in people of every kind, saved and unsaved. At the judgment throne, the Lord, the head of the Church, will separate the saved from the unsaved, and will cast out of His Kingdom all things that offend.

NETHER

Deut. 24:6 (c) We are warned by the Lord not to destroy the usefulness of another man's life. We should not deal with him in such a way that his earning power is hindered and his usefulness prevented.

NETTLE

Isa. 34:13 (b) This is a type of the multitude of little, tiny, sticking, pricking troubles that the Lord would send upon the inhabitants of Idumea because they rejected Him and His Word. (See also brambles, thistles, and thorns.)

NIGHT

Ex. 12:42 (c) The ungodly live in the dark. Paul came to turn men from darkness to light. This darkness in Egypt was just a type and a picture of those who live without the light of life, then are suddenly cut off and taken to the outer dark. When the plague of darkness fell upon Egypt, there was light in all the houses of the Israelites. Those who reject the light of life dwell here and hereafter in darkness.

Lev. 6:9 (c) This represents the night of need. The sinner is living in the dark and so the sacrifice is constantly being offered for him in order that he may be saved any time that he will come to the altar to find the Saviour. There is no time in the sinner's life when he may not come and find the Saviour ready to save him.

Job 35:10 (c) This describes the terrible dark times which Job experienced when he lost all his possessions and only God remained. He sang in the midst of his poverty and boils.

Psa. 16:7 (c) This type represents the dark times in David's life when the shadows fell across his path, and he was constantly in fear for his life.

Psa. 30:5 (c) This probably represents the whole period of this life as contrasted with the time of the coming of the Lord which is the morning hour. It also represents the dark times of some specific sorrow. The Lord gives deliverance and joy follows.

Psa. 42:8 (c) This represents a time of perplexity in which victory is given while the difficulty still remains.

Isa. 21:12 (b) The night which is mentioned no doubt refers to the long night of eternity which is called the "outer dark" in the New Testament. In hell none of the light of God may be seen. The sinner asks about the night. He hardly ever asks, "Is there a heaven?" His inquiry is about hell. The answer in this verse reminds the inquirer of the fact that there is a morning coming, a morning without clouds. It is the time when our precious Lord rules and reigns, and all sin and wickedness has been put away. The saved man enters into the morning time of blessing, while the unsaved man enters into the night of sorrow and suffering.

Jer. 14:8 (b) Israel is going through a time of darkness and despair while scattered over the earth. Some day this night will be past, and Christ, the Sun of Righteousness, will resume His place on the earth, but not as a lowly shepherd, but as the mighty King who will bring light and life to the nation of Israel.

Hosea 7:6 (b) We may learn from this that those in Israel who should have been producing blessing and profit for the nation were not doing so. The leaders were failing in their task as helpers of God's people.

John 13:30 (c) It is always night for those who turn their backs on Christ, go out of His presence to deny Him, and take their place among the enemies of God, and those who wickedly oppose Christ Jesus. (See also John 11:10)

1 Thes. 5:5 (a) This is one of the many ways in which the Lord assures us that those who are His children saved by grace, and brought into His marvelous light, do not belong to the kingdom of darkness, nor do they accept the theology of those who are in the dark.

Rev. 21:25 (a) In heaven where the Lord is the light, there are no times of darkness, no seasons of sorrow or perplexity, no hidden times when the sun goes down and sin comes up. Those who go to heaven dwell in the light constantly, and there are never any shadows there.

NINE

Mark 15:34 (a) This time was 3:00 o'clock in the afternoon, the time of the evening sacrifice, prescribed by Moses. Jesus died at the time of the evening sacrifice.

Luke 17:17 (c) This is the number of insufficiency wherein they failed to return, failed to bring their gratitude, failed to show themselves to the Lord, and were more content with the gift than with the Giver.

NITRE

Jer. 2:22 (b) This is an alcohol used to remove grease and stains but it could not remove the marks of sin.

NOAH

Gen. 6:9 (c) He may be taken as the type of a good man, upright, moral, clean, honest and dependable. However, he learned that he would be under the judgment of God if he did not find a way of salvation. He therefore entered and stayed in the ark which he built, and was saved from the great flood of God's wrath. Every good man must be saved by the Saviour. Everyone outside of Christ will be lost. (See also Heb. 11:7)

NORTH

Job 26:7 (c) There are many ideas about this expression. It is probably best to believe that it represents the great and unknown power of the unseen God. (See also Psa. 48:2; Isa. 14:13) Let us remember that Satan endeavored to occupy God's throne, and that was his great sin.

NOSE

Lev. 21:18 (c) This organ is the organ of discernment by which one can tell whether any substance is spoiled or good, whether an animal is alive or dead, whether anything is sweet or sour. One whose nose is broken has difficulty in discerning by smelling any of these things. In the spiritual sense, it represents one who cannot discern between what has come from God, and what is the product of man's brain. He does not discern that which comes from Satan and that which comes from God. He does not know what is good for the soul, and what is evil. Such a person cannot possibly be a leader of God's people, for he cannot discern right from wrong.

2 Ki. 19:28 (b) In this graphic way the Lord is describing His control over the King of Assyria as when the farmer controls the bull by putting a ring in his nose. God is assuring His people that He will lead the King of Assyria away, back to his own land, and will save Israel from the invader. (See Isa. 37:29)

S. of Sol. 7:4 (a) Solomon is exalting the Person of Christ in some Scriptures and in others He is exalting the Church. In this passage he evidently is talking about the Bride, the Church, and indicates that she has great powers of discernment, able to discern God's ways, and able to judge well the things that are for God's glory, and those that are not.

Isa. 65:5 (b) This figure represents the delicate feelings of God against those who are proud and self-sufficient. They are an offense to God. He has no pleasure in them.

Ezek. 8:17 (b) Our Lord noticed the actions of His enemies. This act of putting the branch of a bush or the twig of a tree to the nose was an expression of contempt, derision and hatred against God. It is the oriental equivalent to the more modern method of thumbing the nose. It also has the same thought as is expressed by Paul in Gal. 6:7. One of the revised renderings of this Scripture is: "God will not let you turn up your nose at Him."

Ezek. 23:25 (a) The Lord is telling us in this passage that the Assyrians will invade Israel and will destroy their ability to serve acceptably, or to hear effectively, or to be of any blessing whatever in their land, or to each other.

NOSTRILS

Ex. 15:8 (c) This is a poetic expression to describe the great power of the Lord in cursing His enemies. (See 2 Sam. 22:9; Psa. 18:8)

NOURISH (and forms)

Gen. 45:11 (b) This expression is used to indicate the helpful care of the Lord in providing for His people, caring for their needs, and supplying all their wants. (See chap. 50:21; Isa. 1:2; Isa. 23:4; Ezek. 19:2)

NUMBER (and forms)

Job 14:16 (c) This seems to indicate that the Lord watches every step that is taken by His child, and knows how many there are, and what is the number of each step that he takes. This indicates the very wonderful care of God for His child.

Psa. 90:12 (b) Evidently the Lord wants us to watch the details of our lives, for we only have a certain number of days to live, and we should know how many days are left in the ordinary course of life. If we do so, we will certainly endeavor to make every day count for eternity.

Matt. 10:30 (b) It does not say that God has counted our hairs, but rather that He has put a number on each hair. The lesson we learn from this is that each hair has its own number as a proof to us that the God of heaven is interested in every detail of our lives. (See also Lu. 12:7)

NURSE

Num. 11:12 (a) Moses uses this type to indicate the sweet, tender relationship which existed between his heart and the people of Israel who are here compared to his children.

Isa. 49:23 (a) This is descriptive of the manner and method by which the Gentile rulers will be made to serve the nation of Israel with their wealth and their power in the day of the millennium.

1 Thes. 2:7 (a) Paul thus describes his loving care for God's people.

NUTS

S. of Sol. 6:11 (b) This probably describes the children of God. They live in heavenly places, not down in the swamps. They are of many colors, like the various races. They have good, sweet hearts. Some have thin shells, and some are hard and thick. They are of various shapes and sizes, according to the way they have grown. There is much about them to be thrown away, but much to be kept that is valuable.

O

OAK

Gen. 35:8 (c) Deborah, the nurse, was buried under an oak tree, and from this we notice that usually the oak tree is a type of the bitterness of sorrow because of death. Notice that in Josh. 24:26 that great leader made a covenant with the people under an oak tree, and then died as we read in v. 29. Notice also that the prophet sat under an oak tree in 1 Ki. 13:14, and immediately thereafter he died, as recorded in v. 24. Absalom was caught by his head in an oak tree, 2 Sam. 18:9. Saul and his sons were buried under an oak tree, 1 Chron. 10:12. In Zech. 11:2 the oaks are said to howl because of death. This verse was used as a text at the funeral of Mr. Spurgeon.

ODOR

Lev. 26:31 (c) The worship which was offered by Israel while they were still living in disobedience and rebellion would not be acceptable to God, nor pleasing to Him.

Phil. 4:18 (a) This describes the fragrance to God of the offerings made by willing, loving hearts.

Rev. 5:8 (b) This type describes the sweetness of the prayers of God's people as their praise ascends to His throne.

OFFERING

All the offerings described in the Scriptures are connected directly or indirectly with Christ Jesus. Most of them are pictures of the work of the Saviour in one form or another. In Ephesians 5:2 we read that Christ is our offering and our sacrifice. The offering is that which we give to God because we love Him, honor Him and trust Him. The sacrifice is that which is given to God in exchange for redemption, forgiveness and His other gifts. The Passover lamb was a sacrifice, not an offering. The offerings and that which they represent are given as follows:

Wave Offering Ex. 29:24 (c) This is typical of presenting before God all the beauties and the virtues of the Lord Jesus Christ as the One in whom we trust and in whom we delight in lieu of anything in ourselves.

Lev. 23:17, 20 (c) You will notice that these loaves are baked with leaven, for they represent the person of the offerer. There is always sin in us. We are never sinless. Therefore, the offering that represents us contains leaven which is always an evil substance. There was no leaven in any of the other offerings which represent the Lord Jesus.

Burnt Offering Lev. 1:3 (c) This represents the offering of the entire person of the Lord Jesus to be accepted instead of our entire person. We receive the blessings of His perfection and God accepts His perfection in the place of our imperfection.

Drink Offering Gen. 35:14 (c) This type represents the utter consecration of the believer who pours out all his life for the service of his Lord.

Meat Offering Lev. 2:1 (c) This is a picture of the beautiful, smooth life of the Lord Jesus Christ offered to God instead of the horrible, rough life that we have lived. (We are saved by His life — Rom. 5:10) The word should be "meal" offering.

Peace Offering Lev. 3:1 (c) By this is illustrated the way in which our Lord Jesus by the sacrifice of Himself made peace for us by the blood of His cross. (Col. 1:20)

Ignorance Offering Lev. 4:2 (c) Here is revealed the sweetness of God's care in that the sacrifice of Christ is efficacious for the sins which are committed unknowingly and therefore are not confessed.

Trespass Offering Lev. 5:6 (c) This offering is for the actual sins which are committed day by day and must be met by the sacrifice of our bessed Lord. "Christ died for our sins" (1 Cor. 15:3). This relates to our conduct rather than to our character.

Sin Offering Lev. 5:17 (c) This type represents the suffering of the Lord Jesus for sinners. This relates to our character rather than to our conduct.

Heave Offering Num. 18:24 (c) This is a type of that which is offered to the Lord of our gifts, talents, activities, etc., which shows Him that we love Him and are happy to give to Him.

All the above types are summed up as pictures and types of our Lord Jesus in Ephesians 5:2, where we read that He "hath given Himself for us an offering and a sacrifice to God for a sweet smelling savour."

OIL

Lev. 14:16 (c) This is no doubt a type of the Holy Spirit Himself. It was to be applied to the ear so that the hearing would be entirely God-ward, and for the Word of God. It was applied to the thumb for the work of the priest was to be for God in the power of the Spirit. It was to be applied to the toe, for his walk was to be with God, and before God, walking in the Spirit. (See vs. 28)

Num. 6:15 (c) In this passage the oil again seems to represent the Holy Spirit actuating the life, filling the soul, and especially the coming of the Spirit upon the Lord Jesus Christ.

Deut. 32:13 (b) It is quite evident in this passage that the oil again represents the Holy Spirit given from and by the Lord Jesus Christ, who is the eternal Rock of ages.

Deut. 33:24 (b) This probably represents a smooth, fragrant and delightful walk in the Spirit of God by this great man of God. An impression would be left behind at each step. So the Spirit-filled man leaves behind him fragrant impressions of his walk with the Lord in the Spirit.

2 Ki. 4:2 (c) Probably this represents the blessings of God which He pours out upon the man or the woman of faith in order that the needs of the life may be met.

Job 29:6 (b) This is an indication of the great wealth and opportunity enjoyed by Job when he lived in prosperity and peace.

Psa. 23:5 (b) This is emblematic of the blessed experience of the believer in which the Spirit of God anoints him for effective service, as a king and as a priest.

Psa. 141:5 (a) By this type we understand the sweet, refreshing effect of the kindly counsel of a godly friend.

Isa. 61:3 (b) The joy of heart, the freedom of soul, and the radiance of spirit are compared to oil because of its sweetness, smoothness and value.

Matt. 25:4 (b) This probably indicates the presence and power of the Holy Spirit in the believer's life.

Luke 10:34 (c) It may be that the oil represents the kind, sweet comforting words that were spoken, and the wine represents the courage and the new hope brought to the heart of this wounded man. It may be that both of these refer to the healing power and the strengthening power of the Holy Spirit, and (or) the Word of God.

Heb. 1:9 (b) This describes the blessed anointing of Christ to be both Lord and Saviour, High Priest and King. The King and the Priest were both inducted into office by this anointing from God.

OINTMENT

Ex. 30:25 (c) Probably we may understand by this perfume that the God of heaven gives to His people the strange fragrance of His presence, which distinguishes them from all other people. No one could use this ointment but those in the tabernacle. Those upon whom it was placed, as well as all the articles on which it was spread, were identified as being holy and belonging exclusively to God. Those who walk with the Lord and live in His presence do have a heavenly fragrance about them that no religion can give.

OLIVE (TREE)

Psa. 133:2 (a) By this we understand the gracious fellowship of God's people as they dwell together and serve with one another.

Eccl. 10:1 (b) This definitely is a type of the godly and wise life of a devoted Christian. This good reputation may be easily spoiled by some act or attitude of folly which may come into the life of that person.

S. of Sol. 1:3 (a) This beautiful picture represents the soothing and blessed effects of the name of the Lord upon the hungry, weary heart of that one who trusts in Christ.

Isa. 1:6 (c) Probably this may be a picture of human efforts which are made to cover up human sins and failures. It may represent God's provision for the sinner.

Matt. 26:7 (c) Perhaps this is a type of the worship and adoration brought to the Lord Jesus because of His loveliness, and because that He is so precious to the heart.

OLIVE (Tree)

Judges 9:8 (b) In this parable probably this tree represents some delightful, refreshing person who might be called to be the leader of the people. You will note that other trees represent other kinds of people in this same parable.

Isa. 17:6 (c) Perhaps this represents the fact that Damascus would not be completely destroyed, but that some families would remain and the city would continue to be a city. This certainly has been the case.

Hosea 14:6 (b) Here we see a picture of Israel restored to her place of prominence and power with the land healed, the rains falling on rich pastures, and the glory of all lands again seen in Palestine.

Zech. 4:3 (a) Plainly the passage indicates that these two olive trees are types of the Holy Spirit of God and the Word of God. The Spirit has, in Himself, might on the one hand, and power on the other. He is able to move mountains out of the life of the believer. Might refers to inward ability. Power refers to outside influence. The Spirit needs neither one. He is able in Himself to give the victory to the believer, and He does it. Some think that these two trees represent Moses and Elijah, Moses the lawgiver, and Elijah the grace giver. Others think that these two trees represent two angelic beings, who stand guard over the believer to protect and preserve him, and make him a radiant conqueror.

Rom. 11:17 (a) This represents God's plan, purpose and program which began with Israel and which continues all through the church. Israel was in that plan as a green tree, and after Pentecost the Gentiles were brought into that same plan. All are saved by grace.

All are redeemed by the blood. All are dependent entirely upon the Lord Jesus for salvation and redemption.

The olive tree represents Israel from a religious aspect, while the fig tree represents Israel from the political aspect. The Lord did not curse an olive tree, for the religion of Israel had God's approval. He did curse the political Israel as a nation and scatter them over the world. It is the fig tree that buds, and is a type of the restoration of Israel from the political standpoint.

Rev. 11:4 (a) The two olive trees in this passage certainly represent the two witnesses. Just who they are we do not know. Most Bible students think they are Moses and Elijah who return to this earth in person with a message from God, and are persecuted. (See Zech 4:3-6)

ONE

Gen. 2:24 (c) Our Lord considers that the husband and wife constitute one unit. This is true even after the family enlarges. It is still one family.

Num. 15:16 (a) Although Israel had many laws, God considers all of it as just one law.

Deut. 6:4 (a) This passage may be easily understood when we remember that it refers to the heavenly family of three, or the heavenly firm of the Father, the Son and the Holy Spirit. We refer to a bank as one bank, though many men operate it. We refer to one family though there may be six members in it. The passage does not speak of "one person." It does speak of one Lord. The three Persons of the Trinity operate together. What is done by any one of the three Persons is agreed to by the others, and is binding on the others. It is one authority, though there are three Persons exercising that authority. These three members of the Godhead are not one Person, but they are one in plan, program, and purpose.

John 10:30 (a) We all know that these two persons are just one person, for we read that the Father sent the Son. In another place, the Father spoke from heaven concerning His Son on the earth. In another place the Son said "I ascend unto My Father." He was telling us that they are one in purpose, one in plan, and one in action. (See John 17:21)

Acts 28:25 (a) Although Paul said that he spoke "one word," or rather Luke said it in this passage, the writer mentioned a great many words that Paul spoke. He was indicating that there was one message for the people, one story to tell, one explanation given.

Gal. 3:28 (a) The church consists of many persons, yet in God's sight it is just one group, one church, one family, one kingdom.

It is not necessary to give the many other references in which the number one represents a group, or a bunch, or a collection, or more than one. From the numerical standpoint the number one represents indivisibility. One cannot be divided. One is not subject to separation. One represents a unit.

ONION

Num. 11:5 (c) This vegetable is a type of that which the world offers to the Christian in the place of manna from heaven. It may consist of pleasures, business, sports, education, music, religion or evil practices. The world seeks to feed on these things rather than on the Lord Jesus Christ, His Word, and His Work. He is the Bread of Life. Those who eat onions carry the effects with them, the odor is unmistakable. So those who participate in the things of the world and have no use for the heavenly manna can easily be distinguished by the effect in their lives.

OPEN

Num. 24:3 (a) This word represents an illuminated vision wherein the one who was blind to the things of God, and the Word of God, has been touched by the Spirit of God so that he now sees things as God sees them, and evaluates things according to the mind of God.

Neh. 1:6 (a) When the servant of God prayed this prayer, it was not that he thought God's eyes were closed, but rather that God would in a special way look upon the destruction of Jerusalem and be moved by the needs of the people in their dire distress. He was asking that God would give special attention at that special time. (See also 1 Ki. 8:29; 2 Chron. 6:20)

Psa. 5:9 (a) The vile things that come out of some people's mouths is compared to the stench that comes from an open grave. This is quoted in Rom. 3:13 as a description of the ungodly.

Psa. 34:15 (a) It is quite evident that God is ready to hear and answer those who live righteously and seek the glory of God, and His interests.

Psa. 81:10 (b) The picture is that of the baby birds in the nest. They hear the fluttering of the wings of the parent bird, and at once stretch open their mouths to receive the food. It is the Lord's desire that we do the same toward Him.

Psa. 118:19 (a) This describes the great welcome which the sinner receives from his loving Lord when he comes to Him to get rid of his sins, and receive the gift of righteousness, as is described in Rom. 5:17.

Isa. 22:22 (a) Our Lord Himself makes the opportunities for service. He describes this same truth in Col. 4:3 and Revelation 3:7.

He sets aside hindrances and removes those who oppose, in order that His Word may enter the hearts and the lives of those for whom He died.

ORACLE

1 Pet. 4:11 (a) Here we see a description of the character, authenticity and forcefulness of the man of God who delivers God's message in the power of the Holy Spirit.

ORCHARD

S. of Sol. 4:13 (c) We may understand this to be a sweet expression which describes the various groups of God's people. In these groups our Lord delights to make His abode, and to enjoy the fruitfulness and the fragrance of their worship.

OVEN

Psa. 21:9 (a) In this way God describes His fierce anger which will bring great suffering upon His enemies.

Hosea 7:4 (a) This strange figure describes the terrible passions that occupy the hearts of ungodly men who burn in their hatred of one another, or in their lusts for one another. God describes it as a heat that so destroys the virtues of the soul that only evil remains.

Mal 4:1 (a) This picture represents the fierce wrath of God which will be poured out on this earth in the day of Jacob's trouble. At this time the Lord will come forth from heaven to rule the nations with a rod of iron.

OVERFLOW

Psa. 69:2 (a) Sometimes sorrows are so heavy, so numerous and so strong that they seem to envelop the whole person's heart, soul and life. Sometimes God's people are submerged under an avalanche of disappointment and defeat that surge over the soul. Christ had that experience at Calvary. David had that experience during the years that Saul persecuted him.

Isa. 8:8 (a) This figure is used to describe the invasion of the King of Assyria into the nation of Israel. The hordes of the enemy would overrun the entire country, destroying as they went, and making slaves of the people. (See also Isa. 10:22; Isa. 28:17; Jer. 47:2; Dan. 11:10.)

Joel 2:24 (a) Here we see a beautiful picture of the great blessings that God would bring to His people Israel in the time of their restoration. There will be an abundance of every good thing, and the hearts of all His people will rejoice and be satisfied.

OWL

Psa. 102:6 (a) This bird represents the Lord Jesus in His solitude and loneliness. As the owl was surrounded by the barren, hot sands, with only reptiles for company, so the Saviour was surrounded by wicked influences and evil enemies. As the owl had no trees in which to make its nest, and rest there, so the Saviour had no place to lay His head, and no resting place for His heart in this life.

OX

Job 1:14 (c) As in other cases where these two animals are mentioned together, the ox represents the believer who has been made clean by the sacrifice of the lamb, while the ass, an unclean animal, represents the unsaved man who has not been redeemed. In this case the oxen were producing value for their owner, and this the Christian does. The ass was eating up what the owner had, and was not producing any value. This is as the sinner does.

Isa. 1:3 (b) This type represents the Christian who is more interested in his blessed Lord than he is in His gifts. The ass represents the unsaved, who is more interested in the gifts than in the Giver.

Isa. 32:20 (c) Our Lord is teaching us that His people should be busy at profitable work for Him among all people (the waters), and that we should have a part in sending forth those who will labor for our Lord in every clime and nation.

Isa. 66:3 (b) Our Lord uses this strange language to express His feelings about those who come to Him with a good offering from a bad heart. These people were enemies of our Lord while they were performing the religious rites prescribed by the law of Moses. They were hypocrites, and the Lord saw through their hypocrisy.

Ezek. 1:10 (b) This symbol represents the Lord Jesus as the servant of God and the servant of man. The ox lives entirely for the service of others. It is a beast of burden and is used for no other purpose. Our Lord Jesus was God's servant, as we read in Isa. 42:1. He also came to serve us, as we read in Luke 22:27. This same figure is used about our Lord in Ezek. 10:14, and again in Rev. 4:7.

1 Cor. 9:9 (b) By this figure the Lord is describing our obligation to the servant of God who preaches and teaches in the church of God. As the animal who works for his owner is entitled to the food, so the servant of God is entitled to remuneration from those whom he serves.

P

PAIN (and forms)

Psa. 55:4 (a) There is some strange connection between the heart and the mind. David was being sorely tried, his difficulties were increasing, and his sorrows were multiplied. He describes his feelings by using this form of speech. (See Psa. 73:16; Isa. 23:5; Jer. 4:19; Joel 2:6)

Isa. 66:7 (a) Evidently Israel was in great trouble just before the Saviour was born in Bethlehem, but they did not realize that their deliverer was so near. Probably the pain referred to was the sorrow she felt when the Roman army captured Jerusalem. The Saviour was born just a little while before this terrible event. Israel did not seem to feel their need of the Messiah; nevertheless He came to save them.

Jer. 51:8 (a) The sorrows of Babylon which overtook her when the Medio-Persian empire conquered her caused untold sorrow inside that magnificent city.

Ezek. 30:4 (a) The great sorrows, the fear and anxiety which overcame the Egyptians and the Ethiopians are thus described. (See also Micah 4:10; Nahum 2:10)

Rom. 8:22 (a) All nature suffers at the present time with the strong injuring the weak, the rich charming the poor, the wild animals destroying the weaker ones, and thorns, thistles and weeds destroying the crops. The earth groans under this torture.

PALACE

Psa. 45:8 (b) This Scripture was probably fulfilled in the following passages: Matt. 2:11, Luke 7:38, Mark 14:3, John 12:3, and Rev. 5:8. This passage may refer to the Christian's mouth from which there pours forth worship, praise, adoration, and thanksgiving, which are compared to the fragrant, sweet incense of the golden altar in the temple. It may also refer to the boundless wealth of the earth which will one day belong to the Lord Jesus and will be presented to Him when He comes to rule and reign.

S. of Sol. 8:9 (b) Probably the wall represents the church, which is solid, substantial, strong and immovable. Since silver is usually a type of redemption, it must refer to the fact that the story of God's redemptive power and the value of the redeeming blood are a very part of the church and is upheld by the church. It is a permanent truth.

Prov. 30:28 (b) The spider probably represents the sinner who desires to enter into the palace of heaven. She watches at the window or the door seeking an opportunity to enter and is not discouraged nor hindered in her quest. So the sinner would be very earnest and persistent in his quest for the Door, which is the Lord Jesus. False doctrines will be offered as a hindrance, religious leaders will give false advice, the devil will bring up many competitors. The truly repentant soul will get past all these evil teachings and get right to the Lord Jesus Himself, for He is the Door, and the only entrance to heaven.

Luke 11:21 (b) The strong man in this passage is the devil. His house refers to the world in all of its various characters. It refers to the religious world, the political world, the social world, the world of sports, the world of travel and beauty, the world of business, of arts and sciences. All of these are very attractive, very interesting, very delightful, and frequently very profitable. The devil uses these to keep his children, the unsaved, from Jesus Christ. He does not want them to find the Saviour, nor even to feel their need of the Saviour. But then the Saviour comes along their way, the Holy Spirit begins to work in the heart, and the friend sees that he is on the broad road and under the control of Satan. The Lord Jesus breaks the chains, loosens the bonds, removes the bands, and sets the prisoner free by means of the gospel of His grace.

PALM (the hand)

1 Sam. 5:4 (c) Apparently the Lord would teach us by this figure that when God's presence is realized, the power of idolatry is broken. (See also 2 Ki. 9:35)

Isa. 49:16 (b) In this beautiful way we are reminded of God's constant thoughtfulness, remembrance, work and ministry for His children. The palm is toward the face. In all the work that He does, His own people are constantly in His mind, and the objects of His care. The graving on the hands was done by the nails of Calvary.

Dan. 10:10 (c) In this passage we are probably being told that the touch of God upon the life, the ministry of the Spirit to the soul leads to an attitude of devotion, reverence and prayer.

PALM (tree)

Ex. 15:27 (c) The seventy trees probably represent the seventy descendants of Jacob who came with Jacob into Egypt (Gen. 46:27). It is typical of their life of separation and of their prosperity in the midst of opposition of every kind. These trees were in association with the twelve wells of water, and this is to teach us that the Word of God and the Spirit of God will sustain the people of God on their journey to their Homeland.

1 Ki. 6:29 (b) This tree is usually a type of the individual Christian life. The tree grows in the desert in very unhappy surroundings and unfavorable conditions. This is true of most true Christians. The tree sends its roots down quite a long way to find an underground supply of water. By means of this it flourishes in the desert. In the same way the believer obtains his source of supply from the Holy Spirit who is the Living Water so that he too can flourish as a believer, a happy Christian, a fruit-bearing child of God in the midst of every adverse condition. Solomon had these palm trees carved in the wood of the temple to ever remind Israel that each one individually was to be responsible for his own individual Christian life. He was not to be influenced by the coldness, nor the rebellion of others around him. (See 2 Chron. 3:5; Ezek. 40:16)

Psa. 92:12 (b) The palm tree in this passage is a type of the life that God expects from the Christian. He is to thrive in the midst of adverse conditions, even though he has no companions of like mind. He should, however, if it is possible, associate with other believers, for the cedar trees grow in forests, each one helping the other.

Jer. 10:5 (a) This is the picture of a hypocrite. He pretends to be a genuine Christian but in reality is not so. It represents also the idol which is made to appear as lifelike as possible. False religions are thus described in Rev. 17:4, and chapter 18, verse 16. The word "decked" in both of those passages may be translated "gilded" or veneered. They look like the genuine article, but are false.

PALMER WORM

Joel 1:4 (a) This is a symbol of the sorrow and suffering sent by the Lord on His disobedient children. (See also Joel 2:25; Amos 4:9)

PALSY

Mark 2:3 (a) This physical ailment may be used to describe the spiritual condittion in which sin paralyzes the life and the activities of a person, and renders him helpless in the things of God.

PANT

Psa. 38:10 (b) In times of distress, weariness and discouragement the heart has a deep desire for someone, or something, to satisfy that craving.

Psa. 42:1 (a) This represents a heart hunger for the presence of God, and the fellowship of the Lord. It is compared to the deep craving of the deer for a drink of water. (See also Isa. 21:4)

Amos 2:7 (a) By this we understand the deep longing of the sinner's heart for the wicked things of earth to satisfy his lusts and desires. It is compared to the thirst of an animal which causes it to seek out the water hole.

PAPS

Ezek. 23:21 (c) This is plainly a type of the lusts of the flesh. These immoralities were always connected with idolatry, and especially so where the idol was a woman or a female. Physical lusts are an integral part of many false religions.

Rev. 1:13 (a) Our Lord Jesus loves His children deeply and eternally. This type is used to reveal to us His wonderful affection, the fullness of His heart toward His church. The golden girdle represents the purity of that love, and the permanence of it.

PARTITION

Eph. 2:14 (a) There is a separation between the Jew and the Gentile. To the Jew was given the oracles of God, but not to the Gentile. The Jews were redeemed by the blood of the passover lamb, but the Gentiles were not. The Jews had God for their Father, but the Gentiles did not. By the coming of Christ and His sacrifice at Calvary, and His ascension to God the Father in His physical body, those differences have been broken down, and now all believers in Christ Jesus, both Jew and Gentile, are made one in Christ. Nothing now needs to separate the Jew and the Gentile. Christ Jesus unites us by the grace of God, and the work of the Holy Spirit.

PARTRIDGE

1 Sam. 26:20 (a) David compares his weakness and helplessness to the condition of the partridge or the quail which has no power against the hunter, nor the wolf.

Jer. 17:11 (a) This is a type of man's work wherein he partly succeeds and partly fails. The quail hatches her eggs in her nest, but the nest is so deep, and there are so many eggs in it that the lower ones in the bottom row may not receive the heat of her body and therefore do not hatch. It is so in Christian work. Some will be successful, and some will fail. There will always be some who believe and some who do not. No work done by man is completely successful. It also means, as given by Moffatt, "like a partridge hatching eggs it never laid, so is the man who makes money unfairly; it leaves him ere his life is over, and in the end he proves himself a fool."

PASSOVER

Ex. 12:11 (a) This is plainly a type of the Lord Jesus, the young man, the young King, sacrificed for us at Calvary and under the protection of whose blood we are safe, as in 1 Cor. 5:7. (See also Lev. 23:5; Deut. 16:2; Matt. 26:19)

PASTURE

Psa. 23:2 (a) This beautifully presents to us the precious truth that God's dear people are made to rest and enjoy His rich provision, His supply, and His goodness. God's sheep receive of God's best. This same truth is found in Psa. 79:13; 95:7; 100:3; Ezek. 34:31; John 10:9.

PATH

Gen. 49:17 (b) Those who study the life of Dan, and the tribe of Dan, will find that he acted just as this type indicates. He was a hindrance in the lives of others. He caused damage to many, and followed idols.

Psa. 16:11 (a) Since none of us know just how we will live, nor just what conditions will arise in our lives, we depend upon the Holy Spirit to show us God's way, and to reveal God's will to our hearts.

Psa. 27:11 (b) The word is used to describe God's way of life for His children. It is called a path because men of every century have traveled the same way, and thus it is established as God's way by experience. (See also Psa. 25:4)

Psa. 77:19 (b) In this way the Lord describes the blessedness of a life that is lived in obedience to God, and fellowship with God. (See also Psa. 119:35; Isa. 26:7)

Prov. 2:19 (b) This indicates that the one who walks in God's way, and along the road God has designed will find his life becoming sweeter, richer and brighter as the years go by. The immoral miss God's ways and God's program of life.

Isa: 42:16 (b) Here we see revealed to us that the way of God, the road He wishes His children to travel, may sometimes lead through very difficult situations, and places that seem to be impossible and impassable. The power of God will be present to enable them to overcome every obstacle.

Heb. 12:13 (a) The Lord is inviting His children by this expression to walk in such a godly way, so upright, so consecrated, that the weak Christian will be encouraged to walk with God, and will not be stumbled by his fellow-believer.

PATTERN

1 Tim. 1:16 (a) Paul's life is compared to a mold into which other lives will be poured so they would live a life like his.

Titus 2:7 (a) This represents a form or mold for the making of other lives.

PAVILION

2 Sam. 22:12 (b) This is a description of the holy and awful presence of God in which He surrounds Himself with an impenetrable darkness secure from all human interference. (See 1 Ki. 8:12)

Psa. 27:5 (a) This is a type of the secret place of prayer and fellowship with God wherein He makes His presence known, and gives a sense of protection and care which quiets the heart. (See also Psa. 31:20)

PEARL

Matt. 7:6 (b) This represents the precious truths of God and the beautiful revelations of His Word which should not be presented to militant atheists nor to hostile, ungodly men.

Matt. 13:45 (b) This gem is a type of the church which is hidden in the world, and sought out by our Lord Jesus Christ who paid the great price at Calvary to purchase us with His own blood.

Rev. 21:21 (b) These gems are probably descriptive of the life experience of the twelve patriarchs. Their names appear on these twelve pearls. (See vvs. 12, 21) In the Old Testament (Ex. 28:21), the names of these same men were on stones. Having lived their lives, and the twelve tribes having gone through the terrible experiences of the centuries, these stones were changed into pearls, for pearls are the product of long suffering. The tiny stone in the shell becomes covered with the pearl substance by the oyster because of suffering.

PEELED

Isa. 18:2 (b) Probably this refers to the fact that the invading enemy would skim off the wealth of the country, as well as its man power. The invaders would take everything that was of value.

Ezek. 29:18 (b) The shoulder that was injured would hinder work and labor. It would be very difficult to work either an animal or a man with an injured shoulder. The Lord is telling us in this passage that Nebuchadnezzar would bruise Tyrus, injure their shipping, and wreck their work.

PEEPED

Isa. 8:19 (b) Spirit mediums, necromancers and others deal with spirit and work in the dark. They cannot see plainly. Therefore, this word is used. It also indicates that there is no intelligence in what they say they see. They cannot see fully nor clearly. Also, the language they use is not familiar. They do not speak plainly. (See also Isa. 10:14, where it indicates the people could not complain.)

PELICAN

Psa. 102:6 (a) This is a type of Christ in His loneliness. He was a stranger in a strange land, and among enemies. The pelican obtained its food from the sea, not in the wilderness. In the wilderness it could find no food and no companionship. It was away from its customary haunts. So Christ was away from heaven, His element, and was among strangers where there was nothing upon which His soul could feed.

PEN

Psa. 45:1 (a) As the pen writes upon the parchment, so David said that his tongue would write upon the hearts and memories of others. He has done so. He has written beautiful stories about his wonderful Lord upon millions of hearts.

PERFECT

Gen. 6:9 Noah was perfect in obedience

Gen. 17:1 Abraham was perfect in trust

Job 1:1 Job was perfect in uprightness

Ezek. 28:15 Satan was perfect in his actions at that time

Matt. 5:48 The Christian is to be perfect in forgiveness of others.

Matt. 19:21 The Christian is to be perfect in devotion to Christ

Luke 6:40 The Christian is to be perfect in discipleship

Luke 13:32 Christ was perfect in His training course on earth

John 17:23 The Christian is to be perfect in his relationship to God

1 Cor. 2:6 The Christian is to be perfect in understanding

2 Cor. 13:11 The Christian is to be perfect in fellowship

Eph. 4:13 The Christian is to be perfect in his development

Phil. 3:15 The Christian is to be perfect in his efforts and desires

Col. 1:28 The Christian is perfect in salvation

Col. 4:12 The Christian is to be perfect in obedience

2 Tim. 3:17 The Christian is to be perfect in instruction

Heb. 2:10 Christ is perfect in His experience (5:9)

Heb. 12:23 The Christian is perfect in the culmination

Jas. 1:4 The Christian is to be perfect in patience

Jas. 3:2 The Christian is to be perfect in conversation

1 Pet. 5:10 The Christian is to be perfect in his training

The word "perfect" as it pertains to the Christian always refers to the subject under consideration. The word is never used in connection with the Christian being sinless, or with all sin eradicated, nor anything else that pertains to the character. It always pertains to the conduct. The word is used in the Old Testament, Isa. 42:19 in regard to the attitude of God's child toward temptation, the call of the world, and the attractions which Satan offers. God always indicates that His child can be perfect in his attitudes, not in sinlessness.

PERFECTING

2 Cor. 7:1 (a) This refers to the growth in grace and godliness of the child of God. He should have the desire to be as near like Christ as it is possible for a redeemed sinner to be.

Eph. 4:12 (a) This indicates clearly that the believer is to grow in usefulness and fruitfulness. The Lord does not want us to drift along and make no progress in our ability to serve Him wisely and intelligently.

PERFECTION

2 Cor. 13:9 (a) Paul had a great desire for the blessing of the saints, and especially in their ability to serve God with vigor, confound the enemy with intelligence, and depend upon God firmly and strongly for all their needs.

Heb. 6:1 (a) This passage refers to the growth of the Christian in his knowledge of the things of God. The believer is not to remain as a baby in the family of God, satisfied just with the elementary truths, but is to grow in his knowledge of God's Word, God's ways, and God's truths.

Heb. 7:11 (a) This evidently refers to being completely saved and cleansed by the salvation which is found alone in Christ Jesus. Under the Old Testament program, the priests could never rest. There was no chair in the tabernacle nor the temple. The priests could never rest from their labors. The sinner was always sinning, and was coming frequently to the priests with his sacrifice to obtain forgiveness. Christ brought in something better. He offered Himself as a sacrifice to God for all the sins, past, present and future. It is not necessary therefore to continue to offer His sacrifice, as is done in the offering of the Mass daily in the Catholic religion. The Lord Jesus put away sin for every generation by His own wonderful sacrifice. There is no need of a repetition as in the Old Testament days.

PERFUME

Ex. 30:35 (b) This sweet fragrance represents the beautiful character of the Lord Jesus which is fragrant to God, and very precious, sweet and fragrant to us. By His sacrifice on the altar. He offered up to God the worship and adoration of His own heart for His Father, and to His God. This is pictured in the incense burning in the Holy place. It could not be used by anyone for personal use (v. 37).

Prov. 7:17 (c) It is always true that Satan makes lustful pleasures very attractive and appealing to the senses. This is true also in Isa. 57:9.

S. of Sol 3:6 (c) This no doubt refers to the loveliness of the Lord Jesus Christ who is admired by His people, and whose Name is as ointment poured forth.

PERISH

This word does not mean annihilation nor obliteration. It always means that the thing under consideration is destroyed from its usefulness.

Deut. 26:5 (c) This refers to a nation that was under condemnation from God because of their idolatry, and therefore was subject to the curse and punishment of God.

Psa. 1:6 (b) The manner of life of the unsaved man brings no blessing to God, and has no value in God's sight.

Matt. 5:29 (b) The member that is cut off is of no further use. It has not been annihilated, nor obliterated, but only incapacitated.

Luke 5:37 (b) The bottles in those days were made of skins. If the bottle was burst, the skin broken, then it could hold no wine, and therefore was of no use. The bottle had not disappeared, nor been annihilated, nor been obliterated, but only incapacitated.

John 3:16 (a) We should note that the passage does not say that the soul will not perish. It says that the person will not perish. It evidently indicates that the voice is saved instead of being wasted. The money is saved instead of being squandered. The time is saved instead of being wasted, and the talents are being put to profitable use. Otherwise, the life has no value to God. Of course, it also means that the soul is saved from hell, and also from judgment.

1 Cor. 1:18 (a) The passage refers to those who are lost in sin. Their lives are of no value to God. They spend their time, talents and treasures on self and on humanitarian projects. These are called "perishing people." (See also 2 Cor. 2:15; 2 Thes. 2:10; 2 Pet. 3:9)

Heb. 1:11 (a) There is coming a day when our Lord will cause the present heavens and the present earth to flee away. We do not understand what happens to them, nor where they go. We do know that they will disappear by the Word of God, and the new heaven and the new earth will take their place. We read in another place "they shall be moved out of their places."

PESTLE

Prov. 27:22 (b) We are assured in this passage that no amount of good associations nor splendid education will change a fool's heart. Only the power of God, only the Spirit of God, only the Word of God, can accomplish this tremendous transformation.

PHARAOH

Gen. 41:44 (c) In this passage the king may be taken as a type of God the Father. He takes the same relationship to Joseph as God the Father takes toward Christ. All "things" are delivered to the Lord Jesus, and all judgment is in Christ's hands. All things were made by Christ. No one can come to the Father except through His Son. We may understand that Pharaoh thus represents God the Father just in this passage.

Ex. 5:2 (c) Here we may see a type of the hardened sinner who rebels against God's Word, and refuses to bow to God's authority. This is true today.

Ex. 7:3 (c) It is still true that those who persist in rebelling against God are bound to their choice by God. He chooses their delusions (Isa. 66:4), and binds their rebellion upon them. Clay when placed in the sun gets hard, so the sinner's heart becomes hardened when it insists on rebelling against the Lord.

Rom. 9:17 (c) In this passage God presents Pharaoh as an example of one in whom He works and deals as He will with all other obstinate sinners.

PHARISEE

Matt. 23:13 (c) These people are held up to us as an example or a symbol of every religious hypocrite. They pretend to be what they are not. They take the place of being devoted, Bible-loving believers, while in their hearts they are seeking to bribe God with their good works.

PHYSICIAN

Job 13:4 (a) These three friends had come to Job as helpers and sympathizers. Their words, however, proved that their diagnosis of this case was erroneous, and therefore the remedies which they suggested were futile and improper.

Jer. 8:22 (c) This indicates that though the Lord is the Great Physician, these people overlook His ministry and His medicine.

Matt. 9:12 (b) Here we find a reminder that the Lord is a great Physician ready to help those who admit their need. (See Mark 2:17; Luke 5:31)

PICTURE

Prov. 25:11 (b) Golden yellow apples present a beautiful picture against a background of shining radiant silver. A proper word spoken at the right moment and under the proper conditions brings about a most blessed sensation to the heart as does the picture to the eye.

PIGEON

Lev. 1:14 (c) This bird represents the Lord Jesus in His sacrificial work. The bird could be had simply by catching it. So Christ may be had simply by appropriation. The bird is a small bird in size, and this indicates that some people must have just a small comprehension of the value of the Saviour. Others have a greater comprehension as is pictured by the larger animal, the sheep. Still others have a very large understanding of the value of Christ, and this is represented by the large animal, the bullock.

Luke 2:24 (c) This type represents the offering of Christ for the pauper. He has no assets and very little understanding of the things of God, yet he trusts the Lord Jesus with the faith that he has, though it be very simple.

PILGRIM

Heb. 11:13 (b) This name is applied to the Christian's attitude toward the world. Though he lives in it, he is not a part of it. He is only occupied with its affairs insofar as this is necessary for proper living. The Christian belongs to heaven. His hopes and ambitions are for the other world. He is a citizen of God's kingdom. The Saviour explains this fully in His prayer in John 17. (See also I Pet. 2:11)

PILLAR

Ex. 33:9 (a) This wonderful cloud so mysterious in its composition, and its actions undoubtedly represents the Holy Spirit. He went with Israel, guiding them before, and protecting them behind. This pillar is more fully revealed as the Holy Spirit in the book of Ezekiel. (See also Psa. 99:7)

Job 9:6 (b) This probably represent the uncertainty of life. In this figurative language, Job is describing the mighty power of God. In the midst of his own unusual losses, he is realizing that God can shake the heaven and the earth, and break all laws that pertain to the hanging of the earth in space. (See also Psa. 75:3)

Prov. 9:1 (a) The seven pillars mentioned here probably are knowledge, discretion, judgment, understanding, equity, righteousness, justice. It is upon these substantial, basic principles that our civilization rests secure and progress is made possible.

S. of Sol. 3:6 (c) This peculiar figure may represent the case and the certainty of the presence of God in one's life. The pillar of smoke drifts easily, without noise, and without effort. So we realize the loving presence of the living God.

S. of Sol. 5:15 (a) It is said that athletes must have firm, substantial legs in order to endure whether it be in wrestling or prize fighting or on the track. Our Lord must be telling us here that the legs of marble represent the stability, firmness and untiring endurance of the Lord Jesus in all His ministry for us, to us, and with us.

Joel 2:30 (b) The chronology of this passage is uncertain. It probably refers to the time of the end when God's judgment will be poured out on the physical earth, and it will be burned up with terrific heat because of the wickedness of rebellious men.

Gal. 2:9 (a) This is a symbol of the substantial and stalwart character of the man of God who occupies a prominent and responsible place in the church.

Rev. 3:12 (a) Here we see a type of the blessed position and condition which will be granted to the Christian who lives for God, honors His Name, and fulfills His requirements as mentioned in this passage.

PILLOW

Ezek. 13:18 (b) This figure describes the path of ease which some people make for the people of God to keep them comfortable and at rest when they should be active in the service of the King, as soldiers of Jesus Christ.

PINE (tree)

Isa. 41:19 (c) This is a type of the Christian who is made useful, profitable and beautiful by the Lord in the midst of unhappy situations and conditions which surround him.

PIPE

Zech. 4:12 (c) We may take this to be a symbol of the ministering Christian who, by faith and prayer, is joined with the resources of heaven. God brings these down to the hearts of men for their help, comfort and encouragement. Each Christian should be a golden pipe to transfer heaven's assets to man's necessities. He should make this pipe as large as possible.

PIT

Num. 16:33 (a) The original word is *sheol,* which in the original Hebrew means hell, or the place of departed spirits. These men and their families and their possessions all went down into hell without dying. They are in hell today in their bodies. God did a new thing. He never did it before, and has never done it since.

Psa. 9:15 (b) The word refers to any trap or device whereby God's child is overtaken by the enemy and made captive. (See also Psa. 35:7; Psa. 119:85; Prov. 28:10)

Psa. 40:2 (b) Any deep trouble may be called a pit. It is so easy to fall in, and so hard to get out. It is always a very unpleasant experience.

Psa. 88:6 (b) Since this was written by the sons of Korah, whose father went down to hell alive, therefore, it may be that these sons are indicating that they too should have been punished by God, but instead were saved by His grace. (See Num. 26:11)

Ezek. 19:4 (b) Probably this refers to the battle plan of the enemy.

PITCHER

Judg. 7:16 (c) Probably this represents the personal plans and purposes of a human soul. These must be laid aside or broken in order that the light of God may shine out freely to those around. Selfishness, self-seeking and greed effectually hide the light of God from others.

Eccl. 12:6 (c) It may be that this is a symbol of the heart of an aged person which at one time beat strong and firm but now fails in its task.

Lam. 4:2 (b) Israel should have been a golden viol full of the precious promises of God, and rich in the experiences of God's grace. Instead of that they are compared to clay, which has little value, is easily broken, and contains nothing of value.

PLAGUE

1 Ki. 8:38 (a) This name is applied to the sins that curse the soul, hinder the life, and hurt the heart.

Psa. 91:10 (a) The believer that walks with the Lord, and dwells in His presence, is safe from the attacks of Satan, and from the thorns and thistles that are in this life to hurt and hinder.

PLANT (verb)

Ex. 15:17 (a) God expected His people to grow in the soil of the new land, and to produce a great crop for His glory. We do not plant anything that is dead, nor anything that is inanimate. We plant things that are living, and expect growth and fruit from it. So Israel had the living God, and the living Word. He placed them in Palestine, and expected a great harvest for the glory of His Name. (See 2 Sam. 7:10; 1 Chron. 17:9; Isa. 5:2; Isa. 60:21; Jer. 2:21; Jer. 32:41.)

Psa. 1:3 (b) This is a type or symbol of the Lord placing a Christian in the church or in the harvest field where He wants him. We say that God planted Livingstone in Africa and Moody in Chicago. God places His child in the part of His harvest field where he can produce the best crop for his Master. (See also Psa. 92:13, Ezek. 17:8). It also expresses the act of placing the Word of God in human hands and hearts by preachers and evangelists. This is evidently the meaning in 1 Cor. 3:6. It is also descriptive of the child of God or even of the sinner in regard to his growth in any city or village where he may live as in Matt. 15:13.

Psa. 128:3 (a) The Lord is promising to the parents that their children will grow as plants grow, and will become able, matured men and women. (See Psa. 144:12.)

PLATTER

Matt. 23:25 (a) This dish is used as a picture of the condition of a hypocrite. This outside is beautiful and clean, but inside he has not been cleansed from his pride and his sin. It may be said that the house has been beautifully repaired, painted and ornamented, but the tenant inside is evil, wicked and unclean. (See also Luke 11:39.)

PLAY

Ex. 32:6 (c) We may consider that this act represents the carelessness and the heedlessness of the sunsaved, who while living in their sins, and enjoying evil pleasures, have no fear of God, no regard for His Word, and no care about their destiny.

PLOW (and forms)

Deut. 22:10 (b) The ox represents the Christian, the ass represents the sinner, yoked together in Christian service. The friend of God and the enemy of God should not try to do the work of God in the harvest fields. The ox is a clean animal, the ass is an unclean animal, and they will not work together.

Judg. 14:18 (a) The picture that is used in this verse describes the association between the Philistines and the wife. The wife is compared to the heifer, and his enemies are compared to those who do the plowing, or conniving with her.

Job. 4:8 (a) The cultivation of sin and sinful programs of evil acts is described as preparing the ground for the seed, as is done in plowing. It is as when one builds a bar in his home that liquor may be served.

Psa. 129:3 (a) The Lord Jesus is telling us about the wicked soldiers who would tear open His blessed back by the use of the flail, or the cat-o-nine-tails. They did this very thing to Him on that fateful night. He was beaten with many stripes.

Hos. 10:11 (b) The passage reads as though God's people of both Judah and Israel would destroy their enemies and break up the ground as with a plow, so that their enemies would be made desolate.

Amos 6:12 (a) The Lord is informing us that some fields of labor will not produce a crop. They are hard and with no good soil. There is no use working in such a place for God. There is no use planting seed there. There is no use plowing the ground there. No crop would be produced, and horses will not want to either work there or feed there. When we find that we are serving in a place where there is no response, or where there is actual enmity, we are expected to move on into a district where the seed will grow.

Isa. 28:24 (b) A beautiful symbol of the evangelist or Bible teacher presenting the form of ministry which is intended to prepare the heart later for the sowing of the gospel seed. It usually refers to preaching messages which will convict of sin, reveal the leprosy in the life, and diagnose the case. The argument in the passage is that no one is to preach that kind of message all the time. He is to get through plowing, then harrow the ground, and then put in the good gospel seed.

Luke 9:62 (b) Putting the hand to the plow is a type of Christians taking hold of the service of the Lord (such as teach a Sunday School class or taking any other Christian work); then instead of going forward, they keep looking back with longing eyes and hearts to the former life.

1 Cor. 9:10 (b) The plowing is done with the hope of a harvest to follow. So the preacher preaches, plows up the ground and plants the seed with a joyful hope that God will give him souls for his hire.

PLOWMAN

Isa. 28:24 (a) The Lord is giving us in this passage a marvelous lesson on evangelism and Christian ministry. The plowman is the servant of God who goes into the harvest field and by his preaching, warning and teaching gets the hearts of the people ready for the gospel message (the wheat). The Lord is telling us that no farmer just plows his field constantly, day after day, and week after week. There is a time to stop plowing, stop harrowing, and put the seed in the ground. So we should do who are preachers or teachers in any group. We must be sure to plant the seed, the wheat, the gospel, or else there will be no crop.

Jer. 14:4 (c) Perhaps this passage may be used to represent the vain endeavors of the visiting evangelists to produce good results for God in a church or community which is barren of spiritual life, and where the Water of Life (the Holy Spirit) has not been free to work because of bad teaching, or no teaching. The evangelist labors in vain. There are no conversions, no restorations, no good results.

Amos 9:13 (b) It is evidently the will of God that hearts should turn to the Lord immediately upon hearing the clear, plain gospel. The plowing, the harrowing, the planting and the reaping may and should take place at the opening of a series of meetings, and not just at the close. (See also John 4:35)

PLUMBLINE

Amos 7:7 (a) The carpenter's plummet for lining up the wall into a perfect vertical line is a type of the care which God exercises in determining that every soul is dealt with in perfect righteousness, justice and equity. (See also Isa. 28:17)

POISON

Deut. 32:33 (a) The terrible story in this verse is to reveal to us that the vine planted by our Lord, which should have produced lovely grapes, was really bringing forth poisonous liquor, such as the wickedness and evil of Sodom. God expected Israel to bring forth good grapes, fragrant flowers, and the sweet graces of heaven. Instead of this, Israel produced hatred, idolatry and lust. See His description of this in Isaiah 5.

Job 6:4 (a) Job thus describes the sorrow of his heart and the distress of his spirit because of what he thought was God's wrath against him. He could not understand why God would thus deal with him when he knew very well he had lived a godly, consistent life. He did not know that his afflictions came from Satan.

Job 20:16 (a) Zophar is telling Job that the reason he is having all these sorrows is because he has been a wicked man. He is comparing Job's troubles to the poison of serpents, which was of course absolutely untrue.

Psa. 58:4 (a) This figure represents the evil words and teachings of the ungodly hypocrite. That which the hypocrite says and does influences for evil those who listen to him. It really refers to the teachings of false religious leaders. (See also Psa. 140:3)

Rom. 3:13 (a) By this we understand that the messages that issued from the lips of ungodly teachers who are leaders of false religions are evil poison. He is also telling us that evil speaking of any kind only hurts, damages and injures those who hear such messages. (See also Jas. 3:8)

POLE

Num. 21:8 (a) The cross of Christ is represented by this figure. Our Lord Jesus said that it represents the cross on which He was lifted up at Calvary as the pole was lifted up in the wilderness, and on which the serpent hung. (See John 3:14)

POLISH

Psa. 144:12 (a) This refers to the beautiful and delightful character of the young people who are raised in the fear of God and in a godly home. They become precious jewels to adorn both their family and the cause of their Lord.

Isa. 49:2 (a) This is a picture of the loveliness, the beauty, the majesty and the glory of our wonderful Saviour, Christ Jesus the Lord. From every angle and in every aspect He is magnificent and beautiful beyond compare.

POMEGRANATE

Ex. 28:34 (c) This fruit was and still is an emblem of fruitfulness. This fruit is quite filled with seeds so that it is able to reproduce itself in a multitude of new plants. It is also a type of sweetness and of satisfaction. These are a fruit of the Spirit of God in the life, bringing about these lovely results. (See S. of S. 4:13)

S. of Sol. 4:3 (c) Solomon is describing the beauty of the church and indicates that the thoughts in the minds of God's people would be beautiful ones and fruitful ones. This of course is true, and perhaps this is the lesson intended.

PORTER

Mark 13:34 (b) This represents the servant of God who is watching constantly for the welfare of God's people and for the interests of his absent Lord.

John 10:3 (b) This is probably a figure of the gracious Spirit of God revealing the open door to the seeking heart. It may refer to a wise servant of God, some Sunday School teacher, pastor, or evangelist, who sees a troubled soul seeking the Saviour and opens the Scriptures of truth to him so that he enters into salvation.

POT

Job 41:20 (c) This animal, the whale, or some other great sea monster blowing the water from the head in some form, is likened to the boiling pot.

Psa. 60:8 (b) The Lord used Moab for the cleansing of Israel when she needed punishment for her idolatry and sin. Moab was one of God's pots in which He washed some of the filth of His people. God uses whomsoever He pleases for His purposes.

Jer. 1:13 (b) This is a type of the great outbreak and overthrow of the armed might from the northern country in the time of God's earthly judgments upon Jerusalem.

Ezek. 24:3 (b) Jerusalem is the pot in which God will destroy His people who have been so rebellious and wicked.

John 2:6 (c) These may be taken as a type of the six people in John who are outstanding in their transformed lives; Nicodemus, the Samaritan woman, the lame man in chapter 5, the blind man, Lazarus, and the nobleman's son in chapter 4.

John 4:28 (c) This may be used as a type of earthly desires and preparations for earthly pleasures which are laid aside as of no further use when the soul trusts Christ and is satisfied with the water of life.

POTSHERD

Psa. 22:15 (b) A potsherd is a piece of a broken clay pot which has no value. The Lord is describing in figurative language the way He would suffer on Calvary, be broken, and apparently have no value to God or to men.

Prov. 26:23 (b) This is a remarkable description of a hypocrite. The potsherd is worthless and the silver dross is worthless, yet the dross on the potsherd is an effort to make it look attractive and appear valuable.

Isa. 45:9 (a) Man is described as a broken piece of gourd fighting with and arguing with another man who is also a piece of a gourd. It is an expression of derision and contempt.

POTTER

Psa. 2:9 (b) This type represents God in His terrible fury breaking the nations of the earth because they have no value to Him, and are an offense to Him. (See also Isa. 30:14; Jer. 19:11; Rev. 2:27)

Lam. 4:2 (a) Those in Israel who should have been as wonderful golden vessels are classed as men of common clay because they had forsaken God, and lived in wickedness.

POUND

Luke 19:13 (b) These pounds represent the quantity of the talents and gifts possessed rather than the quality. One Christian may be able to sing well, play well on an instrument, lead children's meetings, expound the Scriptures, and hold evangelistic services. This one has many "talents." Another Christian may have unusual ability as an evangelist, be outstanding in that particular ministry of Christian service, and not be able to play an instrument or lead singing or handle young people's work. This man's gift is the "pound." Some have less, and some have more of ability in one particular line. So some have one pound of ability, while others may have ten pounds. In the parable of the talents one may have two gifts for ministry and another may have eight or ten gifts in ministry. These are the "talents." (See under TALENTS)

POWDER

Matt. 21:44 (b) Indicates the utter destruction (not annihilation or obliteration) of the one who presumes to stand up in defiance against God.

Luke 20:18 (a) By this figure the Lord is explaining to us the tragedy of being an enemy of Jesus Christ. Christ as the Lord of lords will crush every enemy and render him helpless and hopeless. He will not permit any of His enemies to escape the terrible punishment which He shall bring upon them when He rules over men with a rod of iron.

PRICKED

Psa. 73:21 (b) God's dealings with this dear man of God, Asaph, David's song leader, hurt his mind and conscience, and he thus describes his feelings. The same truth is found in Acts 2:37.

Acts 9:5 (a) It must be that Saul's persecution of the Christians was hurting his own heart and conscience while he was doing it. God's message to the heart has this very result even to this day. (See also Acts 26:14)

PRIEST

Luke 10:31 (c) This clergyman represents the fact that religion has no remedy for the man who has fallen among thieves in his life, and has been robbed of his peace, his joy and his soul's welfare. The Levite represents Christian workers, so-called, who have plenty of religion to give, but no Christ. The Good Samaritan represents the Lord Jesus Himself who alone has the remedy for fallen men.

PRISON

Psa. 142:7 (b) This type represents the soul that is held in bondage by doubts and fears. He has not been set free either by Christ (John 8:36), nor by the truth (John 8:32).

Isa. 42:7 (b) The type in this passage represents the soul that is held in the grip of sin by the Devil. (See Matt. 12:29)

Isa. 53:8 (a) This refers to the fact that our Lord Jesus was bound by His enemies in Gethsemane, and was kept as a prisoner until He was nailed to the Cross.

Isa. 61:1 (b) Our Lord indicates that the unsaved are so bound by their sins and by black darkness in their lives that they are unable to see God's way, nor live according to God's plan. They have not been set free either by the Word of God, or by the Son of God. They are help captive by the will of the Devil, as Christ describes in Luke 11:21.

1 Pet. 3:19 (a) The word is used to describe hell. In the Old Testament hell consisted of two places. One place was a place of comfort, and those in that place were called prisoners of hope, as in Zech. 9:12. They knew they would be delivered by the Lord Jesus after He put their sins away at Calvary. He did so and "led captivity captive." The other section of hell is a place of torment or punishment and no one who enters there is ever delivered. It is a permanent prison, from which there is no escape. (See also Isa. 24:22; Isa. 42:7; Isa. 61:1; Luke 4:18)

PRISONER-S

Job 3:18 (a) He speaks of the grave as a prison. The body is placed there and cannot be removed until the resurrection.

Psa. 69:33 (a) Probably this refers to those who are sold out to the Lord, and are His bond slaves to do only His will, and carry out His purposes.

Psa. 146:7 (a) These may describe those that are in Paradise, which at that time was the place of comfort in Sheol. It may also refer to those who are Satan's slaves bound by sins, iniquities and habits. Both of these are true.

Isa. 10:4 (b) This difficult passage may mean that the unrighteous rulers shall eventually be punished by making such wicked devices that they themselves shall fall, and those who have been their prisoners will become their masters, and they themselves will become the prisoners. Certainly this has happened more than once.

Lam. 3:34 (b) Probably these are those who are bound by Satan, by their habits, and by his seductive snares. Christ will pour out His wrath upon all such.

Zech. 9:11 (a) Because the Lord Jesus had shed His precious blood at Calvary, therefore He could go down to those who were kept in Paradise, and whose sins had been covered by the blood of the animals. Now He could take them right up into His Father's presence, because His own blood had blotted out their sins. (See Eph. 4:8)

PRUDENCE

Prov. 8:12 (a) This is one of the titles of the Lord Jesus Christ. He is called by many wonderful names in the Scripture, and each name represents an attitude or a characteristic or a position which is true of Him, and of no one alse. The other name associated with Him in this passage is "Wisdom."

PRUNE

Isa. 5:6 (b) This describes the blessed action of the Lord in taking away from His people anything that would hinder them from being most fruitful. He sovereignly steps into the life of His child to cut off various things which have developed and which keep him from being all that the Lord wants him to be.

PRUNING HOOK

Joel 3:10 (b) This represents a time when the instruments of peace will be changed into instruments of war because God will take peace away from the earth.

Micah 4:3 (b) By this we understand the opposite of the above in that the instruments of war will be changed into implements of agriculture and God will again give peace to the earth.

PUBLICAN

Matt. 11:19 (b) This name is applied to any evil person as an epithet of contempt. The Pharisees used this name for anyone who failed to agree with their doctrines and their manner of life. (See Luke 7:34)

Luke 18:10 (b) The word here is used to represent any evil person who comes to Christ in repentance and accepts the Saviour to be his Lord and Master.

PULL

Psa. 31:4 (b) This action indicates the way that God delivers His child from the evil plans and wicked ways of the ungodly.

PURE (and forms)

Psa. 12:6 (a) This word is used to indicate that there is no mixture of any kind in the Word of God. There is nothing whatever of man's production, nor thought, in the composition, nor the arrangement of this book. The words are of God (in the original languages). The thoughts are God's thoughts. The arrangement is divine in its construction. No other words could possibly be used to convey God's meaning. These words of the Lord have been tested by men of all calibers and positions. Religious men, men of letters, men in educational circles, atheists, infidels, historians, archeologists, Paleontologists, scientists, chemists, physicists, churches, religions, clergymen have all combined to use their efforts to find a flaw in God's precious Word, but they have utterly failed, and the Word of God stands as a perfect message from heaven. The word pure means "unmixed." The Bible is unmixed with anything of human thought, design or effort. God used only the fingers of a man's hand to write on the wall before Belshazzar. He only uses man's fingers; He does not need man's brains, nor thoughts, nor ideas. (See also Prov. 30:5; Zeph. 3:9)

Matt. 5:8 (a) As in the case of the Scriptures, so it is in the case of the heart of the Christian. It is a heart that is unmixed with worldliness, selfishness or Satan's philosophies. A pure wool suit is one in which there is no cotton, nor silk, nor any other substance except wool. It may be a very poor quality of wool, nevertheless it is pure wool if nothing had been added to it. That butter is pure butter if it is just like it came from the churning of the milk, and no other substance has been added. It may be rancid, and old, nevertheless it is pure butter. Milk is pure milk if nothing has been added to it, and it is just as it comes from the cow, even though it may be greatly lacking in butter fat. The Lord wants us to have a heart that is not divided. He wants our hearts to be wholly devoted to Himself, with no competition, no reservations in our covenant, and no mortgage.

PURGE

Psa. 51:7 (a) This figure is used to describe David's desire for the Lord to remove from his heart sinful thoughts and wicked ways. (See also Psa. 65:3; Heb. 1:3)

Matt. 3:12 (a) This action takes place when our Lord separates the wicked from the just, the chaff from the wheat. He will not always permit evil men to injure, harm and defile His children. (See also Luke 3:17)

1 Cor. 5:7 (a) By this action the wicked church member is expelled from the church until he repents. Upon repentance the church is expected to restore him to membership.

2 Tim. 2:21 (a) In this interesting passage the person separates himself from the evils mentioned in the earlier part of the chapter. He does not separate himself from God's people. The vessels unto honor are like the golden or beautiful china vessels that adorn the parlor. The vessels unto dishonor are those that are used in the kitchen. You can readily see that the kitchen utensils are really more important than those in the parlor. The vessels in the kitchen are to be kept clean and pure just as the ones in the parlor are to be kept clean and dusted.

Heb. 9:14 (a) The word is used in this passage to show how effectively the blood of Christ changes the mind, the thinking and the purposes of the believer. He now is occupied with works that produce living results, and he no longer wastes his time on religious activities that have no value to God, nor to His church.

PURPLE

S. of Sol. 7:5 (c) In this passage the color of our Lord's hair is purple. In the fifth chapter it is black, while in Rev. 1 it is white. These three colors of His hair represent three wonderful characteristics of our Lord. The black hair tells us that He is a young King upon His Throne, with mighty power, vigor, vision and activity. The purple hair reminds us that He is the King of kings, Lord of lords, and the sovereign of eternity. He is part of the royal family. He has a right to wear the purple because of His majestic greatness. The white hair reminds us of His ageless life. He was from the past eternity through the coming eternity. He is the Ancient of days. He has wisdom, knowledge, discretion and understanding. He has experience of every kind. He is the Eternal One.

John 19:2 (c) The purple was placed upon our blessed Lord in mockery. He had claimed to be their King, but the Romans derided His claim, and in order to insult Him and show their hatred they clothed Him in mockery with the royal garments. Thus they exposed the wickedness of their hearts. (See also Mark 15:17)

Rev. 17:4 (c) The royal color on this woman represents apostate Christendom. It indicates that she takes the place of being a royal ruler, even as the Roman Catholic church does today. This church exercises sovereign and supreme power in many countries. Her gorgeous robes, her magnificent processions, her priceless images and idols, her marvelous temples, her cruel power, her secret procedures all tell the story of a church that seeks to be king of kings, and lord of lords in the place of our Lord Jesus Christ. One day she will be utterly destroyed, as this chapter reveals.

Q

QUEEN

Psa. 45:9 (b) This is one of the names applied to the church. She will one day be married to the Bridegroom and will stand at His right hand as His bride forever. She is called a queen because she is married to the King of kings.

Rev. 18:7 (b) This word describes the pride of Babylon (the great false religions of Christendom) in which she takes the place of being the bride of the King of kings, whereas in reality she is really a harlot, and is so named by our Lord.

QUENCH

2 Sam. 14:7 (a) The term is used to describe the destruction of the family name of this hypothetical character.

2 Sam. 21:17 (a) The killing of David is described by this word. His friends felt that if David were killed in the battle, then that one who guided them, directed them and led them to victory would be destroyed and they would be left without a leader.

Isa. 42:3 (a) The word indicates that our lovely Lord would not hinder any believer who is struggling to make progress, to grow in grace, and to become more useful. He would fan the fire in order to encourage the ambitious child of God, and would not criticise destructively, nor adversely, so as to hinder the development of any gift. (See also Matt. 12:20)

Eph. 6:16 (b) We learn from this expression that faith in our blessed Lord and His Word will enable us to conquer Satan and to defeat his purposes and designs.

1 Thes. 5:19 (a) It is the desire of our Lord that we should not in any way hinder the work of the Spirit of God in other people. We may grieve the Spirit in ourselves, but we quench Him in others. If we ridicule a Christian who is seeking to serve the Lord, we hinder the Spirit in that person. We are not to do this.

QUICK

Lev. 13:10 (a) The word is used here to describe proud-flesh, or a similar pathological condition. It indicates a sore that is actively sensitive, and filled with diseased tissue.

Num. 16:30 (a) This word is used to describe the matter of time in regard to the fall of these rebels. Since hell is only eleven miles from the surface of the earth, it did not take long for these rebellious men to go there. It may also refer to the fact that they were alive. In other places it is used in contrast with "the dead." (See Psa. 55:15)

Isa. 11:3 (a) The word is used in this case to indicate an alert mind, one that is apt to understand easily, and to grasp without effort the facts under consideration.

Acts 10:42 (a) This is one of those places in which the word is used to describe those who are living, in contrast with those who have died. (See also 2 Tim. 4:1; 1 Pet. 4:5.)

Heb. 4:12 (a) This is a description which indicates that the Scriptures are searching, living and powerful. They are not ordinary writings. They are not the product of men's minds. Our Lord said "The words that I speak unto you, they are Spirit and they are Life." John 6:63

QUICKEN

The word means to make alive, or to give life more abundant. It is so used and has this meaning in Psa. 71:20; Psa. 80:18; Psa. 119:25; Rom. 8:11; 1 Cor. 15:36; Eph. 2:1; Col. 2:13; I Pet. 3:18.

John 5:21 (a) This word describes the miracle which takes place at the resurrection when our Lord sends life back into the body again. In this passage the Father and the Son accomplish this marvelous transaction. (See Rom. 4:17)

John 6:63 (a) The Spirit Himself is called the Spirit of Life, and He gives life as we read in I Cor. 15:45. He is called the Spirit of Life in Rom. 8:2.

I Tim. 6:13 (a) By this expression we learn that life in all of its forms and expressions, in resurrection and in reproduction, comes from the Lord Jesus Christ in whom is life, and from whom comes life.

QUIVER

Psa. 127:5 (b) The marginal reading of this passage is better. It refers to the fact that the man who has many children, and of course, godly children, is equipped to do great and blessed things for his community and his country. Out of his home, life and atmosphere there will go forth those who will produce blessed results in His name.

Isa. 49:2 (b) This is God's quiver. The subject is the Lord Jesus. God the Father is the owner. Christ is in the hands of God, His Father, that, with Him, God may bring judgment or blessing to those at whom He may direct this arrow. Christ is the arrow.

Jer. 5:16 (a) This quiver is compared to a grave because the terrible invading nation mentioned in verse 15 was to be so very destructive.

R

RACE

Eccl. 9:11 (a) The wise man is telling us that human effort will not accomplish God's purposes. The power of God is necessary to accomplish the work of God.

I Cor. 9:24 (a) This life is like the competition between athletes, each one is endeavoring to get ahead of the other. Each one hopes to get the prize of wealth, honor, fame or power.

Heb. 12:1 (a) The Lord is exhorting us to live wisely, profitably and well. It is His desire that we should seek in every way to gain the prize of the high calling of God in Christ Jesus, the crown, the "well done," and the approval of the Judge.

RAGS

Isa. 64:6 (a) In the Hebrew the word means a body rag on which the vile effusions of the body are found. Nothing is more filthy. So the natural righteousness of people which is made up of the natural effusions of the spirit and mind are an abomination to God. No one would for one moment consider the advisability of giving to another person, as a gift, a cloth on which there were the vile things that come from the human body. The Spirit of God uses this illustration to show that whatever comes out of the human spirit as a natural product of the human spirit is a vile abomination to God. This refers to self-righteousness, religious pride, character-building for salvation, and good works which are offered to God as a reason for salvation and forgiveness.

RAIMENT

Psa. 45:14 (b) These garments represent two things. The golden garment represents the righteousness of God which He gives to His bride as a gift. It is not made by her, but it is made for her. It is not a product of human hands, but of God's heart. The garment of needlework, however, is the white linen garment, and consists of the righteous acts of God's people. By these, their good deeds, they weave a robe to wear, when they meet the Lord in the air. It is not the "robe of righteousness," for that is given to us by God when we trust the Saviour, that is the golden dress. Deeds of righteous living, godly actions, holy ambitions, and saintly words constitute the white robe, and we should be sure it is made full size.

Isa. 14:19 (a) The description given in this portion seems to be a description of the covering of Satan, and of his character. The garments that he wore were gorgeous, magnificent and beautiful, but were not sufficiently strong to offer successful resistance in a day of wrath. In the fateful hour God cast him down.

Isa. 63:3 (a) The garments of our Lord Jesus will be stained with the blood of His enemies as He treads them under His feet in His wrath in the coming day of judgment. His righteous wrath will be revealed by the blood stains on His garments.

Ezek. 16:13 (a) This is a description of the beauty of Israel in the earlier years of their history. The songs of David echoed throughout the empire, there was prosperity, and the fear of God permeated the congregation. The garments represent the character of the people.

Zech. 3:4 (a) The soiled garments represent the evil and wicked life of the ordinary person. In another Scripture He calls these "filthy rags." In the time of the new birth, or salvation, God removes these garments and replaces them with the Robe of Righteousness, which is the Garment of Salvation. This robe makes us presentable to God so that we may come into His presence without hesitation.

Rev. 3:5 (b) This is typical of the beautiful, sinless character of those who are saved by grace, walk with God, and are overcomers of sin and evil. These permit the life also of Jesus to be manifest in their moral bodies. (See also v. 18, and Rev. 4:4)

RAIN

Deut. 32:2 (a) This is a type of the precious blessings of God that will be sent from heaven to revive and restore and refresh His people.

2 Sam. 23:4 (c) In this statement we see a real comparison between the reign of Saul, which was full of sorrow and bitterness, and the reign of David which was to bring such refreshing blessing from heaven to the people.

Psa. 72:6 (a) We see here a picture of the delightful effects of the grace of God, the kindness of our Lord, and the beneficent influence of His presence upon the drooping heart and the weary soul.

Prov. 25:14 (a) The Lord is telling us here of those whose tongue is larger than the hand. They talk big, but do little. They promise much, but produce nothing.

Prov. 28:3 (a) One would think that the poor man would bring a blessing to the poor, seeing they are in the same condition. One would think that the rain would bring fruitfulness and blessing to the ground as it fell upon it. The opposite is true in this picture. The rain destroys the vegetation by its force and power, which is unnatural, and it is quite unnatural for a poor man to oppress others who are poor.

Eccl. 12:2 (a) Here is a wonderful picture of old age. Nothing seems to be right to the one who has become aged. After a rain, the clouds should disappear, and the sun should shine again. With the aged, however, there is no longer a consciousness of joy following sorrow, nor smiles following tears, nor the sun following rain.

Isa. 4:6 (b) This is descriptive of the storms of trouble, and the deluge of sorrow which would overwhelm the soul were it not for the refuge offered by our Lord in Himself. (Se also Matt. 7:25)

Isa. 55:10 (a) The Word of God is compared in this passage to the rain which falls upon the dry ground, and does its work immediately; also to the snow which falls and may lie upon the ground many days to finally soak in and produce a blessing. When we read the Word of God, or hear it preached, some blessing always comes immediately. Other things that we hear or read lie dormant in our souls and minds, sometimes for years; then when the conditions are ripe, that particular message becomes a live message.

Hosea 6:3 (a) The passage no doubt refers to the restoration of Israel in their own land as a nation. It also may be applied to our own lives. The blessing of our Lord is given in the spring to cause the seed to grow, and the fields to flourish. This is true in the early part of our lives when the mind is active, the vision is clear, and there is strength for action. Then at the end of the harvest, as at the end of our lives, the blessing of the Lord is given to soften the ground, and prepare the fields for another season of planting and harvesting. The Lord gives dying grace to those who are dying.

Jas. 5:7 (a) This figure is used to describe the joy that comes to the heart in all our service as we look for and expect and receive the blessings of heaven from the hand of God, both for the inception of our labors, and the progress of them, and the successful conclusion of them.

RAINBOW

Gen. 9:13 (a) Our Lord gives this emblem as a proof of His grace and mercy. It is a sign of the immutability of His Word. Now we never see a complete rainbow. It is always broken at the bottom, and there is a space there where there is no color. So none of us ever see all the grace of God for our lives, all His goodness and mercy, and all the perfect plan He has for us.

Rev. 4:3 (a) The bow in this Scripture is a complete one. There is no break in it. All the colors have disappeared, except the green. Green is the color that represents praise and worship. The complete bow tells us that in the next life we shall see and understand all the goodness of God to us, all His grace in dealing with us, all His measureless mercy which preserved us. Because of this we shall spend eternity in adoring praise and worship.

Rev. 10:1 (a) Since the rainbow appears around the head of this mighty angel just before the judgments begin, it is to tell us that grace always appears before wrath, and God's goodness provides a remedy from the dire results of rebellion.

RAM

Gen. 22:13 (c) This animal is a type of the Lord Jesus, who is available for the sinner as his substitute in a time of need. Isaac was on the altar ready to die, as we too are lost, sinful and on the way to the second death. The animal was found as a substitute taking the place of the boy, and dying in his stead. So the Saviour takes our place, and we go free.

Ex. 25:5 (c) This is a symbol of the blessed protection from God's wrath, which is offered by the death of our Lord and the shedding of His precious blood. The skins had to come from animals that had died. (See also Ex. 26:14; 35:7; 36:19)

Ex. 29:22(c) This ram represents the Lord Jesus Christ as an offering of consecration for us. His life was so perfect that God could accept it, and does accept it, in the place of our's. We give ourselves over to the Lord because we are in Christ, and therefore are acceptable to God.

Lev. 8:21 (c) The burnt offering is a picture of the whole person being offered to God in complete devotion to Him. He is given the body, the mind, the heart, the affections, the talents, and the gifts in complete abandonment to His will. (See chap. 9:2)

Lev. 9:4 (c) This animal represents the Lord Jesus as our peace offering. He made peace by the blood of His cross. He brought peace to us. He is our peace. (See Eph. 2:14)

Lev. 19:21 (c) In this trespass offering we find another picture of the Lord Jesus as the One who gave Himself not only "for us" as a burnt offering, but also "for us" as an offering for our trespasses and transgressions. He died for what we are, that is our character, and He died for what we do, and that is our conduct. As the sin offering is described in Ex. 29:15, wherein the Saviour gave Himself for our own wicked selves, so He gave Himself also for our deeds and doings.

Num. 5:8 (c) This animal paid the debt that was due from the sinner. By the death of the animal, the obligation against the sinner was met, and the sinner could go free. (See also Ezra 10:19) This is a picture of Christ offered for us.

I Sam. 15:22 (c) This picture is to remind us that no amount of outward show will suffice to cover up the truth that is in the inward parts. God would rather have obedience and the love of the soul for Him than gifts and sacrifices from a heart that did not care.

Dan. 8:3 (a) The animal in this case represents the Medio-Persian empire. The two horns represent the power of the two kingdoms. The power of Darius, of the Median Empire, was greater than the power of the Persian empire. Therefore, the greater horn represents Darius.

RANSOM

Job 33:24 (b) The Lord Jesus Christ is the only ransom that can deliver us. Job found that ransom, and it may be that Elihu did as well. Christ is the only one who could pay the debt and set us free. He must belong to us to be our ransom. (See Matt. 20:28)

Job 36:18 (b) This represents the great price which God accepted from the Lord Jesus Christ at Calvary where the Saviour paid the debt for the sinner. The work of Christ does not avail after death.

Psa. 49:7 (b) The redeeming of the soul is by the precious blood of Jesus, and there is no substitute for it. No person, nor priest, can buy salvation for another.

1 Tim. 2:6 (a) Christ is the ransom for the sinner. No woman, no man, no church, no religion, no good works, no money, no prayers can avail for this purpose. Jesus Christ only can pay the debt and set us free.

RAVEN

1 Ki. 17:4 (c) This is a type of any person on earth, but particularly an unsaved person, who naturally would not care for God nor for His people, but who is compelled to minister to God's servant against his own nature.

Isa. 34:11 (c) This is a picture of the unsaved who dwell in desolate places and who have no interest or care for the things of God. The raven was an unclean bird.

Luke 12:24 (b) Here we see a symbol of God's kindness and care. The raven is a worthless bird. It has no particular value and is not cared for by human beings. Yet God meets its needs. So the Lord cares for His own who are certainly far better and more to be considered than this unclean bird. Note also that the raven is black. (Sinners are black in God's sight). Its legs conform in color to its surroundings. Those who live along the ocean have white legs; those around black soil have black legs, those in sandy regions have gray legs. So the sinner conforms his walk to the society in which he moves but he stays black all the time. The little young ravens are as black as their parents. Children are sinners just as their parents. Only God could change a raven and make it white and make it sing. (Only God can change a sinner into a singing saint.)

RAZOR

Psa. 52:2 (a) The tongue of a gossip or a wicked person cuts into the heart and soul of the person who is talked about. It injures easily and hurts deeply.

Isa. 7:20 (a) This is the largest razor in all the world. It is the King of Assyria, who was to take away from Israel much of their possessions and many of their people. God would use this king to punish His people Israel.

REAP

Job 4:8 (a) We shall receive back evil for evil, and trouble for trouble. This is a comparison of spiritual truths with that which is seen on the farm by the farmer. He receives back in the crop whatever he sowed as the seed.

Psa. 126:5 (a) Here we are told of the success that one will have in soul winning if the worker cares enough to weep. This refers not only to ministry among the unsaved, but also to ministry among the believers.

Prov. 22:8 (a) Evil works are not permanently fruitful. We must not cease laboring because of the fear of difficulties.

Hos. 8:7 (a) This figure is used to inform us that a little bit of sin may produce a tremendous lot of evil and harm.

Hos. 10:12 (a) In contrast with Hosea 8:7, the Lord is telling us that a little investment in goodness will produce great and numerous blessings.

Matt. 25:26 (a) The Lord seems to be using this expression in derision and scorn. It is not true that men reap where they have not sowed, except it be that one soweth and another reapeth. It is certainly true that in the case of each convert, at least in civilized countries, someone has preceded the soul winner with messages and godly influences. In this way the one who gathers in the lost soul is reaping that which another prepared.

John 4:38 (a) God had worked in the hearts of the people before the messenger arrived with the closing word. God had been dealing with Israel through the years preparing their hearts for the Messiah. Now the disciples were to go and put on, as we say, "the finishing touches." The prophets had been telling that the Messiah would come, and that they should believe on Him when He arrives. Now the disciples were to go forth pointing to Him and saying, the hour has come, the Messiah has arrived, and you must believe on Him.

1 Cor. 9:11 (a) The lesson we learn here is that those who preach and teach the Word should be well paid for their services. The ox that works for the farmer should be well fed by the farmer. So the servant of God should have his needs well met by those whom he well serves.

2 Cor. 9:6 (a) This statement of fact is a comparison between our ministry to one another with the seed-sowing of the farmer. If we say very little about the Saviour, we shall expect little results. If we say much about Him, we may expect large results. If we spend only a few moments either with Him, or for Him, we may expect that the results may not be very great. The farmer who skimps on the seed may expect a skimpy harvest.

Gal. 6:7 (a) Again our Lord uses the seed-sowing of the farmer, and the resultant harvest as a picture of that which happens in our human lives. The man who gives his life over to whiskey, tobacco, long night hours, careless exposure to the elements, may expect that his body will suffer from it, and his soul will not prosper.

Gal. 6:8 (a) Those who sow to the flesh make provision for the flesh to obtain what it wants. If he is a drinking man he will lay in a stock of liquor so that he may have it easily when he wants it. If he is addicted to tobacco, he will lay in a stock of tobacco, so it will be easy to get when he wants it. This is in contrast to those who sow to the Spirit. These carry a Bible with them so that it will be easy to read the passage suggested by the Spirit. They will have some kind of arrangement whereby they can get alone to pray when the Spirit offers that suggestion. They will make companions of God's people, so that the Spirit can easily engage them in heavenly conversations.

Rev. 14:15 (a) Probably this refers to the time appointed for the death of people. It is compared to the ripened harvest which is ready to be gathered in. With some people this occurs very early in life. With others, it occurs late in life. Only the Lord of heaven knows when the time has arrived. This is a national harvest.

REAPER

Matt. 13:30 (a) The Lord tells us plainly in this passage that "the reapers are the angels." In the day when God will judge the earth, He evidently will send forth His angels and will separate the

Christians, genuine believers, real born-again saints, from the great multitude of the unsaved, the ungodly, religious hypocrites. No one could do this but an angel. No one else can discern the true condition of the heart.

RED

Ex. 25:5 (c) This may be taken to remind us of the sacrifice of Christ and the shedding of His precious blood. The rams had to die before the skins could be obtained. These red ram skins covered all the tabernacle. This may be taken to represent the fact that the precious shed blood of Christ Jesus must cover and protect everything connected with the Christian's life, activity and sacrifice. (See also Ex. 35:23)

Num. 19:2 (c) We may see in this animal a type of Christ Jesus who was made sin for us, and died that we might be presented blameless and guiltless before God.

Isa. 1:18 (a) This color seems to apply to sins in many parts of the Scriptures. We never see sin compared to the color "black." Red seems to be the symbol of sin. (See also Lev. 13:19)

Isa. 63:2 (a) This color represents the terrible wrath and judgment of God when our Lord Jesus, the Judge of all the earth, treads down His enemies. The figure indicates that the blood of His enemies will be splashed up upon His garments making them red. This same truth is found in other passages. Christ is the One who treads upon the grapes in the wine press, and the grapes represent His enemies.

Zech. 1:8 (b) Since the myrtle trees represent those who live a happy life, some think that these horses are a type of Christ riding in power because of the red blood, and because of Calvary to protect and preserve His own people. Others think that these horses represent angels sent among the people to bring upon them the wrath of God because they were indifferent and unconcerned. Others think that these horses are a type of sin that pervades all the land. (See chap. 6:5; Rev. 6:4)

Rev. 12:3 (a) This animal is a type of Satan, the man of sin, who is all evil, sinful and wicked. We should notice that this animal is in heaven. Satan has not yet been cast out of heaven.

REFINE (and forms)

Zech. 13:9 (a) This beautiful type represents the living God dealing with His people and cleansing them from evil ways. (See also Isa. 48:10) It is a type of the bitter experiences through which the Lord permits His people to pass in order to make them better Christians. (See also Mal. 3:2)

REFUGE

Deut. 33:27 (a) This type is used to describe the rest, peace and safety of the child of God who, in the midst of the storms of life, flies to the secret place of prayer and there leans upon the breast of his loving Lord. (See Psa. 46:1; Isa. 25:4)

2 Sam. 22:3 (a) David did not trust in his army, nor in the caves, nor the wilderness, nor men. He trusted only in the protecting care of God. (See Psa. 9:9; Psa. 14:6; Psa. 48:3; Psa. 57:1; Psa. 59:16; Psa. 62:7; Psa. 91:2)

Psa. 142:4 (a) All human devices and plans fail to bring security and peace. David wrote this Psalm while he was in a cave fleeing from Saul. His heart was resting in the Lord, not in the darkness of the cave.

Prov. 14:26 (a) As David, Moses and others of God's great men found a shelter from the storm in the protecting care of God, so this wise man assures us that that protection may be ours also.

Isa. 4:6 (a) God provides in Himself, and for Himself, all the protection from the storms of life that the believer needs. (See also Isa. 25:4; Jer. 16:19; Heb. 6:18)

Isa. 28:17 (b) This is a graphic type of the false position taken by sinners who deceive themselves into thinking they are hidden and protected by false teachings, self-deceptions, and Godless religions.

REIGN

Judg. 9:8 (a) It is not a natural thing for one tree to rule over another tree, and certainly not for a bramble to rule over a big tree. Neither was it right nor natural for Abimelech to rule over Israel, and to destroy the family of Gideon.

Rom. 5:17 (a) The word is used to describe that one who is a conqueror over passion, lust and all evil things.

Rom. 5:21 (a) This word is used to show how that God's grace is more powerful and more evident than sin. When the tide is out, then many rocks and boulders appear on the beach. These represent sins in the life. When the tide comes in, there is far more water than stones, and the tide completely covers all the boulders on the beach. That great incoming tide represents the wonderful grace of God.

Rom. 6:12 (a) By this figure we are admonished to let no evils prevail in the life, so that they direct the life in wrong paths.

I Cor. 4:8 (a) Paul is using sarcasm and irony in this passage to shame the Corinthians into seeing their real condition.

REINS

Job 16:13 (a) The word is used as a type of feelings, experiences, desires and thoughts. (See also Psalm 7:9; 16:7; 26:2; Prov. 23:16; Jer. 11:20; Jer. 17:10; Rev. 2:23)

REND

Eccl. 3:7 (b) The Lord is reminding us that it is not necessary to continue in building something that is not profitable. Sometimes we start on a project which we think will be useful, and then find out we are wasting our time. We should then discontinue that project.

Joel 2:13 (a) By this word we are called upon to feel a deep grief over sin and evil.

Matt. 7:6 (a) If we reveal precious things of God to the ungodly scoffer, he may use it to injure us in many ways. We saw this exemplified in the fact that we helped China in her distress; we also helped Japan at the time of the earthquake; and we helped Russia in the time of the war. We received back bullets, persecution of American citizens, expulsion of American missionaries, and a closed frontier to our travelers. This is a perfect example of the meaning of this passage.

RENT

Matt. 27:51 (a) This torn veil tells the wonderful story of an open way into the presence of God, and also for an open way for God to come forth in blessing to His people Sin had been a terrible hindrance. Now that Christ had died for sin, and for sins, and for sinners, God could come out in grace and kindness to offer salvation to every living person. Now the sinner could enter God's presence because of the precious blood of Jesus. (See Mark 15:38; Luke 23:45; Heb. 10:20)

REST (and forms)

Gen. 2:2 (a) This is a wonderful truth represented in this beautiful word. God rested after He had finished all His work. So the Christian ceases from all his own labors for salvation and efforts to make himself fit for heaven, he comes to the Lord Jesus Christ, the Saviour of sinners, he trusts his soul to that lovely Lord, and at once enters into God's rest. This is described in detail in Hebrews, chapters 3 and 4.

Gen. 8:9 (c) In this picture we may see the truth that the Christian represented by the dove will find no resting place in all the earth's provisions for the soul. Only in Christ, represented by the ark, is there a safe place for rest and peace.

Ex. 33:14 (a) If any man in the world had a right to worry, it was Moses. He had been given the commission and the command to lead about three million people away from their homes, their business, their comforts and conveniences into a desert. There were no bridges, no roads, no stores, no crops, no comforts of any kind. In this tremendously difficult situation, God assured Moses that His provision would be so complete that Moses could rest and not worry about anything. This is one of the greatest promises in the Bible. We may have this rest about our lives.

Ex. 34:21 (a) Most of God's servants get so busy that they have no time to get away for rest with the Lord. (See Mark 6:31)

Ruth 1:9 (a) Naomi gave some very wrong advice to her two daughters-in-law. None of them had found rest down in Moab, and Moab is a type of the world. The "rest" that she spoke about was rest from the sorrows of widowhood, and the grief that always goes with a broken home. The only place they could find real rest would be among the people of God, and under the protecting care of the true God. That kind of rest is the portion of those who lay their burdens at the feet of the Lord, and leave them there.

1 Chron. 6:31 (a) The traveling days of Israel through the wilderness were finished. The ark was to be carried about no more. This is a picture of that which is the blessing of the child of God who, in complete consecration, quits his wandering from the paths of the Lord, and gives his life completely to the Holy Spirit.

Psa. 95:11 (a) The blessing which is spoken of in this passage is described more fully in Heb. 4:5. It is a ceasing from one's own work for salvation, or forgiveness, and a relaxing in God's presence because "Jesus paid it all." The work and Person of Christ are sufficient to satisfy God, and to save the soul. The believer enters into this rest when he ceases from his own works, and trusts fully and entirely in Christ Jesus for His salvation.

Psa. 116:7 (a) This is an appeal David makes to his own heart to quit worrying and fretting over the sins of others, or the sorrows of his own path. The Lord Himself takes the burden, blots out the sins, removes the hindrances, and gives us freedom. David called on his soul to enjoy this blessing.

Isa. 11:10 (a) This is descriptive of the wonderfully blessed condition that shall exist on the earth when all enmity, animosity and antipathy are removed. Man and beast will dwell together in comfort, unity and safety. We may apply this truth now.

Isa. 28:12 (a) Again our blessed Lord invites His people to quit worrying and fretting about the enemy, or about any other adverse situation. He wants his child to let Him handle all the problems, solve the difficulties and gain the victory.

Isa. 66:1 (b) In addition to the prophetic aspect in which Israel was to build a temple again for God, there is a beautiful type here of that sweet experience of the Christian wherein he builds in his life a character and an experience in which God is delighted and in which God feels at home. Jesus said, "We will come unto him, and make Our abode with him" (John 14:23) — thus indicating that God is at rest in the life of a loving, obedient Christian.

RIB

Gen. 2:21 (c) This probably signifies that the act of becoming a Christian is wholly and entirely from and of God as the rib was a part of Adam and was taken out of him. The conviction of sin is from God. Interest in our eternal welfare is from Him. The Word was given by Him and our knowledge of the Word was imprinted by Him. He gives the faith to be saved. He reveals Himself to us and then He gives us His own life. "Salvation is of the Lord" as this rib was "of" Adam. Eve represents the Church. It is a picture also of the fact that the Church (rib) came from Christ, is a part of Christ, the last Adam, and lives because of His life.

Dan. 7:5 (b) Here is indicated the ferocity and devastating effect of this Medio-Persian kingdom in destroying the Babylonian kingdom and retaining some of the fragments of its characteristics. The three ribs represent the three great kings of Babylon.

RIBBAND

Num. 15:38 (c) This ribbon of blue was evidently intended to remind the priest of his heavenly calling. This color of blue is connected with heaven's beauty, and the priest should ever remember that he has a heavenly calling, and is engaged in heavenly business.

RICH (and forms)

Ex. 30:15 (a) We learn from this passage that all are saved by the same price, the precious blood of Christ. There is no respect of persons with God. The rich and the poor must come through the same door, helpless, hopeless and penniless, trusting only in the Saviour of men, Christ Jesus, who paid the price at Calvary.

Prov. 8:18 (c) Here we see a type of all the virtues and graces given by the Lord to His children to adorn society, bless the church, and bring honor and glory to God.

Prov. 10:22 (a) In this is described those who are filled with faith, zeal, earnestness, vision, as well as the graces of the Spirit of God.

Prov. 11:4 (c) This is quite significant in that it typifies all manner of human effort to put away sin, and obtain favor with God. This passage denounces all human efforts to save one's self, or to save another. It repudiates such things as rituals, sacraments, masses, prayers, penance, religious activities, money, time, tears and ecclesiastical powers. None of these have any value at all with regard to the salvation of the soul. They will not avail at the Judgment Throne of God. Only the living Christ and His shed blood do avail to meet God's requirements.

Prov. 13:7 (a) This wonderful truth reveals God's thoughts as contrasted with human ideas. The Lord is telling us that those who lay up riches for themselves and have nothing for God, God's work and God's people, and give nothing for the spread of the gospel, are poor in God's sight. There are others who, out of their poverty, or meager income, give as liberally as possible for the work of the Lord, the building of the church, the spread of the gospel, and these are called rich in God's sight. (See also Prov. 11:24; Luke 12:21.)

Isa. 45:3 (a) The promise made to Cyrus was one of unusual blessing from God. The Lord would let him have the peculiar treasure of kings, the Lord would enable him to obtain the blessings of power, the Lord would give to him unusual experiences of happiness and joy. All of this actually took place.

Matt. 19:23 (a) Those who hold themselves in high estimation and think themselves to be fit for heaven without the robe of righteousness will find themselves deceived and shut outside the door of heaven. This is the same truth as that which is found in Matt. 7:22-23. (See also Mark 10:25; Luke 18:25.)

Luke 1:53 (b) This word describes the condition of those who are religious intellectuals, self-satisfied, self-sufficient, self-made, who feel that they have no need of a Saviour to save them, nor of a Lord to lead them. (See Luke 16:19)

Luke 12:21 (a) This blessing should be enjoyed by all of God's people, the blessing of being rich toward God and for God. We are to have an abundance of good works, of loving kindness, of zeal in the gospel, of earnest care for the church, of increased talents for the Lord, and of usefulness to the people of God.

Luke 16:11 (a) In this place the Lord is evidently referring to the secrets of God as revealed in the truths of His Word. He wants us to be abundantly supplied with grace, mercy, peace, faith, hope, love and all those other sweet graces of heaven which He entrusts to those who are good stewards of the manifold grace of God. (See also Rom. 2:4; 9:23; 11:33; Eph. 1:7, 18; Eph. 3:8; Phil. 4:19.)

Rom. 10:12 (a) God has the blessing of eternal riches. He is said to be rich in mercy. He has an abundance of grace. He has a storehouse of peace and love, with all the attributes that accompany Him. He never is bankrupt in any grace. He is plenteous in mercy and loves to forgive.

1 Cor. 4:8 (a) Paul is using irony and sarcasm in this passage, and is referring to the self-sufficiency of these people wherein they are satisfied with their lot, and seem to have no need of any blessing.

2 Cor. 6:10 (a) The apostle is referring to the fact that his ministry brought much blessing to those who heard him, and who sat under his ministry. He taught them the truth of God which filled their hearts with gladness, their minds with understanding, and their lives with fruitfulness. They were blessed with all spiritual blessings in Christ.

Heb. 11:26 (b) We find here a symbol of the great blessing that comes to the soul through being affiliated with, associated with, and related to the Lord Jesus.

Rev. 2:9 (a) This church had a great deal of spiritual pride and self-sufficiency. They felt they had need of no spiritual blessing or help. (See also Rev. 3:17.)

RISE (up)

Num. 10:35 (b) This is a figure which represents God in action. The same truth is found in Isa. 28:21. It is a prayer for God to work on their behalf.

Jer. 47:2 (b) This is a picture of the enemy organizing a strong army from the northern kingdoms to invade Israel.

Matt. 12:41 (a) We understand, by this expression, the resurrection scene when the witnesses will be brought before the throne of God to testify. (See also Luke 11:32)

Rev. 13:1 (a) Most commentators believe that this is a development of the anti-Christ who emerges from among the common people (the sea), who assumes great power and presents himself as the Christ who is to rule the world.

RING

S. of Sol. 5:14 (a) This is a type of the pure and perfect care which our Lord exercises over His bride because of the intimate relationship between them. It tells of an eternal devotion, which will never be broken. It tells of divine care, which is always sufficient. It tells of the beautiful love that is indescribable, and constant, without end.

Ezek 1:18 (a) It seems that the rings are synonymous with the wheels. They are a picture of God in action, progress, motivations from heaven. The eyes indicate the Holy Spirit, who is Himself always intimately associated with all the works of God the Father and of God the Son. Their height indicates the magnificence and the greatness of the unsearchable ways of God. When we see the might and the majesty of His work in creation, and of His power in keeping the universe in order, this strikes us with awe.

Luke 15:22 (b) Here we see a token of the relationship between the Father and His child. It is a public acknowledgment from God that this one is His Child and His Son. It is a mark of identification in regard to relationship, as well as authority.

RIPE

Jer. 24:2 (b) This word indicates that the time was right for the culmination of God's purposes in regard to His people. God always times His actions to suit His purposes. He knows when the time is right. (See also Hosea 9:10)

Joel 3:13 (b) This type describes the full growth of iniquity and sin in the earth until the righteous God will endure it no longer, and will bring the earth to judgment. (See also Rev. 14:15)

Micah 7:1 (b) The prophet is describing his heart hunger. The evils that were around him, and the wickedness which he saw, gave him a deep longing for something more precious, and more satisfying to the soul than he was able to obtain. It also describes his desire for Israel to be like she was when she came out of Egypt, happy in freedom, and content to walk with God.

Nah. 3:12 (b) The figure used in this case describes the wickedness of Nineveh which made her ready for the judgment of God.

RIVER

Psa. 1:3 (a) The Holy Spirit is thus described. The child of God is planted in the soil for security, close by the water (the river) for inspiration, for refreshing and for the abundant life. (See also Jer. 17:8) The river is the Holy Spirit.

Psa. 36:8 (a) The blessings of God are so abundant, so liberal and so great that no other figure could properly express the value of them. The things that please God are revealed to us in His Word. We enter into those pleasures, and our joy is full.

Psa. 46:4 (b) This type represents the gracious ministry of the Holy Spirit in all His various activities. He brings joy and life more abundant wherever His ministry is given.

Psa. 107:33 (a) This passage is reminding us of the fact that God is able to turn blessings into curses. He tells us this very plainly in Mal. 2:2.

Isa. 32:2 (a) In this beautiful way the Lord is telling us of the tremendous and constant blessings which flow to the soul from the living Christ on the Throne. There is no measuring of His goodness toward us. There is no limit to the supply. (See also Isa. 33: 21; 41:18)

Isa. 43:2 (a) Here we see a type of the great volume and avalanche of sorrow and trouble that sometimes overtakes God's people. The sorrows like sea billows roll. The flood of adversity overwhelms the heart. Then our Lord promises that we will not be submerged by it. He will preserve us and keep us always.

Isa. 43:19 (a) This beautiful promise of our Lord is to inform us that He has an abundance of remedies for all of our barrenness and fruitlessness. He wants us to take advantage of His rich provisions for our lives, so that we will not be barren nor unfruitful. (See 2 Pet. 1:8)

Ezek. 47:5 (b) This is a type of the Holy Spirit issuing out from the door, which is Christ, and coming to the ankles, affecting our walk, then to the knees, affecting our prayer life and devotion, then to the loins, affecting our service, and then enveloping us completely so that we are wholly baptized into Him and He completely controls all of us. Where this river flows, there will be life more abundant. Fishermen will be there fishing for souls and there will be a great multitude of fish to be caught or souls to be saved. Also the salt places will be healed and there will be sweet and blessed experiences among God's people.

John 7:38 (a) Here is a type which represents the gracious spiritual ministry of those who drink in the Holy Spirit, make Him their Lord, and expect Him to fill the life.

Rev. 22:1 (b) It is quite evident that this river represents the fullness of the rich blessings of God revealed in the fulfillment of His Word as it is ministered to the souls of the saved. It tells of refreshing, of life-giving power, of constant supply, and of sweet fruitfulness. All of these are enjoyed to the full when we are in heaven.

ROAR

Psa. 22:1 (a) This undoubtedly refers to the intense suffering of Christ Jesus on the Cross when His soul cried out to God, "Why hast Thou forsaken me?"

Prov. 28:15 (a) This animal roars when it is hungry and seeking more prey. So wicked rulers are never satisfied with that which they have conquered, but are seeking more people to crush and to rule.

1 Pet. 5:8 (a) The Devil is never satisfied with his conquests. He seeks constantly to wreck and to ruin the lives of men, women and children to make them to doubt God, to turn away from the Word of God, and to follow his wicked designs.

ROAST

Prov. 12:27 (a) This exposes the lazy man. He does not finish what he begins. He does not bring to a conclusion the work that he starts. He ends up short of his goal.

ROB

Mal. 3:8 (a) Certainly a part of our possessions and a part of our income belong to God. If we fail to give Him that which is His due, He says that we have become thieves, and have taken that which is His to use on ourselves. He indicates in this question that He is surprised that anyone should do such a thing. It shows a terrible condition of the heart when we embezzle God's property.

ROBE

Job 29:14 (a) Throughout the Scriptures a godly, upright character is represented as a robe or a garment. It is that which people can see. It is that which represents us to the public as our character. Job is indicating that he was righteous in all his ways, his actions, and his words. (See also Isa. 61:10; Rom. 13:14)

Luke 15:22 (b) This garment is called the "best" one for several reasons. It is made in heaven, and therefore is perfect. It is given freely, and no price can purchase it. It always fits every kind of a person. It may be worn in any place. It may be worn at any time. It cannot be stolen from you. It never wears out. It never needs cleaning or mending. It is always appropriate. It is always becoming. It is always in style. It is the only garment which can be worn into heaven, and in the presence of the King. All other garments must be left behind at death. It is the robe of righteousness, the garment of salvation, which God gives to each person who trusts Him fully, and believes in Him implicitly.

Rev. 6:11 (b) These garments represent righteousness which is given as a gift (Rom. 5:17) to those who, coming as lost sinners to God by Jesus Christ, are saved by grace, and washed white in the blood of the Lamb. (See also Rev. 7:9; Rev. 19:8.)

ROCK

Ex. 17:6 (a) This is a type of the Lord Jesus Christ who was smitten at Calvary and from whose precious sacrifice there flows to all mankind the gift of salvation, redemption and pardon. Because of Calvary, Christ also gives the Holy Spirit.

Ex. 33:21-22 (a) This rock represents the Lord Jesus Christ. When we sing "Rock of Ages, Cleft for me, let me hide myself in Thee," that is the thought which we find in this passage of Scripture. God the Father can only look upon us as we are in Christ. It is only as we are in Christ that we can see or understand or enjoy the glory of God.

Num. 20:8, 11 (a) In the first instance God told Moses to strike the rock. That represents the stroke of God on Christ Jesus at Calvary. (Ex. 17:6) In this instance God told him to speak to the rock. That rock is Christ (1 Cor. 10:4). Christ is not to be smitten again, once was sufficient. This completely condemns the Catholic mass. Those who celebrate mass will be shut out of the promised land, as Moses was shut out of Canaan. The rock was to be spoken to the second time, which indicates that we are only to come to Him in prayer and praise with our petitions and receive again the abundance of forgiveness, and the outpouring of the Holy Spirit.

Num. 24:21 (a) This figure is used to represent the Lord Jesus as the hiding place from the storm, the tempest, the wind, and the enemy. (See also Jer. 48:28)

Deut. 32:4 (a) This type represents the sure foundation which we have for our faith. It represents the character of God, His stability, security and firmness. It represents that He is our place of protection and of refuge. (See Psa. 94:22)

Deut. 32:13 (a) Both honey and water are described as coming out of "the Rock" (Christ). The honey is for rich food value, and the water is for refreshing, inspiration and life-giving virtue. (See Psa. 81:16)

Deut. 32:15 — God is the source of our salvation (See Psa. 89:26)

Deut. 32:18 — God is the source of our life

Deut. 32:30 — God is our owner

Deut. 32:31 — God is eternally perfect and unchanging

Deut. 32:37 — The ungodly are not trusting the true Rock

1 Sam. 2:2 (a) Our God and our Saviour can be trusted fully. No one else is dependable except them.

2 Sam. 22:2 (a) David uses this as a type of the strength and stability of the Lord who never changes, never sinks, but is always dependable and safe. (See also Psa. 31:3) Psa. 18:2, 31 and Psa. 92:15)

Psa. 27:5 (a) Whenever David was in trouble he turned to the Lord for security, safety and rest. (See also Psa. 40:2; Psa. 28:1)

Psa. 62:2 (a) The Psalmist learned by experience that there is no hiding place that is secure from trouble except in the presence, the care and the fellowship of his Lord. (See also Psa. 61:2; Psa. 78:35)

Psa. 114:8 (a) Christ never seems to be attractive until after we are saved. Then our Lord becomes the source of all joy and blessing, and the giver of the Holy Spirit.

Prov. 30:26 (c) We are reminded by this that the Rock, Christ Jesus, is a place of refuge for weak, feeble Christians who are unable to resist the enemy, nor stand in the storm.

Isa. 8:14 (a) The Lord Jesus is an offense to all the house of Israel. They resent Him, they reject Him, they crucified Him, and today they will not have Him. He is also an offense to most Gentiles who prefer a false religion, or worldliness, or sinful pleasure rather than to own Him as their Lord, trust in Him as the Redeemer, and follow Him as their Guide.

Isa. 32:2 (a) This describes the sweet, restful experience of the child of God who retires from his busy life, the cares of the home, the distress of business, to rest in the Lord, and to enjoy His fellowship.

Isa. 51:1 (b) Christ Jesus is the Rock and each believer is a chip from that Rock, a very part of Christ. (See Isa. 17:10) It may mean that each sinner is a part and character of this wicked world (which is compared to a rock, with no life), and that only the Divine power of God in the gospel can blast him loose from it, and make him free.

Jer. 23:29 (b) In this passage the rock represents the hardened heart of the sinner. It may represent the hard soil in a church, or the hard feelings in a family. The Word of God is able to break up any of these and make the ground soft for the entrance of His Word.

Jer. 48:28 (b) This is a call for sinners to leave their state of wickedness and give themselves over to Christ Jesus, the Rock of ages, to make Him their dwelling place and their habitation.

Amos 6:12 (b) This verse contains a truth which every Christian worker should observe. The rock represents a hardened condition of the heart which has no desire to receive the Word of God. It represents a class that is being well taught, but does not respond to the teaching. The ground is barren, the minds are not receptive. It represents a church group which resists the teaching of the Word of God, has no interest in the Son of God, and will not listen to the Spirit of God. In every such case, this verse is telling us plainly to move away, find a different location, cease the labor, and find a field or a person who does want the Word of God, and will listen.

Matt. 7:24 (b) Here we see a type of Christ Jesus, the foundation stone for every true believer, a resting place for those who build for eternity. (See also Luke 6:48)

Matt. 16:18 (a) This rock is a type of the Lord Jesus Himself, and is not a type of the Catholic church, nor any other human thing. God never builds anything on the failures of men. He never builds on anything that is not Jewish. The Catholic Popes are Italian, and not Jewish. Most of the officials are Italian or Irish. God never builds anything on men outside the Jewish faith. Christ Jesus is the Rock, He is the foundation, He is the Stone which builders have rejected, and no one else is the Rock. Peter never claimed to be this rock, nor is he ever referred to in the Bible as this rock. "Salvation is of the Jews" (John 4:22).

Matt. 27:51 (c) This is probably a picture of the fate that awaits the foundation of every false religion in the world. Everything upon which men build, every false faith will be utterly broken by the power of our Lord, and only Christ, the eternal Rock, will remain.

Luke 8:6 (a) This rock represents the heart that is hardened by the Devil, so that the seed of the Word of God cannot take root, finds no substance with which to grow, and therefore brings forth no fruit. (See v. 13 for the explanation)

Rom. 9:33 (a) Again Christ Jesus is the Stone. He is an offense to both Jew and Gentile. When they come in contact with Him, through preaching, or through the Scriptures, they stumble and fall. They oppose Christ, but He stands firm while they disappear. It describes the permanent character of Christ. The failure of Israel to receive Christ did not change Him from His purpose, nor remove Him from His place as the Lord and Saviour of the soul. The ungodly might butt their heads against this Rock, might seek to injure or destroy Him, but like the Rock of Gibraltar He stands firm through the ages. He remains on the field of battle to see the burial of His enemies.

1 Cor. 10:4 (a) This passage very clearly states that the Rock which Moses struck the first time, and should have spoken to the second time (but he struck it) was Christ Jesus the Lord. We, too, find that in this desert world where there is so little for the soul of the Christion to enjoy, Christ Jesus is still the Rock from which the Holy Spirit, the Living Water, and the Word of God, the Living Water, flow freely to refresh our hearts and souls.

ROCK OF AGES

Isa. 26:4 (margin) (a) This type represents the Lord Jesus in His strength and permanency. Those of every age may trust in Him. People who are of any age from youth to the aged may safely put their trust in Him. He is the unchanging Christ in a changing world.

ROD

Ex. 4:4 (c) Probably this is an emblem of that which becomes useful to God when it is in the hand of God's servant, although it might have been injurious before being turned over to the Lord. The Lord has a way of turning liabilities into assets.

Num. 17:2 (a) This is an emblem of authority from God. It was a sign and proof to all Israel that Aaron was his chosen high priest to lead the people in their worship, and was His chosen mediator between Himself and the people of Israel. When it budded in the tabernacle, and the others did not, He was showing Israel that He rejected the claims of Korah, Dathan and Abiram, and all others who assumed the place of leadership. He was also revealing the fact that He could take any old dead "stick," bring it into His presence, and change that person into a beautiful and fruitful Christian.

Psa. 2:9 (a) This is a type that reveals God's resistless power. It is unbending, it is irresistible, and will crush all the enemies of our Lord Christ. (See also Psa. 110:2)

Psa. 23:4 (b) This is probably a symbol of the powerful punishment which our Lord will exercise against the enemies of His children. The rod was for the wild animals, while the staff was for the sheep.

Psa. 125:3 (b) This type represents the evil powers of wicked men, and we are assured by the Lord that they shall not be able to conquer nor overcome God's people.

Prov. 14:3 (a) It seems as though pride acts as an injurious influence both for the owner and for those who are hurt by it. It is not a blessing.

Jer. 1:11 (a) We may understand from this type that it represents a condition that had not yet developed. It refers to God's wrath which would come into full force as the slip of the tree would yet bear fruit.

Jer. 10:16 (a) By means of Israel the Lord would get praise, honor and worship through their ministrations and activities. By means of them He would whip many other nations. At times they were quite unfruitful, and not beautiful. Afterward they would be both fruitful and delightful.

Jer. 48:17 (a) At one time Moab was a very strong and vigorous nation. However, they opposed God, and God's people Israel, so that the prophecy is that they were to be destroyed.

Lam. 3:1 (a) Sometimes this is called "a rod iron." Jeremiah had seen God punish Israel terribly, and because of his love for Israel he suffered with them.

Ezek. 7:10 (a) This probably describes the great wickedness of Israel in their pride and self-sufficiency, thinking they could live without God, and could prosper under idolatrous rule. Certain it is that God's wrath had been dormant, but is blossoming out against Israel. In verse 11, the enemy is no longer dormant. He, too, has become active.

Ezek. 19:14 (a) In this lamentation we are told that there is no leader among the people of God who is worthy to rule. All the leaders have been defeated and have gone astray, and bring forth no fruit under God.

Ezek. 20:37 (a) As sheep enter the sheepfold through the gate, and are counted under the rod as they enter, so God will look after each one of His people, and none of those who are His own sheep will ever be overlooked.

Ezek. 21:10 (c) This passage is omitted from most of the various Revised Versions and translations. It may be that the meaning of it is that God's wrath will not be hindered by the power of the rulers of Israel. The nation of Israel is called "His son." (See Isa. 45:11)

Micah 6:9 (b) Here we see a type of the whipping, the punishment and the chastisement which may come upon the child of God. He should pay attention to it, and learn lessons from it. It is probably another way of expressing the truth in Heb. 12:11.

Micah 7:14 (b) Probably this refers to the power of God to bring rich blessings, both material and spiritual, to His people.

1 Cor. 4:21 (a) This type is used to express the scolding that Paul could give these sinning saints, and the reproof he could exercise against them. He did not wish to do so.

Rev. 2:27 (a) We are being told that the conquering Christ will rule every enemy with hard and harsh punishment, which is unmingled with mercy. (See also chap. 19, v. 15)

ROLL (verb)

Micah 1:10 (a) This is the picture of a voluntary humbling of these people.

ROLL (noun)

Ezek. 3:1 (c) This parchment is a type of all the precious Word of God. It is to be appropriated personally, received in the heart, and hidden in the mind of each person.

ROOM

Psa. 31:8 (a) No doubt this refers to the liberty, power and freedom which that soul experiences which meets Jesus Christ, and is set free by the Son of God.

Matt. 23:6 (b) We have here a picture of the pride in man's heart which makes him desire a place of recognition among those with whom he is associated. (See also Luke 14:9)

ROOT

Deut. 29:18 (b) This is a symbol of the hidden, insidious, unseen, wicked influence among the people of God which produces evil results.

Judg. 5:14 (b) It is evident that the men of Ephraim in the past years were enemies of Amalek, as their children became enemies of Amalek. It was a historical hatred.

2 Ki. 19:30 (a) By this we learn that the people of Judah will again embrace the Word of God, the truth of God, and the Rock of Ages, as roots embrace the soil. They will publicly confess their God, and bear fruit to His glory, as the tree grows upward above its roots.

Job 29:19 (a) This figure represents the prosperity and the blessing that were in the life of Job before he was afflicted.

Prov. 12:3 (b) Probably this is a reference to the faith of the Christian. His faith has fastened itself to the eternal Rock of Ages.

Isa. 5:24 (b) This represents a life lived in a sinful atmosphere. These choose their pleasures from sin and evil activities.

Isa. 11:10 (a) The term is used to express the fact that this root which is a type of the Lord Jesus existed before the human Jesus, in the eternal ages, and that Jesse came from Christ, the root.

Isa. 14:29 (a) One kind of sin produces more sin. Evildoers shall cause trouble but God will punish them for it.

Isa. 27:6 (b) Israel will again be established as a nation, and we see this prophecy being fulfilled today in Palestine. (See Isa. 37:31)

Isa. 40:24 (b) By this we learn that God will destroy the wicked leaders of the earth such as Moab, Assyria, et cetera. The temples may remain in ruins, while the worshipers are gone.

Isa. 53:2 (a) This represents the Lord Jesus who, while on earth, was unwanted, and undesired. The people did not believe that He would bring a blessing. Those of every group were apposed to Him. He was despised in the social circles, and by the politicians, by the educators, and by the military forces. He was not attractive to the public.

Jer. 12:2 (b) This lament is from the heart of Jeremiah who could not understand why the wicked seemed to prosper. Asaph had this same difficulty (see Psa. 73:3, 12). Job also raised this question, for he was distressed by it. (See Job 21:7-14)

Ezek. 31:7 (a) The picture represents the great King of Assyria who had access to great wealth and business opportunities, so that he grew to be a mighty monarch.

Dan. 11:7 (b) The Queen of the South had a son and he would supercede and succeed in the battle.

Hosea 9:16 (a) We see by this figure that God's wrath would be poured out upon His people so that their basic supplies would be cut off.

Mal. 4:1 (a) In the great judgment day, whether it be the local one with the nations, or the individual one with Israel, or the eternal one in the last great final day, the wicked are to be removed from the earth, with no posterity. If the time refers to the end time, when the earth is dissolved, then also all the wicked of the earth are sent to the eternal lake of fire, and their memory is blotted out. This has already happened to the seven nations of Canaan. They have been destroyed from off the earth, root and branch.

Matt. 3:10 (b) This prophecy concerns the end of the nation of Israel. Titus came with his Roman army, conquered the country, and scattered the inhabitants. (See also Luke 3:9)

Matt. 13:6 (b) The hearers of God's Word had no convictions and no decision in the soul. They had an outward show of repentance and of faith, but the inner heart was unmoved. (See v. 21; also Mark 4:6; Luke 8:13)

Luke 3:9 (b) It probably expresses the Lord's will and desire for Christians to obliterate and to remove all those hidden evils in the life which would prevent fruit bearing.

Luke 17:6 (b) The lesson learned from this type is that to the man of faith the cause or the causes of his troubles will be removed.

Rom. 11:16 (b) We must be basically right in our faith and in our thinking.

Heb. 12:15 (a) This represents hidden evil thoughts and desires, secret words of animosity and dislike coming from a bitter heart. As this grows in the church, it produces trouble among God's people.

Jude 12 (b) Probably our Lord is reminding us of the fact that the enemies of God will be completely destroyed from off the earth as was Hitler and as was Judas.

Rev. 5:5 (a) The Scripture plainly teaches that the Lord Jesus lived before David, and in His human form descended from David.

Rev. 22:16 (a) Christ is the root which existed before David David came from Christ as Jesse came from Christ. They were both products of the work and plan of the Lord Jesus. He lived before they existed.

ROOTED

Eph. 3:17 (a) It is God's will that we shall be planted in the Word of God, and grounded in the Word of God for stability. As our hearts and minds are filled with the Scriptures, we feed on the Bread of Life, we drink the Living Water, and we grow in our knowledge of the Lord. This understanding of the Scriptures will keep us from being blown about by every wind of doctrine, and the evil schemes of false teachers. (See also Col. 2:7)

ROPE

Isa. 5:18 (b) This is emblematic of schemes and plans which are made to evil purposes and to assist one in committing sins.

ROSE

S. of Sol. 2:1 (c) Some, because of its beauty and fragrance, believe it is a type of the Lord Jesus. Others believe it is a type of the church because of its abundance and because of the presence of thorns in the midst of the flowers. The church, in God's sight, is beautiful and fragrant. It adorns all that is around it.

ROT

Prov. 10:7 (b) This indicates that the work and reputation of ungodly men will become a stench in the nostrils of succeeding generations.

ROTTEN

Job 13:28 (b) Job seems to think that God is working on him as rot works on any substance or as a moth works upon a garment. He feels that he is utterly wrecked and ruined as anything is ruined by rot.

ROTTENNESS

Hab. 3:16 (b) This indicates and describes the terrible feeling of one's own sinfulness and utter helplessness when God speaks and the Spirit works.

ROUGH

Isa. 40:4 (a) God will overcome difficult places in the life in order to make the way of life easy and happy for His child. He smooths out the rocky road, brings down the hills and exalts the valleys to make life a blessing. (See Luke 3:5)

RUBY (stone)

Ex. 28:17 (c) The first stone on the breastplate of the high priest was the ruby. It was red in color to represent the precious blood of Christ. It bore the name of Reuben which has two meanings: "one who hears acceptably," and "one who is the son." All of this signifies that the one who hears the gospel, accepts the Lord Jesus, and takes advantage of the shed blood of Christ at Calvary, becomes as a precious stone for God and will one day be with the Lord when He makes up His jewels. (The word "sardius" means "ruby").

Job 28:18 (a) Here the ruby, which has greater value than the diamond, is contrasted with the great value of wisdom. Wisdom is the most precious of all the gifts of God to men of earth. (See also Prov. 3:15)

RUDDY

So. of Sol. 5:10 (c) This is probably used symbolically to describe the health, vigor, youthfulness and loveliness of the Lord Jesus Christ. This same expression was used of David also in 1 Sam. 16:12.

RUSH (a weed)

Job 8:11 (c) This is a figure to show that the sins of life grow up out of a filthy heart, a defiled soul, a wicked spirit.

Isa. 9:14 (b) This is a description or figure wherein the Lord describes how utterly He will destroy the nation of Israel. The rush represents Israel's national entity and the branch represents the officials, governors, and rulers of the nation of Israel.

S

SABBATH

Col. 2:16 (a) The sabbath day is a shadow and a type of the perfect rest which every sinner finds in Christ Jesus when he ceases to work for his own salvation and trusts the Saviour to blot out all his sins, redeem his soul, bring forgiveness, give him eternal life, and make him a child of God. Immediately this friend rests in the Lord and begins to keep the true sabbath. This same thought is found also in Heb. 4:9 (margin) where the rest which the Lord gives to the trusting soul is compared to the sabbath of the Old Testament. In those days Israel came to the seventh day, and then rested. In our day the Lord Jesus says, "Come unto Me, and I will give you rest." He is the true sabbath, and He is our sabbath.

SACKCLOTH

2 Sam. 3:31 (b) This is a type of sorrow, grief and mourning. Those who wore this cloth publicly announced that they had broken hearts and sorrowing spirits. (See also 1 Kings 20:31; 2 Kings 6:30; Job 16:15; Psalm 35:13; Psalm 69:11; Isa. 32:11; Jer. 4:8; Dan. 9:3; Joel 1:13; Rev. 11:3)

SACRIFICE

Heb. 13:16 (a) By this word is described any praise or worship rendered to God from a grateful heart. (See also 1 Pet. 2:5)

Some of the sacrifices of the Old Testament represented various aspects of the work of Christ on the cross. (See under "OFFERINGS") Other sacrifices represented various attitudes of the Christian in his relationship to God. In some cases the sacrifices represented the attempt of sinners to appease their gods.

SAIL

Isa. 33:23 (b) It indicates that Zion had failed to take advantage of God's provisions to make progress over the sea of life and the ocean of time. Therefore, she had not progressed as she should have.

SALT

Gen. 19:26 (b) This probably represents (1) God's power to change a blessing to a curse as when one is taken out of this life and sent into the eternal dark. (2) Salt is a preservative. The memory of the deed of this woman and her act of rebellion were to be preserved for future generations. (3) Salt is a permanent chemical. The punishment of this woman was to be permanent.

Lev. 2:13 (b) Probably this represents the permanence and durability of Christ's sacrifice for us in all of its aspects. (See also Ezek. 43:24)

Num. 18:19 (b) The covenant which God makes with His people in this verse is characterized by purity, permanence, stability and savour. You will note that the offerings must contain salt as a picture or symbol or type of these characteristics in God, and His Word.

Deut. 29:23 (b) Here is a symbol of God's judgment and curse wherein He prevents the growth of all green things in order to punish the enemy. (See also Judges 9:45 where Abimelech used it as a curse; see also Ezek. 47:11; Zeph. 2:9)

2 Kings 2:20 (b) This is no doubt a type of God's healing and preserving power.

Ezek. 16:4 (b) The story in this chapter reveals that there was no period of preparation in the forming of the nation of Israel. God called Abraham, he obeyed and began the nation of Israel immediately. The salting of the baby at birth showed that God found in Abraham all that he needed for the beginning of a healthy growth for a healthy nation.

Matt. 5:13 (a) This is a type of the believer in the following aspects: Salt (table) is always pure white as the Christian is in God's sight. Every crystal of salt is a perfect cube. It is perfectly square. Each Christian is considered to be "square" toward God. toward his fellowman, toward his family, and toward himself. Salt preserves. The Christian by his godly influence and Christian activities has a salutary and beneficent effect upon those with whom he associates. The presence of Christians in the world preserves the world from the corruption of Satan. When the Christians are removed, the corruption progresses rapidly.

Mark 9:49 (b) Here we see a reference to the preserving power of the eternal fire in Gehenna. Instead of destroving the sinner as it punishes him, it will act as a preservative and keep him alive and conscious of his punishment.

Col. 4:6 (a) It is symbolical of the character of good language, wherein the thoughts expressed, the words spoken, and the attitude of heart in the conversation bring a sweet influence and a preserving power in the lives of those to whom we speak.

SALVATION

Gen. 49:18 (a) This is one of the early pictures of Christ. It is a prophecy concerning the fact that this One who is God's salvation would one day come to those who were waiting for Him. (See also Luke 2:30; Luke 19:9. Christ Jesus Himself is God's "salvation."

SANCTUARY

2 Chron. 30:8 (b) This is a beautiful type of the fellowship and presence of God in the midst of His people. It is a picture of the Church in the New Testament whereby God is able to dwell among us in the Person of the Holy Spirit and feel at home with His children on earth. (See also Psa. 20:2; 68:24; 73:17; 77:13; 96:6)

Psa. 114:2 (a) God refers to the entire people of Judah as a holy place in which He can dwell and walk among them.

Isa. 8:14 (a) God calls Himself a place of holiness. God's people could and should find their place of worship in God's own person, in His presence. (See also Ezek. 11:16)

Ezek. 47:12 (a) This is a type of the Lord Jesus from whom the Holy Spirit comes to work on and in the people of God. The river is a type of the Holy Spirit. (See also under "RIVER.")

SAND

Gen. 22:17 (a) This refers to the prevalence of Israel all over the world, as sand is found all over the world. The nation of Israel is compared not only to sand, but also to dust and to the stars. (See under these words.) (See also Gen. 32:12; Heb. 11:12)

Deut. 33:19 (b) Probably sand is used to convey the thought of a multitude of people throughout the earth from whose enterprise, property and business Zebulon and Issachar would become rich.

Judges 7:12 (a) Here is a type of the very great multitude of the enemy in the army. The enemies were so numerous that they covered the hills, the valleys, the roads and the fields as sand covers all those places. (See also I Sam. 13:5; 2 Sam. 17:11; 1 Kings 4:20; Isa. 10:22; 48:19; Jer. 15:8; 33:22)

Psa. 139:18 (a) This is a description of the great number of God's wonderful thoughts of peace and love toward David. In His mind they were as numerous as the grains of sand.

Hosea 1:10 (a) This represents the great number of people of Israel and their diversified beauty as the grains of sand. Also represents their power to control the nations of the world (the sea and its waves) as will one day be true when Israel is the head of the nations. Only God can make sand, and God Himself made the nation of Israel.

Matt. 7:26 (b) This is a picture of the transient and unsafe character of anything outside of Christ on which men may build their hopes and plans for the future.

Rev. 20:8 (a) This is a type of the countless number of the unsaved, and their prevalence all over the earth. It is also a picture of the shifting and shiftless character of the ungodly.

SAP

Psa. 104:16 (a) This is a type of the live, fresh, sweet character of God's children in whom the water of life (the Spirit) is free to have His own way.

SAPPHIRE

Isa. 54:11 (a) Our Lord Jesus is compared to this beautiful stone because of His holy and heavenly character, and as the foundation of God's Church. It is also a picture of the heavenly character of the nation of Israel as they will appear when God finishes His training of them.

Ezek. 1:26 (a) This is a bright blue stone which is typical of the heavenly and holy character of our Lord. (See also S. of Sol. 5:14; Ezek. 10:1; Rev. 21:19)

SARAH

1 Pet. 3:6 (a) This is a type of the Church, the Bride of Christ, who should be and usually is in obedience to her Lord, the Bridegroom.

SARDINE (Stone)

Ezek. 28:13 (b) Probably the Lord is telling us that all the beauty of heaven's adornments as represented by the different colors of stones was given to this great arch-angel who later fell and became Satan. These stones represent a wide variety in values, so that probably we are being told that Satan in his original exalted position with God had all the values that could be given to a created spirit.

SARDONYX

Rev. 21:20 (b) The beauty and the value of these stones probably represent the beauty and the value of the nation of Israel (the twelve tribes) in God's program of world development. Every blessing we enjoy has come to us through the influence of Israel. These influences were of various kinds and characters, and this fact is represented by the various kinds of stones.

SAVOUR

Matt. 16:23 (a) The influence which Peter sought to have on Jesus is compared to human odor. It did not come from God, but came evidently from Satan. The "odor" of our lives reveals whether we are being activated by motives from heaven, or human influences.

2 Cor. 2:14 (b) This is symbolic of that peculiar influence given out by a person either for good or for evil. In this passage it evidently refers to the sweet presence of the Lord in the soul which may be realized by those about Him. But in verse 16 it refers also to the message for the unsaved concerning their coming punishment.

Eph. 5:2 (a) The life of Christ was so perfect, so beautiful, and so pleasing to God that it is compared to the fragrant incense which ascended from the golden altar in the holy place.

SCAB

Isa. 3:17 (b) This figure is used to describe the results on the nation of Israel when God sends among them invading enemies, the pestilence, and the famine.

SCABBARD

Jer. 47:6 (b) This figure is used to describe the act of God in stopping the outpouring of His wrath, the defeating of the enemy, and the bringing in of peace to Israel.

SCALES

Isa. 40:12 (b) This is a symbol of the power and wisdom of God in putting chemicals together in combination by weight. All chemical combinations are put together by weight and not by volume. All of the combinations of metal, minerals, etc., in the mountains and hills are put together by weight.

SCALP

Psa. 68:21 (b) This is a type of the punishment of all God's enemies. He punishes the head because all sin begins in the thoughts of the mind. The Lord provides the "helmet of salvation" to preserve the thoughts of His children.

SCAPEGOAT

Lev. 16:8 (b) The goats in this story represent two aspects of the sacrifice of the Lord Jesus. The live goat which became the scapegoat is a picture of the Saviour living in glory with the marks of Calvary upon Him, having taken away the sin of the world, and having died at Calvary for our sins. The dead goat represents Christ at Calvary, giving up His life for us.

SCARLET

Gen. 38:30 (a) Since Pharez is found in the genealogy of Christ, this thread may indicate that Zarah would need the blood to redeem him. (See Matt. 1:3)

Ex. 25:4 (c) It may be that this color all through the tabernacle equipment served to remind the Israelites that the blood was always essential in every part of life and service.

Lev. 14:4 (c) This probably is a picture of the value of the blood in every sacrifice for sin. Sins are put away only by and through the blood of Jesus.

Josh. 2:18 (c) This is usually taken to be a picture of the precious blood of Christ. The woman was sheltered because of the red cord. The sinner is sheltered under the red blood of the Saviour.

S. of Sol. 4:3 (a) The smooth, pretty lips of the bride are compared to the scarlet line. It is a picture of the loveliness of the church (the bride) in the sight of the Bridegroom, her Lord.

Isa. 1:18 (a) It is used to describe the stain of sin in contrast with the white garments of salvation.

Matt. 27:28 (c) It is a sign of royalty, though used here in mockery.

Rev. 17:3 (b) It indicates the enormous sin and wickedness of this woman whose stain of sin covered her completely. The woman represents the apostate church.

SCENT

Jer. 48:11 (b) This word is used to describe the unsavory attitude of wicked people. They had a wicked and vile odor in the nostrils of God.

SCEPTER

Gen. 49:10 (b) Here is a symbol of the sovereignty of the Lord Jesus Christ who was to become King of kings, and Lord of lords. In a coming day Jesus Christ will rule the entire earth with a rod of iron.

Num. 24:17 (a) This is a symbol also of the power and authority of Christ Jesus who will one day sit on the throne of David and will rule over not only Israel, but all other nations as well.

Isa. 14:5 (a) This is a type of the power and authority of all wicked rulers on this earth. God will destroy them and Christ will reign.

Ezek. 19:11 (a) These strong rods made into scepters represent the self-made authority of Israel's self-made rulers. God promised that He would destroy all these evil princes and sovereigns. (See also vs. 14))

SCHOOLMASTER

Gal. 3:24 (a) It is said that the schoolmaster was the servant who led the student child to the school or the class where he was to be taught. So the law convicts us of our need of a Saviour, and leads us to come to Him for pardon, forgiveness and eternal life.

SCORPION

1 Kings 12:11 (a) Here is a figure to describe the terrible oppression which Rehoboam intended to bring upon the people over whom he ruled. His father's oppression is compared to a whip. His was to be so much worse that he compared it to the sting of a scorpion. (See also vs. 14 and 2 Chron. 10:11-14)

Ezek. 2:6 (a) The word is used to describe the terrible wickedness and the evil scourge of Israel at this time.

Luke 11:12 (a) The little child, seeing a scorpion rolled up ready to strike, is deceived by its appearance and thinks he is looking at an egg. The Lord is teaching us that often we see something which looks as if it would be good for us to have, but our Lord sees that it would be injurious. Therefore, He does not grant our request for it in prayer.

Rev. 9:10 (b) This may be a symbol of a modern fighting machine such as a tank or a portable cannon pulled by a tractor. Both have power in the rear end.

SCROLL

Isa. 34:4 (a) Evidently the passing away of the heavens, both the first and the second heavens, will be in the form of a roll. Just how this will take place, we do not know. Certainly God will dispose of the heavens in this way. (See also Rev. 6:14) It may be that the Lord is telling us that all the records of things pertaining to our lives on earth and to the activities in heaven will be rolled up as a scroll is rolled, and will be remembered no more. The writings will be hidden from view.

SCUM

Ezek. 24:6 (a) This describes the evil character of the leaders of Jerusalem (the "top" ones) whose lives were wretched and filthy. Some translators think that the Hebrew word here means "rust." (See verses 11 and 12.)

SEA

Ex. 14:2 (c) It may be used to represent extremely difficult problems and situations which arise in the Christian's path and are impossible to conquer unless the Lord performs a miracle.

I Chron. 16:32 (b) This represents peoples, nations and tongues. God is comparing the great praises of the people to the roaring of the ocean. (See Psa. 96:11; 98:7; Rev. 17:15.)

Psa. 80:11 (b) Here is a type which represents Israel as reaching out all her influence to gather and to give blessing for all the earth.

Isa. 23:4 (a) The sea has covered the site of this city and rendered it desolate. Therefore, human activity has ceased on the site. The sea is represented as telling the world of this destruction.

Isa. 43:16 (b) This represents the great difficulties and serious hindrances in life. God opens a path for His child to enter and pass safely through them. Since the ocean seems to typify "people," this figure may represent difficulties caused in the life by relatives or neighbors or enemies, or even officials. In all of these troubles caused by "people," our Lord makes a way of escape and deliverance.

Isa. 48:18 (a) It is a figure of the many blessings and sweet benedictions which God gives to those who walk with Him. They keep coming and never cease.

Isa. 57:20 (a) As the sea is constantly moving and is restless, throwing debris on the shore, so the ungodly live. They too exhibit in their lives the evil of their hearts. They constantly reveal to others the wickedness of their unsatisfied lives.

Lam. 2:13 (a) As the ocean separates lovers who must live far apart, so God is separated oftentimes from His people whom He loves. (See Isa. 59:2)

Nahum 1:4 (c) God is assuring us He has power to rebuke all peoples and to restrain their fury. This picture is seen also in His power to calm the storm, the storms of life. (See also Zech. 10:11)

James 1:6 (a) This is a picture of the professing Christian who is not rooted and grounded in the faith. His life is constantly in a turmoil.

Jude 13 (a) This symbolizes the great power and energy put forth by the enemies of God who rise up out of the great mass of people (the sea) and are leaders in opposing the work of God and the people of God.

Rev. 13:1 (a) The word in this verse evidently refers to the great multitudes of the earth.. (See Rev. 17:15)

Rev. 15:2 (b) The physical ocean hides all that is in its depths; but our Lord will unfold all the hidden sins and iniquities of the human heart so that nothing is hidden from His sight. It is a picture of the wrath of God revealing all secret sins.

SEED

Matt. 13:24 (a) It is the Word of God which, in all of its multitudinous aspects and forms, produces a variety of results. (See vs. 19)

Matt. 13:38 (a) The people of God are the seed in this parable. The Lord takes His children and plants them in soil where they will produce the best results for Him.

2 Cor. 9:10 (b) There are precious portions of the Scripture which can best be used by each individual Christian. The Spirit of God reveals to each person the special truths in His Word which seem particularly adapted to his nature and mentality. The Christian then takes this line of truth and ministers or plants it in the hearts of others.

SEETHE

Deut. 14:21 (b) It is probably used to describe the destructive influences by wrong use of that which should be put to good use. That which should be a blessing to the kid and enable it to grow was used for its destruction. (See also Ex. 23:19 and Ex. 34:26. See under "KID".)

SEPULCHRE

Matt. 23:27 (b) This is a description of the death and decay which the Lord saw in the hearts, minds and lives of these hypocritical, religious leaders.

Rom. 3:13 (a) This is a graphic illustration of God's thoughts about the natural human heart and soul; the stench of which is revealed by the words, the statements and the sayings of the ungodly.

SERPENT

Gen. 3:1 (a) This is a type of Satan for he is so described in Rev. 12:9.

Num. 21:6 (b) It is a type of sin in all of its terrible effect on the people.

Num. 21:8 (a) It is a type of the Lord Jesus when He was made sin for us (2 Cor. 5:21) as He hung on Calvary. (See John 3:14)

Matt. 7:10 (b) This is a symbol of a harmful, injurious thing which the Christian, in his ignorance, thinks is good and profitable. The Lord sees that he is mistaken in his request and so refuses to give it to him because He knows it would harm. God says "no" to the request.

SEVEN

(c) This number is used to represent God's complete provision both in Christ and in His dealings with men. The seven days make a perfect week. The seven colors make a perfect spectrum The seven notes on the piano make a perfect scale. The seven articles of furniture in the tabernacle make a perfect picture of the Christian life. The seven "eyes" describe the perfect omniscience of the Holy Spirit (Zech. 3:9) The number seven occurs very frequently throughout the book of Revelation, and in each case it indicates the perfect character of God, His perfect integrity, equity and justice in all His dealings with men.

SHAVE

Judges 16:17 (c) This represents any action which would destroy fellowship with God and hinder the Spirit from working. Samson deliberately broke his vow with God.

Isa. 7:20 (a) This describes the punishment of Israel when the Assyrians invaded the land.

SHEEP

Psa. 95:7 (a) God's people in their deep poverty and need must come constantly and frequently to the Lord to receive their sustenance and to enjoy His fellowship.

Psa. 100:3 (a) God's people who dwell together in His fold, the church, rejoice in His goodness and continue in fellowship with one another, and with every need supplied.

Isa. 53:7 (a) Here is a type of Jesus brought in weakness before those who were to torment Him and kill Him. He permitted them to do as they pleased with Him.

SHEPHERD

Isa. 44:28 (a) It is used to represent King Cyrus as he took a leading place in the rebuilding of the temple, and restoring Israel to their land.

Ezek. 34:23 (a) This represents King David as he would guide the affairs and the destinies of Israel. Probably it also is prophetic of Christ when He returns to reign.

John 10:14 (a) This is a type of the Lord Jesus. He cares for, protects and leads His people.

SHEWBREAD

Ex. 25:30 (c) It is a type of the rich provision made by the Lord for the sustenance of His people. These loaves were quite large, more than any one person could eat. They were all the same size, revealing that God makes just as much provision for the small tribes as for the large ones. The smallest tribe had just as large a loaf on the table as did the largest tribe. God does not give by measure according to the riches of His grace.

SHIELD

Gen. 15:1 (a) The preserving and protecting care over His children is thus understood.

Eph. 6:16 (b) Here is an attitude of trust in the living God which preserves the heart of the child of God from injury by that which others say and do.

SHILOH

Gen. 49:10 (a) This name is given to the Lord Jesus Christ. The word means "the peacemaker."

Josh. 18:1 (c) The word means "sent." It may be used as a type of the plan and purposes of God for it was at Shiloh that many of God's plans were revealed to His people. (See Judges 21:19, 1 Sam. 1:24, 1 Kings 2:27, 1 Kings 14:2, Jer. 7:12.)

SHIP

Prov. 30:19 (b) This indicates the remarkable guidance of the Lord in directing His own through the trackless lanes of life and bringing them safely to the desired haven.

SHITTIM

Ex. 25:10 (c) It probably represents the deathless, incorruptible body of the Lord Jesus in His humanity. His body could not die except as He deliberately dismissed His Spirit from it. Shittim wood is a wood that resists decay and thus represents the human body of the Saviour.

SHOD

Eph. 6:15 (a) This is symbolical of the act of the Christian who puts on the graces of heaven which makes his life so attractive that it prepares the way for the message from his lips. His walk corresponds with his words.

SHOE

Deut. 33:25 (b) This is a type of the blessed preparation given by God to enable His children to traverse difficult roads without discomfort. He fits our feet for the road.

S. of Sol. 7:1 (c) This indicates that the natural walk represented by natural feet is not beautiful nor acceptable to God unless affected and covered by those graces which He supplies for the work. It must be linked with the death of Christ, for shoes, whether of wood or leather, can only be such after the death of that from which they are made.

Matt. 3:11 (c) These are literal shoes, but symbolical of the Spirit of humility in doing the least and lowliest things for another.

SHOELATCHET

Gen. 14:23 (c) Abraham uses this figure to tell the king that he would have nothing whatever from him, whether it be the least thing, or the greatest. It is a lesson to us that we should depend entirely on the Lord for our prosperity, and not on the favors of this wicked world.

John 1:27 (c) John thus describes his own unworthiness, because the least service one could render would be to kneel at the feet of a monarch and tie his shoe laces. John felt that he was not worthy to do even this.

SHOOT

Psa. 11:2 (b) This figure represents the cutting, stinging words that one might speak against another. The words come quickly in hatred and anger, and deeply wound the person spoken against. (See also Psa. 64:3)

SHOULDER

Ex. 28:12 (c) By this is represented the strength and power of God upon which rests all the burdens and cares of the people of God.

Deut. 18:3 (c) This may represent the fact that Christians give to their High Priest, Christ Jesus, the strength, vigor and power of their shoulders, which represents their work and service. It may mean also that they offer the shoulder to Him that He may put His burdens on them.

Deut. 33:12 (b) This picture indicates that God's people are protected and sheltered by the mighty power of God as the papoose is safe between the shoulders of the Indian mother in a secure resting place.

Neh. 9:29 (b) Here is a graphic picture of the fact that Israel refused to bear God's burdens, and to do His work.

Psa. 81:6 (b) What a beautiful type is seen here of the deliverance that God gives to His child even though He does not remove the difficulty that is in the life. He may leave the affliction in the body or in the home, or in the business, but delivers His child from the burden of it, so that he can sing and be a radiant Christian while under the difficulty.

Isa. 9:6 (b) This is a type of the power, wisdom and judgment of Christ Jesus who is able to bear all the governments of this world because of His sovereign knowledge, power and Deity.

Isa. 11:14 (b) This prophecy reveals the fact that both Judah and Israel will conquer their enemies, make them their servants, and ride upon them as their victors, having them completely under their control. (See also Isa. 49:22)

Isa. 22:22 (b) Here we see a symbol of the responsibility and dependability of Christ Jesus to handle all the affairs of His people.

Zech. 7:11 (b) The refusal of Israel to assume any responsibility for God and His work is thus represented. They would not enter into the program God outlined for them.

Luke 15:5 (a) By this type we understand the loving care and the mighty power of the great Shepherd of the sheep. He restores and returns and protects that one whom He reaches with His love, and who is willing to turn to Him for salvation, or restoration.

SICK

Prov. 13:12 (b) When the heart is depressed and discouraged, it is represented as being ill. It fails to function as it should, and is deeply affected by adversity.

S. of Sol. 2:5 (b) The wise man is telling us by this expression that his whole soul and being is given up to love and loving, so that nothing else in the world matters. It makes him unfit for any other occupation. (See also chap. 5:8)

Isa. 1:5 (a) The Lord is thus describing that which He sees in the minds and thoughts of Israel. They were only evil and wicked continually. Their minds were occupied with rebellion and idolatry, with lust and sin.

SICKLE

Joel 3:13 (b) The sickle is used as a type of God's judging and avenging wrath. The time came when He would endure Israel's rebellion no more. He exercised the same punishment upon the nations that persecuted Israel. One day He will cut down all the wicked nations of the earth, as we read in Rev. 14:14. God permits sinners to run their course, produce their evil fruit, and then He cuts them off, and the day of grace is ended.

SIDE

Num. 33:55 (b) The heart is located in the side of the breast, and the Lord was warning Israel that if they permitted the enemy to remain in the land, then these enemies would strike at their very lives, and wreck their existence. He promised them only trouble from the wicked men of the evil nations if they were not destroyed. (See Josh. 23:13; Judges 2:3)

Dan. 7:5 (b) The Medio-Persian empire is described as a bear. One side of the bear is the Kingdom of the Medes, and the other side is the Kingdom of the Persians. These two kingdoms were united against Babylon, but the side of the Medes was uppermost. represented by their King Darius.

Ezek. 1:17 (b) In this peculiar expression, the Lord is informing us that the Lord Jesus Christ, who is represented by the four animals, and the Holy Spirit, who is represented by the eyes, would influence and affect every part of the earth. The Lord uses the expression "the four sides" and the expression "the four corners" to represent north, south, east and west. No part of the earth would be free from the influence of the Son of God, and the Spirit of God. (See chap. 10:11)

SIEVE

Isa. 30:28 (a) The Lord promised in this passage that He would strain out the nations in such a way that all their boastings, pride and vain glory would prove to be of no value whatever, and would not stand His testings and siftings. The Lord thus describes the helplessness of the proud enemies of Israel.

Amos 9:9 (a) In this promise the Lord assures Israel that He will put them through severe testings and will remove all that is not profitable nor righteous nor good from among them, but He will keep the people eventually for Himself. In the final checkup, those of Israel who remain on the earth will hear the Word of God and believe His message. (See Rom. 11:26)

SIGN

The word is used as a type to represent or express some great truth. Here are some of the signs mentioned in Scripture:

Ex. 4:8 (a) Moses, taking the serpent by the tail, represents the power of God over Satan and the power of the servant of God over the evil powers of earth. Moses' hand in his bosom became leprous. Upon removing it from his bosom it became well. This indicates that man is first wicked within and then through the command and work of God he becomes right within.

Ex. 8:23 (a) The plague of flies demonstrated the power of God over nature and the purpose of God to punish His enemies.

Ex. 13:9 (a) Evidently this refers to the Word of the Lord which was to be bound both upon the hand and the head as a constant reminder of the fulfillment of God's Word in delivering Israel from the bondage of Egypt. (See also Deut. 6:8)

Ex. 31:13 (a) The Sabbath was a sign of that blessed rest which would be offered in its fullness through the Lord Jesus and in His blessed Person when He came and said, "I will give you rest."

Num. 16:38 (a) The brazen censers (of the rebels) which were beaten into broad plates were to remind Israel and also us today that it is fatal to rebel against the Word and the plan of God.

Num. 26:10 (a) The disaster sent upon Korah and his company was ever to remind Israel and us, too, of the punishment of God upon those who rebel against His order.

Judges 6:17 (a) God saw the genuine desire of Gideon to really know His will and therefore granted him the evidence he requested. It is not always so. Very few servants of God ever have asked for a sign to confirm the Word of God. Jesus said about this matter. "An evil and adulterous generation seeketh after a sign." (Mark 8:12) We should believe God's Word without signs.

Isa. 7:14 (a) The coming of Christ was a sign to the world that no other remedy for sin would avail. It was a sign of man's helplessness and inability to save himself. It was a sign of the miraculous gift of a Saviour without human means or device. It was a sign of God's plan and pleasure in sending one who could and would be the Mediator between God and men. It was a sign of God's loving interest in the needs of men.

Isa. 19:20 (a) This prophecy indicates that at some time in the future God's rich grace will reach into the land of Egypt, and hearts will turn to the Lord in that country. The altar which shall be built there will be a testimony to the Egyptians and to the world that they no longer are followers of Mohammed and the Moslem philosophy, but that they have accepted the God of Israel as their God. The altar does not refer to the Pyramids. These are not altars, they are tombs of the dead.

Isa. 20:3 (a) God used the prophet as a living sermon to Israel. What happened to him personally would happen to Israel nationally. The people were to look at Isaiah and learn the lesson of their own future. See that this happened also to Ezekiel in Ezek. 12:6; 14:8; 24:24.

Isa. 55:13 (a) The thorn and the brier are types of wickedness and sinfulness that always work injury to men. They were to be replaced by the fir tree and the myrtle tree which are types of the joyful, beautiful Christian life. These latter growing instead of the former would be a constant testimony to the faithfulness of God and to his restoring power.

Isa. 66:19 (a) Probably this refers to the Lord Jesus Himself ruling and reigning on Mount Zion as Governor of the world. The presence of the Son of God would prove to all men that Christ Jesus has the approval of God.

Jer. 6:1 (b) This sign may represent a destructive fire at this suburb near Bethlehem which would be a warning to Israel that their country would be invaded by the forces of the north, and be destroyed by the local fire. Or, it may refer to the presence of the Lord Jesus Christ coming there, for He will sit one day as a refiner's fire to judge Israel and separate the dross from the silver, or the wicked from the just.

Jer. 44:29 (a) In this exhibition of God's wrath against the people who went down to Egypt from the land of Israel, God is proving to His people His Word is not in vain, but that He will fulfill every promise, whether it be for punishment or for blessing.

Ezek. 4:3 (a) Our Lord used this object lesson as a type or a picture of the manner in which He would deal with the house of Israel in the time of His wrath. It particularly applied to His plan concerning Jerusalem, and was a picture of the destruction of that city.

Matt. 12:39 (a) Wicked people do not usually believe God's Word. They require some kind of evidence. Even when the miracle is performed, the ungodly do not believe God, but raise questions and often show their hatred. God did give them a sign in the Old Testament which was Jonah's experience in the whale. He would repeat that sign in the New Testament by His own experience of going down into the heart of the earth for three days and three nights. That experience of Jonah was a sign that the Israelites represented by Jonah would be swallowed up by nations which are represented by the whale, and then would be thrust out to return to their own land.

Matt. 24:3 (a) Our Lord does give evidences of His purposes, but sometimes we have difficulty in discerning them, or understanding them. The answer He gives to this question concerning the sign is a rather long one, and complicated. It does, however, include the existence of wars, troubles and the putting forth of the leaves of the fig tree. The fig tree is a type of Israel nationally, or politically. This is taking place at the present time. A complete nation has been born in one day. It is growing and flourishing, and shows that a new national existence has begun with this "tree" which has been dormant for a number of centuries.

John 2:11 (a) The word here translated "miracle" is really the word "sign." There are eight of these signs in the Gospel of John. These eight signs teach us four great lessons. In the first sign they had nothing to drink, and in the eighth one they had nothing to eat. Then Jesus came and their needs were satisfied. In the second sign the boy was ready to die, and in the seventh sign the man was dead. Then Jesus came and life, and life more abundant was present to defeat death. In the third sign the man could not walk and in the sixth one the man could not see. Then Jesus came and both men were able to walk with Christ and to see His loveliness. Both of these signs happened on the sabbath day, telling us that those who walk with God and see God by faith, these have rest in their souls and hearts. Both of these signs were at pools. These represent the Word of God and the Spirit of God. They are always preeminent in the salvation of the individual. The fourth sign and the fifth one reveal the presence of fear in the heart. In the fourth one they were afraid of dying of hunger, and in the fifth they were afraid of dying by drowning. Then Jesus came and the fear of death was removed. These eight signs are as follows:

Chapter 2 (b) Water into wine. The Lord can take the ordinary things of life and make them unusually profitable for His glory. There can be no joy in the sweetest scenes of earth unless He is present.

Chapter 4:54 (b) The young man was at the point of death but was not yet dead. The Lord Jesus is able to sustain and to support the life which He gives. He only can keep us from the second death.

Chapter 5:9 (b) This indicates that those who are unable to walk with God and have no power to change their condition need the Saviour to touch them and enable them to walk with God and to live for His glory.

Chapter 6:11 (b) We learn the lesson from this sign that the hunger of the heart and the desires of the soul can only be satisfied and gratified by the presence and power of the Lord Jesus.

Chapter 6:21 (b) This sign teaches us that the storms of life and fears of the soul may be quickly and surely calmed by the presence and the word of the sovereign Lord.

Chapter 9:7 (b) This reveals that only the Lord Jesus can open blind eyes to see their need and to see the sufficiency of the Saviour. It is interesting to note that the lame man was by the pool and the blind man went to the pool. The pool may represent the Word of God or the Spirit of God or both. We should note also that both of these "signs" were given on the sabbath to teach us that when we are able to walk with God and are able to see the things of God as we should, then we have rest in our souls.

Chapter 11:44 (b) This is a blessed sign to teach us that only Jesus Christ can give life to a dead sinner and only the Word of Christ can break open the grave and cause a resurrection. As the young man in John 4 was about to die and needed to be kept alive, so in this case the man was already dead and needed to be restored to life. Only Christ Jesus can do either or both of these blessed miracles in our lives today.

Chapter 21:6 (c) This is to teach us that we cannot be successful in life in the true sense of the word unless the Lord directs our way. We learn also that in the ministry of preaching we shall not gather in a harvest for Him except as He directs both as to the manner and the place. In the first sign, they were lacking wine to drink. Only He could provide. In this, the last sign, they were lacking food to eat and only He could provide. So in these eight signs in John we are told that Christ Jesus is God's answer to every need of the human heart.

Rom. 4:11 (a) The circumcision of the Old Testament was a constant testimony to Israel; first, that they belonged to God; and second, that they were not to live according to the lusts and desires of the flesh, but according to the will of God. (See also Gen. 17:11)

1 Cor. 14:22 (a) The gift of tongues was a gift in which the servants of God were enabled to instantly speak in a different language from the one they knew. The Spirit of God gave them immediately the power to preach the gospel in foreign tongues which had never been learned. This has never been repeated since the apostles' day. Those who today claim to have that "gift" must always learn the language of the country to which they go as missionaries. The message was always an intelligent message, and understandable to those to whom it was addressed. The gift was not given for Christians, but for the heathen. If today those from this country could go to China or Russia and immediately speak freely and fluently in the language of those countries, though they had never learned those languages, that would be a sign to the natives of that country that God was working.

Rev. 15:1 (a) In almost every case the Lord forewarned the earth of impending judgment. He did so in this case. When John saw those seven angels with the seven plagues he knew there was trouble ahead for the inhabitants of the earth. This is written in the Scripture so that all men everywhere will today take heed to this sign and repent and turn to God.

SIGNET

Hag. 2:23 (a) This unusual compliment is probably the greatest given to a man by the living God. He informed Zerubbabel that He would touch his life in such a blessed way that he would leave on every other life he touched the imprint of God and the impress of heaven. His conversation with others and his manner of life with them would make an indelible impression upon their hearts and they would know that he was a man of God.

SILVER

Ex. 36:24 (c) This precious metal is often used as a type of redemption. In this passage it refers probably to redemption as the foundation of the sinner's safety and his standing. The boards represent the Christians, while the silver sockets represent redemption. In the sandy desert, as well as in this wicked world, the sinner needs a sure foundation, a safe resting place. These sockets perhaps weighed one hundred pounds each. The board therefore rested on a solid foundation in the sand. So we "stand on redemption ground." We do not read of silver being in heaven. No one in heaven needs to be redeemed. (See also Ex. 30:15, and other places.)

SINAI

Gal. 4:25 (a) This mountain represents the stern realities of the law. God appeared there in thunder and fire and thick darkness, for the law demands absolute obedience, or else punishment. It is in contrast with Calvary, where God appeared in human form, in tender loving kindness, and in love. The condition of Jerusalem at that time, with its wickedness, sin and the destruction wrought by its enemies was just a plain evidence of the tragedy that follows the broken laws of Sinai. (See Ex. 19:18)

SINEWS

Ezek. 37:6 (b) In this allegory the Lord is describing what we have seen with our own eyes in the restoration of Israel as a political unit. The bones represent the people of Israel. The sinews represent the constitution and laws which have been formed to hold the people together, and enable them to work together in the various departments of their national life. The flesh represents the living conditions of the people, their customs, ways and programs. The skin is that national spirit which holds all of the above together and gives it the form and shape of a nation among the nations.

SINGLE

Matt. 6:22 (b) The expression that is used by our Lord in this passage indicates that the individual is occupied only with the glory of God, the blessing of the people of God, and the growth of the church of God. He does not have one eye that looks out for himself, and the other eye which looks out for God's interests. (See also Luke 11:34)

SINK

Psa. 69:2 (b) This is a Messianic Psalm about the Saviour, but no doubt it also expresses David's feelings about himself when he was in deep trouble. There was none to help in the time of need, and there seemd to be no bottom to the depths of sorrow. This figure is used to describe his feelings at the time of his deep distress.

Luke 9:44 (b) The Saviour is describing in this way the fact that He wanted those who heard Him to accept His words, apply them to their hearts, and let them be permanently impressed upon the mind.

SISTER

S. of Sol. 4:9 (b) In this verse, as well as in the rest of this beautiful, poetical book, this word is used to represent the church. It is a type of the church. Many scholars disagree on the meaning of the various expressions used in these chapters, but it is plainly a description of a love affair between the church and her Lord.

Jer. 3:10 (a) The two nations, Judah and Israel, are represented in this and in other portions as being sisters of each other, as they really were (See Ezek. 16:46)

Ezek. 23:4 (a) Again the two nations of Israel and Samaria are represented as sisters, and they receive new names which describe their character.

Matt. 13:56 These are really the sisters of the Lord Jesus, although the Roman church denies the plain statement of Scripture and teaches that these were really nieces, and not sisters. We do not know how many there were. The statement uses the plural word, which means more than one. Mary gave birth to at least six other children besides Jesus. She was only a virgin in the birth of the Saviour. After that she was a normal mother with her husband Joseph.

SIT (and forms)

The expression is used to denote repose, meditation, laziness, weariness and an attitude of humbleness. Passages will be quoted and the reader will apply the meaning which is plainly indicated in the portion given.

Ruth 3:18 Expectation
2 Ki. 7:3 Discouragement
Job 2:8 Distress
Psa. 1:1 Determination
Psa. 29:10 Power
Psa. 69:12 Authority
Psa. 107:10 Hopelessness
Isa. 40:22 Sovereignty
Isa. 42:7 Helplessness
Isa. 47:1 Humbleness
Jer. 17:11 Industry
Lam. 1:1 Indifference
Mal. 3:3 Attentiveness
Luke 9:14 Anticipation
Eph. 2:6 Security

SIT (Downsitting)

Psa. 139:2 (c) This expression is used to denote the intricate and intimate knowledge of God concerning all of our actions and ways. Probably no one knows how many times he sat down in any one day, nor why he did so. God watches every movement, and is interested whether we are sitting when we should be standing, whether we are resting when we should be working.

Zech. 5:7 (b) Probably the woman represents Israel, while lead represents the heavy burdens and the weight of sorrow in which Israel is sitting. It may also represent the deceitful practices of the people in their commercial life, and this became a weight which held them down from walking with God.

Luke 8:35 (c) We may learn from this posture that when a soul meets Jesus Christ, his restlessness ceases, and he begins to rest in the presence of his Lord. Christ is the anti-type of the sabbath day. He said "Come unto Me, and I will give you rest." This is illustrated in the passage we are considering.

Rev. 17:1 (b) The woman represents the apostate church, while the waters represent peoples, nations and tongues. The great apostate church of Rome, which is undoubtedly intended by the picture of the woman, does rule with vigor, cruelty and power in every country where she controls the government. The rulers and the people must obey the commandments of that church. This is indicated by the fact that she sits on the waters. She is in the place of authority and control.

SIX

This number is used to express man's sufficiency. Six days were sufficient for man's labor. God never intended man to have a five day week, nor an eight hour day. (See Ex. 20:9) Six steps were sufficient to approach the throne of King Solomon, which was the throne of perfect human judgment. (See 1 Ki. 10:19) The loaves on the table of shewbread were in two rows of six each, and this was a sufficient provision to represent all the tribes of Israel. (See Lev. 24:6) The great giant had six fingers on each hand, and six toes on each foot, for he represented the perfect example of that race of giants. (See 2 Sam. 21:20) Six main cities of refuge were sufficient for the protecting care of God over the murderer. (See Num. 35:6) The mystical number of the anti-Christ is six hundred sixty-six, for he represents all that man can produce of human wisdom, power and provision. (See Rev. 13:18) This number is arrived at by adding together the numerical values of the letters in the Greek language which compose his name.

SKIN

Gen. 3:21 (c) Undoubtedly this is a type of the imputed righteousness given as a covering to all who trust Christ Jesus. We are clothed with the garments of salvation, and with the robe of righteousness when we trust Jesus Christ, and He becomes the Lord of our lives. (See Isa. 61:10; Lev. 7:8)

Ex. 25:5 (c) The red skin of the ram reminds us of the life of Christ and the righteousness of God, both of which are given to us because of Calvary. The animal must die that we might be clothed. So the Saviour must die, and did die, so that we might have the righteousness of God put upon us. (See Rom. 3:22)

SKIP

Psa. 29:6 (b) This is a poetical expression which indicates the great joy that the leaders of the kingdoms of this world will have when our Lord rules and reigns, and all His enemies are under His feet. Cedars are usually taken as a type of the great men of God, or great men in other departments of life. Cedars are also taken as a type of the collective Christian life. The Lord is surely telling us of the joy that will fill the heart when He rules in the earth. (See also Psa. 114:4-6)

S. of Sol. 2:8 (b) Again we understand this to represent the feelings of the bride about the poet-King whom she loves so much. The heart cannot express itself in ordinary language when talking about our love for the mighty God, the wonderful Father, or the precious Saviour.

Jer. 48:27 (b) Probably this represents the feelings of the Moabites as they spoke in derision, scorn and hatred of their neighbor, the Israelite.

SKIRT

Ruth 3:9 (c) The action mentioned here probably refers to the sealing of a friendship which was based on relationship. It is an indication that he was accepting her as her near kinsman, and therefore would be her protector. (See also Ezek. 16:8)

SKULL

2 Ki. 9:35 (c) This peculiar incident may teach us the lesson that the thoughts and decisions of the wicked woman Jezebel remained to defile the people after she had gone from the scene. It may be that the palms of the hands remind us that the work which she did in persecuting the believers remained after she was unable to serve because of death.

SLEEP (and forms)

This word is used to describe several different experiences. It is not used about the eternal state of the unsaved who are lost. The ungodly are not usually said to be asleep after death. The exception to this is Dan. 12:2.

1 Ki. 19:5 (c) This experience indicates the carelessness and the indifference of one who forsakes the Lord, lays aside the work of God, and is not exercised about eternal matters.

SLIDE

Psa. 3:5 (c) The type in this case may represent the sweet rest that God gives His child who, though persecuted and in danger, is trusting fully in the living God, and His care.

Psa. 121:4 (c) This is a description of the eternal vigilance and the constant care of the Shepherd for His sheep.

Isa. 56:10 (b) The reference here is to the leaders of Israel who are represented as dogs who do not care about the condition of Israel, nor their danger from enemies that surround them.

Dan. 12:2 (a) Those who have died are referred to in this passage as being asleep and it includes both the godly and the ungodly. Both shall be resurrected for judgment.

Matt. 13:25 (b) Generally speaking, men are not alert to the dangers of the invasion of their rights by the Devil. Satan very cleverly gets into schools with evil doctrines, because the authorities are not on the alert to catch destructive teachings. Satan gets his wicked devices in churches, because the leaders are not awake and careful to discern his tactics. Children learn evil habits and wicked ways because the parents are not alert and watchful over that which their children learn.

John 11:11 (a) The believer is said to be "asleep in Jesus." It indicates that one day the body will be raised from the dead in order to again walk with God in happy fellowship and communion. This is not true of the unsaved. Their bodies are raised in the resurrection, but only for punishment and to be sent away into the outer dark. (See also 1 Cor. 11:30; 1 Thess 4:14)

Eph. 5:14 (b) By this picture we understand the sad condition of many Christians who live so like the ungodly that they appear to be as dead as the unsaved. In reality they do have eternal life, but they are not alert to their work, they are not walking with God, they are not living in happy fellowship with their absent Lord. (See also Rom. 13:11)

SLIDE

Deut. 32:35 (b) In this way the Lord is describing the perilous condition of those who are His enemies. He permits them to prosper for a while, and then in a moment they are cut off and sent into eternity.

Psa. 26:1 (b) David knew that he was in the hands of his loving Lord, and therefore would stand firm and would not fall by the wayside.

Psa. 37:31 (b) It is evident that the Word of God is sufficient to sustain the life and the activity of the child of God. It will keep him walking in a path of uprightness.

Jer. 8:5 (b) The inhabitants of Jerusalem were constantly drifting from the Lord, disobeying His laws, neglecting the sacrifices, and incurring the wrath of God.

Hos. 4:16 (b) This interesting picture describes Israel refusing to come at God's call, and resisting the sweet influences of His Word, and His prophets.

SLIME

Gen. 11:3 (c) We may think of this material as a substitution offered by the religious world for God's revealed truth. God's formula for building His church is quite unlike the systems of men which have devised ways and means of their own to build religious institutions. God's plans are the mortar, while man's plans are the slime.

SLIP

2 Sam. 22:37 (c) This figure indicates that David stood firm on the Rock of ages and kept constantly in the path of the Lord. (See also Psa. 17:5; Psa. 18:36)

Job. 12:5 (c) The description is that of a person who is about to depart from God and to take paths that lead away from the Lord and downward toward destruction. He will fall at any moment under the right conditions and circumstances.

Heb. 2:1 (b) The warning is intended to keep us from listening carelessly to the Word of God. We are to listen attentively and permit the Scriptures to fasten themselves to our hearts and minds.

SLIPPERY

Psa. 35:6 (b) This describes the uncertainty and precarious condition of the wicked who walk in the dark and do not have nor know the Light of Life.

Psa. 73:18 (b) Here is indicated the uncertainty of the life of the sinner who at a moment's notice may be taken off into eternity. (See also Jer. 23:12)

SLING

1 Sam. 25:29 (a) The thought presented here is that God will preserve His servant safely, holding him in His own powerful hand. The enemies of God will be destroyed by the Lord, taken out of the way, and be completely defeated.

Prov. 26:8 (a) This strange illustration describes the foolishness of giving no freedom to the stone which is to be thrown, and in giving a place of prominence to one who cannot fill it.

SLUMBER

Prov. 6:4 (c) The Lord is warning us against laziness and indifference. He expects His people to be alert, vigilant and active, and not "sleeping on the job." (See v. 10)

Isa. 56:10 (a) This is a description of the carelessness, indifference, and laziness of many of the religious leaders of that day and of our day.

Nahum 3:18 (a) The decadence of the leadership of Assyria is thus described.

Rom. 11:8 (a) The indifference and carelessness of Israel in regard to God's provisions is thus described.

2 Pet. 2:3 (a) The Lord is thus revealing to us that the judgment of God is not voided but is quite actively waiting to be engaged against His enemies.

SMELL

Psa. 45:8 (b) It is interesting to note that God uses all of our senses to convey truths concerning Himself. The very sweet effects of fellowship with God are described as fragrant perfumes. It is so in this Scripture and in other passages. Somehow the heart is warmed and the soul is refreshed when the Lord Jesus Christ is presented to us by the Holy Spirit through His Word. (See also S. of Sol. 4:10)

Isa. 3:24 (b) There should have come up to God from Israel the sweet incense of their worship, love, thanksgiving and praise. Instead of that God saw and heard only their worship of idols, their evil practices, their wicked ways, all of which were most distasteful to Him.

Hos. 14:6 (b) This is a prophecy concerning the day when Israel will again be a God-fearing nation, loving the Lord, obeying His Word, and honoring His Name. God compares this to the fragrant perfume from beautiful flowers.

SMOKE

Deut. 29:20 (a) The anger of the living God is described in this graphic way. Smoke is easily seen, it tells of a fire raging somewhere, it tells of destruction. It is an omen of trouble. The wrath of God is all of this. (See 2 Sam. 22:9; Job 41:20; Psa. 18:8; Psa 74:1.)

Psa. 37:20 (b) Here we see the evanescent and transient character of the wicked, who are carried away by the wrath of God, and are seen no more. (See also Psa. 68:2)

Psa. 102:3 (a) It is true that as the days pass in our lives the events of those days are blotted out of our minds and memories. They disappear and cannot be found again.

Psa. 104:32 (b) It may be that our Lord is describing His wonderful power to destroy that which apparently cannot be destroyed. He is the God of the impossible. (See Psa. 144:5)

Psa. 119:83 (a) The Psalmist in the midst of sorrow, difficulty, trial and distress becomes dry, hard and unserviceable as does the skin bottle when it is hung over a fire. It becomes harsh and stiff. The Psalmist did not commit suicide when this happened. He went right to his Bible, the Word of God, to become repaired and become supple and soft in the presence of God.

S. of Sol. 3:6 (c) Poetic license permits the use of words which may have various meanings. This passage may refer to the grace of movement and the ease of performance mingled with the fragrance and sweetness of love which undoubtedly characterizes the Lord Jesus Christ. It may be that this is a prophecy concerning His beauty and character.

Isa. 4:5 (b) The reference is made to the pillar of fire and the cloud that led Israel through the wilderness. In this passage the Lord is reminding them that this will be the precious portion again of His people in a coming day of restoration.

Isa. 6:4 (b) As the incense from the golden altar filled the temple with fragrance, so the worship of God's people ascends to the Throne of God and is as perfume to Him. (See Rev. 5:8)

Isa. 9:18 (a) By this statement the Lord is revealing to Israel that His wrath will be poured out upon the land and upon the people so that their wickedness shall be consumed, and the land will be left desolate.

Isa. 14:31 (a) We understand here that the invasion by a northern enemy will bring destruction and terrible punishment upon Israel because of their sins. The smoke is just an evidence of the presence of the destructive forces of fire.

Isa. 34:10 (a) This may be taken as a picture of the final judgment of God upon the earth and its inhabitants. The eternal character of this punishment is revealed also in Rev. 14:11.

Hosea 13:3 (a) The Lord again warns His people about the tragedy that awaits them because of their wickedness and rebellion against His Word. They will be scattered to the four winds and cease to be a nation.

Joel 2:30 (b) Peter quotes this passage in Acts 2:19 as indicating the great day of the power of the Spirit upon the earth. It probably refers to the wrath of God poured out in fire and judgment because men have rejected the Spirit of God and the Son of God.

Rev. 9:2 (c) Probably we should consider that this expression is used in most of the passages in Revelation to illustrate the terrible power of God in executing vengeance on His enemies. The judgment of God is often revealed as fire, and of course the smoke indicates the presence of the fire. (See Rev. 18:9; 19:3)

Rev. 14:11 (a) The eternal condition of the lost is represented here as being under the continual punishment of the God whom they neglected, or rejected. There is no end to their suffering. The ascending smoke indicates the presence of the burning fire.

Rev. 15:8 (a) The expression "the glory of God" is often used in the Bible as one of the names of the Holy Spirit. His presence is also represented as a cloud which filled the temple in the Old Testament, and here.

SMOKING

Gen. 15:17 (a) The furnace represents Egypt, and the smoke presents the fact that Israel would be punished terribly by the Egyptians in the fire of their oppressing hatred. It describes the four hundred years of suffering which Israel experienced from the Egyptians.

Ex. 20:18 (b) The presence of God in this sinful world is pictured in this way. There must be the fire of God's cleansing judgment at Sinai when He was giving the law to a disobedient people.

Isa. 7:4 (a) These two kings, Rezin, King of Syria, and Pekah, King of Israel, are compared to two wild beasts by our Lord. They are fierce in their anger and destructive in their ways. However, God makes them like two tails of the beast, utterly helpless and impotent to injure Ahaz.

Isa. 42:3 (b) The tenderness and kindness of our blessed Lord are illustrated in this beautiful way. The flax being partly green and damp would be difficult to burn, so the Lord would not despise the effort, but would rather fan the flame and help the flax to burn well. The reed that was bruised would be trying to recover itself and be strong and well again, so He would assist it in recovery, and would not destroy it. The lesson for us is that we should encourage others in their feeble efforts to make progress and to get ahead. We should not discourage others in their ambitions by harsh criticism, and by destructive statements. (See Matt. 12:20)

SMOOTH

1 Sam. 17:40 (c) We may understand from this passage that we too are to select words that may be effectively used in helping others, or in defeating the enemy, and not be careless in our statements. David knew that rough stones would not carry straight when thrown. We must choose expressions that will really go straight home to the heart.

Isa. 30:10 (b) Present day preaching and preachers should be influenced by this passage. Preachers should tell the truth whether or not it hurts. The smooth things mentioned are nice, sweet platitudes, which are intended to hurt no one, and to injure nobody. It is the preaching of the modernist, who fails to warn lost men of the danger that lies ahead. He gives comforting words to those who should have severe denunciation.

Isa. 57:6 (c) This form of idolatry is quite prevalent in our day. Probably the prophet was thinking of the smooth stones of David when he made this statement. Instead of taking the precious words of the Lord from His wonderful book, they take interesting statements of great men or women, beautiful phrases of religious leaders, and make them the law of the life. Thus the words of men supercede the words of God.

Luke 3:5 (b) We read this same expression in Isa. 40:4. It is one of the ways in which our Lord fixes up our lives. He removes troublesome people, or troublesome relatives, or associates who are difficult to work with or live with. He takes out of our lives the things that make living hard and difficult. Sometimes He leaves the path rough, but gives His child shoes of iron and brass. Sometimes He leaves the mountains in the way, but makes the feet of His child like "hind's feet." The hind loves the rough mountains, valleys, cliffs and chasms. She does not want her way to be made smooth.

SMOOTHER

Psa. 55:21 (b) The hypocrite speaks with sweetness and kindness while his heart is filled with hatred and bitterness. His words are soft, but his plans are cruel. (See also Prov. 5:3)

SNARE

Usually this word is used instead of trap. It refers to a device for catching, holding and securing another.

Ex. 34:12 (a) The nations of Canaan had ways of pleasure and sin that would attract the Israelites and soon Israel would be caught in that trap and begin to live as the natives live. The Lord warned them against this path. (See also this same truth in 1 Sam 18:21; Psa. 91:3; Psa. 119:110; Prov. 7:23)

Judges 8:27 (a) This is symbolical of the evil effect of idolatrous worship on the people of Israel. The ephod was a monument to their victory, but they changed it into an idol.

1 Sam. 28:9 (a) The witch thought that these strange men were trying to catch her in a trap so they could have her killed by Saul. She did not know that Saul himself was seeking her help.

2 Sam. 22:6 (b) The plans and schemes of evil men to destroy David are called a snare.

Psa. 69:22 (a) Tthe Lord Jesus is speaking here and asking His Father to change the plans of the enemies in such a way that their evil deeds against Him would be the very evidence that would curse them. The enemies of Christ were planning with great delight to get rid of Him, and their pleasure is compared to a banquet. Certainly their evil plans of that day and night turned to their curse and damnation. They were caught in their own Satanic devices.

Prov. 13:14 (b) Satan has many tricks by which men are deceived and led into paths that end in hell.

1 Cor. 7:35 (a) Paul was not using deceitful words to mislead God's people into a path which he knew would bring sorrow to their hearts. He was open and above board with his statement, for he had only the blessing of God's people in mind.

1 Tim. 3:7 (a) Satan is always making plans and schemes to destroy God's people and especially the leaders of God's people. These devices of the Devil are compared to snares and traps of Satan. (See 2 Tim. 2:26)

SNOUT

Prov. 11:22 (a) What could be more obnoxious than to see a beautiful golden ornament in the nose of a pig? Our Lord compares this with the unhappy acts, or the shameful actions of a beautiful woman who has a place of affection and honor in the minds and hearts of her friends.

SNOW

2 Sam. 23:20 (c) The snow would make the sides of the pit very slippery and dangerous. This great servant of David cared nothing about the hazards to his own life. This was characteristic of him as he fought for David.

Job 9:30 (c) The finest efforts of men and the best means of improvement by man are not sufficient to make and keep any person clean in God's sight.

Isa. 1:18 (a) By this we see the beautiful, stainless character of the one who is cleansed by God through the blood of Jesus Christ, His Son.

Isa. 55:10 (a) There is sometimes a delay in the entrance of God's Word into the heart. Rain falls and does its good work immediately. Snow falls and may remain on the ground quite a long time before it soaks in. So, one may hear a sermon and some parts of it will bless the person immediately, as the rain. Other parts of the message will remain in the heart and mind dormant for years. Then when the proper conditions arise, and the right circumstances exist, the dormant message becomes a living message to the heart.

Rev. 1:14 (c) The white hair of our blessed Lord indicates that He is the Ancient of Days, filled with wisdom, knowledge, understanding and experience. It is in contrast to the black hair described in the Song of Solomon 5:11.

SOAP

Jer. 2:22 (b) By this we understand the human schemes, efforts and plans that men use to get rid of their sins. Soap is a human invention for cleansing purposes. So various religious groups have ways and means which they offer to the public as remedies for the sins of men. These are compared to soap.

Mal. 3:2 (b) This emblem represents the thoroughness and effectiveness of the judgments of God.

SOCKETS

Ex. 26:19 (c) (See under SILVER)

S. of Sol. 5:15 (c) The legs support the body and strong legs are necessary to success for the runner, the wrestler, the prize fighter, and all of those who use the legs constantly in their vocations. Evidently the spiritual meaning of the passage is that our Lord Jesus Christ, concerning whom this passage was written, will never fail, will never weaken, and they in turn are supported by the pure gold of Deity. The sockets sustain the legs and enable them to work properly. The Deity of Christ makes all this true and possible.

SODOM

This city is used by the Holy Spirit to describe the nation of Israel, and also the city of Jerusalem. This city was filled with wickedness, lust and evil of every sort. It was so vile that God destroyed it by fire. Israel and the city of Jerusalem took on the sins of Sodom and practiced their evil ways so that God used that name as a description of the places where His people lived, and of the people themselves. (See Ezek. 16:48; Rom. 9:29; Rev. 11:8)

SOLDIER

2 Tim. 2:3 (a) The child of God is thus described by the Holy Spirit. He is not his own. His time belongs to his Master, so does his body. He goes where he is told, he eats what is given, he wears what is supplied. He has no will of his own, but is an im-

plicit servant of the military forces. He studies the ways of the enemy, he finds means of defense from the enemy, and of offense toward the enemy. This should be true of every believer.

SOLE

Josh. 1:3 (c) The passage indicates that the believer and the follower of our Lord must step out by faith in the service of the King and claim what belongs to him because he is a child of the King.

2 Sam. 14:25 (c) This verse is telling us that all of Absalom's body was perfect and free from any defects of any kind. He had a wicked spirit in a lovely body. The only good thing God could say about him was that he had a good physical body.

Isa. 1:6 (b) The complete wickedness of man is described in this picture. His thoughts in his head are bad, and his walk on his feet is bad. God sees nothing in a natural human being that is good, or right, or pleasant.

Ezek. 1:7 (b) There are four pictures of Christ in this passage, and one of these is the description of His lovely walk, so perfect, and yet so efficient. It is telling us that our Lord in all of His work and service was and is perfect and successful.

SOPE

(See SOAP)

SORE

2 Chron. 6:29 (b) This probably refers to the hurt spirit and the damaged heart that comes because of the mistakes and failures committed by men.

Psa. 38:11 (b) There is no record that David had an actual sore in his body. The statement probably refers to his injured spirit that was hurt so much and so often by his enemies.

Psa. 77:2 (b) This is a symbol of a broken heart that has been hurt somehow by deep sorrow and disappointment.

Isa. 1:6 (b) By this picture we see the terrible sins of Israel breaking out in different acts of wickedness of every kind.

SOUL

This word is used as a picture of, or a type of, many things. Below is a list of some of the things which are covered by this word:

Gen. 2:7	The human life	Lev. 5:2	The person's body
Gen. 34:8	Human feelings	Lev. 17:11	The whole person
Gen. 35:18	The human spirit	Lev. 17:12	The person's body

Deut. 11:13	The human mind or will	2 Chron. 6:38	Purpose of heart
1 Sam. 18:1	Human affections	Heb. 10:39	The whole person
I Ki. 17:21	The spirit of life	Heb. 13:17	The human life

The above types cover practically all of the places where the word "soul" is used throughout the Scriptures. These passages are a guide to other Scriptures.

SOUR

Jer. 31:29 (b) By this peculiar type the Lord is telling us that the evil practices of the father are frequently transmitted to the children. The father may contract a disease which carries over to the child. He may have a bad habit which becomes a part of the life of the child who sees his father do it. Fathers affect their children by their beliefs and practices. (See also Ezek. 18:2)

SOUTH

Psa. 126:4 (c) We may take this as a type of the soft, warm and blessed influences of God which the heart constantly craves. (See also S. of Sol. 4:16)

SOW (animal)

2 Pet. 2:22 (b) We see in this type a picture of an unsaved sinner who has cleansed himself from bad habits and the evil ways in which he has lived. He enters into a Christian group as though he were a Christian. His outward actions are made clean and proper, but his heart remains unchanged. After enduring this religious atmosphere for a while, he turns back to his old ways. There never was a true conversion in his soul, but only a renovation of the outside. (See also Matt. 12:43-45)

SOW (verb)

Lev. 19:19 (c) The mingled seed represents mixed teachings. The Lord forbids orthodox teachings with heterodox teachings. One teacher will be teaching the truth of God concerning the truths of the Bible, while another teacher in an adjoining class is teaching that the Bible is not true, but is mostly fables. One teacher will tell the class that the Lord Jesus was virgin born and was the Son of God. The teacher in the adjoining class will tell the students that Jesus was an ordinary man and not the Son of God. All such mixed teaching as this is forbidden of God. (See also Deut. 22:9-11)

Job 4:8 (b) The actions of wicked people in accomplishing their evil desires is described by this type.

Psa. 97:11 (b) This represents the act of God in bringing the blessings of the light of life to the Christian.

Psa. 126:5 (b) By this we understand the act of the Christian in proclaiming the gospel, distributing tracts, teaching the Word of God, and seeking to place the seed of the Scriptures in the hearts of others. While doing so his own heart is burdened to tears over the lost condition of those around him.

Prov. 11:18 (b) The acts of doing good to others is thus described.

Eccl. 11:4 (c) We may understand from this, the thoughts of those who will not do what they should because they are influenced by circumstances. They imagine that conditions exist which would makes their efforts unprofitable, or useless.

Eccl. 11:6 (b) Here is a command from our Lord to give out the Word of God always, in every place, in joy or in grief, in prosperity or adversity, in wealth or in poverty, nothing is to stop the ministering of God's wonderful Word.

Isa. 28:24 (c) This message is for soul winners. The Lord is telling us that we are not to be plowing up the heart all the time, nor harrowing it all the time. We are to be sure to cast some seed into the ground. Constantly warning the sinner will not lead him to the Lord. He must know God's good gospel.

Isa. 32:20 (c) The waters in this passage represent peoples, nations and tongues, and we should be busy getting the gospel and the Scriptures before all kinds of people, in all parts of the world.

Jer. 4:3 (b) Our Lord would have His people clearly devoted to Himself. He is requesting that Israel would get rid of the things that hinder their walking with God, and prevent their obedience to God.

Jer. 31:27 (b) In a coming day God will again cover the land of Israel with men and women who will believe in Him, will obey Him, and will be occupied with His work and Himself.

Hos. 2:23 (b) This passage is somewhat similar to the one above, except that probably it has reference to the blessing that God will make Israel to be for all the earth. The growth and the enterprise of the nation of Israel will bring peace and prosperity to the whole world some day when Christ will be on the Throne.

Hos. 10:12 (b) The truth revealed in this passage probably is a result of the Scripture above. The Lord wants His people to invest their lives, their talents and gifts in such a way that blessed and happy results will come from the investment.

Zech. 10:9 (b) Probably this refers to the fact that all over the world the Spirit of God will work on and in the hearts of His people in such a way that they will turn back to the living God, and to the Messiah, the Son of God. This same truth is revealed in Ezek. 37, where we read the story of the dry bones.

Matt. 13:3 (a) This action describes the giving out of the Word of God here and there under all circumstances, and all conditions. (See Mark 4:3; Luke 8:5)

Matt. 13:27 (b) In this parable the seed is the child of God, while in the previous parable the seed is the Word of God. The Lord is telling us that when He places a man of God who is truly a saved servant of the Lord, in the harvest field, the Devil will place in the same part of the field one of his children, teaching religion filled with evil doctrines. Thus the people are confounded, their thinking is confused, and the work of the man of God is hindered.

SOWER

Matt. 13:3 (a) Any Christian who goes forth to preach and teach the Word of God is a sower of good seed. (See also 2 Cor. 9:10)

SPARK

Job 5:7 (c) When trouble comes upon the Christian, he should at once fly upward to God. This truth is illustrated by the type of the spark from the bonfire flying upward.

Job 41:19 (c) Probably this is just poetical language to describe the terrible hatred and anger that exists in this case. Some students seem to think that it is a picture of the modern tank which has cannon both in the front and in the rear.

Isa. 1:31 (a) Those who make trouble and cause disturbances are represented by this type.

Isa. 50:11 (b) Sparks and the fire are types of the human reasonings, conclusions and theories which men use to light their path on the way to eternity. These shut out God and substitute their own philosophies for the Scriptures.

SPARROW

Psa. 102:7 (a) Our Lord Himself uses this bird as a type of His loneliness in His life on earth. He had been with angels, archangels, seraphim, cherubim, and with God His Father throughout eternity. Now He was dwelling among those who hardly understood Him, or cared about Him. They could not live the life that He lived. He lived a lonely life for lack of companions who understood Him. The sparrow is seldom seen alone, and rarely on the housetop. It is usually under the eaves, or out in the road, or down in the grass, and always in flocks. This is a picture of the lonely, desolate life of our Lord Jesus on earth.

SPEAR

Psa. 35:3 (b) Here we find a description of God's power to hinder and to hurt every enemy of His people.

Psa. 46:9 (b) It may be that this is emblematic of the peace that the Lord will bring on earth in the millennial day. (See Isa. 2:4)

SPECKLED

Jer. 12:9 (a) As a speckled bird was a subject of attack among other birds, so Israel would be a distasteful and unpleasant people, both toward God and toward the nations round about.

SPICE

Ex. 30:34 (c) The ingredients of this powder made a perfume that was not to be used by anyone else for any other purpose than in the tabernacle. It is emblematic of the beautiful, precious life of the Lord Jesus which was so very pleasing to God, and could not be imitated by another.

S. of Sol. 4:14 (c) We may take this to represent the sweet fragrance to God of the worship and godly living of His people. Believers are compared to a garden, sending out its beauty and fragrance to its owner. (See also chap. 5:1)

SPIDER

Job 8:14 (b) It represents the sinner in his fruitless efforts to provide for himself a refuge from the wrath of God. (See also Isa. 59:5)

Prov. 30:28 (c) We may understand this to represent the seeking sinner who will not be denied the mercy of God. He continues to attend services, to ask questions and finally is saved.

SPIKENARD

S. of Sol. 1:12 (c) The worship of the heart to our Lord, and the fragrant love of the devoted follower of the Saviour, is a sweetsmelling savour to the God of heaven. (See also Mark 14:3)

SPOIL (noun)

Psa. 119:162 (a) The wonderful Word of God is full of rich treasures for the heart, the soul and the mind. The Psalmist felt like he was being greatly enriched as he found these precious jewels in the Scriptures. The Bible is not just a text book, but rather it is a storehouse of food, of jewels, or rich treasures of every kind, and as these are found by the reader, they bring joy to the soul and heart.

SPOIL (NOUN)

S. of Sol. 2:15 (a) The picture presented here represents those little sins, habits and conditions which are called "foxes," and which hinder the Christian from growing in grace and from bearing fruit for God.

Matt. 12:29 (a) Our Lord gives in this parable the story of salvation or conversion. The strong man's house is the Devil's house, or the Devil's territory. The "goods" are the people who are ensnared and enslaved by Satan. The one who enters the house is the Lord Jesus Christ who alone is able to bind and to conquer Satan. He then takes those who have belonged to Satan and delivers them from Satan's power and sets them free. This operation is represented as the spoiling of his (Satan's) house. (See Mark 3:27)

Col. 2:8 (a) The thought presented by this type is that of ruining the testimony and the godly life of a believer through the teaching of false doctrines, or of evil practices.

SPOT

Num. 19:2 (c) By this type we understand the spotless character of our Lord Jesus Christ on whom there was no sin nor fault, and in Him no evil of any kind. (See also Num. 28:3; 29:17; 1 Pet. 1:19)

Deut. 32:5 (b) The Lord brands His people as the Shepherd brands the sheep. In this case those mentioned do not bear the mark of God's ownership. Probably the mark was that of a godly life, holy ambitions, and obedience to the Word of God. (See also Rev. 3:12)

S. of Sol. 4:7 (c) This may be taken as a statement by the Lord concerning His church, or His bride, for He sees no fault nor sin in His people who are washed in the blood of the Lamb. Or, it may be taken as the Word of the bride concerning the Bridegroom, for certainly He is absolutely perfect, beautiful, sinless and stainless. Both things are true.

Eph. 5:27 (b) Here we see a beautiful type of the perfection of God's church, each member of which has been cleansed in the blood of the Saviour, made pure and white in God's sight.

1 Tim. 6:14 (c) Probably the type in this case represents a perfect obedience, in which there is no hypocrisy, and no compulsion. It is an obedience based on the love of God, and from a grateful heart.

Heb. 9:14 (a) By this figure we understand that the Lord Jesus offered Himself to God, with no sin connected with His offering, no pride, no selfishness, no ulterior motives, no evil of any kind. He was a perfect offering in every sense of the word, and therefore was acceptable to God.

2 Pet. 3:14 (a) It is the will of God that the Christian should live a clean, true, pure upright life, with no blemishes that would disfigure his life and cause the people to point to him with scorn. The Christian is to be a good example of a blameless believer.

Jude 12 (b) The presence of an ungodly man among the people of God blots and blurs, hinders and harms the fellowship of God's saints.

Jude 23 (b) This probably refers to any so-called righteousness or plan of salvation, which is contaminated by the works of the flesh, or by depending upon merit in the sight of God.

SPOTS

Jer. 13:23 (b) This is a very interesting type, and it contains a very special truth which we should observe carefully. The Ethiopian is black all over and knows it. It is impossible for him to change it. He may not even want to change it. This represents the sinner who lives in sin and knows that he is all bad, mentally, morally and spiritually. He also knows that he cannot change his condition. The leopard is black in spots. He also knows it, but is is powerless to change his appearance. This represents the sinner who thinks there is a great deal of good in him, and thinks there are just certain bad spots here and there, which he has never been able to change or remove, and perhaps does not care to do so. The case is hopeless with both of these. Only the miracle-working power of God could remove the the black from the Ethiopian, or remove the spots from the other.

2 Pet. 2:13 (a) Our Lord constantly warns against a union between the unsaved and the saved. In this particular warning, He is reminding us and informing us that when the ungodly mingle and mix in the service of the Lord, or the worship of the Lord with God's own people, they smear and blot and disfigure the services in which this takes place. The unrighteous and the unsaved have no place whatever in the service or the worship of the church.

SPRINGS

Psa. 87:7 (a) David is telling us that all the source of his joy, hope, happiness and enrichment comes from the Lord, and not from any earthly conditions, situations or riches. He depended only on the living God to satisfy every longing of his heart.

Prov. 25:26 (a) The righteous man is not supposed to be influenced by the wicked, nor fall down in obedience to the wicked desires. If he does so, then the product of his life is only evil and injurious to others. He becomes a stumbling stone to those who expected better things from him.

S. of Sol. 4:12 (a) It is quite evident that the church of God is under consideration in this passage. She should be giving forth rich blessings to all those around. She should be bringing the Living Water (the Holy Spirit) to every one that she can reach. There should be flowing from the church of God constantly spiritual blessings that will bring light, life and peace to the multitudes. Instead of this the church has in many cases become a social club, with the Word of God neglected, the Spirit of God ignored, and no spiritual blessing being given out to the people.

Isa. 41:18 (c) It is true that our Lord is at the present time changing the desert into a garden in the land of Palestine. It is also true that in a typical sense the Lord does take the weary, worn and dried up Christian and sends into his life the Holy Spirit of God who is the Living Water, so that the life becomes radiant, fruitful and beautiful.

Isa. 58:11 (a) In this beautiful picture we see the story of a child of God who walks with God, loves his Lord, obeys His Word and permits the Holy Spirit, who is the Living Water, to flow through him into the lives of many. That one is satisfied with God's plans. He grows in grace. He shows forth the loveliness of his Lord, and lives a constantly beautiful life. Nothing stops his song, or his service.

SPRINGING

John 4:14 (a) Our Lord reveals in this passage that the Christian may receive from him this wonderful, living Person, the Holy Spirit, who when He is received, recognized and trusted, becomes an active Person in the life of the Christian. This Holy Spirit will reveal His presence in a multitude of ways, will give vision and vigor to the believer, and will enable him to be fruitful, useful and beautiful.

Heb. 12:15 (a) Bitterness cannot be hidden. It reveals itself in many ways, and defiles all of those who see it, hear it, or feel it. Bitterness cannot and will not remain hidden in the heart.

SPRINKLE

Isa. 52:15 (a) In the days of the tabernacle Moses sprinkled the blood on everything in the tabernacle, and this was a sign to all others that God owned these things and had appointed these things for His own purpose and plan. So in the death of Christ He is telling us figuratively that in every nation, and among all peoples He will sprinkle the blood of His Son on hearts and lives to make them His own children, and to save them by His grace.

Ezek. 36:25 (a) Probably the clean water represents the precious, pure Word of God. These pure messages from God will be brought to all the peoples of the world in some way or other, and some will believe and be saved. All will be responsible for the way they treat it.

Heb. 10:22 (b) The teaching in this passage probably is that the Spirit of God works through His Word on the heart and the mind of the believer to remove from him the sense of guilt, because the precious blood of Christ has been shed to put away his sins.

SPROUT

Job 14:7 (b) This is a word of encouragement to those who fall or fail in life. It means that that one may revive and produce real fruit and blessing following the failure, A man may be bankrupt in one business, and then find another in which he is very greatly successful.

STAFF

Ex. 12:11 (c) The Lord's people are pilgrims in this land of sin, sorrow and death. The staff is a sign or a figure of this transient character. It means that the friend was ready for the journey, and prepared to go. We are not to take the place of being citizens here as a finality in our lives.

Psa. 23:4 (c) The rod is for the enemies, while the staff is for the protection and restfulness of the Christian. The staff represents God's promises and the loving care of the Shepherd on which we lean and repose with confidence.

Isa. 3:1 (b) The staff represents the means of protection and provision for Israel. Because of their disobedience the Lord is promising that He will remove all such blessings from that rebellious nation.

Isa. 9:4 (c) We may learn from this that the Lord promised to His people complete deliverance from the burdens imposed by oppressing conquerors, the neighboring nations, so that they would be set free from oppression. Since the coming of Christ is prophesied in verse 6, we probably may believe that He is teaching us that because the Saviour comes into the life, the soul is set free from the bondage of Satan and the oppressing power of sin.

Isa. 10:5 & 15 (c) In this case the staff represents the Assyrian who would be used by the Lord to punish His people Israel. However, He would not permit the Assyrians to boast of their power and victories, for they were only an instrument in the hand of a righteous God.

Isa. 14:5 (b) The broken staff tells the story of the power of God to conquer the enemies of Israel, and to prevent them from injuring His people.

Isa. 30:32 (c) We may learn from this strange passage that the Lord will conquer the Assyrians, and in every place where this enemy has conquered Israel the suffering shall be replaced with the blessing of God, and with musical instruments.

Jer. 48:17 (b) Moab had been a very strong, vigorous nation occupying a beautiful site. Now God's wrath was poured out upon that city, their armies whipped, their strongholds captured.

Ezek. 29:6 (a) Israel had leaned on Egypt for support, but Egypt failed them and did not give the succour and help that Israel expected.

Hos. 4:12 (b) Evidently Israel was depending upon idols for help, and was following the counsel which they received from their divinations. These counsels led them into evil paths.

Zech. 11:10-14 (b) These two staves indicate "authoritative rule and abounding resources." The stave called "beauty" represents God's infinite love and wonderful grace toward His people Israel. He broke this staff to show Israel He was now no longer intending to deal with them kindly, but rather with severity. The breaking of the other staff, bands, revealed that He would now cease giving the necessary resources to these two countries and refuse to further provide for them, or protect them.

STAIRS

S. of Sol. 2:14 (c) It may be that this is a picture of those sweet experiences that the child of God has with His Lord. Whether it be ascending in victory, or descending in defeat, whether it be in ascending with joyfulness or in descending with sadness, there is always the sweet fellowship between the bride and the bridegroom under every condition.

STAKES

Isa. 33:20 (c) By this lovely type we learn how secure is that one who belongs to the Lord Jesus Christ and is kept by the power of God through faith unto salvation.

Isa. 54:2 (b) Probably we learn from this interesting type that the Lord wants us to constantly strengthen our faith through reading His Word, learning all that Christ has done for us, and all that He means to us. Faith is strengthened as we learn from the Scriptures the many things the Lord Jesus does for the soul who trusts Him.

STAR

This word is used as a type of great people. Sometimes these are evil persons, sometimes they are good persons. Sometimes they are real pople, and sometimes they are heavenly persons as angels. Sometimes they are used to represent good, and sometimes evil. We shall consider some of these places. Christ Jesus also is typified by a star.

Gen. 37:9 (a) The explanation of this type is that the eleven stars were the eleven brothers of Joseph, while the sun and moon represented Joseph's father and mother. This dream was a prophecy, and it was fulfilled in Gen. 42:6, and four times following this. These eleven brethren bowed down to their brother Joseph just as he had dreamed.

Num. 24:17 (b) The Lord Jesus is represented by this type. He will one day arise with power, He will come with glory, and He will take charge of the destinies of men.

Dan. 8:10 (b) Alexander the Great was the horn. The stars he cast down were the great generals of opposing armies. He destroyed kings and great powerful leaders in his rapid march from nation to nation.

Dan. 12:3 (a) These are symbols of the honor and glory that will be given to those who are engaged in God's service, and who are used of the Lord to turn men to the Lord. They receive this wonderful position of honor in eternity.

Amos 5:26 (b) Each idol was represented by a high priest or a chief priest who had charge of the worship of that idol. This dignitary is called a "star." (See Acts 7:43)

2 Pet. 1:19 (a) This is not a good rendering of the passage. The meaning really is that the heart is to become phosphorescent. The light of God is to shine out and reveal the presence of the Spirit of God in the soul.

Rev. 2:28 (b) The Lord Jesus is undoubtedly this beautiful orb. He calls Himself by that name. He shines in the heavens, He shines in the darkness, He himself heralds the coming of that day when He will rule and reign.

Rev. 8:12 (b) Since there is rebellion in heaven among the angels and against God, it seems that in this passage we are told that one-third of those great angelic leaders will be cast down from their exalted position because of their enmity to our Lord. The great star that fell in verse 10 is another angelic dignitary who has power to bring bitterness, hatred and evil upon men.

Rev. 12:1 (b) This woman is a type of Israel and the twelve stars represent the twelve patriarchs for whom the twelve tribes are named.

STAVES

Ex. 25:13 (c) These were the two rods covered with gold by which the ark was carried. Other articles of furniture also were furnished with these rods for carrying purposes. In this passage the rods indicate the wandering and movable character of the ark of the covenant. It was to be on the move constantly, therefore the staves were to remain in the rings on the ark. (See v. 15.) However, when it found its permanent resting place (See 1 Ki. 8:8) the staves were removed. The first period is a type of the wandering life of a Christian before he fully gives himself over to the Holy Spirit in complete consecration. The second period is pictured by the removal of the staves in the dedication of the temple. The ark was to wander no more. So God wants His child to get to the place where he is stable, substantial and unmovable in the fellowship of the King. (See 1 Chron. 15:15; 2 Chron. 5:9; see under "STAFF")

STEAL

John 10:10 (b) False teachers do take away from human hearts the possibilities of God's approval and the blessing of God's presence. They take away from Christians the possibility of a reward, and with the unsaved they remove their opportunity to be saved.

STEEL

Jer. 15:12 (b) This is a type of the great strength and power of the northern kingdom.

STEPS

Ex. 20:26 (c) This may be taken as a type of human effort and human plans in making a sacrifice to God for sins. God's altar was to be down where everybody could reach it. It was to be made simple so that anyone might take advantage of it. If there were steps to the altar, the lame, the maimed, the sick, and the infirm would reveal their inability as they sought to reach it. This would hinder their getting to it. God wanted His altar on a level with the people where all could take advantage of the sacrifice easily.

2 Sam. 22:37 (b) David is describing the fact that he knew God so well, and knew the ways of God so perfectly that he was established in the faith, and would not wander from the paths of God. (See Psa. 18:36)

Job 14:16 (c) In this way Job describes the care with which God watched over His servant. He knew how many steps Job took, and why he took them. (See also chap. 31:4, 37)

Job 29:6 (b) In this way Job is telling us that he lived in luxury. He walked as a king, and lacked nothing. He was one of the richest men of the east.

Psa. 37:23 (a) God does direct the manner of life of His child and tells him where to walk, and how to walk.

Psa. 37:31 (b) By this is indicated that the walk of the child of God will be permanently for good, his life will be according to the will of God.

Prov. 5:5 (b) The path of the harlot is always downward, inspired by sinfulness, and results in eternal loss.

Rom. 4:12 (b) The believers in this day follow in the path of Abraham who lived by faith, walked with God, and believed God. These things characterize the godly and believing man in this dispensation.

1 Pet. 2:21 (a) The believer does follow the path of the Saviour. He walks with Him and talks with Him, and his desire is to be like his Lord.

STICK

2 Ki. 6:6 (c) This may be taken to represent the cross by which we recover that which was lost, either through sin, neglect, carelessness or indifference. When Calvary comes into the life, we recover those blessed graces and gifts that make us useful to others.

Ezek. 37:16 (a) These dead sticks represent Judah and Israel who were fruitless, dead, helpless and separated. In the hand of the Lord, they become united and alive. This is being fulfilled at the present time, for the present nation of Israel is one united people, not separated into tribes.

STING (and forms)

Prov. 23:32 (b) The reference is to the terrible after effects of liquor and wine upon the life of those who drink it. The result is very damaging.

1 Cor. 15:55 (b) Death certainly does hurt the hearts of the living, bringing deep wounds, and many sad results. Death is caused by sin, and is the result of sin.

Rev. 9:10 (c) Some commentators think that this Scripture refers to the modern tank which has cannon mounted on the rear, and these guns were referred to as the sting.

STINK

Psa. 38:5 (a) It is not clear whether David referred to some actual ulcers in his body which gave forth a vile odor, or whether he is referring to the injuries received by his soul from his many enemies. We do not read of physical diseases in the case of King David, except indirectly. His enemies spoke of it, and always in derision.

Eccl. 10:1 (b) The unwise actions of an honorable man have a bad effect upon the minds of those who know about it. Ointment or perfume is spoiled by any dead animal being in it, so evil actions injure the hearts of those who hold the actor in honor.

Isa. 3:24 (c) This term is given to the bad living and the evil actions which are a stench in God's nostrils, and which He despises. (See also Isa. 34:3; Joel 2:20; Amos 4:10)

STONE

The stone is used as a type of many things throughout the Scripture. In both the Old Testament and the New, it represents the Lord Jesus Christ, or the child of God, or the truth of God. Sometimes it represents glory and beauty. It stands for solidity and permanence. We will give here some of these typical meanings:

Gen. 11:3 (c) Man-made doctrines are substituted for God's Word.

Gen. 49:24 (a) This represents the Lord Jesus Christ.

Ex. 20:25 (c) The thought in this passage probably is that the stones represent God's truth as revealed in His Word, and man is not to alter it nor change it in any way. False teachers and leaders do take God's Word and twist the meaning to suit their own theology. They take the passage from its text and misuse it. It is this that is forbidden by this type. (See also Deut. 27:6; Josh. 8:31; 1 Ki. 6:7)

Ex. 24:12 (c) The commandments were on stone, not on rubber, which would bend or stretch. It speaks of permanence and durability.

1 Sam. 17:49 (c) This may represent a portion of the Scripture, the Gospel.

Job 28:3 (b) We may understand these to be matters that are difficult to understand, and require much investigation and research.

Psa. 118:22 (b) There is no doubt but that this type represents the Lord Jesus Christ as the One in whom we trust for eternity. Israel rejected him as the foundation of their faith, but God exalted Him as the foundation of the Church. (See Isa. 28:16; 1 Pet. 2:6)

Psa. 144:12 (a) These represent beautiful daughters, refined, cultured, substantial and solid in their faith. They are dependable and trustworthy.

Prov. 26:27 (b) This is probably a type of gossip, malicious lie, or a false report which when started returns to injure the one who told it.

Isa. 8:14 (a) This type represents the Lord Jesus for He stood in the way of Israel. In rejecting Him they fell from their place of power and influence, and have been scattered abroad as a punishment for their sins. His Name and His presence are an offense to the nation of Israel. (See also Matt. 21:42; Mark 12:10)

Isa. 28:16 (a) This type of Christ reveals Him as being tried and tested by men and circumstances, and proving His perfection.

Isa. 34:11 (b) These are types of those matters which look good, but have no value. They make a big show, but have no reality. These things are hypcritical, pretending to be what they are not. They look like stones, but really are puff balls.

Lam. 3:9 (b) God permitted His prophet to be surrounded with wicked men and evil workers so that he could not go about His work easily nor comfortably.

Ezek. 28:14 (b) Satan's glory is thus described. The unsaved follow the Devil's plans and programs, thinking he has permanent value, and will give permanent blessing.

Dan. 2:34 (b) The Lord Jesus is this stone who comes in His sovereign power to crush all opposition, to defeat his enemies, and to set up his own kingdom throughout the earth.

Zech. 3:9 (b) This also is a type of Christ who is brought before men for their trust and confidence. It also represents Christ, Spirit-filled and Spirit-led, and yet the One who sends and gives the Holy Spirit. (See also Zech. 4:7)

Matt. 21:44 (a) Christ Jesus is this stone, the Rock of ages, the foundation of all God's church and kingdom. When He crushes His enemies beneath His feet, they will be utterly broken, but those who, feeling their need, rest their lives and hearts on Him, they are eternally blessed. (See also Luke 20:18)

Luke 20:17 (a) Christ Jesus is this stone. He was rejected by Israel, and is still rejected by that nation. (See also Acts 4:11; 1 Pet. 2:4-7)

1 Cor. 3:12 (b) The good works of God's people carried on for the glory of God, the honor of Christ, and by the leading of the Spirit, are solid, substantial and eternal in their character.

I Pet. 2:5 (a) Christians are reckoned to be a part of Christ, and so they are as small stones broken off from the big stone, the Rock of Ages. They partake of His appearance and character.

Rev. 2:17 (b) Since the Scripture says that no man knows what this represents, we can hardly dare to express an opinion. It certainly represents some pure precious gift solid and eternal in character which the Lord will give to the overcomer.

Rev. 17:4 (b) This type refers to the great wealth and beauty that is seen and adorns false religions. Their magnificence is wonderful and attracts those who do not know our Lord.

Rev. 21:11 (b) This is poetic language which describes the glory of God by telling us of things we can understand, as a comparison to things we cannot understand.

STONY

Psa. 141:6 (b) The reference is to the fact that when trouble comes, the way is rough, and the times are hard, then God's people will hear God's words, and will take heed to His way.

Ezek. 11:19 (b) By this word is described that heart which will not be impressed by God's Word, and does not respond to God's love, nor to His call. (See also Ezek. 36:26)

Matt. 13:5 (a) Jesus thus describes that kind of disposition, or soul, or heart, which sits unmoved under the sound of the gospel and does not respond in a permanent way. The person seems to be moved a little bit, and shows some interest, but this is not permanent. After while he refuses to return to the church, and avoids meeting the Christians. (See v. 20, and Mark 4:5, 16)

STOREHOUSE

Mal. 3:10 (c) We are not to believe that this refers to any local church, for it does not. Israel had only one center of worship, at the temple. The reference evidently is to the Church of God in all its wideness and fullness. We are to invest in God's work and God's business wherever we see the need. We are to place our funds where they will be used for the salvation of souls, and the upbuilding of the saints. This does not need to be only in our own denomination. Of course, the first obligation we should fulfill is to the local work with which we are identified. There is no Scripture at all, nor suggestion, that all the money which is given by God's people should be put into one basket to be spent by others.

STORM

Psa. 55:8 (b) Life's troubles are certainly tempests, turmoil and chaos. We cannot expect to get through life without the winds of adversity. The Lord is to be our place of refuge, and the shelter in the time of storm.

Psa. 107:29 (b) In the time of storm on the sea, the waves mount up with destructive force. The waves represent leaders and rulers who would injure and hurt God's people. Our Lord is telling us that He is able to speak peace on all such occasions and bring rest to the heart with peace in the mind.

Isa. 4:6 (b) Here again our Lord is telling us that we may expect times of trouble in our lives, but He has provided a hiding place in His own presence, resting under the shadow of His wings, and leaving the solution with Him.

Isa. 25:4 (b) Evidently our Lord is referring to the times of great stress and strain that God's people often had to pass through. In the midst of these difficulties the Lord became a hiding place, and a shelter from the conflict. (See Isa. 28:2; 29:6)

Nahum 1:3 (b) This is an assurance to our hearts that when difficulties arise and the problems of life increase, the God of heaven will control every event and make all the difficulties to bow to His will according to His plan.

STRANGE

Ex. 30:9 (c) This peculiar perfume describes natural human sweetness. Many will use beautiful phrases, precious expressions, delightful words, in all of which there is no God, no Holy Spirit, no revelation from heaven. Two great religions use this method of deceiving the people; false leaders frequently take honeyed expressions as a means of attracting the unwary and the untaught souls. (See under "HONEY.")

Lev. 10:1 (c) There are many strange things mentioned in the Scriptures. This one refers to human efforts, human plans and human expedients in the service of our Lord. Perspiration is not inspiration. Excitement, gestures and noise cannot and do not become a substitute for the indescribable and indispensable work of the Holy Spirit. All of these human activities are represented by the term "strange fire." (See Num. 3:4; Num. 26:61)

2 Ki. 19:24 (b) The King of Assyria is boasting of the fact that he had satisfied all his desires by ravaging and robbing other nations, and obtaining their possessions.

Isa. 28:21 (a) God is a God of mercy and grace, but He is also a God of wrath and judgment. He is telling us here that the pouring out of His wrath is not a thing that He loves to do. It is not a thing that He plans to do, but rather to show mercy and to save the soul. When the individual or the nation refuses Him, then He must do that which He calls "His strange work."

Jer. 2:21 (b) Israel should have been a fruitful vine, producing rich blessing for God, glorifying His name, and making glad His heart. Instead of that they produced idolatry, evil and sinful products which were a terrible offense to God.

STREAM

Psa. 46:4 (b) This is a picture of the spiritual ministry placed at the disposal of the people of God as they journey through this desert world.

Psa. 78:16 (b) By this picture we understand the rich blessings for the people of God that flow from the Lord Jesus as the author of eternal life.

Psa. 126:4 (c) Probably this may be considered a type of the flowing waters of the warmer countries which produce such wonderful vegetation, fruits and flowers, in those desert places where the ground is dependent upon the streams, rather than upon the rains.

S. of Sol. 4:15 (c) Here we see a type of the rich and refreshing influence of the church of God. The streams from the mountain of Lebanon are cold, clear and life giving. This should characterize the ministry of God's people as they serve together in the church.

Isa. 30:28 (b) The flow of God's judgment is described in this way, for no power can stop it, and it cannot be hindered nor changed.

Isa. 33:21 (a) By this type we understand the great flow of the blessings of God in which He alone is responsible to carry us along in His everlasting arms, and to provide for every need of our bodies and souls. The ships that are mentioned refer to the fact that God's blessings are not based either on our work (the galley with oars) nor on our fighting ability (the gallant ship).

Isa. 34:9 (b) The Lord is telling us that He will destroy the sources of blessing and dry up the waters of pleasure and profit so that life will become wretched and miserable instead of sweet and pleasant.

Isa. 35:6 (b) The blessings of God flow into the lives of God's people who walk and talk with Him in sweet fellowship, even though they are going through times of barrenness, sorrow and disappointment.

Isa. 66:12 (a) It seems to be God's plan that the wealth of the Gentiles will be brought to His people Israel in great quantities, and in great abundance. We find this same thought in other Scriptures. God's people are to be the head of the nations, and all nations will borrow from her, and she shall lend to all peoples.

Dan. 7:10 (b) This type represents the great outpouring of God's wrath against His enemies in the day when He sets up His throne to judge and to rule the world.

Amos 5:24 (b) This is typical of the abundance and the irresistible power of the righteous judgments of God at the time when men are brought before Him to settle for their deeds. It is typical also of the righteous judgment of God upon Israel for their sins. It is represented as a stream because of its abundance, its permanence, and its continual operation.

Luke 6:48 (b) Here we see a symbol of the powerful and multitudinous troubles that are released in men's lives, and which would overwhelm them if they were not anchored to the Rock of ages.

STREET

Rev. 21:21 (c) This type represents the Lord Jesus Himself, who is the way to heaven, and the way to God. Note that the word is in the singular and not plural. The gold represents the beauty of Christ, the purity of Christ, and the value of Christ. That which men almost worship down here, and constantly seek after, and which is not permanent, may well become insignificant in our sight while Christ Jesus becomes supreme and paramount.

STRETCH

1 Ki. 17:21 (c) This represents the attitude of mind and heart on the part of a soul winner, whereby he seeks to accommodate himself to the kind of person with whom he is dealing. It takes an effort on our part to adjust ourselves, our thinking and our words to those who are not like ourselves, either in age, work, character or disposition. (See also 2 Ki. 4:34)

Isa. 28:20 (b) This represents the desire and the actions of a man who is seeking to accommodate his life and his faith to some proposition which he has devised, or which he has learned from some false teacher. He is trying to find rest for his soul in a doctrine, or a church, or a faith which was never suited to him at all. Only the provision which comes from God in Christ Jesus will enable one to rest. (See Matt. 11:28)

Rom. 10:21 (a) This is a description of God's attitude toward His people in that He pleads with them constantly, and has through the centuries, to turn from their wicked ways and trust Him as their Lord, their leader, and their Saviour.

2 Cor. 10:14 (a) The expression is used in this passage to indicate the fact that Paul was not doing an unusual thing when he came to Corinth with the gospel. He was acting naturally and doing what he should do as God's servant.

STUBBLE

Job 13:25 (b) Job uses this figure to describe himself as one who has been cut down, cast out and is no longer useful.

Isa. 33:11 (b) This is a type of the results of a worthless life spent in sin and in rebellion against God.

1 Cor. 3:12 (a) Many of the works which Christians do in the Name of the Lord have no value. They produce nothing for the glory of God, and will be destroyed at the judgment seat of Christ.

STUMBLE

John 11:9 (b) The light of God's Word reveals God's way, and God's plan so that the child of God who walks in fellowship with God will not stray away from the path.

Rom. 9:32 (b) Israel felt they could get along very well as long as Christ was left out of the picture. When He appeared the Scribes, the Pharisees and the Herodians at once complained, resented and rejected Christ. It revealed their hatred and exposed their evil hearts. (See Rom. 11:11; I Pet. 2:8)

Rom. 14:21 (b) Paul would not have any believer to have a false idea, or come to a wrong conclusion by anything which he would do. A Christian doctor might be going into a saloon as a call of duty to save the life of an injured man. Someone seeing him go might say, "If he can patronize the saloon, so can I." and so that one would be led astray because he did not know the facts. This is Paul's argument. (See I John 2:10)

STUMBLING (block and stone)

Lev. 19:14 (a) We should never teach an unsaved person in such a way that he would be hindered from getting to Christ and becoming a Christian. Neither should we instruct a Christian or do anything to a Christian, or in his presence, that would turn him aside from loving the Lord, and walking with God.

Isa. 8:14 (b) Christ Jesus is called a stumbling stone by God Himself. He is a building stone, a foundation stone for those who believe in Him, but He stands in the way of all others so that they can never find God, nor walk with God, nor have a place in the presence of God, for Christ blocks the way. He is the dividing place in life. (See also Rom. 9:32; I Cor. 1:23) He must be accepted or rejected.

Isa. 57:14 (b) Probably the Lord is requesting the removal of those things which hinder Israel from returning to Him. This may refer to idols, evil associations, wicked practices.

Ezek. 3:20 (a) God does seek to hinder His people from going astray. He puts hindrances in the way, and oppositions, and difficulties in order to keep His people in the right path, walking with Him. (See Zeph. 1:3)

Rom. 14:13 (b) Here again our Lord is requesting His people to do or say nothing that would hinder another Christian in His walk with God, or in His services for God. (See also I Cor. 8:9)

Rev. 2:14 (b) Balak found that he could not persuade Balaam to curse Israel, so he therefore made it easy for the men of Israel to go astray with the women of Moab, and for the men of Moab to entice and attract the women of Israel. This unholy alliance brought about the curse of God upon Israel, and thereby caused the people of God to go astray in their hearts, and to become idolators in their lives.

STUMP

I Sam. 5:4 (c) The head of the image was gone, for God has no use for the thoughts of men, or of idols. The feet were gone, for an idolatrous walk is rejected by God. The hands and arms were gone because God will not have the work of idolators. The only part left was the stump, which was a picture of the helplessness, the uselessness and the worthlessness of idols and those who worship them.

SUCK

Deut. 32:13 (b) The sweetness of Christ is obtained by God's people in very difficult circumstances, and under impossible situations. Out of the hard places of life God grants His people the indescribable sweetness of His love and care.

Deut. 33:19 (b) This prophecy tells how the Jews will obtain their riches from the Gentiles (the sea), and will find riches in strange places, and in strange ways. They will obtain wealth in places and ways that the Gentiles overlooked.

1 Sam. 7:9 (b) In this picture Samuel is describing to the people how helpless they are and how dependent upon God. As the lamb obtained its nourishment from the mother, and its protection from her, so Israel was dependent upon God, for her blessings.

Job 20:16 (b) Zophar is making the statement that the hypocrite and the wicked live on lies and flourish on wicked sayings and evil conversation.

Isa. 66:11 (b) Evidently God's people were told in this prophecy that they would find their enjoyment, their comfort, their delight and their blessing in and from Jerusalem when God restores that city to her former glory.

Ezek. 23:34 (b) By this type the Lord is describing the wickedness of both Israel and Judah. They were revealing in their sins. They were drinking in their iniquities. They were delighting in evil things.

SUMMER

Psa. 32:4 (a) This describes the depressing condition of David's heart, and the lack of joy in his soul.

Prov. 10:5 (b) This figure is used to urge God's people to serve Him actively and efficiently while opportunities abound. It is because there will come a day when either old age or external conditions will make it impossible or permissible to serve Him. (See also Prov. 6:8; Prov. 30:25)

Prov. 26:1 (a) Here we see a figure which shows that things may be as incongrous in society as they are in the elements.

Jer. 8:20 (b) By this picture in nature we see a wonderful truth in human life. In the summer, crops are produced, the fruit ripens, and at the end of summer they are gathered. The grain is saved, but the stubble, chaff and weeds are left in the field to be destroyed. So it is in life. The harvest day is coming, the summertime of opportunity will be ended, and some will be left outside the door because they are of no value to God.

Matt. 24:32 (b) This is a picture of those blessed days that will exist when Israel will be restored as a nation, and like the fig tree will again bear fruit for God. (See also Mark 13:28; Luke 21:30)

SUN

Psa. 19:4 (c) By this illustration we see the gorgeous beauty and the sovereign power of Christ Jesus. As the sun is chief in nature, so Christ is chief in all humanity and in all human affairs.

Psa. 84:11 (a) This is typical of God as the One who gives light and life, warmth and strength to His people, even as the sun gives to vegetation.

Psa. 121:6 (b) This is a promise that the natural forces of earth will be restrained from injuring the children of God who walk in intimate trust with Him.

Jer. 15:9 (b) We may understand from this type that the end of life and of opportunity had come before its time. Punishment came because of disobendience.

Mal. 4:2 (a) This beautiful type represents the Lord Jesus when He shall return to this earth in power to heal all human woes, and to remove all curses from the earth.

Matt. 13:6 (b) Probably this type represents trials, difficulties and opposition which keep the Word of God from being effective in the heart and mind. Sometimes it represents earth's light from human minds, mental arguments and reasonings which destroy the effective power of the Word of God in the soul. (See Mark 4:6)

Rev. 12:1 (b) No doubt this represents Israel, which nation had the light of God, the Word of God, and produced the Son of God who is the Light of the world.

SUPPER

Luke 14:16 (b) It is used to represent the great variety of rich blessings which will become the heritage of the saints as they hear and heed the call of God, in Christ.

Rev. 19:9 (b) Here we see a picture of the times of refreshing and blessing which are in store in heaven for all those who belong to the King of Kings.

Rev. 19:17 (b) This is symbolic of the terrible destruction which awaits those who reject Christ, and who will be punished by God for their rebellion.

SWADDLE (and forms)

Job 38:9 (a) God is describing the fact that He created darkness, or rather He caused darkness to abound by shutting out the light. He surrounded the entire ocean area with darkness, which shows what a miracle-working God He is.

Lam. 2:22 (b) Jeremiah is telling us that the people of Israel who had been his spiritual children under his care were persecuted and destroyed by the enemy.

Ezek. 16:4 (b) Before God took Abram to begin a new nation, he and his family were just rough heathen, with no God, no hope, and no divine law. They were like a little baby that has no care, no protection, and no provision.

SWALLOW (noun)

Psa. 84:3 (c) This bird is used to describe the apostasy of Israel. The altars of God should have been hot with fires for sacrifice. Instead they were so cold, neglected and unused that the birds felt free to make their nests in them.

Prov. 26:2 (a) In this case the bird is used to illustrate God's definite dealings with men. The swallow flies for a purpose, she knows where she is going, and what she is doing. So it is when God punishes sinners. It is an intelligent punishment.

Isa. 38:14 (a) Hezekiah uses the mournful sounds of the swallow to illustrate the sadness of his own heart.

SWALLOW (verb)

Isa. 25:8 (b) When our Lord returns for His people, they will not die, but will be caught up alive into heaven. A victorious ascension will take the place of the sadness of death.

Isa. 28:7 (b) The drunkard is conquered by the liquor. He becomes a slave to that which he drinks. He is submerged under the terrible appetite for wine.

Isa. 49:19 (b) In this prophecy the Lord is informing us that the people who conquered Israel will be driven far away from them, and they will no longer be engulfed by their enemies, but will be free to expand their country.

Lam. 2:2 (b) The wrath of God in conquering Israel and pouring out His wrath over them is described in this way. Israel was helpless in the hands of an angry God, and He consumed them in His wrath. This is in contrast, or perhaps, in comparison with verse 16 in which we find that the enemies of Israel engulfed them. From God's standpoint He did it, but the enemies of Israel were the means and the agents by which God did it. (See also Jer. 51:34)

Hos. 8:8 (b) This action is used to describe the scattering of the Jews among the Gentiles in which they were absorbed after their dispersion.

Amos 8:4 (b) This describes the cruel power of the rich as they destroyed the poor, and the powerful as they destroyed the weak.

Obad. 16 (b) The suicide of the heathen is described in this way. They drink iniquity, they live on their sins, they revel in rioting and drunkenness, and all of this serves to destroy the people.

Matt. 23:24 (b) This figure describes the ease with which hypocrites believe impossible statements, and use them as though they were true.

I Cor. 15:54 (b) Here is a graphic description of the way in which death for the Christian will be abolished when Christ returns to catch up His church in the Rapture. The living Christians will be caught up to heaven without dying.

SWEAT

Ezek. 44:18 (c) Anything that comes out of the body is a defiling thing, unless it is actuated by the Spirit of God. In the service of our Lord, He will not have that which is strictly and only human efforts, human programs, human designs, and carried out in the energy of religious flesh. The garment represents the outward professions made by religious workers.

SWEEP

Isa. 14:23 (b) This picture describes the thorough destruction of Babylon, which was foretold by our Lord, and was completely carried out to the extermination of that great city.

Isa. 28:17 (b) God will destroy all false faiths in Israel in order that the nation may be cleansed of their wickedness, and be godly. Eventually, Israel will be "holiness to the Lord."

Luke 15:8 (b) The wonderful and efficient work of the Holy Spirit is described in this passage. The lost coin represents the Christian who has drifted out of the way of the Lord, and is hiding under home life, or business life, or laziness, and is not being used among God's people. The Holy Spirit seeks out that person by many and various means in order to bring him back into "circulation" where he can be useful again in the service of the King.

SWELLING

Jer. 12:5 (b) This is a picture of the predicament of one who is weary and disgusted with the type of Christianity that he sees around him. Since his distress in the midst of such a weak form of holiness is so great, he would be miserable indeed if he were brought into a situation where holiness abounded, godliness predominated, and the Holy Spirit is working in power. One who is made miserable by the Christians on earth would be far more miserable if he were in heaven where the highest form of pure Christianity prevails.

2 Cor. 12:20 (a) No doubt this refers to the boasting of man in religious circles who are puffed up with their own importance, but who have really nothing substantial to offer. These are clouds without water, and wells that are dry.

2 Pet. 2:18 (a) The reference evidently is to the boastful language used by great religious leaders whose tongues are larger than their hands. They talk much, and do little. They boast of great things, and produce only wind. (See also Jude 16)

SWIM

Psa. 6:6 (b) By this figure we understand the great weeping and the deep sorrow of David. His tears flowed profusely while he lay upon his bed.

Ezek. 47:5 (b) No doubt the flowing river represents the Holy Spirit. It issues from the door, which represents Christ. We see in this picture the story of the Spirit-filled life in which the whole person, spirit, soul and body is abandoned to the blessed Person of the Spirit, and to His prevailing power. First, the Spirit affects the feet, which is the walk; then the knees, which is devotion; then the hips, which is service and work; and finally, the whole person is enveloped by the wonderful Holy Spirit in entire consecration.

SWINE

Isa. 66:3 (b) This type describes the terrible depravity of a man wherein he lives in his filthy sins, and yet offers a sacrifice to God as though he were a godly man.

Matt. 7:6 (b) The ungodly person who wallows in his wickedness is described by this filthy animal. We are not to present the precious truths of God, and His sweet promises to such a vile person. He would not understand, nor appreciate, those messages in which the Christians delight.

Luke 15:15 (b) This wandering boy was mingling with the people of the world who lived in sin, lust and rebellion. Unsaved people are looked upon by God as being in their sins, unrighteous, unholy and stained with evil and wickedness. The Christian has no business seeking to find his satisfaction among them.

SWORD

Deut. 33:29 (a) God Himself takes this name because He alone is able to guard Israel and to preserve them from their enemies.

Josh. 5:13 (b) The man in this passage is the Holy Spirit. The sword in His hand is the Word of God. When the sword is with Christ, it is in His mouth. He speaks the word, and the Holy Spirit uses it effectively, as the Lord of the harvest.

2 Sam. 12:10 (b) The reference here is to war with all of its ravaging and killing effects.

I Chron. 21:16 (b) Again we see the sword of the Spirit which brings a curse upon the people. This same truth is mentioned in Isa. 40:7. The Spirit of God punishes and curses just the same as God the Father, and God the Son.

Psa. 7:12 (b) This is a picture of God's judgments by which He will punish men for their iniquities.

Psa. 45:3 (a) David desired the judgments of the Lord Jesus Christ to be put into effect. He looked forward to the time when Christ would take His place as King of kings, and the Lord of lords.

Psa. 57:4 (a) The tongue is described as being this sharp, cruel instrument that brings damage and injury to many. Terrible destruction of heart, mind and life are brought about by a cruel tongue which cuts deeply into the hearts of the hearers. (See also Psa. 55:21; Psa. 64:3)

Psa. 149:6 (b) The reference here is to the Word of God, the Bible. It does indeed cut down false faith, destroys doubts, and condemns the sinner. (See also Rev. 1:16)

Prov. 5:4 (a) The lips of a strange woman do indeed cut down and permanently injure many a life. That hurts the heart, destroys the family, and often injures the body. (See Prov. 12:18)

Prov. 25:18 (a) The gossiping man who carries tales from one to another injures, harms and hurts as the sword hurts the body. The damage is most severe in many cases as he separates friends, and brings hatred into hearts.

Isa. 49:2 (a) The words that come from the mouth of our precious Lord are indeed a sharp instrument for bringing consternation to His enemies, and punishment to all His foes. (See also Rev. 19:15)

Zech. 9:13 (a) This is a wonderful picture of the way that God will use Israel as a sharp instrument to fight and subdue His enemies on the earth.

Zech. 13:7 (b) In this unusual way God describes how He Himself will bring about the punishment of our Lord Jesus on Calvary when He was made sin for us, and was punished in our stead.

Luke 2:35 (a) By this picture we understand the deep sorrow that would pierce the heart of Mary when she saw her Son, her first-born, mistreated, misunderstood, and crucified on the cross.

Eph. 6:17 (a) This type represents the Word of God which effectually works in the souls of men. (See also Heb. 4:12)

Rev. 1:16 (b) The Bible is this sword. It cuts down its enemies, it cuts the attachments of men to their sins, it conquers the enemy, it brings victory to God's people.

T

TABERNACLE

Psa. 19:4 (a) The great expanse of the heavens is described as a tent in which the sun rules and reigns. It is quite a few million miles wide and high, and is not subject to the whims of men, nor the storms of life.

Psa. 27:5 (a) His presence is described as a tabernacle or tent. As we retire into His presence from the storms of life, we find His preserving care and quietness of spirit. (See also Psa. 61:4; Isa. 4:6; Jer. 10:20)

Psa. 84:1 (b) In this way the Lord describes the holiness and the blessedness of the gatherings of the people of God for worship, praise and service.

Prov. 14:11 (c) Probably this refers to the manner of life of the Christian. Because he walks with God, and seeks to serve his Lord, he is assured of the presence of the Holy Spirit, and this probably is called a "Tabernacle."

Isa. 33:20 (a) Probably the entire city of Jerusalem is called by this name. (See also Lam. 2:4)

2 Cor. 5:1 (a) The human body is called by this name because the spirit dwells in this body in order to serve the Lord, and be a blessing to others. At death the spirit leaves the tabernacle, so that God may repair the building and fix it up new for the return of the spirit in the day of the resurrection. (See also 2 Pet. 1:13)

Heb. 8:2 (b) Probably this is a type of the church of God in which the Spirit of God now dwells, and where the glory of God is revealed.

TABLE

Psa. 23:5 (b) David indicates the rich provision which the Lord makes for His children. He feeds them on heavenly dainties as they travel through this world. They have sources of joy that the world does not have. They feed on the Living Bread, and drink the Living Water, and their hearts are satisfied.

Psa. 69:22 (b) This table represents the sinner's preparations for a good time. The Psalmist asks that their good times be turned into times of sorrow because of their hatred toward him, God's servant.

Psa. 78:19 (b) By this picture we understand that God made provision for food and sustenance in the wilderness where there were no natural supplies.

Isa. 28:8 (b) This is a type of the provision made by false religions for feeding their followers. The food which they offer is called "vomit." It represents good things taken into the person's soul and mind: there it is mixed with their own ideas and notions, and this mixture is given out for others to feed on, and to accept as the doctrine of God. All false religions offer this vomit. The leaders take in some of the Word of God, change the meaning of it, mix it with their own ideas, and then give it out in books and speeches for others to accept and believe.

TACKLINGS

Isa. 33:23 (b) This picture indicates those unseen forces which bind men to their habits and ways which are not pleasing to God.

TAIL

Deut. 28:13 (a) The Lord uses this figure to describe the very low and degraded condition into which Israel would descend when she turned away from the Lord as her leader to follow idols. She would become the lowest of all nations.

Isa. 7:4 (a) Here is another description of God's contempt for the two nations who by God's grace were unable to hurt Israel because He was protecting them.

Isa. 9:15 (a) The false prophet is thus described. By his evil sayings he becomes the object of contempt instead of the object of praise and honor.

Rev. 9:10 (c) We do not know just what is meant by this statement. Some commentators think that perhaps this represents the modern tank which has guns, both in the front and in the tail. It is not definitely known what is represented by this picture.

TALENT

Zech. 5:7 (b) Some students think that this represents the weight of sin that will encompass the business dealings of Israel. It may indicate that false weights and balances are used in their commerce.

Matt. 25:15 (b) The talents represent the quality of the gifts given to Christians for the service of the Lord. Some are unusually gifted for great works and deeds in the gospel and in the church. Others are not so well gifted, but are able to do their work according to their knowledge, education and zeal. (See under "POUND.)

TARES

Matt. 13:25 (a) Our Lord Himself tells us that the tares are the children of Satan. They are religious sinners, who are only professing Christians. They associate with Christians, as the tares grow with the wheat. In the little pods at the top of the wheat stalk, or that which looks like wheat, there are no grains. The pods are empty. So the hypocrite has no value — no eternal life.

TASTE

Psa. 34:8 (a) By this is represented the affectionate love of the Christian for the Lord Himself. The believer seeks to appropriate as much as his heart and mind can hold. It is one of those indescribable experiences which cannot be explained. You may taste an orange, and know at once what it is, but you cannot explain it to another. So the sweetness of knowing Christ can only be experienced by each individual himself.

Psa. 119:103 (a) This picture represents the blessed effects upon the heart and soul of believing and loving the Word of God.

S. of Sol. 2:3 (c) Here is described the complete satisfaction of the believer's heart when he appropriates God's provisions for his life.

Luke 9:27 (a) This unusual expression is used to describe the strange experience of the consciousness of approaching death. (See also Matt. 16:28; Mark 9:1; John 8:52)

Luke 14:24 (b) Our Lord gives a solemn warning here to unsaved people, and to hypocrites. They will never have any experience whatever of the blessings of salvation here, nor of the presence of God hereafter.

Col. 2:21 (b) We are being warned to stay entirely away from the pleasures of the world lest the slightest experience with them entice us to seek more of them.

Heb. 2:9 (a) Our Lord deliberately partook of the experience of death. It did not happen to Him. It was not by accident. It was deliberately planned.

Heb. 6:4 (b) This is a description of the experience of the unsaved sinner when he is brought under the power of the gospel. The Holy Spirit deals with his soul, and the things of eternal life are made vivid to him. After such an experience, the person described in this passage turns away and refuses to accept God's message, either about Himself, or about the Saviour.

1 Pet. 2:3 (b) The Christian has received a little foretaste of the blessings of heaven, and this makes him hungry for more. God gives us glimpses here of the glory that is to follow. We

only get crumbs here, but the full loaf will be given when we see His face.

TAUGHT

Jud. 8:16 (a) Joshua punished these men by thrusting thorns into their bodies, and tortured them in this way because of their rebellion and their refusal to assist him in the hour of his need.

Hos. 10:11 (a) The heifer needed to be broken to work. The prophet speaks of this breaking process as a teaching of the animal to do the kind of work that was expected of him. So the Lord must teach us to do His will.

TEAR (verb)

Psa. 7:2 (b) The feelings of the prophet were injured and he felt it keenly. (See also Psa. 35:15)

Psa. 50:22 (a) This figure represents God's wrath in destroying His enemies, and conquering His foes. (See Jer. 15:3; Hos. 5:14)

Ezek. 13:20 (b) God will remove false cults, false religions and false faiths on which people lean, and in which they trust for comfort and consolation.

Hos. 13:8 (b) This indicates that God will permit the nation to destroy the people of Israel, and to take over their land, their possessions and their persons.

Amos 1:11 (b) By this is described the wrath of Edom against Israel. They constantly sought to invade Israel, destroying the property, taking the people captive.

Nah. 2:12 (b) In this way we learn of the wrath of Nineveh and Assyria against the people of Israel. This nation was constantly at war with the people of God, and sought to destroy them.

TEARS

Psa. 42:3 (b) Some people feed on their sorrows constantly and never seem to be satisfied unless they are grieving over past tragedies. The Lord intends for us to drink the Water of Life, and not be drinking tears of sorrow.

Psa. 80:5 (b) This indicates that God would give to Israel an abundance of sorrow, grief and pain instead of the blessings of good crops, with peace and plenty.

TEETH

Gen. 49:12 (b) By this we may understand that there was to be great wealth and temporal blessings from God. Judah had a special place of blessing from God, and Jacob understood this. He therefore tells in this poetical language how richly God will supply all the needs of Judah.

Job 13:14 (b) Job evidently refers to the extreme pain and distress that he is experiencing in his time of sorrow. It seems as though he was being torn in pieces, distracted and disturbed in body and soul.

Psa. 3:7 (b) This is a type of the evil power of the wicked Absalom. Under God's good hand the evil ones, the rebels, are hindered from hurting His child. (See Psa. 58:6; Psa. 124:6; Prov. 30:14)

Psa. 57:4 (a) At the time David wrote this portion, he was in danger of his life, was hiding in a cave from King Saul, and was in bitterness of spirit because of the enmity of his king. The teeth refer both to the words of Saul, and to his wicked plans and action. Saul was intent on destroying David. He uses the type of teeth to describe his feelings about it.

Prov. 25:19 (b) This indicates the pain brought to the heart of one who has misplaced his trust.

S. of Sol. 4:2 (b) The bridegroom seems to be describing the beauty of his lover, and by means of this type describes the usefulness and attractiveness of his bride. (See also S. of Sol. 6:6)

Jer. 31:29 (b) Sometimes the sins of the fathers are carried through to their children. It is not always so, and yet sometimes we see it. The Lord is telling us in this passage that the children will not suffer for the sins of their fathers in the day when God restores all things to their correct relationship. The children will not be affected by that of which the father is guilty.

Lam. 3:16 (b) Jeremiah uses many figures and types to illustrate his feelings. In this case he probably is telling us that his usefulness has been removed, and in a very painful way. His experiences were not natural in the ordinary course of events. It is not natural to have stones in the mouth in such a way that they would break the teeth.

Dan. 7:5 (a) This is an excellent picture of the complete victory which the Medio-Persian empire won over Babylon. The three ribs probably represent the three kings that had built up so successfully the great Kingdom of Babylon, but now this bear destroys that Kingdom, and the teeth represent the power that accomplished it.

Dan. 7:19 (a) Again we see that this fourth Kingdom had cruel power which was very destructive in character. This kingdom was Rome, which is known in history for its violence and cruelty. The teeth represent that terrible condition of hatred which characterized that nation.

Joel 1:6 (a) This type like those preceding it represents the philosophy and rapacity of the invading nation, which destroyed Israel as the lion destroys its prey.

Micah 3:5 (a) By this type we understand that the false prophets were hypocrites. Publicly they were proclaiming feasts, but privately they were destroying the people by subterfuge and hypocrisy.

Amos 4:6 (b) This is a description of the poverty that had come upon Israel because of her disobedience to God. He sent a famine by withholding rains.

Zech. 9:7 (b) Probably by this type the Lord is telling us that He will eventually conquer the Syrians, and will remove His people from the power of that kingdom, and will enable them to live for the glory of God.

Matt. 22:13 (b) This is a description of the hatred of those hypocrites who thought they would be in heaven, but who found themselves in hell. It should be noted that whenever the expression "gnashing of teeth" occurs, it is always in reference to hypocrites (see under "GNASHING"). These expected God to follow out their own plan, and to save them on their own terms. These had substituted their forms of sacrifice for Christ, and had rejected the Lord Jesus as the only Saviour. Their hatred against God is revealed by the gnashing of their teeth. (See also Matt. 8:12; 13:42; 13:50; 24:51; 25:30; Luke 13:28)

Matt. 27:44 (a) This is a figure of speech in which the contempt of the thieves is revealed, and their attitude of hatred against Christ is seen.

TEMPEST

Job 9:17 (b) This type describes the tremendous, overwhelming sorrow that had come upon Job because of the losses described in the first two chapters of the book.

Psa. 11:6 (b) By this is described the great sorrows which God sends upon His enemies because they will not trust and obey Him.

Psa. 55:8 (b) Evidently David is describing life's troubles, sorrows and perplexities which overwhelmed him, as the storm overwhelms that which is in its path.

Psa. 83:15 (b) The call is for God to send upon His enemies troubles, sorrows, grief and disaster as a punishment for their evil doings.

Isa. 28:2 (b) This is descriptive of the devastation that would be wrought upon Ephriam by the invasion of the enemy.

Isa. 32:2 (a) Here we see a type of the terrible outpouring of God's judgments upon His enemies, but which will not hurt nor harm those who are hidden in the Rock of ages, Christ Jesus.

Isa. 54:11 (b) This type describes the sorrows and afflictions of Israel — pestilence, famine, invasion of hostile armies, internal insurrections, and other troubles which laid Israel low among the nations.

Amos 1:14 (a) God will punish the Ammonites with a terrible destruction when He pours out His wrath upon them because of their wickedness and of their hatred of Israel.

TEMPLE

Psa. 27:4 (a) The presence of God is thus described and David wanted to live in that divine presence constantly, as though it were indeed the house of God.

Psa. 29:9 (b) Probably David was referring both to the actual house of God at Jerusalem and also to the mystical Temple of God which is His people. Every child of God like every piece of the temple in some way represents the majesty, the glory, the beauty, and the usefulness into which we have been called by His grace. It is interesting to note the typology of the temple, for there is a splendid comparison between parts of the temple, and the individuals in the church of God.

John 2:19 (a) The Lord is referring to His own body in which God dwelt. (See also Matt. 26:61 and Mark 15:29)

1 Cor. 3:16 (a) The church is called God's temple. It is a collection and an assembly of God's people. Therefore, it is the habitation of God through the Spirit. In this way it resembles the temple of the Old Testament. (See Eph. 2:21)

1 Cor. 6:19 (a) In the previous reference the whole church is compared to the temple, but in this passage the individual believer is compared to the temple. The Holy Spirit dwells in the church as a collection of God's people, and also in the individual because he is a child of God.

TEN

(c) There are a number of thoughts concerning the typical meaning and the significance of the number ten. I shall use it as a number that represents human infirmity and failure. Here are some examples of this application:

The ten spies failed to see God's power and provision, so they brought back an evil report (Num. 13:32)

The ten tribes failed to walk with God and to bow to His will. Therefore, they established a separate kingdom given to idolatry (1 Ki. 11:31).

The ten day diet of pulse and water which Daniel desired was not sufficient normally to show improvement in the body. It gave God the opportunity of showing His power to bring blessing out of that which humanly and normally insufficient. (Dan. 1:12)

The magicians and astrologers were ten times as weak and insufficient as Daniel. (Dan. 1:20)

The ten virgins all fell asleep, none were awake to their privileges (Matt. 25:1)

The ten lepers were unable to cure themselves, and insufficient because of their leprosy. They needed the Lord Jesus to meet the need. (Luke 17:12)

The ten servants who were given the ten pounds proved to be unfaithful in part, and only two receive their Lord's approbation (Luke 19:13).

TENTS

Deut. 33:18 (b) It is evident that Moses was promising this tribe a happy home life. They were to enjoy that which they had in their own tent and in their family relationships.

Psa. 84:10 (a) The reference in this passage is evidently to the places of sin and to the habitations of wickedness. The Psalmist would not associate with that kind of people.

Psa. 120:5 (b) Kedar was among the Ishmaelites who were enemies of Israel. David had trouble because of Doeg, whose hatred had driven David away into a strange country. The lesson probably is that we should not let difficulties in the church drive us away into the world among the enemies of God.

S. of Sol. 1:5 (c) The two-fold aspect of Christ is found in this passage. He is black and unattractive to the sinner, but He is comely and beautiful to the Christian. The tents of Kedar were black, dusty and unattractive. That is the way Christ looks to the unsaved. The curtains of Solomon are beautiful, attractive, gorgeous, and that is the way Christ looks to His children who are in love with Him.

Hab. 3:7 (b) Cushan was Ethiopia. We learn from this that the home life, the domestic affairs were destroyed by the anger of the Lord. He punished Ethiopia for their hatred of His people.

Zech. 12:7 (b) The domestic life of Judah was to be restored and their peace assured by the mighty God of heaven.

Zech. 14:15 (b) The animals of the enemies of God were to be punished as the people were punished. They would be afflicted in their stables, for evidently the animals were kept in tents of skins.

THICK

Deut. 32:15 (b) This figures describes the healthy and wealthy condition of the nation of Israel in her prosperity.

1 Ki. 12:10 (b) This type is used by Rehoboam to describe the great increase of tax burden and other burdens which he intended to impose upon Israel. He would oppress the people more than his father had done before him. (See also 2 Chron. 10:10)

Hab. 2:6 (See under "CLAY".)

THICKET

Isa. 9:18 (b) This represents the people of Israel in their character before God. They were useless, harmful and injurious, instead of being profitable and attractive.

Jer. 4:7 (b) The word is used to illustrate the evil surroundings and the wicked society of the countries of Assyria, Babylonia and other foreign nations which were to invade Israel and lay it waste. A thicket has no value to a farmer, but is to be destroyed. So these enemies were eventually to be destroyed by the Lord.

THIEF

Luke 10:30 (c) No doubt these wicked men represent the ungodly world which continually seeks to take away everything we have and return to us nothing but trouble. The world welcomes the prize fighter who is winning, but has no use for him when he is losing. The world loves the company of the rich while he can give, but has no use for him when his riches are gone and he has become poor. The world wants the actress who is vivacious, interesting and beautiful. They have no use for her when the beauty has faded, and her skill has ceased. The world has nothing permanent to give, but is always active in taking what we have. Barabbas was a thief, and he represents this wicked world. Christ is a giver, and will always enrich us.

John 10:1 (b) By this picture we see a symbol of the wicked, religious leaders of the world who would take away from God's people their peace, their faith, their time and their money by false teachings.

Rev. 3:3 (a) This type is used by the Lord to describe the manner of His coming. It is not a reference to His character, for He is holy and pure. It refers only to the fact that He will come at a time when He is not expected, and in a way that no one understands.

THIGH

Psa. 45:3 (b) This expression is used to represent the almighty and active power of God in preparing for the judgment of His enemies. As the soldier girds on his sword and is ready for the battle, so the Psalmist asks God to prepare for the great day of the revelation of His majestic power.

Ezek. 21:12 (c) We may use this type to illustrate the rather common practice of striking one's self upon the thigh, or the hip, or the leg, when in anger, or when insisting on some course of action.

Dan. 2:32 (b) Probably this represents the chronology of the kingdoms. The nation of Greece was to be the third after Nebuchadnezzar, even as the head is first, the breast is second, and the thigh is the third in the body.

Rev. 19:16 (b) This is indicative and symbolical of the mighty power and strength of the exalted Christ as He comes forth to rule and reign. The thigh, the place of strength and power in the body, is used to describe the strength and power of Christ when He comes to reign on the earth.

THIN

Gen. 41:27 (a) The Lord uses this symbol to describe the famine and dearth which was to prevail in Egypt for seven years.

THIRD (See under "THREE")

THIRST

Psa. 42:2 (a) It describes the deep desires of the heart for God, a longing for His presence, and the craving for His fellowship.

Psa. 63:1 (a) David was in a cave when He expressed this deep longing. He could not get to Jerusalem because of the armies of Saul. He must seek God as he fled from the enemy and hid here and there in the wilderness and in caves. His heart was hungering for his Lord, and his soul was craving the sweet presence of the God whom he loved. (See Psa. 143:6)

Isa. 55:1 (b) This is typical of the craving of the natural human heart for satisfaction which it fails to find in that which the world offers.

Matt. 5:6 (a) This describes the longing in the hearts of men to be better, to have more goodness, and more holiness.

John 6:35 (b) This is a type of the longing for peace and rest which is fully satisfied when one trusts his soul and life to the Lord Jesus Christ.

Rev. 7:16 (b) The word signifies that those who are in heaven with God have every longing and desire satisfied.

THIRTEEN

(c) This number is generally taken to denote that which is unfortunate, unhappy, unlucky, tragic and sad. It is interesting to note that the chapters in the Bible numbered thirteen are characterized by something that is unhappy and sad. See the following:

Gen. 13 Here we find the first family quarrel, which is certainly a sad event.

Ex. 13:13 This describes the sad ending of either the ass or the lamb.

Lev. 13 What could be more sorrowful than the leper shut out of the camp.

Num. 13 The great tragedy of Israel's history came from the evil report of the ten tribes. In verse 13 the word Sethur means "mystery." The Hebrew letters constituting his name total 666 which is the number of the anti-Christ. Probably this man was the leader of the rebellion of the ten, for the names of all the other leaders had very lovely meanings.

Deut. 13 The punishment of the false prophet or the dreamer is described in this chapter.

Josh. 13 Here is recorded the death of Balaam, the false prophet.

Judges 13 Israel is delivered into the hands of the Philistines.

1 Sam. 13 Saul's sin of presumption lost for him the Kingdom of Israel.

2 Sam. 13 We read here the tragic story of Amon, his sister Tamar, and the murder by Absalom.

1 Ki. 13 The death of the prophet who disobeyed God is described in this chapter.

2 Ki. 13 Israel is delivered into slavery under Hazael, King of Syria.

1 Chron. 13 Uzza is killed by the Lord for touching the ark.

2 Chron. 13 The defeat of the children of Israel by Jeroboam.

Neh. 13 Nehemiah punished those who broke the sabbath.

Job 13 The lament of Job over the persecution of his friends is described with sadness.

Psa. 13 David described the deep sorrow of his heart because of the troubles internally and externally which constantly beset him.

Prov. 13 This sad expression is given "hope deferred maketh the heart sick."

Isa. 13 Here is a description of the destruction of Babylon under the wrath of God.

Jer. 13 This prophecy concerns the ultimate destruction of Judah as indicated by the marred, rotten girdle.

Ezek. 13 This records the wrath of God against the prophets of Israel.

Hosea 13 God describes Himself as a lion, a leopard and as a bear in His judgments against Israel.

Zech. 13 This prophecy concerns the wounds of Christ and the sword of God against His Son.

Matt. 13 Here we read of the seed destroyed by the birds, the tares cast into the fire, the bad fish rejected.

Mark 13 We read here the terrible record of the great tribulation days when the wrath of God shall be poured out on the earth.

Luke 13 Here we read the story of the woman with an infirmity of eighteen years; also the story of the master closing the door against professors who were hypocrites; also the record of Herod, the fox who was to be destroyed by the Lord. We also read of the house of Jerusalem left desolate because they refused to obey God.

John 13 Judas left Jesus and betrayed Him to His enemies.

Acts 13 Elymas, the sorcerer, was cursed with blindness, and the Jews attacked Paul because they hated his message.

Rom. 13 There is a warning here against resisting the powers of God, and the statement is made that the night is far spent.

1 Cor. 13 The sad revelation is made in this chapter that some people are like sounding brass and tinkling symbols. These have no value to God or to man. The Indian said about such a person "Heap big thunder, but no rain."

2 Cor. 13 This is a warning to the Christians that Paul will not spare them when he comes if they continue in their disobedience.

Heb. 13 God warns against divers and strange doctrines, and tells the story of the sufferings of Jesus outside the gate.

Rev. 13 Our Lord reveals that death will be the portion of those who worship the beast, the false prophet, and the anti-Christ, who refuse to obey Jesus Christ, our Lord.

THISTLE

Gen. 3:18 (c) This is a very fitting symbol of the sticking, stinging troubles of life which have come upon us because of the curse. It represents the smallest of our troubles. The briers are larger troubles. Brambles are still larger, and thorns are the largest and the worst of all injuries, sins and difficulties. Thorns were placed upon our Lord Jesus because He suffered the greatest and the most severe of all troubles that come to human beings. (See under BRAMBLE, BRIER and THORN.)

2 Ki. 14:9 (a) Amaziah, the King of Judah, is this thistle. He was an annoying person, as thistles are annoying. He was meddling

with trouble, and causing difficulties that never should have existed. (See 2 Chron. 25:18)

THORN

Num. 33:55 (b) The enemies of Israel were to cause terrible pain, trouble and sorrow as they remained among the people of God. (See also Josh. 23:13; Judges 2:3.)

2 Sam. 23:6 (a) David is describing his enemies. They had a great desire to hurt him and harm him, but God would make them powerless and helpless as He defended David.

Prov. 15:19 (a) There are people who seem more like porcupines than humans. When you get near them, they hurt your feelings and seem bent on doing only things that are injurious. They seem to live in a thorn-patch.

Prov. 26:9 (b) Here is a picture of the carelessness and insensibility of the drunkard. He handles things that will hurt him, and doesn't notice what he is doing. So the fool handles things with which he is not familiar, and gets an injury thereby. The drunkard puts his hand carelessly where it should not be, and is injured by it. So the foolish person says things that injure him.

S. of Sol. 2:2 (c) Probably this means that the church is in God's sight like a beautiful lady, while everything else outside the people of God is of no more value to Him than thorns would be. (See also under THISTLE.)

Isa. 55:13 (c) In the life of the Christian and in the future condition of Israel, the Lord will remove the things that hurt (thorns), and will bring joy, happiness and gladness to the hearts of the people. (See also under BRIER and FIR.)

Jer. 4:3 (b) It has always been God's plan to avoid the mixture of good and evil. He warns us against sowing wheat among weeds. He warns against sowing different kinds of seeds, good seeds and weed seeds. So in this passage, He is calling upon His people to clean house, turn their hearts to the Lord, and have a society or a nation that is altogether for Himself, with no mixture of the heathen.

Jer. 12:13 (c) This sad prophecy is warning Israel in regard to their habits and ways. He is informing them that he will bring weeds instead of grain, and will curse their land instead of blessing it. Instead of the blessing and profit, there will come sorrow and loss.

Ezek. 28:24 (a) This is a very precious promise to Israel, in which God informs them that the enemy will no more be able to cause trouble to invade or to conquer them or their land.

Hosea 2:6 (a) God will see to it that Israel has trouble on every side, and from every source. When they disobey God they may expect tribulation.

Matt. 13:7 (a) Our Lord describes and explains this type in verse 22. The problems that arise in this world and the evils that come with the daily life will be hurtful and harmful to the people.

2 Cor. 12:7 (b) Paul does not tell us just what this particular sorrow or affliction was. Some think it was sore eyes and defective vision. Others think it was the small size of his body. Others think that it was the restraint put upon him in which he was not permitted to tell what he saw in heaven during his visit there. It must have been most difficult for Paul to refrain from describing the glories of that heaven into which he was caught up. (See v. 4)

THREAD

Gen. 14:23 (c) This was the smallest gift of any kind that could be given. Abraham would not receive it. Nothing that was owned by the King of Sodom had any attraction for the man of God. He would not be rewarded by an idolator.

Josh. 2:18 (c) It may be used as a figure of the precious blood of Christ under which the believer takes refuge.

THREE

(c) The threes of the Bible represent triads of completeness. Sometimes it is a triad of good, and sometimes of evil. The Trinity of heaven is the Father, the Son and the Holy Spirit. The trinity of evil is the devil, the anti-Christ and the false prophet. The trinity of blessing is grace, mercy and peace. The trinity of wickedness is the world, the flesh and the devil. It is interesting to note that the books of first and second Thessalonians are built largely around three-fold statements.

Chapter 1:3, "The work of faith, and labor of love, and patience of hope."

Chapter 1:5, "in word . . . in power, and in the Holy Spirit."

Chapter 1:9, 10, "ye turned . . . to serve . . . and to wait."

Chapter 2:10, "Holily, justly and unblameably."

The many triads in both of these books show how fully and completely God has provided for His own people for their daily living.

Man's life also consists of three elements of time — the past, the present and the future.

Our salvation is three-fold. We have been delivered, we are being delivered, and we shall be delivered. (2 Cor. 1:10)

In Bible study there are three time elements as found in Rev. 1:19. John was to write the things he had already seen, and the things that are now transpiring, and the things that are still in the future and shall yet come to pass.

Josh. 1:11 (c) As Jordan was typical of death, the three days are typical of the resurrection assured to the people of Israel. They were to pass through Jordan and come out safely on the third day.

Matt. 12:40 (b) No doubt this is typical of the resurrection, for it was on the third day that Jesus rose.

Matt. 13:33 (b) Probably this is typical of life, for the meal was good food, ready to impart life to those who ate it. (See under "LEAVEN".)

The thought in the number three also indicates the fact that Christ who was typified as meal in the Old Testament would be the living Christ, raised from the dead, to feed His people constantly. Some think it represents the Father, the Son and the Holy Spirit. Others suggest it refers to prophetical, historical and doctrinal aspects of the Bible.

THRESH

Isa. 28:28 (b) In this passage the word represents the climax in dealing with a soul for salvation. As all persons are not saved in the same way, so all grains are not gathered in the same way. Threshing represents just one of the many ways of harvesting. The Lord is teaching in this verse that there are a number of methods to use in releasing a soul from the bonds and bands of sin and Satan until they are born again, redeemed and saved.

Jer. 51:33 (a) The time to destroy Babylon had come. It is described as a threshing because of the tremendous beating she would receive from her enemies. (See also Isa. 21:10)

Amos 1:3 (a) This is a description of the persecution and whipping given to Gilead by the armies of Damascus.

Micah 4:13 (a) By this type we understand that the nation of Israel was to whip her enemies and conquer the opposing nations.

Hab. 3:12 (a) Again this type is used to illustrate the whipping that God gave the heathen for their wicked and hostile attitude toward His people.

1 Cor. 9:10 (b) The thought of being successful in soul winning is indicated by this figure. Certainly there is great joy in the heart of the believer when he sees "the wheat" brought into the garner and separated from the chaff.

THRESHOLD

1 Sam. 5:4 (c) We may learn from this interesting incident that those who approach an idol or the temple of the idol should

see that the idol could neither think (for his head was off), nor work (for his hands were off.) He could be of no use whatever to the idolator. The presence of the God of Israel destroys the idols of men.

Ezek. 9:3 (c) This is the first movement of the Spirit of God as He prepared to leave Israel to the fate of her enemies. It is a picture of the way the Spirit gradually ceases to work with a soul when that person deliberately turns against God and accepts false teachings. The Spirit crossed the threshold of the door of the temple as His first action in departure. (See also Ezek. 10:4)

Ezek. 47:1 (b) No doubt this is a type of our blessed Lord from whom the gracious Holy Spirit is given. Christ is the door. He is the giver of the Spirit. We must first belong to the Lord Jesus before the Spirit can be given to us. Christ must put the sins away before the Spirit can dwell with us. Since the river in this allegory represents the Holy Spirit, it is evident that the threshold of the door represents the Saviour.

THROAT

Psa. 5:9 (a) The picture is that of an open grave from which a terrible stench arises. The filthy talk that comes from many mouths is certainly offensive to every decent person. (See Rom. 3:13)

Prov. 23:2 (b) It represents the appetite or the desire to eat which should be controlled. The Lord does not want us to be gluttons.

THRONE

Psa. 94:20 (a) No doubt this refers to the power of evil purposes and desires, as well as the tragic influence of it.

Isa. 14:9 (a) This seems to teach that in hell thrones are erected for evil and wicked monarchs who have fallen, and who in mockery are given a place on a throne in hell among the people he cursed. It would be a terrible punishment to have such a position and under such conditions.

Isa. 22:23 (a) Christ is the throne, the power, the authority for the universe. God has made Him so. Christians are glad to have Him as their Lord, and the unsaved will be forced to bow the knee to Him.

Jer. 17:12 (a) We may understand that this represents God's great purposes and plans for men. He has the knowledge and wisdom necessary to make such plans, and He has the power to execute them.

Col. 1:16 (a) These probably represent places and positions of power among men, as well as among demons. Christ Jesus has power to control every force and every kind of authority. He is Lord of lords, and King of kings.

Heb. 4:16 (a) Grace does rule and reign in the heart of God, and the lives of His people. There is power in that grace, power to forgive and forget, power to overcome temptation and to be conquerors in the Name of the Lord.

THUMB

Lev. 14:14 (b) This type is used to represent the work and works of the priest. The blood and the oil on the thumb indicate that all the service of the servant of God was henceforth to be dedicated only to God. Jesus' whole hands were covered with blood, for He worked only for the Father. (See also Lev. 8:23; Ex. 29:20)

THUNDER

Job 26:14 (a) This was used to indicate that though our sense of hearing may realize that God is working, our minds are unable to understand the manner of it.

Job 39:19 (b) The type is used to illustrate man's helplessness, either to give strength to the horse, or power to the elements.

Psa. 77:18 (a) In this wonderful way God is telling us of His mighty power which is beyond human control and human comprehension. (See also Psa. 29:3; Psa. 104:7)

Psa. 81:7 (a) God dwells in the high and holy place, but He hears the faintest cry of His child wherever he may be.

Rev. 14:2 (b) It is symbolical of the great and mysterious power of God in that no one can understand it, nor control it.

TIE

Matt. 21:2 (c) This may be taken as a picture of the way that sinners are fastened to their habits and their traditions. Christ comes into the life, breaks the ties that bind one to the old life, and sets him free. Then He can ride upon that delivered one for His glory. (See also Mark 11:2; Luke 19:30)

TIME

Dan. 12:7 (a) This is taken to mean one year. "Times" is taken to means two years. "Half a time" is taken to mean six months. (See also Rev. 12:14)

Rev. 10:6 (a) This passage does not mean that there will be an end to the clocks and that time will be no more. It refers to the fact that what must be done is to be done immediately. There can be no procrastination, no putting off until later, no indecision, every matter must be immediately attended to, without delay. It may be illustrated by the time of the departure of the train. If the train leaves at 9:00 o'clock, then there is no more time to get on board.

TIN

Isa. 1:25 (c) Probably this metal is used as a picture of hypocrisy. It looks like silver, it resembles it in appearance, but is inferior.

Ezek. 22:18 (c) Again this metal is probably used as a picture of hypocrisy. The melting point of silver is 1761 degrees, but the melting point of tin is 449 degrees. It is very easily destroyed by heat, and is not permanent as silver would be. The Lord thus diagnoses the inhabitants of Jerusalem.

TOE

Ex. 29:20 (c) The great toe of the right foot typifies the walk of the child of God. It represents the entire foot, and the foot represents the manner of life. It was anointed with blood to show that the walk of the Christian was to be under the cleansing blood of Christ, and the anointing of oil was to show that the walk was to be devoted to the leading of the Spirit. Jesus' whole feet were covered with blood, for He walked perfectly with God. (See also Lev. 8:23; Lev. 14:14)

2 Sam. 21:20 (c) The ordinary man has five toes. Five is typical of human weakness. The presence of six toes indicates human power and perfection. This man was a superman, greater, stronger and more mighty than his fellows. The number six indicates man's strength and human power. The anti-Christ has the number 666 which indicates that he has power in every department of human life. (See also 1 Chron. 20:6)

Dan. 2:41 (a) These represent the smallest divisions of the kingdom of the Roman empire. It was partly strong, and partly weak. It was very strong in military power, and very weak in moral stamina.

TOKEN

This word represents a pledge or advance payment as proof that the promise will be fulfilled.

Gen. 9:12 (b) The rainbow is God's testimony that He will never again send a universal flood to destroy life upon the earth.

Gen. 17:11 (b) Circumcision is a permanent mark on the men of Israel to remind them of God's unconditional promises to Abraham, and their identification with that covenant.

Ex. 3:12 (b) Moses received this token on Mt. Sinai. The people had been delivered from Egypt, had safely crossed the sea, had been preserved as they traveled through the wilderness. They were now gathered around Moses on the mount. This was the proof that he was God's chosen leader.

Ex. 12:13 (b) The blood of the lamb was the evidence and proof to God that the people within the house believed His Word. It represents the precious blood of Christ, applied by faith to our hearts, wherein we testify that we believe God and His Word.

Num. 17:10 (c) Aaron's rod in the presence of God was the evidence to be used against the rebellious people of Israel, if there should ever be a question of God's righteousness in punishing Korah and his company. It is also a type of the evidence against wicked sinners, manifested in the wounds of Jesus Christ, and His subsequent glory. The wounded Christ on the throne of heaven, exalted by God, is sufficient proof that Christ is God's son, God's servant, even though men reject Him.

Mark 14:44 (c) This may be taken as a type of the false provision and the vain conversation of hypocrites who enter the fold of the church for the sake of making money.

2 Thess. 3:17 (b) Paul's signature on his letters, even though they were dictated by him, was proof that they were genuine and orthodox.

TONGUE

This word is used as a type in a great many ways. Many writers use it to express many and varied meanings. We shall observe some of them here.

Psa. 45:1 (a) It is used as a pen because it makes impressions on hearts.

Psa. 57:4 (a) It is used as a sword because it cuts into people's souls. (See Psa. 64:3)

Psa. 73:9 (a) It is like a detective searching people's lives.

Prov. 10:20 (a) It is like silver because it produces valuable results.

Prov. 15:4 (a) It is like a tree because it adds to the joys of life.

Isa. 30:27 (a) It is like fire which destroys evil things in the lives of others.

Jer. 9:3 (a) It is like a bow because it sends forth sharp words. (See vs. 8)

Rev. 5:9 (a) The tongue is used for language in its general aspect. (See Gen. 10:5)

Tongues have many descriptions:

The lying tongue Psa. 109:2; Prov. 6:17

The false tongue Psa. 120:3.

The sharpened tongue Psa. 140:3

The froward tongue Prov. 10:31.
The wholesome tongue Prov. 15:4
The naughty tongue Prov. 17:4
The perverse tongue Prov. 17:20
The soft tongue Prov. 25:15
The backbiting tongue Prov. 25:23
The stammering tongue Isa. 33:19
The fiery tongue Jas. 3:6.

TOOL

Ex. 20:25 (c) There are to be no human schemes nor designs used in the service of God. The Lord has told how to handle His work, and He expects it to be done by His people in His way. An illustration is found in the way David tried to bring up the ark on a new cart. It was a plan of the Philistines, but it was not God's plan. God's work must be done in God's way. (See Deut. 27:5; 1 Ki. 6:7)

TOOTH

Prov. 25:19 (a) The unfaithfulness of a friend in time of need hurts the soul, breaks the heart, and causes mental pain.

TORCH

Nahum 2:3 (c) Some think that this refers to the headlights used on automobiles, tanks and other vehicles. The real meaning is not clear.

Zech. 12:6 (a) God is prophesying that the rulers of Jerusalem will some day destroy all their enemies, as the fire destroys the wood.

John 18:3 (c) We may understand that this is a type of human intelligence, research and reasoning by means of which men seek to find the Lord Jesus, who is the light of life. "Reason is the natural sun in the mental world." Men with the feeble light of their intelligence seek to find the One who made "the sun to rule by day, and the moon by night."

TOW

Isa. 1:31 (a) God is assuring the world that His enemies will be easily destroyed. No one can harden himself against God and prosper. God always will have the last word.

TOWER

2 Sam. 22:51 (b) The tower is a type of the high and safe place occupied by the children of God who hide in Christ and dwell in the secret place of the Most High. (See also Psa. 18:2; Psa. 61:3; Psa. 144:2; Prov. 18:10.)

S. of Sol. 7:4 (a) Ivory is very valuable and beautiful. A tower is firm and substantial. These qualities are evidently referred to as characteristic of the bride. The tower of Lebanon was evidently a lookout tower, facing Syria where the watchman could discern quickly the coming of the enemy. It probably means that the bride had a great sense of discernment and could easily and quickly discern that which was evil or wrong, or was from the enemy.

Jer. 6:27 (a) Jeremiah was the center of God's work and power among the people of Israel. From him came the words of warning and entreaty. Through him God sent His messages, His commands, and made known His desires.

Micah 4:8 (a) Mount Zion is a high, rocky fortress, quite difficult to ascend, very steep. It was recognized as the very center of the defense of Jerusalem and of Judah.

Matt. 21:33 (b) This tower probably represents Mount Zion in the midst of Israel, and of Jerusalem, and was a watch-tower from which the enemy could be seen for many miles away. Christ is referring partly to the history of Israel, and partly to the present time when He is away in the far country.

Luke 14:28 (b) This is a type of any great work of God which a man of God builds for the honor of the Lord Jesus Christ. This is illustrated in the great school built by Moody in Chicago, the great work in China built by Hudson Taylor, and the wonderful work in the Sudan built by R. V. Bingham. God would have all His children building something for His glory.

TRANSPARENT

Rev. 21:21 (a) The gold which we see and use is far from transparent. It covers many sins, and evil motives. It is used to bribe and to deceive. Gold plating is used to cover the iron that is beneath. It is hypocritical in many cases. Gold may make a man appear to be a wonderful citizen, when he really is a criminal at heart. The gold of heaven hides no hypocrisy, no sham, no evil. It is pure in its character, and transparent in its effects.

TRAP

Josh. 23:13 (a) These evil people who should have been exterminated would by their charms, attractions and reasonings catch the people of God, and make them idolators, living in wickedness.

Psa. 69:22 (a) In this Messianic prophecy our Lord is telling us that His presence should have been a blessing to them, but instead of that it excited their evil hearts and they became murderers of the One who loved them, and would have saved them. Their treatment of the Lord Jesus revealed their wicked hearts, and their hatred against the sweetest and best man in the world. (See also Rom. 11:9)

TRAVAIL

Psa. 7:14 (a) The wicked man has a tremendous urge in his soul to do wrong, and gets no relief until he executes his evil designs.

Psa. 48:6 (a)The sons of Korah are describing the sudden outpouring of God's wrath on the nations, so that they are filled with fear and can find no relief. (See Jer. 6:24; Jer. 13:21; Jer. 22:23; Micah 4:9)

Eccl. 1:13 (a) Solomon seems to indicate that all kinds of labor and investigation are a burden to men. They never seem to get the job done, and therefore never rest. He uses this expression all through this book of Ecclesiastes.

Isa. 53:11 (a) Christ's terrible sufferings and sorrows are compared to the pains of a woman in childbirth.

Isa. 54:1 (a) There is a comparison here between the Law and Grace, between Israel and the Church, between the bondage of the Old Testament, and the freedom of the New. Hagar gave birth to a child through the scheme and plan of Abraham. In contrast with this, Isaac was the child of Sarah by promise and by miracle. So it is with the Old Testament plan. Men sought by many ways (given by God) to better themselves and increase their usefulness They failed and were set aside. Then Christ Jesus came to bring betterment, goodness, and the salvation of the soul by the sacrifice and the resurrection of Himself. Millions have been set free by the Saviour, far in excess of that which came from Israel.

Isa. 66:7 (b) Christ Jesus came to Israel, but they were not ready for Him, and did not want Him. The nation of Israel was formed in a day, but they did not want their King, they were not ready for their Messiah.

Rom. 8:22 (a) All of nature is indeed suffering with the things that exist on the earth. Plant life and animal life suffer the depredations of enemies, and are finally overcome by death. All human beings have sorrow, the wealthy as well as the poor. All minerals and metals suffer with rust and decay. Nothing improves with age. Sorrow abounds in every realm.

Gal. 4:19 (a) Paul was deeply exercised in his soul about the spiritual welfare of the Galatians. They had become so occupied with lawkeeping, that they had forgotten the precious presence of the Lord Jesus Christ. Paul wanted them to make Christ Jesus Lord of all, and preeminent in their thinking and their worship. His soul was deeply exercised about this.

1 Thes. 2:9 (a) Paul was a marvelous example of one who accompanied his faith by his works. He worked with his hands

day and night to pay all of his own bills, and also the expenses of the nine men who were with him. He demanded no salary, and took no offerings from these people. It was not an easy task. It was most burdensome and difficult, as he indicates by using the word travail.

TREASURE

Ex. 19:5 (a) The people of Israel were especially precious to God. They were His valued possession. He cared for them as the merchant cares for his diamonds. In them and through them He was to reveal His wonderful character, His patience, His longsuffering and His marvelous power. He therefore considered them priceless.

Deut. 28:12 (a) God Himself calls the blessings which He gives as treasures from Him. It is a good name for them, for what would we do without the sunshine, and what would we do without the rain? (See also Psa. 17:14)

Isa. 33:6 (a) It certainly is true that the fear of God makes one rich in his life. It is not riches that can be stolen by another, nor does it decrease in value with time. The man who fears God is rich in faith, in character and in good works.

Matt. 6:20:21 (b) This describes the gracious gifts for the Lord's work which are done in the name of the Lord Jesus, and for His glory. God records these in heaven, for they have great value to Him. The money that we send to the Lord, and give for His service is also included in the treasure, and this is recorded in heaven. The money we give, as well as the time and talents we expend for our Lord, reveal the attitude of our hearts.

Matt. 13:44 (b) This type represents the Kingdom of God, which consists of love, joy, peace, salvation and righteousness. These virtues are found in the hearts of God's people who are scattered and hidden throughout the earth. Throughout the world there are those who are called according to His purpose. There are the "other sheep," those who "should be saved," those who are "ordained unto eternal life." All of these, together with the blessings that accompany God's gospel, are referred to as "a treasure." (See under "KINGDOM.") The Kingdom of God is the church, His family.

2 Cor. 4:7 (a) The treasure is the gift of eternal life, divine grace, the knowledge of God, and belonging to Jesus Christ, the Saviour.

TREE

This beautiful plant of God's design and creation is used in many ways in the Scripture. Each type of tree represents a different truth. Trees are also used to represent positions of great power, or of lesser power. Trees represent God's people in some cases, while they represent Satan's product in other cases.

Gen. 2:17 (c) It has been suggested that this tree represents human reasonings, searchings and conclusions about God's matters. Men today prefer psychological investigations and mental processes rather than to believe God and His Word. The Devil offers many philosophies and theories which men eagerly grasp and prefer them to God's revealed truth. (See also Gen. 3:3)

Ex. 15:25 (c) Perhaps this tree represents the Lord Jesus Christ who certainly does sweeten the bitter things of life, and make the sorrows of earth a blessing to the soul.

Ex. 15:27 (c) Strangely enough, these trees may, and possibly do, represent the seventy persons who came down to Egypt from the land of Israel. The twelve springs may represent the twelve tribes. Certainly they were to be a blessing to the whole earth.

Num. 24:6 (a) It is a type of the people of God seen in the light of God's thoughts, as His own choice planting, and bearing fruit for His glory. (See Jer. 17:8)

Job 14:7 (c) The teaching of this passage is that though a man may fail in business, or fall as a sinner, it is quite possible for him to be restored and to recover and to end his days in blessing, and with God's approval.

Psa. 1:3 (a) This is the child of God who is rooted and grounded in the Word of God, and is having his soul and life permeated by the Holy Spirit (the river). He is not planted in the river, but by the river. The finest tree will not grow in the best of soil unless there is water available. The water represents the Holy Spirit.

Prov. 3:18 (a) God is giving us here a picture of "wisdom." Those who exercise this virtue certainly save themselves from much trouble, and become a rich blessing to many. Christ bears this name.

Prov. 11:30 (a) The tree represents a fruitful life lived for the glory of God and the blessing of men.

Prov. 13:12 (a) The Lord uses this picture to illustrate the blessings of answered prayer, and the receiving of the desires of the heart.

Prov. 15:4 (a) Good talk and wise words certainly do bring the blessings that a tree of life would bring. The Lord tells us to let our conversation be always with grace. The Psalmist also requested that "the words of my mouth" might be acceptable to God.

Isa. 56:3 (a) The eunuch had no power to propagate himself, he could have no posterity. He is like the dry tree in that there would be no fruit in his life that might produce posterity.

Isa. 66:17 (b) Probably this tree represents some particular wicked religion which permits abominations and wicked practices. The self-righteous person is satisfied with that kind of arrangement.

Ezek. 17:24 (a) God uses this strange illustration to describe His power in bringing down the important men of the nation, and exalting the obscure man. He wrecks the life of the great man, and promotes the welfare of the small man. The trees here represent people. (See also Ezek. 21:10)

Ezek. 31:8 (a) This allegory describes Satan in his original beauty and glory. The description of Satan begins at verse 3. It runs through verse 9.

Dan. 4:10 (a) This tree is King Nebuchadnezzar. Daniel explains this fully.

Matt. 3:10 (b) The primary application of this type is to Israel. The application is also to the individual. God did lay the ax to the root of Israel and destroyed the nation. The roots, however, remain in the earth, and are even now producing a new tree. This happens also to individuals who, because their lives are so utterly given over to the Devil and there is no fruit for God, that one is cut off and sent to hell. (See also Luke 6:43)

Matt. 12:33 (a) The Lord is propounding here a very deep truth, which should stir every heart. The individual must be born again to become a good tree, which will bring forth good fruit. No man is naturally a Christian. The tree itself must be made before the fruit can be right. An unsaved person lives the life of an unsaved person. If he is transformed by the power and grace of God, then he becomes a Christian and lives the life of a Christian. (See Luke 6:44)

Matt. 13:32 (a) Mustard does not grow on trees. There is no such things as a mustard tree. The mustard grows on a bush. Therefore, this tree is an unnatural thing, and it represents the great, unnatural religious system, which consists of many denominations having a multitude of beliefs, many of them grotesque, and even wicked. God never intended that His church should be of this sort. Those who really trust Jesus Christ and are true Christians form only a very small part of that great institution we call Christendom. The birds in this story represent evil spirits. They are made to feel at home in this great unnatural religous system, which is a curse to the earth. (See Luke 13:19)

Luke 17:6 (b) The reference is to any trouble or difficulty in the life, which seems like a mountain that cannot be moved by any human means. Our Lord is able to do it, and therefore He gives us the privilege of bringing the problem to Him. (See "SEED")

Rev. 2:7 (b) We find no indication of the meaning of this type, but we may assume that it refers to the blessings that come from the Lord Jesus Christ to those who walk with God, dwell in His presence, and are planted in His courts.

TREES

Deut. 16:21 (b) These groves were very immoral and vile inventions of wicked men. They were not groves of trees, as we understand a grove. They were human creations to arouse the passions and lead to vile immoralities. (See under "GROVE".)

Jud. 9:8 (a) This is an interesting allegory. The olive tree represents a leader who was wise, kind, helpful and fruitful. The fig tree represents an Israelite who was busy and useful in the service of his people. The people could not find a worthwhile man to rule over them, and so they took the bramble, which was Abimelech, to be their King. They chose a man who brought them into terrible trouble.

1 Chron. 16:33 (b) This is a poetic picture of all the people of Israel who would rejoice and sing when their King, the Messiah, returns to be their Lord and leader. (See Psa. 96:12)

Psa. 74:5 (b) This is a case of irony. It is equivalent to the woman who boasted that she had made more quilts in the sewing circle than anybody else. When questioned about her spiritual condition, she had never been born again, knew nothing about the Scriptures, and had no spiritual experience. It is like the man who wore 42 Sunday school medals on his coat for faithful attendance, and yet could not quote a verse of Scripture, and had no experience of meeting the Saviour.

Psa. 104:16 (b) It is quite evident that those who are the "planting of the Lord" and know the Holy Spirit are vigorous, active Christians as a tree is filled with leaves and fruit when the sap is flowing.

Psa. 148:9 (b) Those praise God in song and worship who are living fruitful, useful, valuable lives for their Lord.

S. of Sol. 2:3 (a) Christ is the apple tree in this verse. Those who love Him love to be with Him, and to partake of the riches of His grace which He gives so freely.

Isa. 10:19 (b) God promises to destroy the leaders of Israel until they are few in number. The leaders are the trees.

Isa. 55:12 (b) These trees represent the happy people of God and their leaders because of the restoration of Israel under the good hand of their God. As there are many kinds of trees, and many sizes of trees, so the verse indicates that all kinds of people in the nation of Israel will enjoy the presence of the Lord and His blessings.

Isa. 61:3 (a) The people of God are called "trees of righteousness" when they are restored, and are again a growing, fruitful nation.

Ezek. 47:7 (b) The river which represents the Holy Spirit, when operating freely, produces converts, saved people who become trees of righteousness, planted by the river, and bearing fruit. This should be true in every orthodox, evangelical church.

Matt. 3:10 (b) Our Lord indicates in this verse that God gets at the bottom of things and examines thoroughly the motives and purposes of those He judges. (See Luke 3:9)

Mark 8:24 (a) In Oriental countries where the houses are made of branches of trees, men go to the water courses, cut down branches of willows, and other trees, and carry these home to be used for thatch. As the men walk along the road carrying these great masses of leafy branches, it is difficult to see their feet or legs. This blind man had never seen such a sight. When he saw the mass of trees going down the road, and could not see the legs of the carriers, he thought that the trees were walking. As he became more accustomed to looking, he finally discerned beneath the branches the bodies of the men who were carrying them. This is a picture of the way untaught Christians misinterpret the Scriptures. Not knowing the Holy Spirit as their teacher they get wrong impressions from various portions of the Word, and so come to wrong conclusions. This leads to the establishment of false religions.

Mark 11:13 (b) The fig tree always represents Israel in her national position. (The olive tree represents Israel from the religious viewpoint. See under "FIG".) Our Lord had come to Israel expecting to receive from them a royal welcome as their King. They should have rendered to Him praise, worship and obedience. He found nothing but a profession of faith in God (the leaves). He therefore cursed the nation of Israel, and they became dispersed throughout the whole world.

Luke 21:29 (a) Our Lord describes in this passage the beginning of the restoration of Israel which we see today. The fig tree is Israel. It has been revived as a nation. All the other nations are busy seeking to reject Israel as a nation, and refuse all her claims.

Jude 12 (a) By this figure the Lord is telling us of His hatred of the hypocrite who intrudes himself into God's church and infiltrates the people of God with his hypocrisy. He produces no fruit for God. His influence wanes. He is dead to God and useless to his fellowmen, and has no posterity.

Each type of a tree represents a different truth as follows:

Palm tree — it represents the individual Christian life living for God in the midst of adverse conditions such as the palm tree has in the desert. It sends its tap root down a great distance until it finds water, and then flourishes. So the Christian finds the secret place of fellowship with God, drinks the water of life from the Word of God, walks with the Spirit of God, and so is a radiant believer. (See Psa. 92:12)

Cedar tree — it represents the collective Christian life, for cedars grow in forests and not as the palm tree which dwells almost alone. Cedars help each other. They support each other. They protect each other. So Christians seek the fellowship of other Christians.

Fig tree — it represents Israel from the political standpoint as a nation.

Olive tree — it represents Israel from the religious standpoint as the people of God.

Willow tree — it represents the sorrowing believer because of separation from loved ones, or from the homeland.

Oak tree — it represents sorrow because of death. Deborah was buried under an oak tree. (Gen. 35:8) Absalom died in an oak tree. (2 Sam. 18:14) Saul was buried under an oak tree. (1 Chron. 10:12) The bitterness of the oak tree is compared to the bitterness of death.

Fir tree — it represents the happy, radiant Christian life under every circumstance and throughout the year.

Myrtle tree — it represents joyous experiences in the Christian life.

Pine tree — it represents prosperity for those who walk with God, and believe Him.

Thorn tree — it represents the disagreeable life filled with antagonisms, criticisms and hatreds.

TRIM

Jer. 2:33 (b) This expression is used to describe the preparations which men make to obtain that which they desire.

Matt. 25:7 (c) This illustrates the way that the Lord's people should remove from their lives anything that would keep their testimony from shining out brightly for the Lord.

TURTLEDOVE

Lev. 1:14 (c) This bird probably is used to indicate a very small and narrow view of the person of Christ as our sacrifice.

It is almost the smallest of all the offerings. The sparrow is the only one that is smaller. The lamb was a larger offering and indicates a more comprehensive view of the value of Christ in His sacrificial work. The bullock is the largest of the offerings, and indicates a wide and deep knowledge of the work and the person of the Lord Jesus in His sacrifice for us. Thus the Lord makes provision for every kind of person, none needs to be excluded.

Psa. 74:19 (b) It is typical of the weakness felt by God's people in the presence of their enemies.

TWELVE

(c) This number denotes God's governmental control of His people. In the twelve tribes, He controlled their politics; in the twelve loaves, He sustained and provided enough for all; in the twelve spies, He controlled their knowledge and information, even though some disobeyed; in the twelve disciples, He showed His lordship over the church and His ability to provide the gifts the church needs; in the twelve gates to Jerusalem, He manifested His control over who and what entered the kingdom.

Twelve Patriarchs. Gen. 42:13 (c) The meanings of the names of these twelve men constitute a wonderful story of God's dealings with His people.

Reuben means sonship.
Simeon means scholarship.
Levi means lordship
Judah means worship
Dan means judgeship
Naphtali means workmanship
Gad means companionship
Asher means fellowship
Issachar means partnership
Zebulon means comradeship
Joseph means leadership
Benjamin means heirship

Twelve Stones in the Breastplate of the High Priest: (Exodus 28:17-20) (c)

1. Sardius, the ruby or red stone on which was placed Reuben's name. As we hear about the blood and accept the Saviour, we become children of God.

2. Topaz, a greenish, yellow stone on which was engraved the name of Simeon. The revelations he received from God were to be eternal in duration and divine in character.

3. Carbuncle, a green stone really known as the "emerald" on which was engraved the name of Levi. The lordship of God continues forever and ever and is the means of producing blessing in this life and in the next.

4. Emerald, not the emerald of today. The word was used for several brilliant red stones probably the garnet. On this stone was engraved the name of Judah, for worship is based on the efficacy of the blood.

5. Sapphire, beautiful, clear, and sparkling on which was engraved the name of Dan, for the throne of judgment must be transparent with no taint or stain upon it.

6. Diamond, not the diamond of our day, for records would indicate that the Hebrews had no means of engraving on this hard stone. It probably was alabaster for the name of Naphtali was engraved upon it and this unusual workmanship made it most attractive.

7. Ligure, probably the opal on which appeared the name of Gad. Companionship involves so many beautiful attributes and attitudes that the flashing colors of the opal beautifully represent it.

8. Agate, beautifully striped with white, red and green. On this was placed the name of Asher for fellowship is white in its character, green in its perpetuity and red in its fidelity.

9. Amethyst. This beautiful blue stone had the name of Issachar upon it for in every partnership, there is true fidelity and faithful devotion.

10. Beryl, sometimes called the arrow stone. It was the hardest substance for cutting known to the ancients. The name Zebulon was engraved upon it for comradeship is to be firmly fixed and not easily disappointed.

11. The onyx, the banded carnelian, beautifully striped with black and white, and brown and white. Upon this was engraved the name of Joseph for leadership is certainly varied in its character and diversified in its expressions.

12. Jasper, the chalcedony, a dark green stone. Upon this was the name of Benjamin for we are to be eternally heirs of God and to enjoy in perfect bliss the blessings of that happy relationship.

It is interesting to note that in Rev. 21:19 these stones are found in the foundation of the New Jerusalem, while the names of the twelve patriarchs are found upon the pearls which constitute the gates (see verses 12 and 21). Pearls are the result of suffering. They are produced by the anguish of the oyster. Thus we see that the twelve patriarchs through their sorrows and sufferings were promoted and elevated to be pearls when the Lord had finished with their training. The meaning of the names is given here:—

The Twelve Disciples — Mark 3:16-19 (c)

1. Simon: hearing with acceptance. Evidently it is hearing the gospel message about the Lord Jesus which saves the soul. This

is the beginning of the Christian life and is the beginning of the story of the Twelve.

Peter — a rock. As soon as one hears with acceptance, he immediately becomes a part of the body of Christ and partakes of His nature.

Cephas — a stone. The one who hears acceptably becomes united to Christ and is at once useful in the house that God is building.

2. James: supplanter. The things of God have supplanted the things of earth and the path of separation is begun. This first James is the Son of Zebedee.

3. John: the Lord hath begun to speak. How true it is that when one is delivered from the world and the devil, he becomes God's mouthpiece to carry God's message.

4. Andrew: a strong man. God gives strength to His children to continue in the service of the King and in the path of separation.

5. Phillip: loving. The Christian loves his Lord, loves the Word of God, loves the people of God, and loves the service of God.

6. Bartholomew: son of his father. Those who are separated to the Lord and love the things of heaven are soon known as members of God's family for they become more and more like their Lord.

7. Matthew: gift of the Lord. It is true that God's people are gifted from God for the various works which they are privileged to do.

8. Thomas: a twin. It speaks of companionship and comradeship for the Lord sent them out two and two. He said, "Two are better than one." (Eccl. 4:9)

9. James, the son of Alphaeus: the supplanter. In this case, it is a godly Christian supplanting what may have remained of the old life with the blessed provisions of the new life.

10. Thaddeus: (Lebbeaus, Judas, the brother of James, son of Alphaeus). The word means praise of God. The one who is wholly devoted to the Lord finds much occasion for praise, worship, gladness and thanksgiving.

11. Simon: (Zelotes, also Simon the Canaanite). Again the word means "hearing acceptably." In this instance, it is hearing God's voice in directing the path, guiding the way, revealing His will, and instructing the Christian concerning his service.

12. Judas Iscariot: the traitor. He is always named last. It is always said of him, "who also betrayed Him." The outstanding sin of rejecting Christ marks him for time and eternity.

The Twelve Spies: Numbers 13:4,15 (c)

1. Shammuah: hearing of the Lord. This is the beginning of the life of faith. The ears are closed to other voices to hear and believe the call of God.

2. Shaphat: a judge. As soon as one listens to God, he judges his path, and turns from evil to obey God.

3. Caleb: as the heart. Out of the heart proceed the issues of life. Those whose hearts are right with God will receive God's blessings.

4. Igal: whom God will avenge. The believer whose heart is right with God leaves his judgments in God's hands.

5. Joshua: a saviour. Those who listen to God, have their hearts filled with God's love, and have turned their lives over to the Lord, become interested in the salvation of others.

6. Palti: deliverance of the Lord. Those who go about as saviours of men by their ministry and service are delivered by the Lord from their enemies and from want.

7. Gaddiel: the Lord is my happiness. Those who listen to God and are busy in His service find their joy in the things of God.

8. Gaddi: a troop of God. God's servant is entitled to receive and does receive his assets and reinforcements from heaven.

9. Ammiel: one of the people of God. Those who are walking with the Lord and are busy in His service soon get a reputation for being one of God's children.

10. Sethur: mysterious or hidden. This is the only man among the spies whose name is not a glorious one revealing some blessing from heaven. Strangely enough, the Hebrew letters making up his name produce the number 666. It may be that this man headed up the insurrection of the ten spies and instigated the evil report.

11. Nahbi: hidden of the Lord. How true it is that those who are persecuted for the Lord's sake are hidden by Him in His pavilion from the strife of tongues.

12. Geuel: majesty of God. After all the walk of faith represented by these names, God is victorious at the end and His glory will fill heaven and earth.

Twelve Sons of Ishmael: Gen. 25:13-15 (c) God told Abraham in Genesis 17:20 that Ishmael would be blessed with twelve princes. This is an unusual case in which God foretold how many sons a man would have. This prophecy was fulfilled.

1. Nebajoth: high places. This is one of the marks of the ungodly. They are filled with pride, and desire to run their own lives, and the lives of others as well.

2. Kedar: black skinned. Those who are unsaved are black in God's sight and need to be washed in the blood of the lamb to make them whiter than snow.

3. Adbeel: miracle of God. It is indeed a miracle of God that He supplies the needs of the ungodly and particularly that He has preserved the Ishmaelites through all the centuries until this present day.

4. Mibsam: sweet odour. Frequently there is found among the unsaved and the ungodly attractive qualities which make them delightful citizens though they are strangers to the grace of God.

5. Mishma: report. Strangely enough the believers of false religions are unusually busy propagating their faith in far greater measure than the true Christians.

6. Dumah: silence. Among the ungodly there is only silence regarding the grace of God, the loveliness of Christ, the value of the blood, and all those precious themes which are loved by the Christians.

7. Massa: burden. The unrighteous are constantly burdened for they have no one to lift the load and no means of getting rid of their sins.

8. Hadar: enclosure. Those who are strangers to God live for themselves and shut out the Word of God, the love of God, and the people of God. They surround themselves with darkness and erect bars lest the gospel should intrude into their lives.

9. Tema: a desert. Truly the unrighteous do live in a desert. Their voices are fleeting, their happiness is transient, their way is a way of tears and they know not the river of the water of life nor the green pastures provided by the good Shepherd.

10. Jetur: an enclosure. As the social life of the unsaved is inclosed in order to eliminate and exclude God's religion, God's Word, and God's people, so the mind also is closed lest they should see, hear, understand and be saved.

11. Naphish: cheerful. The world of the ungodly is filled with multitudinous and multivarious methods of providing happiness for those who have shut out God and desire not the blessings of Christianity.

12. Kedemah: eastward. The sun rises in the east. They imitated Isaac as sinners often imitate Christians in their religious activities. The Mohammedans who are the descendants of Ishmael always face eastward when they pray.

TWIG

Ezek. 17:4 (b) This is typical, because of their position in the top of the tree, of the kings, nobles, and the rulers of Israel. In their size as twigs, they are emblematic of weakness and helplessness.

TWO

Gen. 2:24 (c) This is an emblem of union in that the husband and wife are made one. The number also denotes division. It divides because it is the smallest number that may be divided. Israel was divided into two camps; the spies were divided into two groups. Even the two brothers, Cain and Abel, were divided and separated from each other.

U

UNACCUSTOMED

Jer. 31:18 (a) This is a splendid picture of the sinner in his natural state. He does not submit to authority, he is unbroken, unruly, and in rebellion against God, and His laws.

UNBLAMEABLE

Col. 1:22 (a) This interesting word means that the Christian will not be challenged at the gate of heaven. He will not need a password to enter. He will not be stopped and examined to see if he is fit to enter. Those who enter a lodge hall are challenged at the door, and must give the sign required. Those who enter the army camp are challenged at the gate. This word "unblameable" refers to that form of procedure. It tells us that the Saviour, who is the Lord of glory, does such a complete work in the soul of the child of God, that he enters immediately into the presence of God when his spirit leaves the body, and there is no challenge. (See also 1 Thes. 3:13)

UNCERTAIN-LY

1 Cor. 9:26 (a) There are those who seem to go through life like a butterfly. When the butterfly leaves the flower, you never can tell where it is going. It flies in an erratic way, here and there, and not "as the crow flies." Many people live the same way. They are in church one Sunday, and in the theater the next Sunday. They are for some kinds of religion, and also for some kinds of sin. They are headed nowhere, and make no progress in life. The exhortation in this passage is to have a godly and good goal in life, and make every effort to arrive at it.

1 Cor. 14:8 (a) Here we see the picture of many preachers and teachers of the Bible. When they finish their message, you do not know what point they were making. They give no clear explanation of the gospel, nor do they reveal God's truth about Christ. No wonder the people who listen to such preaching have no peace in their hearts, and no knowledge of God in their souls.

1 Tim. 6:17 (a) It has been proved many times that riches do not bring the peace and the blessing that was expected of them. One wealthy man who lost a great deal of money was asked, "Do you not worry about the money you have lost?" He answered, "No, it was my money that got me into trouble." Misery and money often go together.

UNCIRCUMCISED

This word is applied in a number of ways, but always with the thought of being antagonistic to God, rebelling against His rule, and refusing His authority. All peoples who were not Jews are called in the Bible "the uncircumcised."

Ex. 6:12, 30 (a) Moses evidently thought he knew God so little, and also was among the enemies of Pharaoh, that his message would not be acceptable to Pharaoh, and would lack authority. He had rejected the power of Egypt, and he had no official promotion to be God's messenger in the sight of Pharaoh, and therefore he spoke as he did about his own lips. It is a figure of one who speaks without knowing God's restraining and transforming power. Moses evidently felt that this was his condition.

Lev. 19:23 (a) The food in this case was reckoned to be unacceptable to God or to men. God ordained that this particular food should be classed as outside the realm of His acceptance, and could not be used either as an offering to God, or as useful fruit to men.

Lev. 26:41 (a) These hearts were at enmity with God. They had not been subject to the law of God, and were in rebellion against God.

Jer. 6:10 (b) This figure is used to denote that these people had not been converted from the things of earth to the things of God. They had no desire to hear God's voice. They refused His commands. Their fleshly desires were not cut off so that godly desires could be developed.

Ezek. 44:7, 9 (a) These hearts and these people have never come under the judgment and the will of God as represented by circumcision. They therefore were reckoned to be enemies of God, and were not permitted to be in the house of God.

Acts 7:51 (a) The hearts and the ears of these people were not subject to the law of God, nor had they believed the Word of God. They refused to hear God's Word and refused to love the Lord of glory. Circumcision was a sign of obedience and confidence.

Rom. 2:25, 26 (a) Circumcision was a physical evidence of submission to God. It very frequently failed to prove the true condition of the heart. If a man was circumcised and rebelled against God, his circumcision was rejected. If, however, an uncircumcised man kept the law of God, he was accepted because his heart was right.

Col. 2:13 (a) The Lord uses this figure to describe the condition of the unsaved man. His soul was dead to God, and he was disobedient to God's laws.

UNCLEAN

Isa. 6:5 (a) The reference is to the fact that the prophet felt that his words were not what they should be; his messages were not as clear and true as they should be. He felt that from his lips came some things that did not have God's approval. He realized that this also was true of the Israelites among whom he dwelt.

Isa. 64:6 (b) This word reveals our condition before God in relationship to Him and others. What we are and what we say very often defiles other people. What we are naturally in our sins prevents us from coming into God's holy presence. We defile holy things when we contact them in our natural state.

Hag. 2:13 (b) Our Lord is revealing to us that holiness and godliness cannot be transmitted to another by contact. Sinful things are transmitted to others easily. The saved father and mother do not pass on their godly character in Christ to their children, but they certainly do pass on their evils to their children.

Acts 10:28 (a) The "animals" that Peter saw in the sheet represent peoples who had been cleansed by the sacrifice of Christ, the blood had put away their evil, and they were fit for heaven. The Lord shows them in the sheet as animals because that was our natural state. Now Peter is to be sent to the Gentiles, who were considered only as unclean animals in the sight of the Jews. Peter was being taught that every man is eligible to be made clean by the gospel of our Lord Jesus Christ. None are excluded. (See Acts 11:8) In this passage Peter is referring to foods that God permitted to be eaten, and other foods which were prohibited. He was very careful about keeping all the law.

Rom. 14:14 (c) In this passage the word seems to be used to indicate our thoughts about various matters in the Christian life. The converted Jew thinks that pork is unclean for him to eat, and he refuses it. The devout Catholic thinks that all meat is unclean on certain occasions. These words indicate the attitude of mind toward certain matters which are given prominence in some religions.

2 Cor. 6:17 (a) The unclean people here represent all unsaved people of every kind no matter how nice, beautiful or religious. Only those who have been born again, saved by grace, and washed in the blood of the Lamb, are reckoned as "clean" in God's sight. They have been given the gift of righteousness.

Rev. 18:2 (b) Birds in the Scripture are usually connected with Satan and his angels. This Scripture is informing us that the great apostate religions, and evil religious systems of the world are occupied by demons who control the teachings and the practices of those religions.

UNCLOTHED

2 Cor. 5:4 (a) By this we understand the state of the spirit after it leaves the body. The body is represented as the clothing of the spirit. Four times in the Old Testament we read that "the spirit of God clothed Himself with . . ." The person becomes the house in which the Spirit of God lives. That person is always and only one who belongs to the Lord, and has been redeemed by the blood of the Lamb.

UNCOVER

Isa. 47:3 (a) The Lord is informing Israel that He will strip them as a nation so that their conveniences will be taken from them, their comforts of living, their prestige and power, and they will be left helpless before their enemies. (See also Jer. 49:10)

UNDONE

Isa. 6:5 (a) This is a type of a cake that is only partially cooked. Isaiah realized that he was not what he should be in God's sight, and he cried out for more of that which would enable him to be conformed to the will of God. This thought is expressed also in Hosea 7:8.

UNEQUAL

2 Cor. 6:14 (a) The yoke that is used on animals is always an equal one. It should not be larger on one side than on the other. It is not to be put on a large animal and a small one together. The ox and the ass were not to be yoked together, for it would be an unequal yoke. So the Christian and the sinner, the unsaved person, are not to be joined together in marriage, in business, or in anything that constitutes a yoke, for they are not equal.

UNFRUITFUL

1 Cor. 14:14 (a) It represents a mind that is educated, but not along lines that will produce good results. It indicates a zeal that is not supported by knowledge.

Eph. 5:11 (a) By this we understand works which produce no good results for God. These are activities which do not result in spiritual blessings. Usually it is religious works which have no spiritual significance, and produce no value in the soul.

UNGODLY

Psa. 1:1 (b) This word has the same meaning in every place where it is used. The prefix "un" means to be without. Joined to the word "godly," it means that the person, the nation or the subject under consideration is without God. The ungodly person may be beautiful in character, attractive in manner, cultivated, refined and educated, but he is living without God. He has no faith in God, and may be rebellious toward God. He may be quite religious in his outward actions, and yet have no knowledge personally of Jesus Christ. Such a person is *un*-godly.

UNHOLY

Heb. 10:29 (a) Certain Jews considered the blood of Jesus to be in direct opposition to the blood of the sacrifices, and was therefore not of God and not to be accepted by them.

UNICORN

Num. 24:8 (a) The power and strength of Israel in her prosperity is represented by this animal. We do not know just what animal it was, but from the description it must have been some prehistoric monster built like the rhinoceros. From the fact that it had just one horn, we may understand that this represents just the one Person who could strengthen and use Israel, and that one was their God.

Deut. 33:17 (a) This figure represents one who has unusual strength and power. It probably represents Joseph, with his great influence for the benefit of his children.

Psa. 22:21 (b) Here we see the figure which is used by our Lord to represent the terrible power of His enemies, who had Him under their control and were putting Him to death at Calvary.

Psa. 92:10 (b) This describes the great power and invincible might which the Psalmist knew would be his because he believed God, and walked with Him.

UNLEAVENED

1 Cor. 5:7 (a) Since the word is used to describe the bread in which there is no fermenting yeast, so now it is used to describe the church in which there are no ungodly sinners, none of the Devil's children, but only those who have been washed in the blood of the Lamb, made pure and beautiful in Christ. No evil doctrines would be permitted in such a church.

UNREPROVEABLE

Col. 1:22 (a) This word has a very interesting meaning for the Christian. It means that there will be no final examinations at the end of the journey. Our Lord Jesus is so effective in His work in the soul that the person is completely prepared in this life for the entrance into God's presence. The Christian does not get an examination, when he dies, to see where he is going. That point is settled the moment Jesus Christ becomes the Lord and the Saviour of the believer.

UNRIPE (grapes)

Job 15:33 (b) This describes the unfinished labor and the untimely destruction of the works of wicked men.

UNSHOD

Jer. 2:25 (b) The Lord is inviting His people to be well equipped for the journey through life. The feet should be shod with the preparation of the gospel of peace. We should have shoes of iron and brass because the road will be rough.

UNSKILLFUL

Heb. 5:13 (a) Many of God's people who know their Bibles fairly well are not skillful in using them. What is written in the Word is clear, but how to use the message to help others is not clear. The Lord wants us both to know what He says in His Word, and also how to use His Word effectively and helpfully in the hearts of others.

UNSPOTTED

Jas. 1:27 (b) This is a picture of the defilement which the Christian may encounter during his day's duties as he mingles and mixes in a world filled with sin. The Lord would have us guard our lives daily lest we be contaminated by the evils that surround us.

UNSTABLE

Jas. 1:8 (b) Many Christians are not rooted and grounded in the truth of God; therefore, they vacillate and change with the winds of doctrine, and with altered circumstances.

2 Pet. 3:16 (a) The term is used to describe those who are easily swayed by emotion, circumstances and false teachers. They do not stand their ground under pressure, or under the cunning schemes of evil men.

UNTEMPERED

Ezek. 13:10 (b) The term is taken from building materials to describe careless methods or wrong teachings in building God's people as a nation. Faulty building materials will not stand the test of the storms of years. They will crumble under pressure. So, the nation of Israel, and also the church, must be built according to God's provisions and His divine will. (See also Ezek. 22:28)

UNTIMELY

Psa. 58:8 (b) It may be that this refers to the premature disaster and death which will overtake the wicked in their sinful ways. They are cut off by the Lord because of their wickedness and their rebellion against Him.

USURY

Matt. 25:27 (a) The Lord gives to His children and to His servants certain gifts and talents. He expects these to be put into use so that they will increase in value and in quantity. It is this increase that is termed "usury." Many gifts are given to Christians, and they should be used for the glory of God in the lives of others. (See also Luke 19:23)

V

VAIL

Isa. 25:7 (b) This is typical of the blindness which Satan has brought over the minds and hearts of the Gentile nations. It is described more fully under the figure of blindness in 2 Cor. 4:4.

2 Cor. 3:14 (a) This represents the peculiar unbelief which fills the hearts and minds of the people of Israel as they read the Old Testament and cannot see Christ depicted there.

Heb. 6:19 (b) The word is used to describe that mysterious space that separate us from God, but through which by faith we come to God.

VALLEY

Psa. 23:4 (b) David describes in this way the deep sorrow and perplexity which comes upon a person as he nears the portals of death. It may refer also to the times of deep sorrow and trouble through which persons pass along life's pathway.

S. of Sol. 2:1 (c) No doubt this is descriptive of the deeply distressing experiences of life into which the Lord brings the fragrance of His presence, the comfort of His words, and the sweetness of His fellowship to His own people. We should note that the word is in the plural, for there are many valleys between the cradle and the grave.

Isa. 22:1 (c) This probably represents the feelings of the prophet when he was depressed in spirit, and felt quite crushed beneath the burden of Israel's future. He was looking forward to the terrible destruction that awaited His people and it brought him low before the Lord.

Isa. 40:4 (c) It may be that this is literal, and yet it may indicate that deep sorrows and perplexities may be overcome and great difficulties may be removed. It probably is a figure of the smooth, blessed life in which Christians may walk when God is present in power. (See also Luke 3:5)

Jer. 2:23 (a) It seems as though these enemies of God were hiding in secret places to carry out their wicked designs. Where there should have been happiness under God's blessing, they were sinning and inviting God's wrath.

Ezek. 37:1 (a) God sees all the nation of Israel as gathered together in one place, and that a low place. We see Israel scattered all over the world, and found in every country. No doubt they are in the valley, for they are the subjects of other people when they should be citizens of their own country, with their own king. God sees all of Israel, every person of Israel as though they were in one place constituting one unit. (See under "BONES") for a description of this truth found in this passage.)

VAPOUR

Jas. 4:14 (a) This describes the transient character of our lives. We live for a while and are known in the community, then we die, and we are soon forgotten. We move from one house to another part of the city, and in a very short time those in the old neighborhood forget that we ever lived there; even the name is forgotten. (See Lam. 4:8)

VENOM

Deut. 32:33 (b) This describes the evil and wicked effect of Israel's activities as they worshiped idols and forsook the Lord.

VESSEL

Psa. 31:12 (a) It is used by David to describe his feelings of weakness and unfitness for the great position he occupied as a leader of God's people.

Prov. 25:4 (b) God will remove evil things from our lives in order to make us fit for the Master's use.

Isa. 66:20 (a) The teaching is that Israel will again become the repository of God's truth.

Jer. 18:4 (a) Israel has been marred by sinful practices, and individuals have suffered in the same way. God would like to make each of His children a vessel meet for His purposes and use, but wicked ways and sinful practices hinder. (See also chap. 22, vs. 28) (See also Rom. 9:22, 23)

Jer. 48:11 (a) Moab had one success after another and had not been defeated nor suffered from other calamities. For this reason he became full of pride and self-sufficiency. The vessels evidently represent troubles of different kinds. Moab had experienced none of them.

Jer. 51:34 (a) This king had taken away the wealth of Israel and ruined the crops. Israel is the vessel mentioned in the passage.

Hosea 8:8 (a) It describes the failure of Israel to be a receptacle for God's glory and God's Word.

Hosea 13:15 (b) These vessels represent the excellent qualities of the leaders of Israel which God would take away and destroy.

Matt. 13:48 (c) This probably is descriptive of heaven and the various mansions into which God's people will be gathered when they go to be with the Lord.

Matt. 25:4 (b) It may mean that these wise virgins were really in touch with heaven, and all of God's supply of the Spirit. The other five had simply been worked upon by the Spirit, whereby certain good results had been obtained, but not that complete act of linking them with heaven and God, called the "new birth."

Luke 8:16 (a) No real Christian will hide his light, nor smother his testimony under his business enterprises, nor in laziness. (See also Matt. 5:15; Mark 4:21)

Acts 9:15 (a) This is a beautiful type of Paul, and of any other believer into whom the Lord has put His Spirit. God makes the believer the receptacle for the gifts and graces of the Spirit for the use and glory of His great name. (See also 2 Cor. 4:7)

2 Tim. 2:20 (a) These vessels represent people. The vessels unto honor are those in the parlor, made of gold, silver and expensive china. The vessels unto dishonor are those in the kitchen that are used for cooking and other purposes. These represent two kinds of Christians; the beautiful ones with lovely attractive lives are like the vase in the parlor and have little value to the household, and are not usually useful. Those in the kitchen attract little attention, if any, but they are of the most use to the family. It would be easier to get along without those in the parlor than those in the kitchen. The Lord is telling us that if we purge ourselves from the evils described in the first part of the chapter, then we shall be clean vessels that are fit for God's use and will be beautiful in His sight.

1 Pet. 3:7 (a) It is emblematic of the position occupied by the wife in whom reposes precious graces which she sweetly expresses in her home to make the presence of God felt there.

Rev. 2:27 (a) The Lord compares His destruction of the enemy to that destruction which the potter executes upon a vessel that is not made right.

VIAL

Rev. 5:8 (a) These golden receptacles are evidently pictures of the value our Lord places upon the worship and the prayers which ascend to God from the hearts of His children. None of the prayers are lost. They are kept as valuable treasures.

Rev. 15:7 (a) These golden receptacles contain God's wrath. The lesson we learn is that the wrath of God is just as precious and valuable as His mercy and grace. We give just as much honor to the judge who properly punishes the guilty as we give when the innocent is set free. His wrath is preserved as a treasure in the golden casket. This wrath is poured out in the next chapter, verses 1 and 2. (See also Rev. 17:1)

VINE

This plant is used as a type of the nation of Israel, and of other nations. Sometimes it is spoken of as a good vine, and in other passages as a vine that was unprofitable and that brought forth evil fruit. God speaks of this vine as His own planting, when it refers to Israel. He expected it to bring forth good fruit that would be for His glory, and would bring joy to His heart. Instead of doing so, it brought forth evil fruit in most of the cases where it refers to Israel.

Gen. 49:11 (b) This vine is Israel. Judah was tied to Israel by blood bonds, and his children also bore the same relationship.

Deut. 32:32 (a) The vine in this case refers to the wicked cities of Sodom and Gomorrah. It is in contrast with what they should be, the vine of Israel. God is telling us that Israel had become so corrupt that they were more like those two wicked cities than like His city, and their works were as evil as those of Sodom.

Judg. 9:12 (b) Jotham is telling the people of Israel that they have invited a weak, helpless person to be their king, because he considered that Abimelech was an incompetent man.

Psa. 80:8 (a) The nation of Israel is compared to the vine. God brought them from Egypt and placed them in the land of Palestine. They replaced the heathen nations whom God enabled Joshua to conquer.

Psa. 128:3 (a) In this case the wife is compared to a vine because she would be beautiful in her life, and fruitful in her conduct. Children would be born into the family, and they would be a blessing to the mother, to the father, and to the nation.

Jer. 2:21 (a) Here we read the sad lament of the Lord because of the evil conduct of His people. The vine is Israel. They did not act like a good vine bearing grapes, but as an evil vine, bearing useless fruit, or poisonous fruit.

Ezek. 17:6 (b) This vine is probably the apostate Kingdom of Israel. The first great eagle, the King of Babylon, invaded Israel and took some of the people away as captives to his own land. The second eagle was the King of Egypt. Israel sent messengers to Egypt to obtain help, but Egypt failed and Israel was destroyed. It is a wonderful allegory which is described in verses 12 to 18. (See also Isa. 5:2; Jer. 2:21; Ezek. 15:2)

Hosea 10:1 (a) God expected fruit from His people Israel. He received none. Israel turned to idolatry and to wicked practices learned from the people of the land. They served themselves, and satisfied their own lusts, while God's Word was neglected, and His service ignored.

John 15:1 (a) In this case the Lord Jesus Himself is the vine. Those who are saved by His grace are the branches. God sees the believer as a very part of Christ Jesus Himself. The branch bears the likeness of the vine, and has the same living sap flowing through it constantly. It bears the kind of fruit that characterizes the vine. All the fruit on the vine is found on the branches. Let us be bearing fruit for Him.

Rev. 14:18 (a) This vine refers to the people of the earth of every kindred and nation who are enemies of God, enemies of Israel, and reject the authority of Jesus Christ.

VINEYARD

Deut. 22:9 (c) This vineyard represents any field of service in which the soul winner seeks to sow the seed of the Word of God. The Lord is warning against mixing truths or doctrines in any service. If one Sunday-school teacher is teaching her class the true gospel of salvation by grace alone, and the teacher in the next class is teaching salvation by morals or forgiveness by merit, then there is little expectation of gathering a crop for God. The seeds are mixed. If the farmer sows wheat in his field, but another one sows weeds in among the wheat, there will be no wheat crop gathered. The weeds will succeed. Corn is planted by itself, and potatoes by themselves, and wheat by itself. So it must be with God's gospel. It must be taught and given where there will be an opportunity for a crop.

Psa. 80:15 (a) The vineyard is God's people gathered as a nation in Palestine. The vines are the individual Jews.

S. of Sol. 1:6 (c) In this strange passage, probably there is some irony. The people rather often during the life of Christ indicated that they believed He could do wonderful things. Some acknowledged Him as a sovereign ruler. Others indicated their faith in His power. He was not allowed, however, to be the ruler of His people Israel, to deliver them from their enemies, and to be their Messiah. They rejected His Lordship, although they claimed to be the people of God.

Isa. 1:8 (b) The vineyard is the nation of Israel, and the daugh ter represents the people in that nation. They were desolate because they had rejected the Lord of their lives.

Matt. 20:1 (b) This type represents any field of labor where God may place His servants to labor for Him.

Matt. 21:33 (b) The vineyard is Israel, the householder is God Himself, the husbandmen are the rulers and leaders of the nation of Israel. (See also Mark 12:1; Luke 13:6; Luke 20:9)

VIPER

Isa. 59:5 (b) This indicates the product of the works and the plans of wicked Israel in producing evil and harmful results.

Matt. 3:7 (a) This type represents wicked teachers whose messages from their mouths poison those who hear them so that they are eternally lost. Not all snakes are vipers. Vipers are snakes which kill with the poison from their fangs, such as the cobra and the rattlesnake. Vipers are a type of false teachers of false cults, who damage and destroy the souls of all who believe their teachings. (See also Matt. 23:33; Luke 3:7)

VIRGIN

2 Ki. 19:21 (a) Our Lord uses this expression to describe the duty, the sweetness and the loveliness of the children of Israel in His sight. It was used to show the enemy how He despised them, and loved Israel. (See also Isa. 37:22; Jer. 14:17; Jer. 18:13; Jer. 31:4)

Isa. 47:1 (a) In derision our Lord calls this wicked city by that beautiful name of virgin. He knew and they knew how wicked the city was, and He used this name in derision.

Jer. 46:11 (a) Again our Lord speaks in derision of the evil nation of Egypt which was living in wickedness and sin, and was held up to ridicule by the God of Israel.

Matt. 25:1 (b) Probably these women are called virgins to represent that they are professing Christians. It is generally thought by Bible students that five of these represent true Christians, who are real believers, and the other represent professing Christians, who are not really saved.

VOICE

This word is usd to describe many sounds and noises. It is not always a human voice that is intended.

Ex. 4:8 (a) God intended that this sign should carry a message to the hearts of all who observed it. It failed to do so. Pharaoh would not believe.

2 Sam. 22:14 (a) It is quite probable that the thunder was God's word of warning concerning His power and His might. (See also Job 40:9; Psa. 46:6; Psa. 77:18; Psa. 104:7)

Psa. 93:3 (a) The power of water, the irresistible waves, and the force of the flood are called the voice of God, because they are supposed to bring a warning message to the people of the power of God. (See also Jer. 10:13; Jer. 51:16; Ezek. 43:2; Rev. 1:15; Rev. 19:6)

VOMIT

Prov. 26:11 (a) Vomit is good food that has been mixed with the juices of the body, and is then thrown out for consumption by another. It represents doctrines that are taken from the Word of God into the human mind, are mixed with human ideas, and then given out for others to believe and accept. That which emanates from the pens and the lips of false teachers who present a false faith is "vomit" in the Bible sense of the word. (See also 2 Pet. 2:22)

VULTURE

Isa. 34:15 (b) This bird is a type of the voracious, hungry nations who are to come down on Idumea, and devour her assets.

W

WAGES

Hag. 1:6 (a) This is a reference to the results obtained from labor which in this case are not permanent. The wages are lost instead of saved because they are not invested for the glory of God.

John 4:36 (b) It refers to the eternal rewards which will be given to those who work for the Lord in His service. The reward of the wicked is found in Rom. 6:23.

2 Pet. 2:15 (b) Here we see the results of living a wicked life. It describes the satisfaction that is received by the sinner from yielding to evil desires. (See Rom. 6:23)

WALK

This word in its typical meaning refers to the manner of life and to the path pursued through life.

Gen. 24:40 (a) This man of God lived a life according to the will of God, and kept himself by faith in the presence of God. The same is true of Enoch as in Gen. 5:22. Also of Noah in Gen. 6:9.

1 Ki. 6:12 (a) The same thought is found in this passage. The manner of life of Israel was to be in observance of the Word of God, and the will of God, as revealed in the law. (See also Ezek. 33:15; Zech. 3:7)

Gal. 5:16 (a) Again the manner of life is described in this passage, as also in Eph. 5:2, and Eph. 5:8.

WALLOW

Jer. 6:26 (b) This type represents the attitude of deep humility before God because of sin. (See also Jer. 25:34)

2 Pet. 2:22 (b) Here we see a type of the wicked who revel in their own filthy sins and iniquities.

WASH

Jer. 4:14 (a) The cleansing of the soul and heart from evil sin is compared to a washing. It is the thought of taking advantage of the blood of the sacrifices, or of the Word of God, or of the Spirit of God, to put away things that are wrong in the sight of God in order that the person may be cleansed from the evil. It occurs many times throughout the Scriptures. (See also Job 29:6; Psa. 51:2, 7; Isa. 1:16; Jer. 2:22)

Matt. 27:24 (a) Pilate evidently thought that by this procedure he could take away the sin of his soul. He was using a Jewish custom.

Eph. 5:26 (b) The cleansing effect of the Word of God on the ways and activities of His Church is thus described.

1 Tim. 5:10 (b) This type represents any gracious hospitality rendered by a godly hostess to her Christian guest.

Heb. 10:22 (b) By this type is described the cleansing of the Word of God on the habits and activities of the person whose body is given to the Holy Spirit as His temple. (See also Psa. 119:9)

2 Pet. 2:22 (b) This represents the moral cleansing brought about in the lives of those who seek by their own efforts to get rid of their evil ways and habits, thinking that thereby they will be Christians. The pig that is washed still stays a pig.

Rev. 7:14 (b) It represents the act of faith whereby the believing sinner trusts in the Lord Jesus Christ who, by His own blood, makes the believer clean and white in God's sight.

WASHPOT

Psa. 60:8 (a) The mighty God of Israel is describing how completely He will conquer the country of Moab and make it to become His servant.

WATCH

Gen. 31:49 (b) In this way God describes His gracious supervision over His people individually and collectively.

Psa. 102:7 (b) Here we see the sorrow of soul in the Lord Jesus when He looked for some to take pity in His lonely sojourn and in the time of His great sorrow, only to find that all had forsaken Him and fled.

Psa. 130:6 (b) This is emblematic of an earnest heart's desire for the return of the Lord. (See also Matt. 24:42; 25:13; Mark 13:35; Luke 21:36; Acts 20:31)

Prov. 8:34 (b) This probably represents the attitude of heart wherein the soul seeks the Lord and expects constantly to see His face, and to hear His voice in sweet fellowship.

Mark 13:33 (b) This is an attitude of heart wherein one is attentive to the possibilities of Satan's hindrances and to the opportunities for serving Christ.

Heb. 13:17 (b) This is typical of the careful attention which the elders of the church should show for the welfare of those entrusted to their care in the church.

WATCHMAN

Psa. 127:1 (b) He is a type of the activity of a Christian leader in whom the power of God is lacking in his service.

Isa. 21:11 (b) This watchman represents the servant of God who faithfully brings God's message to the people, without changing it or altering it.

Ezek. 3:17 (b) In this case the watchman is a type of the prophet in Israel who is set to bring God's message of warning to the people. He watches for some word from heaven and then watches for the opportunities to deliver it.

WATER

This type is sometimes presented as a river as in Psa. 1:3; Ezek. 47:5; John 7:38. In these cases the water undoubtedly represents the Holy Spirit. It is plainly indicated. He is constantly working, blessing, enriching, and those who permit Him to be a living personal power in their lives do flourish for God, grow in grace, and bear much fruit.

This type is sometimes presented as a fountain, as in John 4:14. Again, the Spirit of God is the one thus described. He does not stay dormant in the soul, but works up and out in the life, and produces evidences of His presence.

Sometimes water is presented as a drink, as in John 7:37. This also represents the Holy Spirit, and we drink Him into our souls and lives, as the living Lord, who satisfies the cravings of the heart for the things of God. (See also 1 Cor. 12:13)

Prov. 11:25 (a) In this wonderful passage the Lord is telling us plainly that if we will give blessings to others, they in turn will give blessings to us.

Isa. 58:11 (a) The soul that is blessed by God, who walks with God, and loves the Word of God will be filled with joy and gladness, his life will be beautiful in character, and he will be a blessing to many. (See also Jer. 31:12)

Jer. 2:13 (b) Our Lord is the giver of the Holy Spirit who is the living Water. Those who turn away from God and refuse His life and His gifts find that the things in which they trust, and on which they lean, will fail them and they are left at the end of the journey with no peace, no eternal life, no hope, no joy, and only the outer dark.

1 Cor. 3:6 (a) The work of ministering the Word of God to others has a two-fold aspect. The seed is the Word of God, and Paul planted it. No seed, however, will grow without water, no matter how good the seed, nor fertile the soil. Therefore, Apollos came ministering the Spirit of God to those who had heard the

Word of God. The Holy Spirit is the water, and when He is present in power, recognized and trusted, then the seed of the Word of God grows and prospers in the hearts of the people.

Eph. 5:26 (b) This type represents the cleansing effect of the Word of God on the habits and ways of the people of God. As the Christian studies the Scripture against temper, he will become sweet-spirited. As he reads the Scriptural warning against liquor and profanity, he will avoid it. In this way, evil ways are cleansed from a Christian's life.

Jude 12 (b) Water is typical of the refreshment and blessing that should characterize the ministry of one who claims to be the servant of God. In this Scripture the blessing is lacking, and the message is dry and unfruitful.

WAVES

Psa. 42:7 (a) Our Lord Jesus in describing His second baptism said in Luke 12:50, "I have a baptism to be baptized with." He had already been baptized in water, but now He was to be baptized under the wrath of God. This passage in Psa. 42:7 describes His experience in going through that baptism. God's terrible judgment and the overwhelming sorrows which came from God's wrath poured over the soul of His Son at Calvary, where He died for us. It was His baptism under the wrath of God that saves our souls. (See also Jonah 2:3; 1 Pet. 3:21)

Psa. 65:7 (b) Waves are frequently used as a type of leaders among the people. The waves of the sea are made of the same material as the rest of the waters, but they merely rise to a greater height than the rest of the waters. So, the leaders of the people are made of the same material, and come up from among the other people. They simply rise higher in power, position and authority than others. They soon recede, and disappear. In this passage the Lord is telling us that the great boastings of the leaders will soon be made silent, and their voices will be heard no more. (See also Psa. 89:9; Psa. 107:29)

Psa. 88:7 (a) The Psalmist is comparing the punishing blows of God to the waves of the sea. They beat against him unmercifully. This Psalm was written by the "sons of Korah." It is recorded that Korah and his family, with the exception of his sons, went down alive into hell. That was a terrible blow, and it may be that the sons are referring to this in the passage before us.

Isa. 48:18 (b) This type represents the honor and power conferred by the Lord upon those who are true to His Word, and who live for His glory.

Jude 13 (b) These waves are typical of ungodly leaders who, in their hatred of the Lord, and their enmity against the church, become vociferous in their denunciations, and seek wide publicity for their ungodly teachings.

WAX

Psa. 22:14 (b) In this peculiar way the Lord describes His feelings when stricken with the terrible agony, sorrow and grief at Calvary. He was becoming as wicked as we, and it brought about these terrible feelings in His righteous soul.

WAY

This word is used to describe the manner of life which is lived by both saved and unsaved. Sometimes it is a good way called the "narrow way." Sometimes it is the road which the wicked travel down to destruction. Some samples are given of these two ways.

Gen. 24:42 (a) The servant of Abraham is referring to the path he took and the course he pursued in carrying out the instructions of Abraham. (See v. 27.)

Psa. 110:7 (b) This is a reference to the life of our Lord as He walked through the desolate scenes of earth. He refreshed His heart from the ministry of the Spirit and communion with His Father.

Psa. 119:1 (b) By this is described the general path of life which the Christian enters at the new birth and pursues on his way to heaven. Christianity is a way of living, a manner of life. (See also Acts 9:2)

Psa. 119:29 (a) There are those who persistently live a life of deceit in seeking to obtain position, power and wealth. This is the course referred to in this verse. (See also Psa. 139:24)

Prov. 14:12 (a) Satan is very clever in devising a path of life that seems to be the right way to heaven. Every false religion teaches one of the ways of Satan. These paths or programs appear to be all right to the person who does not know God, nor the teachings of the Scriptures. Everyone of these paths of living are opposed to the one way which is Christ Jesus. Every one is a substitute for Christ Jesus. These seem right to men, but they end in hell. (See also Prov. 16:25)

Isa. 59:8 (a) God has a path for His people in which peace with God rules and reigns. It is a way of rest in which Christ blots out the sins, God the Father justifies the soul, the Holy Spirit directs the path, and there is no fretting nor worrying. It is God's path for every one of His children. (See also Rom. 3:17)

John 14:6 (a) Here we see a beautiful description of the Person of the Lord Jesus Christ, the only one who can bring us to the Father. He only can make us fit for heaven, He only has the right and the power to take us to God.

WEANED

Psa. 131:2 (a) The heart of the Psalmist, and his life, had been so changed by God that he lived in heavenly places and walked with his Lord separate from the world. His desires were heavenly, and not earthly. His plans were for God's glory, and not his own. Unsaved people obtain their satisfaction and promote their plans for the blessings of earth. At salvation we are weaned from that source of blessing, and our affections are set on things above.

WEAPON

Isa. 13:5 (a) God describes His anger and His power as being weapons of destruction against His enemies. Sometimes it is pestilence, and sometimes famine. It might be disease, or the invading army. It might be the plague of locusts, frogs or flies. God knows how best to punish those who oppose Him. (See Jer. 50:25)

Jer. 51:20 (a) This type is used to describe the nation of Babylon which God used as an instrument for destroying other nations that were rebellious against Him, including Israel.

2 Cor. 10:4 (b) This is descriptive of the gifts and graces of the Spirit; the spiritual armour, the spiritual sword, the Word of God, prayer, zeal, wisdom, godliness, earnestness, knowledge of the Word of God, all of these are used by the believer to defeat the enemies of our souls.

WEAVE

Isa. 59:5 (a) The Lord in this place describes the labors, schemes and plans of religious people to manufacture a protection for themselves against the wrath of God, while ignoring God's way and God's plan. The failure of these plans is as sure as the failure of the spider's web to protect from an enemy.

WEB

Job 8:14 (a) In this typical way the Lord describes the frail and worthless character of the expedience used by the unsaved as a false trust for future peace. (See also Isa. 59:5-6)

WEDDING

Matt. 22:3 (a) Our Lord is referring in this passage to the meeting between a sinner and his Saviour individually, and perhaps also between the church and her Lord collectively. When the individual comes to the Lord Jesus, falls in love with Him and trusts Him, it is described as a marriage, as in Rom. 7:4. When the church is caught up to meet the Lord in the air to be actually, personally and physically in His presence forever, that also is described as a marriage, as in Rev. 19:7. Everything has been prepared by the

Lord Jesus, both for the reception of the individual, and for the reception of the entire church. He invites everyone to come and gives a royal welcome and rich provision to those who do come. (See also Luke 12:36)

WEIGHT

Job 6:2 (a) Certain it is that the loving God of heaven knows just how much sorrow we can bear. He says about our griefs, pains and troubles "thus far shalt thou go, and no farther." He never deals unjustly with His people.

Psa. 58:2 (a) It seems that these wicked men planned deliberately to accomplish certain evil purposes, and decided on the limits of their wicked plans and intentions.

Isa. 26:7 (a) God is well acquainted with every detail of our lives, and He knows the value of what we are doing, what we are saying, where we are going, and our manner of life. He makes a record of this to use at the Judgment Seat.

Isa. 40:12 (a) It is an actual fact that all chemical elements are put together by weight, and not by volume. So, in every mountain and hill, the chemicals that compose that mass of earth are put together by weight, and thus are made the various compounds found there. In addition to this, God must know the weight of the mountains, because the earth is a ball and must rotate on an axis without bursting and flying to pieces. It is well known that nothing will rotate safely on an axis unless it is perfectly balanced. Our Lord has therefore determined exactly the weights of the mountains, the plains, the oceans, and every part of this earth in order that it may rotate safely.

Dan. 5:27 (a) Before we die, and while we are still living, God estimates the value and the worth of each soul. This king had been placed in God's scales while he was still living and serving on the throne. The estimate of his value was made before he died. This is true of every human being. The decision concerning our destiny is made by God while we are still living. This should make us seriously consider our relationship to God.

WELL

Gen. 21:19 (c) We may use this as a type of that sweet experience of the soul wherein the desolate and distracted Christian finds precious truths in the Word of God. Water may represent blessed promises, in which relief and refreshment are found.

Gen. 24:11 (c) We may consider this as a type of the Word of God and the Spirit of God. The believer, living in the blessings of both of these, may expect to be led into paths of profit and usefulness in his journey. (See also Gen. 49:22)

Psa. 84:6 (a) It is the privilege of the child of God, to turn deserts into gardens. Many times in our lives dry, deserted valleys are changed into sweet, rich mountain tops of joy and peace, as the grace of God is seen and experienced.

Prov. 5:15 (a) This well refers to the privileges and blessings of one's own home. There, with the wife of his youth, he may enjoy all that his heart desires, instead of seeking for satisfaction elsewhere.

Prov. 10:11 (a) The Lord expects that the man of God will be a source of rich blessing for his neighbors, and those who observe him, or have contact with him. Out of the life of the godly man there should emanate the blessings of helpfulness, sympathy and kindness which enrich the lives of others.

Isa. 12:3 (a) There are unlimited treasures found in the Christian life. They are called "wells" in this passage, because they bring untold blessings to the hearts of the people of God who come into God's family. These may consist of love, joy, peace, rest, comfort, happiness, gladness, zeal, vision, confidence and trust. Faith is prominent and greatly enriches the life. Fruitfulness also is present and the life becomes radiant with usefulness. These are the wells of salvation. Let us drink deeply from them.

John 4:14 (a) This is plainly a type of the Holy Spirit abounding abundantly in the soul of the Christian. When He is acknowledged and given the place of Lordship in the heart and life, He will make His presence felt. He fills the heart with the joy of the Lord, and sweet hopefulness in service.

2 Pet. 2:17 (b) This type beautifully represents the ungodly leader or teacher who has a religious message, but with no power from heaven, and no life for those who listen. He may have a muscular christianity, with lots of noise, illustrations and activities, but he gives no living water to those who listen. He disappoints his hearers.

WELLSPRING

Prov. 16:22 (a) God gives a fertile brain and an understanding heart so that we may draw from it the needed help for every problem and need that arises. Of course, there are many who do not have such a mind, and therefore are of little value to society. (See also Prov. 18:4)

WEN

Lev. 22:22 (c) This may be considered as a type of any defect in the Christian's life which would hinder him from being a true servant of God, faithful, useful and devoted to the Lord.

WHALE

Ezek. 32:2 (b) This great fish is a type of the nations that swallowed Israel, will keep them suffering in bondage, and afterwards expel them out of the many countries back into their own land. This type is seen more graphically illustrated in the book of Jonah. Egypt was one of those nations that endeavored to swallow up Israel.

Matt. 12:40 (b) This again is a type of the nations of the world who have swallowed up Israel, but have not been able to digest her, nor absorb her. One day all the nations will expel the Jewish people, and send them back into their own land.

WHEAT

Psa. 81:16 (c) We may learn from this that those who harken to the Lord and seek to obey His Word may expect to receive God's richest blessings that will make them strong, able and happy Christian servants. (See also Psa. 147:14)

Jer. 23:28 (a) The wheat in this case represents the Word of God, while the chaff represents the ideas, notions and dreams of men.

Matt. 3:12 (a) Our Lord Jesus, as well as others, used "wheat" as a type of Christians, believers in the Lord Jesus. The chaff represents hypocrites, who are raised among the wheat, and close to the wheat, but never become "wheat." In the final day, God takes the Christians (the wheat) into His home in glory, while the unsaved are shut out. (See also Luke 3:17)

Matt. 13:25 (a) The grain in this verse represents the Word of God as the wheat, and false doctrines and false writings as the tares. There are always those in every community who would bring evil doctrines in among God's people in order to hinder the salvation of souls. The field in which these mixed seeds are sown is the world. In God's true church, only the precious Word of God is preached and taught.

John 12:24 (a) This grain is the Lord Jesus Himself. He was cut down and was buried, but came forth from the tomb to produce a tremendous crop of believers for eternity.

WHEEL

Psa. 83:13 (a) We may believe that it is a type of a rolling, moving mass, with no anchorage, no certain dwelling place, and no goal. It describes the enemies of God, and their fickle character.

Eccl. 12:6 (c) It is generally believed that this refers to the human heart which fails at the end of the journey, and therefore cannot again pump the blood. It occurs in the midst of the story of old age in which various parts of the body become unfit for service.

Jer. 18:3 (a) This type represents the processes of God wherein He molds and shapes either a person or a nation into the kind of vessel He desires. It represents the training He gives, and sometimes the whipping necessary in order that He may obtain the result He wishes to have.

Ezek. 1:15 (b) Wheels always represent progress, motion, purpose, accomplishment. In this Scripture the wheels represent the power of God in action. The wheel within a wheel represents the inner motions, purposes and desires of our Lord within Himself. These cause the outer actions which we see, and which are represented by the big wheels. The rims of these wheels reach unto heaven to inform us that the purposes and works of God are higher than ours, too high for our comprehension. The eyes on the wheels represent the omniscience of the Spirit of God, who knows full well what He is doing, and understands all the purposes of God. He sees the end from the beginning, and nothing is hidden from His sight. (See also Dan. 7:9)

WHELP

Gen. 49:9 (a) This type represents Judah as the offspring of Jacob. Jacob is the lion, and Judah is his puppy. Jacob is informing us that he has imparted to Judah his own cunning, power, knowledge of God and ability.

Job 4:11 (c) Probably this type may represent the descendants of great men, especially kings. These sons do not have the power of their father, but are scattered, persecuted and killed by their enemies.

Ezek. 19:2 (a) The Lord describes the children of Israel's kings and leaders as being nourished and brought up as wild animals, rebellious against God, and fierce in their attitudes. They should have been as lambs, raised among the sheep, but were wild instead.

Ezek. 19:3 (a) This young lion was the King of Israel who was taken prisoner by Pharaoh and carried in chains into Egypt. His name was Jehoahaz whose mother was Hamutal.

Ezek. 19:5 (a) The whelp mentioned in this verse was the king of Israel whose name was Jehoiakim. He was captured by the King of Babylon and was carried as a prisoner to Babylon.

Nahum 2:11 (b) This type represents the generals of the Assyrian army who lived and are called "old lions." The captains and other officers who worked under these generals are called "young lions."

WHET

Deut. 32:41 (a) In this way our Lord describes the preparations which He makes for executing judgment upon His enemies. He prepares the disaster Himself, and executes His plans deliberately. (See also Psa. 7:12)

Psa. 64:3 (a) Evil men prepare cutting words and lying statements by which they intend to injure others. They meditate beforehand on their wicked statements.

WHIP

1 Ki. 12:11 (b) The expression is used to illustrate the burdens and distressing conditions imposed upon the people of Israel by King Solomon, who probably oppressed them by imposing severe taxes, and causing them to do difficult work.

Prov. 26:3 (c) We may use this type to describe the pressure which God sometimes brings upon His people to cause them to make progress in His service.

WHIRLWIND

Hosea 8:7 (b) We have proved that this is typical of the experience in the life of some of God's people. They indulge in sinful practices (the wind), but forget that the results may be tremendously great and damaging as a result of that indulgence (the whirlwind).

WHITE

Gen. 40:16 (b) This is a picture of the death of the baker. It typifies the absence of life, health, strength and vigor.

Lev. 13:3 (c) We may consider this as a type of the absence of life, nutriment and power. It fits in with the picture of leprosy as a type of sin and death to God.

Eccl. 9:8 (c) By this we may understand the purity and the beauty of the life of that one who walks with God in righteousness and godliness.

S. of Sol. 5:10 (c) In this way we may understand the sinless character of the Lord Jesus Christ in all His perfection. He was stainless, spotless, harmless and holy.

Isa. 1:18 (a) The blood of the Lord Jesus Christ removes all the stain of sin that is on the soul, and all the record of sin that is in the book.

Dan. 7:9 (b) Here is a beautiful type of the holiness of the Judge in whom is no spot nor shadow of turning. All His decisions are true, equitable, right and without prejudice. (See also Dan. 12:10)

Joel 1:7 (b) The prophet is expressing his great sorrow because his people have been spoiled and robbed by the invading enemy. Nothing is left of the beauty or the wealth of Israel. The enemy has taken it all.

Zech. 1:8 (b) It is generally thought among Bible students that the white horse represents famine in some cases, and power in other cases. In this passage, it seems to represent the famine that follows war, pestilence and drouth. (See also Zech. 6:6)

John 4:35 (b) The picture used by our Lord represents the culmination of the life of the sinner, wherein he is ready for the judgment, having run a full course of rebellion against God. It indicates also the preparation of a sinner's heart for judgment through the years in which he lived in his sins. It may represent also the sorrow, disappointment, ill health and other such troubles that prepare him for the grave. During all these times he has perhaps read gospel literature, been prayed for by his friends, and heard sermons which declared the gospel. All of these things working together have prepared the sinner for the reaping. The Lord indicates that he is ready now for the gospel, so that he will meet and trust the Saviour when Christ is preached.

Rev. 1:14 (a) This white hair indicates that the Lord Jesus is the Judge who is the Ancient of Days. He has had centuries of experience and therefore has knowledge and understanding more than others. He is the Eternal Judge, with omnipotent power.

Rev. 6:2 (b) Some Bible students believe that this represents the Lord Jesus going forth with power to conquer. Others believe it represents the power of famine which conquers men of all ages and positions in life.

Rev. 6:11 (b) These are evidently the robes of righteousness, pure and stainless, which are given to the saints of God because they are washed in the blood of the Lamb. This is quite evidently the meaning found in chapter 19, verse 8.

Rev. 20:11 (c) No doubt we are to understand that this Throne of God was not stained in any way by prejudice, injustice, unrighteousness or bribery. The judgments issued from it will be perfect in every espect.

WHOLE

This word is used to describe the perfection of the person as regards his physical condition. Those who were made whole were restored to their original condition of health and strength, with all damage removed, and all marks or evidences of disease taken away. The body was restored to normal. Those who were healed by our Lord Jesus were completely healed. Not only was the disease stopped, but the effects of the disease were removed. We do not see that type of divine healing exhibited today. When the maimed were made whole, the part of the body that had been lost was restored. They came to Christ with one leg, and went away with two. They came with one eye, and went away with two. They came with one arm, and went away with two. The Lord is not doing this today. Note the following Scriptures: Matt. 9:12; Matt. 15:31; Luke 6:10; Luke 7:10; John 5:14; Acts 9:34)

Luke 5:31 (b) There are those who think that they are so good, righteous and holy that they do not need the Saviour. These are the ones who are called "whole." Not until one realizes his sinful condition and his need of the power of God will he come to Jesus Christ for salvation, admitting that he is helpless and hopeless.

John 5:6 (c) Probably this is a type of the condition of Israel for the thirty-eight years during which they wandered in the wilderness. They too were helpless and hopeless. They needed God to work a miracle for them, and deliver them from their predicament. This man is a splendid picture of that great event.

WHORE

Jer. 3:3 (a) God is comparing the brazen effrontery of Israel to that type of a wicked woman. They sinned against God, and did not hide it. They rebelled against God's Word, and His law, with no regrets. (See also Ezek. 16:28)

Rev. 17:1 (a) God spares no language in exposing the wickedness of the great false religions of the world, and particularly that cruel, voracious one that has its seat and headquarters in Rome. This religion has corrupted the nations of the world through the centuries. It offers its followers pleasure and protection from God's wrath while taking from them their money, their persons, their possessions, and their souls. (See also Rev. 19:2; Rev. 17:15)

WIDOW

Lam. 1:1 (b) By this we understand the condition of Jerusalem and Israel who had turned their backs on God (the husband), and sought other lovers, idolatrous nations, upon whom they lavished their gifts and affections.

Rev. 18:7 (b) This is Babylon. It is a term which is used to describe the great unrighteous religious world, which boasts that she has sufficient prosperity and power to take care of herself. Because of this she denies that she is like a widow, who has no support, no one to love her, nor care for her. She really lives independent of God.

WIFE

Rev. 19:7 (b) This is a type of the church. Here we find the real Church of God, which has been prepared for the meeting with the Lord by the new birth, by redemption, and by salvation. She has also lived a godly life, filled with zealous service and trustful belief.

WILDERNESS

Psa. 102:6 (a) This type represents the lonely, desolate condition of the blessed Lord as He walked about among sinful men and wicked enemies on the earth. (See under PELICAN.)

Prov. 21:19 (a) It is better for one to go without many comforts, and to deny himself many pleasures if thereby he can live as he pleases. This is to be preferred to living the life with one who is constantly a source of sorrow and trouble to the heart.

Isa. 32:15 (b) This is a wonderful type of the barren Christian life, which is filled with sorrow, difficulty, disappointment and grief, but which, by the ministry of the Spirit, becomes a life filled with fruitfulness, beauty and joy.

Isa. 43:19 (b) This word describes the deliverance which God is able to bring into the tangled affairs of human life, straightens out the difficulties, delivers from perplexities, and brings His child safely through to a life of peace.

Rev. 12:6 (b) Probably this refers to the condition of Israel as scattered throughout the world, where they have weary feet, longing eyes, and heavy hearts. God will bring them out of this condition, and out of these nations, to inhabit again their own land.

Rev. 17:3 (b) This wilderness no doubt represents the various nations of the world in which the great apostate and religious system operates. This church produces nothing but tragedy and sin in the lives of the people who become members of their group. It really is a wilderness in every sense of the word.

WILLOW (tree)

Psa. 137:2 (c) We may use this as a type of sorrow in separation. Its drooping leaves and branches indicate the depressed and drooping spirit of those who have been separated from the things they love.

WIND

Job 7:7 (a) This poor man, in his affliction, felt that his life had no stability nor permanence. His soul was cast about with reasonings, philosophies and conclusions, which gave him no peace.

Psa. 135:7 (c) We may understand from this that the events that happen in our life which seem to be above and beyond our control, as is the wind, these come out of God's heart of love, because we are precious in His sight. He sees that these will be a blessing to us.

Prov. 11:29 (b) No doubt the writer referred to the transient character of that which falls to the lot of the evil man. If he stirs up trouble, it will come back on him twice fold.

Prov. 25:14 (a) There are those who claim to have great gifts, but when they stand before the audience, they fall flat. The audience is disappointed. The people expected great things from the advertising, but they wasted their time in listening to the speaker.

Eccl. 11:4 (b) We are advised in this passage to work diligently and earnestly at our work regardless of conditions and situations which seem to be unfavorable.

Isa. 26:18 (a) This remarkable illustration certainly fits in many cases. A meeting is advertised largely, the speaker is extolled for his ability, the proper music is arranged, the crowd has arrived, and then the whole meeting falls "flat." Things do not move smoothly, the speaker has no message worth listening to, and there is a general feeling that the meeting was an utter failure. This is the picture in this verse.

Ezek. 37:9 (a) In many cases throughout the Scripture, the Greek or Hebrew word for wind really refers to the Holy Spirit of God. It is so in this case, as is revealed in verse 14. The picture is quite clear, for the wind is not seen, and usually the Holy Spirit is not seen. The wind cannot be controlled, and neither can the Spirit. The wind is sent by God, and so is the Spirit. The wind has resistless power sometimes, and so does the Spirit. The wind is sometimes soft, balmy and delightful, and so is God's Spirit. The wind is necessary for cleansing the atmosphere, and the Holy Spirit is necessary for cleaning up our lives. He is "the Spirit of Life." He must be present to give Life Eternal.

Matt. 7:25 (b) Here the wind is an emblem of the adverse conditions that arise, with various density and force in the human life.

John 3:8 (a) As has already been described, the wind is a type of the Holy Spirit, in that it and He are invisible, and yet forcible. The wind is sovereign in its actions, uncontroled by human mandate, and undirected by human minds; so is the Spirit of God.

Eph. 4:14 (a) This indicates the strange power of evil teachings, which, in their sophistry and clever logic, lead away from the truth of the Scriptures into error, and a false faith.

Jude 12 (b) By this type we understand the many false religions and evil teachings which abound, which easily deceive the ungodly, and carry them off into false religions.

WINDOW

Isa. 24:18 (b) God uses this figure to describe the pouring out of the wrath of God from heaven as though one were shooting arrows or throwing stones from the apertures of a fort.

Mal. 3:10 (b) This type probably is based on the fact that the windows, or upper doors of the buildings, were often open to throw out feed for the animals. I have a photograph of a flock of sheep in a barnyard looking up at a closed window in a large barn, from which presently the farmer will throw out their feed. In like manner, God, in a spiritual way, opens up the windows of heaven to pour out great blessings and good things for His people. He expects us to be waiting under those windows, with large baskets, to receive the rich things which He will throw out. This is the truth represented in the above Scripture.

WINE

Gen. 49:11 (b) Jacob used this figure to describe the wonderful wealth that would accrue to Judah. It is similar to the statement by Job when he said "I washed my steps in butter." It is a description of great wealth, comfort and blessing.

Prov.9:2 (b) Probably this is typical of the sweet experiences of those who feel their own weakness, and then partake of the truths of God, as revealed in His precious Word.

Isa. 55:1 (b) This symbol represents the joy of the Christian life which God gives to those who trust Jesus Christ, and honor the Holy Spirit.

Matt 9:17 (b) This may be taken as a type of the new life which God does not put into the old nature. The Lord does not try to fix up "the old man." Instead He gives a new birth so that the new-born soul, with a new life and a new nature may enjoy heaven's blessings.

John 2:3 (c) We may take this wine to represent that peculiar joy and peace which only Christ can give to human hearts. The wedding is the sweetest of all human experiences, but even that could not be completely satisfactory unless Christ Jesus came to bring the peculiar blessing of heaven, which only He can give.

Rev. 16:19 (a) This wine represents the wrath of God which emanates from His own righteous heart, and is given to His enemies to drink. It is the product of the holy anger of the righteous Judge.

Rev. 17:2 (a) The wine in this case represents the evil practices of the apostate church. The teachings and the practices of this wicked group offers to the rulers of earth and to the great men of the lands pleasures and comforts in their lives of sin and wickedness. The nations receive the false teachings of this evil church which makes it easy to live in every kind of sinfulness, and yet be comforted by the assurance that the church can forgive. and has the power to send the soul to heaven.

WINEPRESS

Rev. 19:15 (a) This is typical of the acts of the Lord Jesus Christ wherein He will tread down all His enemies, crush His opponents, and in His anger would tread upon all those who live in rebellion against Him. It is the picture of grapes crushed in the vat as men trod upon them.

WING

Ex. 19:4 (a) How wonderfully our Lord took care of Israël through those rough days in the wilderness. They should have been at ease in their hearts and minds, as the baby bird is at rest on the mother's back. There should have been no fear. (See Deut. 32:11)

Ruth 2:12 (a) In this sweet way is described the precious feeling of comfort, rest and safety that is experienced by those who trust their lives to the Lord of glory, and rest their souls in His care. (See also Psa. 17:8; Psa. 63:7; Psa. 91:4)

Prov. 23:5 (a) Wealth, money and riches certainly do disappear, sometimes gradually, and sometimes suddenly. We may start out with a big bank account, but it gradually gets smaller and smaller until the tiny bit that is left disappears. This is as the eagle flies. It also gets smaller and smaller to the vision until it is lost in the skies. The eagle on our dollar certainly acts like this.

Ezek. 1:6 (b) These wings are emblematic of the great activity of the Lord Jesus, and the speed with which He works His will. This is indicated in the Gospel of Mark, the "servant" book, where we find the words "immediately," "at once," "forthwith," "straightway," as they occur constantly throughout that Gospel. (See also Rev. 4:8)

Ezek. 10:12 (a) These are the same wings referred to in Ezek. 1:6. The eyes indicate that these wings of power, speed and purpose are guided by the omniscience of the Holy Spirit who sees and knows, who directs and guides in all the activities of the Lord Jesus.

Ezek. 17:3 (b) The wings mentioned on these two eagles described in the passage represent speed, swiftness and ability in progress. These two kings (of Egypt and of Babylon) conquered easily and quickly the people of Israel, as the hawk swoops down onto its prey.

Dan. 7:4 (b) The lion represents the King of Babylon, and the wings represent the power and swiftness, as well as the ease with which this king operated his kingdom and conquered his enemies.

Dan. 7:6 (b) The leopard represents the King of Greece, Alexander the Great. The four wings represents the four generals who enabled him to fly from country to country in conquering power swiftly and speedily. The leopard is one of the swiftest of beasts, and when the wings are added it is to tell that he was unusually swift, and acted with unusual speed. History confirms this.

Zech. 5:9 (b) It may be that the two women represent Israel and Judah. The wings undoubtedly represent their ability to undertake great matters, and to carry heavy loads in their program, and to succeed in establishing a mighty work in their own land. The stork has very large wings capable of carrying heavy burdens.

Mal. 4:2 (a) This type probably informs us that when our blessed Lord returns to heal the hurt that exists everywhere on this earth it will be with quickness and suddenness. The seraphim flew with the live coal to Isaiah. The father ran to greet the prodigal son. God hurries with His blessings. "The king's business requireth haste." I Sam. 21:8

Rev. 12:14 (b) This mysterious passage is not clearly understood. The woman undoubtedly is Israel. The wings probably represent speed and ability to overcome obstacles and hindrances. The wilderness probably refers to desolate places where the Jews are driven during that period. One cannot dogmatize on the meaning of this passage.

WINTER

S. of Sol. 2:11 (c) We may use this type as a picture of the long life of hardship, sorrow, darkness and difficulty which one may live on this earth. In the case of the Christian this time is followed by God's blessing, care and recovery, both in the millennium, in heaven, or in the individual experience here on earth.

John 10:22 (c) We may use this as a picture of the cold, repelling and unhappy atmosphere which exists outside the house of God, and outside the fellowship of God's people.

WIPE

2 Ki. 21:13 (a) God gives a graphic description of the way He will destroy Jerusalem. He will leave not a vestige remaining, and certainly this was done when Titus, with his Roman army, completely destroyed that city.

WISDOM

Prov. 8:12 (b) It is quite clear that this word is used to describe the Lord Jesus Christ Himself. The description that follows in this chapter shows clearly that it is none other than our Saviour who is being described. It is a lovely picture of our wonderful Lord in His pre-natal glory.

WOLF

Ezek. 22:27 (a) It was a most unhappy situation that existed when the leaders became beasts to destroy the people over whom they were supposed to rule beneficently. The wicked rulers of Israel were suppressing, robbing and injuring the people whom they should have been protecting and preserving. (See also Zeph. 3:3)

Matt. 7:15 (a) This animal represents religious leaders of the present day, who pretend to be God's servants, but who rob the people of their faith, their peace, and their money.

Matt. 10:16 (a) The Lord knew that His disciples would be subject to persecution wherever they went. The people who prosecuted and sought to execute the servants of the Saviour are described as these wild beasts. (See also Luke 10:3)

Acts 20:29 (a) The wolf is used in this case to represent wicked, cruel leaders who, in the name of Christianity and the Church, will burn, maim, torture, kill and seek to destroy God's people and God's testimony. History reveals that this is the course pursued by the great apostate church.

WOMAN

Lam. 1:17 (a) The city where God had placed His name had become a vile, filthy community. That which emanated from this city was offensive to God, and shameful in every aspect. Her manners and her ways were repulsive to the holy God who had chosen her. (See also Ezek. 16:30; Ezek. 23:44; Ezek. 36:17)

Zech. 5:7 (b) This woman represents Israel from the commercial standpoint. The ephah, which was a measure, represents her business enterprises. It was the burden of the nation, as it still is. Their object in life was to make money, gain power, and rise to places of distinction.

Matt. 13:33 (b) Here is a type of apostate christendom, and false religions. They use much of the Word of God (the meal), but they mingle with it their false and evil explanations which poison the souls of those who partake of it. Every false religion, in so-called christendom, uses much of the Bible in their writings and utterances. They poison these messages by interjecting their own explanation and false deductions which produce wrong conclusions. The result is that Christ Jesus is not honored and the Word of God is dishonored.

Rev. 12:1 (b) This woman represents the nation of Israel with her twelve patriarchs (or tribes), and Jesus was the child born from Israel.

Rev. 17:3 (b) The Lord represents apostate christendom as the woman. She grows wealthy, proud, arrogant, wicked and tremendously powerful by her demands upon people, and her control of the heads of government.

WOMB

Psa. 110:3 (a) This is a beautiful emblem of the attractive emergence of the sun from the dark gray mists of the east. It may also refer to the bright coming of our Lord Jesus when He returns to dispel the darkness of this earth.

WOOD

I Cor. 3:12 (b) The word is used to represent Christian activities, which look big, but have little value in God's sight. "Wood" (works) make a big pile in men's eyes, but will not stand the searching judgment of God.

WOOL

Lev. 19:19 (c) We may use this as a type of human works mixed with divine provision. God condemns it. The garment described in this passage is quite typical of many religious professors. The linen represents the good works of man, for linen is made by men. The wool represents the divine work of God, for only God can make it. Man cannot cover himself with a religious garment, which is made partly of God's provision in Christ, and partly of his own provision in character building. Salvation must be all of God, with no mixture of human merit whatever.

WORD

John 1:1 (a) This is a personification of the Lord Jesus Christ. Jesus spoke and His Godhead and Deity were revealed at once. His words revealed His character. When He spoke everyone knew at once that it was the voice of God. He spoke with life-giving power. He spoke with transforming power. It is as when one speaks on the telephone to a friend many miles away. The moment the voice is heard, the friend recognizes the person, and visualizes his appearance. Christ is the Word of God.

WORD OF GOD

Below are given some of the types which are used to describe the Word of God, which is the Bible:

Bow, Habakkuk 3:9 (a`
Buckler, Psa. 18:30 (a)
Fire, Jer. 23:29 (a)
Hammer, Jer. 23:29 (a
Judge, John 12:48 (a)
Lamp, Psa. 119:105 (a)
Laver, Ex. 30:18 (c)
Light, Psa. 119:105 (a)

Meat, 1 Cor. 3:2 (b)
Milk, 1 Pet. 2:2 (a)
Rain, Isa. 55:10-11 (a)
Seed, Luke 8:11 (a)
Shield, Psa. 91:4 (a)
Snow, Isa. 55:10-11 (a)
Spoil, Psa. 119:162 (a)
Sword, Eph. 6:17 (a)
Truth, John 17:17 (a)
Water, Eph. 5:26 (a)

WORM

Psa. 22:6 (a) This type represents the utter degradation and worthlessness of human beings in God's sight. When Jesus took the sinner's place, He called Himself a worm because the one for whom He died was considered by God as a worm. (See also Isa. 41:14)

Isa. 66:24 (b) No doubt this is an emblem of the gnawing pains of conscience which must be endured constantly and forever by those who are lost, and are in the lake of fire. (See also Mark 9:48)

WORMWOOD

Jer. 9:15 (b) This is certainly a description of the bitterness which comes into the soul of those who refuse to worship the Lord, and who reject His Word. (See also Jer. 23:15)

Lam. 3:15 (b) By this we understand the great depression of spirit, and the bitterness of soul which was experienced by Jeremiah, the prophet, when he was so cruelly rejected by Israel.

Amos 5:7 (a) The judgments of God were so severe, and Israel was so evil in their minds, that they were made bitter by God's decisions against them.

Rev. 8:11 (b) The curses of God, which He will send upon this earth, are bitter to the heart and the soul of His enemies. He will make the so-called pleasures and attraction of the world bitter and offensive in the eyes of those who indulge in them.

WOUND

Job 34:6 (a) This suffering man called his affliction and sorrow a wound, for which there was no remedy.

Jer. 10:19 (a) The prophet felt that the sorrows he was undergoing because he was true to God were making a wound in his life. He was hurt deeply by the words of the people. (See also Jer. 15:18; Jer. 30:12; Micah 1:9; Nahum 3:19)

WRAP

Isa. 28:20 (b) We may understand from this that the unrighteousness of men, their pride and their self-sufficiency, are not adequate to satisfy even their own hearts, much less the demands of God.

Micah 7:3 (b) Here we see the care with which wicked men seek to cover up their evil actions, and to prevent the public from seeing what they are doing.

WRESTLE

Eph. 6:12 (a) Here we see the exercise of soul in a child of God as he opposes the powers of darkness. Frequently it is difficult for the Christian when in prayer to get through the multitude of hindrances until he feels he is in the presence of God.

WRINKLE

Eph. 5:27 (a) This word indicates any lack in the believer's life which would make his life rough, unpleasant or unattractive in the sight of God, or in the sight of the saints. The spots in his life are removed by washing, and the wrinkles are removed by the hot iron of circumstances sent from God.

Y

YOKE

Gen. 27:40 (b) This type is used to indicate the oppression and repression placed upon one person by another person, or upon one nation by another nation.

Matt. 11:29 (b) This term is used to indicate the blessed union for service which the Lord desires on the part of His people. The Christian, walking with the Lord and serving Him, finds the work to be easy, and the load is light.

2 Cor. 6:14 (b) In this case the yoke represents an unhappy union of those who are saved with those who are unsaved in any service or work. The Lord commands His people to be linked up only with Christians, and not with those who belong to Satan's family. This refers to marriage, to business, and to every other form of union. This situation is complicated frequently by those who are saved, born again, after the union is made. God made provision for this situation in various parts of His Word.